The Internet and Health in Brazil

André Pereira Neto • Matthew B. Flynn
Editors

The Internet and Health in Brazil

Challenges and Trends

Springer

Editors
André Pereira Neto
National School of Public Health
Oswaldo Cruz Foundation
Rio de Janeiro, Brazil

Matthew B. Flynn
Department of Political Science
and International Studies & Department
of Sociology and Anthropology
Georgia Southern University
Statesboro, GA, USA

ISBN 978-3-030-07587-3 ISBN 978-3-319-99289-1 (eBook)
https://doi.org/10.1007/978-3-319-99289-1

Softcover re-print of the Hardcover 1st edition 2019

This Springer imprint is published by the registered company Springer Nature Switzerland AG
The registered company address is: Gewerbestrasse 11, 6330 Cham, Switzerland

This book is dedicated to Bia, Rafael, Pedro, and Gabriela, who closely followed the pain and delight of this dream that becomes reality.

The book is also dedicated to Lucas who is a true digital native.

Foreword: Internet and e-Health Care – An Interdigital Field of Study

Introduction

The use of the Internet for health-related purposes has reached overall massive proportions, although local national realities still largely differ one from the other around the world. The Internet, with its open design allowing communication among current and future technology, and the World Wide Web open architecture, enabling easy access and popular participation, need no presentation: their importance can hardly be overstated. But, as this chapter illustrates, e-health – or health-related Internet-based technology – and the implications associated to its diffusion go well beyond the technological scale, to include multidimensional means of connecting, accessing, and delivering health care and well-being from multiple agents. Nowadays, more and more people and things are connected to one another than at any other point in human history. The implications of the broad adoption of the Internet and the web are so important that we are living in a new phase of the digital era: an "Internet-based digital" or interdigital era (Murero 2012, 2018a). Information and communication technologies (ICTs), and in particular the Internet, have been supporting the development of unprecedented practices for accessing, receiving, providing, and seeking health care.

What Is Health?

Most popular accounts focus on an overgeneralization of the concept of health as simple absence of disease. In truth, health is a multidimensional concept. It is not only a physical condition related to the absence of disease but also a status of mental and social well-being.

Given its multidimensionality, health is not only a physical status, or the simple absence of sickness; it includes mental and social well-being. In other words, health equates to well-being.

The World Health Organization (WHO), a United Nations specialized agency that is concerned with international public health and represents hundreds of Member States, including Brazil, offers a multidimensional definition of health in its constitution. Since 1948, the definition of health guides WHO's policies and programs, affecting Member States and their Ministry of Health systems:

> [...] Health is a state of complete physical, mental and social well-being and not merely the absence of disease or infirmity. (WHO 2018)

What Is Health Care?

What role are new technologies playing in the development of current scenarios, and in this context, what is health care? When considering health from a well-being perspective, as I am proposing in this chapter, health care results from multiple determinants affecting both patients and health-care providers. In this context, health care is mainly concerned with the maintenance or restoration of a multidimensional state of physical, mental, and social well-being by trained and licensed providers. Therefore, health care becomes the result of multiple variables that include, but are not limited to, the use of high-tech diagnostic instruments, professional skills, effective medical treatments, but also prevention. Moreover, health care determining factors may also include education, the quality of the environment, personal lifestyle, genetics, nutrition, family culture and values, available resources, online information, and more. The socioeconomic determinants of health are the conditions in which people live, grow, work, and receive health care. Socioeconomic conditions are mainly responsible for health status, equities, and inequities between countries. These conditions are largely affected by the economy of distribution of the resources available at the local, regional, national, and international levels. In this context, the availability of information and communication technologies (ICTs) to access information and care, maintain, and restore health is becoming an essential dimension affecting the quality of individual and social well-being.

The majority of the world's health-care systems are mainly concerned with treating and preventing diseases rather than promoting well-being. When observing how users of ICTs meet their health-care needs online, a definition closer to the concept of well-being, rather than the notion of "absence of sickness," emerges (Murero and Rice 2006).

From e-Health to e-Health Care

E-health is a broad term encompassing a wide variety of technologies and socio-communicative practices used by health-care providers, patients, and "health seekers." The academic literature shows that there is no general consensus on a standardized terminology for defining the field of the Internet and health: this is due, in part, to the dynamic of a rapidly evolving field both in terms of new tools, applications, and online practices (Eysenbach 2001; Oh et al. 2005; Murero and Rice 2006). Current popular terms include e-health or eHealth, Medical Informatics, Consumer Health Informatics, Medicine 2.0, Digital Health, mHealth, Health 2.0, and more. While each of these terms defines specific aspects of Internet-mediated access to health practices, they may overlap only in part. Some scholars focus on the technological dimensions of the phenomenon, some on the sociological aspects, and others offer an interdisciplinary approach, like the one I am developing in this chapter. Internet-based technologies consist of a wide variety of telecommunication infrastructures, architectures, protocols, platform services, and smartphone-based apps. The popularization of the Internet and the invention of the World Wide Web date only to the early 1990s.

Historically, several macro-factors have contributed to the popularization of the Internet and the revolutionary access to health-care information and knowledge, particularly for the nonmedical population.

Early computerized systems for processing information and code-breaking signed the beginning of computer science during the 1940s (Hodges 2014). After World War II, rapid developments in computing applications offered unprecedented opportunities to public health-care analysis, particularly during the 1950s and the 1960s. For example, in early epidemiologic applications (like in the 1950s), mainframe programs were able to identify the variables causing diseases according to age, gender, and location (Shortliffe 2001). Later on, the development of the first personal computer and the diffusion of digitalization contributed to the informatization of society during the 1970s and the 1980s. For the first time in history, the use of information technology for health-care management made possible not only the use of digitalization for archiving information on a computer but also for retrieving and distributing digitalized medical data, in a large majority of the world's health-care systems, including Brazil.

From a purely technological point of view, the increase in speed, memory, and mass data storage (e.g., servers) played a crucial role in the development of unprecedented opportunities for early health-care management systems. In the last 30 years, the exponential proliferation of digitalized network infrastructures and telecommunication, allowing the communication and exchange of large amounts of data among computers – thanks to the Internet – was a crucial passage not only for archiving patient's records on digital supports and exchange them over the net but also to deliver new forms of health-care treatments through early telemedicine solutions; these made the provision of health care in remote areas of North America and Australia at the beginning of 2000s possible (Heaton 2006; Murero and Rice 2006).

Internet-mediated technology, social platforms, and mobile applications currently support and affect online practices such as searching, exchanging, and receiving health-care information and also others' opinions about medical treatments, products, and services. More recently, body sensors technology for remote body monitoring, Internet of Things (IoT), and artificial intelligence (AI) solutions are offering new perspectives to e-health and particularly to health care (Murero 2018a).

In this chapter, I specifically focus on e-health care. Although I will analyze multiple technological solutions available to patients, caregivers, and "health seekers," it is important to keep in mind that the availability of smart and advanced technological devices is only one side of the current e-health phenomenon. One of the most interesting developments in the field of the Internet and health accounts for what millions of agents do with new technologies over time and what needs they are satisfying, thanks to 24/7 accessibility and use. I would like to emphasize this central concept, as it contributes to the definition of the health-related, Internet-based technology, or e-health, as a field of study.

As I mentioned at the beginning of the chapter, it is important to differentiate the current phase of the digital era from its origin, in the 1970s, when the first digital calculators and the personal computer became available to the public for the first time. Today our multimedia smartphones and wireless tablets are thousands of times faster and powerful than the first stand-alone personal computer, which by the way had no Internet connection – besides those networked computers available to a few lucky users in limited academic environments.

Becoming Interdigital: The Internet-Mediated Digital Era

Compared to the early beginning of the digital era, the current phase of digitalization presents a completely different scenario from every perspective, not only from a technological standpoint but more interestingly for the adoption of new socio-communicative practices among millions of Internet-connected people around the world, which have affected every sector of society, including health care. The current digital era is interdigital or Internet-mediated digital society (Murero 2012). Online interdigital agents of course use the Internet and web-based digitalized platforms for communicating and staying connected.

In the context of using the Internet for health-related purposes, interdigital agents may include the following:

- *Health-care providers (hospital, medical care centers, pharmaceutical companies, etc.).*
- *Health-care receivers (patients).*
- *Health-care seekers (actively search information for themselves or on behalf of someone else; may include family members, friends, caregivers, or significant others).*
- *Computerized agents (software programs, chatbot, robots). Nonhuman agents connected to the Internet (interdigital agents) (Murero 2012) are programmed to perform specific tasks online, such as publishing, receiving, and analyzing information through the Internet; to interact via chatbot; and more.*

It is important to remark that the uses of health-related Internet-based technologies and their implications are interdisciplinary and broad. For example, thanks to the Internet, patients can access vast information about a specific disease, stay in touch with other patients via social media, share their treatment experiences, keep up with a diet via an app, engage in a chatbot conversation with a computerized agent, and even diffuse wrong information about a disease or a medical condition.

Why ICT Always Matters

Technology plays a facilitating role in the development of socio-communicative dynamics and relations for e-health. At the current stage, some of the most interesting challenges are happening in the field of mobile health-care applications (mHealth).[1] For example, millions of people in South America and all over the world have the possibility to control their sleep habits on their smartphone, follow a yoga course or a diet via an app, and even share with friends their running performances through online social platforms. The use of mobile solutions for personal health care has grown exponentially in any field of medicine, from birth control to heart failure. Moreover, thanks to ICTs, health-care providers can offer remote monitoring and tele-counseling and new means to access reliable medical education and new research findings for the scientific community.

As previously stated, the field of Internet and health does not only refer to technological tools and platforms supporting health care but also to socio-communicative practices that agents exchange online. The use of new technology plays a facilitating role in platform-mediated communication exchange that overcomes space, time, and costs barriers. Human communication happens more and more via new media platforms. The amount of data – big data – that millions of agents are generating online every single day, over time, are creating new challenges and debates regarding their use. Millions of agents using ICTs for e-health generate large quantities of data and facilitate the development of new forms of online power and control where such social production and exchange occur. These have the potential to affect not only the characteristics of platforms where social media communities for mutual support meet or offline patient-doctor relations but also the socioeconomic dynamics of the health-care and well-being sectors, including their regulation. Internet-mediated practices and their implications are currently challenging the field of health-care provision in many countries, including Brazil. From experimental telemedicine systems to massive education courses, the debate on the future uses of ICTs for e-health affects every aspect of the phenomenon and its specific characteristics, including policymakers.

In the current international scenario, expensive solutions and low-cost applications for remote patient care coexist. For example, patients and their families living in Western countries, particularly in North America, may benefit from complex and costly technology for remote home care management. Advanced e-health solutions combine telemedicine, tele-homecare, wearable sensors, multiple databases such as Electronic Health Records (EHR), clinical information, picture archiving and

[1] This aspect is discussed in Chap. 17, which addresses the topic of mHealth.

communication system (PACS), and even nonclinical applications (system administration, doctor's payroll, etc.).

On the other hand, an emerging trend shows that when hospitals do not offer efficient, rapid, and expensive solutions for rapid and convenient patient's care management, do-it-yourself e-health systems for instant messaging communication emerge, mainly via WhatsApp (Murero 2012).

Current Trends and Challenges in e-Health Care

WhatsApp is an instant messaging multiplatform app for smartphone – and computer desktop – that offers inexpensive ways of communicating and exchanging multimedia data. The recent popularization of instant messaging applications like WhatsApp tends to facilitate the exchange of patients' medical information via smartphone (RX pictures, lab test results, diagnostic videos, text, emoji, recorded audio) for medical decision-making (Follis et al. 2012). Based on end-to-end encrypted technology, WhatsApp is becoming a pretty popular and easy-to-use mobile application, allowing for instant communication of multimedia contents (RX pictures, audio, video) over the Internet and supporting rapid interaction by overcoming space limitations. Small groups of caregivers using their private smartphone and Internet connection can exchange information via WhatsApp and communicate urgent orders regarding patient treatment. Examples include, but are not limited to, diagnosis and decision-making in emergency care, orthopedics evaluation, or acute heart disease. When a medical emergency occurs, and a patient's sensible data need to be evaluated by a group of experts, some of which might not be physically present in the hospital, smartphone-based systems of communication may offer an efficient alternative to make immediate professional consultations, send multimedia contents, and increase efficiency in decision-making. Once patient data is digitalized, multimedia contents can be conveniently exchanged over the Internet including blood test results, X-ray pictures, videos, and diagnostic reports. The exchange of medical information via smartphone becomes a convenient alternative to overcome space or time limitations. Moreover, the use of multiplatform solutions like WhatsApp is also reported in doctor-patient interaction or doctor-patient's caregiver interactions, particularly when an urgent medical need emerges. Also, instant messaging helps co-workers and medical professionals to engage and keep in touch with their peers.

The use of WhatsApp as a local-made telemedicine communication system among small groups of health-care professionals and collaborators is still a little-investigated phenomenon (Murero 2018b). However, its rapid diffusion may be due to a number of partially related reasons. For example, Brazil is the country where free messaging services like MSN Messenger and Orkut, one of the oldest online social networks in the world, both became largely popular, while telecommunication companies kept charging telephone users for sending SMS. Moreover, the increased availability of personal smartphones constantly connected to the Internet among health-care professionals, the popularization of easy-to-use mobile applications for messaging, and social networking that is already in use for communicating with family and friends are other factors that facilitated the rapid adoption of WhatsApp not only in private but also in professional settings. In particular, the convenience of exchanging diagnostic pictures among professionals and co-workers, like X-rays, in a relatively safe and rapid manner contributes to the emergence of new forms of interaction that are free and convenient. These emergent practices of e-health may support the daily routine of medical practice.

The trend is not limited to communication among health-care providers. For example, the literature shows that more and more physicians, physiotherapists, and mental health professionals use WhatsApp all over the world to directly communicate with patients and their caregivers, exchange information, and offer rapid feedback and medical indications as needed.

Sensible Data Exchange, Security, and Electronic Health Records (EHRS)

Controversial limits regarding privacy and security of patients' sensitive data do not appear to be a matter of concern for caregivers interacting via WhatsApp. Health caregivers may take and circulate pictures of patient's lab results or X-rays that often do not show personal data (patient's name) but sensitive information that may be available in the patient's Electronic Health Records (body lab tests and screening results, previous diseases, and more). Electronic Health Records or electronic medical records consist of patient's digitalized information usually collected by points of health care – like hospitals – that collect demographic data, previous medical history, medical lab reports, body images or video taken for diagnostic purposes, vital signs monitoring, financial and administrative information, and other sensitive information.

When Electronic Health Records are digitally available, data can be used to acquire, analyze, process, archive, and communicate information to a variety of other information-keepers over the Internet, including the Ministry of Health or any other third parties. Data privacy and security are crucial issues when safeguarding patient information in a distributed system. Other issues may include regulation of access to different levels of data confidentiality and information at each point of care (secretary, nurse, doctor, commodification of data, etc.), difficulties for physicians doing EHR data entry, and challenges in integrating different databases into a central information system from each point of care.

The use of EHRs has several advantages. For example, newly admitted patients, especially those who may be unresponsive as a consequence of a trauma, may largely benefit from a central system providing previous medical records. Also, people unable to provide valid medical information or who are impaired may benefit from convenient portability of their medical history, reliable and precise medical information, and protections against data loss as well as data durability over time once digitalized and easy duplicability of records. Health organizations accessing EMR EHRs may have the possibility of conducting medical studies on a large population to assess the quality of a treatment provided, the evaluation of a clinical trial, etc. Policymakers may also benefit from public health epidemiologic analysis, health data analysis for policy decision-making, and improved quality of care.

From Telemedicine to Tele-Homecare

Citizens living in underdeveloped areas of the world experience shortages in health-care professionals. Exchanging digitalized medical information among distant points of care in order to evaluate single cases and provide access to adequate medical care is crucial for remote diagnosis. In particular, telemedicine and tele-homecare solutions have been relying upon complex systems of health-care management that requires challenging maintenance of and investments in infrastructure. Telemedicine consists in the remote provision of health care through specific ICTs architectures and platforms that rely on fast and high-quality Internet connection for video communication and multimedia data exchange. For example, patients might receive a real-time dermatological visit while sitting hundreds of kilometers away from the hospital that provides the service. Practical examples include several medical practices, from psychiatrics and dermatology to radiology.

Early telemedicine pioneering systems tested the possibility of delivering emergency telesurgery care via robot to astronauts in space (Kilpatrick 2004). Nowadays, telemedicine encompasses several clinical applications in wealthy nations. For example, it is useful in supporting the medical decision-making process based on remote imaging exchange (like high-quality pictures of the derma, X-ray evaluation in an orthopedic emergency, psychiatric and psychological consultancy, etc.). Whenever professional expertise is missing at the point of care, even within a large city area, telemedicine systems may be useful to provide access to patient records, evaluation, and care. Because telemedicine architectures may offer multiple forms of communication in a single virtual point of care, several health providers and the patients can simultaneously audio-video interact and access and exchange data, all from different physical locations. Telemedicine systems may offer virtual visits and several other services through a sophisticated Internet-based, two-way communication system. Benefits associated with telemedicine systems are very valuable for patients and doctors, although only a minority of health-care facilities are able to offer such complex services, since they require large investments over time in management, staff education, and high-cost maintenance and administration.

While telemedicine manly offers remote assistance if expert consultations is locally missing, or because an acute problem emerges, a specific branch of telemedicine, tele-homecare, seeks to offer continuous health-care assistance to patients with chronic conditions at their home, by monitoring their vital signs remotely. Chronically sick patients, who may suffer from diabetes, acute health failure, or severe asthma, do not need hospitalization. They need to follow their doctor's instructions in terms of lifestyle and medication at their home. However, chronic patients need to be regularly checked to make sure their health is fine. If early signs of deterioration occur, these patients may need immediate professional evaluation and, if it is the case, even hospitalization. Tele-homecare devices are installed in the patient's house. Tele-homecare may alert an urgent medical treatment by combining Internet-based telemedicine technology, continuous home monitoring through sensor-based technology, and remote analysis of body signs, even without a patient's knowledge. When the tele-homecare system records an abnormal situation, it alerts the point of care over the Internet. Also, according to the specific situation, the health-care provider may contact the patient to receive more information and evaluate the case and decide the type of treatment needed.

By exchanging information and checking symptoms as well as vital signs in real-time, complex systems for tracking patient health over the Internet can help doctors provide medical evaluations and assist with treatments in areas where expertise and services are unavailable. Tele-homecare may prevent health deterioration and improve patients' quality of life through accurate data analysis protocols and life-saving procedures.

Advanced Integrated Systems for Interdigital Health Care

In advanced e-health care contexts, particularly in North America, significant investments allowed for the development of complex systems of information management for health-care organizations, like hospital chains. These integrated systems use Internet-based technology to gather, process, integrate, and archive multiple sources of data and applications for managing health-care services. Since the 1990s, the early information system for handling hospital's financial matters and billing patients have drastically improved to include more and more areas of organizational health management, integrating both clinical and nonclinical solutions to the point of care. Examples of multiservice systems of interdigital health management include the following:

- *Applications providing different levels of security for accessing patient's information and EHRs (e.g., transcribed diagnostic reports, blood lab results, X-ray archiving, internal communication systems, and PACS)*
- *Physicians' orders (e.g., adding and consulting other's orders, ordering of medical materials and drugs for hospitalized patients)*
- *Monitoring patients' vital signs, inside and outside the hospital, through an Internet-based system of patient surveillance, including systems for sensors' activity, digital devices, and applications*
- *Creation of internal databases for conducting medical research, academic activity, clinical trials, and international collaborations*

- *Hospital administrative management (e.g., purchase and inventory of materials, patient information and payment management, internal auditing to verify the quality of treatments and procedures provided, access security and financial management systems, including managing payrolls and payments of internal staff)*
- *Technological devices to internal staff like smartphones, ad hoc application for care provision, office automation programs (e.g., word, excel)*
- *Internal systems providing access to mandatory online continuing education and scholarly information (e.g., drug information database, scientific medical literature)*

The health-care technology industry and policymakers should consider that the lack of sufficient resources from health-care providers may ultimately result in maintaining old technology rather than embracing innovative e-health solutions that may largely benefit patients and their families – like tele-homecare. In the last two decades, information and communication technology and health information systems (HIS) have been offering new challenges for in-house and remote clinical applications to benefit patients and their families. However, because technology evolves very fast when new solutions become available, policymakers and health-care institutions are faced with the continuous need to anticipate future demands and provide for adequate hardware investments and resources, also in educational terms. It is important to keep in mind that the availability of smart and advanced technological devices is only one side of the current e-health phenomenon. Although the focus of this chapter is to define e-health care in the context of multiple technological solutions available to patients, caregivers, and "health seekers," it is important considering what millions of interdigital agents do with new technologies over time and what platforms they use to satisfy what types of needs. Moreover, what third parties do with user data is a matter of concern given limited regulation on the topic.

Past, Present, and Future of e-Health

In the last 20 years, e-health advantages and disadvantages, barriers, and facilitators have been a matter of study, concern, and debate. For example, online health-care optimists have been claiming that investing in new ICTs can reduce costs, provide access to an immense range of information and practices, and improve efficiency and quality of care. On the other side, there are concerns over liability, security, privacy, and confidentiality of sensitive data and their use (big data), as the chapters of this book show. When observing how the use of the Internet has affected millions of people around the world, including both health-care providers and patients, advantages and disadvantages emerge. For example, when patients educate themselves about their disease online, the use of the Internet can potentially empower patients and help doctors better manage health-care processes and challenges; patients can better participate to the decision-making process. On the other hand, assessing the quality and the sources of online health contents is still a major issue for the nonmedical population because anyone can potentially publish online content without following any particular regulation. Even when a country has regulation in place, the distributed nature of online information may allow exceptions. This is a matter of concern because according to academic evidence, online info affects the health decision-making process of the nonmedical population. The HONcode logo guarantees online users that health-care information is safe and reliable. The Health On the Net Foundation (HON),[2] a not-for-profit organization based in Genève, issued a code of conduct (HONcode) for websites that publish health-related content.

A Pew survey indicated that artificial intelligence and robotics are expected to have enormous implications on e-health in the next 10 years (Smith and Anderson 2014). The rapid introduction of new ICTs devices like smart assistive robotics for disabled and seniors, artificial intelligence (AI) supporting medical diagnosis and care, and new tools to remotely manage patients with chronic conditions may offer unique opportunities. However, they also generate new challenges related to access and provision of e-health. Huge challenges are expected to impact crucial sectors of society, like work, governance, education, socio-communicative practices, and of course health and well-being. Among these challenges, the Internet of Things (IoT) is expected to largely impact the field of health in the next three decades because an enormous number of medical objects connected via the Internet and communicating with each other are expected to grow exponentially from embedded smart sensors for remote monitoring to smart medical devices for home integration and fitness activities. The diffusion of intelligent mobile devices for health care and social robots companions for patients needing home assistance and care will pose new challenges particularly to hospital's IT facilities in terms of securing privacy of sensitive data, managing the enormous quantity of data they collect, and constant surveillance.

The commodification of huge amounts of sensitive data and their use by companies providing techno platforms and Internet services is still a challenge that is expected to grow in future years and is currently lacking adequate regulation from policymakers. In fact, the ability to generate, transmit, and capture huge amounts of personal data (big data) through sensors, webcams, smartphones apps, and wearable devices is an ongoing reality. Analytical models that evaluate big data for public health purposes have the potential to expand government's capabilities in terms of disease prevention campaigns, health-care provisions, and rationalization of scarce resources. But, the need for adequate regulation to address current disadvantages, threats, and barriers on the one hand and to develop benefits and facilitators, on the other hand, is likely to face additional challenges in years to come.

Health is a multidimensional concept. It is not only a physical condition related to the absence of disease but also a status of mental and social well-being. The implications of the broad adoption of the Internet are so significant that we can define a phase of the digitalization era, an "Internet-based digital" or interdigital era

[2] Health on the Net Foundation (HON): https://www.hon.ch/

(Murero 2012, 2018a). Nowadays, more and more people – and things – exchanging trillions of data are connected technologically to one another. In this context, the use of the Internet for health-related purposes and well-being has reached overall massive proportions, although local national realities differ one from the other. But as this chapter illustrates, e-health – or health-related Internet-based technology – and the implications associated to its diffusion go well beyond the technological scale, to include multidimensional means of connecting, accessing, and delivering health care and well-being from multiple agents.

When analyzing how e-health stakeholders meet their needs online and the controversial effects related to emerging online e-health behaviors, certain patterns emerge. A major point in the international debate is that while the provision of health care within hospitals and points of care is highly regulated by governments all over the world, e-health is still largely unregulated. Health data collection, security, protection, and different levels of access to sensitive information still require government and international debate and regulation.

While innovative technologies try to conquer e-health consumers, inadequate regulation of online practices remains common in many countries. For example, the implications of exchanging personal health information through online platforms and their commodification from third parties are still a matter of debate with little action taken by industry stakeholders, policymakers, and academics. Online virtual environments and home care sensor-based technology, Internet of Things, and artificial intelligence are rapidly evolving. The gap between industry innovation for e-health and regulation is still a challenge. As per the provision of health care within hospitals and points of care, that is, currently highly regulated by governments all over the world, innovative tech-based solutions for e-health such as companion robotics and even do-it-yourself instant telemedicine should be regulated and safeguarded to guarantee the fundamental right to health to anyone.

Monica Murero
Department of Social Sciences
University of Naples Federico II
Naples, Italy
monica.murero@unina.it

References

Eysenbach, Gunther. 2001. What is e-health? *Journal of Medical Internet Research* 3: e20.

Follis, Fabrizio, Monica Murero, Giuseppe D'Ancona, Elio Pieri, and Marco Follis. 2014. Sharing medical data: An easy way through interdigital mobile communication. *Journal of Telemedicine and Telecare* 20: 157–158.

Heaton, Lorna. 2006. Telehealth in indigenous communities in the far north: Challenges for continued development. In *Internet and health care*, ed. M. Murero and R. Rice, 335–336. LEA: New Jersey.

Hodges, Andrew. 2014. *Alan Turing*: The enigma. New Jersey: Princeton University Press.

Kilpatrick, Ken. 2004. Telemedicine: On, under and out of this world. *Canadian Medical Association Journal* 171: 716.

Murero, Monica. 2012. *Interdigital Communication Theory*. Padova: Libreriauniversitaria.it.

———. 2018a. Internet and health care. In *SAGE Encyclopedia of the Internet*, ed. B. Warf, B. London: Sage (in press).

———. 2018b. Wearable Internet. In *SAGE Encyclopedia of the Internet*, ed. B. Warf, B. London: Sage (in press).

Murero, Monica, and Ronald Rice. 2006. *Internet and health care*. LEA: New Jersey.

Oh, Hans, Carlos Rizo, Murray Enkin, and Alejandro Jadad. 2005. What is ehealth (3): A systematic review of published definitions. *Journal of Medical Internet Research* 7: e1.

Shortliffe, Edward, and Marsden Blois. 2001. The computer meets medicine and biology: Emergence of a discipline. In *Medical informatics*: Computer applications in health care and biomedicine, ed. E. Shortliffe et al., 3–40. New York: Springer.

Smith, Aaron, and Janna Anderson. 2014. *AI, robotics, and the future of jobs*. Pew Research Center, Washington. Report. http://www.pewinternet.org/2014/08/06/future-of-jobs/. Accessed 12 October. 2016.

WHO – World Health Organization. 2018. Constitution of the World Health Organization: Principles. http://www.who.int/about/mission/en/. Accessed June 6 2017.

Acknowledgments

This book began to be conceived in May of 2016. From that moment, we began organizing its structure and invited some of the most important Brazilian authors who study the different interfaces of the social phenomenon of the Internet and health. We knew some authors in person; others we did not. In the case of the latter, we made contact through the Internet/email. After Springer approved the project, we began the process of producing this work. During the year 2017, some authors had to exit the endeavor for different reasons. Other authors were immediately contacted to fill the space they left. Since the beginning, we aimed to have a book with 20 chapters in order to cover the varied set of questions and perspectives on the subject.

Practically all the chapters were initially written in Portuguese – the native language of the contributors. As the book's editors, we reviewed the chapters individually to determine whether the contents fit within our criteria and scope. We also invited outside referees to provide additional feedback. After the authors incorporated our suggestions, we gave them permission to translate their work into English. We then reviewed the English translations to guarantee uniformity across chapters and ensure quality and readability for both experts in the field and new-comers interested in the topic. To crown our project, we invited two internationally renowned scholars to write the foreword and the afterword. Here it is. A book that analyzes different trends and challenges of the Internet and the phenomenon of health in Brazil.

We would like to thank all the authors who contributed to this effort and the editors at Springer who allowed us to bring the social phenomenon of the Internet and health in Brazil to an international audience. It is worth mentioning the participation of the researcher Leticia Barbosa who kindly offered to assist with the final process of producing this work by reviewing each chapter in terms of formatting, length, and bibliographic standards. We also would like to thank Kendra Cooper who helped with the initial revisions of many of the chapters that had been translated into English.

Contents

Author Biographies

Dolores Abreu is a veterinarian with a PhD in Public Health from the National School of Public Health of the Oswaldo Cruz Foundation (2018) where she is a collaborating researcher. She is also a health worker at the State Health Secretariat of Rio de Janeiro. Her academic interests include monitoring and evaluation, health education, health surveillance, health management and planning, and health information.

Natália Fernandes Andrade has a degree in Health Management, a master's in Collective Health from the University of Brasilia (2018) and is a researcher of the "Group of Studies and Research in Information and Communication in Collective Health". Her academic interests include information management and health education and communication.

Zelia Andrade is a biologist with a master's in Biology from the State University of Rio de Janeiro (1982). She has worked at the Secretary of Health of the State of Rio de Janeiro, the State Institute of Public Health Louis Pasteur, and the Oswaldo Cruz Institute of the Oswaldo Cruz Foundation. Currently, she is the pedagogical coordinator of the "Laboratory Internet Health Society" (LaISS) of the Oswaldo Cruz Foundation and a researcher in public health with activities in teaching and research focusing on methodologies of health intervention and promotion for digital and social inclusion. Her academic interests include health promotion and digital literacy.

Inesita Soares de Araujo has a degree in Social Communication and a PhD in Communication and Culture from the Federal University of Rio de Janeiro (2002). She is a professor at the Graduate Program in Information, Communication, and Health at the Institute of Communication and Scientific and Technological Information in Health of the Oswaldo Cruz Foundation. She also heads the "Communication and Health Research Group" and coordinates the "Communication and Health Working Group" of the Latin American Association of Communication

Researchers. She has experience in the area of communication and public policy. Her main academic interests include communication and health, in its political, epistemological, theoretical-methodological, institutional dimensions, and its agents and practices, as well as the methodological and political approaches guided by "epistemologies of the south."

Larissa Barão is an undergraduate law student and currently has a Scholarship for Scientific Initiation and the "Scientific Vocation Program" at the Oswaldo Cruz Foundation. Her academic interests include the digital born, cyberbullying, and online advocacy.

Allan Claudius Queiroz Barbosa is an economist with a PhD in Administration from the University of São Paulo (1995). He was a postdoctoral fellow at the Higher Institute of Economics and Management of the University of Lisbon (2006). Currently, he is a professor in the Graduate Program in Technological and Biopharmaceutical Innovation at the Federal University of Minas Gerais, where he is a member of the Research and Extension Teaching Council, and a professor at the University of Porto, Portugal, where he is a researcher at the Institute of Sociology. His academic interests include management of (non) corporate organizations and human resources in health.

Leticia Barbosa has a degree in Media Studies and a master's in Information, Communication, and Health from the Institute of Communication and Scientific and Technological Information in Health that is part of the Oswaldo Cruz Foundation (2017). She is a researcher at "Laboratory Internet Health Society" (LaISS) that is part of the Oswaldo Cruz Foundation. Her academic interests include social media, the empowerment process, physician-patient relationship, and cyber-activism and advocacy.

Elias Bitencourt is an industrial designer with a master's in Culture and Society from the Federal University of Bahia where he is a researcher at the "Digital Media, Networks and Space Research Laboratory." He is also a professor in the Department of Hard Sciences and Earth Sciences at the State University of Bahia where he is the coordinator of "Ubiquitous Media Laboratory." He researches the relationship between the body, Internet of Things, wearables, and big data. His academic interests include digital culture, actor-network theory, object-oriented ontology, and new materialism.

Vânia Coutinho Q. Borges is a psychologist with a master's in Information, Communication, and Health at the Institute of Communication and Scientific and Technological Information in Health of the Oswaldo Cruz Foundation (2015). Her academic interests include subjects related to psychology, with an emphasis on chemical dependency.

Wilson Couto Borges has a degree in Social Communication and a PhD in Communication from Fluminense Federal University (2009). He is a professor in the Graduate Program in Information, Communication, and Health at the Institute of Communication and Scientific and Technological Information in Health of the Oswaldo Cruz Foundation. He coordinates the Oswaldo Cruz Foundation's "Communication and Health Research Laboratory" and is an associate researcher with the "Health Media Observatory." His academic interests include political science, history, psychoanalysis, and health.

Liara Saldanha Brites is a speech therapist with a master's in Collective Health from Federal University of Rio Grande do Sul (2017). Currently, she is a speech and hearing therapist at the 18th Regional Health Coordination of the State Health Secretariat of Rio Grande do Sul and is a professor of Collective Health in the Nursing Technical Course at the "Centro Universitário Cenecista" in Osório, state of Rio Grande do Sul. Her work experience encompasses state primary care management, interdisciplinary team coordination, family health matrix support, and institutional support. Her academic interests include educational and vocational training and new information and communication technologies.

Claudio Luis de Camargo Penteado is a sociologist with a PhD in Social Sciences from the Pontifical Catholic University of São Paulo (2005). Currently, he is a professor at the Federal University of ABC in the state of São Paulo where he works in the Graduate Program in Human and Social Sciences and the "Laboratory of Free Technologies." He is also a researcher at the "Studies Center of Art, Media and Power" at the Pontifical Catholic University of São Paulo. He has experience in the area of political science, with an emphasis on Internet and politics. His academic interests include the Internet, democracy, blogs, public policies, political marketing, cyber-activism, and digital culture.

Gisela Cardoso is a psychologist with a PhD in Collective Health from the Institute of Social Medicine at the State University of Rio de Janeiro (2008). She was a postdoctoral fellow in Health Sciences at Tulane University in the USA (2012). Currently, she is a researcher in the Samuel Pessoa Department of Endemics at the National School of Public Health at the Oswaldo Cruz Foundation. She is also the coordinator of the "Laboratory of Evaluation of Regional Endemic Situations" and researches health evaluation focusing on disease control programs. Her academic interests include the evaluation of the training processes and monitoring and evaluation of public policies.

Flávia Garcia de Carvalho is a graphics designer and artist with a master's in Information, Communication, and Health from the Institute of Communication and Scientific and Technological Information in Health that is part of the Oswaldo Cruz Foundation (2016). She studies the relationship between health institutions and populations in their processes of production, circulation, and appropriation of information, discourses, and knowledge. She is interested in studying the emergence and development of new communication spaces, especially those that develop from new technologies, especially virtual technologies.

Lung Wen Chao is a physician with a PhD from the Faculty of Medicine at the University of São Paulo (2000). Currently, he directs the Discipline of Telemedicine in the School of Medicine at the University of São Paulo; is coordinator of the Interactive Educational Technologies Project for health education; the leader of the Research Group on Telemedicine and Telehealth in the research directory of the National Research Council; the coordinator for the Virtual Man Project, Digital Media, and use of 3D printing and the "Young Doctor Networks Program"; and member of the Technical Chamber of Informatics and Health of the Federal Council of Medicine. His academic interests include telemedicine, medical professional training, health information and communication technologies, and telehealth.

Maíra Lie Chao has a degree in Social Communication with a specialization in Art Direction in Communication from the Centro Universitário Belas Artes de São Paulo (2012). She works as an instructional designer, educational designer, and educational communication designer. Her academic interests include planning and application of educational methodologies and the management of interactive educational platforms and of educational learning objects.

Tiago Coutinho is an anthropologist with a PhD in Human Sciences with a concentration in Sociology and Anthropology from the Federal University of Rio de Janeiro. He has experience in Anthropology and Sociology, with an emphasis in the Anthropology/Sociology of Health, and in Urban Anthropology/Sociology. He studies the consumption of psychoactive substances in urban centers and teaches in the Department of Anthropology of Federal University of Rio de Janeiro and in the Department of Sociology of Fluminense Federal University, at Niteroi, Rio de Janeiro State.

Evelyn Eisenstein is a physician with a PhD in Nutrition from the Paulista School of Medicine, Federal University of São Paulo (1999). Currently, she is a professor in the Faculty of Medical Sciences at the State University of Rio de Janeiro where she coordinates the Telemedicine Program. She is also the scientific editor of the *Adolescence & Health Magazine*, a member of the Society for Adolescent Health and Medicine, and a consultant for the Medical Missions for Children. She has experience in the areas of Medicine, Pediatrics, and Adolescent Care. Her academic interests include adolescence, risks, prevention actions, and the growth and development of children and adolescents.

Cyrus Elahi has a degree in Biology from Texas Christian University in Fort Worth, Texas. Currently, he is a 4th-year medical student and 2nd-year global health master's student at Duke University interested in pursuing neurosurgery. His interests include health information technology and the intersection of technology and neurosurgery.

Matthew B. Flynn has an MSc in Sociology from the London School of Economics, United Kingdom, and a PhD in Sociology at the University of Texas at Austin (2010). He is currently an associate professor of Sociology and International Studies at Georgia Southern University. His interests include globalization, development, pharmaceuticals, immigration, and global health.

Heloísa Cristina Figueiredo Frizzo is an occupational therapist with a PhD in Nursing from the University of São Paulo (2015). She did a postdoctorate in the Graduate Program in Science, Technology, and Society at the Federal University of São Carlos in the state of São Paulo. Currently, she is a professor at the Federal University of Triângulo Mineiro in the state of Minas Gerais where she heads the "Interdisciplinary Nucleus in Technologies in the Daily Life." She is also the founder of the "Scientific Association of Occupational Therapy in Hospital Settings" and has experience in physical and occupational therapy. Her academic interests include adult health, occupational therapy, professional training, hospital contexts, palliative care, loss and mourning, and technologies.

Ariadne Chloe Furnival is a librarian with a PhD in Scientific and Technological Policy from the State University of Campinas (2001). She is a professor in the Information Science Department of the Center for Education and Human Sciences at the Federal University of São Carlos, in the state of São Paulo, where she is the coordinator of the Working Group for the Implementation of the Institutional Repository. She has experience in the area of information science with an emphasis on communication processes. Her academic interests include open access, public understanding of science and technology, sustainable development and communication, information users and informational competencies, and scientific communication.

Estélio Gomberg is a sociologist with a PhD in Public Health from the Federal University of Bahia (2008). He was a postdoctoral fellow in Social Sciences at the Federal University of Bahia (2011). Currently, he is a professor at the State University of Santa Cruz in Bahia with experience teaching and researching in the areas of Social Sciences and Collective Health. His academic interests include health, religiosities, science, and technology.

Denise Cristina Ayres Gomes has a degree in Social Communication and a PhD in Social Communication from the Pontifical Catholic University of Rio Grande do Sul (2016). She did a postdoctorate in Media and Quotidian at the Fluminense Federal University in the state of Rio de Janeiro (2018). Currently, she is a professor and researcher at the Federal University of Maranhão where she coordinates the "Imaginarium Research Group – Communication, Culture, Imaginary and Society" and is a researcher in the "Journalism, Media and Memory Group." She is also a researcher in the "Humanitas Digitalis Group" at the University of São Paulo and in the "Multis - Center for Audiovisual Studies and Experiences in the Multimedia Context" at Fluminense Federal University. She worked as a communications consultant and reporter. Her academic interests include Digital Culture Journalism, Imaginary and Health.

Elizabeth Alves de Jesus Prado has a degree in Collective Health and a master's in Collective Health from the University of Brasilia (2016) and works in the areas of Health Policy, Planning, and Management. Currently, she is a lecturer in Health Policy of the Ceilandia Faculty, University of Brasília, and a professor of the Training Course of Community Health Agents and Agents to Fight Endemics in the state of Goiás. Her academic interests include primary care, policies of equity, and health economics.

Luís Velez Lapão is an Engineer with a PhD in Systems Engineering (Health Management) from the Technical University of Lisbon. He is a senior researcher and professor of International Public Health at the Institute of Public Health and Tropical Medicine – Universidade NOVA de Lisboa. He is an active member of the World Health Organization Collaborating Centre for Health Workforce Policy and Planning and an auditor of the European Commission for the Healthcare Information Systems and works in the areas of Health Innovation and Health Information Systems, with emphasis in the areas of Organization and Project Management and Management of Information Systems in Health and Telemedicine.

André Lemos is a mechanical engineer with a PhD in Sociology from the Université René Descartes, Paris V, Sorbonne (1995). He was a postdoctoral fellow at the National University of Maynooth, Ireland (2016); at McGill University, Canada (2008); and at the University of Alberta, Canada (2007). Currently, he is professor in the Communication Department and in the Graduate Program in Contemporary Communication and Culture that are part the Communication Faculty at the Federal University of Bahia. He is also the director of the "Research Laboratory in Digital Media, Networks and Space" at the Federal University of Bahia and founder of the "Brazilian Association of Researchers in Cyberculture." His academic interests include communication and sociology, with an emphasis on digital culture or cyberculture.

Julyane Felipette Lima is a nurse. She has a PhD in Nursing from the Federal University of Pelotas (2016). Currently, she is a professor at the Fronteira Sul Federal University, Chapecó, Santa Catarina, and a member of the "Group of Studies and Interdisciplinary Research of Health and Care" at the Federal University of Pelotas in Rio Grande do Sul and the "Laboratory Internet Health Society" (LaISS) of the Oswaldo Cruz Foundation. Her academic interests include social media, empowerment process, physician-patient relationship, cyber-activism, and advocacy.

Vera Lucia Luiza is a pharmacist with a PhD in Public Health from the Oswaldo Cruz Foundation (2003) and was postdoctoral fellow in Health Sciences at Harvard University (2009). As a public health researcher at the "Department of Medicines and Pharmaceutical Policies" in the National School of Public Health at Oswaldo Cruz Foundation, she has participated in or coordinated research projects on topics such as access to medicines, health evaluation, evaluation of pharmaceutical assistance, and primary health care in Brazil as well as in Latin America and Africa. She works in the area of collective health, with emphasis on pharmaceutical assistance and drug policy. Her academic interests include pharmaceutical services, rational use of medicines, drug policy, health evaluation, access to medicines, hospital pharmacy, study of drug use, and management of essential medicines.

Dilton C. S. Maynard has a PhD in History from the Federal University of Pernambuco (2008). He was postdoctoral fellow in History at the Federal University of Rio de Janeiro (2013) and an associate professor in the Graduate Program in Comparative History of the Federal University of Rio de Janeiro. Currently, he is a professor of the Graduate Program in Education at the Federal University of Sergipe. His academic interests include cyberculture and its appropriations by the new South American extreme right.

Ana Valéria M. Mendonça has a degree in Social Communication and a PhD in Information Sciences from the University of Brasília (2007), and completed a post-doctorate at the "Center de Recherche sur la Communication et la Santé" (ComSanté), Université du Québec à Montréal (2015). Currently, she is a professor in the Department of Collective Health at the University of Brasília where she is the coordinator of the Professional Masters in Public Health and the "Nucleus of Studies in Public Health" and heads the "Group of Studies and Research in Communication Information in Collective Health." She has experience in the areas of Information Science and Communication in Health. Her academic interests include health information and communication, digital inclusion, information and communication literacy, networks and social media, and distance learning.

Donizete Moreira has a degree in Information Systems (2006). He is a system analyst and administrator of distance education platforms in free software as well as produces material for virtual environments. His academic interest focuses on virtual learning environments.

Stephanie Muci has a MPH from the Bloomberg School of Public Health (2018) and an MBA from the Carey Business School (2018), both located at Johns Hopkins University where she worked as a researcher at the Women's and Children's Health Policy Center. She is a member of the American Public Health Association and Healthcare Business Association.

Monica Murero holds a PhD from New York University and is an associate professor at the University of Firenze, Federico II, where she is the director of "e-Life International Institute." She is the beneficiary of the "Rientro Cervelli Award" – the most prestigious Italian prize for distinguished international academics. Her research interests focus on innovative socio-technologies for health care, new media communication theory, online literacy, and the effects of the diffusion of information, communication, and technology in the society. During the last 20 years, she has been doing extensive research, professional consulting including for the World

Health Organization, and academic teaching in 6 countries. The comm-tech controversial effects of innovation upon human behavior and their steady encroachment into crucial aspect of everyday life appear in her work since the 1990s.

Márcia Niituma Ogata is a nurse with a PhD in Nursing from the University of São Paulo (2000). She did a postdoctorate in Health Sciences at the State University of Rio de Janeiro (2013). Currently, she is a professor in the Nursing Department at the Federal University of São Carlos, in the state of São Paulo, where she develops a line of research on public health policies, knowledge, representations, and practices. Her academic interests include permanent education in health, health policies and practices and their symbolic constructions, and quality of life of people living with HIV.

Brunela Della Maggiori Orlandi is a gerontologist with a PhD in Science, Technology, and Society from the Federal University of São Carlos, in the state of São Paulo (2018). She develops activities related to healthy aging and has an academic interest in active aging, public policy, info-inclusion, gerotechnology, and science and technology and health.

Rafael de Paula Aguiar Araújo is a sociologist with a PhD in Social Sciences from the Pontifical Catholic University of São Paulo (2009). He was postdoctoral fellow in Communication Sciences at the Autonomous University of Lisbon (2016). Currently, he is a researcher at the "Center for Studies in Art, Media and Politics" at the Pontifical Catholic University of São Paulo and a professor in the Graduate Studies Program in Social Sciences at the Pontifical Catholic University of São Paulo. He researches the areas of Political Science and Sociology, with emphasis on the sociology of technology, urban sociology, modern political theory, and media theory. His academic interests include public policies, communication and information technologies, and art, politics, and society.

Wilson José Alves Pedro is a sociologist with a PhD in Social Psychology from the Pontifical Catholic University of São Paulo (2002). Currently, he is a professor in the Graduate Program in Gerontology and in the Graduate Program in Science, Technology and Society at the Federal University of São Carlos in the state of São Paulo where heads the "Interdisciplinary Nucleus of Studies and Research in Gerontology." He is also a member of the Board of Directors of the "Association of Studies and Research on Aging" and the "Council of the Brazilian Society of Gerontotechnology." His academic interests include active aging, gerontechnology, management, work and retirement, lifelong learning, social protagonism, science, technology, and aging as well as culture and gender.

André Pereira Neto is a historian with a PhD in Collective Health from the State University of Rio de Janeiro (1997). He was a postdoctoral fellow in Sociology of Health at California University, San Francisco (2006). Currently, he is also professor of the Graduate Program in Information, Communication and Health at the Institute of Communication and Scientific and Technological Information in Health of the Oswaldo Cruz Foundation and coordinator of the "Laboratory Internet Health Society" (LaISS) linked to the Germano Sinval de Faria School Health Center of the National School of Public Health of the Oswaldo Cruz Foundation. His academic interests include empowerment process, expert patient, physician-patient relationship, evaluating the quality of information on health web sites, digital natives, and cyberbullying.

Rodolfo Paolucci has a degree in Computer Science and a master's in Information, Communication, and Health at the Institute of Communication and Scientific and Technological Information in Health of the Oswaldo Cruz Foundation (2015). Currently, he is a professor of Informatics at the State Technical School Oscar Tenório at the Foundation of Support to the Technical School of the Government of the State of Rio de Janeiro and is a researcher at the "Laboratory Internet Health Society" (LaISS) that is part of the Oswaldo Cruz Foundation. His academic interests include web development, applied technologies in the education, and evaluating quality of the information of health websites.

Lise Renaud is a sociologist with a PhD in Education and Health from the University of Montreal, Canada (1987). Currently, she is a professor in the Department of Social and Public Communication at the University of Quebec in Montreal, Canada. She has received diverse prizes including "Leadership Capacity: Framework for Implementing" offered by the "National Public Health Leadership Development Network," Chicago (2003). She researches how games and simulations are interventions and evaluates their capacity to achieve changes in individual attitudes and behaviors. Her academic interests include media and health, health promotion, the prevention of cardiovascular disease, and youth and communities.

Cristianne Maria Famer Rocha has a degree in Social Communication and a PhD in Education from the Federal University of Rio Grande do Sul (2005). She was a postdoctoral fellow at the Pan American Health Organization (2005) and at the National University of Distance Education, Spain (2013). Currently, she is a professor at the School of Nursing at the Federal University of Rio Grande do Sul. She works as a consultant for the Pan American Health Organization in different projects in Brazil and abroad. Her academic interests include health education, health communication, and collective health.

Thiago Augusto Hernandes Rocha is a psychologist with a master's in Business Administration from the Federal University of Minas Gerais (2011). He works with projects in the area of public health, with an emphasis on public policy evaluation and health data mining, and is a member of the Brazilian Society of Health Informatics. He has complementary training in spatial analysis, database analysis and development, machine learning, and business process modeling notation. His academic interests include public policy evaluation, the development of performance evaluation methodologies, data mining, geoprocessing, performance management, mapping processes, organizational restructuring, mHealth, business intelligence, big data, and data science applied to management.

Celita Almeida Rosário is a psychologist with a master's in Public Health from the Oswaldo Cruz Foundation (2015). She researches health policies, planning, management, and practices. Her academic interests include collective health, humanization policies, health training, health policies, and health evaluation.

Elizabeth Moreira dos Santos is a physician with a PhD in Community Health from the University of Illinois at Champaign-Urbana (1985). She has more than 20 years of experience in research, teaching, and consulting in evaluation and health, with an emphasis on program evaluation aimed at prevention, control, and eradication of endemic diseases and processes in Brazil and in African countries, particularly in Ethiopia. Her career combines academic experiences with practices in evaluation in different contexts. She plays a leading role in curriculum development and innovative teaching modalities at different levels of training in Monitoring and Evaluation in Brazil and Africa and coordinated the first Professional Master's Degree in Monitoring and Evaluation in Brazil, in partnership with the Ministry of Health, the Centers for Disease Control and Prevention and Tulane University (USA) that integrates the "Technical Reference Group on Global Fund Assessment." Her academic interests include the evaluation of the training processes and monitoring and evaluation of public policies.

Marcelo Burgos Pimentel dos Santos is a sociologist with a PhD in Social Sciences from the Pontifical Catholic University of São Paulo (2012). Currently, he is professor in the Department of Social Sciences and in the Graduate Program in Political Science and International Relations at the Federal University of Paraíba. He is also a researcher at the "Center for Post-Graduate Studies in Social Sciences" at the Pontifical Catholic University of São Paulo and the leader of the "Research Group on Aesthetics, Technique and Society" in the Department of Social Sciences at the Federal University of Paraíba. His academic interests include the use of information communication technologies by civil society, democratic participation, and municipal political processes.

Eda Schwartz is a nurse with a PhD in Nursing from the Federal University of Santa Catarina (2002). She is a professor in the Graduate Program in Nursing and in the Professional Masters and Family Health at the Federal University of Pelotas. Besides her membership in the International Family Nursing Association, she has experience in the area of nursing with emphasis in medical-surgical nursing. Her academic interests include nursing, family, nephrology, oncology, neoplasias, and chemotherapy.

Rosemary Segurado is a sociologist with a PhD in Social Sciences from the Pontifical Catholic University of São Paulo (2002). She was a postdoctoral fellow in Political Communication at the Rey Juan Carlos University of Madrid (2008). Currently, she is a professor and researcher at the Pontifical Catholic University of São Paulo; coordinator of the Media, Politics and Society Course at the School of

Sociology and Politics at the Foundation School of São Paulo; researcher at the "Center for Studies in Art, Media and Politics" of the Pontifical Catholic University of São Paulo; and editor of the "Aurora Magazine" of the Graduate Program in Social Sciences at the Pontifical Catholic University of São Paulo. Her academic interests include media and politics, the Internet and politics, political behavior, and the politics of the common.

Eduardo Jorge Custódio da Silva is a physician with a PhD in Children's Health from the "Fernandes Figueira Institute" at the Oswaldo Cruz Foundation (2002). Currently, he works as neurophysiologist at the Pedro Ernesto University Hospital of the State University of Rio de Janeiro and as a physician at the Institute of Psychiatry, Federal University of Rio de Janeiro. He has experience in medicine with an emphasis on neuropediatrics. His academic interests include deafness, epidemiology, hearing impairment, special education, and neurophysiology.

João Paulo Fernandes da Silva has a degree in Information Systems and a master's in Collective Health from the University of Brasília (2016) where he currently works as an administrative technician and researcher. His academic interests include social participation, collective health, health technology assessment, information technology, and public policy.

Nubia Cristina da Silva has a degree in Administration and a PhD in Administration from the Federal University of Minas Gerais (2014). She is a Researcher and Consultant of the "Interdisciplinary Nucleus in Management of (non) Business Organizations" at the Federal University of Minas Gerais and the "Observatory Workstation of the Health Work Labor Market in Health" of the State Health Department of Minas Gerais. She has complementary training in spatial analysis, database analysis, and development and in "Business Process Modeling Notation." She is also a consultant for the Pan American Health Organization. Her academic interests include public policy evaluation; development of performance evaluation methodologies; career management and salary policy; mapping processes in administration, with emphasis on human resources administration; and organizational restructuring.

Maria Fátima de Sousa is a nurse with a PhD in Health Sciences from the University of Brasília (2007). She was a postdoctoral fellow at the "Center de Recherche sur la Communication et la Santé" (ComSanté), Université du Québec à Montréal (2015). Currently, she is a professor in the Department of Collective Health and the Graduate Program in Collective Health in Faculty of Health Sciences at the University of Brasília where she was the director of the Faculty of Health Sciences. She was also vice-president of the Brazilian Association of Collective Health. Her academic interests include public health policies, models of health care, and management of local health systems.

Marcelo Simão de Vasconcellos is an industrial designer with a PhD in the Graduate Program in Information, Communication, and Health at the Institute of Communication and Scientific and Technological Information in Health of the Oswaldo Cruz Foundation (2013). His a health technologist at the Institute of Communication and Scientific and Technological Information in Health and professor in the Masters in Dissemination of Science, Technology, and Health program. He has experience in the area of visual programming, having worked mainly in graphic design, visual identity, and web design. He also researches and develops digital games for health, focusing on communication and health. His academic interests include social participation, serious games, and games applied to health.

João Ricardo Nickenig Vissoci is a psychologist with a PhD in Social Psychology from the Pontifical Catholic University of São Paulo (2015). He is a postdoctoral fellow at the University of São Paulo and at the Duke Global Health Institute at Duke University where he is a researcher in the Emergency Medicine Division of the Department of Surgery and research director at the Duke Global Neurosurgery and Neuroscience Division in the Department of Neurosurgery. He is also a leader of the "Methods, Analytics and Technology for Health" consortium and coordinator of the Global Emergency Medicine section. His academic interests include global health and human development and data analysis and implementation applied to global health.

Chapter 1
The Internet and Health in Brazil: Trends and Challenges

André Pereira Neto and Matthew B. Flynn

Abstract New information and communication technologies are increasingly present in our daily lives. Change occurred very fast. The sensation is that we live in another world. This new digital reality is where all or almost all economic, social, political, and cultural activities develop. They can be everywhere at the same time in people's everyday lives. However, digital exclusion and privacy on the Internet are some of the challenges that compromise the initial design of new information and communication technologies as universal, free, and secure by their very nature. In the field of health, the presence of the Internet transcends the technological realm. It is an emerging field characterized by the intersection of different spheres, practices, and knowledge (such as medical informatics), public health, and business. It can be considered a state of mind, a way of thinking, and an attitude that can improve health care. This chapter looks at where Brazil stands in this process, especially in the health field. It also presents the parts in which this book is divided.

New information and communication technologies are increasingly present in our daily lives. In recent years, they have converged into a single place: the modern-day cell phone. Originally intended only for conversation between two people, this device has gradually acquired several additional functionalities. We can send and receive messages by email, install a communication application such as WhatsApp to send text messages and images and even talk to another person anywhere in the world for free, take pictures and make videos, and then send them to another person anywhere in the world at no additional cost. We can also listen to music and watch a movie. Alarms can be set to wake us up in the morning and an agenda used to schedule and remind us about appointments. With the help of a search engine, we can visit a library or search for a school. If we get lost in a city, we will be able to

A. Pereira Neto (✉)
National School of Public Health, Oswaldo Cruz Foundation, Rio de Janeiro, Brazil

M. B. Flynn
Department of Political Science and International Studies & Department of Sociology and Anthropology, Georgia Southern University, Statesboro, GA, USA
e-mail: mflynn@georgiasouthern.edu

A. Pereira Neto, M. B. Flynn (eds.), *The Internet and Health in Brazil*,
https://doi.org/10.1007/978-3-319-99289-1_1

locate ourselves and be guided by the fastest route to reach our destination. We can receive news that interests us, as well as enter social networks and share information, experiences, and knowledge with many people. Smartphones have become small pocket-sized computers with Wi-Fi capabilities. There is an increasing trend in the number of applications that serve the most diverse interests. Access to these services occurs in fractions of a second. Spatial distance matters little. Thanks to the mobility inherent to the mobile device and the network infrastructure, we can receive or send information regardless of location. So, the cell phone currently assists in countless activities, besides talking on the phone.

Change occurred very fast, and those born before 1970 followed this unfolding closely. Fifty years ago, no one imagined that a device with so many functionalities would be in the palm of their hands. In this short period of time, the cell phone began to store increasingly more memory and operate at an increasingly faster speed. Most impressively, memory, speed, and features improve even more with each new device released. All these innovations have been accompanied by the progressive decline in prices of this equipment. Not surprisingly, there are currently about as many cell phones as there are people in the world, including in Brazil. According to data from the Brazilian Institute of Geography and Statistics (IBGE), there are 194.4 million cell phones in operation in a country with 185.7 million inhabitants. The data for 2017 also indicate that Brazil holds the fourth spot in the global ranking of nations with the largest number on online gamers.

Michael Haneke, 76, acclaimed Austrian director and screenwriter, winner of the Oscar for the best foreign movie in 2013, recently said that the smartphone has become an extension of our bodies. Haneke's view aligns with the results of "The Phone-Life Balance Study" (Etcoff 2018), conducted between November 30 and December 26, 2017. The survey, designed to gather information on the behavior of mobile phone users, involved 1100 users aged 16–65 in four countries, namely, Brazil, France, India, and the United States. The results suggest specific trends. A third (33%) of the respondents said that they prefer to use their cell phone instead of paying attention to people around them. Half of the respondents (53%) describe the smartphone as their best friend. Only 48% of Brazilians think they need to have a life separate from the smartphone, compared to 62% of French, 60% of Indians, and 69% of Americans. Another fact that has caught our attention relates to the feeling that users have when they think they have lost their cell phone: 56% of Brazilians panic, against 59% of French, 66% of Americans, and 77% of Indians.

As we mentioned earlier, the presence of smartphones in our lives is relatively recent. We are still living in a time when digital natives mingle with those born before the Internet and computers. Behavioral patterns and social perceptions of people's relationships with new information and communication technologies blend into a tangle that deserves in-depth understanding.

Are these new information and communication technologies, the epitome of which is the smartphone, different from traditional means of communication? We believe so. Let us see why.

Television, radio, and print media all have an information production center. Following this communication model, the users' role is restricted to receiving this information. Media owners decide what users should or should not know. With the new media, this power has increasingly shifted to our hands. We now have more power to choose what we want to know and see! If we access, for example, YouTube or Netflix, we decide which movie we want to watch. The channels geared to specific interests in these platforms multiply incessantly. The traditional media has been renamed mass media because it is targeted toward an undefined population. In contrast, post-mass media, such as through the Internet, deals with niches: fragmenting the traditional mass media consumer population into increasingly isolated audiences. Also, the media in mass media are limited, although there are hundreds of cable channels or radio stations. On the Internet, this number is incalculable. Furthermore, digital users are not just passive participants of streams of information. They comment, direct, and actively produce more content. In theory, they can dominate the entire creative process by building their community of users, establishing open links between them, neutralizing intermediation, and interacting directly with a market full of niches. These are a few of the differences that lead us to conclude that mass media are entirely different from post-mass media.

In Brazil, we use the verb "navigate" when we refer to accessing the Internet and looking for something or trying to communicate with someone. Brazilians believe the Internet is like the sea. In 1997, Brazilian singer-songwriter Gilberto Gil announced in his song "Pela Internet" that he would like to "create his website" and make his homepage to have "a boat that sails through this *infomar*": a word he created by joining two words, namely, *info* for information and *mar* for sea. He wanted to get into the "network and promote a debate." He wanted to gather "groupies from Connecticut" via the Internet and send an "email to Calcutta." He hoped "to contact the homes of Nepal and the bars of Gabon" through the network. This was the first song streamed live over the Internet in Brazil. In 2018, 21 years after the first edition, Gil released a second version with the same melody but with revised lyrics.[1] Before his presentation on a YouTube channel, the composer, born in 1942, said: "That's the way it goes: we're getting old, and the world is getting new." He admitted, in his new composition, that "everything is very well planned on the Internet!" In the 1997 lyrics, he stated that he could create a boat that sailed the *infomar* with 5 gigabytes. Now, 21 years later, his new fan page needs a terabyte.[2] "Each day is a new invention" – says the composer.

Statistics suggest that the desire to navigate the *infomar* is not restricted to the Brazilian musician. At the start of the century, the Internet had only 400 million users or 6.5% of the world's population. In 2015, according to the International Telecommunication Union (ITU) – a body linked to the United Nations – the number of Internet users in the world already reached 3.2 billion people, which is 43% of the world's population. The proportion of homes connected to the network reached 46% that year. The ITU also released data on the mobile Internet use. It reports that, in 2000, there were 738 million mobile connection subscriptions worldwide. By 2015, the cell phone was used by 4.4 billion people. This number is expected to reach 5.07 billion people by 2019 (Statista 2018).

[1] Pela Internet: https://www.youtube.com/watch?v=pGONgrm3mEU

[2] Terabyte is the measurement unit used for data storage in the computing area, equivalent to 1024 gigabytes.

Gilberto Gil and Michael Haneke are right: new information and communication technologies are becoming more and more pervasive. They tend to spread, infiltrate, propagate, or diffuse throughout human life. They bind us. They integrate different realms of people's lives throughout the world. Gil announces: "I am trapped in the net, like a fish when caught."

The sensation is that we live in another world. This new digital reality is where all or almost all economic, social, political, and cultural activities develop through new information and communication technologies.

In political terms, we can mention the "*Movimento Cinque Stelle*" in Italy, the "*Podemos*" in Spain, and the "*En Marche!*" in France. Ideologically different, all three share the fact that they carried out their political campaigns based mainly on digital communication. In 2009, Iranian youths took to the streets organizing themselves through the Bluetooth of cell phones. In 2010 and 2011, the "Arab Spring" was organized via Twitter. In 2013, it was Brazil's turn. Castells (2015) and many other social thinkers around the world have emphasized the singularities of social movements via the Internet.

The impact of digital networks affects not only political mobilization but also new economic opportunities. The *Forbes*' list of billionaires (2018) can serve as a yardstick for measuring the economic importance of new information and communication technologies. Who is the richest citizen in the world? Jeff Bezos who was born in 1964. Does he own a factory? Is he a farmer? No. He owns *Amazon* – the leading e-commerce company in the world. He became the richest man in the world, surpassing Bill Gates, founder of Microsoft because his company's stocks soared 59% in 2017. His fortune went from $72.8 billion to $112 billion.

Another example can be identified in collective financing. Crowdfunding has become a feasible alternative to obtain financing and to achieve successful new ventures. In fact, companies built with collective financing ensure a significant share of new jobs generated each year. This funding model has not only created a billion-dollar global market but has added value to projects by drawing businesses and consumers even closer together. The company comes to know firsthand the tastes and needs of its customer. It often invites its potential clients to participate in the development of a new project. The consumer becomes a collaborator and an investor, who receives exclusive benefits, pre-acquires products, engages in social causes, and may even own a stake in the company.

The United Nations' Sustainable Development Goals (2020/2030) consist of 17 goals aimed at eradicating poverty and promoting economic growth, social inclusion, environmental sustainability, and world peace through collective partnerships. In a broadcast available on the Internet (ITU 2018), Ban Ki-moon (UN Secretary-General) said that "people everywhere can reap the benefits of connectivity." He concludes by stating: "We will empower individuals with these transformative technologies so they can advocate and innovate for our common future."

Ubiquitous. This word means that something is or can be everywhere at the same time. Omnipresent. This is another expression that has been associated with the reality of new information and communication technologies in people's everyday lives. The emerging trend is the "Internet of Things" that connects items used in our daily routines to the World Wide Web.

However, let us not be naive! The expansion of new information and communication technologies is taking place in a turbulent sea with numerous storms. It involves tense, complex navigation, where caution is necessary.

One of the obstacles is the important social dimension: not everyone has access to the Internet. Despite the aforementioned growth, barriers to connect online are almost always associated with peoples' living conditions. The ITU warns that, although access has increased over the past 15 years, 4 billion people are still disconnected worldwide. Digital exclusion is highest in less developed countries, where only 89 million people have a connection out of a total of 940 million. They reside in places where wireless networks do not reach them. Also, many people do not access the Internet due to its high cost. Considered the creator of the World Wide Web, Tim Berners-Lee recently stated that "unsurprisingly, you're more likely to be offline if you are female, poor, live in a rural area or a low-income country, or some combination of the above."

There is also a substantial proportion of users with access to the network but do not know how to deal with the innumerable functionalities inherent to the new information and communication technologies.

Thus, digital exclusion is also associated with mastering specific skills required to use these technologies. In this group, worth noting is the illiterate population residing in the impoverished parts of the planet and not taking advantage of these technologies. Either way, digital exclusion is the current metaphor of social exclusion. Also, the sea of information is turning into a deluge. It is the arena where correct information clashes with incorrect and unreliable information. In many cases, fraud is virulent. Recently, the issue of fake news involves political personalities in Brazil and the United States and has become a weapon for those interested in interfering in a country's political debate.

Another problem is associated with the IP (Internet Protocol) of each computer or cell phone. When a user sends information over the Internet, someone knows. For example, when we buy a plane ticket to a specific location over the Internet, we immediately receive restaurant ads that we should go to in the city we are visiting. If we send many messages related to the environment, we will soon receive product promotions for extreme sports or organic or macrobiotic food. These agencies build our profile and start selling our IP according to our standard of production and consumption of information. That is why people with an environmental profile will hardly receive messages or advertisements advocating genetically modified agricultural production. Gradually, a bubble is formed where green-oriented people only receive messages that value organic and natural production. These ads and messages are not sent to adepts of pesticides.

Information has currently become the primary asset in the economic environment. Data that each of us unpretentiously makes available daily is transformed into value and generates fortunes. Its importance is so evident that it is often referred to as the "Information Society." In this context, the richest companies in the world are those who know best how to manage and convert information we inject daily on the

Internet into money and competitive advantage. Thus, information posted or obtained on the Internet is collected and stored by information and business agencies such as Google and Facebook. This information is sold to other companies. For this reason, they are two of the most profitable companies in the world. Tim Berners-Lee stated that "what was once a rich selection of blogs and websites has been compressed under the powerful weight of a few dominant platforms."

Digital information does not only have a commercial value. Government bureaucratic systems appropriate information flows and communications for the interests of national security, surveillance, and political control. In this regard, Edward Snowden is an exemplary case. He made public the details of the programs used by the information system of the United States' intelligence agencies to establish a global surveillance program of each of us, especially public persons. One thing seems increasingly clear: our privacy is strongly threatened. The freedom to insert and send messages, found in the original design of the Internet, seems to be in jeopardy, as it has become a high-value commodity. Furthermore, autocratic regimes are also known to track dissidents' online activities and police web content perceived as threatening. If political unrest occurs, the first move by repressive governments is to shut down Twitter and other social media.

In these terms, digital exclusion and privacy on the Internet are some of the challenges that compromise the initial design of new information and communication technologies as universal, free, and secure by their very nature.

Where does Brazil stand in this process? How is access to the Internet evolving? Two different trends converge in this country: digital exclusion and increased access. Digital exclusion is closely associated with the structural problems of Brazilian society. Recent data released by IBGE indicate that 25% of the population lives on or below a household income equivalent to US$ 5.50. Class differences intersect with racial hierarchies. In the bottom quartile of the population comprised of some 50 million, the African-descendant population makes up 78.5% of this strata compared to whites who account for 20.8%. Despite recent efforts in the opposite direction, Brazil continues to be a country with high levels of income inequality, even when compared to other Latin-American nations. Furthermore, illiteracy rates are incredibly high. In 2016, IBGE's National Household Sample Survey (PNAD) revealed that the illiteracy rate reached 7.2%, which translates into approximately 11.8 million illiterates aged 15 years or more living in Brazil.

Digital exclusion can be measured in numbers. The "Internet Steering Committee (CGI.br)" frequently conducts national surveys to verify the expansion of the Internet in the country. Data of the study published in 2017 show that only 59% of households in urban centers are connected. This rate drops to 26% in rural areas. The population's income levels and years of schooling explain in part this reality. The CGI.br data indicate that the Internet is present in 29% of households with income of up to one Brazilian minimum wage per month (which corresponds to approximately US$ 300), against a rate of 97% in those earning up to 10 minimum wages. Also, private telephone companies must cover 80% of the urban area from the center of the municipalities that encompass up to 30 square kilometers. As a result, companies concerned about their profits disregard places where the population is small and resides far from urban centers.

Increasing access can also be verified. The data provided by the United Nations Conference on Trade and Development (UNCTAD 2017) places Brazil fourth in the world ranking of Internet users: 120 million Brazilians are connected, which corresponds approximately to 57% of the population! In absolute numbers, Brazil lags behind only China (705 million), India (333 million), and the United States (242 million). After Brazil, we find Japan (118 million), Russia (104 million), Nigeria (87 million), Germany (72 million), Mexico (72 million), and the United Kingdom (59 million). The same report also evaluated the growth rate of Internet access in recent years, considering the 2012–2015 period. According to this study, Brazil's average growth in the period was 3.5%, behind Mexico (5.9% %), Nigeria (4.9%), Japan (4.6%), and India (4.5%) (UNCTAD 2017). Rich countries, such as the United States, Germany, and the United Kingdom, have seen a slower Internet access growth pace, as most of the population already has access.

The "Brazilian Telecommunications Association" (Telebrasil 2018) released a survey conducted in the third quarter of 2017, which indicates that data revenues (e.g., over the Internet) from mobile operators surpassed voice revenues (i.e., phone calls). It also found that there are already 95 million 4G and 92 million 3G cell phone handsets in Brazil.

What role can new information and communication technologies play in health?

In a premonitory text, Eysenbach (2001) sought to answer this question by defining the concept e-health. Stating that the Internet-health interface transcends the technological realm, he argues that it is an emerging field characterized by the intersection of different spheres, practices, and knowledge (such as medical informatics), public health, and business. His vision of e-health, therefore, surpasses the mere technological realm and highlights a state of mind, a way of thinking, and an attitude. Finally, he emphasizes that using information and communication over the Internet can improve health care.

In the same text, the author associates ten other expressions, beginning with the letter "e," like e-health, which would characterize this emerging field. We grouped them into two categories of questions and concerns the author had 17 years ago.

The first group refers to the quality, efficiency, and comprehensiveness of health care through the Internet. The author advocates that e-health should translate into efficiency and thus lead toward decreasing costs. Also, he argues that e-health is based on evidence proven through rigorous scientific evaluation. Internet-based medical care, now called telemedicine, could extend the scope of health care beyond its conventional boundaries. This is meant in both a geographical sense and in a conceptual sense. These services, in his view, can range from simple advice to more complex interventions or pharmaceutical products. New information and communication technologies could allow for standardized exchange of information and communication between health-care establishments.

The second group of questions and concerns considers the impact that changes in access and use of the information obtained and shared over the Internet have on the doctor-patient relationship. Eysenbach (2001) highlighted the empowerment of consumers and patients. In this case, e-health opens new avenues for patient-centered medicine and enables evidence-based patient choice. He further said that information and communication technologies encourage a new relationship between the patient and health professional, toward a true partnership, where decisions are shared. Accordingly, Eysenbach predicted that the treatment decisions adopted would be in the hands of the patient or would be shared with the doctor. The doctor-patient relationship would not be asymmetric. Therefore, education would be necessary for both physicians through online sources (continuing medical education) and consumers (health education, tailored preventive information for consumers, etc.). This new relationship should impose new types of ethical conduct, insofar as e-health involves new forms of patient-physician interaction and poses new challenges and threats to moral issues, such as online professional practice, informed consent, privacy, and equity issues. Accordingly, health professionals, ranging from primary physicians, specialists, pharmacists, and other caregivers, can share vital patient information to ensure complementary health care. With a lot of information at their disposal, individuals could compare the services provided and choose the one that suits them best. Where health services are rendered in a market governed by the free competition between companies, this attitude is seen as something that enhances the quality of care.

Dr. Muir Gray, director of United Kingdom's National Health Service, believes we are in the "midst of the Third Health Revolution."[3] The first was public health, and the second was the revolution promoted by high-tech medicine. Now, the three revolutionary forces are knowledge, the Internet, and the patient. He concludes his interview by stating: "We have to recognize that the Internet changes everything, including clinical practice." Many of his warnings have turned into questions or problems.

The decreasing costs resulting from the efficiency of e-health remain a controversial issue. Health information available on the Internet is not always based on the rigorous scientific evaluation. The problem concerning the quality of health information on websites is constant. Despite this, many people follow these guidelines. Some medical practitioners, represented by professional associations, often resist telemedicine, especially for the diverse set of services it can provide. The changes in the doctor-patient relationship advocated by the Eysenbach (2001) are still in the making. Patient empowerment through online information is increasing, but the decision about the most appropriate treatment is hardly shared. The survival of the asymmetrical doctor-patient relationship seems evident to us.

In our view, the weight of tradition is the main challenge to be faced in Brazil by those who understand that new information and communication technologies play a prominent role when it comes to health.

In the first place, it is crucial to highlight mass media's current hegemony in Brazil. This leadership has been conquered over the last two centuries. The ordinary citizen continues to prefer information obtained through television broadcasts. In fact, it should be noted that the situation is very critical in Brazil since five families

[3] Interview with Sir Muir Gray: https://www.youtube.com/watch?v=AQjsS9K8-cQ&t=8s

control the main communication vehicles with the largest audience in the country. The case of the Globo Group stands out. It maintains the largest audience on open channels, cable channels, radio stations, and various print media. Globo's audience is larger than the sum of the four other groups (Intervozes 2018).

This tradition extends to health managers, who still print paper leaflets that are distributed to people gathering in public places, as they have done for over a hundred years. In government agencies, online communication continues to play a residual role. Tuberculosis is a case in point. Brazil is included in the list of the 22 countries that concentrate 80% of the cases of this disease in the world. In spite of this, only 12 of the 27 state health secretariats in the country had a tuberculosis website or webpage. In municipal health departments, the situation is even worse. Of the 5570 municipal health secretariats in Brazil, only 8 had a tuberculosis website or webpage.

The "Internet, Health and Society Laboratory" (LaISS) of the Oswaldo Cruz Foundation in Rio de Janeiro researched the quality of information on 20 dengue, 12 tuberculosis, and 19 breastfeeding sites linked to public and private institutions. The results showed that only 14 of these sites achieved 60–70% of the compliance criteria and indicators used in the assessment (LaISS 2018).

The weight of tradition can also be observed in Brazil's academic sphere. Research and debate about the interfaces between the Internet and health are practically ignored in scientific associations and journals related to public health.

Despite the weight of tradition in Brazil, some initiatives related to new information and communication technologies deserve to be highlighted. They reveal current trends and challenges to those who work in and analyze this social phenomenon. Many of these issues are covered in this book that examines these trends and delves into some of the problems mentioned above. To begin this journey, Monica Murero, an Italian Internet researcher, introduces her vison about the Internet and e-health care as an interdigital field of study in the foreword text preceding this chapter.

The subsequent body of this book is divided into six parts.

The first part will address the emergence and development of the Internet in Brazil. It consists of four chapters. The second chapter analyzes the construction of Brazil's Internet between 1995 and 2015 to contextualize its origins and growth amidst the global spread of the web. The third shows how Brazil succeeded in passing progressive legislation establishing principles, warranties, rights, and duties governing the Internet. The fourth describes one of the first cities to offer free access to the Internet in the world – Piraí, a small city in Brazil's interior. The fifth analyzes a political experiment in e-participation, focused on the "*Nossas Cidades*" (Our Cities) network, that was developed to facilitate civil society groups' demand-making on local public authorities. They are, thus, chapters that highlight Brazil's uniqueness and pioneering efforts in the expansion and consolidation of the Internet.

In the second part, we will explore four key audiences at the interface of the Internet and health: the patient, the young, the elderly, and the social media user. In the first case, the impact of available and shared information on the Internet and the emergence of the "expert patient" are addressed. In this case, action profiles of virtual communities that gather patients with chronic diseases will be shown. The next chapter concerns how young people from different social classes access the Internet and use the available health information. The third chapter in this section discusses how the elderly should access the Internet for active aging. The last chapter in this section details the most popular Facebook page about health and the Internet.

In the third part, we will discuss some of the main challenges related to the expansion and use of the Internet throughout the world by covering important health topics: information quality, safety, cyberbullying, and medicines. The four chapters that integrate this third part adopt different theoretical perspectives. The chapter on the quality of information shows Brazil's innovative experiences on the subject. The next two chapters provide conceptual reviews of health risks associated with the Internet. The first reviews various problematic issues that excessive online activity has on the cognitive and physiological development of young people. The next chapter illuminates the Brazilian experience of how digital technologies mediate bullying and cyberbullying. The following chapter highlights the new opportunities and risks the Internet offers in relation to medicines by considering its global dimension and contrasting cases of the United States and Brazil.

The fourth part is devoted to experiences in health education conducted through the Internet. It consists of four chapters. The first describes an e-learning experience and shows some of the challenges it faced to achieve its goals. The second shows Brazilian massive open online courses (MOOC) initiatives in the field of health. The third details about the experience of the University of São Paulo Medical School in the training physicians using digital innovations. The fourth shows the impact of an online professional training course on community health workers enrolled in the class.

The fifth part of this book highlights and analyzes some practical applications of new information and communication technologies in health. This part consists of four chapters. The first examines smart wearable devices and the barriers toward their widespread adoption given a challenging local context. The second showcases Brazilian experiences using new information and communication technologies for health promotion. The third demonstrates Brazil's contribution in the use of online games and their importance for health. The next chapter discusses the Internet of Things (IoT) applied to health in Brazil.

The last part and final chapter provides a global overview of future trends and challenges along with an overview of how to evaluate the introduction of new digital technologies.

The majority of authors include professors and researchers from Brazilian academic institutions of excellence located in different regions of the country. Some have written more critical and reflective texts. Others highlight new and innovative experiences. Some chapters analyze the academic research and publications in a particular field of knowledge or action.

In sum, the chapters offer an overview of Brazil's unique experiences with the Internet in general and its relationship to health in particular. They show the various trends and challenges faced by multiple stakeholders, including civil society groups, government officials, corporate interests, and individual end users. The rollout of new digital technologies in Brazil will retain a dynamic unto itself.

Nonetheless, the trends illustrated throughout this book are not exclusive to the country. Like any new technology, the hopes and promises, as well as the challenges and pitfalls, the Internet encompasses will continue to play out throughout much of the developing world and even parts of the developed world. The lessons provided throughout should help illuminate others interested in navigating this complex digital web that draws us together in new ways but that also continues to highlight essential differences in our society as well as in our health and well-being.

References

Castells, Manuel. 2015. *Networks of outrage and hope: Social movements in the internet age*. Cambridge: Polity.

Etcoff, Nancy. 2018. Motorola phone-life balance study: Data report by generations. https://www.ipsos.com/sites/default/files/ct/news/documents/2018-02/motorola-phone-life-balance-study-topline-2018-02-21.pdf. Accessed 26 June 2018.

Eysenbach, Gunther. 2001. What is e-health? *Journal of Medical Internet Research* 3: e20.

Intervozes – Coletivo Brasil de Comunicação Social. Media Ownership Monitor – Brazil. 2018. http://brazil.mom-rsf.org/en/. Accessed 16 June 2018.

ITU – International Telecommunication Union. 2018. ICTs for a Sustainable World #ICT4SDG. https://www.itu.int/en/sustainable-world/Pages/default.aspx. Accessed 26 June 2018.

LaISS – Laboratório Internet, Saúde e Sociedade. 2018. Avaliação de Sites – Resultados. http://laiss.ensp.fiocruz.br/pesquisa/buscar. Accessed 26 June 2018.

Statista. 2018. Number of mobile phone users worldwide from 2015 to 2020 (in billions). https://www.statista.com/statistics/274774/forecast-of-mobile-phone-users-worldwide/. Accessed 26 June 2018.

Telebrasil. 2018. Telebrasil – Associação Brasileira de Telecomunicações. http://www.telebrasil.org.br/. Accessed 26 June 2018.

UNCTAD – United Nations Conference on Trade and Development. 2017. *Information economy report: Digitalization, trade and development*. Geneva: United Nations.

Part I
The Emergence and Development of the Internet in Brazil

Chapter 2
An Introduction to the History of the Internet: A Brazilian Perspective

Dilton C. S. Maynard

> *The second flood will be endless. There is no solid bed beneath the ocean of information. We should accept this as our new reality. We have to teach our children to swim, to float, perhaps to navigate.*
>
> *Lévy (2000, 15)*

Abstract In the twenty-first century, the world has been restructured around the Internet. From economies, cultural activities, government policies, commercial enterprises, military action, sporting events, and educational policies to health policies and procedures are all conceived from the starting point of their presence on the web. Thus, considering its growth and the impact of the global computer network on our day-to-day lives, the purpose of this chapter is to present a historical perspective of the implementation and popularization of the Internet, with particular attention to the situation in Brazil. This chapter covers the construction of the Internet, revealing a process that began at the end of the 1950s, and focuses on the transformations it went through between 1995 and 2017. From the formative nodes that grew into what is now the Internet, the chapter traces the path of how its adoption and its popularization in Brazil resulted from the tension between the different sectors involved in its installation and in the efforts to expand the global computer network.

D. C. S. Maynard (✉)
Education of Human Sciences Center, Federal University of Sergipe, Aracaju, Brazil
e-mail: dilton@getempo.org

A. Pereira Neto, M. B. Flynn (eds.), *The Internet and Health in Brazil*,
https://doi.org/10.1007/978-3-319-99289-1_2

2.1 Memories of the Second Flood[1]

The physicist Albert Einstein (1879–1955) once stated that the twentieth century had experienced three great explosions: the demographic, the atomic, and that of telecommunications. Roy Ascott[2] termed this last "bomb" the "second flood," to say that, as in the first flood described in the Bible, humanity had experienced an overwhelming and unavoidable phenomenon, something that had changed the world. However, unlike the times of Noah, the waters of this new flood are made up of data, news, images, music, and everything else which circulates in the electronic universe. The ocean is now made of information.[3] This new place is what we call the Internet.

While the Internet originated in the 1960s, for most people it began in 1995. And, since its "birth," this innovation has networked our lives. But what is this? What is this means of communication that seems omnipotent and incessantly revolutionary? Put basically, it is "the network of the networks; the collection of hundreds of networks of connected computers in diverse countries in six continents," the Internet – an abbreviation of INTERaction or INTERconnection between computer NETworks, the equivalent of an information highway – or, more accurately, an information superhighway (Gates 1995), a term coined by the former senator Al Gore (Senior) in 1978, in a reference to the highways opened in the USA by President Dwight D. Eisenhower during his terms of office (1953–1961).

The idea for what we now call the Internet came about as a result of experiments with the ARPANET, a network of computers set up in September 1969 by ARPA – *Advanced Research Projects Agency*, an institution founded in 1958 by the US Defense Department. ARPA had the job of managing research resources, principally in the university sphere, with the aim of attaining technological military superiority over the Union of Soviet Socialist Republics (USSR), serving as a type of North American institutional response to the launch of the first satellite, Sputnik,[4] in 1957.

> In those times, when the dispute between the two post-war superpowers – USA and USSR – was tied to technological achievements in space, "astronauts were idolized as typical American heroes by taking on the cold-war enemy in the heavens," according to Richard

---

[1] This chapter is an updated version of the initial text of the book *Writings on History and the Internet*, published by the author (Maynard 2011).

[2] Roy Ascott, British artist and theoretician. Since the 1960s, he has pioneered the interaction between cybernetics, telematics, and art. Ascott undertook several projects in global network and published more than 70 texts. Professor of technology at the University of Plymouth, England, and adjunct professor of design/media arts at the University of California Los Angeles

[3] Chapter 10 addresses the theme of online health information.

[4] Launched on October 4, 1957, Sputnik was the first in a series of artificial satellites created by the Soviet Union. Among its purposes was the contribution in collecting information for a possible space travel. As Heitor Shimizu (2006, 18) explains, "today, with so much equipment in orbit of the earth, sending signals to all parts of the planet, it is difficult to understand the importance of its precursor. But in 1957, only 12 years after the end of World War II, when television became popular and rock rehearsed its first steps, the little metal ball thrown at his was a shock."

Barbrook (2009). Despite this, for a time the Soviets were in the lead. Not content with putting the first satellite in orbit, the Soviets went on to send the first cosmonaut, Yuri Gagarin (1934–1968) into space. To the horror of the Americans, this soldier became a celebrity. In 1961, "the Russian visited Rio de Janeiro and São Paulo, where he was greeted by crowds, and Brasilia, where he was decorated by the then President Janio Quadros." (Shimizu 2006)

As such, the emergence of the Internet simultaneously has its roots in two worlds (Castells 2003). In one way, it was designed in the bipolarized scenario generated by the Cold War (1945–1991) and, at the same time, in a decentralized environment, teeming with pacifist protests and counterculture (Willer 2009). Placing the creation of the global network in this environment is essential because, as Roy Rosenzweig claims, "Understanding this dual heritage enables us to better understand current controversies over whether the Internet will be 'open' or 'closed'—over whether the Net will foster democratic dialogue or centralized hierarchy, community or capitalism, or some mixture of both" (Rosenzweig 2006). And, from within this opaque zone, with its illusory sensation of immediacy, it is essential to tell the story, though still provisional and introductory, of the global computer network.

An initial observation is the Internet resulted from the work of different institutions. Universities, software companies, governmental organizations, and military corporations have been involved, with different intensities, in the construction of the nodes than became the network of networks. After almost four decades of existence, this great innovation became viable for commercial uses in the 1990s. This innovation was the result of the fusion of three fundamental processes:

1. Economic demands for administrative flexibility and globalization of capital for production and commerce
2. Social demands in which the values of individual liberty and communication became supreme
3. The microelectronic revolution that permitted important advances in telecommunications and computing

However, the concept of the Internet was not only down to ARPANET. Considering other important contributions is necessary including those which Manuel Castells called the "traditional foundation of computer networks" (Castells 2003, 6). One of these contributors was the *Bulletin Board Systems*, a system of notice boards which arose from the interconnection of personal computers at the end of the 1970s. This system, together with programs such as MODEM, created in 1977 by Ward Christensen and Randy Suess, students at Chicago University, enabled files to be transferred between personal computers. One year later, the same students wrote another program, named the *Computer Bulletin Board System*, allowing messages to be stored and transmitted between personal computers.

Years before the appearance of the program mentioned above, in 1975, ARPANET was transferred to the DCA – *Defense Communication Agency*. One and a half decades later, in 1990, the network was put under the control of the *National Science Foundation*, and shortly, other networks with a similar structure, but now with commercial bases, appeared. According to Manuel Castells:

> From then on, the Internet grew rapidly as a global computer network. What made this possible was the original Project of ARPANET, based on a multiple layer architecture and open communication protocols. Under these conditions, the Net could expand by adding new nodes and by the infinite reconfiguration of the network to meet communication needs. (Castells 2003)

ARPANET was a small program within ARPA, connected to the *Information Processing Techniques Office* (IPTO), created in 1962, one of ARPA's departments. This department was under the control of Joseph Licklider, a psychologist from the *Massachusetts Institute of Technology* (MIT). The idea was to increase research into interactive computing. Due to this collaborative focus, ARPANET allowed various departments to exchange information. Sharing was to be done by packet switching, following the procedure developed by Paul Baran of the Rand Corporation, a research and policy institute affiliated with the Pentagon. Donnal Davies, from the *British National Physical Laboratory*, was also involved. But what did this project consist of?

2.2 A Novel on Postcards

Baran's switching project proposed a flexible military communication network, capable of surviving a nuclear attack, something that seemed quite probable given the level of antagonism between the two Cold War superpowers. The information that was divided up into packets would arrive gradually at its destination. In this way, Baran started telematic communication. It was, as he explained, like writing a novel on postcards. Instead of sending the receiver the content of a novel, all bound, the idea was to send the text in pieces. Only after receiving the final package could it be assembled and understood.

For this, Paul Baran proposed a hybrid system which made use of telephone, satellite, and radio communication. Then, in 1973 came the Transmission Control Protocol (TCP).[5] A revolutionary model emerged. Instead of centralized communication, the inverse was proposed, investing in decentralization and flexibility (Cyclades 2000). In this way, the protocol enabled machines with individual characteristics, and even with different languages, to communicate. Later, in 1978, this convention was divided into two parts, and an intranet protocol (IP) was added. This addition generated the TCP/IP network protocol – standard on the Internet to this day.

However, it is important to note that the ARPANET project did not have explicit military objectives. The conception of a decentralized network involved several

[5] "On a TCP/IP network, each equipment must have an individual address, capable of identifying it on the network. Those addresses, called IP addresses, are 32-bit numbers, represented by 4 fields of integer decimal numbers, separated by the dot character. Each field can assume values from 0 to 225 and corresponds to 1 byte of the IP address in the form of bits. Each IP address contains the network address to which the device belongs and the address of the device itself within that network." See Cyclades (2000, 8).

institutions, such as the University of California in Los Angeles, the Stanford Research Institute (SRI), the University of California in Santa Barbara, and the University of Utah. From this cooperative work came the idea of connecting ARPANET to two other networks, PRNET (Packet Radio Network, developed for switching packages in a military tactical environment) and to SATNET (intended for satellite control). With its implementation, the concept of a network of networks was more clearly defined as "a kind of serpent's nest with thousands of heads and at the same time without any head" (Mazzeo 2000, 7).

This connection is important, because it transformed the Internet – something that was previously limited to hackers, scientists, and the military, eager to overthrow others, especially if these "others" were the Soviet enemy– into a platform for the new world that was developing: a networked society. Therefore, in summary, the Internet emerged due to a unique convergence: military research, cutting-edge science, and a culture of freedom (expressed, e.g., by the anti-war movements of the 1960s). As fundamental components of this process, 15 "nodes" formed the network in 1971. They were all basically university research centers, institutions that led this field until the early 1980s.

2.3 The Paths to the World Wide Web

The ARPA project was carried out by *Bolt, Beranek, and Newman* (BBN), an acoustic engineering firm from Boston that started to work in the field of applied computer science. Professors from MIT founded the firm, and engineers and scientists from both MIT and Harvard staffed it.

In 1975 ARPANET was transferred to the *Defense Communication Agency* (DCA). But, with a view to working on communication between the computers on the various networks under its control, the DCA created the *Defense Data Network*, operating with the TCP/IP network protocols. However, in 1983, worried about possible security breaches, the Defense Department decided to create MILNET, an independent network with specific military objectives. Consequently, the ARPANET became the ARPANET-Internet, to be used solely for research.

Shortly after the creation of the MILNET, and after the Internet had been transferred to the *National Science Foundation* (NSF) in 1984, the latter established its computer communications network (called NSFnet). In 1988, the ARPANET-Internet began to be used as a *backbone* (physical network infrastructure through which electric currents known as signals pass) of the NSF. Years later, in 1989, the World Wide Web (also known as WWW, or web) was ready, having been created in the CERN Nuclear Research Laboratory in Geneva, Switzerland. A strategic part of the commercial success of the web came from a project to interconnect researchers in various institutions via the Internet. These days, the WWW is, without doubt, the main reason for the recent growth of the network. It makes things easier for network users because it is an application that runs on the "previous layers" of the Internet (Lévy 2000, 27).[6] It creates a "web" that is capable of connecting documents via the Internet.

In 1990, the ARPANET, long considered obsolete, was taken out of service. Finally, the Internet was free from the military sphere. After being transferred to the NSF, the Internet became attractive to service providers, who built their networks and established commercial communication gateways. As a result, the Internet snowballed. But what made this dizzying growth possible? Probably, the original ARPANET project. It was based on multilayer architecture, which was decentralized and had open communication protocols. These protocols enabled the network to expand with new nodes, an ability for infinite reconfiguration to take account of communication needs (Cyclades 2000). As a consequence of this, the Internet has a capacity for almost nonstop self-redesign.

The Cold War created a favorable context for applying scientific resources. The goal was to beat the Soviets. However, it is important to note that ARPA had considerable autonomy, even though it was linked to the military. The staff were scientists, as well as their friends and students. The researchers' objective was to produce something that was simultaneously important for the military and profitable for the economy. So, since the 1980s, the Department of Defense has encouraged manufacturers to include the TCP/IP network protocols on their computers.

We should also consider the political impulse that the network gained as a result of the election of Bill Clinton, whose vice was Al Gore Jr. Defeating the incumbent president George Bush (Senior), Clinton included the popularization of the Internet as one of his campaign promises. The Internet became part of the political landscape as the most visible part of what was called the Information Society.

Eventually, in 1995 the Internet became a private business, too. At the end of its first year of operation, 16 million users had navigated the electronic ocean. In 2001, this had already become around 400 million. In December 2017 the figure of 4 billion people connected to the Internet had been reached, according to Miniwatts Marketing Group, who administers the website Internet World Stats (2018).[7] This growth was accompanied by another significant change, as over the years, the web, initially based in the USA, established itself as global media:

> An interesting statistic revealed in the research is that the internet is no longer a USA-centric media and has instead become global. Presently, 21% of people accessing the web are from the USA, whereas in 1966 the figure was 66%.
>
> […]
>
> According to the study, the number of people using social network sites such as Orkut, MySpace, Facebook e LinkedIn, reached 530 million a year, which corresponds to a growth of 34%. The numbers become even more impressive when comScore claims that these sites attract more than 100 million visitors a month, and that two out of every three people that

[6] For Pierre Lévy (2000, 27) the WWW is "an Internet function that brings together all the documents and hypertexts that feed it in a single hypertext or hyperdocument (comprising images and sounds)."

[7] The number presented by the website for December 31, 2017 is 4,156,932,140 users, 54% of the world population.

use the internet navigate on social network sites, principally YouTube, which attracted more than 250 million users world wide in January. (Internet World Stats 2009)

Here is some more data: according to Pierre Lévy, in the 1970s, the ARPANET network possessed, in the USA, nodes which supported 56,000 bits per second.[8] Later, in the 1980s, the lines on the networks connecting American scientists could transport 1.5 million bits per second. This growth continued, and in 1992, "lines on the same network could transmit 45 million bits per second" (Lévy 2000, 36). This is the same as saying that it was possible to transmit the equivalent of an encyclopedia per minute.

The importance of the web goes beyond numbers. As Nicholas Negroponte (1995, 11) wrote, "information no longer has anything to do with computers. It has to do with people's lives." So, economies, cultural activities, government policies, commercial enterprises, health policies, and procedures are all conceived from the starting point of their presence on the web. As such, Castells (2003, 8) claims that "to be excluded from these networks is to suffer one of the most damaging forms of exclusion in our economy and in our culture." In Brazil, the difficulty of overcoming this problem is demonstrated by the long way there is still to go to reduce the exclusion of millions of people with computers yet without the Internet (Santana 2009).

2.4 The Internet: Brazilian Style

In Brazil the Internet began commercially in 1995, accompanying what was happening in other parts of the world. However, years before, the São Paulo State Research Support Foundation (FAPESP) and the Federal University of Rio de Janeiro (UFRJ) already used a network, supported by international partners, principally laboratories and universities, mainly in the USA. As can be seen, the academic environment was almost an isolated "locus" of the network until then.

In truth, efforts to include Brazil in an international network date back in the 1970s. The Brazilian Telecommunications Company (EMBRATEL) commanded a monopoly of the sector, as was true of other state companies at the time. At the end of 1979, the National Laboratory of Computer Networks (*Laboratório Nacional de Redes de Computadores* – LARC) was created. This network was later renamed the National Research Network (*Rede Nacional de Pesquisa* – RNP) in 1989, with the objective of giving international networks access to Brazilian academic systems. In the following decade, acting as an academic backbone provider, RNP included 600 institutions and served approximately 65,000 users.[9]

Before consolidation, the initial advances were apparently fundamental but straightforward for the development of the network. In 1989, Brazil received ".br"

[8] Bit stands for "binary digit" and is the smallest unit of data used in computing.

[9] For more information about the history of the Brazilian Internet, see the following: Alves (2013), Balboni (2007), Motta (2011), Penteado et al. (2011), Prado (2011), and Schlegel (2009).

as its country domain code, giving the country's web operations a national identity. Shortly after, in 1994, the first IP blocks were authorized. The year 1995 also saw the birth of the Brazilian Internet Steering Committee (Comitê Gestor da Internet – CGI).[10] The increase of .com.br domains strengthened the commercial side of the web. The success of the spread of these addresses is seen in the increase in registrations. In 1996 Brazil had a little over 850 domains, and in 2016 the country had around 3.8 million, and, for the first time, sales on the web overtook sales in physical shops. The second half of 2010s revealed the power of the "cybertide."

In the first years of the twentieth century, a combination of factors contributed to the expansion of the Internet in Brazil. After the privatization of telecommunications which from 1998 onward gave different companies access to the infrastructure and millions of potential clients, tax program incentivized the acquisition of computers, making the equipment cheaper, as with smartphones and tablets, thereby increasing Brazilians' access to the network.

So, in five decades of existence, the Internet in Brazil and the world has undergone continuous transformations, some subtle – one such transformation being interface development – others more explicit. With the advent of what is known as Web 2.0, the process of producing information underwent necessary changes. It ceased to be rigidly hierarchical and became the receiver and the producer of information. The explosion of social networks transformed the ordinary citizen into a potential celebrity. Relationship pages such as Facebook,[11] Orkut, and Instagram, sites such as YouTube, and the invasion of weblogs, videologs, and microblogs, such as Twitter, revealed the unique need of everybody speaking at the same time. In the same way, specific moments such as the invasion of the Complexo do Alemão[12] shantytown, known as a *favela* in Portuguese, in Rio de Janeiro, in November of 2011, or the demonstrations calling for the resignation of Hosni

[10] In Brazil, the Internet Steering Committee was created by Inter-ministerial Ordinance n.147, dated May 31, 1995, and implemented by Decree No. 4829, dated March 09, 2003. Its mission is to define strategic guidelines for the use and development of the Internet in the country, consider security procedures for the network, conduct surveys, as well as respond to the guidelines and execution of the registration of domain names and Internet Protocol (IP) addresses. To learn more about CGI, see https://www.cgi.br

[11] Chapter 6 analyzes activity profiles in virtual communities of chronic kidney patients, organized in Facebook.

[12] On November 25, 2010, after a police operation to combat trafficking in the neighborhood of Vila Cruzeiro, traffickers who managed to escape the siege organized by the police forces of Rio de Janeiro took refuge in Complexo do Alemão. Seeking to arrest the criminals, on November 26 the Military Police and the Civil Police took access points of access Complex. The response of the traffickers came with attacks in different parts of the metropolitan region of Rio de Janeiro (bus burnings, vehicle assaults, commercial establishments and to passersby, destruction of ATMs). In response, on November 28, on a Sunday morning, the security forces decided to invade the Complex with a force of 800 soldiers from the Army Parachute Infantry Brigade, 300 Federal Police (PF) officers, and 1300 Military and Civil Police. The agents had tactical support from Army and Navy armored vehicles, as well as vehicles from the Special Operations Battalion of the PM (Bope). At the time, the expectation was that between 500 and 600 traffickers were in the Complexo do Alemão. For more information, see G1 (2010).

Mubarak in Cairo and other cities in Egypt could be followed not only from the perspective of the international press.[13] Those directly involved in the situation – in the case of Rio, a supposed "soldier" of the drug traffickers had a slanging match on Orkut with internauts demanding bodies and the "elimination" of the trafficker, while in Egypt it was possible to follow the developments of events via Twitter or Facebook. With the Internet, the world emerges as incredibly new and absurdly small. That sensation that we are tramps in a world of tourists seems to disappear (Bauman 1999).

2.5 Perspectives

In this digital landscape, what can we expect? The twenty-first century holds many challenges for Brazil concerning the Internet. Possibly the greatest of these lies in reducing the asymmetry of access to the Internet within social classes and those living in rural areas. While those with more considerable resources, the so-called "A" class, show Internet access rates of around 97%, the disparity is shocking when it is considered that only 6% of what is known as classes "D" and "E" have access to the network.[14] The exclusion of these groups means that no fewer than 68 million people ever use the Internet (RSN 2013).

There is still a need for substantial investment in infrastructure to enable better quality access to the Internet in the countryside. A high number of rural residents are excluded, with only 10% of homes there having access to the web. There are also cases of the scarcity of points of access and problems with the quality of the signal offered. On the other hand, the ability to undertake digital inclusion programs in deprived areas of large cities is also critical, especially considering the demands that the labor market has established with the increase in the use of electronic environments in recent years.

A similar problem becomes apparent when one considers age groups. The Brazilian population has aged, and today it is necessary to work longer into life, and the use of the world computer network cannot be discarded. However, only 23% of the elderly have Internet access.[15]

---

[13] See Ghonim (2013).

[14] In Brazil, government and private research agencies use this classification in alphabetical order to frame social stratification, considering average family incomes. Basically, the relationship between income and social class is distributed in the following groups: A1, A2, B1, B2, C1, C2, D, and E. While in group A1 we have the families with the highest income, at the other end, D and E, we have widely recognized situations of social vulnerability. Therefore, in strata D and E we have the poorest segments of the Brazilian population, possibly being the main targets to be reached in public policies that aim at changes in the country's human development indexes. See Kamakura and Mazzon (2013).

[15] Chapter 8 discusses the use of information and communication technologies to promote active aging.

Another important aspect of the problem is that more effective and ambitious proposals have to be considered for basic education. For a long time now, Brazilian classrooms have educated a vast majority of boys and girls who were born after the advent of the commercial Internet and the explosion of social networks. This difference means that for students the use of keyboards and computer screens, cell phones, and tablets, regardless of prices or brands, is something almost natural. Schools can no longer distance themselves from this.

Actions intending to promote the concept of citizenship via the global computer network will have to be carefully planned. If the Brazilian state supplies its citizens with electronic tools which allow them to follow public spending and the actions of various government organs, there will be a need to improve responses and update legislation.

Cybercrime will also become a significant challenge. However, if over recent years banks and other private businesses have offered examples of how to avoid and track criminals who use the net to steal credit card data resulting in losses for their clients, Brazilian society needs to learn how to deal with other types of crime, principally those linked with intolerance.[16] Bullying, fake news, racist attacks, increasing racism, hate speech, and fundamentalism were unleashed with the expansion of the Internet in Brazil. It will be necessary to educate our young navigators, to show them that the web is not a no man's land. We will need to show them the virtues and the limits of democracy.

Meanwhile, the number of computers increases in giant steps. After all, they are vital to the Internet which advances relentlessly into all areas of life within society. Cell phones, iPads, and watches are just a few of the different devices that allow access to the world of networks, the electronic tide, that is, to the cyberspace imagined by William Gibson in the classic *Neuromancer* (1984). And if we observe this calmly, we will see that making networks is nothing new. In truth, for a long time, humanity has been establishing connections. Robert Darnton (2005) reminds us that every era has had its own "Information Society." Computers and the Internet are the most visible points in the times in which we live.

As Lévy showed, networks used to belong in the private domain while the hierarchical world was in the public sphere. But the systems in breaking the hierarchy have come up against problems when dealing with this flexibility to coordinate tasks. The web appeared to resolve such a dilemma. It seems to be seen as a blessing, but can become something of a curse:

> New pharmakon, the intelligence collective that favours cyberculture is, at the same time a poison for those that don't participate (and nobody can participate fully, so vast and multiforme as it is), and a medicine for those that dive into its whirlpools and manage to control their drift in its currents. (Lévy 2000, 30)

However, it has become vital to understand that the question is not to be either for or against the Internet. It is essential to understand its qualitative changes. Spreading over us, flooding our daily lives, the global computer network puts us up against

[16] The issue of bullying and cybebullying is addressed in Chap. 12.

the wall. It makes demands on us to reflect yet denies us time to do so. We need to understand its rhythm, question its certainties, and to peek between its bits and clicks, a difficult task, challenging to the most seasoned of historians. Researching on the Internet, just like navigating, is a precise art.

References

Alves, Ludmila. 2013. Redes de comunicação e território: a formação e organização socioespacial da internet no Brasil. Master's thesis, Universidade de São Paulo, São Paulo.

Balboni, Mariana R. 2007. Por detrás da inclusão digital: uma reflexão sobre o consumo e a produção de informação em centros públicos de acesso à internet no Brasil. PhD diss., Universidade de São Paulo, São Paulo.

Barbrook, Richard. 2009. The American century. In *Imaginary futures: From thinking machines to the global village*. São Paulo: Petrópolis.

Bauman, Zygmunt. 1999. *Globalização: as consequências humanas*. Rio de Janeiro: Jorge Zahar Editor.

Castells, Manuel. 2003. *A Galáxia da Internet: reflexões sobre a Internet, os negócios e a sociedade*. Rio de Janeiro: Jorge Zahar Ed.

Cyclades. 2000. *Guia Internet de conectividade*. São Paulo: Editora SENAC São Paulo.

Darnton, Robert. 2005. As notícias em Paris: uma pioneira sociedade da informação. In *Os dentes falsos de George Washington: um guia não convencional para o século XVIII*, 40–90. São Paulo: Companhia das Letras.

G1. 2010. A ocupação das Favelas do Alemão. Globo Comunicação e Participações. http://g1.globo.com/rio-de-janeiro/rio-contra-o-crime/noticia/2010/11/ocupacao-das-favelas-do-alemao.html. Accessed 12 Oct 2017.

Gates, Bill. 1995. *A estrada para o futuro*. São Paulo: Companhia das Letras.

Ghonim, Wael. 2013. *Revolution 2.0: The power of the people is greater than the people in power: A memoir*. Boston: Houghton Mifflin Harcourt.

Internet World Stats. 2009. http://www.internetworldstats.com/sa/br.htm. Accessed 14 Nov 2009.

———. 2018. Internet usage statistics – The Internet big picture https://www.internetworldstats.com/stats.htm. Accessed 10 Mar 2018.

Kamakura, Wagner, and José Afonso Mazzon. 2013. *Estratificação socioeconômica e consumo no Brasil*. São Paulo: Editora Blucher.

Lévy, Pierre. 2000. *Cibercultura*. Rio de Janeiro: Editora 34.

Maynard, Dilton. 2011. *Escritos sobre história e internet*. Rio de Janeiro: Multifoco.

Mazzeo, Luzia Maria. 2000. Evolução da Internet no Brasil e no Mundo. Ministério da Ciência e Tecnologia/Secretaria de Política de Informática e Automação. http://www.faeterj-rio.edu.br/downloads/bbv/0032.pdf. Accessed 8 June 2018.

Motta, Marcelo Paiva. 2011. Geografia da Internet no Brasil: redes técnicas e espaço. Universidade Federal do Rio de Janeiro. Available at http://objdig.ufrj.br/16/teses/773302.pdf

Negroponte, Nicholas. 1995. *A vida digital*. São Paulo: Companhia das Letras.

Penteado, Cláudio Luis de Camargo, Marcelo Burgos Pimentel dos Santos, Rafael Aguiar de Paula Araújo, and Sidney Jar da Silva. 2011. Ação política na Internet brasileira. *Perspectivas em ciência da informacao* 16: 111–132.

Prado, Luciana Tavares. 2011. Estrutura e evolução da Internet no Brasil: subsídios à análise econômica – 1996 a 2009. Master's thesis, Pontifícia Universidade Católica – São Paulo, São Paulo.

Rosenzweig, Roy. 2006. Wizards, bureaucrats, warriors & hackers: Writing the history of the Internet. http://chnm.gmu.edu/resources/essays/d/25. Accessed 15 Mar 2006.

RSN – Rede Sul de Notícias. 2013. Brasil tem 80,9 milhões de usuários de internet, mas expansão nas classes D e E e nas zonas rurais ainda é desafio. Rede Sul de Noticias. https://redesuldenoticias.com.br/noticias/brasil-tem-809-milhoes-de-usuarios-de-internet-mas-expansao-nas-classes-d-e-e-e-nas-zonas-rurais-ainda-e-desafio/ Accessed 12 Oct 2017.

Santana, Rogério. 2009. Cresce o acesso às TICs, mas ainda é grande o desafio de democratizá-las a todos os brasileiros. In *Pesquisa sobre o uso das tecnologias da informação e da comunicação*, ed. Comitê Gestor da Internet (CGI), 45–48. São Paulo: Comitê Gestor da Internet.

Schlegel, Rogerio. 2009. Internauta brasileiro: perfil diferenciado, opiniões indiferenciadas. *Revista de Sociologia e Politica* 17: 137–157.

Shimizu, Heitor. 2006. *Aventura espacial: um grande fracasso?* São Paulo: Editora Terceiro Nome.

Willer, Claudio. 2009. *Geração Beat*. Porto Alegre: L&PM.

Chapter 3
The Brazilian Civil Rights Framework for the Internet: A Pioneering Experience in Internet Governance

Rosemary Segurado

Abstract The Global Multistakeholder Meeting on the Future of Internet Governance (NETmundial) held in Sao Paulo, Brazil, on April 23 and 24, 2014, confirmed Brazil's leading role in formulating progressive rules on Internet governance. On this occasion, Bill No. 12.965 – the Brazilian Internet "Bill of Rights" – passed. The bill, developed through a collaborative platform involving several sectors of civil society, became law. This chapter discusses Internet governance as it relates to the functioning of the global computer network of which Brazil has played a leading role in this process, especially after the approval of the regulatory framework which contains principles, assurances, rights, and duties for Internet users and providers in the country. The Brazilian Civil Rights Framework for the Internet is the first national legislation that works like a "Constitution" for network users. This paper outlines the influence of Brazil's Internet "Bill of Rights" on the global Internet governance debate as well as the main actors and agencies involved. The findings show Brazil as a relevant player in discussing processes about rules governing the Web.

3.1 Introduction

In this article, we will analyze the main aspects of the process involved in elaborating Brazil's Civil Rights Framework for the Internet. Considering this, we will highlight civil society's participation along with the way in which this process had placed Brazil in a prominent position among the international community involved in this debate.

On April 24, 2014, President Dilma Rousseff sanctioned Bill No. 12.965/14 and announced at the opening of the NETmundial meeting that Brazil had just approved the first "Internet Constitution" containing the rights and duties of Internet users and companies.

R. Segurado (✉)
Social Sciences Faculty, Pontifical Catholic University of São Paulo, São Paulo, Brazil

A. Pereira Neto, M. B. Flynn (eds.), *The Internet and Health in Brazil*,
https://doi.org/10.1007/978-3-319-99289-1_3

The meeting, organized by the Brazilian Internet Steering Committee (CGI.br)[1] along with 1NET – a global Internet governance platform – named NETmundial, debated 188 proposals from 46 countries on the future of the Internet according to the following themes: security, privacy, neutrality, freedom of expression, freedom of association, government roles, and policy. The primary objective was to allow an open platform with undeniable access to content, applications, and services. In other words, the bottom line was transparency and isonomy. Therefore, servers could not interfere with digital connections whether the user is watching a video, listening to a song, or reading a text. Internet service providers must also guarantee service quality for any and all forms of online access.

In this way, with 1480 representatives from 97 countries, the Brazilian Civil Rights Framework for the Internet was announced and voted by the Congress on the day before the meeting began. The bill was received as the most advanced proposal about Internet regulation in the world and became a reference for debates concerning Internet governance.

Before we reflect on Brazil's role in this debate, it is essential to review some key terms and concepts, such as the meaning of Internet governance. According to Kurbalija (2016, 18)[2]:

> Internet governance is the development and application by governments, the private sector, and civil society, in their respective roles, of shared principles, norms, rules, decision-making procedures, and common programs that shape the evolution and use of the Internet.

Internet governance is commonly related to the technical features of the network's structure. According to Benkler (2000), three layers divide governance: physical infrastructure, code or logic, and content. It means that each of these spheres points to challenges at local and global levels. In other words: "A significant global Internet governance concern related to keeping the Internet accessible and universal is the question of how independent networks conjoin to form the global Internet" (Denardis 2013, 10).

Internet data can travel through various means, including telephone wires, fiber-optic cables, satellites, microwaves, and wireless connections. In this regard, it is important to emphasize that the regulation of telecommunications has a direct impact on Internet governance.

Regarding the physical structure, it is important to clarify that having servers capable of storing content that travels through the Web as well as routers and cables to assure information conveyance is necessary. This issue implies infrastructure investments able to guarantee information flow. Otherwise, Internet access is not viable, and that is why in some countries there are regions without Internet access, precisely because of the lack of infrastructure.

---

[1] The Brazilian Internet Steering Committee is responsible for outlining strategic guidelines related to the Internet's development in Brazil and also for the execution of the domain name and Internet Protocol (IP) address assignments. The Committee also conducts studies on Internet security, technical quality, and innovation.

[2] Jovan Kurbalija is the founder director of the DiploFoundation and head of the Geneva Internet Platform.

Infrastructure is also responsible for access quality, that is, bandwidth,[3] which is one of the central technical features to achieve such excellence. Brazil has not yet solved problems related to digital inclusion,[4] despite a government decree created to bring Internet connection to underprivileged regions.[5] Research carried out by the Regional Center for Studies on the Development of the Information Society (CETIC.br 2017) mapped access to information and communication technology infrastructure in urban and rural households:

> In Brazil, 54% of households are connected to the Internet, which represents 36.7 million households - an increase of three percentage points compared to 2015. The patterns of inequality revealed by the research mentioned above persist: only 23% of the lower middle class and the lowest class are connected to the Internet, while in rural areas this proportion is 26%. Internet access is more present in urban areas (59%), in the upper class (98%) and upper middle class (91%).

On the other hand, the logical sphere is related to the production and maintenance of protocols regulating data that travels across the Internet, so-called Internet Protocol (IP). Protocol is a language used for two or more computers to talk to each other. This communication is possible by using TCP/IP (Transmission Control Protocol/Internet Protocol), which is a kind of protocol stack and is responsible for information flows across the Internet.

One analogy is the classic exchange of messages through the postal system. To send a letter, we need to put it in an envelope with the full address of the senders and receivers. Physical addresses are equivalent to a protocol; without this information, the letter does not reach the desired destination. The Internet is also like this; every message – let us call it a data packet – is involved in an IP that would act as a kind of "envelope" in which we have the address of the sender (IP address) and the receiver.

Each computer has its IP address. Consequently, there is no possibility of two networks having the same IP address, just as it is similar to the logic of the physical or postal address, which includes name, surname, street, house number, postal code of the city, the state, the country, etc.

After the letter arrives at the post office, it is sent to a sorting center until it reaches its final destination. Similarly, on the Internet, messages are placed in an IP packet, and this packet travels from computer to computer until it reaches its final address, the destination port. There are many ports on each network, such as a browser, specific e-mail software, and another one just to listen to music, among other functions. In this context, some questions arise: How should the computer proceed? For which software should the IP packet be forwarded? Will it go to the correct port?

---

[3] Created by Decree No. 7.175/2010, the National Broadband Plan (PNBL) is an initiative of the federal government. Its main objective is to increase broadband Internet access in the country, especially in those regions most in need of this technology. See Brazil (2010).

[4] Chapter 4 discusses a pioneering digital inclusion project in Brazil.

[5] Chapter 2 addresses the history of the Internet in Brazil.

Each software program receives a number on the computer, which we could associate to the mail that arrives at an apartment building. Each apartment would be a specific port. The address is the same for all, but each one has a particular number. The IP address specifies to which port the information must be sent, and this address allows the message to arrive at a specific computer, where the port number determines which computer software to forward it to.

The size of information packets has its limits, so it is not possible to send files with a lot of information. There is a limit to this submission. The TCP was precisely developed to ascertain the receipt of the data by the receiver to fragment the large packets later, number each one, and check its integrity. In this way, TCP/IP makes communication between operating systems located in different computers reliable.

Indeed, this whole communication process is quite complicated, involving multiple layers, numerous decision-makers, and social and political players. Earlier, we specified a fundamental part of this process in order to arrive at the importance of Internet governance and regulatory dynamics.

> There is no unitary system that oversees and coordinates the Internet. Some administrative tasks and policies are carried out by private industry operating as part of markets; some tasks are overseen by relatively new institutions such as the Internet Corporation for Assigned Names and Numbers (ICANN), and some administrative jurisdiction resides with sovereign nation states or multilateral governmental coordination. Explanations of the various components of Internet governance have filled entire volumes and there are many possible taxonomies for describing these functions. One way to understand the Internet governance ecosystem is to divide its main functions into six areas: (I) control of "critical Internet resources," (II) setting Internet standards, (III) access and interconnection coordination, (IV) cybersecurity governance, (V) the policy role of information intermediaries, and (VI) architecture-based intellectual property rights enforcement. (Denardis and Raymond 2013, 3)

3.2 Multistakeholder Governance Model

It is important to emphasize that the NETmundial meeting was fundamental to reaffirm Brazil's leading role in global Internet governance. This meeting was also crucial for collaborating in the formulation of the Brazilian Internet "Bill of Rights," with the use of online and offline tools to facilitate the debate among the various sectors involved, confirming the multistakeholder character consolidated by CGI Brazil. The government, telecommunication companies, civil society, academics, and technical community attended this arrangement, interacting equally in decision-making processes. Their attendance means that the event ratified the country's experience and expertise in procedures managing a participatory process, making it as a critical player in global Internet governance. The CGI Brazil legislation reveals the multistakeholder character, as presented below in its internal regulations:

> On the composition of the CGI.[6]

---

[6] It is possible to see the internal regiment of the Brazilian Internet Steering Committee at the CGI.br website at https://cgi.br/pagina/regimento-interno-do-comite-gestor-da-Internet-no-brasil/308

Art. 3° The CGI.br has the following members in its composition:

I. A representative of the National Forum of State Secretaries for Science and Technology Affairs;
II. A well-known expert in Internet affairs;
IV. Four representatives and four surrogates from the business sector in the following segments: one holder and one surrogate from Internet Access and Content Providers; one holder and one surrogate from Telecommunication Infrastructure Providers; one holder and one surrogate from the Computer and Electronic Product Manufacturing industries as well as from telecommunication and software industries; one holder and one surrogate member from the business sector;
V. Four representatives and four surrogates from the tertiary sector;
VI. Three representatives and three surrogates from the scientific and technological community.

CGI.br adopted the multistakeholder governance model since its inception, meaning that from the outset, there was always a particular concern about multi-participatory Internet governance that could be considered a pioneering model since it was unprecedented.

> The efforts of the scientific and technological community, the tertiary sector, business community, and government with their proposals for network development converged with the publication of Interministerial Ordinance N°. 147 on May 31, 1995. The Ordinance defined the creation of the Committee to coordinate and integrate all Internet service initiatives in the country, promoting technical quality, innovation and dissemination of the services offered.
>
> According to Augusto Cesar Gadelha Vieira, coordinator of CGI.br since 2005, the Brazilian Internet governance model pioneered the creation of a multi-stakeholder forum, being a model for other countries and a milestone in Internet history. "The fact that 21 representatives from different segments meet monthly to discuss the Internet in Brazil is remarkable. Those meetings resulted in extremely important actions and initiatives, such as the constitution of NIC.br, our executive arm, the establishment of general principles for governance that guide public policies and legal procedures as well as an evaluation of the use of ICTs in the country" (...) Since 2004, elections have been held for Civil Society seats (scientific and technological community, tertiary sector, and business community). Government representatives are indicated according to their respective areas of activity or expertise and announced through interministerial ordinances. (CGI.br 2017)[7]

Through a collaborative process aimed to prepare the meeting's reference document, the NETmundial Multistakeholder Statement[8] generated 1370 participants' comments. The statement also had the input of 200 daily viewers, who followed the arguments in real time in more than 30 hubs,[9] a kind of discussion center spread all over the world.

> Brazil is modern with respect to the Internet. The country is at the forefront in formulating and implementing public policies for global Internet governance, policies that value

[7] Currently, this model is being questioned, and it is possible that changes will happen soon. Currently, CGI.br is conducting several discussions. There are many differences about the permanence of the current governance model, considering that the business community and government representatives are increasingly seeking influence in the voting process.

[8] See the NETmundial Multistakeholder Statement at http://netmundial.br/wp-content/uploads/2014/04/NETmundial-Multistakeholder-Document.pdf

[9] In general, a hub is a device that has the function of connecting computers to a network.

> multi-stakeholder models, involving government and society. The Brazilian Civil Rights Framework for the Internet, the Internet Steering Committee, and the NETMundial meeting are Brazilian initiatives with broad international recognition. These are concrete examples of Brazilian modernity in cyberspace (...) CGI.br and several international organizations, such as ICANN, among others, worked on the construction of this multistakeholder meeting; NETmundial, notably, with the aim of discussing the evolution of global Internet governance. The results were clearly positive. Brazil's leadership in the matter was clear, confirmed by the significant presence of representatives from all sectors involved, representing almost 1,000 representatives from 110 countries. (Almeida 2014, 4)

The international community's recognition of Brazil's role in Internet governance debates demonstrates the importance of the Brazilian Internet "Bill of Rights" in this whole process. We could say that after the meeting, Internet regulation entered another level of discussion.

One of the first aspects to be clarified in addressing Internet governance is the necessary distinction between Internet management and control. Although they are two separate issues, they are closely intertwined. The management of the Internet's technical resources has significant political inferences, and there must be a dialogue between governmental and nongovernmental actors to understand the complexity of the Internet governance ecosystem.

Such an understanding is of paramount significance, considering that the Internet cannot be treated as unidimensional, as we can see in the words of Wolfgang Kleinwächter, professor of International Policy and Regulation, Department of Media and Information Sciences, University of Aarhus, Denmark:

> The Internet governance ecosystem can be partially compared to that of a rainforest. In the rainforest, an untold amount of distinct plants and animals coexist in a very complex system. In the "virtual forest," we also have an endless and growing diversity of networks, services, applications, regimes and other properties that cohabit, collaborate, contradict and conflict each other (...) In the Internet governance ecosystem, many actors with quite different legal status operate multilaterally at local, national, regional and international levels, driven by technical innovation, user needs, market opportunities and political interests. (Kleinwächter 2014, 33)

According to Kleinwächter, it is necessary to overcome the clashes between the United States and China in order to avoid unilateral measures. This joint action must prevail to overcome what he defines as a "lame consensus." Thus, Netmundial was seen as a kind of third way that allowed "Internet actors, including governments, to stop having to make a choice between US surveillance and China's censorship" (Kleinwächter 2014, 37).

3.3 The Collaborative Process of Drafting the Brazilian Civil Rights Framework for the Internet

First of all, it is important to briefly review some steps in the process of drafting the Internet "Bill of Rights" to understand Brazil's leadership, not only at the NETmundial conference but in the increasingly crucial global debate about the Internet.

The debate about drafting the regulatory framework began in the second half of 2009. The Secretariat of Legislative Affairs of the Ministry of Justice initiated the development framework in partnership with the Technology and Society Center of the Getúlio Vargas Foundation (CTS/FGV).

The debate developed through a collaborative platform explicitly created for the elaboration of this project. Undoubtedly, it was a pioneering way of using digital devices to formulate public policy. This innovation led to the expansion and diversification of partners in the debate, without excluding participation in face-to-face forums organized by the Ministry of Justice.

In the first phase of the process, the Ministry of Justice invited participants to collaboratively build the Internet regulatory framework through a public consultation held at the address http://culturadigital.br/marcocivil. The primary goal was to receive the demands and opinions from various segments of civil society for grounding the legislative text and regulation of the matter. The first phase of the consultation was structured around the following axes:

> (I) to adapt and consolidate the fundamental rights of individuals in the context of electronic communication; (II) to clearly define the civil responsibility of the various actors involved in Internet communication processes; and (III) to establish convergent guidelines for the performance of both in the formulation of public policies in eventual subsequent regulations. Topics such as the right to access, freedom of expression and privacy, non-discrimination of content and resolution of conflicts related to the network, among others, are being discussed. (Abramovay 2009)

From suggestions sent to the collaborative platform, the Ministry of Justice systematized and made an initial text available for discussion. Contributions came from various sectors, such as network users, academics, companies, public and private institutions, as well as government representatives interested in this topic.

The debate ensued with the development of the following phases:

1. Drafting discussion prepared by the Ministry of Justice

At this stage of discussion – scheduled to last 45 days – users were able to post their comments and proposals.[10] These comments were open to all those who accessed the central plan. The more lengthy posts were directed to another forum at the same website in order to deepen the debate and to contemplate the totality of the recorded comments.

At the end of this first phase, a summary of the main discussion topics, along with a draft, was moved to the second phase of the debate.

2. In the second phase, the selection was scheduled to be discussed and divided as follows:

   Chapter I – Preliminary provisions, containing five articles.
   Chapter II – On the users' rights and guarantees, containing three articles.
   Chapter III – Internet connection and services, containing 18 articles.
   Chapter IV – Public power performance, containing five articles.
   Chapter V – General provisions, containing two articles.

[10] Each piece of this legislation was open for comments on the Web portal. For more details, see http://culturadigital.br

This stage of discussion was similar to that of the first one. However, the text from the *Cultural Digital* Web portal, on this consultation procedure, strictly affirmed the need for users to appropriate information and communication technologies to engage in the legislative decision-making process.

Based on data gathering on the website about the collaborative process, people posted approximately 2000 comments through articles, subsections, and paragraphs with the aid of various sectors of civil society, such as companies, organizations, activists, and the technical community. Besides the recorded comments, the netizens could also express themselves through blogs and Twitter.[11]

A related point to consider is that the draft review was conceived as a reaction against the bill on Internet crimes (Bill No. 84/99), authored by Deputy Luiz Piauhylino. Senator Eduardo Azeredo amended the bill, and it became known as "Azeredo Amendment" or "AI 5 Digital," referring to the Institutional Act Number Five, a significant decree issued on December 13, 1968, inaugurating the most authoritarian period of the Brazilian military dictatorship.

In an article published in the daily newspaper *Folha de São Paulo* in May 2007, Ronaldo Lemos – one of the collaborative platform coordinators – affirmed the importance of a regulatory framework for the Internet:

> This was the first time the term came out publicly. The notion that a "Regulatory Framework" could oppose criminal or repressive initiatives, previously dominant in the National Congress, still needed to be recognized by the government so that it could move forward with greater force. Already supported by members of the academic sector and civil society, the speech in support of the regulatory framework reached the government and effectively consolidated in 2009. (Souza and Lemos 2016, 18)

The debate was controversial, and it was hard to reach consensus, partly because of the diversity of actors involved, often with antagonistic interests. Among the controversial points are the critical disagreements by some participants contrary to any form of Internet regulation which they viewed as an attempt to control users' freedom.

The preliminary question was about regulation or nonregulation. In other words, there were questions about even the need for a law to address specific issues regarding rights on the Web. This debate takes us back to the 1990s when John Perry Barlow[12] wrote the Declaration of Independence of Cyberspace. The aim was to prevent government interference in the development of the Internet with any regulatory design. In this debate, Lawrence Lessig (2006) and Alexander Galloway (2004) made important contributions. For Lessig (2006), what governs life in cyberspace are the codes (i.e., software). Therefore, codes are the law of the Internet, which means that the network architecture is composed of a set of codes that regulates cyberspace, just as a constitution governs life in offline world. For him, the central issue is the fact of defining who controls the code; that is, the one who controls the

---

[11] To know more about the use of Twitter in the making of the Brazilian Internet Bill of Rights, see Bragatto et al. (2015).

[12] Barlow wrote the Declaration of Independence of Cyberspace in 1996. For more information, see https://en.wikipedia.org/wiki/A_Declaration_of_the_Independence_of_Cyberspace

code will have more power over the Internet, raising concerns about the private sector's increasing control of the Web.

On the other hand, Galloway (2009) says that the very engineering of the Internet is in and of itself already a form of regulation. Therefore, the argument in favor of private control is a false premise. Thus, we believe the following statement is accurate:

> It is fundamentally redundant to say a "regulated Internet." The Internet is regulation and nothing else. Just look at the protocols. The "C" in TCP/IP stands for "Control." I am against the notion, which is still quite common, that the Internet is a force that fundamentally eliminates regulation, hierarchy, organization, control, etc. Distributed networks are never "out of control" -- this is the worst kind of ideological delusion. The key question, therefore, is never whether control does or does not exist, but rather to ask: What is the quality of this control? Where does it come from? Is it being wielded by governments, or is it deployed at the level of machine infrastructure? I don't pretend to answer the question about government power, for there are decades and centuries of writings devoted to the excesses of state power. We can still read those books. My contribution is merely at the machine and infrastructural level. What is the specific character of informatic organization? This is the basic question of protocol. (Galloway 2009)

Authors like Lessig and Galloway were fundamental in defining the debate around drafting of Brazil's regulatory framework, including clarification about the meaning of a free Internet. Indeed, free Internet is not Internet without law:

> Contrary to the above idea, the Brazilian Civil Rights Framework for the Internet presents a new scenario in which the concept of "free Internet" is linked not to the absence of laws, but to the existence of laws that can guarantee and preserve the freedom that is enjoyed by all, precisely because of technology and more specifically, the development of the Internet. The Brazilian Civil Rights Framework for the Internet was conceived as a law capable of preserving the foundations for the promotion of freedom and rights on the Internet. Dissociating from a repressive regulation, Brazil offered one of the most symbolic examples that encourages global debates on Internet regulation that has human rights as its guiding principle, maintaining its main character to avoid an early expiration of its legal devices. (Souza and Lemos 2016, 16)

As a scholar of communication, Dominique Wolton (2003) has noted that it is essential to distinguish between censorship and regulation. According to the author, there is no guarantee of freedom in communication without some form of control. In this way, it is understood that the complete absence of laws that specifically regulate Internet usage can let the logic of the market and the economic forces prevail:

> […] there is no freedom of communication without regulation, that is, without protection of this freedom. In fact, the heralds of deregulation are favorable to a kind regulation: that of the market, that is to say, of economic relations, that of the laws of the jungle. (Wolton 2003, 122)

Wolton's understanding points to an imperative that questions whose interests would serve deregulation. Therefore, the author is emphatic in stating that it is only with some regulation that freedom of expression and communication can be guaranteed to prevent any form of censorship.

Concern over censorship found in several comments mobilized the participants in the debate. Even among those in favor of creating specific rules for the use of the Internet, there was a need to discuss appropriate legal mechanisms with the aim of avoiding any censorship or vigilantism. They had in mind the "AI5 Digital," as we mentioned above, the amendment proposed by Senator Eduardo Azeredo, as an example of censorship.

On the other hand, the regulatory and procedural dynamics, articulated by the Ministry of Justice, presented a new perspective for public policy formulation and stakeholder engagement. The collaborative process and the incorporation of information and communication technologies (ICTs) in the debate about issues relevant to civil society encouraged the inclusion of diverse social actors and were seen as an advance in the consolidation of democracy. Thus, we note that digital tools were appropriate to encourage debate and arrange political actions.

In the Brazilian case, studies on political culture indicate that engagement of individuals does not occupy a central place in political dynamics. This means that the incorporation of digital technologies – according to the Ministry of Justice's initiative – must be understood as a means to increase participation and inclusion of a significant number of individuals who are currently far from the decision-making process. For Javier Cremades (2009, 35):

> [...] citizens' awareness of micro-power is the key to a new political action capable of administering globalized and plural society, by managing the previous energies to the process of institutionalization. It could be possible to describe this action with the adjective "relational," which has already been used when talking about the network of human relations maintained through a constant dialogue (speaking and listening) made possible by new technologies.

Because it is an open platform, and considering the multistakeholder nature of the Internet, it should be remembered that telecommunication companies also had significant participation in the collaborative process. This is part of the CGI.br experience, as we can see below:

> The Brazilian Internet Governance model, conducted by the Internet Steering Committee in Brazil (CGI.br), is a worldwide reference. Based on principles of multi-stakeholder participation and transparency, CGI.br represents a model of multi-participatory and democratic Internet governance, enabling diverse sectors of society to equally participate in debates and decisions about the Internet in Brazil. In nearly 20 years of history, representatives from all over the country, with diverse backgrounds and interests, have put CGI.br on firm grounding and contributed to building the history of the Brazilian Internet as well as preparing it for the future. (CGI.br 2014)

Although it is important to note the complexity of the discussion in multistakeholder environments, it is also valuable to understand this space as a fundamental field of contention. Telecommunication companies involved in the collaborative process were against the most controversial point of the regulatory framework: net neutrality. The companies considered that this item would interfere directly with their business models. Regarding the importance of this issue, there is a need to understand the meaning of a neutral Internet in which no type of data packet can take priority over other network traffic. Neutrality ensures that all transmissions, regardless the issuer, are subject to the same rules and criteria.

> Vehicles ride over a highway, and datagrams ride over Internet circuits (the data "packets" that compose each e-mail message, video, voice over IP, etc.). As in a highway, the

concessionaire cannot discriminate between a blue and a red car (...), on the Internet, [and] operators should not interfere in the traffic of any datagram (...) If they interfere in some way, causing datagrams to be delayed, lost, or even copied for some sort of espionage, they will be violating the principles of net neutrality. (Afonso 2010, 101)

The difference with the Internet lies in the decentralized shape of content creation and delivery. Proposals that interfere with net neutrality, in fact, mean changing its elements that guide its configuration and define its development.

The loss of net neutrality can transform the Internet into cable TV, that is, the user pays for different packages of channels distinguished by the type of information. Such an outcome increases the cost of accessing the network. Those with more resources can get more expensive packages, which is in disagreement with the nature of a distributed network that characterizes the structure of the Internet.

For Lessig (2006, 74), it is essential to consider the multiplicity of ways that define the architecture of the network.

There is certainly a way that cyberspace is. But how cyberspace is not how cyberspace has to be. There is no single way that the Net has to be; no single architecture that defines the nature of the Net. The possible architectures of something that we would call "the Net" are many, and the character of life within those different architectures is diverse.

At this point, consumer protection agencies also actively participated in the discussion. It is worth remembering that consumers always complain about the services offered by the providers. Among the most frequent complaints are those concerning contracted speed service in relation to the one provided. Consumer protection agencies affirm that it is a citizen's right to receive contracted service in the same way that providers cannot slow internal connections by increasing speed for large companies. Consequently, net neutrality must also ensure this principle of isonomy.

On the one hand, it is vital that the proposal contained in the Brazilian Internet "Bill of Rights" ensures that the principle of neutrality is not violated. On the other hand, the transnational nature of the Internet makes it possible to change other countries' protocols, allowing communication flow in places where neutrality is not provided by law. It is worth mentioning that the only country that approved net neutrality, before Brazil, was Chile, regulated by the Law No. 20,453/11. This lies at the center of the debate around global Internet governance. Currently, several countries from the European Union, South America, and part of the Asian continent have shown some intention to discuss the matter more deeply. Until December 2017, net neutrality was also a reality in the United States, but the Federal Communications Commission (FCC) – the US's top media regulator – voted to end rules protecting an open Internet. The voting section, held on December 14, 2017, had the score of three votes in favoring of ending neutrality and two for its maintenance. Jessica Rosenworcel (apud Gomes 2017), one of the councilors who voted against the end of neutrality, made the following statement:

They will have the right to discriminate and favor the Internet traffic of those companies with whom they have a pay-for-play arrangement and the right to consign all others to a slow and bumpy road (...) Our broadband providers will tell you they will never do these things. They say just trust us. But know this: they have the technical ability and business incentive to discriminate and manipulate your Internet traffic. And now this agency gives

> them the legal green light to go ahead and do so. This is not good. Not good for consumers. Not good for businesses. Not good for anyone who connects and creates online. Not good for the democratizing force that depends on openness to thrive.

On the other hand, FCC Chairman, Ajit Pai (apud Gomes 2017), voted to repeal net neutrality protections, arguing in favor of freedom of enterprise:

> Investment in high-speed networks has declined by billions of dollars. Notably, this is the first time that such investment has declined outside of a recession in the Internet era (...) that means fewer next-generation networks are built, less competition; fewer jobs for Americans building those networks; and that means more Americans are left on the wrong side of the digital divide (...) Online traffic is exploding, and we consume exponentially more data over time. And we are imposing ever more demands on the network with the dawn of the Internet of Things, with the development of high bit-rate applications like virtual reality, and with new activities like high-volume bitcoin mining that we can't yet fully grasp.

In practice, broadband will once again be classified as an information service, while the mobile Internet will be considered as an interconnection service. By being organized in different ways, it may be marketed at different prices, depending on market interests, and because of the importance of the United States in the network regulatory discussions, there will undoubtedly be impacts on other countries. This discussion is already underway in Brazil, threatening the achievements gained with the introduction of net neutrality in the Civil Rights Framework for the Internet.

There is a conflict between the flow of information without blockages or national filters and regulation made in each country. In countries where media corporations are powerful, as in the United States, there is a strong commitment to limit communication practices and technological creations, subordinating them to the laws of the market. The greater the control by large media corporations over production and distribution of content and technology, the higher the profitability of their business.

Another controversial issue in the drafting process was the article that regulates user identity. The possibility of giving control over user identity within the regulatory framework was cause for concern. Anonymity was seen as a necessary condition to guarantee freedom of expression.

In addition to the complex technical aspect related to registration access records, there is a concern regarding the possibility of tracking Internet users' access, a factor that would affect the loss of users' anonymity. Protecting navigation logs was not foreseen in the original project and was considered as problematic and as a possible form of privacy invasion.

3.4 The Debate About Approving the Law

While the bill (No. 2.126/2011) was prepared collaboratively through collective authorship, President Dilma Rousseff took ownership and presented it to Congress at the end of August 2011. The proposal, establishing the set of principles, guaranties, rights, and duties related to the use of the Internet, was submitted to National Congress on a priority basis.

The process approving the bill was not easy. Despite given a priority basis, it took 3 years to be approved, even under pressure from civil society, with public hearings in various states, among other proceedings, such as petitions, online applications, etc.

Net neutrality was one of the bill's most controversial points. Several representatives, especially those connected to the telecommunication sectors, did not agree with this article. In this context, these representatives prevented the bill from being voted upon in its original version.

On September 11, 2013, President Dilma Rousseff[13] requested a vote on the bill under constitutional urgency. Regarding this legal provision, Senate and Chamber of Deputies had 45 days to approve the project. Otherwise, no bill could be voted. That is, in legislative jargon, when an issue ends in stalemate, there is a legislative gridlock, meaning that Congressional agenda is locked and no bill could be voted.

Given the urgency, parliamentarians would have until the end of October to vote, but that was not what happened. There was a lot of pressure from the telecommunication sectors, considering that they were radically opposed to the approval of network neutrality. This sector has powerful representation in Congress that was able to manipulate various politics interests and thus to gain enough votes for repealing the article dealing with neutrality. Given the gravity of the situation, this was the most critical moment of the whole process; thus, the government decided to withdraw the bill, believing that it would lose the vote, and the possibility of developing democratic legislation would be lost.

After regaining sufficing political support, the bill was again presented and approved in the Chamber of Deputies and later in the Senate before the NETmundial meeting. Several celebrities as well as social and political leaders expressed support for approving the legislation.

> The regulatory framework gained support not only from the president and several politicians but also from some celebrities. Among those who favored approving the bill were singer and former Minister of Culture, Gilberto Gil, comedians Gregorio Duviver and Rafinha Bastos, actor Wagner Moura, French philosopher Pierry Lévy and British Tim Berners-Lee, considered the inventor of the World Wide Web, the WWW. (Carvalho 2014)

Support from national and international celebrities – in addition to those civil society groups who mobilized in favor of the legislation – was vital for its approval. Received with enthusiasm by the international community, its approval was held at NETmundial by President Dilma Rousseff.

> President Dilma Rousseff signs the Civil Rights Framework for the Internet into law during NETMundial, a meeting held in São Paulo that brings together representatives of more than

[13] At that point, former President Dilma Rousseff was already aware of the allegations made by former CIA employee, Edward Snowden, when he revealed details of some surveillance programs used to monitor the former president's talks with her advisors. These revelations were essential to raising awareness about the importance of approving the regulatory framework, especially by ensuring the rights of Internet users.

> 90 countries, including 27 ministers. "The Internet we want is only possible in a scenario based on respect for human rights, in particular privacy and freedom of expression. The rights that people have offline should also be protected online," Rousseff said. (Araujo 2014)

To understand the exact position occupied by Brazil at that time, we stress the presence of Tim Berners-Lee alongside the president during the passage of the Internet regulatory framework. Lee severely criticized the US's spying on the former president and said plainly that other countries should follow Brazil's example by creating laws that protect the rights of users on the Web and also the form of Internet governance practiced in the country, affirming that "Brazil defends that Internet governance be, by its very nature, multisectorial, multilateral, democratic, and transparent."

The meeting also discussed other Internet-related issues, such as the need for a new governance form regarding ICANN (Internet Corporation for Assigned Names and Numbers) to follow multistakeholder and multilateral dynamics, ensuring the transparency of the agency's actions.

3.5 Implementing the Civil Rights Framework for the Internet

Tim Berners-Lee sent a letter to federal deputies defending the regulatory framework and reaffirming the role of the "Brazilian Internet Constitution" in network governance:

> Brazil loves the Internet. Over half of the Brazilian population is online, and this number is rising fast (...) Your country became the first to take the bold step of putting in place a 'Bill of Rights' for the Internet – or Civil Rights Framework for the Internet. This visionary approach has already had global impacts. From Italy to Nigeria, other countries are seeking to emulate Brazil. And for this, the Internet loves Brazil. This is why I am saddened to learn that the principles enshrined in the Marco Civil may be under threat following a new report on combatting cybercrime which you are being asked to consider (...) Proposals that threaten net neutrality by providing new powers to block applications or throttle content are deeply worrying, as they would deal a hammer blow to freedom of speech online – at a time when freedom of speech and robust debate is needed more than ever. I urge you to reject the proposals in the report before you, consider alternative ways to combat cybercrime, and recommit to the principles of *Marco Civil* that protect the Internet as it should be – an open, collaborative space for all to benefit from. (Berners-Lee 2016)

Civil society also played a crucial part in the implementing of the new law despite the fact that it was a prerogative of the presidency of the republic and included vital input from CGI.br during various debates.

On May 11, 2016, Decree No. 8871/16[14] implementing the Civil Rights Framework for the Internet was published. It was one of the last measures taken by

[14] Decree No. 8871/16 is available at https://www.planalto.gov.br/ccivil_03/_ato2015-2018/2016/decreto/d8771.htm

former President Dilma Rousseff before her impeachment. Although this is not our primary focus here, it is important to emphasize that the country was experiencing an adverse political situation, taking into account the strategic interests and specific points of the legislation.

The Decree dealt explicitly with network neutrality as well as procedures related to the storage and protection of personal data by Internet service providers. Articles No. 17 to No. 21 in Decree No. 8.771/16 are especially noteworthy: Chapter IV – On Supervision and Transparency, the possibility of regulation by National Telecommunications Agency (Anatel) (Article No. 17), the National Consumer Secretariat (Senacom) (Article No. 18), and the Brazilian System for the Defense of Competition and other bodies (Article No. 18 to No. 21). However, the whole chapter does not specify the role of each agency concerning activities that involve personal data. By leaving vacant this section, the new law did not define the regulatory model and its instruments to safeguard this data, bypassing what should be specified.

This imprecision regarding the role of regulatory bodies leaves a gap that can be a real problem for law enforcement. Also, it is important to note that the Brazilian Agency of Telecommunications (Anatel) does not have regulatory competency involving personal data in the same way that of the National Consumer Secretariat (Senacom) and its bodies. The Consumer Protection Code provides protection and has acted as a consumer ally, especially in clarifying information on the terms of use and licenses related to the Internet.

It is also essential to make the character of CGI.br clear. Although it plays a key role in the debate over Internet regulation, it is mainly an agency regarding technical matters and has no regulatory power. In this sense, one of the enormous problems of the Brazilian Civil Rights Framework for the Internet is that there is no specific regulatory body capable of protecting the privacy of personal data.

Another critical point is the breakdown of net neutrality due to technical reasons. One of the arguments alleged by telecommunication companies contrary to neutrality rests concerns new investments in infrastructure capable of providing quality services to users. Brazil offers meager broadband quality at a high cost. Consumers pay 100% and receive 10% of the speed hired. The regulatory framework has become an essential tool for demanding better services.

Another controversial issue is in Article No. 15, Chapter III in Law No. 12.965/14.

> Chapter III: On the Provision of Internet Connection and Applications
>
> ART 15. The Internet application provider established as a legal entity, and carrying out this activity in an organized, professional and economic manner, shall maintain the respective records of access to Internet applications, under secrecy, in a controlled environment, and secure for a period of six (6) months, pursuant to the regulation.
>
> § 1 A Court order may oblige, for a certain time, Internet application providers that are not subject to the provisions of the caput to keep records of access to Internet applications, provided that they are records related to specific facts in a given period.
>
> § 2 The police authority, administrative authority, or the Public Prosecutor's Office may om a precautionary way request any Internet application provider that access records for Internet applications be stored, including for a period longer than expected in the caput, subject to the provisions of subsections 3 and 4 of art. 13.

§ 3 In any case, the provision to the applicant of the records referred to in this article shall be preceded by judicial authorization, as provided in Section IV of this Chapter.

§ 4o In the case of penalties for non-compliance with the provisions of this article, the nature and gravity of the infraction, the damages resulting therefrom, any advantage obtained by the violator, the aggravating circumstances, the offender's history and recidivism shall be considered. (Brazil 2014)[15]

Recent reports of US surveillance and spying at an international level have further reinforced the need to create parameters and rules in global Internet governance to safeguard against such measures.

It is worth mentioning that the US government's espionage allegations made by former Central Intelligence Agency employee Edward Snowden, including monitoring Rousseff's conversations with key advisors, initiated an important debate regarding the privacy of users on the Internet. This revelation drew Rousseff's attention to the issues of Internet regulation, specifically the regulatory framework.

In light of these complaints, Brazil played a prominent role in placing this issue on the international agenda and promoting the discussion of new rules for governance and the functioning of the Internet as well as the commitment to approve the regulatory framework when President Dilma Rousseff spoke at the United Nations Assembly in 2013.

The Decree assures that access and application providers cannot discriminate in data package traffic management, thus ensuring their expected isonomic treatment. It means that no provider can favor some service for some people at the expense of others.

Data traffic may have some bias only in exceptional circumstances or when there is a need to prioritize emergency services, such as when the government needs to send messages to users with some information about environmental disasters. In this item – even if at a slow pace, given the urgency – it is important to note that Bill No. 5276/2016, which regulates access to personal data in the country, is running in Congress. Most scholars consider this bill be modern form of legislation.

3.6 Final Considerations

With the regulatory framework approval, Brazil consolidates its reputation as the leader of democracy, contributing to a new era in which the rights of the citizens of the world will be protected by digital constitutions (Berners-Lee apud Lima 2014).

Tim Berners-Lee statement above reveals the country's importance in the global debates on Internet governance and reaffirms that it is possible to innovatively develop public policies with input from civil society. Brazil's interest in Internet

[15] The original, in Portuguese, is available at http://www.planalto.gov.br/ccivil_03/_ato2011-2014/2014/lei/l12965.htm

governance is not so recent, given the work of the Internet Governance Committee (CGI.br) created approximately 20 years ago that involves multistakeholder participation, an open and transparent arrangement, and compelling civil society involvement. The approval of the Brazilian Internet "Bill of Rights" has attracted the attention of the international community involved in Internet regulation. The country has demonstrated that it is possible to develop an advanced public policy along with civil society.

This article sought to recover the main aspects of the drafting process regarding the Brazilian Internet regulatory framework. Internet regulation is currently a very controversial and complex issue, comprised of governments, civil society, Internet communities, and the private sector who formulate the principles, norms, rules, and decision-making procedures that define how networks should function. However, it is a field with considerable contestation, bringing together actors with the divergent interests and positions regarding the Internet, notwithstanding its possibly free and collaborative architecture that aims to assure freedom of expression.

Central points of contention include the following: (1) net neutrality; (2) privacy, security, and vigilance; and (3) freedom of expression. The only countries that have passed laws ensuring net neutrality are Brazil and Chile, two countries that present the most advanced rules on civil rights, citizenship, and the standard use of the Internet.

Despite the passing progressive legislation to govern the Internet, there are no guarantees that such legal protections cannot be reversed or weakened. Currently, Brazil is facing one of the most severe political crises in its history, involving allegations of corruption, influence peddling, and illicit enrichment by prominent political leaders from the three branches of government (executive, legislative, and judiciary). In fact, its deep distrust involves not only these government bodies but the political system as a whole.

In this complex scenario, conservative political forces have emerged and assured private companies broad powers to define their business models in various sectors of the economy. More specifically, telecommunication companies have been able to align with the conservative sectors in the National Congress to impose a political agenda that promotes profound setback in several economic sectors with significant impacts for the majority of the people. For example, the Ministry of Communications was extinguished and its responsibilities assumed by the Ministry of Science and Technology.

In December 2017, another major threat to the maintenance of the open Internet occurred with the end of net neutrality in the United States, which will undoubtedly cause a massive impact on countries such as Brazil. According to the lawyer Flávia Lefèvre, from the Brazilian Association of Consumer Protection (Proteste), ending net neutrality in Brazil would require a change in legislation:

> Institutionally and legally, the situation of Brazilian and American Internet services are very different. The US, with its leading role, certainly influences the whole world. But, whoever says there will be an immediate reaction is being opportunistic (...) Breaking this principle would be disaster in a country where 50% of households do not have Internet access, and even among the 50% that has it, only 23% have access to fixed broadband. You would be going against another right which is the right of digital inclusion. (Lefèvre apud Mendonça 2017)

According to Lefèvre, civil society is still absorbing the Civil Rights Framework for the Internet. It is in this context that the achievements of the new legislation are under threat. Although the law is already implemented, the strategy of the conservative sectors is focused on presenting bills that challenge fundamental aspects of the regulatory framework, such as protection of freedom of expression and net neutrality. If these bills are approved, they will overrule the established regulation, which implies a profound setback, not only for democratically constructed legislation but also in regard to weakening the position of the principal position acquired by Brazil in the debate on global Internet governance.

References

Abramovay, Pedro Vieira. 2009. Marco Civil da Internet. Cultural Digital. http://culturadigital.br/marcocivil/tag/convite/. Accessed 4 Apr 2018.

Afonso, Carlos. 2010. Neutralidade no trânsito da Internet? In *Cidadania e Redes Digitais*, ed. Sergio A. Silveira. São Paulo: Comitê Gestor da Internet no Brasil/Maracá – Educação e Tecnologias.

Almeida, Virgílio A.F. 2014. Marco Civil, NETmundial e a modernidade do Brasil na Internet. Politics. https://www.politics.org.br/edicoes/marco-civil-netmundial-e-modernidade-do-brasil-na-internet. Accessed 6 June 2018.

Araujo, Bruno. 2014. Dilma sanciona o Marco Civil da Internet na abertura da NETMundial. Globo.com. http://g1.globo.com/tecnologia/noticia/2014/04/netmundial-inicia-com-obrigado-snowden-e-defesa-da-Internet-livre.html. Accessed 5 Dec 2017.

Benkler, Yionchai. 2000. From consumers to users: Shifting the deeper structures of regulation toward sustainable commons and user access. *Federal Communication Law Journal* 52 (561): 579.

Berners-Lee, Tim. 2016. An open letter to Brazilian lawmakers. World Wide Web Foundation. https://webfoundation.org/2016/04/uma-carta-aberta-aos-legisladores-brasileiros-an-open-letter-to-brazilian-lawmakers/. Accessed 12 Dec 2017.

Bragatto, Rachel C., Rafael C. Sampaio, and Maria A. Nicolas. 2015. Inovadora e democrática. Mas e aí? Uma análise da primeira fase da consulta online sobre o Marco Civil da Internet. *Revista Política & Sociedade* 14: 125–150.

Brazil. Presidência da República. Casa Civil. 2010. Decreto n° 7.175, de 12 de maio de 2010. Institui o Programa Nacional de Banda Larda – PNBL e dá outras providências. Diário Oficial da União, Seção 3, 13 Maio 2010.

———. 2014. Lei n° 12.965, de 23 de abril de 2014. Estabelece princípios, garantias, direitos e deveres para o uso da Internet no Brasil. Diário Oficial da União, Seção 1, 24 Abril 2014.

Carvalho, Caio. 2014. O Marco Civil foi aprovado. E agora, o que vai mudar na Internet brasileira?. Canaltech.br. https://canaltech.com.br/Internet/O-Marco-Civil-foi-aprovado-E-agora-o-que-vai-mudar-na-Internet-brasileira/. Accessed 5 Jan 2017.

Cetic.br – Centro Regional de Estudos para o Desenvolvimento da Sociedade da Informação. 2017. TIC Domicílios 2016 aponta estabilidade no número de domicílios conectados por meio de Banda Larga Fixa. Centro de Estudos sobre as Tecnologias da Informação e da Comunicação. http://cetic.br/noticia/tic-domicilios-2016-aponta-estabilidade-no-numero-de-domicilios-conectados-por-meio-de-banda-larga-fixa/. Accessed 15 July 2017.

CGI.br – Comitê Gestor da Internet no Brasil. 2014. Governança multissetorial e pluriparticipativa da Internet no Brasil. https://www.cgi.br/noticia/videos/cgi-br-governanca-multissetorial-e-pluriparticipativa-da-Internet-no-brasil/10062. Comitê Gestor da Internet no Brasil. Accessed 4 Apr 2018.

———. 2017. Comitê Gestor da Internet no Brasil completa 15 anos. Comitê Gestor da Internet no Brasil. https://www.cgi.br/noticia/releases/comite-gestor-da-Internet-no-brasil-completa-15-anos/. Accessed 12 Oct 2017.

Cremades, Javier. 2009. *Micropoder: a força do cidadão na era digital*. São Paulo: SENAC.

Denardis, Laura. 2013. *Internet points of control as global governance*. Internet Governance Papers no. 2, Centre for International Governance. https://www.cigionline.org/sites/default/files/no2_3.pdf. Accessed 6 June 2018.

Denardis, Laura, and Mark Raymond. 2013. Thinking clearly about multistakeholder internet governance. Eighth annual GigaNet symposium, Bali.

Galloway, A.R. 2004. *Protocol: How control exists after decentralization*. Cambridge, MA: The MIT Press.

Galloway, Alexander R. 2009. Rede é regulação e nada mais – Alexander Galloway interview at Fórum da Cultura Digital Brasileira. http://culturadigital.br/blog/2009/10/30/entrevista-com-alexander-galloway/. Accessed 7 Mar 2010.

Gomes, Helton S. 2017. EUA decretam 'fim' da neutralidade de rede e decidem que provedor pode controlar acesso à Internet. Globo.com. https://g1.globo.com/economia/tecnologia/noticia/eua-decretam-fim-da-neutralidade-de-rede-e-decidem-que-provedor-pode-controlar-acesso-a-Internet.ghtml. Accessed 20 Dec 2017.

Lessig, Lawrence. 2006. *El código 2.0*. Madrid: Traficantes Del Sueño.

Lima, Luís. 2014. Dilma destaca defesa a Marco Civil feita por Berners-Lee. Estado de São Paulo. http://politica.estadao.com.br/noticias/geral,dilma-destaca-defesa-a-marco-civil-feita-por-berners-lee,1148991. Accessed 20 Sept 2014.

Kleinwächter, Wolfgan. 2014. Netmundial: divisor de águas na regulamentação da Internet? Politics. https://www.politics.org.br/edicoes/netmundial-divisor-de-%C3%A1guas-na-regulamenta%C3%A7%C3%A3o-da-internet. Accessed 6 June 2018.

Kurbalija, Jovan. 2016. *Uma introdução à governança da internet*. São Paulo: Comitê Gestor da Internet no Brasil.

Mendonça, Heloísa. 2017. O fim da neutralidade da Internet nos EUA pode afetar o Brasil? El País. https://brasil.elpais.com/brasil/2017/12/15/politica/1513351293_438759.html. Accessed 4 Apr 2018.

Souza, Carlos Affonso, and Ronaldo Lemos. 2016. *Marco Civil da Internet: construção e aplicação*. Juiz de Fora: Editar.

Wolton, Dominique. 2003. *Internet, e depois? Uma teoria crítica das novas mídias*. São Paulo: Sulinas.

Chapter 4
Piraí Digital: A Pioneering Experience in Digital Inclusion

Wilson Couto Borges, Estélio Gomberg, and Vânia Coutinho Q. Borges

Abstract Free access to the Internet is widespread, and open networks are expanding to address digital inclusion. But few know that Piraí was one of the first cities to offer free Internet access in Brazil. Piraí has about 25,000 inhabitants, located almost 100 km (kilometers) from the state capital of Rio de Janeiro. In 2004, the "Piraí Digital Program" began. It sought to disseminate digital culture, involving initiatives of digital inclusion, media education, and information technology management. Although located in a hilly area, the city achieved expansive wireless Internet coverage in a relatively short time. This chapter provides an analysis of the experience based on published materials in the press, statements, and academic papers about the program. This pioneering project in the field of digital inclusion around the world included an interdisciplinary character based on the emancipatory vision of technology.

4.1 Introduction

The 1970s represented a kind of symbolic landmark in the transformation of information and communication environments, especially with the Internet. The potential of connecting a global computer network, bringing subjects, organisms, and institutes together, seemed to lie in the possibility of shortening special and temporal distances, conforming to what the Canadian philosopher Marshall McLuhan (2011, 2013) proposed with the designation global village, that is, a world where everyone could potentially be connected. However, one cannot ignore the fact that much of the impetus associated with the development of what Armand Mattelart (2000)

W. C. Borges (✉) · V. C. Q. Borges
Institute of Communication and Scientific and Technological Information in Health, Oswaldo Cruz Foundation, Rio de Janeiro, Brazil
e-mail: wilson.borges@icict.fiocruz.br

E. Gomberg
Department of Philosophy and Human Sciences, State University of Santa Cruz, Ilhéus, Brazil

A. Pereira Neto, M. B. Flynn (eds.), *The Internet and Health in Brazil*,
https://doi.org/10.1007/978-3-319-99289-1_4

called the "new immaterial resource" was associated with a simultaneously occurring double movement. The first of these was the need to expand markets as an alternative to overcoming the oil crisis that marked the first half of the 1970s; the second was the overlap between the conception of the Information Society and the phenomenon characterized as globalization. For this reason, we agree with the diagnosis produced by this French sociologist when he points out that:

> The "exit crisis" imperative called for new technologies to be planted "at the head" of the economies of the large industrial countries. The notion of the "information society" appeared in the research programs of governments and international institutions since 1975 in the Organization for Economic Co-operation and Development (OCDE) and four years later in the European Union. With the advance of deregulation and privatization, the myths of the information age would cross the path of the "global age." (Mattelart 2000, 1)

This broader scenario propelled a global movement to encourage the generation of the so-called Information Society. Brazil, as well as other developing countries, has become a fertile soil so that, as Azevedo (2012) observed, new entities could enroll in the "Information Society and the world economic system" (Azevedo 2012, 42). With this more general picture, the 1990s, but especially in the first decade of the 2000s, was the scene of the acceleration in the transformations of the processes of interaction between individuals and of these with organizations through so-called information and communication technologies (ICTs) that held a primordial role in this new social configuration. In these terms, Brazil arrived in the worldwide wave of dissemination of a digital culture, defined by Manuel Castells according to the following:

> i) ability to communicate or merge any product based on a common digital language; ii) ability to communicate from the local to the global in real time and, vice versa, to dilute the interaction process; iii) the existence of multiple modes of communication; iv) interconnection of all digitized networks of databases (…) with the data storage and retrieval system; v) ability to reconfigure all configurations creating a new meaning in the different layers of the communication process; and vi) gradual constitution of the collective mind by networking, through a set of brains with no limits, at this point I refer to the connections between networked brains and the collective mind. (Castells 2009, 3)

Even if we can speak of a certain irreversibility of the dissemination of digital culture, it is not a stable process, nor is it developed in the same way in the most varied countries, especially in developing countries, as in Brazil. In these cases, between the end of the twentieth century and mid-twenty-first century, digital exclusion predominated, mainly affecting low-income people who did not have the resources to buy a computer and pay for access to the network. Also, their knowledge and skills in dealing with these new technologies were scarce. In this context, the expansion of the Internet depended in no small extent on "public policies for digital inclusion, and joint actions between the State, civil society, and private companies, for individuals to be included in this Society" (Lemos 2007, 30).

Thus, this chapter aims to present and analyze one of the first experiences of digital inclusion in Brazil – the "Piraí Digital Program" started in 2004, in the municipality of Piraí, in the state of Rio de Janeiro. To do so, we will be using information produced by the press, as well as statements from those responsible for the creation and implementation of the project, and academic works that have taken Piraí Digital as an empirical object of investigation. Then, we will use such references to reflect on how the process of digital inclusion in the region occurred, primarily from two perspectives: the availability of access and appropriation that the population makes of information and communication technologies (ICTs) within their reach. Finally, we will dwell on one axis of Piraí Digital, which is health. For us, the choice seems to be justified by the understanding that health (whether in that municipality or Brazil as a whole) is a necessary field to debate both in terms of public policies and especially in terms of citizenship.

The political, social, educational, and informational architecture of the "Piraí Digital Program" sought to democratize access to information and communication media in order to generate opportunities for professional, social, and economic development. This aspect made it a pioneering effort both nationally and internationally. In a historical moment and in a region where the material conditions were very adverse for its execution and maintenance, the dissemination of a digital culture characterizes the program, through actions of digital inclusion, education for new media, and the computerization of management.

4.2 Piraí: Local Development Program, International Highlight

Piraí has an area of approximately 506 m^2 (square meters), whose population, according to the last census (IBGE/2010), totaled 26,309 inhabitants. It lies 89 km (kilometers) from the capital of the state of Rio de Janeiro (Southeastern Brazil); the municipality composes the microregion of the Paraíba Fluminense Valley and the South Fluminense mesoregion. It borders the cities of Barra do Piraí, Paracambi, Pinheiral, Rio Claro, Volta Redonda, and Mendes.

In 1996, an unemployment crisis struck the city. This crisis was due to the dismissal of a large number of employees from the newly privatized Light and Pirahy Paper Factory (a supplier to the Souza Cruz company and sold to a foreign group). In the face of the crisis, public administrators hoped to create alternative sources of revenue and income generation (Coelho 2004; Teles 2010, 109). As described by Teles (2010):

> At that time, the agricultural and peripheral economy (in relation to Volta Redonda and Rio de Janeiro, especially), in the words of Professor Franklin Coelho, was drastically battered and government leaders felt compelled to act with force and speed. The Local Development Program of Piraí was launched in January 1997 to combat an unemployment rate of 10% of the economically active population and a fall in agricultural production. The municipal tax revenue needed a substantial increase to meet the obligations of public administration. Light (an electric power supply company) was called upon to pay taxes on its property in the municipality, and the city was granted the right to collect taxes on electricity generation, which were previously collected in the [state] capital. (Teles 2010, 109)

Piraí sought to create a market encompassing the Paraíba Valley region by providing opportunities for cooperation between municipalities, whose diagnoses pointed to the formation of productive chains and groups supported by labor and income policies. The universalization of access to ICTs was perceived as an important amalgam for socioeconomic development. Teles (2010, 109), in this sense, affirms the following:

> Stimulation of economic enterprises; integration of popular enterprises into production chains; guarantee of access to credit, training and promotion of technical assistance to informal economic sectors; fair-trade efforts; monitoring of the economic profile of the municipality and creation of means of access to the Internet to enhance relations between the market and the territorialized economy of these communities.

From this point of view, the 1997 Computer Master Plan (drawn up in 1996) began to develop the "Piraí Digital Program." The proposal to democratize access to information and communication as a way to generate opportunities for economic and social development formed the basis for the program's strategy. In this sense, the plan sought to establish a relationship between ICTs, local development, and citizenship. Created in 2004, the "Piraí Digital Program"[1] was born with the strategic vision of a "local information society in which the citizen becomes the protagonist in the production, management, and enjoyment of the benefits of new information and communication technologies" (Iizuka 2004, 21).[2] This program was structured through the use of the hybrid system with wireless support (HSWS) and the use of free software (SoL). This system deserves emphasis because, according to Teles (2010):

> This network installed in Piraí (HSWS - hybrid system with wireless support, which operated at a minimum speed of 54 Mbps in its wireless portion) interconnected all the public buildings in which other local networks were available, and was used as the communication support phone number IP. There were 23 wireless, 68 wired, and three satellite connected points in rural areas with limited access.

It is important to highlight that the adoption of HSWS emerged as an alternative in the face of the refusal by Brazil's National Bank for Economic and Social Development (BNDES)[3] to finance Internet expansion in the city. The first request

---

[1] The pioneering aspect of the "Piraí Digital Program" was not initially associated only with the year of its implementation. Unlike other similar initiatives, such as Sampa.org (held in São Paulo), the digital inclusion movement in Piraí did not occur mainly through telecenters (as in the case of São Paulo). The city of Rio de Janeiro connected telecenters, schools, health units, and libraries, proliferating access points – either by cabling or wireless – providing coverage in almost 100% of the city.

[2] Later we will return to this premise of the citizen as the main actor in the production, management, and usufruct of the project's benefits. A central question in this process will need to be answered: What conception of citizenship is the "Piraí Digital Program"?

[3] Brazil's National Bank for Economic and Social Development (BNDES) is the federal government's main instrument for long-term financing and investment in all segments of the Brazilian economy, whether for modernization, expansion plans, or realization of new businesses with the goal of generating jobs, income, and social inclusion for the country. For more information, see https://www.bndes.gov.br/wps/portal/site/home/quem-somos/.

for funding was rejected by the bank, which considered the proposed technology solution very expensive. However, once a subsequent request was approved, the municipality received approximately US$ 370,000 to boost the computerization process through the bank's Tax Administration Modernization Program (PMTA).[4] However, it is important not to lose sight of the fact that the "Piraí Digital Program" had, as Iizuka (2004) and Teles (2010) point out, "tributary and efficiency-related genes,"[5] focused on "decentralization of services to the taxpayer, integration of systems, control of public expenditures with management support software, training of employees and increasing the efficiency and transparency of public management" (Teles 2010, 114).

The democratization of access to information and communication media in Piraí should also be associated with the integration of governmental, corporate, and community networks. These networks also produced (or facilitated) the promotion of IT actions on five fronts, promoting "global development: government, education, community, business and health" (Teles 2010, 114). In this scenario, we can see the construction of an Information Society through, as demonstrated by Marques (2010), "a strong technological determinism [where] the ICT artifacts are often taken as being neutral in relation to the effects they produce" (Marques 2010, 5). Critically, the author notes that such a movement ends up producing, as one of its effects, the construction of the notion that "countries, regions or individuals that do not adhere to the inexorable race towards the 'Information Society' would be part of a new category of exclusion, now based on digital criteria" (Marques 2010, 5).

Given this scenario, it is possible that the "Piraí Digital" initiative lies between two perspectives: one more focused on the sophistication of diffusion/dissemination and the other more related to appropriation/uses. In the case of the former, the following would be necessary:

> The sustainability of economic, political, ethical and legal processes, the existence of physical infrastructure, and the availability of accessing computers and the internet, the existence

[4]The Program for the Modernization of Tax Administration and Management of the Basic Social Sectors (PMTA), by the National Bank for Economic and Social Development (BNDES), has been used as a step for digital cities' project by financing various technological updating activities. Created in August 1997, it has served approximately 330 Brazilian municipalities. "At the time of its creation, the PMTA's main objective was to stimulate an increase in revenues, in order to reduce the municipal dependence in relation to federal and state transfers." Later, in May 1999, the PMTA was renamed the Modernization Program of Tax Administration and Management of the Basic Social Sectors. "The original objectives were to improve the quality of citizen service and greater transparency in government action" (for more information, see http://www.bit.ly/gcd-pmat). In 2000, Piraí had already been included in PMTA. It was the first small municipality to be a part of this program, which was mainly aimed at cities with more than 500,000 inhabitants. In May 2001, about $370,000 was released to the city through the PMTA.

[5]As highlighted by Teles (2010), between 2003 and 2005, the resources of the Program of Modernization of the Tax Administration sustained progress training civil servants, contracting services, and constructing the physical structure in the municipality. During that period, the SHSW system connected 29 public buildings where internal networks were installed. In addition, the city government purchased administrative systems and computers and started the geoprocessing of the city.

> of content produced locally and/or adapted for local use, and education focused on the autonomy of individuals and their capacities to take advantage of the opportunities of the information society. (Teles 2010, 79)

The perspective involves:

> A creative and social process of appropriation that transcended the diffusion of products and services of individual consumer goods. This process can be understood as a continuous interaction between the assimilation and reinvention of meanings and uses of ICTs by individual or social actors, significantly influenced by the contexts in which it occurs and transforms itself. (Marques 2010, 5)

The process of creating the "Piraí Digital Program" represented a true watershed in both the relationships between municipal public bodies as well as in altering the population's routines. However, one of the issues that emerged at this juncture is precisely the role ICTs played in this context. More specifically, would expanding access to the Internet be sufficient to profoundly transform social practices built on other parameters?

4.3 Digital Inclusion: Providing Access or Social Appropriation of ICTs?

The "Piraí case" deserved prominence both nationally and internationally as it became a symbol of a model whose longevity came to attract the attention of several organizations. A report published by the newspaper *O Globo*,[6] 10 years after the creation of Piraí Digital, showed that the initiative became a concrete reality and gain international acclaim. With the title "TEDx celebrates ten years of project that took the internet to the streets of Piraí" (Wrede 2014), the newspaper emphasized the pioneering nature and singularity of the project: "In 2004, the residents of Piraí did not know what the internet was. In the municipality of the State of Rio, there was not even a provider. After ten years, the city enters the digital world, hosting one of the editions of TEDx" (Wrede 2014, 1).[7] All the theses and dissertations about Piraí Digital we reviewed (Azevedo 2012; Teles 2010; Iizuka 2004, 2008; Castro 2007; Coelho 2004) are unanimous in pointing out that the project's main impact was promoting the democratization of access to information and knowledge, especially in terms of taking the web to the municipality's streets, houses, and institutions. This perspective seems to be confirmed when internationally recognized personalities and authorities visit Piraí. As described by *O Globo* newspaper:

[6] Founded in 1925, *O Globo* is one of the three leading newspapers in Brazil. With a circulation of approximately 130 thousand (Monday to Saturday) and 170 thousand (Sunday) copies per day, according to the latest research by the Circulation Verification Institute (CVI), it is one of most economically and politically consolidated newspapers considered credible and shaping public opinion.

[7] For more references on TEDx Piraí, see http://tedxpirai.com.br/sobre-o-tedx-pirai/.

> TEDx is a local version of TED (acronym for Technology, Entertainment, Design) project, created in the USA in 1984, and has had lectures by celebrities like Al Gore, Bill Clinton, Bill Gates and Bono Vox. Osni Silva, a former trainee of Piraí Digital, told the city's Secretary of Science and Technology that the event crowns the city's efforts to enter the online world:
>
> – We did not have any access, broadband, provider, nothing. It was just the same rural town. The city then decided to embrace the idea and spread the internet. Piraí Digital promotes the dissemination of digital culture. (Wrede 2014, 1)

It is entirely possible that a considerable part of the success of the "Piraí Digital Program" is associated with three dimensions. The first one, as described by Teles (2010), is related to the fact that this project encompasses "a range of initiatives in five areas – government, education, health, business, and citizenship[8] – with the objective of overcoming digital exclusion in the municipality and contribute to its development" (Teles 2010, 8). The second relates to what Teles describes as the result of an "association of artifacts – computer networks, telecenters, Master Plans and others – and people in efforts to overcome digital exclusion and contribute to local development" (Teles 2010, 8). The final dimension concerns the participation of the three spheres of government (municipal, state, and federal), like the movement that occurred in the adoption of 1:1[9] computing, in the area of education, from 2007.

We believe that it is plausible to affirm that the dimensions described in the previous paragraph are directly related to the assumption that "digital exclusion is a set of social, economic and cultural consequences of unequal distribution in access to computers and the internet" (Castro 2007, 29). Thus, it seems to make sense that the entry of ICT in Piraí accompanied the training of public officials, teachers, and students in the use of these devices, notably amidst the expansion of telecommunications products and services. Thus, we agree with Castro (2007) when he states that "digital exclusion must be understood as a process of broader social exclusion, feeding and being nourished by it" (Castro 2007, 30). At the limit, what Piraí Digital intended was to enhance citizenship for a relatively significant portion of its population by including them digitally. But, would access (granted) to public services by local authorities be enough to strengthen the citizenship of the city's residents?

It is in this context that an idea of emancipatory communicational practice begins to give the residents of Piraí an opportunity to possess communicative citizenship guaranteed by the democratization of communication using available digital resources. With this vision, works such as those of Castro (2007) and Marques (2010) understand that the consequences of introducing ICTs seem to have contrib-

[8]Of these areas, health will be highlighted. We will dedicate a section to it, since in Brazil the notion of the right to communication and information is inherent to the right to health. Since the 1988 Constitution, all three are considered citizenship goods.

[9]The project of incorporating technology in the field of education established the 1:1 ratio of One Computer Per Student (OCS). The pilot project took place in the Arrozal neighborhood in the municipal education network (more specifically in CIEP 477) since 2007 (considered an acceleration phase of the project).

uted more with improving communication between municipal agencies than in fostering the interaction between citizens and government. Castro (2007) is even more radical when he states that "the application of ICTs in Piraí has served more the objective of improving the efficiency of service provision and dissemination of government acts than in increasing social control and citizen participation in municipal management" (Castro 2007, 63). This statement reinforced the population's forgetfulness even of the creation of the "city council" as a tool of social accountability for the program. It is important to emphasize that this does not minimize the fact that the "Piraí Digital Program" is a state-based initiative (in this case, in the municipal sphere), which, centered its articulation with various celebrities/actors (national and international organizations, civil society, civil servants, education professionals), sought to promote a broad process of digital inclusion.

However, the authors reviewed in this study insist that the increase in participatory governance and social appropriation of ICTs did not take place in equal proportions, insomuch as the project could not guarantee the capacity to appropriate the new digital technologies nor accessibility and ineligibility of content and interfaces (Marques 2010, 5). Such an understanding of the process also led Castro to state that "the supply of services and technology were not sufficient factors to confirm the hypothesis that ICTs have increased the exercise of citizenship in the municipality" (Castro 2007, 48). It is worth mentioning, from structuring the process, the creation of the "city council" to accompany the execution of the "Digital City Master Plan" (Teles 2010), as a social control device, did not guarantee that the Digital City has become more socially inclusive. Thus, these authors did not observe, in the case of Piraí, a direct relationship between the increase in the presence of ICTs and an increase in the exercise of citizenship.

Yet, the academic studies we reviewed do not fail to highlight the advances contained in the "Piraí Digital Program," especially in addressing digital exclusion. One of the most positive effects, either through interviews granted by representatives of the municipal government or by other devices used in the research carried out by Teles (2010), is a "significant increase in the Basic Education Development Index (BEDI) in the first municipal school that provided each of its students with a personal computer in September 2007" (Teles 2010, 19). At the same time, recognition for the city's achievements was neither negligible nor insignificant, including awards granted by the "Getúlio Vargas Foundation (Public Management and Citizenship Award in 2001) (Teixeira et al. 2004), the success in the area of information technology – IT, in 2005) and the Intelligent Community Forum (Top Seven Intelligent Communities, 2005)" (Teles 2010, 20).[10]

[10] The prize granted to the city of Piraí in 2001 (public management and citizenship) demonstrated that the Master Plan of the Digital City was beginning to show a successful experience. Already as "Piraí Digital Program," the 2005 awards celebrated the singularity of the initiative. But it would be from 2007, with the One Computer Per Student Project (UCA) that Piraí would gain national and international prominence, attracting the curiosity of the world for digital inclusion practiced in the municipality, especially with the visits of the president of Brazil and a former US president.

Another critical element of the "Piraí Digital Program" is associated with computerizing government processes. That is, from its implementation, there was an increase in the capacity to make government actions more transparent. This aspect enhances the participation of the population to engage and oversee public entities through virtual spaces. This participation opens up the possibility of citizen power over state action to the extent that such information is made public. However, since the emphasis on governance was sometimes greater in aspects related to the measurement of efficiency and effectiveness of government (to the detriment of the citizen), it is more likely that disseminating digital culture had greater potential in terms of economic development than in social development (Teles 2010). Still, this does not seem like an important shortcoming. Beforehand, we had seen in this process the possibility for constructing new spaces of public debate.

What seems to be a fundamental element of the Piraí project is sustaining a process of broad digital inclusion, as described by Teles (2010), especially when affirming that such sustainability "should not only be economic-financial. It is necessary to guarantee the continuity of the programs beyond the political transitions of the governments, providing regulatory frameworks and an ethical environment to include those at the margins of the digital society" (Teles 2010, 81). In this way, would it be possible to understand this ethical environment, described by this author, as an environment in which there would be a transition between the habilitation for use and the appropriation of the technologies by the citizens? If the answer is positive, we can suggest that Piraí initiated an "information-inclusion" (inclusion of information) process, but not of "commu-inclusion" (inclusion of communication).

Based on our reflection on the relationship between communication and citizenship, this process of "commu-inclusion" would need to be the basis of a new type of social engagement that leads to an increase in the exercise of citizenship. For us, in a scenario in which ICTs help shape human relationships in high modernity, we cannot think of communication only from the technical devices (i.e., special channels, new platforms) of information transmission. It is essential to incorporate communication as an element of interaction, dialogue, exchange of information, and knowledge. In this sense, when we propose the notion of "commu-inclusion," we want to think about the relationship between ICTs and the citizen, not only because of the possibilities they open up but mainly because of the way in which people are summoned to use them. With this perspective, what we seek to perceive is how technology in use enhances human actions.

Another aspect of Teles' (2010) research, which allows us to emphasize a specific hypertrophy of the technological dimension of the "Piraí Digital Program," is the conclusion that there was a shallow "level of knowledge by the population about the municipality's digital inclusion initiatives, including its actions in the sense of becoming a digital city" (Teles 2010, 107). In one aspect, this (un)familiarity of the project may have represented an obstacle to the very notion of digital citizenship – understood here as an action driven by the existence of devices that allow some interaction with government agencies. When Teles points out that "for the general population, the digital city is not well understood and its manifestations are not fully understood" (Teles 2010, 107), it is possible to infer that the first motivation may not have been digital inclusion, but the search for management efficiency in public administration through the use of the ICT, as seems to have been the case for health. In this regard, the main objective was "to reduce the number of cesarean sections and eradicate child malnutrition" (Teles 2010, 110). It was, therefore, a relative dynamic (even digital) relationship between public authorities and the population in promoting citizenship.

Based on reports, dissertations, theses, and press reports, we present the following hypothesis: Piraí Digital was a democratization project through access to the means of information and communication launched as an alternative to address economic adversity. In fact, it is undeniable that such democratization occurred, mainly due to the universality of network coverage, which reached almost 100% of the city's districts. However, we still tend to agree with Teles, when he emphasizes that "The DNA of Piraí Digital has tributary genes and links to efficiency" (Teles 2010, 114).[11] These genes indclibly mark the "Piraí case" in the overvaluation (and hypervisibility) of state actions. They also underscore the political decision that the municipality's own network should serve schools and health posts, for example, to the detriment of the creation of other spaces for the use of ICTs. In our view, it is necessary to pass a verdict about whether Piraí Digital was good or bad for the city or the population, but to highlight its innovativeness and singularity, as well as its capacity to open space for the possible exercise of citizenship.

It is important to state that, for us, access to ICTs via the Internet, in particular neighborhoods aimed at integrating information systems, is less important than how the user/citizen can access them. This vision is not trivial, nor does it represent a play on words. The area of health, within the "Piraí Digital Program," is not "the best known or even one in which the main events make the program noteworthy. Such characteristics mark the area of education" (Teles 2010, 153). However, insofar as the project's image is strongly linked to education,[12] one of the most noticeable effects is that the school ends up representing the space for direct digital inclusion, secondary to other spaces. As a result, an understanding emerges that in health such an addition would take place indirectly:

> Exactly those who do not directly use or operate computers and other components of the intelligent digital layer superimposed on the city become the main benefactors (…) the elderly, illiterate, sick, technophobic or uninterested in technology and other categories of citizens that, although not being able or willing to use computers for example, are served by the health system or receive the benefits of improved tax collection. (Teles 2010, 210)

[11] The recurrence to Teles is justified by the more detailed research (doctoral thesis) on Piraí Digital. With it, the author not only takes the process of digital inclusion as an objective of research but problematizes it in light of economic, social, technological, and cultural elements. In parallel, IT and Internet actions are analyzed on five fronts: government, education, community, business, and health. It is last, as we have already mentioned in the previous note, places the dimension of citizenship as the structuring element of the field.

[12] Chapter 14 discusses the issue of e-learning.

4.4 ICTs and Health: Emancipation and Direct Citizenship

A considerable part of the success of Piraí Digital, as we have already pointed out, is attributed to the articulation between five great original areas of the program, which sustained the program and allowed the subsequent advances. These are the area of government (.gov), education (.edu), health (.health), business (.com), and community (.org).[13] For Teles (2010), as already mentioned by Castro (2007) and Marques (2010), the .org and .com areas were the least advanced in terms of digital inclusion. These areas were not included in the program because financing halted the process of universal access process because the National Telecommunications Agency (Anatel), the federal regulatory body, denied the city of Piraí the right to charge for access. One of the observed effects was that job creation was less than desired. At the same time, to the extent that a large part of the population also lacked Internet access coverage, there were few signs of social participation.

As regards the area of government (.gov), it was responsible for the political support of the development process of Piraí, especially its digital face, based on the Computer Master Plan (thanks to a partnership between Piraí and the University of Brasília [UnB], Rio de Janeiro State University [RJSU], Fluminense Federal University [FFU], and the Federal University of Rio de Janeiro [FURJ]). With this, the municipality built an Internet network that served administrative bodies but included schools and health posts. One of the main contributions made with such an initiative was the city's contribution to the construction of a regulatory framework for telecommunications in Brazil. The opportunity proposed a type of license that allowed municipalities to operate their own networks (Teles 2010, 120). Network expansion to schools ended up putting the .edu area at the forefront of Piraí Digital for the incorporation of public education in the process. Thus, the image of the program is linked to the adoption of ICTs in education.[14]

Despite some areas having greater prominence (.gov) or visibility (.edu) and those in which there were notably fewer advances (.org and .com), we would like to focus our attention on what we see as an intermediary category, that is, where although there was no prominence or visibility, there were some advances: health. This area, for us, has (or should have) a place in the debate on the process of incorporation and broadening access to ICTs associated with the dimension of citizenship. At the same time, as we are professionals and intellectuals that take health as a right, a citizen's asset, some of the considerations/observations produced along these pages will not necessarily be negated. Starting from this perspective, we reject the thesis that health can be represented (as in the case of the Piraí Digital) only as some form of indirect inclusion of the population, that is, citizens only feel the effects of technology and do not use, do not appropriate, or do not directly participate

[13] Its structure and projects can be accessed at https://www.piraidigital.com.br/.

[14] As we mentioned in note 6, as of 2007, the One Computer Per Student Project placed Piraí on national and international stage to the extent that authorities like former president Luís Inácio Lula da Silva was present at a ceremony delivering computers to students or that former US President Bill Clinton and former presidential candidate Al Gore were present at the TEDx event.

in the project. From this perspective, we aim to present the foundations of the incorporation of health as a citizen's asset, as we did with recovering the bases of Piraí Digital (materialized in the Computer Engineering Master Plan).

As part of the process in which several countries sought new ways of organizing health systems – as a result of their high cost, increasing complexity, and low resolution – the World Health Organization (WHO) and the United Nations Children's Fund (UNICEF) carried out the First International Conference on Primary Health Care in 1978 in Alma-Ata. This Conference proposed that the highest possible level of health in the world will be achieved by the year 2000. Such a policy became known as Health for All in the year 2000. Matta and Morosini (2008) emphasize that the Alma-Ata Declaration is a proposal that covers more than actions geared toward primary health care. It highlights the need for health systems that are universal and thus understand health as a citizen's right[15]:

> Health is the result of economic and social conditions, and inequalities between countries; and also stipulates that national governments should lead the management of health systems, stimulating international technological, economic and political exchange and support. (Matta and Morosini 2008)

During the 1970s and 1980s, significant political mobilization against dictatorships plaguing Latin-American countries and to address important crises in public health systems characterized the region. In Brazil, this mobilization contributed to the creation of the expanded concept of health during the 8th National Health Conference (NHC) held in 1986. Accompanying the processes of redemocratization and the health workers reform movement (*movimento sanitarista*) in the country, which coexisted with new agendas for confronting economic crises, the expanded concept of health became a framework of citizenship and was integrated into the Brazil's Constitution of 1988.

> In a broad sense, health is the result of the conditions of food, housing, education, income, environment, work, transportation, employment, leisure, freedom, access to and possession of land and access to health services. Thus, it is mainly a result of the forms of social organization, of production, which can generate great inequalities in the levels of life. (Brazil 1986, 4)

Considered as a historical milestone for health and citizenship, the 8th NHC also recognized that, for the full exercise of the right to health, education, *information, and participation of the population should be guaranteed in the organization, management, and control of services and health actions* (National Council of Health 2005). In this historical context, the Piraí Digital Program began to develop. The Conferences of 2000 and 2003 (11th and 12th, respectively) reaffirmed the strategic importance of communication and information actions as a way to guarantee social control and the participation of society in public health efforts and policies. This movement eventually included communication as one of the ten thematic axes

---

[15] It does not seem inappropriate for us to remember that part of the "Piraí Digital Program," as far as the health area is concerned (organization of the system, skills, distribution, incorporation, and increase of information systems) is based on current policy.

for discussion at the 12th health conference. This fact demonstrates the value and importance of communication, information, and social participation in the construction and maintenance of the Unified Health System (known by its acronym in Portuguese *Sistema Único de Saúde* – SUS).

SUS' principle of universality guarantees all citizens, as a right, access to health, public, free, and integral. The conquest of democracy in Brazil, after a significant period of military dictatorship, brought the possibility of change, allowing the exercise of citizenship through, for example, social control through the participation of the population. In addressing the issue of citizenship and modernity, Coutinho (2008) draws attention to the fact that popular sovereignty, democracy, and citizenship have synonyms. He also points out that we can define them as "the effective presence of social and institutional conditions that enable all citizens to participate actively in the formation of government and, consequently, in the control of social life" (Coutinho 2008, 50).

When we look at the creation and development of the health dimension in the "Piraí Digital Program," we note that the element of citizenship appears timid, not to say fragile, in the same way, for example, that the existence of the aforementioned city council remained unknown. If the reference is the municipal health council, even in this case, what happened was, at most, a protected citizenship right, insofar as its deliberations were guided by information provided by the state executing agency (the municipal health department) and not through broad debates about health services with the population since citizens are not aware of the spaces where such discussions should take place. At most, the municipal health council[16] was just a co-manager, failing to fulfill/occupy its role of social participation and social control of the local health system.[17]

In discussing the concept of law, Coutinho (2008) points out that, in the first place, it arises from a demand formulated by certain classes or groups. It is a social phenomenon; it has a history. Therefore, the requirements for law arise at a given historical moment, which is why we identify the Piraí Digital initiative with the

[16] This institute, as Neto and de Faria (2012a, b) pointed out, was created based on a particular notion of social control, not that traditionally linked to state control over society but that of society over the state. In Brazil, as highlighted by the researcher, "social control is associated with the struggle for participation in the decision-making process and the democratization process" and has in its architecture "health councils composed of representatives of users, professionals and managers of services of the Unified Health System (SUS) at the municipal, state and federal levels. The users started to have equal representation in relation to the other two stakeholders. Currently, all the states of the federation and all the municipalities of the country have Health Councils" (Neto and de Faria 2012a, 442).

[17] We agree with the assertion that one of the main characteristics of information in general, and health information in particular, consists of decision-making at whatever level. However, it cannot be neglected that it is from reality itself (and from the phenomena observed in this reality) that data are gathered, later transformed into indicators and then into information, which will serve for decision-making. In this sense, it is necessary to problematize a process where such data are already mediated by professionals who observe (and soon interfere) in that same reality. To a certain extent, a space for debates and constructions of alternatives for health ends up being a space for a referendum about the actions developed by the municipal manager.

potential to strengthen citizenship. Our vision is based on the fact that the program increased the access points to the Internet and thus not only increased the possibility for consuming information but also the population's participation and social control. What could represent the effort achievement seems to be the open door for widening and consolidating the principles of citizenship. Thus, in the modern world, there is a space to promote a tendency toward the universalization of citizenship and also the inclusion of civil rights in the agenda. In addition to previously acknowledged political rights (such as the right to vote and to be voted, the right of association and organization), which were not universal, and modern civil rights[18] (such as the right to life, freedom of thought, to come and go, property, etc.), we also have social rights[19]: achievements that enable a citizen's participation, albeit minimal, in the wealth created by the community. In this way, we have rights to health, communication, and information as part of a set of social rights.

There are authors, such as Torres (2012), who point out that usually, the field of health presents the themes of communication, information, and education in an associated and sometimes interconnected way. Thus, the relationship between health and communication can be, for example, through the communication products and press, advisory activities of institutions, and entities linked to the sector. However, they would only be their instrumental expression. Going beyond this vision, the author emphasizes that, according to this expanded concept of health, all three – information, communication, and health – are related, in the field of rights, as an expression of citizenship. Still, in relationship to rights, Torres (2012) cites Araújo and Cardoso (2007) to highlight that communication at its interface with health is associated with the notion of rights. The objective of this interface is to improve the public health system, by establishing a "public debate on topics of interest and guaranteeing people the expansion of their citizen participation in health policies" (Araújo and Cardoso 2007, 61).

For this reason, Teles (2010) affirms that there is an indirect digital inclusion when we "feel the effects" of what we do not participate in directly. The very notion of "an intelligent digital layer superimposed on the city" (Teles 2010, 210) empowers the potential of exercising citizenship[20] through the construction of the "Piraí Digital Program." After all, was the increase in participation and social control not a structural element of the program? Was this not the sense of universal access to the Internet in the municipality? Toward this end, it is possible that we can still find some glimpses that add the right to communication and information (as with the right to health) to the "freedom of public expression of cultural, political and cultural agendas and demands with equal access to channels of expression - means of communication" (Pitta 2007, 48). It seems plausible to think that the process in Piraí stems from the extension of digital access points. But, did this mean concomitantly, for example, increased channels for expression?

[18] Chapter 3 discusses the Brazilian Civil Rights Framework for the Internet.

[19] According to Coutinho, there is a risk of misunderstanding here, since "all rights, including civil and political rights, are social because of their origin and validity" (Coutinho 2008, 63).

[20] The issue of civil society and online citizen participation is addressed in Chap. 11.

For Oliveira (2004), the terms communication, information, and social participation interconnect; communication and information are the way in which the third can be operationalized – social participation. Thus, it is understood that the variables communication and information can not only intervene in social relations but also contribute to the execution of public health policies involving widespread participation. When we understand that information and communication in health assist decision-making and that there are different ways of interpreting them, it becomes fundamental to question how they have been produced, made available, and used. Therefore, once again we wonder if such information has reached the user, how it has been accessed (if it has been) by the citizen. We ask: Are modern information and communication technologies capable of dealing with the intense interaction between technology and society today?

Observing the "Piraí Digital Program" from the prism of information production, the observation that "transmitting knowledge to those who need it is a social responsibility" (Saracevic 1996, 43) appears appropriate. For this reason, knowledge management as the basis of the "Piraí Digital Program" is not forgotten. Thereby, it would be incumbent upon information science to "confront the problem of effective communication of knowledge and its records among human beings, in the institutional or individual context of the use and information needs" (Saracevic 1996, 47). To the extent that the production (and dissemination) of scientific knowledge helps in decision-making – particularly crucial in the case of social participation and decision-making for public policy-making – we again ask ourselves: To what extent is information contextualized to meet the information needs of those who access the system?

4.5 A New Possible World: The Relevance of Utopia[21]

There is no denying the pioneering aspects of the "Piraí Digital Program." The innovative process provided free access to the Internet in both urban and rural environments, interconnected public buildings (such as schools, libraries, health units), telecenters, created access points (through cables, where possible, and wireless), and covered almost the entire city, in a region far from the capital of the state of Rio de Janeiro. To a large extent, this project disseminating digital culture is a tributary of a broader movement to use ICTs. It is closely associated with the phenomenon of globalization, amidst economic crises, which Brazil acutely faced in the 1990s during a time that combined the end of a dictatorship, the incorporation of a neoliberal agenda, and the arrival from the Internet.

[21] The title of this section is a direct homage to the great Brazilian intellectual Milton Santos who, in *Another Globalization: From Single Thought to Universal Consciousness* (Santos 2000), traces a diagnosis of a largely excluding development model, which has in the diffusion of technology one of its most powerful arms, without losing sight of the gaps opened by this same model for human emancipation.

In our view, there were three factors that allowed Piraí to achieve this novel status: the first was the role of the local executive in the construction of the program, from the point of view of financial support (budget forecasting, seeking funding from other sources) or searching for partnerships (universities, state, and federal governments).

The second was valuing the relationship between ICTs and education. Although the One Computer Per Student Project was a very important achievement for the "Piraí Digital Program," this project would have not succeeded if the necessary infrastructure had not been built. That is, without the Internet having arrived at schools, there would be no way in which each student would be able to use a netbook to access the network.

The third point is the model and the adoption of an infrastructure such as the hybrid system with wireless support (HSWS) linking all public administration buildings, schools, health centers, and telecenters, as well as the use of freeware. This choice cheapened the cost of the program since the municipal government did not have to pay for the software.

These three pillars allowed the city to rapidly expand wireless Internet coverage as a state policy. One of the strengths of the program was the view that technology could be emancipatory, that is, allow Piraí's population be included in digital culture. Our perception is that it was precisely here that the central point of this experience resided: Piraí Digital inaugurates, as described by Santos (2000), the realm of possibilities. However, realizing that the residents of Piraí would experience digital inclusion by feeling the effects of the process and not acting as citizens, the program seems to have not left the field of possibilities. This is the sense, for example, of the fact that health in Brazil is a field involving social participation and exercise of citizenship.

In discussing the social causes of health inequities in Brazil, the National Commission on Social Determinants of Health reported that overcoming the problem of information inequities depends on policies that are specific to achieving that end and that the same should "be based on the recognition that knowledge, information and the Internet are public goods and should therefore be the object of public policies" (CNDSS 2008, 78). Thus, its report not only recognizes that communication and information are central elements to prevent a population's health problems from worsening but also points out that ICTs, especially the Internet, are valid strategies for access to health information. By incorporating the Piraí Digital Program as a policy of the state, the city government has taken a significant step toward reducing health inequities and, at the same time, enhancing this dimension of citizenship.

However, this movement was not automatic and is not complete. One cannot speak of citizenship, popular participation, and social control only by increasing access points to the Internet[22] nor by arguing that the indirect benefits (for groups

[22] The example of laptops given to students is a clear example of this. We are not going to consider the fact that the students cannot take the equipment home. But the determination of use at school restricts the uses that families could make to the technology if they could accompany some activities of their sons and daughters in the home.

below the intelligent digital layer superimposed on the city) are sufficient to ensure that the population is included digitally. What is worth mentioning in the "Piraí Digital Program" was the premise that systems used by hegemonic actors can be liberating and emancipatory. In the words of Santos (2000):

> The families of emerging techniques at the end of the twentieth century – combining computer science and electronics – offer the possibility of overcoming the imperative of hegemonic technology and at the same time admit the proliferation of new arrangements, with the resumption of creativity (...) consumption and indulging in the pursuit of citizenship. (Santos 2000, 165–166)

The possibilities are open for their use, "combining computing and electronics," states Santos (2000, 168). However, alternatives have to be found to transform information and knowledge into action. This means that it is not enough that expertise empowers if this empowerment continues to be asymmetric. Agreeing once again with Araújo and Cardoso (2007), we must confront the challenge of getting social actors to seize the knowledge produced in a combination of empowering/empowerment so that unequal positions in a dispute process are reduced. Thus, the utopia of citizenship will finally find ground to germinate.

References

Araújo, Inesita, and Janine Cardoso. 2007. *Comunicação e saúde*. Rio de Janeiro: Ed. Fiocruz.

Azevedo, Maria de Lourdes Pinheiro. 2012. Cidade Digital e as novas espacialidades urbanas: o caso de Piraí, RJ. Master's thesis, Federal University of Viçosa, Viçosa.

Brazil. 1986. *Ministry of health. 8ª Conferência Nacional de Saúde*. Brasília: Ministry of Health.

Castells, Manuel. 2009. Creativity, innovation and digital culture a map of interactions. *Telos Magazine*. https://telos.fundaciontelefonica.com/telos/articulocuaderno.asp@idarticulo=3.htm. Accessed 1 Jan 2018.

Castro, Paulo Alexandre Batista. 2007. Tecnologias de Informação e Comunicação, desenvolvimento local e cidadania: o caso do município de Piraí. Master's thesis, University of Brasília, Brasília.

CNDSS – Comissão Nacional sobre os Determinantes Sociais da Saúde. 2008. *As causas sociais das iniquidades em saúde no Brasil*. Rio de Janeiro: CNDSS.

Coelho, Franklin Dias. 2004. Ambiência produtiva e construção social no território: o programa de desenvolvimento local no município de Piraí. In *Congreso Internacional del Clad sobre Reforma del Estado y de la Administracion Pública*, vol. 9. Madrid: CLAD.

Coutinho, Carlos Nelson. 2008. Notas sobre cidadania e modernidade. In *Contra a corrente: ensaios sobre democracia e socialismo*. São Paulo: Cortez Editora.

Iizuka, Edson Sadao. 2004. Piraí: Município digital. http://inovando.fgvsp.br/conteudo/documentos/20experiencias2004/3Pirai-Municipio_Digital.pdf. Accessed 1 Aug 2017.

———. 2008. Fluxos de ações e processos decisórios na gestão pública local: estudos de casos de projetos e programas inovadores em municípios de pequeno porte populacional. PhD dissertation, Fundação Getúlio Vargas, Rio de Janeiro.

Lemos, André, ed. 2007. *Cidade Digital: portais, inclusão e redes no Brasil*. Salvador: Edufba.

Marques, Marcos de Carvalho. 2010. Sociedade da Informação e inclusão digital: do discurso à prática. Master's thesis, Universidade Estadual de Campinas, Campinas.

Matta, Gustavo, and Márcia Valéria Morosini. 2008. Atenção Primária à Saúde. In *Dicionário da Educação Profissional em Saúde*, ed. I.B. Pereira and J.C.F. Lima. Rio de Janeiro: EPSJV/Fiocruz.

Mattelart, Armand. August, 2000. Cómo nació el mito de internet. Le Monde Diplomatique.
Mcluhan, Marshall. 2011. *The Gutenberg galaxy: the making of typographic man*. Toronto: University of Toronto Press.
———. 2013. *Understanding media: the extension of man*. Berkeley: Gingko Press.
National Council of Health. 2005. History of the National Health Council. http://conselho.saude.gov.br/apresentacao/historia.htm. Accessed 1 Aug 2017.
Neto, Pereira, and André de Faria. 2012a. A representação dos usuários nos Conselhos de Saúde: uma contribuição para o debate. *Physis* 22: 441–462.
———. 2012b. *Conselho de favores: controle social na saúde: a voz dos seus gestores*. Rio de Janeiro: Editora Garamond.
Oliveira, Valdir de Castro. 2004. Comunicação, informação e participação popular nos conselhos de saúde. *Revista Saúde & Sociedade* 13: 56–69.
Pitta, Aurea Maria da Rocha. 2007. Políticas de comunicação comparadas: comunicação e democracia na saúde em dois municípios em gestão plena. *ECO-PÓS* 10: 45–63.
Santos, Milton. 2000. *Por uma outra globalização: do pensamento único à consciência universal*. Rio de Janeiro: Record.
Saracevic, Tefko. 1996. Ciência da informação: origem, evolução e relações. *Perspectiva em Ciência da Informação* 1: 41–62.
Teixeira, Marco Antônio, Melissa Godoy, and Carla Coelho. 2004. *20 experiences of public management and citizenship*. Rio de Janeiro: Fundação Getúlio Vargas.
Teles, Adonai. 2010. Piraí Digital e a Teoria Ator-Rede: a trajetória de inclusão e desenvolvimento de Piraí. PhD dissertation, Fundação Getúlio Vargas, Rio de Janeiro.
Torres, Rodrigo Murtinho de Martinez. 2012. Estado, comunicação e cidadania: diálogos pertinentes sobre a relação entre direito à saúde e direito à comunicação. PhD dissertation, Universidade Federal Fluminense, Niterói.
Wrede, Catharina. 2014. TEDx celebra dez anos de projeto que levou internet às ruas de Piraí. *O Globo*, .March 14. https://oglobo.globo.com/rio/tedx-celebra-dez-anos-de-projeto-que-levou-internet-as-ruas-de-pirai-11877375. Accessed 27 Apr 2017.

Chapter 5
Civil Society and Online Citizen Participation: A Case Study of the Nossas Cidades Network

Claudio Luis de Camargo Penteado, Marcelo Burgos Pimentel dos Santos, and Rafael de Paula Aguiar Araújo

Abstract The article presents a study of civil society's use of Information and Communication Technologies (ICTs) to promote e-participation. The focus is on the *Nossas Cidades* [Our Cities] network (www.nossas.org) formed to facilitate civil society groups' advocacy on local public authorities. Based on the paradigm of networked society, organizations act by meeting the institutional norms through ICTs to promote different types of activism. The *Nossas* network uses interactive and collaborative technological tools to broaden political participation in cities' civic affairs. To evaluate Rede Nossas Cidades, the methodology of the "Index of Political Participation and Influence" (IPPI) of civil society was used to identify the effectiveness and efficacy of the organization in the policy-making process. The results demonstrate that Nossas Cidades represents an important experience of e-participation toward the development and practices of digital activism.

5.1 Introduction

The development of Information and Communication Technologies (ICTs) has introduced essential transformations in sociability and human activities. Although a significant part of the world population still has no access to the Internet and other digital communication devices, Web-based technologies already belong to more

C. L. de Camargo Penteado (✉)
Department of Engineering and Social Sciences, Federal University of ABC, Alameda da Universidade, s/n, São Bernardo do Campo 09606-045, SP, Brazil

M. B. P. dos Santos
Department of Social Sciences, Federal University of Paraíba, Conj. Pres. Castelo Branco III, João Pessoa 58033-455, PB, Brazil

R. de Paula Aguiar Araújo
Department of Politics, Pontifical Catholic University of São Paulo, R. Monte Alegre, 984, São Paulo 05014-901, SP, Brazil

A. Pereira Neto, M. B. Flynn (eds.), *The Internet and Health in Brazil*,
https://doi.org/10.1007/978-3-319-99289-1_5

than half the world's population.[1] Indirectly, almost all people are affected in some ways by the use of these technologies either by governments offering public services and computerizing bureaucracies or by commercial enterprises (be they information technology or traditional companies) that have gradually been adopting ICTs in their various activities. Additionally, new digital communication channels shape the context of contemporary human sociability.

Data from the 2015 International Telecommunications Union show that the number of users on the Internet has rapidly increased in the last 15 years. In 2000 the number of people able to access the network was 400 million, and in 2015 it had already reached 3.2 billion people all over the world (ONUBR 2015), thus pointing out an essential change in the communication structure of contemporary society.

In Brazil, there are already over 36 million (57%) households able to access the Internet according to a recent survey by TIC Domicílios of 2016.[2] However, an important factor for the increase in Internet users, mainly in Brazil, is connections through mobile devices. The survey shows that the number of digital accesses per mobile phone has grown by over 50% in the last 2 years, reaching 43% of the total number of accesses in 2016. TIC Domicílios points out that in 2016, 69% of the individuals had already used the Internet at a particular moment in their life, a figure 5% bigger than 2013 data (CETIC 2018).

The daily use of digital technologies in different activities and human practices has led to the digitalization of social life by introducing new ways of sociability and behaviors[3] (Lupton 2014). For the people connected, using and appropriating ICTs are part of their work, leisure, entertainment, personal communications, access to services and information, among others. Software programs, applications, platforms, and social media already comprise daily activities of this connected population, which creates jobs, means of social interaction, and fields of knowledge.

Interactivity and collaborative practices through the Internet have enabled the appearance of social actions developed by using information networks of communication (Benkler 2006). The emergence of a networked society restructures the material and symbolic practices of production carried out by the flow of information within a large global network in which information has become the raw material (Castells 1999). Similarly, it inaugurates social interactions that take place through ICTs using communicational processes where users now occupy a more active role in the process of production, transmission, and circulation of information.

---

[1] According to data of Internet World Stats (2018), 54.4% of the world population has access to the Internet.

[2] The data presented next have been obtained from the *TIC Domicilios* ["which refers to Information Communication Technology Household"] survey conducted annually by the CETIC (Portuguese acronym of the *Centro de Estudos sobre as Tecnologias da Informação e da Comunicação*, or Regional Center of Studies for Development of the Information Society), a part of the Brazilian Internet Steering Committee (CGI.br), the body in charge of Internet governance in the country, of defining guidelines for registration of domains, allocation of IP (Internet Protocol), and management of the .br domain. It also promotes studies and research geared toward the development of technical quality and innovation. For more information about CETIC, see www.cetic.br

[3] Chapter 6 discusses the issue of virtual communities of chronic kidney patients.

The composition of an interconnected public sphere has broadened communication mechanisms, enabled political events to gain more visibility (Castells 1999), and allowed for an unlimited discursive space through which Internet users can express or share their opinions (Rasmussen 2013) or manifest indignation and hope by organizing public protests using social networks. According to Castells (2013), this is what happened in the protests involving the Arab Spring, *Los Indignados* (in Spain), and Occupy Wall Street movements, as well as other protests from around the world, including those that took place in Brazil in 2013.

The sociotechnical characteristics of Internet interactivity have broadened the possibilities for citizens' political participation. In addition to active involvement in the communication process inside informational networks, digital technologies now create possibilities for online deliberation and engagement (Coleman and Gøtze 2001), online participation practices (Macintosh 2008), ways of online activism by using the social networks for spontaneous political mobilization (Anduiza et al. 2014), participation through online petitions (Wright 2015), and slacktivism[4] (Vie 2014).

Participation through communicational devices, i.e., e-participation, is a hybrid field of knowledge related to interdisciplinary studies, including democracy theory (known as a way of deepening democracy through online participation), communication studies (via the development of mediation models and channels), technology studies (design and operation of digital tools for participation), and information science (concerned with the ways through which data and knowledge are socially produced and distributed). With the development of ICTs and an increase in the number of people connected, governments at local, regional, and national levels are experimenting with several forms of e-participation (Macintosh et al. 2009).

Within the expansion of the Internet and use of communication devices to broaden participation, civil society organizations have also been using online communication channels in their sociopolitical practices to promote political debate and involvement beyond formal institutional channels and to influence public policies (Araújo et al. 2015).

In this article, we present a study about the *Nossas Cidades* [which translates into "Our Cities"] network, a civil society organization that is structured within network dynamics and mainly acts by using digital participatory tools to advocate social, cultural, and political campaigns and causes by pressuring public agents and institutions. The objective of this study is to present an example of how civil society has been using digital technologies to promote e-participation and influence public policies.

The article has four parts. In the first part, we present a brief discussion on the use of ICTs to promote participation and democratization of the society. Next, the article offers a description of the *Nossas Cidades* network and identifies the digital tools used to encourage e-participation. In the third part, the influence of the *Nossas Cidades* network is analyzed by applying and gauging the Political Participation and Influence Index developed by the authors. Finally, we discuss the findings in light of the digital technologies used by the *Nossas Cidades* network.

---

[4] Neologism in the English idiom to define the "slack activism" done at virtual social networks

5.2 Democracy, Participation, and ICT

The re-democratization process in Brazil started in the second half of the 1980s, and citizens' participation in the political process began to be a fundamental element for consolidating and increasing and the quality of the democracy (Diamond and Morlino 2005). The Constitution enacted in 1988 embraced the principle of participation by institutionalizing forums and creating regional and citizens' councils in specific sectors, in addition to other ways of promoting civil society's participation within the political process (Moisés 1990, 2010). Such involvement has made room for the community to get involved in the development of public policies. In this sense, the creation of ombudsmanship bodies at public institutions and other mechanisms of transparency and accountability, including some of which became laws to make the government more responsive to citizens, has been important.

With the appearance of ICTs, the possibilities for political participation have increased. Contemplating emerging themes of citizenship and carrying out creative political actions have become possible, including civil society's involvement in political and decision-making arenas. The number of these tools has increased and, in a way, has altered the possibilities of exchange and debates about collective and public topics.

ICTs have connected local citizens to a global network of digital information that helps to develop new institutional designs and favors interactions between public officials and citizens. There are now more possibilities for increasing the number of consultations, debates, deliberations, follow-ups, access to information, and social control. According to Castells (1999, 2009, 2013), in a networked society, there is the possibility of incorporating the Internet's communicational devices and mechanisms to broaden citizens' participation in public life through social groups, thus decreasing the costs of participation and making it more interactive and democratic.

These structural changes have occurred as a result of the presence of technologies that started to permeate citizens' daily life[5] and, at the same time, their relationship with the State. As to public administration, the Brazilian government has begun to articulate new ways of political participation inside institutional arenas by using new tools to discuss and develop different designs and formats to administer public policies in an attempt to increase cost-efficiency as a way to limit expenditures (making adjustments and/or fiscal austerity), mainly to social programs.

The institutionalization of participatory policy channels in Brazil has led to, for example, to the creation of Councils of Managers of Public Policies Managers Councils, spaces for the civil society to participate in the development of policies, mainly in the process of formulating, implementing, and evaluating them (Pereira et al. 2016). Another example for increasing participation in public administration is experiments in participatory budgeting (*Orçamento Participativo* – OP), which began in Porto Alegre in 1989 and spread to other Brazilian cities and around the

[5] Chapter 17 addresses a pioneering digital inclusion project in Brazil.

world as a model of good governance and interaction between public officials and citizens (Wampler 2008). OPs have become a reference and included in agendas of international agencies, where they have assumed different meanings (Oliveira 2016). OPs have been studied as a case of citizen participation in several places in Brazil and worldwide and won the UN-Habitat Award of good governance practice in 1996 (Avritzer 2003).

Therefore, the re-democratization process in the 1980s, whereby civil society organizations played a more active role in their relationship to the State and in developing public policies, shaped political participation in contemporary Brazil. In a second instance, from the 1990s onward, marked by globalization and neoliberalism, citizen participation in public policies has become one of the organizational principles advocated by national and international agencies as a mechanism to improve efficiency in public administration, accountability, and transparency (Milani 2008).

The development of ICTs has brought profound changes in the operating dynamics of the society, creating conditions for broadening citizen participation through interactive and collaborative communication channels. Political involvement through these communicational devices, such as e-participation, can be understood as the means through which different institutions, organizations, and citizens use technological tools to support and render support to a democratic decision-making process by creating opportunities for consultation and dialog between government and citizens (Medaglia 2012).

Archon Fung et al. (2013, 30) developed:

> Six models of how digital technologies might affect democratic policies: the empowered public sphere, displacement of traditional organizations by new digitally self-organized groups, digitally direct democracy, truth-based advocacy, constituent mobilization, and crowd-sourced social monitoring.

Some recently published academic studies deal with the use of ICTs in the Brazilian political field. Whether because of the possibility in participating and being involved in decision-making processes about the development of public policies or because citizens are empowered when they participate, these papers discuss and examine actions proposed both by the State and by civil society. As examples, the cases of the *Nossa São Paulo* network, *Instituto Pólis*, *Mobilize Brasil, and MCCE* (Movement to Combat Electoral Corruption) can be mentioned, among other examples of interest groups that use ICTs (Silva and Araújo 2014; Santos et al. 2013; Araújo et al. 2014). The same thing occurs with the *Nossas Cidades* network analyzed herein.

Civil society, in its various ways of association and organization, has started to play a more active role inside the political process, in social mobilization and in pressuring public officials, which Gohn (2005) calls civil society protagonism. Supported by the Internet, people have organized themselves into political advocacy groups, including Avaaz or Change that are proposing laws, such as the *Ficha Limpa* Law (Clean Records Law) (Santos 2016; Wright 2015) and gathering names to support online petitions.

Using ICTs enables ordinary citizens to participate in the political field through actions promoting common interests, and additionally it helps to develop the idea of belonging, whether to encourage association and community practices or to make room and give voice to xenophobic groups. The potential of interaction and articulation through ICTs points toward the possibility of having citizens act locally based on national or international markings. Local actions achieved prominence due to their effectiveness with public administration precisely because public policies are geared more toward people's daily lives, motivating citizens to fight for their right to the city and to develop their civic culture.

The data presented in the next section assesses civil society's use of ICTs to promote citizen participation and influence in public policies. Ten local autonomous networks composing the *Nossas Cidades* network were analyzed, to wit: *Meu Rio, Minha Sampa, Meu Recife, Minha Campinas, Minha Garopaba, Minha Porto Alegre, Minha Ouro Preto, Minha Jampa, Minha Blumenau, and Meu Oiapoque*[6] and their influences within the development of local public policies.

To this end, a two-phase methodology was used: initially the use of the tools available at *Nossas Cidades* network was identified and analyzed descriptively and qualitatively, and then the actions taken were evaluated by applying the Political Participation and Influence Index (*Índice de Participação Política e Influência* – IPPI) (Araújo et al. 2014) that measures civil society's participation and influence in the development of public policies. Since it is a complex phenomenon, the IPPI includes six analytical dimensions about ICT uses and resources in order to evaluate initiatives concerning the interactions between the State and civil society. The dimensions deal with Internet uses and resources (D1), actors and social capital (D2), e-participation (D3), strategies of social mobilization (D4), how advocacy evolves and its relation to public policies (D5), and repercussions on the traditional media (D6).[7]

5.3 The Nossas Cidades Network

Civil society organizations have employed cyberspace to create new communication channels and to develop new formats of participation and mobilization through software programs, applications, and platforms, available via the Internet. The case of the *Nossas Cidades* network is a notable example of an organization that uses the principles of the networked society and ICTs to promote online citizen participation, mixing online and offline actions, i.e., virtual and real ones.

---

[6] These networks listed in their original Portuguese names literally translate into the following, all of which refer to cities in Brazil: My Rio de Janeiro, My São Paulo, My Recife, My Campinas, My Garopaba, My Porto Alegre, My Ouro Preto, My Jampa, My Blumenau, and My Oiapoque. The *Meu Oiapoque* network is still being implemented, and *Minha Blumenau* did not engage in any actions in 2017, and that is why the IPPI was not used.

[7] The reference table of each dimension can be found at Penteado et al. (2014).

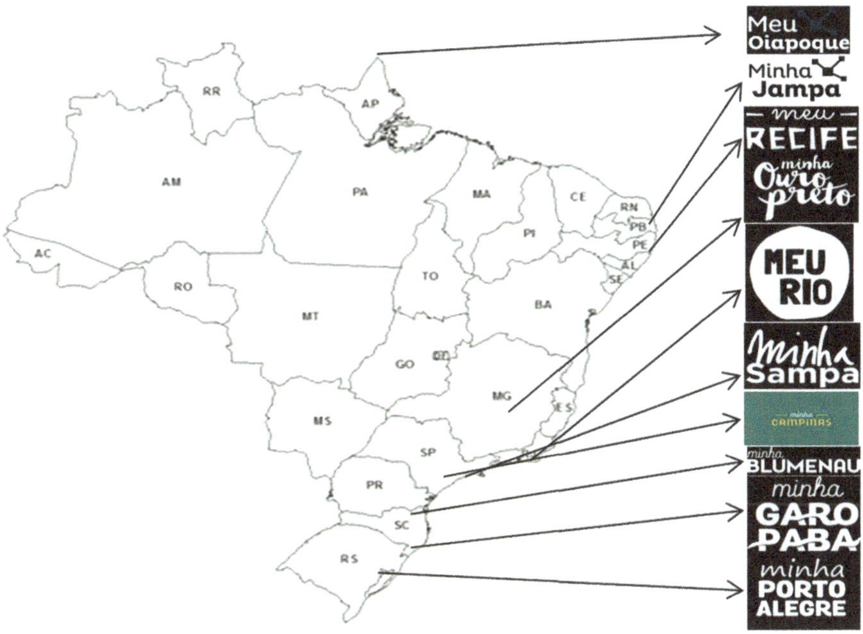

Fig. 5.1 Locations of *Nossas Cidades* local networks. (Source: Prepared by authors 2018)

The *Nossas Cidades* network[8] is a civil society organization that appeared in Rio de Janeiro in 2011, with the system *Meu Rio*, and today is present in ten cities located in all regions of Brazil except the center-western region.

Figure 5.1 shows the local networks spread all over Brazil but with certain concentrations in the coastal area of the country where the largest cities are also located (Table 5.1).

Local networks are located in four out of the five Brazilian regions. They are present in the large metropolises of São Paulo and Rio de Janeiro; the large cities of Recife, Campinas, and Porto Alegre; and medium-size cities including João Pessoa and Blumenau; but they are also present in smaller cities of Oiapoque, Ouro Preto, and Garopaba. The highest number of affiliates are in the southeastern region with four local networks, followed by the south region, with three affiliates, both being the most developed regions in Brazil.

The *Nossas Cidades* network consists of independent local networks connected through software platforms for collaboration, sharing, and participation. Every member city has its organization and its website, where they present and divulge campaigns, collect funds, and promote other activates. However, all of them follow the same structure and maintain the visual identity of the overarching network.

[8] Nossas Cidades – Quem somos. http://nossas.org

Table 5.1 *Nossas Cidades* local networks

Local network	Population	State	Region
Meu Oiapoque	25,514	Amapá	North
Minha Jampa	769,607	Paraíba	Northeast
Minha Recife	1,625,583	Pernambuco	Northeast
Minha Ouro Preto	70,281	Minas Gerais	Southeast
Meu Rio	6,498,837	Rio de Janeiro	Southeast
Minha Sampa	12,038,175	São Paulo	Southeast
Minha Campinas	1,173,370	São Paulo	Southeast
Minha Blumenau	348,513	Santa Catarina	South
Minha Garopaba	22,082	Santa Catarina	South
Minha Porto Alegre	1,481,019	Rio Grande do Sul	South

Source: Author's elaboration based on information from IBGE (2018)

Currently, the website of the *Nossas Cidades* network has a video[9] to present its objectives, its way of acting, platforms for participation, and some of the campaigns it has carried out. The material emphasizes the importance of democracy and citizen participation in Brazil's political life. There are comments about the current crisis of representation based on political parties and politicians in general, and about the population's willingness to participate by any means, but without actually knowing what to do. The audiovisual material highlights the importance of acting locally and new formats for participation through campaigning and use of ICTs, with reports and testimonies about successful initiatives and online tools for political involvement combined with offline actions.

As stated on its website, the network's objective is to develop new ways of having people "influence and give new meaning to politics," by stimulating campaigns and using tools for digital activism. *Nossas Cidades* network works as an intermediary between ordinary citizens and their political representatives. By supporting the "networked citizen," they share methodologies, technologies, and opportunities for actions to strengthen "the potency of distributing power."

In its "manifesto," the organization proposes to reinvent and strengthen politics by mobilizing citizens "willing to have impact on their realities" and developing technologies to increase activism. For this civil society organization, politics should be carried out through "citizens' effective participation." Based on nonpartisanship, the *Nossas Cidades* network advocates independence, transparency, pacifism, and respect for human rights.

Its activities started with the local *Meu Rio* network. This network began its actions through practices aimed at making the citizens of Rio de Janeiro city come closer to local politics and to stimulate activism by developing applications and organizing campaigns, linking online actions with offline ones. During its first 2 years, *Meu Rio* succeeded in promoting its campaigns and making significant "victories," reaching 100,000 people registered on its activism platform.

[9] NOSSAS – um laboratório de outros futuros: https://youtu.be/LtxKJ-rIVyk

In 2014, *Meu Rio* expanded and formed the *Nossas* network after being granted an international award.[10] As a strategy to increase and create a new national network, the Founders' Program[11] was launched to select and train citizens to start their own cities' activist affiliates linked to *Nossas Cidades*, thus developing a network of multiplying activists. Currently, present in ten locations, the networks' objective is to increase new member registrations and promote new activist models mainly targeting young people.

The *Nossas Cidades* team is currently composed of more than 30 people, who have executive functions, assume specific coordination activities, and work as staff, including designers and programmers. According to its website, the objective of the organization is "reconstructing politics" in three performance areas: (i) incubations, the activism laboratory, which incubates organizations and tests activist models and strategies; (ii) forming networks, making links between and training of local networks; and (iii) development and use of digital tools, using online activism tools. Additionally, they understand politics as a "space of tension, interaction, and intermediation" where there is room for society to act according to the following principles: nonpartisanship, strong fundamentals, independence, pacifism, respect for human rights, and transparency.

An important strategy for spreading its message is to use links to stories aired in popular channels of communication (i.e., Zeitgeist, CNN, UOL, BuzzFeed, TED, NEXO, etc.) that mention the *Nossas Cidades* network and its regional partnerships, thus increasing the visibility of its practices and of its advocacy "victories." This communication strategy serves as publicity and signals its participants and sympathizers that the actions executed by the network are effective and are reverberating throughout society, which may help generate more social capital for future collective actions (cf. Putman 1995).

The network has many programmatic actions. In general, the primary format of action is the aforementioned Founders' Program. That program gathers people interested in taking the *Nossas Cidades* proposal to their respective cities. This includes a screening and training process for new founding members of local networks to perform as "leaders of mobilization networks" which use offline actions and online tools to increase citizen participation. These founders have the following mission[12]: (1) mapping mobilization opportunities to improve the city, (2) developing tactics and strategies for action, (3) engaging and mobilizing people to join in their campaigns and actions, (4) divulging causes through networks and on the streets, (5) articulating solutions with local partners, and (6) training and managing volunteers.

Additionally, the *network* offers participants in the Founders' Program the following support: residency at his headquarters in Rio de Janeiro during the training period, access to the digital tools developed by the network' team of activists, contact and exchange of experiences and learning with other participants in the network, and transfer of rights to use the trademark when creating local networks in the future.

---

[10] Nossas Cidades – O que fazemos. https://www.nossas.org/#block-2551

[11] Nossas Cidades – Programa Fundadores. http://www.fundadores.nossas.org/

[12] Nossas Cidades – Papel dos Fundadores. https://www.fundadores.nossas.org/#block-2178

The *Nossas Cidades* network follows a network dynamic when creating new local affiliates through the Founders' Program. Even with local autonomy to develop projects and campaigns, each participant in the network has to act by complying with the paradigm of action defined by the central organization, as stated in the founders' missions, in order to increase the network's power of mobilizing resources (political, technological, human, etc.) by forming partnerships and sharing experiences and learning.

Any ordinary citizen can participate in local actions carried out by local affiliates of the *Nossas Cidades* network in two ways: by creating a cause (campaign) and/or joining in an ongoing campaign. Any citizen can create a cause, provided that he/she respects the principles of the *Nossas Cidades* network. The creators of an advocacy campaign are called "cooks" because they use the Pressure Cooker application (described next) as a mobilization tool and form political pressure on authorities. Some local causes are selected by the network's general team to be given technical support by teams from the *Meu Rio* and *Minha Sampa* networks (network nodes with more technical resources).

The causes and campaigns are found on Facebook, Twitter, Instagram, YouTube, and on its portal. Every campaign has a website with information about the cause, how to join in, proposals, supporters, and stories about the topic. Based on this information, an ordinary citizen can support a cause or join an ongoing campaign. Forms of e-participation vary according to the characteristics of every campaign, but in general, they work by using the Pressure Cooker device.

In both actions (cause or support), participation occurs by using the software programs developed. There can also be some political mobilizations for offline actions, such as protests and street manifestations. Below are the main ways for participating using ICTs:

5.3.1 Pressure Cooker[13]

The Pressure Cooker, created and managed by the technical team of the Nossas Cidades network, is an application for mobilization that enables direct contact with government authorities, public administrators, members of Congress, providers of public services, politicians in general, and other decision-makers in the city. It is not a website for online petitions; it works as a digital system to put pressure on the authorities in charge, which can be done as follows: (i) by email (by clicking, a user will send an email from his/her electronic address to the target's electronic address), (ii) by Facebook (by clicking, a user will post with his/her profile directly on the target's mural), (iii) by Twitter (by clicking, a user will send a message directly to the target with his/her profile), and (iv) by phone (by clicking, an electronic operator will call the user's mobile phone and complete the call with the target, putting her/him in direct contact). In other words, these are pressure mechanisms that are different from lists of signatures because they put citizens in direct contact with their representatives and politicians in general.

[13] Nossas Cidades – Panela de Pressão. http://paneladepressao.nossascidades.org/

5.3.2 *DefeZap*[14]

Created in 2016, DefeZap is a digital system to send anonymous audiovisual materials with complaints about the excessive use of violence by State agents[15] in the state of Rio de Janeiro (*Meu Rio*). The DefeZap team receives the audiovisual materials and activates its network of collaborative assessors to confirm the complaint and then demands action from the authorities in charge, ensuring the complainant's privacy. In addition to demanding actions from the authorities, the audiovisual materials feed a database available to the media to publish stories. DefeZap bulletins are also published containing information and data about complaints filed (However, an analysis of the bulletins reveals that the last update took place in December 2016). E-participation may take place by sending a video complaint, by participating in the team that assesses the complaints, or by receiving and sharing the information published in the DefeZap Bulletin.

5.3.3 *Sheltering Map*[16]

Based on a partnership of the *Nossas Cidades* network and the collective #AgoraÉQueSãoElas, the Sheltering Map is a digital platform created in June 2016 to "shelter" women who are victims of sexual violence. At the platform, therapists, lawyers, and other people can register as volunteers to participate in sheltering people who are victims of sexual violence. According to the data available at the website, the initiative already has 540 therapists, 1578 volunteers, and 16 lawyers registered in the program.[17] The victims can also register online to receive support from the project. E-participation can also be done through financial support (e.g., crowdfunding).

5.3.4 *Beta*[18]

Beta is a feminist chatbot, i.e., an Internet robot created in 2017 that is dedicated to defending feminism and protecting women's rights. The chatbot interacts with female users through a private message box on a social network. Communicating with Beta allows people to receive updates about feminist debates online and on the streets and creates a database on the subject. Chatbot, geared toward protecting women's rights in Brazil, also issues online warnings when an agenda or theme requires political mobilization.

---

[14] Nossas Cidades – Defezap. https://www.defezap.org.br/

[15] Policial violence is a serious problem in the city of Rio de Janeiro.

[16] Nossas Cidades – Mapa do Acolhimento. https://www.mapadoacolhimento.org/

[17] Data collected on January 22, 2018.

[18] Nossas Cidades – Beta: um robô feminista. https://www.beta.org.br/#block-5812

The *Nossas Cidades* network has used other applications which have since been deactivated: *Legislando* (a digital platform to create bills for future laws), *Multitude* (an application offering volunteer work), *Imagine*, *De olho* (a blog that follows up the City Council of Rio de Janeiro – the last update was 3 years ago), *De guarda* (collective electronic vigilance; projects *De Guarda na Friedenreich* and *De Guarda no Bondinho*, *Meu Rio*), and *Compartilhaço*. The *Legislando* platform has become *Mudamos*, developed in a partnership with the Institute Technology & Society in Rio de Janeiro. Currently, it has expanded to several cities.

5.3.4.1 Description of the Portal

The website of the *Nossas Cidades* network undergoes constant revisions and updates; however, it keeps the same visual identity as do its local affiliated networks. Currently, the website has the following structure (Table 5.2).[19]

By analyzing the website, it is apparent that important elements guided the formation of the network's social identity and principles governing *Nossas Cidades* network's political activities. It was also possible to identify a communication strategy oriented toward divulging the results achieved and their repercussion in the media.

All the affiliated websites comprising the *Nossas* network have an appearance similar to that of the *Nossas Cidades* portal, with some variations related to the number of sections and texts. According to the network's principles, every member of the *Nossas Cidades* network is free to define its profile, but all of them are supposed to follow the same visual identity and maintain a general uniformity.

However, it is worth highlighting that, despite websites' easy navigation, it is tough to find information about other actions and background information about campaigns (either successful or otherwise).

It is worth stressing that some of the local networks are still being organized, such as *Minha Garopaba*, *Minha Blumenau*, and *Meu Oiapoque*. (They are in the process of choosing people to be founding members.) *Minha Jampa*, for instance, was recently formed, in 2016, and it is undergoing consolidation; however, it has held advocacy campaigns and achieved victories in some of them, such as *Do not drown 80 million reais and 27 council members and one secret.*

5.3.4.2 Nossas Cidades on Social Networks

The *Nossas Cidades* network is present on Brazil's most popular social network, Facebook, and has a video channel on YouTube. The profile on Facebook[20] received 1486 likes (January 2018). The number of likes illustrates that the *Nossas Cidades* network's profile is not very popular on the social network, and its posts, in general,

---

[19] Data collected on September 25, 2017.

[20] *Nossas Cidades* profile at Facebook. https://www.facebook.com/nossas.org

Table 5.2 Description of the *Nossas Cidades* portal

Section	Description
Vision	Presentation of the phase (format .gif) "We want to live in a society where," which can be completed with the following alternating phrases: "The power of I does not eliminate the potency of We" "The power of the core does not diminish the potency of the periphery" "The power of hatred does not eliminate the potency of affection" "Power of patriarchy does not eliminate the potency of women" "Power of information does not eliminate the potency of privacy" "The power of some does not eliminate the potency of others" "The power of teachers does not eliminate the curiosity of children" "The power of whiteness does not eliminate the potency of diversity" "The power of adults does not eliminate the potency of children" "The power of politicians does not eliminate the potency of the multitude" "The power of propaganda power does not eliminate the potency of art"
Who we are	Video (Laboratory of alternative futures) and phrase: "NOSSAS *IS A LABORATORY OF ACTIVISM. WE ARE CREATING #OUTROSFUTUROS. Here we invent new ways of having people INFLUENCE and GIVE NEW MEANING to politics*"
What we do	Photo with people protesting (caption: "Linking up networked citizens") Text clarifying that *Nossas* is a nonprofit organization performing in the field of politics oriented toward mediating citizen empowerment and institutions by sharing methodology, technology, and opportunities for action
Timeline	An image of a timeline describing *Nossas'* main actions and projects, such as the creation of *Meu Rio* in 2011, *Minha Sampa* and *Nossas Cidades* networks in 2014, scholarship about activism in 2017, among others
Achievements	Images (links) and videos of some successful campaigns by the network's members
To act now	Images (links) of some ongoing campaigns by network members
Join us	Statements encouraging people to join the *Nossas* network and an online registration form
Transparency	Text clarifying its main organizational principles, links for interested parties to make donations, and a link to an audit report of the network's accounts
Team	Text informing that the network is composed of over 30 people who do different tasks and try to transform the world to make it a fairer, more inclusive, and sustainable place. In the background, there is a photo with all the team members
In the media	Links to stories about the *Nossas* network in different media in Brazil and abroad

Source: Prepared by authors (2018)

have received just a few likes, comments, and shares.[21] On YouTube, however, the channel has 130 subscriptions and has aired 31 videos. Different types of audiovisual materials can be seen, including promotional videos from the local networks. The most watched video is "*Rede Nossas Cidades – A Revolução da Participação*" [*Nossas Cidades* Network – A Participatory Revolution][22] with 2858

[21] At the time the article was written, January 2018, the profile had not been updated for 1 month.

[22] Rede Nossas Cidades – A revolução da Participação. https://www.youtube.com/watch?v=NuMg8KDzyLE

Table 5.3 Local networks on social media[a]

Local network	Facebook	Twitter	Instagram	YouTube
Meu Rio	122,879 likes	4520 followers 2977 tweets	2840 followers 253 posts	244 subscriptions 80 videos
Minha Sampa	71,796 likes	1234 followers 1159 tweets	4820 followers 295 posts	2130 subscriptions 25 videos
Minha Campinas	7561 likes	148 followers 838 tweets	659 followers 153 posts	12 subscriptions 26 videos
Minha Porto Alegre	5856 likes	It does not have a profile	514 followers 220 posts	26 subscriptions 14 videos
Minha Jampa	3462 likes	9 followers 2 tweets	542 followers 102 posts	10 subscriptions 1 video
Meu Recife	14,650 likes	702 followers 642 tweets	1532 followers 399 posts	1 subscription 7 videos
Minha Ouro Preto	2661 likes	Profile unavailable	It does not have a profile	11 subscriptions 5 videos
Minha Garopaba	1976 likes	Profile unavailable	269 followers 8 posts	It does not have a channel
Minha Blumenau	1901 likes	33 followers 5 tweets	405 followers 28 posts	It does not have a channel
Meu Oiapoque	Profile unavailable	Profile unavailable	Profile unavailable	Channel unavailable

Source: Prepared by the authors (2018)
[a]Data collected in January 2018

views (data from January 2018). The video, which lasts barely 2 min, presents an animation encouraging local participation as a way to transform the world through technologies and networks. It also shows a brief history and some achievements of the founding network *Minha Rio* (Table 5.3).

Strategies to use social media vary according to the profile of every local network. The networks in the largest cities (i.e., São Paulo and Rio de Janeiro) are more popular on social media. All networks use Facebook, but *Meu Oiapoque*, which is still in construction, does not have a page on that social network. Six local networks use Twitter, but some have few followers and posts. Only the *Minha Ouro Preto* and *Meu Oiapoque* networks do not use Instagram.

The *Meu Rio* network has the highest number of likes on Facebook and followers on Twitter. *Minha Sampa* network, on the other hand, has the highest number of followers on Instagram and subscriptions on YouTube. The *Minha Sampa*, *Minha Campinas*, and *Minha Jampa* networks also use the *Medium* social media. However, all have few followers and posts.

5.4 Use of the IPPI

To assess the effectiveness and efficacy of the *Nossas Cidades* network, this chapter uses the methodology embodied in the Political Participation and Influence Index (*Índice de Participação Política e Influência* – IPPI). Araújo et al. (2014) developed this index to study contemporary phenomena such as civil society's impact on shaping public policies using ICTs. The index is a valuable tool to study the actions and practices in today's information society since it measures civil society organizations' capacity to influence policy by examining different dimensions involving the use of ICTs.

The IPPI has six analytical dimensions created based on a review of the literature about collective action, the Internet and society, public policies, and cyber-activism. Below is a brief description of its dimensions (Araújo et al. 2015):

1. D1 – Use of internet resources: Identifying and assessing communicational devices that the group/collective uses in an activism.
2. D2 – Actors and social capital: Identifying and ranking the actors involved in their social capital for mobilizing financial resources and mobilizing people.
3. D3 – E-participation: Identifying and classifying different ways of e-participation Web-activism [based on the categories developed by Tamborius et al. (2007) and Araújo et al. (2014)].
4. D4 – Mobilization strategies: Identifying and assessing strategies to use cyberspace's resources for mobilizing resources.
5. D5 – How an action evolves and its relationship to public policies: Checking whether after actions or mobilization there has been any political impact though a public policy proposal, influence in the formation of an agenda, etc.
6. D6 – Repercussion in the media: Identifying whether an action or mobilization has had any repercussion in traditional media outlets and in cyberspace.

The IPPI was applied to all local networks forming the *Nossas Cidades* network to analyze their capacity to influence. The outcome can be seen in the Table 5.4 presented below.

The *Minha Blumenau* network did not record any actions in 2017, and that is why the IPPI was not used. Nevertheless, it is valid to record a mobilization and campaigns in 2015 and 2016. The *Meu Oiapoque* network is still in construction, so the IPPI was also not applied to this case.

The results show that there is significant variation in the scores of the local networks. The *Minha Sampa* affiliate presents the best performance, followed by the founding network *Meu Rio*, *Meu Recife*, and *Minha Jampa*. On the other hand, the *Minha Garopaba* and *Minha Ouro Preto* affiliates scored very low. Here it is worth observing that they both exist in small cities whose socialization easily occurs on a personal level and, as such, online engagement is hardly necessary.

In terms of other dimensions, *Use of Internet Resources (D1)* scored well in all local networks, which is the main characteristic of the *Nossas Cidade*s network. The dimension *Actions in relation to public policies (D5)*, measuring campaign outputs, ranked the worst, illustrating that effectiveness is the main area that needs to be developed.

When comparing the means of every one of the scores in the IPPI dimensions obtained based on analyses of the networks separately, some variations were observed, which can be explained by local specificities, such as the size of the population, number of equipment present in the cities, size of local media, etc.

Table 5.4 IPPI assessment of *Nossas Cidades*

Dimension	*Meu Rio*	*Minha Sampa*	*Minha Porto Alegre*	*Minha Campinas*	*Meu Recife*	*Minha Jampa*	*Minha Ouro Preto*	*Minha Garopaba*	Weighted averages
D1 – Use of Internet resources	5	5	5	5	5	5	4	3	4.62
D2 – Actors and social capital	4	5	4	4	4	4	2	2	3.62
D3 – e-participation	4	5	3	3	4	4	2	2	3.37
D4 – Mobilization strategies	5	5	3	5	5	5	2	2	3.75
D5 – Actions in relation to public policies	4	4	4	4	4	4	0	0	3.25
D6 – Repercussion in the media	5	5	4	4	5	5	0	0	3.5
Weighted averages	4.5	4.8	3.8	4.1	4.5	4.5	1.6	1.5	3.68

Source: Prepared by the authors (2017)

5.5 Final Considerations

The development of the Information and Communication Technologies (ICTs) has enabled new means for citizen participation, such as in the case of the *Nossas Cidades* network and its local networks. Improvements made in online platforms and software programs by *Nossas'* activities team allows citizens to engage in different campaigns and projects, thus stimulating a paradigm of participation through online devices (e-participation) and new models of sociopolitical activism.

The findings confirm the thesis that the success of online actions taken by civil society organizations is directly associated to a combination of actions taken offline, including the formation of (online and offline) networks, and/or joint actions through traditional means of communication. These results are found in other studies, such as an analysis on the *Nossa São Paulo* network or, under a different perspective, the analysis of the strategies of the movements *Vem pra Rua* and *Movimento Brasil Livre* (*MBL*)[23] in the protests that led to the impeachment of Dilma Rousseff (Araújo et al. 2012, 2016).

In the case of the *Nossas Cidades* network, there are observable differences related to local networks. *Meu Rio* and *Minha Sampa* have more than 200,000 registered members, while *Minha Garopaba* and *Minha Ouro Preto* have about 2000. It is worth remembering that both are located in the two most prominent cities in Brazil – Rio de Janeiro and São Paulo, places where civic events, both protest-based and participatory actions, typically occur.

The development of each institution inside the *Nossas Cidades* network is also quite different, partly because they are newer but essentially because of local differences. This indicates an intrinsic relation between the concrete and virtual worlds. Such a characteristic, which may seem obvious, goes against a trend in the literature when considering the advancements made by online activism independent from the development of the offline reality. As much as one can realize that the networks' success is directly related to the possibilities of establishing partnerships with local institutions, it is necessary to recognize that the success of mobilization and engagement in online actions is related to the specifics of political culture.

The political deficit in the use of the Internet is associated to a deficit in political culture resulting from different historical and conjunctural facts, such as the appearance of metropolises, an increase in the world of work, the advent and strengthening of the cultural industry, and the emptying of political parties and unions. The popularity of the Internet does not alter this structural factor, so much so that the increase in its use does not necessarily imply that the increasing use of networks is associated with the development of civic culture. However, for the last few years, civil society organizations, despite depoliticization of the majority of the population, have been able to strategically use ICTs and have established relatively efficient political action programs. The case of the *Nossas Cidades* network is an example.

[23] Those two political movements appeared in the protests in 2013 in Brazil. They are classified as rightwing movements, and they intensely used ICTs to mobilize and divulge its values and actions.

In spite of the differences among the local networks analyzed herein, the results show that the *Nossas Cidades* network is an innovative platform for online citizen participation, by offering digital devices and creative methodologies to develop new formats for applying pressure on and presenting proposals to public agents.

In the area of public healthcare, studies also point out that the use of ICTs in parallel with traditional advocacy has helped groups obtain treatments and medical drugs that had been denied or were difficult to get. One case that can be mentioned in Brazil is the users' association of medical drugs, such as cannabidiol and others derived from marijuana, which used to be prohibited. Battles and claims made by groups of family members and users through online and offline actions have succeeded in having their use cleared by ANVISA,[24] along with some facilities receiving approval to import such medical drugs not manufactured in Brazil (Santos et al. 2015). ICTs have also changed the relationship between users and healthcare providers because new tools have been developed and used, helping professionals and their patients to communicate via ICTs (Machado et al. 2010).

References

Anduiza, Eva, Camilo Cristancho, and José Sabucedo. 2014. Mobilization through online social networks: The political protest of the indignados in Spain. *Information, Communication & Society* 17: 750–764.

Araújo, R., C. Penteado, and M. R. Santos. 2012. Sociedade Civil e políticas públicas: o uso da internet pela Rede Nossa São Paulo na articulação política. *36° Encontro Anual da ANPOCS*, Caxambu.

Araújo, Rafael, Claudio Penteado, and Marcelo Burgos Santos. 2014. Sociedade Civil e a eParticipação em Políticas Públicas: o Índice de Participação Política e Influência (IPPI) do Instituto Pólis e do Portal mobilize Brasil. *38° Encontro Anual da ANPOCS*, Caxambu.

———. 2015. Democracia Digital e experiências de e-participação: webativismo e políticas públicas. *História, Ciências, Saúde-Manguinhos* 22: 1597–1619.

———. 2016. Movimentos políticos pelo impeachment de Dilma Rousseff e suas organizações na internet. *40° Encontro Anual da ANPOCS*, Caxambu.

Avritzer, Leonardo. 2003. *O orçamento participativo e a teoria democrática: um balanço crítico. A inovação democrática no Brasil*. São Paulo: Cortez.

Benkler, Yochai. 2006. *The wealth of networks: How social production transforms markets and freedom*. New Haven: Yale University Press.

Castells, Manuel. 1999. *A sociedade em rede – a era da informação: economia, sociedade e cultura*. Vol. 1. São Paulo: Paz e Terra.

———. 2008. The new public sphere: Global civil society, communication networks, and global governance. *The Annals of the American Academy of Political and Social Science* 616: 78–93.

———. 2009. *Comunicación y poder*. Barcelona: Alianza Editorial.

———. 2013. *Redes de indignação e esperança*. Rio de Janeiro: J. Zahar.

CETIC – Centro Regional de Estudos para o Desenvolvimento da Sociedade da Informação. 2018. Data Portal. Centro de Estudos sobre as Tecnologias da Informação e da Comunicação. http://

[24] ANVISA (Agência Nacional de Vigilância Sanitária) is Brazil's federal regulatory body for medical products, similar to the US Food and Drug Administration.

data.cetic.br/cetic/explore?idPesquisa=TIC_DOM&idUnidadeAnalise=Usuarios&ano=2013. Accessed 5 June 2018.

Coleman, Stephen, and John Gotze. 2001. *Bowling together: Online public engagement in policy deliberation*. London: Hansard Society.

Diamond, Larry, and Leonardo Morlino, eds. 2005. *Assessing the quality of democracy*. Baltimore: Johns Hopkins University Press.

Fung, Archon, Hollie Gilman, and Jennifer Shkabatur. 2013. Six models for the internet + policies. *International Studies Review* 15: 30–47.

Gohn, Maria da Glória Marcondes. 2005. *O protagonismo da sociedade civil: movimentos sociais, ONGs e redes solidárias*. São Paulo: Cortez Editora.

IBGE – Brazilian Institute of Geography and Statistics. 2018. Instituto Brasileiro de Geografia e Estatística. http://www.ibge.gov.br. Accessed 15 Jan 2018.

Internet World Stats. 2018. World internet usage and population statistics, December 31, 2017 – Update. http://www.internetworldstats.com/stats.htm. Accessed 15 Jan 2018.

Lupton, Deborah. 2014. *Digital sociology*. New York: Routledge.

Machado, Eliara, Jerusa Haddad, and Elma Zoboli. 2010. A comunicação como tecnologia leve para humanizar a relação enfermeiro-usuário na Atenção Básica. *Revista BioEthikos* 4: 447–452.

Macintosh, Ann. 2008. E-democracy and e-participation research in Europe. In *Digital government: Integrated series in information systems*, ed. H. Chen et al., 85–102. Boston: Springer.

Macintosh, Ann, Stephen Coleman, and Agnes Schneeberger. 2009. eParticipation: the research gaps. In *Electronic participation – ePart 2009 – lecture notes in computer science*, ed. A. Macintosh and E. Tambouris, 1–11. Heidelberg: Springer.

Medaglia, Rony. 2012. eParticipation research: Moving characterization forward (2006–2011). *Government Information Quarterly* 29: 346–360.

Milani, Carlos R.S. 2008. O princípio da participação social na gestão de políticas públicas locais: uma análise de experiências latino-americanas e europeias. *Revista de Administração Pública* 42: 551–579.

Moisés, José Álvaro. 1990. *Cidadania e Participação - ensaios sobre o plebiscito, o referendo e a iniciativa popular na nova Constituição*. São Paulo: Editora Marco Zero.

———. 2010. *Democracia e confiança*. São Paulo: EDUSP.

Oliveira, Osmany Porto. 2016. Mecanismos da difusão global do Orçamento Participativo: indução internacional, construção social e circulação de indivíduos. *Opinião Pública* 22: 219–249.

Organização das Nações Unidas – Brasil (ONUBR). 2015. Em 15 anos, número de usuários de internet passou de 400 milhões para 3,2 bilhões, revela ONU. Nações Unidas no Brasil. https://nacoesunidas.org/em-15-anos-numero-de-usuarios-de-internet-passou-de-400-milhoes-para-32-bilhoes-revela-onu/. Accessed 8 Dec 2016.

Pereira, Rafael Morais, Rúbia Fonseca Roberto, Rodrigo Gava, and Edson Arlindo Silva. 2016. Conselhos gestores de políticas públicas: relações entre Estado e sociedade civil no contexto local. *Revista de Gestão em Sistemas de Saúde* 5: 29–40.

Penteado, Cláudio Luis Camargo, Marcelo Burgos Pimentel Santos, and Rafael de Paula Aguiar Araújo. 2014. Sociedade civil e a eParticipação em políticas Públicas: o Índice de Participação Política e Influência (IPPI) do Instituto Pólis e do Portal Mobilize. CLACSO Library. http://biblioteca.clacso.edu.ar/gsdl/collect/clacso/index/assoc/D10234.dir/paper_CLACSO_Penteado_Santos_Araujo.pdf. Accessed 15 Jan 2018.

Putman, Robert D. 1995. Bowling alone: America's declining social capital. *Journal of Democracy* 6: 65–78.

Rasmussen, Terje. 2013. Internet-based media, Europe and the political public sphere. *Media, Culture & Society* 35: 97–104.

Santos, Marcelo B.P. 2016. Lei da Ficha Limpa: entre a sociedade civil e arranjos estatais. In *Brasil: 25 anos de democracia – Participação, Sociedade Civil e Cultura Política*, ed. N. Mesquita. Rio de Janeiro: Fundação Konrad Adenauer.

Santos, Marcelo, Claudio Penteado, and Rafael Araújo. 2013. Sociedade Civil y participación ciudadana en São Paulo. *VII Congreso Latinoamericano de Ciencia Politica*, Bogotá.
Santos, Marcelo, Rosemary Segurado, and Pedro Malino. 2015. Movimentos sociais e a contestação pública sobre os usos da maconha no Brasil. *39° Encontro Anual da ANPOCS*, Caxambu.
Silva, Suylan Midlej, and Suely Araújo. 2014. O combate à corrupção eleitoral no Brasil e a relação sociedade e Estado: em defesa de uma nova cultura política. *38° Encontro Anual da ANPOCS*, Caxambu.
Tambouris, E., Macintosh, A., Coleman, S., Wimmer, M., Vedel, T., Westholm, H., ... & Aichholzer, G. (2007). Introducing eparticipation. DEMO-net The Democracy Network. DEMO-net booklet series, 1.
Vie, Stephanie. 2014. In defense of "slacktivism": The human rights campaign Facebook logo as digital activism. *First Monday*, 19.
Wampler, Brian. 2008. A difusão do Orçamento Participativo brasileiro: "boas práticas" devem ser promovidas? *Opinião Pública* 14: 65–95.
Wright, Scott. 2015. Populism and downing street e-petitions: Connective action, hybridity, and the changing nature of organizing. *Political Communication* 2: 414–433.

Part II
Internet Audience and Health in Brazil

Chapter 6
Internet, Expert Patient, and Empowerment: Activity Profiles in Virtual Communities of Chronic Kidney Patients

André Pereira Neto, Julyane Felipette Lima, Leticia Barbosa, and Eda Schwartz

Abstract In recent decades, the Internet has become an integral part of the daily lives of millions of people around the world, engendering multiple transformations. In the health sector, it is increasingly used as a source of information and advice. In this context, the "expert patient" stands out. This is an individual who becomes a specialist by conducting an extensive search for information about his health condition online and sharing his experiences in virtual communities. In the face of this setting, this chapter reflects on the relationship between empowerment, "expert patient," and the biomedical model by examining two online groups on Facebook that include chronic kidney patients and their relatives, friends, and caregivers. It identifies the activity profiles of participants posting messages – the posters. We identify three "ideal types" of posters: one has a supportive nature, another is concerned with the clinical realm of the disease, and the third is committed to patient's rights. The results indicate that supportive and clinical posters reiterate the biomedical order, while the citizen poster is concerned with the patient's rights as a citizen.

6.1 Introduction

In recent decades, the media landscape has been restructured following the establishment and expansion of the Internet: a worldwide network that connects millions of computers around the world, of various types, sizes, brands, models, and with

A. Pereira Neto (✉)
National School of Public Health, Oswaldo Cruz Foundation, Rio de Janeiro, Brazil

J. F. Lima
Faculty of Nursing, Federal University of the Southern Frontier, Chapecó, Brazil

L. Barbosa
Institute of Scientific and Technological Communication and Information in Health, Oswaldo Cruz Foundation, Rio de Janeiro, Brazil

E. Schwartz
Faculty of Nursing, Federal University of Pelotas, Pelotas, Brazil

A. Pereira Neto, M. B. Flynn (eds.), *The Internet and Health in Brazil*,
https://doi.org/10.1007/978-3-319-99289-1_6

different operating systems (Bimber et al. 2012). The Internet has facilitated access to different communication and information services that have gradually become an integral part of the lives of millions of people around the world. Internet universalization encourages the establishment of new sociocultural, political, and economic practices (Jordan 2014; Srinivasan and Fish 2017). It furthermore promotes new understandings, concepts, and assumptions about the role of information and communication for the contemporary individual.

According to Lévy (2001), the proliferation of vast amounts of data, the overgrowing interconnection of informative contents, and the increased cross-cutting contacts between individuals through the Internet have prompted a flood, that is to say, an overflow of chaotic information. Flows of information have become pervasive and capillary, as they spread through different spheres of society, engendering different social transformations. Health is no exception to this new digital reality.

In recent years, the emergence and dissemination of the World Wide Web, online search engines, and social media have contributed to making websites, blogs, and portals increasingly used as a source of information and advice on health (Li et al. 2015; Lin et al. 2016). The amount of health information that is produced and shared in virtual networks is growing (Kim 2015). Such information is available in multiple formats and platforms and from different independent content producers – whether government agencies, companies, groups with common interests, or individuals. In this context, the term "expert patient" was coined to designate an individual who practically becomes a specialist in a given subject by conducting an extensive search on his health condition, mainly through virtual sites and communities (Fox et al. 2005).

In recent decades, the medical-scientific community's response to this new stakeholder in the field of health has fluctuated between optimism and pessimism. Although some professionals are not receptive to the "expert patient," others incorporate the existence of this social player into their practice. To do so, they move from a position that has been paternalistic, imposing, and top-down to more of a model based on the Internet as a way to support treatment compliance (Ahluwalia et al. 2010; Fox et al. 2005).

The figure of the "expert patient" is associated, in our view, with the notion of empowerment – a comprehensive, multifaceted, and difficult concept to define. It is generally used to refer to individuals or groups in a situation of vulnerability, inequality, or impotence that are transformed and are given greater autonomy, self-determination, and political awareness. This change can be boosted with the help of different resources, among which information and knowledge stand out (Zimmerman 1995).

Virtual communities play a unique role in the process of empowering individuals with their health. Participants in these online communities can share information and obtain knowledge derived from people's daily life experiences with a disease. By doing so, he can learn about treatment alternatives, know the adverse effects of certain medications, and share decisions about his therapeutic process with peers.

Empowerment can simultaneously favor an individual's independence and facilitate adherence to a treatment style that submits to the biomedical paradigm (Wilson et al. 2007; McAllister et al. 2012; Fox et al. 2005).

Given this context, this paper will discuss this topic by analyzing the particular case of chronic kidney disease: a chronic noncommunicable disease characterized by the kidney's failure to perform its function for 3 months or more (National Kidney Foundation 2013).

Upon receiving the diagnosis, the patient may undergo conservative treatment based on diets, water restrictions, and medications. From the moment that renal function failure reaches a stage incompatible with the maintenance of the organ's function, this treatment is supplanted by "renal replacement therapy," which is performed using equipment or surgical procedures that replace renal functions such as transplantation, peritoneal dialysis, or hemodialysis, according to each case. The next step in treatment involves a kidney transplant, although it is challenging to find a compatible donor (Jay et al. 2016). Peritoneal dialysis is a procedure that consists of the infusion of a balanced and heated solution at a temperature close to that of the body inside the abdomen (i.e., peritoneum). In this case, the patient assumes responsibility for treatment (García-Llana et al. 2013). Hemodialysis is the cleansing method by which blood obtained through vascular access (e.g., catheters, shunts, or arteriovenous fistulas) comes into contact with a dialysis solution and a particular filter using an artificial semipermeable membrane bound to a machine. Hemodialysis requires the patient to visit health center on average three times a week. Each procedure lasts around 4 h and may vary according to the patient's clinical condition (National Kidney Foundation 2013). Therefore, hemodialysis promotes a series of restrictions and forces sick citizens to substantially modify their daily behaviors.

Currently, there are about 100,000 chronic kidney patients in Brazil who require renal replacement therapy treatment – 85% of whom are assisted exclusively by the Unified Health System (SUS), which provides free and indiscriminate care to all people (Ministry of Health 2018). They are also included in the social security system which provides payments to people with disabilities (Brazil 2015).

Patients with chronic kidney disease are in a profound state of vulnerability, since they depend on the hemodialysis machine and the full functioning of public systems of health care and social security to survive. This disease is irremediable and produces residual incapacity/disability. It is caused by irreversible underlying diseases and demands constant patient dedication to rehabilitation, generally requiring an extended period of supervision, observation, and care.

Given this context, this chapter intends to reflect on the relationship between empowerment, the "expert patient," and the biomedical model of health in two Facebook groups where chronic kidney patients, their relatives, friends, and caregivers interact. We are particularly interested in identifying possible models or patterns of social participation in these virtual environments.

This chapter is divided into three parts. In the first one, we will review conceptual aspects of empowerment, resorting to the current debate on the subject in the international academic literature. In the second one, we will show the methodological procedures for choosing and analyzing two Brazilian virtual communities that gather chronic kidney patients, professionals, and caregivers. Finally, we will investigate the empirical material and discuss how empowerment can be perceived in this context and what patterns of participation could be observed.

6.2 Empowerment: A Conceptual Reflection

The discussion of empowerment dates back to the nineteenth century (Lincoln et al. 2002). Currently, part of the international academic literature concerned with the definition of this concept discusses whether empowerment is individual, collective, or both. Let us look at some elements of this controversy.

Authors who emphasize the individual realm of empowerment usually refer to the sense of power and control experienced by individuals in the decision-making process on issues affecting personal life. Individual empowerment would thus be associated with modern individualism and the reflexive construction of the "I" (Giddens 1991).

Zimmerman (1995, 582) criticizes the emphasis given to the individual level of empowerment by stating that it "should not be taken to mean that sociopolitical or contextual factors are overlooked." Rissel (1994) affirms that life experienced by the individual is inscribed in a social, political, economic, and cultural context that conforms him and on which he has the possibility of transforming. According to Riger (1993), ignoring this more collective or social realm encompassing each of us contributes to the individual being seen as a free, self-sufficient, and self-determining agent, without suffering any social constraints.

The authors who emphasize the collective realm of empowerment define it as "an active, participatory process through which individuals, organizations, and communities gain greater control, efficacy, and social justice" (Mo and Coulson 2014, 984).

Further pursuing this debate, Ryhänen et al. (2012) present the "empowering theory of knowledge" according to which empowerment is perceived as a cognitive state in which individuals feel as if they have more control over their life. While focused on the individual as a unit of analysis, this realm does not consider that empowerment is a decontextualized phenomenon, which is isolated from the influences and relationships subjects can establish between themselves and with society.

The collective realm of empowerment is to a large extent influenced by the ideas of Brazilian pedagogue Paulo Freire[1] (2015). Thus, inspired by Freire's ideas, the

[1] Paulo Freire (1921–1997) was a Brazilian educator and thinker, whose intellectual work was nationally and internationally recognized. He is considered, in the academic environment, a reference in the fields of "critical pedagogy, popular education and participatory action-research, as well as a basic reference of liberation theology, of Latin American critical theory and a precursor of the epistemologies of the South" (Altamirano 2016). In his extensive intellectual production, we highlight *Pedagogy of the Oppressed* (Freire 2015) and *Pedagogy of Hope: Reliving Pedagogy of the Oppressed* (Freire 1994).

concept of empowerment departs from the individual-psychological perspective toward the other necessarily collective, social, and political perspective.

In any case, individual and collective empowerment can promote changes in power relationships (Page and Czuba 1999). In our view, empowerment is an integral part of reciprocal and simultaneous processes of loss, gain, sharing, and strengthening of power relationships between individuals and institutions. In this perspective, although empowerment may have an individual level and encompass the feeling of greater control and mastery, it is necessary to look at such reciprocal and simultaneous underpinning processes.

The individual and collective realms of empowerment have been increasingly used in the field of health. One of its primary uses has been in the organization and consolidation of health promotion goals, strategies, and practices (Wallerstein 2006; Rissel 1994).

The definition of "health promotion" is, to this day, the subject of debates that generate numerous controversies.[2] According to the World Health Organization, this is a new conception on health and the process of illness that aims at "enabling people to increase control over, and to improve, their health" (WHO 2009, 29). One of its main theoretical axes is the concept of "empowerment." Health promotion involves creating the conditions for increased individual and community control over the social determinants that affect their health.

Thus, health promotion is enhanced when individual/psychological empowerment is articulated with community empowerment. According to Rissel (1994), this community empowerment encompasses the mental strengthening and personal development of community members, as well as collective action and political mobilization around the redistribution of resources favorable to the development of the group to which the individual belongs. It can, therefore, promote improved health of populations and increase their quality of life through collectively engendered social transformations.

In the field of health, empowerment is closely related to information. In a report prepared for the World Health Organization, Wallerstein (2006) points out that health inequalities are increasing around the world. The researcher argues that, given this setting, empowerment can be understood as a feasible strategy for public health, which can improve health and curb disparities.

To ensure a successful empowerment strategy, Wallerstein (2006) mentions some necessary elements, identified by Deepa Narayan (2002)[3] in her report published with the support of the World Bank. In this 280-page paper, the author shows "four key elements" for economic growth and poverty reduction, namely, "inclusion/participation, accountability, local organizational capacity, and access to information" (Narayan 2002, VI-VII). Regarding this last element, the author states that:

> Information is power. Informed citizens are better equipped to take advantage of opportunity, access services, exercise their rights, and hold state and nonstate actors accountable.

---

[2] Chapter 19 is dedicated to the issue of new information and communication technologies in health promotion.

[3] Deepa Narayan is a senior adviser of "Poverty Reduction and Economic Management" (PREM) at the World Bank in Washington, D.C.

> [...] Information and communication technologies often play a pivotal role in broadening access to information. (Narayan 2002, VI)

Information and communication technologies (ICTs), especially those available through the Internet, can play a crucial role in accessing and disseminating information and, consequently, in empowering individuals and communities:

> Connectivity through telephones, radio, television, and the Internet can enable the voices of even the most marginal and excluded citizens to be heard, promoting greater government responsiveness. ICT can thus help to overcome poor people's powerlessness and voicelessness even while structural inequities exist in the distribution of traditional assets such as education, land, and finance. (Narayan 2002, 73)

Choudhury (2009) affirmed that the ability to produce content, establish digital social networks globally, and access a myriad of information sources makes the Internet an essential means of empowerment.

According to Amichai-Hamburger et al. (2008), the phenomenon of empowering through digital media available on the Internet can be termed as *e*-empowerment. These authors argue that several possibilities would be provided by virtual networks to increase well-being, mutual aid, and autonomy, both individually and collectively. The authors emphasize flexibility in identity performance and self-construction, increased self-efficacy, combating and reducing stigmata, setting up supportive and self-help digital social networks, sharing decision-making processes, and promoting participation in government processes and decisions. They also point out that, while the Internet may facilitate citizen empowerment, the empowerment process is not given a priori with technology.

The Internet's decentralized structure that allows content production by users, access to several sources of information, and the possibility of communicating with people at a potentially global level is one of the aspects that digital Internet media can contribute to increase individual and collective empowerment.

In this case, we highlight citizens and groups of individuals with some disease or health problem. Patients, their families, friends, and caregivers often resort to collaborative environments on the Internet to address the consequences of a given diagnosis and treatment. They thus quickly and remotely obtain information about their illness and comfort for their distress from other people who live or have experienced similar problems. Also, patients who use the Internet can search for information at their own convenience about when, how, and where disease symptoms occur. They can search for self-prescribed drugs and learn about their side effects. Last but not least, they can find alternative treatments and obtain recommendations from health professionals (Mano 2014; Lin et al. 2016).

According to a survey conducted by the Pew Research Center, individuals diagnosed with chronic diseases are one of the leading groups that access the Internet to establish social networks among themselves: one in four uses the Internet to find people with the same health condition (Fox 2011).

In this chapter, we will analyze the empowerment process in two virtual communities of patients undergoing renal replacement therapy. The next section describes how we selected the virtual communities and how they were analyzed.

6.3 Methods

As mentioned earlier, much of the anxiety, stress, and depression resulting from the sudden changes experienced by chronic kidney patients is associated with a lack of information about the disease, treatment, and survival (Torchi et al. 2014). Thus, the information obtained and shared through social media can play a central role.

Virtual communities have experienced exponential growth in recent years (Kosinski et al. 2015). They provide attractive means for interaction and communication, but they also highlight the problem of privacy and information security.[4] Its emergence and expansion are associated with the increase of Web 2.0 (Kaplan and Haenlein 2010): a term used to designate virtual communities where information is produced and shared by users and developers. Web 2.0 therefore refers to an environment of interaction and participation that encompasses many languages.

In this chapter, we will devote our attention to the online social media site Facebook. It allows its users to post information and build relationships with other users with whom they can identify. Facebook contains pages, personal profiles, and groups (Coutinho 2014).

These pages have, in general, a professional or even commercial character, representing, in general, a company, brand, or product. They enable engagement with a broad audience and have the resources to manage, monitor, and control interaction with their users. A personal profile can share information, in a limited or indiscriminate way, through a timeline (Facebook 2018). A group is a name given by Facebook for the affiliation of people with common interests who build, attend, and participate in a particular virtual environment (Facebook 2010).

In this study, we analyze the behavior of people who meet in an online group, because they are interested in the topics and problems related to renal replacement therapy.

We used Netvizz,[5] a tool that extracts data from different sections of Facebook's platform (including online groups and webpages) for research purposes (Rieder 2013) in order to select the Facebook groups to be analyzed in this study. The tool compiles group data by generating a table that contains the names or descriptions and the keywords chosen for a given search.

In Facebook, we searched for two groups that had recent online activities, had the word hemodialysis in their name or description (in Portuguese), and had a large number of members. Thus, groups *Eu faço hemodiálise Brasil*[6] ("I do hemodialysis Brazil") and *Hemodiálise – Uma dádiva de vida*[7] (Hemodialysis – a life gift) were selected in July 2016, which resulted in the following Table 6.1.

---

[4] Issues of privacy and information security on the Internet are addressed in Chaps. 3 and 11 of this book.

[5] For more about Netvizz, see https://apps.facebook.com/netvizz/

[6] Available at: https://www.facebook.com/groups/1489994287957985/?ref=bookmarks

[7] Available at: https://www.facebook.com/groups/hemodialisevida/

Table 6.1 Comparison of the two groups investigated

Group	Type	Members	Moderators
Eu faço hemodiálise Brasil	Private	570	2
Hemodiálise – Uma dádiva de Vida	Public	4448	1

The public group *Hemodiálise – Uma dádiva de vida* is a space for people to clarify matters about hemodialysis procedures. The homepage contains a large picture where some people in white uniforms can be seen hugging in a semicircle. In the center is a person in a blue outfit. We can guess that they are health professionals around a patient. In the background, serum supports can be identified with hanging bottles and in the distant background a bed with a person lying down. Therefore, we can deduce that the picture was taken in a hospital setting that provides care to patients undergoing hemodialysis. The private group *Eu faço hemodiálise Brasil* identifies itself as a "group set up to address renal failure issues," aimed at "preventing more people from reaching renal failure." When you open the page, a centered photo with a logo with the word AMPARUS[8] appears, which stands for "Association of Patients, Recipients, Donors, and Organ- and Tissue-Transplanted People." This association has a website,[9] which includes the address of its physical headquarters and bank details for financial contributions.

Differences were also identified with regard to the number of members and moderators. These gaps will not be considered in our analysis.

To carry out the research that has developed in this chapter, we follow the recommendations outlined in the Association of Internet Researchers (AoIR) document created for this purpose, namely, the "Ethical Decision-Making and Internet Research: Recommendations from the AoIR Ethics Working Committee." The anonymity of those who made posts in public or private access environments was thus ensured (Markham and Buchanan 2012). The document also emphasizes that "data aggregators or search tools make information accessible to a wider public than what might have been intended" (Markham and Buchanan 2012, 6).

Thus, posts' contents were copied in the form of text so that authors would not be identified. Frequenters were identified with letter "F," followed by an Arabic numeral. This numbering follows the order in which the person appears in each group. Moderators were referenced with letter "M."

In virtual communities, Kozinets (2010) identifies two types of visitors, namely, lurkers and posters. Lurkers are participants with little or no activity in the group. They benefit from this access because they participate in the activities and follow the group's posts. Posters often insert information in the group and join in the debates, clearly stating their positions. Mo and Coulson (2010) estimate that approximately half of the community users consist of posters. They can be compared to opinion-makers or leaders of a particular social group. They also participate and engage in group activities by commenting on or reacting to what has been posted.

[8] *Amparus* is a word written in Latin and means support.

[9] Association of Patients, Recipients, Donors, and Organ- and Tissue-Transplanted People (AMPARUS): http://amparus.org/

Our analysis aimed to identify possible models or patterns of participation in these patient groups with chronic renal failure. To do so, we focused on the performance of posters.

The construction of these models or patterns of participation followed, in general, the proposed "ideal type" conceived by Weber (1949). The construction of ideal types allows the researcher to rationalize univocally the phenomena studied from the analysis of behaviors. This analytical category does not conform to the explanatory ideal or profile of a given social phenomenon. They are types built for research purposes. They exist in the realm of ideas. This means that, after a reflexive, interpretive, and analytical process, ideal types that explain certain phenomena (Aron 1999) can be constructed. The "ideal type" is a theoretical construct that allows us to operate a kind of abstraction that converts reality into a constructed object. Through a process of categorization while developing the analysis, the researcher gathers essential aspects of a particular behavior and establishes ideal models and explanatory typologies for them. Thus, this scholar can show a clear vision of the studied reality (Aron 1999).

In the research for this chapter, we were able to construct three ideal types of posters found on the two chronic kidney patients' groups on Facebook: one has a supportive character, another is concerned with the clinical realm of this disease, while the third is interested in the rights of the patient undergoing renal replacement therapy. We will see in more detail the characteristics of each poster next.

6.4 Results

6.4.1 The Supportive Poster

The supportive poster is one that systematically comments on what other people report about their everyday challenges with the disease and treatment, particularly their experiences at the onset. These posters publicly take an optimistic view of the condition of having to live with the disease and undergo treatment, particularly hemodialysis. They make clear the internal processes and changes they had to experience in order to find another meaning to life. One of them states:

> A lot of things have happened and I learned many things too in my four years of treatment. […] I do not regret *accepting this treatment*. On the contrary, today I see that it enables me to learn new things, *see the other side of life* and that not everything is easy. I have learned that we must always have hope and faith, because we can get anywhere that way. And so I go on living, doing my treatment, helping those in need, giving them advice, that hemodialysis is not the end, but an *opportunity for us to live longer…* Stop and think before you say you can't do it! *We all can.* One must have faith and hope (F85) (our emphasis).

When this poster admits "seeing the other side of life," he shows the processes endured until he was able to accept the limitations imposed by the disease and the treatment. To see this "other side," the poster provides the temporal dimension by using the present continuous – "to have accepted that treatment." The use of this verbal tense suggests the time interval between the person accepting his condition, undergoing this new routine, and becoming familiar with the treatment, particularly hemodialysis, perceiving it as "an opportunity to live longer," a period that has lasted 4 years. In the end, the poster utters words of hope: "We all can."

We note that supportive posts appear when someone makes a post mentioning a difficulty or adversity experienced by a member of the group that initiates the treatment.

The case of a daughter of a chronic kidney patient can serve as an example. She admits that she does not know how to cope with her father's pressure levels and asks the group whether anyone has ever experienced a similar situation. This daughter-caregiver of a chronic kidney patient is a new member of the group: someone who has a relative who was diagnosed with chronic kidney disease and started hemodialysis treatment. Inexperienced and insecure with the new condition of her father's life, she seeks support among her peers. She admits not "accepting doing hemodialysis." She concludes her post by stating: "I am terrified" (F22).

The daughter-caregiver's post received 18 likes and 21 comments. The supportive poster reacts, in this case, as follows:

> Good evening my friend. I have to tell you that it is not scary. [...] when I went to do hemodialysis, I felt that way, I cried over the machine for four hours, but then I began to realize that the machine is a precious thing and that it only does us good. [...] Before hemodialysis, I did not even have desire to eat. Then I improved a lot. [...] You will see that life does not end with hemodialysis... it is only transformed. It is up to each of us to choose to mourn or struggle to continue to live well. (F90)

The supportive poster reveals, in this instance, compassion for the suffering. At the same time, he provides his opinion and submits his recommendations as to the best way to overcome the adversities mentioned. The F90 post reinforces the supportive interface of this type of ideal poster. Thanks to him, the person emotionally shaken by the disease – its limitations and treatment – has his concerns addressed by another person who has faced the same challenges. Participants talk horizontally about their health needs. The supportive poster describes how he tackled the problems faced by the new member. The posts show solutions empathically, based on the processes that the most experienced chronic kidney patients have lived. Motivational posts try to influence new patients to believe that it is possible to live well despite the hemodialytic treatment. Following the same logic, another supportive poster concludes his post with the following words of encouragement: "The machine is not your enemy. It is one that will help you live. Gather your strengths, warrior!" (F23).

According to the National Kidney Foundation (2013), the ideal dose of hemodialysis is three times a week with each session lasting for 4 h each but varying according to the patient's clinical condition. According to Lins et al. (2017), adherence to treatment presupposes a cultural adaptation. They admit that:

> The cultural adaptation of a tool is usually not a simple and easy process, because it demands not only the literal translation of words but also respect for the culture of the individuals for whom the tool is being translated. Particular attention should be paid to the translation of words and even to semantic, idiomatic, experimental and conceptual equivalences. (Lins et al. 2017, 1174)

In this respect, this chapter resumes the question that motivated the study of Fox et al. (2005, 1299): "Do 'informed' or 'expert' patients challenge dominant traditions in biomedicine or merely adopt these as conventional ways of thinking about body shape and size, illness, and health?"

The words stimulating the practice of hemodialysis can be understood as facilitating submission to the biomedical approach and may play an inhibitory role in avoiding treatment.

This can only be possible because, in the groups analyzed, frequenters can interact with the perspective of other people who live in the same health condition and face the same restrictions imposed by the disease and treatment. They are environments where kidney patients, professionals, and caregivers are free to describe their experiences with the disease without a biased or adverse reaction. They are experiences shared with those who experience the same health condition.

Following the interactionist perspective, we can conclude that the supportive poster writes a post in which he places himself in the other's shoes. He already felt the pain of the other. He has had previous similar experiences (Charon 2010). Then, the moment the supportive poster identifies himself with other people's suffering, he puts himself in their place. His post is intended to ease the pain of the other. Reciprocal support was the thread of the supporting poster. His orientation follows the biomedical parameters and may contribute to lower treatment avoidance.

Another characteristic of the supportive poster deserves attention: faith.

Facing the limitations imposed by treatment and illness, Schwartz et al. (2009, 200) have shown that the ill, caregivers, and patients often resort to faith. According to these authors:

> Faith is a tool that assists in treatment and also acts as a driving force, giving us the strength to move forward and bringing hope for a better tomorrow. (Schwartz et al. 2009, 200)

In our research, a supportive poster expressed the following:

> [...] And so I go on living: doing my treatment, helping those who need it, saying to them that hemodialysis is not the end. It is an opportunity for you to live longer ... Stop and think before you say you can't. We all can do it. And we need to have faith and hope. (F85) (Our emphasis)

Resorting to spiritual forces may be associated with the high mortality rate of chronic kidney patients.

Silva et al. (2012) concluded that one-third of patients with chronic kidney disease due to hypertension and diabetes and who initiate renal replacement therapy in an unplanned way die during the period between hospital admission and transfer to hemodialysis clinics. In Brazil, life expectancy of chronic kidney patients is lower than that of the general population. This phenomenon is explained by the high rate of cardiovascular events and the greater predisposition to infections and neoplasms (Canziani 2004). Kidney transplantation plays a vital role in reducing such rates. However, cardiovascular mortality remains, on average, ten times higher than in the general population (Arantes 2008).

The systematic review by Murray et al. (2005) revealed that simply identifying through online discussion networks with cases or symptoms experienced by patients with similar problems could provide improvements in health and promote greater patient autonomy. According to this argument, Moretti and Barsottini (2017) observed that participation in social networks could improve the patient's social life and reduce hopelessness.

In this chapter, we want to show that there are three ideal types of posters. They reveal, in our view, three different ways of being an "expert patient" and three different ways to expose empowerment.

This first ideal type of poster has a supportive nature.

Only those who undergo renal replacement therapy know how much it hurts physically and psychologically to be diagnosed with this disease and begin treatment. No health professional has this same experience. As much as this professional studies and specializes in this disease, he will never be able to feel it, because he never had to live with the limitations that it imposes on his body. This is the not the case of the supportive poster. He went through this ordeal. The onset of renal replacement therapy can be seen as a terrible situation, with much suffering that tests individuals' ability to overcome and their willingness to continue to live. At this moment, the statement of the supportive poster plays a decisive role. It encourages unbelieving spirits and, with his testimony, helps his virtual friend to live. He is an "expert patient" with a more psychological character, which highlights the importance of submission to hemodialysis – an ideal procedure according to biomedicine today. He is empowered with emotions and feelings of those who, like him, have gone through existentially difficult situations.

In the clinical poster, the "expert patient" plays another role.

6.4.2 *The Clinical Poster*

The clinical poster is one that shares information in the Facebook group on issues involving different therapeutic aspects of chronic kidney treatment. This includes information about renal replacement therapy that he disseminates because he is undergoing treatment, diet, and medications for a more extended period than those who demand information and clarification. He has knowledge derived from the experience of living with the disease and coping with the countless limitations inherent in the treatment and everything that it involves about his body and social behavior. It is, therefore, someone who has experiential learning.

Experiential learning (Kolb 1984) is a learning process that derives from concrete experience and reflection that, in general, occurs during a given activity. It differs from traditional knowledge in which the learner plays a relatively passive role in the teaching-learning process. In experiential learning, the educator assumes a prominent role. Kolb (1984) recognizes the role that emotion and feelings, derived from learning from experience, have in experiential learning. This author believes that the direct engagement of the individual in the experience and his later reflection, using analytical tools, allow the learner to understand better what happened and retain the information for a longer time. Thus, he can pass on this knowledge as well.

The clinical poster profile is, to no small extent, close to someone who exercises experiential learning (Kolb 1984). He responds to people who have just begun treatment and are eager for information and clarification about hemodialysis and other issues and problems that arise during renal replacement therapy. For this reason, they answer questions, clarify doubts, and share their experiences with members of the Facebook groups investigated.

The clinical poster responds to the demands of his colleagues. He is an "expert patient," that is, a person "expert in managing their disease, and this could be used to encourage others to become key decision makers in the treatment process" (Tattersall 2002).

As described by Pereira Neto et al. (2015), the "expert patient" is the individual who seeks information and knowledge to solve his health needs. The phenomenon of the "expert patient" is linked to the processes of empowerment since the intense and extensive research of information about his pathology allows the individual to have access to a larger field of choices about his health condition.

In this regard, this chapter resumes the question that motivated the study of Fox et al. (2005, 1299): "Do 'informed' or 'expert' patients challenge dominant traditions in biomedicine or merely adopt these as conventional ways of thinking about body shape and size, illness, and health?"

To answer this question, we will see how the clinical poster submits and answers concerns online.

One of the passages found in our research refers to a recommendation made by two clinical posters to another person, possibly less versed in dealing with hemodialysis. One recommends: "Take one additional set of clothes with you... I threw up a lot ... but it will soon pass" (F12). Another suggests:

> Whenever you drink water and other [liquids] never fill the glass. Always fill the size of a couple of fingers. Drink it. You can control better this way. *At least, it worked for me.* (F19) (our emphasis)

Vomiting is a recurrent complication in people undergoing hemodialysis. Chronic kidney patients face severe restrictions on water intake because the kidney no longer has the same filtration capacity (Terra et al. 2010).

These postings illustrate how clinical posters act on group members' demands. We realize that these recommendations are based on the patient's personal experiences throughout his treatment – an initiative that "at least worked" for her. Only someone undergoing renal replacement therapy has the competency to give such guidelines. It is a knowledge derived from the experience itself that may favor a better coping strategy for patients who are starting treatment.

Knowledge derived from experience seems to have credibility among the participants who initiate the treatment. One of the frequenters said:

> Thank you so much for answering me. Everything is handy. As we are in the process of adaptation, we need information. God bless you! (F12)

The clinical poster's adherence to the biomedical treatment is such that he feels capable of convincing others about the success of hemodialysis in order to improve quality of life of kidney patients, reduce the debilitating signs, and ameliorate symptoms that derive from chronic renal failure. One of them even extolled the existence of hemodialysis, stating:

> Man has had the wisdom to create a machine that gives us a little better quality of life and that helps us to feel a bit better. Can you imagine that years ago people did not have access to what we have today? (F112)

The first hemodialysis machines were tested in humans around the 1940s. The first record of the procedure dates back to 1945. However, several attempts were made before achieving success in treatment. Today, with technological advances in the manufacture of hemodialysis machines, and especially with the development of vascular access surgical techniques, thousands of people benefit from renal replacement therapy (Xavier et al. 2012).

The clinical poster is mostly not a health professional. However, he can translate medical knowledge into a simple and understandable way for the user. We were able to perceive, responding to the question by Fox et al. (2005), that conventional forms of treatment are faithfully reproduced by her. His adherence is such that the clinical poster comes to encourages new patients to practice hemodialysis.

He also knows how the procedure should be at the time of hemodialysis. One of them explained this process as follows:

> From the moment the blood leaves the body, it (the blood) tries to coagulate. That is why heparin[10] is used. The more concentrated it is, the faster it will coagulate (Hematocrit[11] too high). Doctors and nurses should update their dose of heparin and the use of an oral anticoagulant. (F20)

The above passage reveals that the clinical poster masters hemodialysis procedures. He is someone familiar with the scientific terminology. He goes on to say how healthcare professionals should proceed. Thus, He can establish a more horizontal relationship with the doctor and other health professionals. Traditionally, this relationship was based on the professionals' knowledge and patient's ignorance, one subjecting herself to the authority of the other.

In analyzing these dialogues from an interactionist point of view, we observe that, even in computer-mediated communication, in which language stands out as a way to help understand the other's perspective, people make themselves understood by affirming that they are sure about what they are saying (Charon 2010). The tone of advice often assumes a taxing character. One of them says, "You *should* control your dry weight. *Only in this way* will you improve" (F155) (our emphasis). This argument with the air of authority can be perceived by the use of terms, such as: *only this way* and *should*. Even in the form of writing, it is possible to understand the tone that people want to give their speech: an imperative tone. These posts can be considered an authoritative argument. In general, this expression refers to the presentation of an argument sustained by the citation of a reliable source, which can be a specialist, a leader, a politician, an artist, or a thinker, in short, an authority on

---

[10] Heparin is the most commonly used anticoagulant in Brazil. It is indicated to avoid blood coagulation and the formation of thrombi that can obstruct the blood's passage or form emboli that can end up in the lungs, leading to death.

[11] Hematocrit is a test that measures the percentage of red blood cells.

the subject under discussion. In the case mentioned above, the clinical poster gives power to his argument based on his experience with hemodialysis and the treatment of chronic renal failure. In a way, he reproduces the physician's authoritative argument when advising treatment to a patient.

Thus, although the clinical poster seeks to establish a less asymmetric relationship with the health professional, the centrality of physician and medicine[12] in the treatment of chronic kidney disease seems evident in the clinical poster's discourse:

> [...] Has anyone ever had a sore throat with a terrible cough? What decongestant can we take? Does anyone have a good idea? [...] I'll see to this with the doctor today, but it's always good to exchange ideas. (F209)

When analyzing the meetings between physicians and patients in hospital wards, Araujo (2013) concluded that patients' passivity toward the medical discourse results from the social construction on the supremacy of the medical professionals' knowledge. This fact can also be observed in some of dialogues and recommendations given on the Facebook platform. The centrality of biomedical power can also be perceived in them. One of them suggests: "You should ask your doctor: it may be excess fluid" (F204).

This second ideal type of poster has a clinical character.

Only those who undergo chronic kidney therapy know how their devices should be handled. He knows how to measure the amount of water in the glass so that the patient does not get sick. She's had too much water. They already inserted the cannula into his and he felt pain. The health professional does not have this same experience. He did not have any cannulas inserted into his body, nor did he know how to measure the best amount of water to drink. This is knowledge derived from practical experience, which differentiates the clinical poster from other chronic kidney patients and health professionals, including physicians. Although his guidance is biomedical, only he can translate exoteric scientific knowledge into a comprehensible and straightforward way to the user.

The clinical poster is empowered with knowledge derived from the practical experience of living with the disease and undergoing treatment. With the citizen poster, the "expert patient" still submits to the biomedical order but attempts to occupy a more horizontal relationship toward health professionals.

In the citizen poster, the "expert patient" plays another role.

6.4.3 *The Citizen Poster*

In Brazil, citizens who rely on renal replacement therapy have some civil rights guaranteed by law. These rights are associated with the high lethality of terminal chronic renal failure (CRF), despite the available treatments (Louvison et al. 2011).[13]

[12] Chapter 13 addresses the issue of Internet and medicines.

[13] Brazilian law guarantees that patients with chronic kidney problems receive sick pay, disability retirement (without a grace period), and exemption from payment of many taxes, including the income tax.

In addition to these civil rights achieved over time, the public health policies of patients undergoing renal replacement therapy deserve attention.

Firstly, it should be remembered that the Unified Health System (SUS) in Brazil establishes that:

> Health is the right of all and the duty of the State, guaranteed through social and economic policies aimed at reducing the risk of disease and other illnesses and universal and equal access to actions and services for their promotion, protection and recovery.[14]

Regarding the chronic kidney patient, the Unified Health System (SUS) provides several free and universal renal replacement therapy treatments, namely, peritoneal dialysis, hemodialysis, and transplantation.[15]

How many people are undergoing renal replacement therapy in Brazil?

In 2006, Brazil had a rate of 531 patients per million population (pmp) and the United States, 363 patients pmp (Louvison et al. 2011). Brazil's rate is considered low compared to Chile (750 patients pmp) and Uruguay (800 patients pmp).

Therefore, these are kidney patients' rights and the health policies that aim to guarantee comprehensive care to patients in renal replacement therapy.

Also, the country's Constitution formally advocates "community participation." "Social control," one of the fundamental principles of SUS, involves different levels of political representation of society supported by various legal provisions. "Social control" facilitates and encourages advocacy actions that may include press campaigns, public events, and lobbying activities to pressure the legislative, executive, and judicial branches (Stafford and Mitchell 2009). Thus, advocacy has a broader meaning, denoting those types of initiatives ranging from political pressure, promotion, and defense of a cause and interest through various actions mobilized by civil society organizations aimed at giving greater visibility to specific topics or issues in public debate and thereby influence policy (Libardoni 2000).

The citizen poster on websites is one that knows the country's civil rights and health policies that affect chronic kidney patients. He is present in many different ways. He is often enlightening. Some patients under renal replacement therapy are unaware of these rights or do not know what bureaucratic procedures they should adopt to enjoy these legal prerogatives.

One of the most common requests in these virtual environments is social security. A patient in renal replacement therapy who receives "sick pay" asks what should be done to obtain the "Social Integration Program"[16] (*Programa Integração Social* or PIS), as follows:

> I'm getting sick pay. I do not get PIS. Has anyone ever received it? Here I know people here who already have… Who received it? How did you apply for it? (F19)

---

[14] Article 196 of the 1988 Brazilian Federal Constitution.

[15] Ordinance 1.168 of the Ministry of Health of June 15, 2004.

[16] The "Social Integration Program" (PIS) is aimed at employees of private companies. This is a social contribution tax, paid by a legal entity, aimed at financing unemployment insurance, bonus payments, and employee participation in the revenue of the companies in which they work.

The enlightening citizen poster is aware of the legislation relating to the PIS grant states:

> I began receiving sick pay in May last year. In March, I received the PIS. Why is that? In 2015, I paid my contributions until February. People who have not worked for at least a month last year do not receive it. No application required. The grant is automatically credited to your bank account. To be entitled to PIS, you must have worked 30 days in 2015. This is because PIS refers to last year. Next year, I will not receive this payment anymore. (F26)

The explanations of the citizen poster follow the established regulations. It was a post made by someone who is up-to-date about the legal-political universe in which the rights of citizens undergoing renal replacement therapy are found, particularly regarding the PIS grant. This information must have been useful to the requesting party.

The citizen poster also exercises oversight and plays a role in social mobilization.

The following complaint is made: "Good morning. I thank you in advance for any help you may provide. Hemodialysis patients do not deserve to be treated that way" (F2). Next you can find a video posted on YouTube[17] with the title:

> The municipality of Amélia Rodrigues does not carry out maintenance on the hemodialysis patient's car. This neglect with patients is absurd. (F2)

The images show a pickup truck with patients sitting and waiting for a vehicle to take them to the nearest city for hemodialysis. This video was made by users themselves. The first image shows the torn tire of a truck. A man who holds the tire and shows the tear says: "It almost killed everyone. A lot of accidents would have happened were it not for the slow driving speed." Then a lady reveals that the attendant warned that the tire was in bad shape, but that the driver came anyway. He concludes by saying, "There! I have said it!" The same man complements what the lady denounced, stating: "It has been denounced! Now he has to face the Public Prosecutor[18]!" Finally, the filmmaker does a close-up, filling the whole screen, of the inscription where one could read: "Municipality of Amélia Rodrigues. A city of all." This was not the only post on the poor transport of patients undergoing renal replacement therapy. Many complaints are accompanied by photos and videos thanks to smartphones facilities.

Amélia Rodrigues is a Brazilian municipality in the inland region of the state of Bahia with little more than 20,000 inhabitants. The chronic kidney patients of this city live a reality similar to that of patients residing in many small municipalities of the country: hemodialysis services are not included in the health services structure of the municipality. Thus, they must be transported to another nearby municipality. In this case, we can assume that patients are being transported to the municipality of Feira de Santana, with 600,000 inhabitants, 30 kilometers away from Amélia Rodrigues.

---

[17] Available at https://www.youtube.com/watch?v=7tqApuvexhU

[18] The mission of the Public Prosecutor's Office, part of the Brazilian judiciary, is to defend the rights of citizens in relation to the offenses made by government representatives.

By seeing this video available on YouTube, group members who agree with their content can share it with others. In this perspective, we reiterate the vision of Belfort and Sena (2015, 33) when they affirm that "citizenship demands greater participation and pressure and this can be exercised online."

It should be noted, however, that the renal replacement therapy service and other care services provided by the Unified Health System are currently undergoing a financial crisis. Complaints about the scraping of the renal replacement therapy public service were not limited to the issue of transport.

> We are experiencing a real collapse in hemodialysis clinics. If the authorities responsible for PUBLIC health do not take URGENT steps regarding the transfer of money to clinics, renal life will be extinct in roughly one year.[19] (F104)

Then there is the image of a bond, similar to that found in the AIDS campaign that suggests solidarity with patients and commitment to preserving public, free, and quality treatment. In the case of chronic kidney patients, green replaces red. In this post, the green bow is accompanied by the black bow – an explicit mention of announced death.

In Brazil, the Ministry of Health is responsible for 87% of patients in renal replacement therapy (Lugon 2009). In 2014, an observational study by Gouveia et al. (2017) in the city of Curitiba, State of Paraná (Brazil), concluded that:

> The lowest cost of a kidney transplant in the first year was R$ 40,743 when cyclosporine was used, and the highest was R$ 48,388 with the use of tacrolimus. In the second-year post-transplant, hemodialysis and peritoneal dialysis have a higher cost compared to kidney transplant. Transplantation with a deceased donor, treated with tacrolimus is R$ 67,023.39; Hemodialysis R$ 71,717.51 and automated peritoneal dialysis R$ 69,527.03. (Gouveia et al. 2017, 162)[20]

It is, therefore, a costly treatment, which in Brazil must be provided free of charge by the Ministry of Health. The service can be found in public (federal, state, and municipal health care facilities) and private institutions. In the second case, treatment is subsidized by the government budget.

The third ideal type of poster described here has a citizen character.

Only those who are chronic kidney patients know the importance of fighting for the rights of those with this disease. The limitations imposed by the disease require the full exercise of constitutionally guaranteed rights. In these terms, this "expert patient" plays different and complementary roles: he provides guidance to other members of the virtual community on how to obtain their rights and denounces where they are not being fulfilled. He knows that inefficiency of the free and universal public renal care system in Brazil can lead many patients to death. Few have the financial means to pay for this treatment. He is a politically conscious "expert patient" who is fighting for the rights of chronic kidney patients from the "bottom-up" (Turner 1994). We believe that patients have more legitimacy

---

[19] We kept the original spelling in the box when it was in capital letters.

[20] In 2014, a dollar was worth 2.30 reals, the name of Brazil's currency. Information was obtained on April 14, 2018, on the website http://www.acinh.com.br/servicos/cotacao-dolar

to denounce and claim their rights than people who study and specialize in this subject. The sense of belonging makes the words of the citizen poster no longer just his. He believes that he is not speaking for himself, but for a community. His words translate values and aspirations of a group, showing empowerment in the collective realm. He is empowered with information and political awareness derived from the daily struggle to ensure quality care services and the preservation of the civil rights of patients undergoing renal replacement therapy.

6.5 Final Considerations

The search for health information, the configuration of support networks, and the struggle for the recognition of civil rights of disease-carrying patients did not begin with the Internet. After all, until very recently, individuals discussed their issues with a friend, relative, or some acquaintance and sought solace from another patient like them about the anguish involving renal replacement therapy. They had to find the assistance of lawyers if they wanted to report or claim any of their rights as the chronic disease's carriers.

Now, with the Internet, it all got easier and faster. Individuals with access to the network and skills in handling this tool can obtain a vast amount of informative content. Without leaving home, they can access at any time, with a single click, many sources of information, with content that is updated and available in different languages and formats, which may have different perspectives and opinions on the same topic (Miller and Bell 2012; Riggare et al. 2017). In social networks available online, they can share ideas, knowledge, and apprehensions with people who experience the same problem. With the Internet, researching health information has shifted from being an uncommon practice to another that is part of one's daily routine (Holmes et al. 2017).

In one of the pioneering studies about online support groups, Feenberg et al. (1996) suggest that these virtual environments could represent a new form of patient empowerment. According to the authors, "the larger implications of these online patient meetings have to do with their potential for changing the accessibility, the scale, and the speed of interaction of patient groups" (Feenberg et al. 1996, 130). These authors also affirm that support groups formed through virtual networks would allow hundreds or thousands of people to approach and share views with a credibility that is similar to that of a physician. They warn:

> Groups with hundreds, even thousands, of members can form rapidly and inexpensively, and present views that have credibility as representative. We may well be witnessing the beginning of a new kind of empowerment of patients. (Feenberg et al. 1996, 131)

In this context, some studies on Internet and health have discussed the characteristics of the "expert patient." On the one hand, such a patient has been seen as a confident individual, with skills, information, and knowledge to play a central role in managing his pathology. In these terms, he is seen as a patient who, to some extent, defies medical authority (Shaw and Baker 2004; Kopelson 2009). However, some researchers look for the process of continuity present in the empowerment of the "expert patient." McAllister et al. (2012), for example, point out that patient empowerment in and of itself does not subvert the biomedical order, since it is associated with the idea of adherence: the individual tends to voluntarily agree with the proposals specified by medical care – possibly formulated in a shared way.

The issue of "expert patient" empowerment and the biomedical order was also discussed by Fox et al. (2005). In their paper, the researchers looked at whether the "expert patient" would challenge biomedical traditions or adopt them as a conventional model in thinking about body, health, and disease. The researchers concluded that participation in virtual environments helps participants to become "expert patients" rooted in the biomedical paradigm.

In this paper, we have been more concerned with the "ideal types" of intervention in two chronic kidney disease online groups that gather people interested in the subject, whether patients, caregivers, or relatives.

The three ideal types identified in the research portrayed throughout this chapter gravitate around the authority of biomedicine and the medical professional.

The supportive poster encourages new entrants based on the idea that renal replacement therapies prolong life. Ultimately, he reiterates biomedical treatment. By sharing the suffering and anguish of the patients and their families, the supportive poster plays a role that doctors and medicine have ceased to exercise: welcoming, listening, and comforting. He establishes a horizontal relationship with others based on trust and solidarity. He is the only one who can occupy this place. The fact of having experienced what others went through gives the supportive poster a legitimacy among his peers. He becomes a unique "expert patient": sharing the pain he has already endured with those who are now suffering. The supportive poster becomes a central actor in the initial process of adherence to renal replacement therapies.

The clinical poster also appears to be under the orbit of biomedicine. However, he does not dutifully submit to the physician's professional authority. The knowledge he gains from the daily practice of treatment and Internet searches and sharing on social networks brings him closer to the typical "expert patient." Tattersall (2002, 227) had already pointed out that the "expert patient" would be "a new approach to chronic disease management for the twenty-first century." By 2002, these ideas were relatively new. Our work has confirmed this viewpoint. Since then, Tattersall (2002) admitted that a cultural change was necessary for the way healthcare professionals deal with the "expert patient." His perspective proposed a horizontal relationship: an underprivileged topic in medical schools in Brazil and many parts of the world. In 2004, Shaw and Baker (2004) questioned whether the "expert patient" would be a dream or a nightmare. Our chapter revealed that it is increasingly a reality nowadays.

The third ideal type of social media poster transcends the standards of biomedicine and does not affect the doctor-patient relationship. This poster is aware of his rights, denounces irregularities, guides his peers, and summons them to action. He is a mobilizer and is engaged. The citizen poster plays a role that the traditional doctor is far from exercising. His action exceeds clinical care and self-management of the disease. He devotes his attention to the civic realm of the chronic disease. The renal replacement therapy does not only mean adopting routines of self-care, but it also imposes some changes and limitations on the patient's life. In this context, the citizen poster reminds the other users of the online group that they are all part of a social security network formally guaranteed by the State. Their messages highlight the condition of participants in the virtual environment as holders of rights recognized by law. He encourages them to seek the fulfillment of what is legally guaranteed to them. He denounces situations in which the rights of patients undergoing chronic kidney therapy are disrespected.

From the analysis of two chronic kidney disease online groups, this chapter contributes insights to and debates about empowerment, the "expert patient," and the biomedical order that deserves to be presented.

A first point deserves attention. The construction of the "expert patient" does not necessarily imply a break with the hegemony of biomedical knowledge and power. Our findings in this chapter coincide with the results obtained in the academic literature on the subject. The supportive and clinical posters reiterate the procedures accepted and adopted by biomedicine and construct arguments that value these practices and encourage their full and unchallenged adoption.

A second point is also worth mentioning. We identified different performance styles between posters in these two virtual environments. Some take a more accommodating stance, triggering their experience to comfort other participants in times of distress or doubt and offering a word of comfort in a moment of despair and tension. Others who are more concerned with the clinical realm clarify doubts and questions based on the knowledge they have developed from the practical experience of living with the disease. In general terms, they base their recommendations on the biomedical model, since their statements reiterate results obtained by medicine in the treatment of the disease or the information validated by the medical knowledge. The third option of participation in online groups emphasized the civic realm. This poster extrapolates beyond the realm of care and assistance, paying attention to the importance of civic participation of the chronic kidney patient and his condition of citizen protected by the State and bearer of social rights.

The results of our study point not only to the centrality that the Internet, as a means of information and communication, has assumed in the life of the patient, but also to the performance of the "expert patient" in one of the virtual environments most sought by people interested in discussing health: online groups. Participation in patient groups organized in virtual networks today is an obvious reality. Additional research needs to be carried out. We recommend reflections on the place of the "expert patient" not only about the doctor but also to the health system and public policies. Thus, this new social player's social and political role will be recognized and analyzed.

References

Ahluwalia, Sanjiv, Elizabeth Murray, Fiona Stevenson, Cicely Kerr, and Jo Burns. 2010. A heartbeat moment': Qualitative study of GP views of patients bringing health information from the internet to a consultation. *The British Journal of General Practice* 60: 80–94.

Altamirano, Ana Fernández-Aballí. 2016. Where is Paulo Freire. In *The international communication gazette*, vol. 78, 1–7.

Amichai-Hamburger, Yair, Katelyn Y.A. McKenna, and Samuel-Azran Tald. 2008. E-empowerment: Empowerment by the internet. *Computers in Human Behavior* 24: 1776–1789.

Arantes, Rodolfo L. 2008. Avaliação do risco cardiovascular em pacientes com doença renal crônica: importância e limitação dos diferentes métodos. *Rev Bras Hipertens* 15: 173–176.

Araujo, James. 2013. A análise do discurso no contexto da comunicação na saúde: elementos para uma abordagem do direito à informação na interação entre médico e paciente. *C&S* 34: 121–140.

Aron, Raymond. 1999. *Main currents of sociological thought: Durkheim, Pareto, Weber*. New Brunswick: Transaction Publishers.

Belfort, Maíra, and Arcângela Sena. 2015. Cibercidadania: um estudo de caso do site vakinha.com.br Puçá 2: 1–35

Bimber, Bruce, Andrew Flanagin, and Cynthia Stohl. 2012. *Collective action in organizations: Interactions and engagement in an era of technological change*. Nova York: Cambridge University Press.

Brazil. Presidência da República. Casa Civil. 2015. *Lei n° 13.146, de 6 de julho de 2015*. Institui a Lei Brasileira de Inclusão da Pessoa com Deficiência (Estatuto da Pessoa com Deficiência). Diário Oficial da República Federativa do Brasil, 7 jul 2015.

Canziani, Maria Eugênia F. 2004. Doenças cardiovasculares na doença renal crônica. *Jornal Brasileiro de Nefrologia* 26: 20–21.

Charon, Joel M. 2010. *Symbolic Interactionism: An introduction, an interpretation, an integration*. Englewood Cliffs: Prentice Hall.

Choudhury, Naziat. 2009. The question of empowerment: Women's perspective on their internet use. *Gender, Technology and Development* 13: 341–363.

Coutinho, Virgínia. 2014. *The social book: tudo o que precisa saber sobre Facebook*. Coimbra: Conjuntura Actual.

Facebook. 2010. Facebook tips: What's the difference between a Facebook page and group? https://www.facebook.com/notes/facebook/facebook-tips-whats-the-difference-between-a-facebook-page-and-group/324706977130/. Accessed 2 Jan 2018.

———. 2018. Criar e gerenciar uma página. https://www.facebook.com/help/135275340210354/?helpref=hc_fnav. Accessed 30 Mar 2018.

Feenberg, Andrew L., Jonathan M. Licht, Kathleen P. Kane, Kay Moran, and Richard A. Smith. 1996. The online patient meeting. *Journal of the Neurological Sciences* 139: 129–131.

Fox, Susannah. 2011. *Peer-to-peer healthcare*. Washington, DC: Pew Research Center.

Fox, N., K.J. Ward, and A.J. O'rourke. 2005. The 'expert patient': Empowerment or medical dominance? The case of weight loss, pharmaceutical drugs and the Internet. *Social Science & Medicine* 60: 1299–1309.

Freire, Paulo. 1994. *Pedagogy of hope: reliving pedagogy of the oppressed*. New York: Continuum.

———. 2015. *Pedagogy of the oppressed*. New York: Continuum.

García-Llana, Helena, Eduardo Remor, and Rafael Selgas. 2013. Adherence to treatment, emotional state and quality of life in patients with end-stage renal disease undergoing dialysis. *Psicothema* 25: 79–86.

Giddens, Anthony. 1991. *Modernity and self-identity: Self and society in late modern age*. Cambridge: Polity Press.

Gouveia, Denise, Alexandre Tortoza Bignelli, Silvia Regina Hokazono, Itamara Danucalov, Tobias August Siemens, et al. 2017. Analysis of economic impact between the modality of renal replacement therapy. *Jornal Brasileiro de Nefrologia* 39: 162–171.

Holmes, Michelle, Felicity L. Bishop, and Lynn Calman. 2017. "I just googled and read everything": Exploring breast cancer survivors' use of the internet to find information on complementary medicine. *Complementary Therapies in Medicine* 33: 78–84.

Jay, Colleen, Patrick G. Dean, Ryan A. Helmick, and Mark D. Stegall. 2016. Reassessing preemptive kidney transplantation in the United States: Are we making progress? *Transplantation* 100: 1120–1127.

Jordan, Tim. 2014. *Internet, society and culture: Communicative practices before and after the internet*. London: Bloomsbury.

Kaplan, Andreas, and Michael Haenlein. 2010. Users of the world, unite!: The challenges and opportunities of social media. *Business Horizons* 53: 59–68.

Kim, Yong-Mi. 2015. Is seeking health information online different from seeking general information online? *Journal of Information Science* 41: 228–241.

Kolb, David. 1984. *Experiential learning: experience as the source of learning and development*. Englewood Cliffs: Prentice Hall.

Kopelson, Karen. 2009. Writing patients' wrongs: The rhetoric and reality of information age medicine. *JAC* 29: 353–404.

Kosinski, Michal, Sandra C. Matz, Samuel D. Gosling, Vesselin Popov, and David Stillwell. 2015. Facebook as a research tool for the social sciences: Opportunities, challenges, ethical considerations, and practical guidelines. *The American Psychologist* 70: 543–556.

Kozinets, Robert V. 2010. *Netnography: doing ethnographic research online*. Thousand Oaks: Sage.

Lévy, Pierre. 2001. *Cyberculture*. Minneapolis: University of Minnesota Press.

Li, Jinhui, Yin-Leng Theng, and Schubert Foo. 2015. Predictors of online health information seeking behavior: Changes between 2002 and 2012. *Health Informatics Journal* 22: 1–11.

Libardoni, Marlene. 2000. Fundamentos teóricos e visão estratégica da Advocacy. *Revista Estudos Feministas* 8: 1–15.

Lin, Wan-Ying, Xinzhi Zhang, Hayeon Song, and Kikuko Omori. 2016. Health information seeking in the Web 2.0 age: Trust in social media, uncertainty reduction, and self-disclosure. *Computers in Human Behavior* 56: 289–294.

Lincoln, Nicola Denham, Cheryl Travers, Peter Ackers, and Adrian Wilkinson. 2002. The meaning of empowerment: The interdisciplinary etymology of a new management concept. *International Journal of Management Reviews* 4: 271–990.

Lins, Silvia Maria de Sá Basilio, Josete Luzia Leite, Simone de Godoy, Patrícia dos Santos Claro Fuly, Silvia Teresa Carvalho de Araújo, and Ítalo Rodolfo Silva. 2017. Cultural adaptation of the end-stage renal disease adherence questionnaire for hemodialysis patients. *Revista Brasileira de Enfermagem* 70: 1169–1175.

Louvison, Marilia Cristina Prado, Mônica Aparecida Marcondes Cecilio, Vera Lucia Lopes Rodrigues Osiano, Silvany Lemes Cruvinel Portas, and Ricardo Sesso. 2011. Prevalência de pacientes em terapia renal substitutiva no Estado de São Paulo. *Bol epidemiol paul* 8: 23–42.

Lugon, Jocemir R. 2009. Doença renal crônica no Brasil: um problema de saúde pública. *Brazilian Journal of Nephrology* 31: 2–5.

Mano, Rita S. 2014. Social media and online health services: A health empowerment perspective to online health information. *Computers in Human Behavior* 39: 404–412.

Markham, Annette, and Elizabeth Buchanan. 2012. Ethical decision-making and internet research: Recommendations from the AoIR ethics working committee (Version 2.0). https://aoir.org/reports/ethics2.pdf

McAllister, Marion, Graham Dunn, Katherine Payne, Linda Davies, and Chris Todd. 2012. Patient empowerment: The need to consider it as a measurable patient-reported outcome for chronic conditions. *BMC Health Services Research* 12: 1–8.

Miller, Lisa M.S., and Robert A. Bell. 2012. Online health information seeking: The influence of age, information trustworthiness, and search challenges. *Journal of Aging and Health* 24: 525–541.

Ministry of Health. 2018. Saúde incorpora procedimento de hemodiálise para pacientes em trânsito. http://portalms.saude.gov.br/noticias/agencia-saude/42715-saude-incorpora-procedimento-de-hemodialise-para-pacientes-em-transito. Accessed 20 Apr 2018.

Mo, Phoenix K.H., and Neil S. Coulson. 2010. Empowering processes in online support groups among people living with HIV/AIDS: A comparative analysis of 'lurkers' and 'posters'. *Computers in Human Behavior* 26: 1183–1193.

———. 2014. Are online support groups always beneficial?: A qualitative exploration of the empowering and disempowering processes of participation within HIV/AIDS-related online support groups. *International Journal of Nursing Studies* 51: 983–993.

Moretti, Felipe Azevedo, and Claudia Barsottini. 2017. Support, attention and distant guidance for chronic pain patients: Case report. *Revista Dor* 18: 85–87.

Murray, Elizabeth, Joanne Burns, Sharon See Tai, Rosalind Lai, and Irwin Nazareth. 2005. Interactive health communication applications for people with chronic disease. *Cochrane Database of Systematic Reviews*. https://doi.org/10.1002/14651858.CD004274.pub4.

Narayan, Deepa. 2002. *Empowerment and poverty reduction: A sourcebook*. World Bank Publications.

National Kidney Foundation. 2013. KDIGO 2012 clinical practice guideline for the evaluation and Management of Chronic Kidney Disease. *Kidney International Supplements* 3: 1–163.

Pereira Neto, André, Letícia Barbosa, Adriano da Silva, and Monica Lucia Gomes Dantas. 2015. O paciente informado e os saberes médicos: um estudo de etnografia virtual em comunidades de doentes no Facebook. *História, Ciências, Saúde – Manguinhos* 22: 1653–1671.

Page, Nanette, and Cheryl Czuba. 1999. Empowerment: What is it? *Journal of Extension* 37.

Rieder, Bernhard. 2013. Studying Facebook via data extraction: The Netvizz application. 5th annual ACM web science conference, ACM, 346–355.

Riger, Stephanie. 1993. What's wrong with empowerment. *American Journal of Community Psychology* 21: 279–292.

Riggare, Sara, Pär J. Höglund, Helena Hvitfeldt Forsberg, Elena Eftimovska, Per Svenningsson, and Maria Hägglund. 2017. Patients are doing it for themselves: A survey on disease-specific knowledge acquisition among people with Parkinson's disease in Sweden. *Health Informatics Journal*. https://doi.org/10.1177/1460458217704248.

Rissel, Christopher. 1994. Empowerment: The holy grail of health promotion? *Health Promotion International* 9: 39–47.

Ryhänen, Anne M., Sirkku Rankinen, Mervi Siekkinen, Maiju Saarinen, Heikki Korvenranta, and Helena Leino-Kilpi. 2012. The impact of an empowering Internet-based breast Cancer patient pathway programme on breast cancer patients' knowledge: A randomised control trial. *Patient Education and Counseling* 88: 224–231.

Schwartz, Eda, Rosani Manfrin Muniz, Andréia Burille, Juliana Graciela Vestena Zillmer, Danubia Andressa da Silva, Aline Machado Feijó, and Maria Emília Nunes Bueno. 2009. As redes de apoio no enfrentamento da doença renal crônica. *REME – Revista Mineira de Enfermagem* 13: 183–192.

Shaw, Joanne, and Mary Baker. 2004. "Expert patient": dream or nightmare? The concept of a well informed patient is welcome, but a new name is needed. *British Medical Journal* 328: 723–724.

Silva, Letícia Krauss, Rachel Bregman, Dulce Lessi, Beatriz Leimann, and Mariane Branco Alves. 2012. Ensaio sobre a cegueira: mortalidade de pacientes com doença renal crônica em hemodiálise de emergência. *Ciênc saúde coletiva* 17: 2971–2980.

Srinivasan, Ramesh, and Adam Fish. 2017. *After the Internet*. Cambridge: Polity Press.

Stafford, J., and H. Mitchell. 2009. *Advocacy in action: A toolkit for public health professionals*. Perth: Public Health Advocacy Institute of Western Australia.

Tattersall, Robert. 2002. The expert patient: A new approach to chronic disease management for the twenty-first century. *Clinical Medicine (London, England)* 2: 227–229.

Terra, Fábio de Souza, Ana Maria Duarte Dias Costa, Estevão Tavares de Figueiredo, Alline Moterani de Morais, Marina Dias Costa, and Rosane Dias Costa. 2010. As principais complicações apresentadas pelos pacientes renais crônicos durante as sessões de hemodiálise. *Rev Bras Clin Med* 8: 187–192.

Torchi, Thalita Souza, Sílvia Teresa Carvalho de Araújo, Alessandra Guimarães Monteiro Moreira, Giselle Barcellos Oliveira Koeppe, and Bruna Tavares Uchoa dos Santos. 2014. Condições clínicas e comportamento de procura de cuidados de saúde pelo paciente renal crônico. *Acta Paulista Enfermagem* 27: 585–590.

Turner, Bryan. 1994. Outline of a theory of citizenship. In *Citizenship: Critical concepts*, ed. Bryan S. Turner and Peter Hamilton. New York: Routledge.

Wallerstein, N. 2006. *What is the evidence on effectiveness of empowerment to improve health?: Health evidence network report*. Copenhagen: WHO Regional Office for Europe.

Weber, Max. 1949. *The methodology of the social sciences*. New York: The Free Press.

WHO - World Health Organization. 2009. *Milestones in health promotion: Statements from global conferences*. Geneva: World Health Organization.

Wilson, Patricia, Sally Kendall, and Fiona Brooks. 2007. The expert patients Programme: A paradox of patient empowerment and medical dominance. *Health & Social Care in the Community* 15: 426–438.

Xavier, Aline, Ana Oliveira, and Marislei Brasileiro. 2012. Evolução histórica da hemodiálise e dos acessos vasculares para a assistência ao doente renal crônico. *Rev Eletr Enferm Centro Estudos Enferm e Nut* 4: 1–15.

Zimmerman, Marc A. 1995. Psychological empowerment: Issues and illustrations. *American Journal of Community Psychology* 23: 581–599.

Chapter 7
Digital Natives and Health: An Exploratory Study with Young Brazilians of Different Socioeconomic Profiles

André Pereira Neto, Leticia Barbosa, Larissa Barão, and Stephanie Muci

Abstract Digital Native. Although debated in the international literature, this term refers to a new generation of individuals embedded in a context highly permeated by "New Information and Communications Technologies" (NICTs). In this chapter, we intend to analyze specificities and possible diversities of Brazilian "Digital Natives." Research indicates that socioeconomic status can restrict access to NICTs, preventing generalization of the term Digital Native. To verify whether this was applicable to the Brazilian context, we conducted an exploratory study with young people in three distinct environments with different socioeconomic statuses. Results suggest that among the young, low-income people participating in the study, their socioeconomic status did not prevent or restrict access to the Internet. On the contrary, we found that they spend more time on the Internet than young, high-income people do. The frequency of online access identified among the participants suggests the central role of NICTs in the lives of "Digital Natives," as well as in their searches for health information.

7.1 Introduction

The emergence and popularization of "New Information and Communications Technologies" (NICTs) from the turn of the twentieth century to the twenty-first century has contributed to a series of transformations and reconfigurations of

A. Pereira Neto (✉)
National School of Public Health, Oswaldo Cruz Foundation, Rio de Janeiro, Brazil

L. Barbosa
Institute of Scientific and Technological Communication and Information in Health, Oswaldo Cruz Foundation, Rio de Janeiro, Brazil

L. Barão
Law School, State University of Rio de Janeiro, Rio de Janeiro, Brazil

S. Muci
Department of International Health, Georgetown University, Washington, DC, USA

A. Pereira Neto, M. B. Flynn (eds.), *The Internet and Health in Brazil*,
https://doi.org/10.1007/978-3-319-99289-1_7

practices, organizational structures, and behaviors in various fields of society (Fuchs 2008). This atmosphere derived from two main aspects. One is ubiquity: at any given time, individuals enjoy the possibility of connecting to social networks. Another realm closely related is the capacity for social, political, and intellectual relationships individuals can establish with each other, thanks to the technical ease of sharing information and experiences on the Internet (Bimber et al. 2012). Thus, the communicational setting established in this context is characterized by many-to-many communication, at any time and on a global scale (Castells 2001). The chaotic overflow of information (Lévy 2001) and the possibility of being both producers and consumers of information (Ritzer and Jurgenson 2010) are also imprints of this new era.

In this context, it is increasingly common to find in the literature, whether scientific or not, reports and analyses on the establishment of a new generation of individuals called "Digital Natives" (Prensky 2001a). This term has been used to define people born after the 1980s, who grew up surrounded by digital technologies such as video games, cellphones, and computers. NICTs are part of the daily life of these people who do not admit living without them (Akçayir et al. 2016). Their massive use of NICTs would singularize them from previous generations. Some authors argue that this habit tends to engender and affect, to a greater or lesser extent, their interests, values, behaviors, and skills (Bennett et al. 2008). The first mention of children native to the cyberspace world was found in John Perry Barlow's "Declaration of the Independence of Cyberspace" (Barlow 1996).[1] A few years later, in his book, Prensky (2001a) coined the term "Digital Natives" when analyzing the singularities of the first generations that grew in a context where digital technologies were created and began to be disseminated.[2]

Over the past decades, different terms have been constructed to designate this unique group of individuals, such as "net generation" (Tapscott 1998), "I-generation" (Rosen 2010), and "Y-Generation" (Bolton et al. 2013). While elaborated by different authors, these expressions seek to emphasize the central role of digital technologies in the lives of this generation and the differences compared to previous ones (Gibbons 2007). In this chapter, we will use the term "Digital Native" because it best expresses the behavior of people who were born and grew up in a world in which interpersonal relationships have become increasingly mediated by digital technologies.

According to these authors, "Digital Natives" would consist of individuals with a set of common characteristics. One would be the sophisticated knowledge and skillful use of NICTs. Prensky (2001a, 1) argues that, since they are immersed in these technologies, they would be "native speakers" of the digital language. According to Akçayir et al. (2016, 435), "They frequently use technological products,

[1] In an excerpt from this Declaration, addressing the rulers of the industrialized world, meeting at the World Economic Forum in Davos, Switzerland, Barlow (1996) stated: "You are terrified of your own children, since they are natives in a world where you will always be immigrants." https://www.eff.org/cyberspace-independence

[2] Palfrey and Gasser (2010) also adopted this concept in their studies.

and do not experience difficulties with the use of complex technological products." The permanent use of NICTs would also reveal another characteristic of this generation: the ability to be multitasking, that is, to perform different activities simultaneously (Calderwood et al. 2016). The close relationship with digital technologies would help them to prefer visual highly graphical language to the detriment of textual language. According to Akçayir et al. (2016) "[...] digital natives are prone to communicate using visual images, such as pictures or videos taken with their mobile devices" (Akçayir et al. 2016, 435). This aspect also helps them think and process "information fundamentally differently from their predecessors" (Prensky 2001a, 1). Additionally, Prensky (2001b, 1) says the brains of Digital Natives are very likely to be "physically different" due to the "digital input they received growing up."

As students, "Digital Natives" feel bored by traditional teaching methods (Oblinger and Hagner 2005). They are particularly "active experiential learners" (Bennett et al. 2008, 776), preferring discovery-based methods that allow them to actively explore and test their ideas (Brown 2000). They would also learn at a faster and more interactive speed than previous generations. They would be able to establish multiple linkages between different contents as well as process a huge amount of visual information and respond positively to the games-based activities in their learning process.[3] Prensky (2001b) argues that because of these characteristics, school and teachers would be unprepared to deal with the behavioral and cognitive uniqueness of "Digital Natives."

These studies reached these conclusions and built this definition based on the analysis of the behavior of young people who were born between the 1980s and 1990s. Generations that were born before this period have been denominated as Digital Immigrants. Prensky (2001a) says they needed to learn the language of NICTs to manipulate it and adapt it to a sociocultural environment profoundly affected by the massive use of such technologies. He adds by stating that "digital immigrants [...] always retain, to some degree, their 'accent', that is, their foot in the past" (Prensky 2001a, 2), for example, textual language, printed material, and analog media.

While increasingly common, the concept of "Digital Natives" has been criticized. One criticism refers to the age group attributed to these individuals: the fact that they were born after 1980 would not be enough to characterize "Digital Natives." Moreover, the social realm should not be neglected. It is common for people who were born after 1980 not to have access to NICTs because of their low income and/or their poor schooling.

The context – cultural and gender – has also been pointed out as a factor that affects the access to and use of NICTs. Finally, poor conditions of access to the network, due to either the lack of infrastructure or slow connection speeds, have also been mentioned as hurdles to younger people's permanent contact with digital

[3] For more information on the subject of Internet, games, and health, please read Chap. 20 of this book.

technologies (Akçayir et al. 2016). Bennett et al. (2008) point out that many people born after 1980 may not master this technology. They claim that:

> The research evidence to date indicates that a proportion of young people are highly adept with technology and rely on it for a range of information gathering and communication activities. However, there also appears to be a significant proportion of young people who do not have the levels of access or technology skills predicted by proponents of the digital native idea. (Bennett et al. 2008, 778–779)

Thus, some young people who do not have access to the Internet and financial resources, knowledge, and skills to manipulate NICTs could not be termed "Digital Natives," although they were born between 1980 and 1990.

Moreover, some critics of the "Digital Natives" concept point out that there is scarce empirical evidence in the scientific literature that corroborates with the specific terms regarding the abilities and behaviors of these individuals (Akçayir et al. 2016). Thus, the way this notion is addressed would tend to generalize individuals who, despite sharing the same age group, would be very different due to their sociocultural and economic conditions. Therefore, this idea tends to ignore the existing diversity within this generation (Bennett et al. 2008).

Some institutions have conducted research to understand the habits, behaviors, and values of "Digital Natives" in the world. We have identified studies with this objective in Brazil, the United States, Europe, and globally. Let us take a closer look at this research.

In Brazil, some academic efforts have sought to understand the behaviors, values, and attitudes of "Digital Natives." The "Brazilian Internet Steering Committee (CGI)"[4] is the main research institution in this field. Among CGI's research is one that focuses on understanding how the population aged 9–17 years uses the Internet and how it deals with the risks and opportunities arising from this activity. This is the "TIC Kids Online Brazil" research program. It aims to produce estimates on Internet access by children and adolescents, investigate the profile of nonusers of the network, and understand how children and adolescents access and use the Internet and how they perceive the content accessed.

The last "TIC Kids Online Brazil" study was published in 2016.[5] It included structured questionnaires, with closed-ended questions and predefined answers (single or multiple answers). Children and adolescents aged 9–17 years answered two different questionnaires: one carried out face-to-face by one interviewer (in face-to-face interaction) and the other a questionnaire in which respondents filled in answers.

---

[4]The "Brazilian Internet Steering Committee in Brazil" was established with the enactment of Decree No. 4.829, dated September 3, 2003 (Brazil 2003). It conducts research to support the formulation, implementation, and evaluation of public policies to promote the use of information and communication technologies. The indicators and analyses generated by these investigations are an important tool for monitoring the information society and the progress of the network in the country. Thus, the "Brazilian Internet Steering Committee" produces reliable and internationally comparable statistics. https://cgi.br/

[5]To date, the CGI has published six issues of this study. All are available in full, in Portuguese and English, at the following link: http://cetic.br/pesquisa/kids-online/publicacoes

Thirty-three thousand permanent private households were sampled in this research[6] (CGI 2016a).

The United States of America has an institution that performs research activities that can be compared to those carried out by the CGI in Brazil. It is the "Pew Research Center," a nonpartisan think tank that informs the public about the issues, attitudes, and trends shaping America and the world. It does not take a policy stance. It conducts public opinion polling, demographic research, media content analysis, and other empirical social science research (Lenhart et al. 2015, 1).

In 2015, the "Pew Research Center" published a report titled "Teen, Social Media, and Technology Overview 2015." This was the first report that this institution produced in order to understand the use of information and communication technologies by adolescents in that country. It focuses on "how American adolescents use social media and mobile phones to create, maintain and end their friendships and romantic relationships" (Lenhart et al. 2015, 1).

In Europe, "EU Kids Online" is organized by a network of 33 countries coordinating and stimulating quantitative and qualitative studies on children to observe how they use digital technologies. Their research is funded by the "EC Better Internet for Kids" program and aims to provide evidence that risk factors can affect children navigating virtual networks. In 2014, "EU Kids Online" released the results of a survey conducted in 25 European countries with children and young people between 9 and 16 years. This study sought to identify participants' main uses of the new media, their online activities, the risks they face when using the Internet and how they deal with it, and the role of parents in their relationships with children and young people establishing virtual networks (EU Kids Online 2014).

In global terms, the "Global Kids Online Research Synthesis": a collaborative initiative between the UNICEF Office of Research – Innocenti, the London School of Economics and Political Science, and the EU Kids Online Network (Byrne et al. 2016) was published in 2016.

> The project developed a global research toolkit that would enable academics, governments, civil society and other actors to carry out reliable and standardized national research with children and their parents on the opportunities, risks and protective factors of children's internet use. (Byrne et al. 2016, 6)

The empirical part of this work coordinated by UNICEF was held in Argentina, the Philippines, Serbia, and South Africa.[7]

In this chapter, we intend to analyze some behavioral characteristics specific to Brazilian "Digital Natives." In order to assess the diversity within this generation, as critics point out to the generalization of the concept "Digital Natives," young people were selected in three different sociodemographic environments.

---

[6] The criteria for designing, stratifying, selecting, and allocating the sample are detailed in the research report (Lenhart et al. 2015). Available from: http://www.pewinternet.org/2015/04/09/teens-social-media-technology-2015

[7] The criteria for designing, stratifying, selecting, and allocating the sample are detailed in the research report (Byrne et al. 2016). Available from: www.globalkidsonline.net

The first group of young people lives in a district called Manguinhos, in the northern part of the city of Rio de Janeiro.

According to official data (IPP 2013), Manguinhos is a territory with more than 36 thousand inhabitants. It is located in an area that was originally dominated by mangroves – a geographical condition that inspired its name.[8] The area generally referred to as Manguinhos exceeds the limits corresponding to the district with the same name established in 1998. In this region of the city, many people attracted by the benefits derived from the construction of two railroads, proximity to industries, and the city center that provides work opportunities converged. The region was occupied during the twentiethand twenty-first centuries through informal housing resulting from individual and collective actions and public housing policies. Manguinhos now encompasses 15 communities with different names (Fernandes and Costa 2013).

Since the 1980s, the area has been suffering from economic depletion, since the few industries that existed in its surroundings were extinguished or transferred to other locations, such as the Central Cooperative of Milk Producers and Gillette do Brasil (Soares 2010).

In general, the population of Manguinhos shares the same reality characterized by social exclusion, unemployment, illiteracy, government neglect, and violence. The region is the setting of numerous armed clashes between police officers, drug traffickers, and militias.[9] Leopoldo Bulhões Street, which traverses the whole area and touches the train line, is known as the "Gaza Strip," referring to the homonymous region in Palestine, famous for violence (Frúgoli Junior and Cavalcanti 2012).

Manguinhos has one of the worst "Human Development Indexes" among the districts of the municipality of Rio de Janeiro. In general, the local population has poor schooling and low purchasing power, with a life expectancy below the Brazilian average in years. About 78% of households have a per capita income up to one minimum wage[10] (IPP 2017). Despite public works carried out by the state and federal governments in the region, problems with polluted rivers, clogged culverts, garbage dumps, and a poor sanitation network still persist, causing residents to be exposed to extremely degrading environmental and housing conditions (Lima 2010).

In the study that was the basis for the production of this chapter, young people who make up the first group investigated reside in Manguinhos and were

---

[8] In Portuguese, "Manguinhos" is the plural diminutive of the word "mangue," which means "mangrove" in English, thus, "small mangrove."

[9] Militia is the generic name of military or paramilitary organizations, not legally recognized, composed of ordinary armed citizens who fight with drug traffickers and police over power in the favelas of various Brazilian cities (Misse 2011).

[10] The minimum wage is the lowest legally defined monetary payment that a worker must receive in a company for his services in Brazil for 1 month's work. The minimum wage amount is defined by federal law and is reassessed annually based on the current cost of living of the population. Currently, the monthly minimum wage in Brazil is 954 reais, approximately 297 US dollars, or 10 US dollars per day.

approached in the waiting room of two primary care centers in the region: one is the Germano Sinval School Health Center Faria[11] and the other is the Victor Valla[12] Family Clinic.

In Brazil, primary health care (PHC) works as the main gateway to the "Unified Health System" (SUS).[13] The "National Primary Care Policy" (PNAB) defines it as:

> A set of health actions, both individually and collectively, covering health promotion and protection, disease prevention, diagnosis, treatment, rehabilitation, harm reduction and health maintenance aiming at developing comprehensive care that affects the health situation and the autonomy of the people and the health determinants and conditionants of communities. (Ministry of Health 2012, 19)

In this context, the "Family Health Strategy" appears as the main means of organizing primary care, contributing to its qualification, expansion, and consolidation.

In our study, the first group of young people participated in the study while waiting for their consultations in the waiting room of these two health facilities. It should be noted that users of these two primary care units must show some documentation attesting to their residence in Manguinhos in order to enjoy the services provided by these two establishments. Thus, this first group of respondents is formally inserted into the public system of primary health care – a condition that is not shared by all young people living in low-income communities.[14] These are, therefore, young people served by primary care residing in Manguinhos.

The second group of young people is composed of secondary school students from the Professor Clóvis Monteiro State College.

This college is part of the state public education network of Rio de Janeiro, developing regular secondary school educational activities in three shifts: morning, afternoon, and night (CEPCM 2014). According to data from the State Education Secretariat of Rio de Janeiro, the school has 1426 students, divided into 71 classes

---

[11] The Germano Sinval Faria School Health Center (CSEGSF) is one of the departments of the National School of Public Health (ENSP) of the Oswaldo Cruz Foundation. It coordinates, in partnership with the Municipal Health Secretariat of Rio de Janeiro, the "Teias-Escola Manguinhos' Project." This project is responsible for the management of primary health care in the region. It adopts the Family Health Strategy (ESF) as a regulator of the local health system. Both the Victor Valla Family Clinic and the Health Center provide primary care and services for residents of Manguinhos (Teias 2014).

[12] Victor Valla Family Clinic: http://smsdc-csf-victorvalla.blogspot.com.br/

[13] The Unified Health System (SUS) is the name given to the public health system in Brazil. According to Law 8080, the SUS consists of "a set of actions and health services provided by federal, state and municipal public bodies and institutions of the direct and indirect administration and foundations maintained by the public power" (Brazil 1990). Its scope includes medical care, disease prevention, and health promotion, as well as covering policies and strategies in areas such as health surveillance and pharmaceutical care. Its services are provided free-of-charge to all Brazilians (Ministry of Health 2007; Paim 2015).

[14] Not all Brazilian municipalities are covered by the "Family Health Program." In one municipality, not all locations are served by this governmental program. Today, the Family Health Strategy is found in 94% of the municipalities (29,000 teams and population coverage of 48%, corresponding to 92 million people).

and 108 servers (SEEDUC 2017). It has basic infrastructure such as classrooms, restrooms, Internet access, indoor sports court, school meals for students, kitchen, and library.

Brazil is a Federative Republic. According to Brazil's educational legislation, municipal governments are responsible for basic and elementary education and state governments for secondary education.[15] It is incumbent upon these public authorities to provide all Brazilians aged 4–17 years with compulsory basic education free-of-charge.[16] Thus, both preschool and elementary and secondary schools are a universal right available to any Brazilian citizen, including those who did not complete their schooling within an expected age range. Teachers must submit to a public examination (Brazil 1996) to be able to perform their activities in these establishments. At the same time, there is a large and complex network of private institutions at all three levels of education throughout the country.

This organizational structure, however, does not ensure universally accessible and high-quality public education. In recent decades, advances have been observed in the Brazilian education system. According to the 2016 School Census, there are 186.1 thousand primary education schools in Brazil, of which 21.5% belong to the private education system (INEP 2017). However, universal access to basic education in terms of quantity and quality and increased investment in the education system are still challenges faced by the country (UNESCO 2015). The last survey of the School Census found that secondary education is provided in only 28.5% of the basic educational institutions in the country, and of these only 10.2% are located in rural areas (INEP 2017).[17]

The "Education at a Glance" report published by the Organisation for Economic Co-operation and Development (OECD 2017) indicates that investment in secondary education in Brazil is approximately US$ 3.8 per student per year. This is the third lowest value in world rankings. In this case, Brazil is behind only Colombia and Indonesia. Another point raised by the OECD report was the low salary paid to Brazilian teachers, referred to as the "backbone of the educational system." The text states that wages are low compared to other full-time workers with a similar educational level. In addition to the low financial reward, the report points out that Brazilian teachers are responsible for a relatively large number of classes. This reduces the time they have to devote to activities outside the classroom, interdisciplinary practices, lesson preparation, and the more attentive follow-up of underachieving students. These aspects make teaching careers unattractive in Brazil.

The Professor Clóvis Monteiro State College is located in the favela called "Agricultural Community of Higienópolis." It is a small underprivileged community with about 2400 inhabitants where unemployment predominates. This condition leads residents to seek a source of income in self-employment. One of the great

[15] The federal public power is responsible for higher education in most of the national territory, although some universities are subsidized by the state public power and are all free.

[16] According to the Law of Guidelines and Bases (N° 9394/1996), elementary school and early childhood education and secondary education make up basic education.

[17] In Brazil, primary- and secondary-level education are typically offered in the same building but at different times of the day.

Table 7.1 Socioeconomic indicators – Gávea and Manguinhos

Indicator/district	Life expectancy at birth/years	School attendance rate	Per capita income
Gávea	80.45	100.00	710 U$
Manguinhos	66.30	69.64	62 U$

problems faced by the families of this shantytown (known as *favela* in Brazil) is the difficulty in reconciling work demands with their children's upbringing and schooling. This college mainly receives students residing in Manguinhos and the neighboring territory of the "Agricultural Community of Higienópolis."

Young people who are waiting for a consultation in a primary care center and students of the state college have, therefore, the same socioeconomic profile. They differ from each other because the first group is formally inserted into a public primary care service and the second possibly not. On the other hand, the second group is inserted in a public school and the first is probably not.

The third group of young people interviewed differs from the previous two because it consists of students enrolled in a private secondary school system. This group comprises secondary school students from Escola Parque: a private establishment that serves the part of the economic elite of Rio de Janeiro and is located in one of the most sophisticated districts of the city, namely, Gávea.

The Escola Parque develops its pedagogical activities from kindergarten through secondary school. It stands out for the excellent quality of teaching provided, an excellence that is not affordable to everyone. The monthly fee paid by the families who enroll their children at the Escola Parque is just over US$ 500 per month for 4 h of activity. This amount does not include transportation and food. The high monthly fee is even more evident if we consider that the national minimum wage is approximately 300 dollars per month (IBGE 2017). Thus, we can, without embarrassment, conclude that the Escola Parque is attended by students of the city's economic elite, since only families with high purchasing power can enroll their children in this institution. It has units in the districts of Barra da Tijuca and Gávea. The research in question was held in the Gávea unit, a district located in the south zone of Rio de Janeiro.

In these terms, it is necessary to establish a comparison between Gávea and Manguinhos. To do so, we will use the "Social Development Index" (IDS) of the municipality of Rio de Janeiro (2008).

This index was inspired by the Human Development Index (HDI), calculated by the UN (UNDP) for several countries in the world. Its aims to measure the degree of social development of a particular geographical area compared to others of the same nature. The IDS used 10 indicators built from variables of the 2000 Demographic Census of the Brazilian Institute of Geography and Statistics (IBGE)[18] for the composition of the Social Development Index (IDS). Briefly, we have constructed the table below with some of these indicators.

[18] The Brazilian Institute of Geography and Statistics (IBGE) is a public institute of the Brazilian federal administration created in 1934. It is the country's main data and information provider, which serves the needs of the most diverse segments of civil society, as well as the federal, state, and municipal governmental levels (IBGE 2018).

Looking at Table 7.1, the social differences between the first two groups of respondents and the third group are evident. Differences in life expectancy and income reveal that these groups belong to very different social strata.

Another way to compare the two secondary schools is through the results obtained in the "National Secondary Education Exam" (ENEM).

In Brazil, the secondary school student who is interested in entering a university must take the ENEM. The average result of students who took the exam in 2015 reveals the abyss between public and private school systems. ENEM scores indicate that results of students from state public institutions are increasingly worse. Of the hundred schools with the highest scores in the country, 17 are from the State of Rio de Janeiro and none of them public. Escola Parque is ranked 24th in this list, whereas the Clovis Monteiro State College is not listed (INEP 2015).

Despite all these differences, research participants are young "Digital Born," as they were born after the New Information and Communication Technologies (NICTs) were already a palpable reality to many citizens.

The first group consists of young people living in Manguinhos who were waiting for a consultation or examination in a waiting room of a public primary care clinic. For this first group, the research tool was applied during 5 weeks between October and November 2013. Young people had to meet the following four criteria to participate in the research: (1) be an Internet user, (2) be male/female aged 16–24 years, (3) reside in Manguinhos, and (4) agree to participate in the study. In this sample, 201 participants completed the questionnaires.

In relation to the other two groups, 225 people completed the questionnaire, of which 116 were from Escola Parque da Gávea and 109 from the Professor Clóvis Monteiro State College. These are students regularly enrolled in each of the two institutions in the first year of secondary school on June 9, September 2, and September 14, 2015.[19]

We aimed to verify whether Brazilian young people with low income[20] and/or poor schooling face greater difficulty in accessing the NICTs than young people of the privileged social strata. We wanted to see whether the context – cultural and gender – somehow interferes with this process in such different social realities. The guiding question of this study discusses whether individuals of the same age group use and own NICTs differently due to their sociocultural and economic conditions.

---

[19] This research was submitted and approved by the Research Ethics Committee (CEP) of the National School of Public Health, in Rio de Janeiro, Brazil, under opinion N° 460.098. The Research Ethics Committee (CEP) is an interdisciplinary and independent collegial body in Brazilian institutions that conduct human research. It aims to evaluate the ethics of the research projects submitted, defending the interests and integrity of research subjects, within current ethical standards (Muccioli et al. 2008). The studies were also supported by the Germano Sinval Faria School Health Center (CSEGSF), the Victor Valla Family Clinic, the Clóvis Monteiro State College, and the Escola Parque da Gávea.

[20] The World Bank defines that citizens living on less than $1.90 a day as below the poverty line. In Brazil, 8.9 million people are in this condition. The new poverty line will be set at $3.20 a day. If this index were to be applied, 1/5 of Brazil's population would be living below the poverty line (Cunha and Fagundes 2017).

Thus, we intended to verify differences within this generation, as recommended by Bennett et al. (2008). In this case, particular emphasis was given to their ownership of health-related themes and issues.

To analyze the findings of the research, we used as reference the values and attitudes of young people using the Internet found in the results of the national survey "TIC Kids Online Brasil" – 2015, a study by the US' Pew Research Center, an international UNESCO study dubbed "Global Kids Online Research Synthesis," and research conducted in Europe. However, we were not limited to that.

The research that gave rise to this chapter takes into account these national and international parameters to know the behavior and the attitudes of a small group of young people who were born in the city of Rio de Janeiro in the late twentieth and early twenty-first century in Brazil. It is, therefore, the result of an exploratory empirical study that aims to discuss the specificities of "Digital Natives" by analyzing the abilities and behaviors of a small group of individuals in relation to the use of NICTs. In all three cases, young people interviewed were aged 16–24 years. Therefore, it is an exploratory study with different samples. A study of this nature facilitates the understanding of human behavior in its social context, especially in realities that are still poorly studied, providing a greater familiarity with the context investigated.

The exploratory study also allows the development of hypotheses and propositions, which may be objects of future studies, thus establishing a research agenda (Baxter and Jack 2008, Yin 2003). According to Yin (2003, 21), "instead of stating propositions, the design for an exploratory study should state a purpose, as well as the criteria by which an exploration will be judged successful." Thus, although the exploratory study does not start from a proposition or hypothesis to be investigated, its realization presupposes the definition of three fundamental methodological components: what will be explored, the purpose for the research being conducted, and the criteria for evaluating the success of the study (Yin 2003). As an exploratory study, its tendency to generalization is therefore limited.

7.2 Methods

Data was collected with a closed-ended questionnaire consisting of 13 questions, divided into 3 sections, namely, "identification," "Internet access," and "Internet access for health information."

The first section aimed to identify the participant's profile, especially age and gender. These two questions are important because they are the two main categories specified in the research identified in the literature on the subject (CGI 2016a; Lenhart et al. 2015; EU Kids Online 2014; Byrne et al. 2016).

The second section of the questionnaire aimed to map how these young people accessed the Internet. One of the questions in this section aimed to identify how many respondents had (or did not have) access to the internet. Another question intended to identify what equipment is used by young people (highlighting smartphone access). A question about the frequency of Internet use was also added.

The third section aimed to investigate the behavior of young people searching for health information on the Internet. One of the questions in this section was to identify when and how often this search is performed. Thus, we wanted to verify whether the doctor-patient relationship is affected by the consumption of online health information. Another question introduced in this section of the questionnaire refers to the factors that motivate young people to seek health information on the Internet. We also included a question about the level of trust in the information obtained on the Internet. With this item, we sought to understand how young people perceive the quality of information obtained online, especially in the context of "information deluge" (Lévy 2001), typical of digital communication and information networks.

The results are shown in a comparative table for each topic discussed. Thus, we hope to facilitate readers' understanding and to raise explanatory hypotheses. The analysis dialogues between our findings and research on the subject conducted by the Brazilian Internet Steering Committee (CGI 2016a), EC Better Internet for Kids (EU Kids Online 2014), and UNICEF (Byrne et al. 2016), while others were based on analyses in the international scientific literature (González et al. 2011; Hughes-Hassell et al. 2008).

7.3 Results and Discussion

Our analysis is divided into three parts. In the first part, we show the profile of study participants, taking into account their socioeconomic status. This framework serves as a basis for further reflection. Next, we discuss how Internet access and use among young people occurs. At that moment, we analyze whether or not the Internet access and use profile of the participants of our research is closer to what is generally attributed to the "Digital Native." We also discuss to what extent access is affected by the socioeconomic status in each group of young users. Finally, we examine the profile of the consumption of online health information on the Internet. We aim to understand how these young people who are seen in the scientific literature as "Digital Natives" take ownership of NICTs in their self-care process.

7.3.1 Profile of Participants

As mentioned earlier, we applied the questionnaire to three distinct groups of young people: 201 young people were in the waiting rooms of the two primary care clinics (CAP) in Manguinhos, 109 responded to the questionnaire at the Clóvis Monteiro State College (CCM), and 116 were in classrooms at the Escola Parque da Gávea (EPG). The data obtained allowed the construction of Table 7.2.

The above data allow us to note a difference in access to primary care services based on gender. At the primary care centers investigated, 74.1% of women and 25.9% of men participated in our research.

Table 7.2 Profile of respondents

Location	Mean age	Men (%)	Women (%)
CAP	21 years	25.9	74.1
CCM	17 years	42	56
EPG	16 years	52	48

Gomes et al. (2007) carried out a study aimed at analyzing the explanations in male discourses for the low demand of men for primary care services in Brazil. They found that male respondents understand that health care is a feminine task. In addition, some men see themselves as invulnerable. Gomes et al. (2007) conclude their study stating that:

> Health services are also considered unfit to absorb men's demand, since their organization does not stimulate access and the public health campaigns themselves do not turn to this segment. (Gomes et al. 2007, 571)

It should also be noted that primary care centers in Brazil operate during business hours (Monday through Friday, from 8:00 am to 5:00 pm). These working hours hinder workers with formal employment to access health services.

Another aspect of the date in the table above drew our attention: female predominance among public school students. This phenomenon is explained by the growth of women's education in the world in recent years. Beltrão (2002) concludes his study by affirming that:

> According to the World Bank report [...], there has been a considerable improvement in the situation of women in most countries in recent decades. The educational level of women increased significantly, and so did their presence in the job market. However, in the future, part of the way forward must include the elimination of gender inequalities, in terms of their rights, resources and voice. (Beltrão 2002, 17)

Another important aspect of the data is the mean age of participants. The similar result between the two educational institutions hides a reality worth noting. At the Escola Parque, 78% of the students in the second year of secondary education were 16 years of age or less. At the Clóvis Monteiro College, this profile is reversed: 72% of the sampled population was over 16 years old at the time they completed the questionnaire. It is possible, therefore, to conclude that the Clóvis Monteiro State College students participating in the study are outside of the ideal age range for the secondary education cycle. It should be noted that this delay could be due to cases of abandonment and repetition associated with early entry into the labor market, in order to complement family income or demotivation.

Recent research in Brazil indicates that "school dropout and poverty are closely linked and that child labor impairs the achievement of better educational levels" (Néri 2015, 21). The same study found that school dropout among young low-income people aged 15–17 years (23.25%) is higher than in the total population (17.8%). Among the rich young people, this rate is extremely low (5.8%).

It should also be pointed out that 78% of young people of the state college survive with a family income equal to or less than two minimum wages (about 600 dollars a month).

Table 7.3 Internet access

	Internet access	
Location	Yes (%)	No (%)
CAP	87.8	12.2
CCM	97	3
EPG	98	2

The brief description of the profile of respondents that underpinned this chapter reveals that the sample, albeit statistically inexpressive, draws us nearer to the reality found in Brazil as a whole. It also suggests a significant socioeconomic difference between students of the Escola Parque and the other respondents. Thus, this study will transform this socioeconomic difference as a variable for the analysis of the data obtained. In this work, we are interested in knowing the effects of social stratification on the use of online media among Brazilian adolescents.

7.3.2 *Internet Access and Use*

One of the main motivations of this study was to verify whether more or less access to the Internet by young Brazilians who participated in this investigation was associated with their socioeconomic status. Table 7.3 shows the results that seem relevant to us.

The exploratory study that we conducted may provide greater familiarity with the issue investigated. In this case, the results suggest that there are no notable percentage differences in relation to the young people attending public and private schools who have access to the Internet. The rate of Internet access was a little lower for young people waiting for the consultation in primary care waiting rooms of Manguinhos. It may be that the percentage was higher among secondary school students due to the dynamics and routine of the school setting. Schools are socialization spaces for young students; they provide frequent contact between young people through several activities (Moura and Zucchetti 2014). Thus, it may be that young students, in this context, discover new digital technologies through this socialization process and end up using the Internet to communicate with each other during the period they spend in and out of school at greater rates.

As the reality of the life of these communities is unknown, this type of study imposes itself as an alternative for the formulation of hypotheses and questions for future research. The comparison with the results obtained in the national research carried out by the Brazilian Internet Steering Committee (CGI) can feed our analysis.

The percentage of Internet access among low-income young people participating in our study is higher than that shown by CGI (2016a, b) TIC Online Kids survey. Data collected between 2015 and 2016 indicate that 79% of children and adolescents aged 9–17 years access the Internet. This indicator corresponds to 23.4 million

Table 7.4 Internet use frequency

	Use frequency				
Location	5 or more daily hours (%)	3–4 daily hours (%)	1–2 daily hours (%)	Less than 1 daily hour (%)	Do not access every day or did not reply (%)
CCM	51	30	13	6	0
EPG	28	44	19	5	4

individuals throughout the country (CGI 2016a). If we include the socioeconomic variable, the result of CGI research is quite different: "In 2015, one-half of children belonging to classes D and E (51%) were Internet users. This proportion rose to 84% among children from class C and 97% among those in classes A and B" (CGI 2016a, 330).[21]

Our research with class D/E young people from a poor region of Rio de Janeiro identified access rates of 87.8% among primary care users and 97% among public school students. These levels were similar to those obtained among the young students of Escola Parque da Gávea.

It may be that this observed difference between the CGI result and ours is related to the fact that Manguinhos, where we conducted our research, is located in an urban center. As pointed out in the CGI report (2016a), Internet access in urban areas is high, reaching 84%. Thus, results obtained in Manguinhos may be associated with the availability of infrastructure and easy access to Wi-Fi networks or signals from telephone providers where young participants of the research circulate.

Table 7.4 shows the number of Internet hours used by young secondary school students.

Data obtained in our research reveal that poor young people of public schools spend more time on the Internet than those of private schools. We can deduce that class D/E students of the Clovis Monteiro State College access the Internet more than once a day.

These results differ from those shown by the national CGI survey, which identified that 80% of class A/B children and adolescents accessed the Internet more than once a day, whereas among class D/E individuals, this rate fell to 51% (CGI 2016a).

Results related to the frequency of Internet access indicate that young people of Manguinhos have practices similar to young people in the United States. According to the Pew Research Center report (Lenhart et al. 2015, 16), "92% of teens report going online daily – with 24% using the internet 'almost constantly,' 56% going online several times a day, and 12% reporting once-a-day use. Just 6% of teens report going online weekly, and 2% go online less often." Our data indicate that

[21] IBGE, the federal government's census bureau, classifies social classes based on the official minimum monthly salary. At the time of this publication, the minimum monthly salary was R$ 954, which is approximately US$ 300. Therefore, those who make between two to four minimum salaries (i.e., about US$ 600 to US$ 1200 a month) would be in the D class, from 4 to 10 minimum salaries in class C, from 10 to 20 minimum salaries in class B, and above 20 salaries in class A.

young students from Manguinhos access the Internet more often and stay connected longer than young North Americans do.

It should be noted that 51% of Clóvis Monteiro State College students access the Internet for 5 h or more on a daily basis, while 28% of the Escola Parque students spend the same time online.

This difference may have at least three explanatory hypotheses.

It may be that this percentage gap observed between public and private school students is related to the difference of social and cultural equipment they access. The region of the city where Parque Escola students live provides a significant amount of cultural and leisure activities. The region of the city where public school students reside is not equipped with the same cultural and leisure diversity.

In São Paulo, the most populous city in Brazil, the urban reality is no different. When reflecting on the role of culture in the establishment of collective identity and cultural policies as a development tool in the city of São Paulo, Caiado (2001) found that:

> […] there is a large concentration of cultural offerings in the city's center and in the districts where the high and middle-income population resides. Districts where most residents are low-income are deprived of cultural facilities or have them in very small proportions. (Caiado 2001, 65)

Thus, Escola Parque students can perform other cultural and sporting activities instead of spending their time accessing the Internet, an opportunity that is not available to Clovis Monteiro College students. Thus, this statistical difference may be related to leisure and cultural opportunities enjoyed by these two groups of young people.

Another explanatory hypothesis for the greater time that state college students have for Internet access is associated with their socioeconomic profile. The high purchasing power of parents of the Escola Parque young people allows them to attend music, dance, and foreign languages private courses and to perform physical activities in private institutions for this purpose. The socioeconomic status of parents of public school children does not allow them to partake in the same activities for young people.

Finally, it is worth highlighting the supply of complementary educational actions or extracurricular activities provided by each of the educational establishments. These activities contribute to pedagogical training. They are often carried out in accordance with the school's political-pedagogical project, contributing to the processes of personal development, social promotion, and strengthening of self-esteem.

The private school selected for the study has an excellent infrastructure, while the public school faces a number of structural problems. Monteiro and Silva (2015) describe the educational supplies available at a public school in the state of Ceará and found:

> Inadequate buildings and facilities, lack of libraries, sports venues and laboratories, lack of access to textbooks, reading materials, inadequate classroom sizes, and the number of students are problems that directly influence the performance of students. (Monteiro and Silva 2015, 23)

This setting is similar to that found at Clovis Monteiro State College. It should be noted that teaching activities are often interrupted due to "crossfire" involving the police, traffickers, and militia members on a daily basis (Alves and Evanson 2013).

Under these conditions, students in the state education system may feel discouraged to study and use the Internet as a way to fill their free time. Leisure of these young people lies, almost exclusively, in the palm of their hands: the cellphone.

However, there is one commonality across these three groups.

New Information and Communication Technologies play a central role in the daily lives of young people. In our study, 81% of public school students and 72% of private school students spend 4 h or more online.

By allocating a significant part of their day to go on the Internet, it is possible to verify that the use of NICTs plays an important role in the daily life of young people, permeating various aspects of their routine. Schoolwork, communication with friends and family, and a source of information and entertainment, among others, can be activities performed each time by these young people through digital technologies. Digital technologies, especially cellphones, increasingly intermingle with the daily lives of youngsters, enabling a permanent connection to virtual networks and mediating a large extent of interpersonal relationships.

The central figure that NICTs seem to assume in adolescent life upholds the perspective in the "Global Kids Go Online" report that young people and the Internet are, in the current setting, a two-way street. On the one hand, they represent a significant portion of Internet users around the world, playing an important role in the way that the Internet develops. On the other hand, the Internet plays an important role in shaping the lives, identities, and cultures of these same young people (Byrne et al. 2016).

Another aspect to be emphasized regarding the frequency of children and adolescents' Internet access refers to the role of parents and guardians. The American Pediatric Association (AAP 2016) recommends monitoring the time spent with different types of media. They must keep track of the time and activities that children and adolescents do in virtual networks. They can prevent the use of cellphones, computers, video games, and other technological gadgets from overcoming physical activity, adequate sleep, and other behaviors that are important to the well-being and quality of life. We can deduce that this monitoring is not in place, since a large part of the young people surveyed spends more than 5 h a day on the Internet.

In our research, we observed that young people with lower income spend more time on the Internet than young people with higher social strata. It may be that this data is associated not only with the different opportunities of leisure and culture to which these young people can access (or not) but also with the poor monitoring of their parents and guardians concerning the use of these technologies.[22]

What is the technological device that these young people, with so different socioeconomic profiles, use to access the Internet?

[22] The problems related to the risks inherent in the use of the Internet by young people will be explored further in Chaps. 11 and 12, dedicated, respectively, to cyberbullying and Internet risks.

Data obtained in our research revealed that 68% of students interviewed at the Clovis Monteiro College access the Internet through smartphones. In private schools, the same rate reaches 57%. Among primary care center users, this rate is only 42%.

The prevalence of mobile Internet technologies observed among low-income young people participating in the study is consistent with data obtained from the CGI national survey and international surveys.

According to the CGI (2016a, 334), "in line with the trend toward mobility of Internet access observed in the general population, the growing use of mobile devices has been highlighted in the TIC Kids Online Brazil survey in recent years." Data from research carried out by the institution shows that 85% of children and adolescents use the mobile phone to access the Internet. Of this amount, the share identified among class D/E young people was 86%.

The use of smartphones as main access to the Internet was also observed at international level. The survey conducted by the "Pew Research Center" in the United States found 88% of young people own a cellphone. Of these, 73% access the Internet via smartphones (Lenhart et al. 2015). The "EU Kids Online" (EU Kids Online 2014, 6) research report pointed out that young people "go online on more personal and mobile devices." The prevailing use of smartphones to access the Internet was also identified in the "Global Kids Online" survey:

> Smartphones are the most common device used by children to go online while desktops and laptop computers are used less frequently. Over 80 per cent of children in Argentina, Serbia and South Africa report going online via smartphones at least every month or more often. This number is lower in the Philippines (61 per cent), but smartphones are still the most common device used by Filipino children to go online. (Byrne et al. 2016, 37)

The predominant use of mobile phones to connect to virtual networks observed among low-income young people who participated in the study may be one of the factors explaining the levels of Internet use and frequency identified among this group.

In the contemporary setting, smartphones are increasingly the main technology to access the Internet. Wireless communication networks have spread rapidly, and the global dissemination of mobile telephony in recent decades is the most visible aspect of this growth (Castells et al. 2007; Kalba 2008).

If smartphones were initially a technological luxury item, their affordability and popularization made them central to the identity of contemporary individuals, causing profound changes in sociability, space-time perception, and urban practices (Fidalgo and Canavilhas 2009; Lemos 2004). More than a technical object, the smartphone has become a social object, traversing several aspects and practices of the personal, professional, and academic routines of its users (Srivastava 2005). The spread of mobile telephony is associated with the constant and rapid transformation of mobile telephony, both in its hardware and software. Current smartphone models, even smaller devices, already have the same power and can perform many of the functions performed by a desktop computer. In the coming years, its processing capacity and performance is likely to increase (Srivastava 2005).

Table 7.5 Internet access connection type

	Internet access connection type		
Location	Wireless network (Wi-Fi) (%)	3G/4G postpaid package (%)	Buy credits as needed (prepaid) (%)
CCM	52	32	16
EPG	10	83	7

Research conducted by the "Brazilian Telecommunications Association" indicates that the number of cellphones connected to 4G technology exceeded those of 3G handsets for the first time in Brazil. Currently, the 4G network reaches 3363 municipalities, where 90% of the Brazilian population lives. In all, there are now 205.5 million accesses to the Internet through the mobile network in Brazil (Telebrasil 2017).

This number is even more surprising given that, according to data from the 2010 Demographic Census conducted by the Brazilian Institute of Geography and Statistics (IBGE), Brazil had a population of 190,755,799 inhabitants.

New content interaction and production forms, coupled with the multiple uses aggregated in a single device, have made smartphones an expression of digital media convergence (Jenkins 2008). Growing adherence to mobile telephony is also consonant with mobile, ubiquitous, and pervasive computing that characterizes the twenty-first century: in urban settings, increasingly marked by mobility and connection, cellphones stand out as easily mobile, with high processing capacity and easy connections to the Internet.

For low-income young people, such as those interviewed in health facilities and public schools, cellphones seem to be a strategic device to ensure access to the Internet.

Features and functions, ease of use, and cost are factors that are contributing to massive adherence to smartphones. While the price of smartphones in Brazil is high,[23] the acquisition of this type of device may show a better value for money than a desktop computer or laptop. When arriving at home, private school young people should be able to access the Internet through other devices, leaving cellphones aside.

How do these young people connect to the Internet? Table 7.5 shows some important data to that effect.

In this case, a clear disparity can be identified in the way the two groups of students access the Internet. The difference between the proportions found in schools can be attributed to the social class of individuals that circulate in these spaces.

In the private school attended by class A/B young people, the prevalent type of connection is postpaid 3G/4G: usually purchased by their guardian at high prices from telephone providers. In the public school attended mainly by class D/E young people, wireless network connection predominates. It may be that these young people who cannot afford mobile data plans use public wireless networks spread around the city or access some kind of shared network wherever they live.

[23] In the United States, it is possible to buy a new smartphone in an online store for U$ 50 or less. In Brazil, the lowest value in the market for a cellphone with the same conditions can be double or triple in price.

We could observe the popular use of smartphones as a priority access to the Internet both in the research with users waiting for treatment and in that with secondary school students, an access that occurs mostly by wireless networks, especially among the poorest. Thus, despite their poor socioeconomic conditions, low-income young people have typical "Digital Native" behaviors. These behaviors resemble those observed among young people of higher social classes. However, this does not imply that socioeconomic inequalities do not affect access to ICTs or that all young people from the lower classes are necessarily "Digital Natives" because of their age, as discussed at the beginning of this chapter.

7.3.3 Search and Consumption of Online Health Information

The results of the exploratory study that has developed into this chapter point out that the Internet is an important source of health information for young people. Table 7.6 shows the results obtained:

These results deserve some comments.

First of all, 60% of young people in primary care center waiting rooms search for health information on the Internet and 40% do not. This gap can perhaps be explained by the fact that they are formally inserted in the health system. It may be that health professionals hold a prominent place for these young people when it comes to providing health information.

The results obtained with young people in their schools were very different: almost everyone seeks health information on the Internet. There was no significant difference between public school (90%) and private school (89%).

This result is consonant with international literature, reporting adolescents as active seekers of health information on the Internet. In a study on UK adolescents, Gray et al. (2005, 1470) found that "a significant number of adolescents had actively sought health information online." These authors argue that one of the reasons for young people actively seeking online health information may be associated with the fact that the Internet allows access to unpublished information that is not casual or unknown to them. This realm increases motivation to search for information on the Internet.

For students who participated in our study, the main motivation to search for health information online is the diversity and coverage of subjects available on the Internet. At the Escola Parque, 53% of students consider this reason "very important." The vast and diversified amount of health information available in virtual

Table 7.6 Consumption of health information on the Internet

	Seek health information on the Internet	
Location	Yes (%)	No (%)
CAP	60	40
CCM	90	10
EPG	89	11

networks was also the main reason given by young people interviewed in the waiting rooms: 94.5% of participants say it is important to find information on any subject on the Internet. Thus, it is possible to observe that access to the countless sources of information facilitated by the Internet is one of the main attractions for Digital Natives to search for health matters online, regardless of their social classes.

Finally, it should be noted that the percentages found in this exploratory study are higher than those obtained by CGI's (2016a) "ICT Households" survey in Brazil. In the national territory, the search for information related to health or health services is the second information search activity performed by young people on the Internet. It is outweighed by the demand for information and services in general: 13% of young people between the ages of 10 and 15 and 40% of those between the ages of 16 and 24 seek health information online.

The questionnaire used in our research also sought to know how often these young people sought health information on the Internet. Table 7.7 shows the result of this question.

These rates seemed low to us. It may be that rates observed among young people of the study are associated with how they address their health and self-care. Participants can search for information only when they have a disease or health problem. If young people perceived that access to information about health on the Internet could help them manage their well-being and increase their quality of life, perhaps the identified frequency rates would be higher.

It should be noted, however, that data obtained in our research are close to those of the "Global Kids Go Online" report (Byrne et al. 2016). In a study organized by UNICEF, one third (33%) of children and adolescents in Serbia and South Africa and a quarter (25%) of those in the Philippines search for health information on the Internet at least once a week (Byrne et al. 2016).

How could we compare results obtained in our sample and results of a global survey? If we consider "at least once a week" as "few times," the numbers obtained in our research (30 and 24%) are close to those obtained globally (33 and 25%).

Despite these low global rates, one of the UNICEF study participants said: "It was funny: I was saying that I had some health problem and they asked me if I had visited a doctor, I said no, I visited the Internet. (Girl aged 15)" (Byrne et al. 2016).

Table 7.8 can help us understand why young people surveyed do not seek health information, especially on the Internet.

One aspect caught our attention by looking at the table above. Doctor's prominence for school students is in contrast to the emphasis given to family and friends as a source of information for resolving a health problem.

Table 7.7 Search for health information frequency

	Search for health information frequency			
Location	Often (%)	Sometimes (%)	Few times (%)	Never (%)
EPG	6	13	30	51
CCM	12	12	24	52

Table 7.8 Source of information for a health problem

Location	Source of information for a health problem				
	Family and/or friends (%)	Doctor (%)	Internet (and then seek a doctor) (%)	Internet only (%)	Do nothing (%)
CCM	24	44	15	13	4
EPG	58	19	16	7	0

Table 7.9 Trust in the health information obtained on the Internet

Location	Level of trust in online health information				
	Always (%)	Often (%)	Sometimes (%)	Few times (%)	Never (%)
CCM	3	16	58	21	2
EPG	0	23	59	17	1

The differences observed between these two groups of students may be related young people's access to health services. Public school students may be placed in the primary care network where they reside and, much in the same way as young people in waiting rooms, have the doctor's figure as a reference for information and health problems. It may be that the poor level of education, common among lower social classes, contributes to these young people choosing the guidance of the medical professional rather than people that are closest to them. The high proportion of students at the Escola Parque seeking information with relatives and/or friends can also be associated with their socioeconomic context. It may be that many of the students' relatives at that school are doctors or doctors' friends. In addition, due to the higher socioeconomic context, relatives and friends of these young people may have more academic education, making these class A/B young people seek health information with their closest social relationships.

As we can see in the table above, the Internet did not rank first in the search for health information in neither of the two school environments surveyed. One possible explanation for this result may be related to the level of trust of these young people in the information available on the Internet.

Table 7.9 shows the level of trust of each group of young people in the health information obtained on the Internet.

In both sociocultural contexts, most students do not fully rely on health information obtained on the Internet. Thus, the results suggest that the information available does not deserve the user's trust.[24]

Research participants' concern with the quality of information obtained online is consonant with results of international studies. In a survey of UK public and private school students, Gray et al. (2005) identified that young people highly value getting accurate online health information, and one of their major concerns about seeking health information on the Internet is reliability of the content consulted.

[24] Chapter 10 will analyze the issue of quality of information in health websites.

7.4 Final Considerations

The age we are currently experiencing is increasingly marked by the popularization of NICTs, global communication, and floods of information in digital networks. "Digital Natives" have grown in this context. They are the young people who were born after the 1980s, who do not know a world without the Internet. There are many features that are attributed to "Digital Natives," such as the ability to be native speakers of the digital language, simultaneous multitaskers, and "active experiential learners."

While the concept of "Digital Natives" has spread widely in recent years, few researchers refer to this term. They note that the application of the concept is oftentimes restricted to the age group of individuals, disregarding the socioeconomic and cultural conditions that can affect and shape the use of NITCs (Bennett et al. 2008).

Inspired by this caveat, we conducted this exploratory study. Thus, we applied a questionnaire to young Brazilian people located in different sociocultural contexts. Some of the survey participants live in a low-income setting, while other participants are extremely privileged. In selecting the groups of young people, we aimed to investigate whether socioeconomic status would have an effect on their use of digital technologies. We questioned whether these individuals, from different social strata, who were born at the beginning of the twenty-first century, could be considered "Digital Natives."

The results indicate that among the low-income young people who participated in the study, socioeconomic status did not prevent or restrict their Internet access. On the contrary, we found that young people attending public schools spend more time on the Internet than young people attending private schools. This should be highlighted because the socioeconomic status has been pointed out as one of the main reasons that prevent generalization of the term "Digital Natives."

We also identified that young people attending public schools frequently access and spend more time on the Internet. Thus, we could say that low-income young people have more intense "Digital Native" behavior than high-income young people do. It should be noted that this result might be associated with socioeconomic conditions. In their spare time, young people attending private schools have better access to cultural programs, while young people attending public schools have much more restricted options in these terms. Therefore, we may consider that, for the low-income young people of our study, the frequent use of the Internet is a means for accessing options of entertainment and consumption of cultural products that they do not have in their physical environment.

For the specific group of young low-income people who participated in the study, the concept of "Digital Natives" can be applied regardless of factors such as income. However, we do not intend to generalize this condition. The young people interviewed live in the urban area of one of Brazil's major cities. If the study had been conducted in another city, results may have been different: the socioeconomic profile of young people could be a barrier to access the Internet and other digital technologies. The structural conditions of virtual network access could overly hamper this access. The Brazilian National Telecommunications Agency (ANATEL), in partnership with the Brazilian Institute of Applied Economic Research (IPEA), recently released a report containing a "prioritization assessment for the expansion of the broadband access network in Brazilian municipalities" and concluded that 20% of all 10,000 municipalities in the country do not have access to the Internet. It is estimated that around 4.5 million Brazilians cannot access the Internet due to structural network problems. The study found that hard-to-reach places are located in rural areas or in regions where low-purchasing power populations live, even in large urban centers (IPEA 2017). The district of Manguinhos, thanks to its location near the center of the city of Rio de Janeiro, should be considered an exception.

The frequency in accessing the Internet identified among survey participants suggests the central role of NITCs in the life of "Digital Natives." A significant proportion of young people interviewed spend 4 h or more on virtual networks. This suggests that digital technologies permeate different aspects of the routine of these young people. In this context, it is possible to consider that interpersonal relationships become one of the main realms in the lives of these young people mediated by digital technologies: they spend increasingly more time connected to the Internet, especially to talk and interact with other people. According to the perspective of Oliveira (2017, 297), the young participants of our exploratory study can be seen as "adolescents who, above all, measure time in a new way. This is the 'touch generation,' always linked to internet-connected cellphones, which has evolved in the use of digital technologies from interaction to integration."

Regarding the devices used to connect to the Internet, the results of our study reiterate the centrality of cellphones as a connecting device pointed out in the TIC Kids Online (CGI 2016a), Global Kids Online (Byrne et al. 2016), EU Kids Online 2014), and Pew Research Center (Lenhart et al. 2015).

The results shown by young low-income people indicate that, because of their affordability and the availability of an increasingly wider range of applications and possibilities of use, cellphones favored digital inclusion of this group and their development as "Digital Natives." They showed behaviors and habits similar to those of the privileged social strata.

While cellphones may have expanded Internet access, it is necessary to emphasize that the massive use of these devices poses important issues for young people. According to Byrne et al. (2016, 36–37):

> Mobile access may be positive in terms of flexibility and privacy, but it could also reduce opportunities for parents to mediate or support their children as they explore the internet [...]. The quality of experience for a child who accesses the internet only through a mobile phone may differ from that of children who also use desktops or laptops: the small screen limits the amount and complexity of content that can be readily viewed, and when searching information online mobile users tend to scan content rather than to process and analyse it more deeply.

The results of our study show that the Internet is an important source of health information for young people. Due to the countless sources of information available, the participants of our research, regardless of their socioeconomic profile, are motivated to access health information on the Internet. However, the Internet is not their only resource, depending on the socioeconomic status of respondents. In fact, the medical profession appears to play are more central role in the lives of disadvantaged young people. Among those interviewed in health facility waiting rooms, only 1.7% of those who access health information reported that they would use the Internet instead of consulting their doctor. Young people in the waiting room are formally inserted in the local primary care network, whose services are administered by the Oswaldo Cruz Foundation. In a survey carried out in 2012 by Hollanda et al. (2012), users indicated high satisfaction with Fiocruz primary care services. While not ascertained, it may be that public school students are also formally enrolled in the primary care network where they live. In turn, private school students come from high-income families. We can presume their economic condition facilitates access to health services, especially in the private network. In this context, important considerations are that regular access to the primary care services, regular monitoring by health professionals, and satisfaction with the services provided are important factors in determining whether the Internet and online health information occupy a secondary place in the life of users waiting for a consultation in waiting rooms. For them, the physician's standing and authority continue to prevail.

In the contemporary setting, the technological environment tends to increase in daily life. Children and adolescents are not oblivious to the effects and implications of this atmosphere. Instead, they find themselves in the virtual environment. This exploratory study suggests that socioeconomic conditions may interfere with the way in which these young people relate to digital technologies. However, the spread of wireless networks, especially in urban areas, and the increased affordability of cellphones seem to have been crucial elements to narrow gaps between social classes on the use and appropriation of NICTs, allowing both groups to be perceived as members of the "Digital Native" generation.

As ICTs become increasingly present in the daily lives of young people, the Internet emerges as a major source of health information. In this context, it is important to understand not only how digital technologies affect and shape the different realms of young people's lives but also to look at the opportunities, challenges, and issues related to health, self-care, and well-being of Digital Natives.

Finally, it should be noted that this exploratory study was imposed before a reality that is still not well known in Brazil and in the world. This work enabled us to show some explanatory hypotheses and formulate questions for future research, avoiding hasty conclusions. We believe that the exploratory study shown in this chapter provides an introductory analysis about the place and use that New Information and Communication Technologies play in the life of young people and further encourages future investigations with similar objectives.

References

Alves, Maria Helena, and P. Evanson. 2013. *Vivendo no fogo cruzado: Moradores de favela, traficantes de droga e violência policial no Rio de Janeiro*. São Paulo: Unesp.

AAP – American Academy of Pediatrics. 2016. American Academy of Pediatrics announces new recommendations for children's media use. https://www.aap.org/en-us/about-the-aap/aap-press-room/pages/american-academy-of-pediatrics-announces-new-recommendations-for-childrens-media-use.aspx. Accessed 10 Nov 2017.

Akçayir, Murat, Hakan Dündar, and Gökçe Akçayırc. 2016. What makes you a digital native? Is it enough to be born after 1980? *Computers in Human Behavior* 60: 435–440.

Barlow, John. 1996. A declaration of the independence of cyberspace. https://www.eff.org/pt-br/cyberspace-independence. Accessed 20 Oct 2017.

Baxter, Pamela, and Susan Jack. 2008. Qualitative case study methodology: Study design and implementation for novice researchers. *The Qualitative Report* 13: 544–559.

Beltrão, Kaizô. 2002. *Acesso à educação: diferenciais entre os sexos*. Brasília: Ipea.

Bennett, Sue, Karl Maton, and Lisa Kervin. 2008. The 'digital natives' debate: A critical review of the evidence. *British Journal of Educational Technology* 39: 775–786.

Bimber, Bruce, Andrew Flanagin, and Cynthia Stohl. 2012. *Collective action in organizations: Interactions and engagement in an era of technological change*. Nova York: Cambridge University Press.

Bolton, Ruth, A. Parasuraman, Ankie Hoefnagels, Nanne Migchels, Sertan Kabadayi, et al. 2013. Understanding generation Y and their use of social media: a review and research agenda. *Journal of Service Management* 24: 245–267.

Brazil. Presidência da República. Casa Civil. 1990. *Lei n° 8.080, de 19 de setembro de 1990. Dispõe sobre as condições para a promoção, proteção e recuperação da saúde, a organização e o funcionamento dos serviços correspondentes e dá outras providências*. Diário Oficial da República Federativa do Brasil, 19 set. 1990.

———. 1996. *Lei n° 9.394, de 20 de dezembro de 1996. Estabelece as diretrizes e bases da educação nacional*. Diário Oficial da República Federativa do Brasil, 20 dez. 1996.

———. 2003. *Decreto n° 4.829, de 3 de setembro de 2003. Dispõe sobre a criação do Brazilian Internet Steering Committee – CGIbr, sobre o modelo de governança da Internet no Brasil, e dá outras providências*. Diário Oficial da República Federativa do Brasil, 3 set. 2003.

Brown, John. 2000. Growing up digital: how the web changes work, education, and the ways people learn. *Change*: 10–20.

Byrne, Jasmina, Daniel Kardefelt Winther, Sonia Livingstone, and Mariya Stoilova. 2016. *Global kids online research synthesis, 2015–2016*. Florence: UNICEF Office of Research Innocenti.

Caiado, Aurílio. 2001. O espaço da cultura: guia cultural do estado de São Paulo. *São Paulo em Perspectiva* 15: 55–65.

Calderwood, Charles, Jeffrey D. Green, Jennifer A. Joy-Gaba, and Jaclyn M. Moloney. 2016. Forecasting errors in student media multitasking during homework completion. *Computers & Education* 94: 37–48.

Castells, Manuel. 2001. *The internet galaxy: Reflections on the internet, business, and society*. Oxford: Oxford University Press.

Castells, M., Mireia Fernández-Ardèvol, Jack Linchuan Qiu, and Araba Sey. 2007. *Mobile communication and society: A global perspective*. Cambridge, MA: MIT Press.

CEPCM – Colégio Estadual Professor Clóvis Monteiro. 2014. Colégio Estadual Prof. Clóvis Monteiro: desde 1950 formando cidadãos. http://cepcm.blogspot.com.br/. Accessed 10 Nov 2017.

CGI – Comitê Gestor da Internet. 2016a. *Survey on internet use by children in Brazil: ICT kids online Brazil*. São Paulo: Brazilian Internet Steering Committee.

———. 2016b. *Survey on the use of information and communication technologies in Brazilian households: ICT households 2015*. São Paulo: Brazilian Internet Steering Committee.

Cunha, Joana, and Álvaro Fagundes. 2017. 22% dos brasileiros vivem abaixo da linha da pobreza, diz estudo. http://www1.folha.uol.com.br/mercado/2017/10/1931680-22-dos-brasileiros-vivem-abaixo-da-linha-da-pobreza-diz-estudo.shtml. Accessed 19 Jan 2018.

EU Kids Online. 2014. Eu Kids Online: findings, methods and recommendations.https://lsedesignunit.com/EUKidsOnline/html5/index.html?page=1&noflash. Accessed 2 Dec 2017.

Fernandes, Tania, and Renato Gama-Rosa Costa. 2013. As comunidades de Manguinhos na história das favelas no Rio de Janeiro. *Tempo* 19: 117–133.

Fidalgo, António, and João Canavilhas. 2009. Todos os jornais no bolso: pensando o jornalismo na era do celular. In *Jornalismo on-line: modos de fazer*, ed. Carla Rodrigues, 99–117. Rio de Janeiro: Sulina.

Frúgoli Junior, Heitor, and Mariana Cavalcanti. 2012. Territorialidades da(s) cracolândia(s)em São Paulo e no Rio de Janeiro. *Anuário Antropológico* 2: 73–97.

Fuchs, Christian. 2008. *Internet and society: Social theory in the information age*. New York: Routledge.

Gibbons, Susan. 2007. *The academic library and the net gen student: Making the connections*. Chicago: American Library Association.

Gomes, Romeu, Elaine Ferreira do Nascimento, and Fábio Carvalho de Araujo. 2007. Por que os homens buscam menos os serviços de saúde do que as mulheres? As explicações de homens com baixa escolaridade e homens com ensino superior. *Cadernos de Saúde Pública* 23: 565–574.

González, Irene Miguel, Cristina Echevarría Broz, Elena Ferrero Fernández, and Patricio Suárez Gil. 2011. Uso de Internet por parte de los adolescentes de Gijón (Asturias) como fuente de información sobre salud. *Atención Primaria* 43: 281–286.

Gray, Nicola J., Jonathan D. Klein, Peter R. Noyce, Tracy S. Sesselberg, and Judith A. Cantrill. 2005. Health information seeking behavior in adolescence: The place of the internet. *Social Science & Medicine* 60: 1467–1478.

Hollanda, Eliane, Sandra Aparecida Venâncio de Siqueira, Gabriela Rieveres Borges de Andrade, Alex Molinaro, and Jeni Vaitsman. 2012. Satisfação e responsividade em serviços de atenção à saúde da Fundação Oswaldo Cruz. *Ciência & Saúde Coletiva* 17: 3343–3352.

Hughes-Hassell, Sandra, Dana Hanson-Baldauf, and Jennifer Burke. 2008. Urban teenagers, health information, and public library web sites. *Young Adult Library Services* 6: 3–42.

IBGE – Brazilian Institute of Geography and Statistics. 2017. Estatísticas Econômicas. https://cnae.ibge.gov.br/home-por/9865-ibge-divulga-o-rendimento-domiciliar-per-capita-de-2017.html. Accessed 10 Nov 2017.

———. 2018. O IBGE. https://www.ibge.gov.br/institucional/o-ibge.html. Accessed 19 Jan 2018.

INEP – National Institute for Educational Studies and Research "Anísio Teixeira". 2015. Enem por escola. http://portal.inep.gov.br/web/guest/enem-por-escola. Accessed 10 Nov 2017.

———. 2017. Censo escolar da educação básica 2016: notas estatísticas. http://download.inep.gov.br/educacao_basica/censo_escolar/notas_estatisticas/2017/notas_estatisticas_censo_escolar_da_educacao_basica_2016.pdf. Accessed 10 Nov 2017.

IPP – Instituto Pereira Passos. 2013. Bairros cariocas. http://pcrj.maps.arcgis.com/apps/MapJournal/index.html?appid=096ae1e5497145838ca64191be66f3e3. Accessed 10 Nov 2017.

———. 2017. *Data-Rio*. http://www.data.rio/. Accessed 10 Nov 2017.

IPEA – Instituto de Pesquisa Econômica Aplicada. 2017. *Avaliação da priorização para a expansão da rede de acesso a banda larga nos municípios brasileiros*. Rio de Janeiro: IPEA.

Jenkins, Henry. 2008. *Convergence culture: Where old and new media colide*. New York: NYU Press.

Kalba, Kas. 2008. The adoption of mobile phones in emerging markets: Global diffusion and the rural challenge. *International Journal of Communication* 2: 631–661.

Lemos, André. 2004. Cibercultura e mobilidade: a era da conexão. *Razón y Palabra* 41: 107–133.

Lenhart, Amanda, Maeve Duggan, Andrew Perrin, Renee Stepler, Lee Rainie, and Kim Parker. 2015. Teen, social media and technology overview 2015. Pew Research Center. http://www.pewinternet.org/2015/04/09/teens-social-media-technology-2015. Accessed 10 Nov 2017.

Lévy, Pierre. 2001. *Cyberculture*. Minnesota: University of Minnesota Press.
Lima, Carla. 2010. Vozes de quem sofre: discutindo a Saúde Ambiental na Bacia do Canal do Cunha. In *Território, participação popular e saúde: Manguinhos em debate*, ed. Carla Lima and Leonardo Bueno, 63–80. Rio de Janeiro: ENSP/Fiocruz.
Ministry of Health. 2007. Entendendo o SUS. http://portalarquivossaudegovbr/images/pdf/2013/agosto/28/cartilha-entendendo-o-sus-2007pdf. Accessed 10 Nov 2017.
———. 2012. *Política Nacional de Atenção Básica (PNAB)*. Brasília: Ministério da Saúde.
Misse, Michel. 2011. Crime organizado e crime comum no Rio de Janeiro: diferenças e afinidades. *Revista Sociologia Politica* 19: 13–25.
Monteiro, Jéssica, and Diego Silva. 2015. A influência da estrutura escolar no processo de ensino-aprendizagem: uma análise baseada nas experiências do estágio supervisionado em Geografia. *Geografia Ensino & Pesquisa* 19: 19–28.
Moura, Eliana, and Dinora Zucchetti. 2014. Socialização escolar, educação não escolar e (con) formação de sujeitos. *Revista Contrapontos* 14: 339–352.
Muccioli, Cristina, Paulo E.C. Dantas, Mauro Campos, and Harley E.A. Bicas. 2008. Relevância do Comitê de Ética em Pesquisa nas publicações científicas. *Arquivos Brasileiros de Oftalmologia* 71: 773–774.
Néri, Marcelo. 2015. *Motivos para evasão escolar*. Rio de Janeiro: Fundação Getúlio Vargas.
Oblinger, Diane, and P. Hagner, 2005. Seminar on educating the net generation. http://www.innovateonline.info/pdf/vol3_issue4/teaching_and_learning_with_the_net_generation.pdf. Accessed 10 Nov 2017.
Oliveira, Eloiza. 2017. Adolescência, internet e tempo: desafios para a Educação. *Educar em Revista* 64: 283–298.
OECD – Organisation for Economic Cooperation and Development. 2017. Education at a Glance 2017. http://www.oecd-ilibrary.org/education/education-at-a-glance-2017_eag-2017-en;jsessionid=1oy4g4byvx4gu.x-oecd-live-03. Accessed 10 Nov 2017.
Paim, Jairnilson. 2015. *O que é o SUS?* Rio de Janeiro: Editora Fiocruz.
Palfrey, John, and Urs Gasser. 2010. *Born digital: Understanding the first generation of digital natives*. New York: Basic Books.
Prensky, Marc. 2001a. Digital natives, digital immigrants: Part 1. *On the Horizon* 9: 1–6.
———. 2001b. Digital natives, digital immigrants: Part 2. *On the Horizon* 9: 1–6.
Ritzer, George, and Nathan Jurgenson. 2010. Production, consumption, prosumption: The nature of capitalism in the age of the digital 'prosumer'. *Journal of Consumer Culture* 10: 13–36.
Rosen, Larry. 2010. *Rewired: understanding the iGeneration and the way they learn*. New York: Macmillan.
SEEDUC – Secretária de Educação do Estado. 2017. Quadro de Horários 2017 das Escolas do Rio de Janeiro. http://consultaqh.educacao.rj.gov.br/ConsultaQHIGestao.aspx. Accessed 10 Nov 2017.
Soares, Daniel. 2010. Análise crítica do Plano de Desenvolvimento Urbanístico do Complexo de Manguinhos. In *Território, participação popular e saúde: Manguinhos em debate*, ed. Carla Lima and Leonardo Bueno, 15–36. Rio de Janeiro: ENSP/Fiocruz.
Srivastava, L. 2005. Mobile phones and the evolution of social behaviour. *Behaviour & Information Technology* 24: 111–129.
Tapscott, Don. 1998. *Growing up digital: the rise of the net generation*. New York: McGraw-Hill.
Telebrasil. 2017. Número de celulares com tecnologia 4G já supera o de 3G no Brasil. http://www.telebrasil.org.br/sala-de-imprensa/releases/8384-numero-de-celulares-com-tecnologia-4g-ja-supera-o-de-3g-no-brasil. Accessed 10 Nov 2017.
TEIAS – Território Escola Manguinhos. 2014. Quem somos. http://andromeda.ensp.fiocruz.br/teias/quem-somos. Accessed 10 Nov 2017
UNESCO – United Nations Educational, Scientific and Cultural Organization. 2015. Report education for all in Brazil: 2000–2015. http://unesdoc.unesco.org/images/0023/002300/230021e.pdf. Accessed 10 Nov 2017.
Yin, Robert K. 2003. *Case study research: Design and methods*. Thousand Oaks: Sage.

Chapter 8
Access and Use of Information and Communication Technologies to Promote Active Ageing: For What? For Whom?

Wilson José Alves Pedro, Márcia Niituma Ogata, Heloísa Cristina Figueiredo Frizzo, Ariadne Chloe Furnival, and Brunela Della Maggiori Orlandi

Abstract Considering the specificities and demands arising from demographic changes, this chapter analyzes dimensions and aspects of the access and use of information and communication technologies to promote active ageing. Inserted in the interdisciplinary field of science, technology, and society (STS), we show from a review of studies and research (1) the importance of access to and difficulties arising from health information seeking, (2) some strategies adopted by elderly people using social networks, (3) the development of new capabilities and competencies for elderly people to access and use ICTs autonomously and independently, (4) the emergence of public policies and strategies for the socio-educational inclusion of the elderly population, and (5) the relevance of studies on the use of gerotechnological technologies pointing to new alternatives for the promotion of active ageing.

W. J. A. Pedro (✉)
Department of Gerontology, Federal University of São Carlos, São Carlos, Brazil
e-mail: wilsonpedro@ufscar.br

M. N. Ogata
Department of Nursing, Federal University of São Carlos, São Carlos, Brazil

H. C. F. Frizzo
Department of Occupational Therapy, Federal University of the Triângulo Mineiro, Uberaba, Brazil

A. C. Furnival
Department of Information Science, Federal University of São Carlos, São Carlos, Brazil

B. D. M. Orlandi
Department of Technology and Society, Federal University of São Carlos, São Carlos, Brazil

A. Pereira Neto, M. B. Flynn (eds.), *The Internet and Health in Brazil*,
https://doi.org/10.1007/978-3-319-99289-1_8

8.1 Introduction

In the award-winning film, *I, Daniel Blake*, directed by Ken Loach (2016), there is a scene that creates an impact and can make the viewer reflect on contemporary scenarios of access and use of information and communication technologies (ICTs) by elderly people.[1] In this scene, the eponymous protagonist goes into a public library to use a computer to fill out a social services form, which exists exclusively in online format. But, the usability of the system is lamentable, placing people with little familiarity with its use at a great disadvantage. Confronted with this difficulty, Daniel soon finds himself obliged to ask for help from strangers around him – notably all much younger than him – to fill out the form. The scene brilliantly captures how excluded an elderly person can feel when unable to deal with new ICTs. With this scene, the director invites the viewer to reflect simultaneously on how the state can routinely employ these technologies to (sometimes unwittingly) propagate the exclusion of citizens at the very moment that they are trying to rightfully demand services from the state.

This scene thus describes an important moment in the life of many inhabitants of the planet in the twenty-first century. The case of Daniel Blake is emblematic, for researchers in the field of science, technology, and society (STS) like us, for it encourages us to apprehend how these technologies impact peoples' daily lives and what their potential might be in actually promoting "active ageing."

In this chapter, we bring together some of our reflections from the Brazilian context: namely, How is knowledge concerning access and use of ICTs produced, disseminated, and appropriated by people and, more specifically, by more elderly people? What are the objective and subjective conditions of access and use of these technologies? How do teaching and learning processes – be they formal, informal, and nonformal – occur over the life course and especially from adulthood onward? What roles do public policies and management have in these processes? And how do professionals, workers, and managers act in this dynamic? In short, when the subject is ageing, we can ask: Technologies for what and for whom?

To answer these questions, we will present and analyze the Brazilian context of elderly people and the difficulties they sometimes confront in having to deal with this set of new technologies – the ICTs.

[1] The World Health Organization (WHO) defines the elderly person according to their chronological age, so that a person of 60 or above in a developing country is considered elderly, whereas in developed countries, this age is 65 years old or more (WHO 2002).

8.2 Active Ageing: Inputs and Interconnections with Science, Technology, and Society

The concept of "active ageing," disseminated by the World Health Organization (WHO), was developed in the Second United Nations World Assembly on Ageing in 2002 held in Madrid, Spain. Since then, the term active ageing is used to refer to:

> […] the process of optimizing opportunities for health, participation and security in order to enhance quality of life as people age. Active ageing applies to both individuals and population groups. It allows people to realize their potential for physical, social, and mental well being throughout the life course and to participate in society according to their needs, desires and capacities, while providing them with adequate protection, security and care when they require assistance. (WHO 2002, 12)

It is estimated that by the year 2050, there will be a "demographic watershed" (Centro Internacional de Longevidade Brasil 2015). The expectation is that 21% of the world population will be 60 years old or more, that is, more than two billion people, and furthermore it is likely that this demographic will be concentrated in 64 countries (mainly in Latin America, Asia, and China) representing 30% of the world population. Access and use of ICTs for social participation, security, and health promotion will form the structural pillars of these societies. For this reason, older persons like Daniel Blake need to have a minimum set of skills when dealing with ICTs. For researchers like us, investigating ageing in the Brazilian context, the understanding of these processes and contexts is always challenging.

To think about the access and use of ICTs for promoting active ageing necessarily implies thinking about the multiple contexts and possibilities of ageing, its complexity, and multidetermination (WHO 2002). It implies thinking of new forms of social interaction and new possibilities of teaching how to learn that respects the diverse expressions of ageing and old age: active, autonomous, independent, plural but also fragile, pre-fragile, and dependent. It implies thinking about users, community, workers, and managers in all types of organizations, programs, and services through which this population group interacts.

The increase in life expectancy is, without doubt, a conquest for humanity that brings us continual demands and challenges, be they from scientific and technological advances that have contributed to the reduction of fecundity and mortality and be they the impacts from changes in lifestyle dynamics, as well as from multidimensional factors that the ageing process combines in all their diversity and complexity. Today, this issue is firmly placed on the academic and public policy agenda (WHO 2017). Scientific and technological advances impact upon longevity. On the one hand, they contribute toward innovations that increase life expectancy; and on the other, and complementing the former, they provoke anxieties, needs, and prospects for improvements in the conditions and quality of life among the ageing population.

Having as the theoretical and methodological framework studies from the field of STS, this chapter resulted from a meeting of researchers linked to the Graduate Program in Science, Technology, and Society at the Federal University of São

Carlos (PPGCTS/UFSCar), Brazil, who are aware of the impacts that scientific and technological advancements have on the day-to-day life of elderly people. The STS field is historically configured as a privileged locus of research and interventions that study the interactions and social determinations of science and technology, the analysis of its sociohistorical and cultural factors, and the implications of technoscientific changes. Originating in the 1960s and consolidating in the 1970s in Europe and the USA, the field has expanded into Latin American countries and especially in Brazil. It is an interdisciplinary field, sustained by theoretical and epistemological frameworks from philosophy and the sociology of science and history of technology, showing how all scientific and technological development is socially constructed, the consequences of which affect social life and environmental dimensions of existence (Bloor 1991; Bijker et al. 1987; Fuller 1993; Jasanoff et al. 1994; Latour 1987). The STS field seeks to investigate the social dimensions of science and technology with the aim of apprehending phenomena from the perspective of their social antecedents, critically analyzing their consequences, and repercussions of technological changes from an ethical, environmental, and cultural perspective. In STS, the relevance of social actors is made evident in the context of scientific development and in the production and dissemination of technological artifacts, as well as in the democratization of decision-making processes in issues concerning science and technology (Bijker and Law 1994; Leach et al. 2004; Jasanoff 2005). The field of STS contributes, then, to the deconstruction of the traditional viewpoint – essentialist and triumphalist – of science and technology, which can be summarized in the so-called linear model of development: + science = +technology = +wealth = +social well-being, a model that still prevails and often goes unquestioned and which is still present in academia and in science communication (Mayr 1982; Irwin 1995).

In this STS context, we have prioritized studies in gerontology as an interdisciplinary science that focuses on ageing processes and established connections with the field of STS (Maddox 1987; Johnson 1997; Alkema and Alley 2006). The ageing process is understood to be a dialectical one, on an individual and/or collective level – retrospective and/or prospective – based on experiences that do not occur in an isolated way and which is influenced by social networks and life conditions (Cabral et al. 2013). Thus, the phenomenon-object "ageing processes" is multidetermined and demands interdisciplinary frameworks for the construction of knowledge that can apprehend the individual, intra-subjective, and intersubjective dimensions, as well as the social, historical, and cultural dimensions and their respective interactions, including their consequences and impacts on the course of life (Whitbourne 2008; Johnson 2005).

One of our main concerns in the field of gerontology is understanding the way in which the individual interacts with society throughout life, especially in the phase or stage in which they are getting old, and how social structures influence the ageing process (Johnson 2005; Whitbourne 2008). On studying human beings, "it should be clear that one is always studying a determined material formation, whatever the perspective assumed in the universality of reciprocal relations in which one is inserted" (Ciampa 1993, 150). We should restate our assumptions that scientific and technological knowledge should contribute to improve the place of old age in our society. We corroborate the thesis that:

> [...] it is against democratic values to accept the exclusion or marginalization of elderly people, or even to define old age as a social condition of dependence. Elderly people should take on the effective right of representation and social and political participation. To reposition old people in the set of the system of intergenerational relations is a democratic imperative and a political challenge that ageing societies face. (Cabral et al. 2013, 12)

Thus, to universalize access and free choice with ICTs is a challenge that is continually being renewed.

The emerging specificities of human-technology interactions, when delimited in the context of ageing, also make up a field of study, research, and clinical and psychosocial interventions called "gerontechnology." Internationally, the term gerontechnology (Bouma et al. 2007) has been used to refer to a branch of auxiliary technologies in health and social domains in search of quality of life, comfort, and security of elderly people. Gerontechnology is an interdisciplinary academic, professional, and research field in which technology is directed to the aspirations and opportunities of elderly people. It aims for good health, social participation, and independent lives for ageing people. In this sense, it seeks the sustainability of an ageing society through the creation of technological environments, including assistive technology, inclusive design for life and social participation, innovating and independent for elderly people in good health, comfort, and safety.

Gerontechnology refers to the development of technological environments for health, habilitation, mobility, communication, leisure, and work of elderly people (Bouma et al. 2007). Sale (2018) points out that gerontechnology has been developing new appliances to help people who experience limitations in their activities of daily living (ADLs, e.g., bathing, eating, using the toilet) and in their instrumental activities for daily living (IADLs, e.g., shopping, housework, meal preparation). It also seeks to improve activities related to daily living (ADLs), along with memory and monitoring functions, thereby reducing, too, their dependency. Specifically, gerontechnology contributes to the development and distribution of products, environments, and services, using more appropriate technologies to improve the daily life of ageing people, and particularly elderly people, with the aim of providing living conditions for quality, dignified ageing that is autonomous and independent. It is evident that today, technologies are a necessary resource to optimize the social and functional performance of elderly people. However, many challenges remain regarding cultural assimilation, the process of learning, access, and use, as well as human-machine interactions. Of which technologies are we talking? In which contexts? We need to clearly delimitate in order to advance cautiously with our discussion.

The term technology (from the Greek *teck-nologia*) means systematic treatment or description of one or more *teknai* (practical art, craft). Following this Greek translation, Weber employed the term *technik* in German, but for him, it referred to physical products and artifacts and intellectual ideas (Schatzberg 2006). Today, technology is seen as inseparable from the sociocultural and economic context in which it is generated, including, or not, scientific knowledge. Technology, knowledge, government, and economy form constituent and interdependent parts in the productive infrastructure: they make up structured sociotechnical systems that are networked with actors being people, institutions, as well as artifacts and objects (Bijker and Law 1994; Bijker et al. 1987). Palacios et al. (2001) define the term technology in the field of STS, explaining that:

> Technology is a projection of human beings onto their surroundings, but it is important to maintain a critical position regarding technology because it has not always produced the desired effects, turning against us in the same way that the monster turned against Victor Frankenstein. In the final instance, we develop forms of living with technology in today's world, ways that allow us to correct the mistakes of the past – expressed so eloquently by the Luddite movement – and to adapt machines, needs and aspirations of human beings. (Palacios et al. 2001, 75)

When juxtaposed with the prefix "geronto-," the word "technology" brings within it a legacy that also needs to be contextualized and (re)signified.

It was in the eighteenth century that technology was used to signify rational improvement of the arts (techniques), and especially those that were used in industry, through their scientific study (Mayr 1982). But it is in the twentieth century, with the technological advances associated with the demands of demographic transition, that gerontechnology gradually emerged as an interdisciplinary area that brings together scholars and researchers to improve and optimize technologies for ageing processes. As Bouma et al. (2007, 210) note:

> In the second half of the 20th century, efforts were initially directed at two important fields: ergonomics or human factors for ageing persons and aids for the handicapped. From the nineties, the knowledge base has been expanded as other ambitions and needs of ageing persons have been taken into account as well. This is the field of Gerontechnology, bringing gerontology and technology together for the purpose of a good life for ageing persons, most of whom can be independent and integrated in society.

Several technological resources are currently available for elderly people, but they lack studies, dissemination of information, and interventions with the elderly public. Among them are the following: technologies for work and employment (changes and technological innovations in a variety of occupations and careers); technologies for social participation (electronic voting urns, banking transactions, emission of personal documents and ID); education technologies (making the multiple forms of formal, informal, and nonformal education viable); entertainment technologies (closed caption, games, e-books, social networks, sound, and image capture and production); technologies for day-to-day life (machines and instruments that characterize these activities like cars, coffee machines, subscription TV, remote controls); social interaction (social networks); assistive technologies (that promote functional abilities for contexts of pre-fragility and fragility, aiming for independence and inclusion); and technologies for health self-care (gadgets for monitoring and control of state of health, remote interactions with health services).

Many of these technologies work through the use of the computer or smartphone, using the Internet, which implies minimum competency and familiarity with these devices and media. ICTs are technical resources used to treat information and help with communication. They include computer hardware, networks, mobile phones, as well as all the necessary software to fulfill their functions. ICTs correspond to most of the technologies that interfere and mediate communicative and informational processes of human beings (Briggs and Burke 2004). ICTs make up a set of integrated technological resources that provide, through the functions of hardware, software, and telecommunications, the automation and communication of business processes, and those of scientific research, teaching, and learning, among others. ICTs are, therefore, present in day-to-day human life, including in the life of elderly people like Daniel Blake, from the eponymous film. His was a predicament (evoked in the description of a scene from the film at the beginning of this chapter) common to many elderly people today: not knowing how to deal with ICTs placed him in a condition of profound vulnerability and dependency in today's society.

The demographic situation in Brazil is not different from that observed in other developing countries in the world. The Brazilian "age pyramid" has undergone notable modifications over recent decades. In the 1980s, there was a wide base and narrow apex, representing the fact that there were more children and young people than elderly people. However, considering the present age pyramid, and the projection for 2050, there is a narrowing of the base and a widening of the apex, which means that the population is ageing as a consequence of demographic transitions observed worldwide. The issue of ageing in Brazil and in developing countries relates to social issues that have still not been resolved, such as extreme poverty, giving rise to even more inequality and exclusion of this demographic group (Costa et al. 2000).

In this more general context, the World Health Organization (WHO) poses the following questions:

> How do we help people remain independent and active as they age?
> How can we strengthen health promotion and prevention policies, especially those directed to older people? As people are living longer, how can the quality of life in old age be improved? Will large numbers of older people bankrupt our health care and social security systems? How do we best balance the role of the family and the state when it comes to caring for people who need assistance, as they grow older? How do we acknowledge and support the major role that people play as they age in caring for others? (WHO 2002, 5)

One answer to such questions could be possible through what is conventionally called "active ageing," which is "the process of optimizing opportunities for health, participation, and security in order to enhance quality of life as people age" (WHO 2002, 12).

8.3 Profile of Elderly People and Access to ICTS: Some Evidence

It is still difficult to locate data on the use of ICTs segmented by age, especially for those over their 60s. We will here illustrate access by elderly people with data collected and published by the UK's Office for National Statistics. In that country,

74.1% and 78% of elderly people from 65 to 74 years old and 38.7% and 41% over 75 years old used the Internet in 2016 and 2017, respectively. There is also greater access by elderly men in these age ranges for both years, but we note a significant growth in access to the Internet by the elderly population in general. In 6 years (between 2011 and 2017), the growth of elderly users of the Internet in the UK was significant: between the age ranges of 65–74, it grew from 52% to 77.5%, and for the age range above 75 years old, it increased from 19.9% to 40.5% (ONS 2016, 2017).

In the case of Brazil, the "National Home Sample Survey" (*Pesquisa Nacional de Amostra de Domicílios* – PNAD), carried out by the Brazilian Institute of Geography and Statistics – IBGE (2014), for the year 2013, revealed that the relative participation of elderly people of 60+ was 13% of the total population, being that this indicator was greater for the southern region of the country (14.5%) and less for the northern region (8.8%).[2] The same study showed that the most common (30.6%) family arrangement for elderly people was made up of elderly people living with children of 25 years old or more, cohabitating with or without other relatives or family members. More elderly women (33.3%) were in this situation, compared to 27.3% of elderly men.

A challenge related to populational ageing is related to social security. For the group of people of 60+ years old, 23.9% did not receive a retirement pension, compared to 7.8% who did. The high proportion of elderly 60+ people who do not receive a pension is possibly related to their insertion in the workplace, given that 27.4% in this age range still work, but for those who were not retired or receiving pension, this rate was 45.1%.

In Brazil, according to the 2012 National Home Sample Survey, of the people above 50 years old, only 20.5% used the Internet in that year, with those in the southeast (26%) and southern (21.4%) regions of the country accessing networks the most. As we mentioned above, men predominate in the use of the Internet with an average of 22.2% for men above 50, compared to 19.1% for women in the same age group. The southeast and southern regions also have the greatest number of elderly users of the Internet (IBGE 2012, 2017).

8.4 ICTS in the Context of Ageing

ICTs favor the inclusion of the elderly population in society as active members of society, given that they can help to spread information about voluntary work and assist in the acquisition of new knowledge, in accessing information, and in socialization and participation in artistic and cultural manifestations – contributions that are much more than mere pastimes. ICTs make communication faster with friends and relatives anywhere, from the comfort of the homes of elderly people, which

[2] The population with more wealth and education are found in the southeast, center-west, and southern regions of Brazil.

constitutes a great incentive for the use of these resources for this age group. Access to ICTs can help foment positive feelings among elderly people, potentially reducing loneliness, depression, and anxiety. Some studies have pointed out that as well as having the potential to reduce isolation, this access improves organizational involvement, especially for those elderly people who have reduced mobility (Etchemendy et al. 2011).

The digital tools most used by elderly people are those that provide access to information and promote social interaction, such as social networks that allow information sharing, as well as the sharing of ideas, images, photos, videos, and audio. A study carried out by Miné (2014) concluded that social networks[3] have begun to penetrate and mold the daily life of elderly people, who are increasingly connected and have begun changing their ways of communicating, entertaining themselves, and interacting socially. The author points out that the "third age" Facebook page seeks to break with the stereotype of valuing the "cult of youth" which is so present in Brazilian culture. The publications on this page reinforce the issue of physical and mental autonomy, and financial and social independence, and subjects that are extremely relevant for this group. Miné (2014) asks if identifying with the image of a successful old age is one of the reasons why this Facebook page has so many fans. The study also emphasizes the way in which the "third age" page gets close to the reality of elderly people via themes of memory, tangentially related to other aspects like times gone by, of friends, relatives, and people who have passed away and of the nostalgia typical of this phase in life. In this sense, it could be alleged that this page tends to actually reinforce a distorted view of old age, but in conclusion, Miné (2014) asserts that this Facebook page in general seeks to challenge existing stereotypes in relation to the third age, addressing topics that reinforce happiness and memory and projecting a positive image of active elderly people.

Chepe and Adamatti (2015) observe that the use of social networks by elderly people facilitates social interaction contributing to learning and consequently to human development, given that these networks are mediating instruments for human communication. Associated to this issue, these authors highlight that communication and the acquisition of knowledge in the digital environment, through Facebook, constitute ways of maintaining the cognitive functions of elderly people, contributing to successful ageing. Social networks emerge as social tools that permit the widening of communication forms and information sharing. Páscoa (2012) presented a case study carried out at the Universidade Sénior Albicastrense in Portugal, analyzing the contribution of Facebook to promote active ageing. The study revealed that elderly people consider Facebook as a facilitating digital tool that is very helpful for forming relationships in the context of active ageing because "it increases the quality of life, fights isolation, promotes socialization, it is a complement to leisure and entertainment, and brings together generations in which grandparents and grandchildren speak the same language" (Páscoa 2012, 53). In the research, the participants see Facebook as a life project to age better because they feel "info-included"

[3] Chapter 6 addresses the theme of virtual communities of patients.

in the digital environment, with greater participation in society and of value to the community. On conducting research on the use of digital social networks, Lewis and Ariyachandra (2010) also found that they possess the potential to improve the quality of life for elderly people, acting as a medium that facilitates interaction with peers in the community.

Today, the use of ICTs is considered one of the fundamental aspects of citizenship.[4] They effectively permeate the course of life in the context of old age, whether in the workplace and/or in the context of retirement, in interpersonal networks, in support and neighborhood relationships, in social participation, and in health care and well-being, and for entertainment – within and outside the home, in leisure time activities and occupations (Cabral et al. 2013; Pedro 2013). However, there is no consensus in the research already conducted with both the elderly and the general population regarding a possible relationship between regular ICT use and the reduction of loneliness (a subjective experience of negative feelings regarding social contact) and social isolation, which is the objective experience of the absence of contact with other people (Cotten et al. 2013). Some research has demonstrated that the use of ICTs can even increase feelings of social isolation, especially if the interactions forged in the use of ICTs are superficial or if they are perceived as not compensating for those social relationships already lost in the elderly person's life (Cotten et al. 2013). On the other hand, it is possible that increased access to information, and the possibility of being able to communicate easily with friends and family on a regular basis, can help diminish perceived loneliness (Azevedo 2017). There is a need for more research that goes beyond mere measures of Internet use but which examines the type, quantity, moment in time, and for what reason the Internet is being used by elderly people (Cotten et al. 2013). For example, if it is being used for non-communicative purposes regularly, it is possible that its use contributes to greater social isolation and a sense of loneliness.

Doll et al. (2011) discuss initiatives aimed at digital inclusion of elderly people which are still rare and require strengthening networks to better contribute to access by this population and preparing courses that consider aspects important for ageing. The present trend in the growth of the elderly population has led countries like the USA and Holland to make sites available specifically for this demographic (Alpay et al. 2004; Campbell and Nolfi 2005). In the state of São Paulo, in the southeast region of Brazil, there is a program called *AcessaSP* ("AccesSãoPaulo") created in the year 2000 by Decree 45.057 and reformulated in 2016 by Decree number 62.306 (Brasil 2016). *AcessaSP* is until today the main and largest free program of digital inclusion for the population of that state, and its mission is "to promote the digital empowerment of citizens offering free technological and communication infrastructure, guidance, information and training, in a collaborative way," via 800 centers throughout the state (Governo do Estado de São Paulo 2017). It is a strong policy which, to date, has very probably contributed to the digital inclusion of the population of the state of São Paulo.

[4]The issue of online citizen participation is addressed in Chap. 5.

8.5 eHealth, eHealth Literacy, and the Elderly

The increasing expansion of Internet use brings with it growing interest in defining how health information will be found and accessed (Brodie et al. 2000). Eysenbach (2001) observes how the term "eHealth" rapidly became present when speaking of growing Internet use to find health information on the Web. It is a field located at the intersection of medical informatics, public health, and business and refers to the delivery point of health services and information over the Internet and related technologies. For Eysenbach (2001), the concept of eHealth goes beyond the mere use of ICTs, in the sense that these are used to inculcate values of a global, networked thinking with the aim of improving health services delivery at regional and local levels.

The author lists and defines the "10 Es" of eHealth, among which there are the "empowerment of health services consumers" and – perhaps the most relevant for elderly populations – "equality" because there is the potential for eHealth to lessen the gap between the "haves" and "have-nots." Those people who do not have access to computers and networks, and that do not have the ability to use them, are usually those who would benefit most from having such access to health information. The digital divide reinforces the divide between urban and rural populations, the rich and poor, males and females, old and young, and common and rare diseases (Eysenbach 2001). Etchemendy et al. (2011) developed an eHealth platform with the aim of helping elderly people and carers to detect early stage changes in emotional states and physical aspects. The system works in a way to investigate, through steps, small changes noted in the elderly person's mood. Monitoring the platform, and from the results presented (on a scale of slight to serious, considering the elderly person's age), therapeutic and recreational choices of activities are provided. Another aspect of the platform is that each time an elderly person activates the assessment and chooses a given therapeutic course of action, their doctor receives a report and is able to interact with the elderly person through the platform should it be deemed necessary.

Among the reasons given by elderly people for their use of the Internet is searching for health information (Laganà 2008; Koopman-Boyden and Reid 2009). A study with 2084 people of 50+ years old, carried out on the North American site *SeniorNet*, demonstrates that 70% of those interviewed used the site to obtain health-related information, because it allowed them to access it at the moment that they found most appropriate and convenient (Tak and Hong 2005). Another study reported that although only 22% of North American adults aged 65 or more searched online, 66% looked for information related to health or medical matters (Fox 2004). Deursen (2012) reports that getting health-related information on the Internet can help in the early detection of health problems and even improve treatments. According to data collected by the Brazilian Internet Management Committee (*Comitê Gestor da Internet*) for 2016, the search for health information occupies second place in terms of the type of information sought by this group, with searches for products and services being in first place (CGI 2017, 341).

The fact that information available on the Internet is often incomplete, or represents unreliable sources,[5] alongside the difficulty of assimilating the information and putting it into practice, catalyzes and permeates the international research agendas on the phenomena of "health literacy," "health information literacy," and "eHealth literacy." According to the Medical Library Association, "health literacy" refers to the "ability to read, understand, and act on health information" (Pfizer 2002, *apud* MLA 2007), with "to act on" referring to the ability to make health-related decisions. Nutbeam (2008, *apud* Watkins and Xie 2014) observes that the concept of "health literacy" has evolved from two perspectives: that of clinical care and that of public health. From the former, health literacy is a determining factor that influences the choices of treatments and their possible outcomes: a low level of health literacy can influence, for example, the way in which a patient adheres to clinical recommendations, having a potentially negative impact on clinical treatment. On the other hand, the public health perspective positions health literacy as a result of the patient's interest in seeking and presenting the information found as a possible input into the decision-making process. Hirvonen et al. (2015) report that research shows that health literacy at inadequate levels is more prevalent among the male population, poorer groups, ethnic minorities, people with long-term disabilities, and elderly people.

In turn, the definition of "health information literacy" formulated by the Medical Library Association (MLA 2007) is:

> […] the set of abilities needed to: recognize a health information need; identify likely information sources and use them to retrieve relevant information; assess the quality of the information and its applicability to a specific situation; and analyze, understand, and use the information to make good health decisions.

Niemelä et al. (2012) developed a framework to gauge people's everyday health information literacy that incorporates the MLA definition of health information literacy and which was used by the same researchers on a sample of Finnish students and also by Hirvonen et al. (2015) in a study of young Finnish men. But there is a dearth of studies that apply this framework specifically to elderly groups.

With the current omnipresence of ICTs in everyday life, the definition of health information literacy is seamlessly intertwined with these technologies, giving rise to another concept, which is that of "eHealth literacy" involving "a mixture of literacies in health, information, science, media, computers and Internet" (Watkins and Xie 2014). Despite being a concept with increasing recognition in the literature, as revealed in the systematic review conducted by Watkins and Xie (2014), these authors also observe that there is still a lack of more theoretical research in the field of eHealth literacy to validate these models empirically, not least because the generability of such models to elderly populations needs to be established. There is also the eHEALS framework, which measures (subjective) self-reported scales of eHealth literacy (Norman and Skinner 2006) but which needs to be updated to explicitly incorporate Web 2.0 (Watkins and Xie 2014).

[5] Chapter 10 discusses the theme of health information on the Web.

In the systematic review of the literature on eHealth literacy and elderly people, Watkins and Xie (2014) identified only 23 articles extracted from 28 databases covering 9 relevant knowledge fields. They identified a fault in most of the collected studies, for not having identified income, ethnicity, race, and education level of the elderly people who took part, these being the sociodemographic variables known to influence levels of health literacy. In most of the studies analyzed by the authors, the eHealth literacy interventions were composed of institutional material developed by the National Institutes of Health (USA), or websites dedicated to a specific condition like stroke, or multimedia tutorials, like radio programs, among others. Most of the interventions occurred in nonformal contexts, such as in public libraries or leisure centers for the elderly, with only 17% of the interventions occurring in clinical contexts. None of the studies identified by Watkins and Xie (2014) had eHealth literacy interventions that resulted in a positive health outcome as a measured result, because they were not carried out in clinical contexts. The authors identify this as a fault of the interventions to promote eHealth literacy, recognizing, at the same time, that it would be difficult to administer certain interventions of eHealth literacy in clinical contexts precisely because they require that the participants use computers. The review also identified a prevalent gap in the eHealth literacy interventions for not including access to information via mobile devices and for neither having dealt with the issue of Web 2.0 for such interventions.

Arief et al. (2013) examine the advantages and barriers in relation to the use of eHealth from the perspective of elderly people by identifying strong and weak points, threats, and opportunities in order to assist in the formulation of future strategies concerning access to such technologies. The results of that research led to an understanding that the use of eHealth resources improves access to health services and has potential benefits by economizing on costs. From this perspective, a positive attitude was observed among the elderly in relation to the use of the technologies. However, there are significant weaknesses related to the lack of evidence-based research to prove their benefits and physical limitations. The authors emphasize that the quality of eHealth is still questionable in comparison to traditional services. The study shows that the main threats include data protection, privacy, and the digital divide. Finally, their research points out that the opportunity to implement eHealth strategies for elderly people is still promising, since economic growth, education, and technological advances can all improve, alongside the improvement of evidence-based practices in health informatics. The article emphasizes that associated weaknesses and threats can be overcome by reinforcing and investing resources in the positive aspects of eHealth.

In the Brazilian context, there has been an increase in the number of studies and amount of research involving the use of technologies for health and in the social domains of elderly people, mainly in the context of the I and II Brazilian Conference of Gerontechnology (Revista de Medicina Ribeirão Preto 2016, 2017) which covered the themes of environment, multi-sensorial stimulation, design, closed caption, assistive environments and technologies, games, literacy, work, mobility, apps, mobile phones, tablets, and virtual environments. In what follows, aspects of some specific studies will be delineated and discussed.

8.6 Some Evidence on ICTS and Elderly People in the Brazilian Context

A study conducted by Orlandi and Pedro (2014) analyzes some aspects of geriatric syndromes and focuses on access and use of health information on the Internet by a group of elderly people who take part in a program of digital inclusion in a municipality in the state of São Paulo. This study points to the fact that as people age, they concomitantly become more worried about health and illness but that the Internet can be a facilitating and liberating means through which information can be obtained. In the case of this study, accessing health information on the Internet reduced concerns regarding the ageing process among the participants. The study also saw a reduction in tendencies toward social isolation and renewed sense of individuals' social roles and of intergenerational meetings on the Web.

The theme of mourning has been explored using ICTs, more specifically blogs constituting a strategy adopted by elderly people. Studies carried out by Frizzo et al. (2017a) sought to understand, using a science, technology, and society framework, blogs as a space for the production of interaction and social ties between mothers mourning loss. Through virtual ethnography, by means of an analysis of thematic blogs written by mothers mourning the loss of a child, six blogs were identified and analyzed, using participant observation in the virtual environment and the application of a questionnaire to analyze the blogs. The data collected were systematized into categories. The study found that the blogs constituted a strategy to express personal narratives of the mothers' experiences of losing a child. Over time, the blogs afforded a space for social interactions, validated quantitatively by numeric indicators, as well as qualitatively, through the interactions among the blog's readership. The intra-blog social interactions were registered in the comments section. Gradually, interactions beyond the blogs were initiated, establishing communication between authors of different blogs; in social networks, via personal profiles of the blog's author; and/or in communities and groups, with the aim of supporting other people mourning such losses. The blogs facilitated potential resources for self-expression for the constitution of a social support network and the reassumption of daily life in the context of mourning and loss.

More recently, research has addressed the topic of virtual communities on Facebook pages (Frizzo et al. 2017b) made up of groups of mothers of deceased children, where a number of mothers conduct public discussions or share feelings about the loss of a child for enough time to establish personal networks. These communities are characterized by their interactivity, permanence, and feelings of belonging. Also adopting virtual ethnography carried out in cyberspace, specifically in virtual communities on Facebook pages created by mothers of deceased children, the study investigated the virtual social interactions produced in these groups. A total of 56 such communities/pages were found. Data analysis identified five themes: mourning processes, memory and homage processes, social activism processes, self-help processes, and support processes. The research illustrated death and mourning processes in contemporary society, and how the use of ICTs can help to express such a personal and unique process like the loss of a loved one, through social interaction and creation of support networks.

There is the belief that ICTs, and particularly the quick and easy communication that they facilitate, can contribute to the reduction of inequalities in health, if supporting the promotion of health, self-care (health management), in the prevention of illnesses and in the management of disease, by accessing information on the Internet (Bertera et al. 2007). So that this occurs, it is necessary to pay attention to the quality of the information being transmitted, since it is easy to use health information resources found on the Internet, but which may not be secure (Tak and Hong 2005). It is necessary to establish indicators of website trustworthiness, alongside developing navigation abilities and competencies for searching, accessing, and using information found on the Internet, so that the information sought can be used appropriately. In order for elderly people to assess sites and the information found on them, fomenting continued learning initiatives in the use of the ICTs, which can be contextualized by the concept of lifelong learning, is also needed. The European Community memorandum on lifelong learning contains a definition of the concept (established in the context of the European Strategy for Employment) which is: "all purposeful learning activity, undertaken on an ongoing basis with the aim of improving knowledge, skills and competence" (Comissão das Comunidades Europeias 2000, 3). The broadness of this definition draws attention to the spectrum of basic categories of activities concerning learning, be it formal, nonformal, or informal, going beyond the inclusion of all phases of learning from childhood to retirement.

Lifelong learning aims toward a positive solution in the debate on unemployment in Europe and of a situation in which updating of professional knowledge becomes an imperative for all citizens. This means that, if a person wants to learn, s/he will have the conditions to do so, independently of where and when this occurs. To this end, the confluence of three factors is necessary: that the person has the predisposition for learning, that there are learning environments (centers, schools, companies, etc.) which are adequately organized, and that there are people who can help the learner in the learning process (i.e., learning agents). What should be emphasized is that learning that occurs in school or during professional life should be an extension of learning that took place in childhood or will take place in the third age. People should have the means to continue to learn, interacting with the world and receiving help from learning agents. The question therefore is: how should these learning opportunities be created so that people can construct knowledge as part of their day-to-day life, from birth extending throughout life?

Analyzing knowledge production on the theme of gerontechnology, Ogata et al. (2016) corroborate the tendencies identified in these studies on ICTs. These authors observe that gaps in studies continue, alongside a scarcity of research groups and human resources, indicating that there is still a need for training support, as well as the formation of researcher networks for advances in this area in Brazil.

8.7 ICTS and Public Policies for Ageing

The World Conference that elaborated the "International Plan of Action on Ageing," which took place in Madrid in 2002, defined central themes in its objectives, aims, and commitments. Among them are:

(a) Guarantee human rights in their entirety and fundamental freedoms for elderly people.
(b) Promote secure ageing, eliminating poverty in old age, based on the United Nations Principles in favor of elderly people.
(c) Empower elderly people so that they can participate effectively and integrally in economic, political, and social dimensions wherever they are.
(d) Guarantee access to lifelong learning, and participation in their communities, showing their heterogeneity as a group and asserting opportunities for development, personal self-fulfillment, and well-being, including individuals and groups.
(e) Elimination of any kind of violence and discrimination against elderly people, guaranteeing them economic, social, civic, political, and cultural rights.
(f) Guarantee equality between the sexes, through the elimination of gender-based discrimination.
(g) Recognize the important role of the family for social development, interdependence, solidarity, and reciprocity between the generations.
(h) Promote health aid, support, and the social protection of elderly people, including preventative health care and rehabilitation.
(i) Detect individual, social, and public health consequences of ageing, making use of scientific research and the use of technological resources, considering the differential aspects of developing countries.
(j) Observe and recognize the presence of elderly people in indigenous populations and give them an active voice in the decisions in which they are involved (WHO 2002).

Besides this, the document asserts that, to transform the plan of action into practice, collaboration between government, society, the private sector, and elderly populations will be necessary (WHO 2002). In line with the principles and guidelines of the International Plan of Action on Ageing, Brazil has laid out the National Policy of Health for Elderly Persons, through the Decree GM/MS n° 2.528, of October 19, 2006. This policy aims to reclaim, maintain, and promote the autonomy and independence of elderly people, and so the Decree lays out eleven guidelines to direct the policy, the first two of which highlight the promotion of active and healthy ageing, and integrated health care of this population (Brasil 2006). We should remember that ageing is taken to be a process that includes opportunities, participation, and safety, involving positive experiences: the concept of active ageing should be valued (WHO 2002).

With the widespread development and proliferation of ICTs at the beginning of the twentieth century, the open-access movement emerged to promote different alternatives for mainly scientific information – the basis of all scientific and technological development and advance/progress – to be freely accessible to all sectors of the population. From the Declaration of Berlin on access to knowledge in the sciences and humanities (Max Planck Open Access 2003), these concerns were at the base of many international guidelines and mobilized the political and scientific agendas in several countries. Following this movement, in Brazil, the "Brazilian Manifesto in Support of Free Access to Scientific Information" was launched in 2005. Its main aim is to promote open-access principles throughout Brazil, including support for public universities in establishing their open-access repositories (IBICT 2005).

Among the Brazilian guidelines, the Statute of Elderly Persons via Law 10.741/2003 advocates for the establishment of mechanisms that favor the dissemination of educational information on aspects related to biopsychosocial aspects of ageing and designates public authorities to create opportunities for elderly people to access education, adjusting curricula, methodologies, and didactic materials accordingly. In this context, ICTs should promote elderly people's social participation and also their protagonism by recognizing their condition as citizens as well as agents for the preservation of memory and of cultural identity (Brasil 2003).

8.8 Conclusion

This chapter is located at the crossroads of the demographic transition with scientific and technological advances. Not only is the movie protagonist Daniel Blake an emblematic subject who encapsulates and catalyzed some of the issues and reflections discussed here, but the evidence, scenarios, and contexts examined have allowed us to reflect on access and use of information and communication technologies (ICTs) in relation to content and debates on active ageing (WHO 2002) and its proximity with frameworks and debates in the area of science, technology, and society. It has been a challenging but fertile exercise, since it has allowed us to visualize potential paths and strengths, as well as weaknesses and gaps around this issue.

The growth of ICTs worldwide is also evident, revealing international tendencies of elderly people accessing them and also prioritizing knowledge production concerning ICTs through various apps, platforms, devices, in the context of ageing, and access to health information for elderly people, implying the need for initiatives around eHealth literacies. In the case of Brazil, incipient research and knowledge production that articulate ICTs with ageing populations is advancing. More efforts in constructing a public research agenda that connects institutes, professionals, and citizens are needed. ICTs and public policies on ageing have general guidelines that would be able to capitalize and have implications on local policy agendas.

Questions and issues were problematized at the beginning of this chapter, questions that renew themselves in the process and that certainly will help us to advance in this line of research: How has knowledge on the access and use of ICTs been produced, disseminated, and appropriated by people, particularly by elderly people? Which are the objective and subjective conditions of access and use of these technologies? Who accesses and how do they access these technologies? How do teaching and learning processes occur over the life course, especially from adulthood onward through formal, informal, and nonformal learning? How do public policies and public administration perform in these processes? As for professionals, workers, managers, how do they act in these scenarios and dynamics? Finally, when the subject is ageing, we can continue asking: Technologies – for what? For whom?

References

Alkema, Gretchen E., and Dawn E. Alley. 2006. Gerontology's future: An integrative model for disciplinary advancement. *The Gerontologist* 46: 574–582.

Alpay, Laurence L., Pieter J. Toussaint, Nicole P.M. Ezendam, Ton A.J.M. Rövekamp, Wilco C. Graafmans, and Rudi G.J. Westendorp. 2004. Easing Internet access of health information for elderly users. *Health Informatics Journal* 10: 185–194.

Arief, Muzawir, Nguyen Thi Thanh Hai, and Kaija Saranto. 2013. Barriers to and advantages of e-health from the perspective of elderly people: A literature review. *Finnish Journal of eHealth and eWelfare* 5: 50–56.

Azevedo, Celiana. 2017. TIC e sociedades cada vez mais envelhecidas: uma contextualização de estudos no Brasil, em Portugal e em outros países. *Verso e Reverso revista da comunicação* 31: 14–25.

Bertera, Elizabeth M., Robert L. Bertera, Russell Morgan, Ellen Wuertz, and Alfred M.O. Attey. 2007. Training older adults to access health information. *Educational Gerontology* 33: 483–500.

Bijker, Wiebe, and John Law, eds. 1994. *Shaping technology/building society: Studies in socio-technical change*. Cambridge: MIT Press.

Bijker, Wiebe, Thomas P. Hughes, and Trevor Pinch, eds. 1987. *The social construction of technological systems: New directions in the sociology and history of technology*. Cambridge: MIT Press.

Bloor, David. 1991. *Knowledge and social imagery*. Chicago: Chicago University Press.

Bouma, Herman, James L. Fozard, Don G. Bouwhuis, and Vappu Taipale. 2007. Gerontechnology in perspective. *Geron* 6: 190–216.

Brasil. Assembleia Legislativa de São Paulo. 2016. *Decreto 62.306 de 14 de dezembro de 2016. Dispõe sobre a reformulação do Programa Acessa São Paulo, reestruturado pelo Decreto n° 52.897, de 2008, e dá providências correlatas*. Diário Oficial – Poder Executivo, Seção 1, 15 dez. 2016.

Brasil. Presidência da República. Casa Civil. 2003. *Lei n° 10.741, de 1° de Outubro de 2003. Dispõe sobre o Estatuto do Idoso e dá outras providências*. Diário Oficial da União, 3 out. 2003.

Brasil. Ministério da Saúde. 2006. *Portaria GM n° 2528, de 19 de outubro de 2006. Aprova a Política nacional de Saúde da pessoa Idosa*. Diário Oficial da União, 20 out 2006.

Briggs, Asa, and Peter Burke. 2004. *Uma história social da mídia: de Gutenberg à internet*. Rio de Janeiro: Jorge Zahar.

Brodie, Mollyann, Rebecca E. Flournoy, Drew E. Altman, Robert J. Blendon, John M. Benson, and Marcus D. Rosenbaum. 2000. Health information, the Internet, and the digital divide. *Health Affairs* 19: 255–265.

Cabral, Manuel Villaverde, Pedro Moura Ferreira, Pedro Alcântara da Silva, Paula Jerónimo, and Tatiana Marques, eds. 2013. *Processos de Envelhecimento em Portugal: usos do tempo, redes sociais e condições de vida*. Lisboa: Fundação Francisco Manuel dos Santos.

Campbell, Robert J., and David A. Nolfi. 2005. Teaching elderly adults to use the internet access health care information: Before-after study. *Journal of Medical Internet Research* 7: e19.
Centro Internacional de Longevidade Brasil. 2015. *Envelhecimento ativo: um marco político em resposta à revolução da Longevidade*. Rio de Janeiro: Centro Internacional de Longevidade Brasil.
Chepe, Lucélia Moreira, and Diana Francisca Adamatti. 2015. Estudo sobre a interação de idosos em Redes Sociais Digitais. *Informática na educação: teoria & prática* 18: 177–198.
Ciampa, Antônio C. 1993. *A estória de Severino, a história de Severina: um ensaio de psicologia social*. São Paulo: Brasiliense.
CGI – Comitê Gestor da Internet no Brasil. 2017. *Survey on the use of information and communication technologies in Brazilian households: ICT households*, 2016. São Paulo: Comitê Gestor da Internet no Brasil.
Comissão das Comunidades Europeias. 2000. Memorando sobre Aprendizagem ao Longo da Vida. https://infoeuropa.eurocid.pt/files/database/000033001-000034000/000033814.pdf. Accessed 11 June 2018.
Costa, Maria Fernanda F.L., Elizabeth Uchoa, Henrique L. Guerra, Josélia O.A. Firmo, Pedro G. Vidigal, and Sandhi M. Barreto. 2000. The Bambuí health and ageing study (BHAS): Methodological approach and preliminary results of a population-based cohort study of the elderly in Brazil. *Revista de Saúde Pública* 34: 126–135.
Cotten, Shelia R., William A. Anderson, and Brandi M. McCullough. 2013. Impact of Internet use on loneliness and contact with others among older adults: Cross-sectional analysis. *Journal of Medical Internet Research* 15: e39.
Deursen, Alexander J.A.M. 2012. Internet skill-related problems in accessing online health information. *International Journal of Medical Informatics* 81: 61–72.
Doll, Johannes, Letícia Rocha Machado, and Meire Cachioni. 2011. O idoso e as novas tecnologias. In *Tratado de Geriatria e Gerontologia*, ed. Elizabete V. Freitas and Ligia Py, 1664–1671. Rio de Janeiro: Guanabara Koogan.
Etchemendy, Ernestina, Rosa María Baños, Cristina Botella, Diana Castilla, Mariano Alcañíz, Paloma Rasal, and Luis Farfallini. 2011. An e-health platform for the elderly population: The butler system. *Computers & Education* 56: 275–279.
Eysenbach, Gunther. 2001. What is e-health? *Journal of Medical Internet Research* 3: e20.
Fox, Susannah. 2004. *Older Americans and the Internet*. Washington DC: Pew Internet & American Life Project.
Frizzo, Heloisa Cristina Figueiredo, Wilson José Alves Pedro, and Regina Szylit. 2017a. Blogs: espaço de produção de interações e laços sociais frente o luto. *VI Congresso - O luto em Portugal/ I Congresso Luso-Brasileiro do Luto*, Lisboa.
Frizzo, Heloisa Cristina Figueiredo, Regina Szylit, Pedro Moura Ferreira, and Wilson José Alves Pedro. 2017b. Luto e comunidades virtuais: Interatividade das redes sociais nas páginas do Facebook. *VI Congresso - O luto em Portugal/ I Congresso Luso-Brasileiro* do Luto, Lisboa.
Fuller, Steve. 1993. *Philosophy, rhetoric, and the end of knowledge: The coming of science and technology studies*. Madison: University of Wisconsin Press.
Hirvonen, Noora, Stefan Ek, Raimo Niemelä, Raija Korpelainen, and Maija-Leena Huotari. 2015. Socio-demographic characteristics associated with the everyday health information literacy of young men. *Information Research* 20: paper 25.
Governo do Estado de São Paulo. 2017. Sobre o AcessaSP. Acessa São Paulo. http://www.acessasp.sp.gov.br/sobre-o-acessasp/. Accessed 11 June 2018.
IBGE – Brazilian Institute of Geography and Statistics. 2012. *Pesquisa Nacional por Amostra de Domicílios – 2012*. Rio de Janeiro: IBGE.
———. 2014. *Uma análise das condições de vida da população brasileira - Pesquisa Nacional de Amostra de Domicílios - 2014*. Rio de Janeiro: IBGE.
———. 2017. *Pesquisa Nacional por Amostra de Domicílios, 2017*. Rio de Janeiro: IBGE.
IBICT – Brazilian Institute of Information in Science and Technology. 2005. Manifesto brasileiro de apoio ao acesso livre da informação científica. http://livroaberto.ibict.br/Manifesto.pdf. Accessed 11 June 2018.

Irwin, Alan. 1995. *Citizen science: A study of people, expertise and sustainable development*. London: Routledge.

Jasanoff, Sheila. 2005. *Designs on nature: Science and democracy in Europe and the United States*. Princeton: Princeton University Press.

Jasanoff, Sheila, Gerald Markle, James Petersen, and Trevor Pinch, eds. 1994. *Handbook of science and technology studies*. Thousand Oaks: Sage.

Johnson, Allan G. 1997. *Dicionário de sociologia: guia prático da linguagem sociológica*. Rio de Janeiro: Jorge Zahar.

Johnson, Malcom L. 2005. *The Cambridge handbook of age and ageing*. Cambridge: Cambridge University Press.

Koopman-Boyden, Peggy G., and Sarah L. Reid. 2009. Internet/e-mail usage and Well-being among 65–84 year olds in New Zealand: Policy implications. *Educational Gerontology* 35: 990–1000.

Laganà, Luciana. 2008. Enhancing the attitudes and self-efficacy of older adults toward computers and the internet: Results of a pilot study. *Educational Gerontology* 34: 831–843.

Latour, Bruno. 1987. *Science in action: How to follow scientists and engineers through society*. Cambridge: Harvard University Press.

Leach, Melissa, Ian Scoones, and Brian Wynne, eds. 2004. *Science and citizens: Globalization and the challenge of engagement*. London: Zed Books.

Lewis, Sam, and Thilini Ariyachandra. 2010. Seniors and online social network use. In *Proceedings of the 2010 Conference on Information Systems Applied Research (CONISAR)* 3: 1522.

Loach, Ken, director. 2016. I, Daniel Blake. 101 minutes. United Kingdon, France, Belgium. Film.

MADDOX, George Lamar, SCHULZ, Richard. 1987. *The encyclopedia of aging*. Yorque: Spring, 1987.

Max Planck Open Access. 2003. Berlin declaration on open access to knowledge in the sciences and humanities. https://openaccess.mpg.de/Berlin-Declaration. Accessed 11 June 2018.

Mayr, Otto. 1982. The science-technology relationship. In *Science in context: Readings in the sociology of science*, ed. B. Barnes and D.O. Edge, 155–164. Milton Keynes: Open University Press.

Miné, Tania Zahar. 2014. De bem com a vida: idosos no Facebook. In *4° Congresso Internacional em Comunicação e Consumo*, São Paulo.

MLA – Medical Library Association. 2007. Health Information Literacy: Definitions. http://www.mlanet.org/resources/healthlit/define.html. Accessed 25 Aug 2010.

Niemelä, Raimo, Stefan Ek, Kristina Eriksson-Backa, and Maija-Leena Huotari. 2012. A screening tool for assessing everyday health information literacy. *Libri* 62: 125–134.

Norman, Cameron D., and Harvey A. Skinner. 2006. eHEALS: The eHealth literacy scale. *Journal of Medical Internet Research* 8: e27.

Nutbeam, Don. 2008. The evolving concept of health literacy. *Social Science & Medicine* 67: 2072–2078.

Ogata, Márcia Niituma, Melisa Cristina Silva, Lidia B. Anitelli, and Wilson José Alves Pedro. 2016. Research priorities agenda for the health of the elderly: Reflections from STS (Science, Technology & Society) social dimensions. *Gerontotechnology* 15: 96–97.

ONS – Office for National Statistics. 2016. Internet users in the UK. https://www.ons.gov.uk/releases/internetusersintheuk2016. Accessed 11 June 2018.

———. 2017. Internet users in the UK. https://www.ons.gov.uk/releases/internetusersintheuk2017. Accessed 11 June 2018.

Orlandi, Brunela Della Maggiori, and Wilson José Alves Pedro. 2014. Pessoas idosas e a busca por informação em saúde por meio da internet. *Revista Kairós Gerontologia* 17: 279–293.

Palacios, Eduardo Marino García, Juan Carlos González Galbarte, José Antonio López Cerezo, José Luis Luján, Mariano Martín Gordillo, Carlos Osorio, and Célida Valdés, eds. 2001. *Ciencia, Tecnología y Sociedad: una aparoximáción conceputal*. Madrid: Organización de Estados Iberoamericanos para la Educación, la Ciência y la Cultura.

Páscoa, Gina Maria Gouveia. 2012. *O contributo da web social – rede social Facebook – para a promoção do envelhecimento ativo: estudo de caso realizado na USALBI*. Lisboa: Universidade Técnica de Lisboa.

Pedro, Wilson José Alves. 2013. Reflexões sobre a promoção do envelhecimento ativo. *Revista Kairós Gerontologia* 16: 009–032.

Revista de Medicina Ribeirão Preto. 2016. I Congresso Brasileiro de Gerontotecnologia. *Revista de Medicina Ribeirão Preto* 49: supl. 2.

———. 2017. II Congresso Brasileiro de Gerontotecnologia. *Revista de Medicina Ribeirão Preto* 50: supl. 3.

Sale, Patrizio. 2018. Gerontechonology, domotics and robotics. In *Rehabilitation medicine for elderly patients*, ed. S. Masiero and U. Carrato, 161–169. Basel: Springer.

Schatzberg, Eric. 2006. Technik comes to america: Changing meanings of technology before 1930. *Technology and Culture* 47: 486–512.

Tak, Sunghee H., and Song Hee Hong. 2005. Use of the Internet for health information by older adults with arthritis. *Orthopaedic Nursing* 24: 134–138.

Watkins, Ivan, and Bo Xie. 2014. eHealth literacy interventions for older adults: A systematic review of the literature. *Journal of Medical Internet Research* 16: e225.

Whitbourne, Susan Krauss. 2008. *Adult development and aging: Biopsychosocial perspectives*. Hoboken: Wiley.

WHO – World Health Organization. 2002. *Active ageing: A policy framework*. Geneva: World Health Organization.

———. 2017. *Global Health Observatory (GHO) data: Life expectancy*. http://www.who.int/gho/mortality_burden_disease/life_tables/situation_trends/en/. Accessed 11 June 2018.

Chapter 9
Health in the Social Network: An Exploratory Study of the Fan Page "*Melhor com Saúde*" ("Better with Health")

Denise Cristina Ayres Gomes

Abstract This study aims to understand the symbolic dimension of health in the digital environment. We conducted an exploratory study of the fan page "*Melhor com Saúde*" ("Better with Health") that has 8.5 million followers on Facebook. We selected the two most commented posts, described the content, and analyzed the first 50 comments for each. We used content analysis by thematic category proposed by Bardin (*Análise de conteúdo*. Edições, Lisboa, 2004). The fan page focuses on daily issues that tend to affect the body and spiritual balance. Based on an analysis of the most commented posts, we can observe how digital social media reconfigure the meaning of health. The topic expands in the social realm, creating a network of solidarity around new thematic ideas. Today, health becomes associated with well-being and the hedonistic enjoyment of life. Going beyond modern sense of rationality, it encompasses an ethos that is aesthetic, circumstantial, erected, and shared through a communication network.

9.1 Introduction[1]

The development of means of communication and networked capillarization has radically changed the way we live. The Internet has become an integral device of postmodern sociability, operating as a privileged space for the social production of meaning. The virtual age allows instantaneous, continuous, and interactive communication that affects our ways of being, acting, feeling, and suffering. In other words, it establishes subjectivity, social practices, and the very definitions of reality. This new way of being/existing in the world is called postmodernity.

[1]This research is financed by the Maranhão Foundation to Support Research and Scientific and Technological (FAPEMA); Maranhão State Secretary for Science, Technology, and Innovation (SECTI); and the State Government of Maranhão.

D. C. A. Gomes (✉)
Social Sciences, Health and Technology Center, Federal University of Maranhão, Imperatriz, Brazil

A. Pereira Neto, M. B. Flynn (eds.), *The Internet and Health in Brazil*,
https://doi.org/10.1007/978-3-319-99289-1_9

The modern imaginary, based on totalizing schemes, has now given way to relativism and paradox. Instead of an absolute truth, there are now several possible interpretations for a given phenomenon. The truth is put into perspective. We live the failure of metanarratives (Lyotard 2011), in which the explanatory schemes of reality lose their legitimizing and universalizing appeal and are replaced by volatile and relative concepts and references.

Science itself is a metanarrative and questionable, resulting from a historical-cultural process. "To put it simply to the extreme, disbelief over meta-narratives is considered 'postmodern.' It is undoubtedly an effect of the progress of sciences; but this progress, in turn, supposes it" (Lyotard 2011, XVI). The saturation of the rational and mechanical model provokes a return to a transcendental approach to the world, a return to the supernatural. This implies considering the divine not as a transcendent being, but permeating all things, a kind of "natural mystique." "Today's culture, first of all, projects into the divine its weak epistemology, which is made of the crisis of science and the rational world in general [...]" (Terrin 1996, 75).

The networked communicative model is typical of postmodernity, in which social actors interact in a decentralized way. The Internet modifies what we traditionally understand by public and private spheres. Intimate aspects are exposed in society and arouse people's interest. We participate in a "confessional society" (Bauman 2013), where exteriorizing intimacy produces collective recognition.

The private sphere invades and dominates the public arena, acting on our ways of being. Continued and excessive life exposure is a means of becoming visible, achieving social existence. In this confessional society, the public interest turns to particular and atomized stories that feed daily conversations. The struggle for equality and collective action gives way to the primacy of individuals and searches for self-affirmation.

Again, according to the author (Bauman 2013), the media society transforms the traditional concept of community, where individuals have affective ties and belonging. Today's community has weak and ephemeral relations and disputes the economy of attention, sharing some transient interest that is soon replaced by another. Individuals have the urge to connect and disconnect without restraint or compromise. The temporary nature of communities allows people to change their minds, leave a group, and contact people without commitments or substantial losses.

Transient relationships can be understood from the emergence of a new emotional sensitivity (Maffesoli 1995, 2018). Postmodernity experiences the mutation of the concept of the individual, an identity linked fundamentally to work, and provides the return of the feeling of belonging to a group and to a place. Emotions impel us to intensified communion because of easy connections between people.

According to Maffesoli, we appreciate the roles each person represents in the group. We live in the times of tribes, groups of empathic, organic origin and driven by the need to live in the now. Postmodernity restores the importance of shared affections, experiences, and emotions capable of aggregating people, myths, and other narratives that transcend the purely rational and utilitarian realm. The environment now constituted points to instability, the preeminence of the emotional domain, and the transience of relationships. Life is not woven by great shocks and achievements but, based on the trivial, on the evidence of daily life.

The postmodern environment, made up of the synergy between old and cutting-edge technology (Maffesoli 1995, 2018), reconfigures the individual and collective realms. The concept of health becomes increasingly symbolic, unstable, tied to the moods of the market, reappropriated, and continuously shared by social stakeholders. Being or feeling healthy concerns not only the individual sphere but acquires a collective dimension when shared through the network (Gomes 2017). Cyberspace extends the symbolic realm because it expands our mental potentiality and connects us with the other (Davis 2015).

The virtual space or cyberspace (Lévy 1995) has become the primary catalyst of the contemporary health imaginary, driving beliefs, values, myths, rituals, and desires. Online media promotes easy and abundant access to knowledge. Multiple health-related issues translate the pervasive character of this topic in postmodernity. As Le Breton (2013) points out, health mobilizes society, becoming the new religion, resulting from intimate aspirations, discourses, and collective investments. Being healthy amounts to a categorical imperative, a code indicating effective self-management.

The fan page of the magazine "*Melhor com Saúde*" is symptomatic of the postmodern ambiance. The webpage engages more than 8.5 million followers on Facebook,[2] making it the largest Brazilian community with the word "health" in the title. Users enjoy the fan page and become part of a group that not only receives content but interacts through the like, share, and comment tools. The webpage is a platform for interaction and conversation, a symptom of postmodern sociability.

This study aims to understand the symbolic realm of health in the digital environment. We start from the following research questions: Which focus on health most attracts the interest of Internet users in the fan page? What are the positions of web users vis-à-vis the fan page posts? Research is essential to understand the health imaginary in postmodernity. Herein, meanings are reconfigured, reappropriated, and tend to modulate practices, worldviews, values, and behaviors.

9.2 Methods and Techniques

This research is an exploratory study of a qualitative nature that aims to identify explanatory hypotheses to understand the notion of health shown on the fan page "*Melhor com Saúde*" and the views of netizens on the topic, based on the comments posted on the page.

> Exploratory research, as the name suggests, is often conducted to explore the research issue and is usually done when the alternative options have not been clearly defined or their scope is unclear. (Singh 2007, 63)

[2] Chapter 6 addresses the issue of Facebook and the "expert patient."

The fan page was selected through a Facebook search with the Portuguese word "*saúde*" ("health"). We noted that the page has 8.5 million likes, well above other pages listed by the search engine, thus our interest of studying the phenomenon to understand the reason why so many people gather around this fan page. As an initial approach to the event, the study does not pretend to be exhaustive. Additional research should further analyze the subject.

The "*Melhor com Saúde*" page has 8.5 million followers. Between January 1 and March 1, 2018, we used the digital extraction tool Netvizz to collect Facebook data about postings and comments on the fan page.

To understand the notion of health on the "*Melhor com Saúde*" page and what generated the most interest in online discussions, we selected the two posts with the highest number of comments. These are the video entitled "Being left-handed is a privilege" with 18,842 hits, followed by the video titled "Tequila has an interesting slimming effect" with 6815 comments. Both aroused the interest of followers who engaged in conversations about these topics.

We described the videos' content and reviewed the first 50 comments for each of the posts. To verify the position of Internet users who commented on the content displayed in the videos, we used content analysis organized by topic categories as proposed by Bardin (2004). The technique consists of classifying a set of elements through a process of differentiation and regrouping them by analogy based on predefined criteria. We stipulated two categories for comments, "agree" and "disagree" with the content of the video. Because it is a qualitative research, we chose not to quantify the observations according to these categories. We also did not establish typologies, because we wanted to identify whether or not there was agreement with the posted issues.

9.3 Health Imaginary in Postmodernity

Since the mid-twentieth century, a new sensitivity that expresses the saturation of modern values has emerged. The concept of health, developed by the World Health Organization (WHO), expresses this modified understanding of the topic.[3] For the first time, a consensus among several countries sought to define what it is to be/feel healthy. Until then, diseases were the concern, finding a cure or alleviation of sickness. As such, the WHO Charter defines health as "[…] a state of complete physical, mental and social well-being, and not merely the absence of disease and infirmity…" (WHO 1946, 1).

Although the definition has been criticized as being an unreachable condition and of difficult objectification, we understand the concept of health as a symptom of a transformation of sensibility that was already outlined in the middle of the twentieth century and is enhanced by the advent of new information and communication technologies from the 1980s onward. Accordingly, the mechanistic

[3] Chapter 19 discusses the issue of ICTs and health promotion.

of health view has thus given way to a holistic conception, which implies equilibrium with the environment.

> [...] at the end of the century, we witness a return of the so-called spiritual vision; a vision that grows ever wider until it leads to a crisis in the institutional apparatus that gained unprecedented fame and prestige in the name of accuracy, experimentation, verification, and many results that have been achieved. (Terrin 1996, 186)

This postmodernity entails a return to the transcendent, the organic union provided by cutting-edge technology. It is the recognition of affective and elective groups, the so-called tribes (Maffesoli 1995, 2018), in which the individual subscribes to a collective whole. The individual body, therefore, is a tributary of the community.

Postmodernity surpasses the rational sphere and enhances myths and transcendences. We understand health as a symbolic phenomenon that integrates the social, the imaginary that is configured from the relentless flow of information disseminated and shared in a network. The imaginary is, thus, an atmosphere, a mental construct that binds people, an involving aura.

The imaginary precedes the individual; he/she modifies it. It is something rational and irrational and comprises the playful, dreamlike, affective, and symbolic realms. Such spheres mobilize individuals around common feelings and values, establishing "a true spiritual infrastructure, ensuring the principles and foundation of all life in society" (Maffesoli 2016, 13).

Social networking sites are symptomatic of a new way of being/existing in the world called postmodernity. Ties tend to be established by empathy, affinities, and willingness to share and collaborate. In other words, it is an "emotional pact," which we call tribalism (Maffesoli 1995, 2018). Linkages happen deliberately and circumstantially, so they are ephemeral and can break up at any time.

> This tribalism is no longer an exception, but a daily reality. Social networks are helping; everything is done to share various and diverse tastes: sexual, religious, sports, musical, cultural, and dietary. The marketing of tribes has become inescapably evident. (Maffesoli 2018, 191)

The conceptions of health are revealed in narratives shared on the Internet. The discourse conveyed on a fan page promotes interaction, creates bonds, and makes ordinary different ways of being. Information opens up to a multiplicity of meanings that exceeds the intellectual sphere, awakens sensations, and acts upon daily life.

The media modulate the contemporary experience of health, intervene in ways of addressing the phenomenon, and modify personal propensity and decisions. Cyberspace is a repository and stimulator of beliefs, values, myths, rituals, and aspirations. Virtual space has a spiritual realm because it enhances the symbolic and connects us to the other.

> Because cyberspace embodies and extends our symbol-making minds, it can mediate these sacred communications with each other, as well as with the entities–the divine parts of ourselves–that we invoke in that space. (Davis 2015, 202)

Health includes the typical unstable, ephemeral, conflicting, paradoxical, and dynamic atmosphere of postmodernity. Sharing experiences, moods, aspirations, feelings, and viewpoints in a digital social network produces an environment that mobilizes people and reconfigures the ways of being and feeling healthy.

9.4 Social Network Websites and the "Melhor Com Saúde" Fan Page

The advent of the Internet has brought about profound changes in society. Communicative flows have become capillary and interactive, modifying the traditional structure of the process that polarized emitter and receiver. The network provides a dynamic, continuous, and abundant exchange of information. It is estimated that around 58% of Internet users consult health-related issues on the web (Atkinson et al. 2009). This percentage is equivalent to about 6.75 million daily search sessions on the subject (Eysenbach and Kohler 2003), highlighting the centrality of health in daily life. The current numbers tend to be much more significant considering the advent of Facebook and expanded access to the network. New technologies transform our perception of reality and the way we relate.

Virtual social networks are human clusters set in the digital sphere that change with the mediation of communication-enabling technologies and tools. The network consists of actors, that is, people, organizations, or groups and their connections (Recuero 2012). Social networks are places where connections are established through shared information, whether through texts, pictures, videos, and memes, among others.

Increased access to the Internet has given rise to new practices that have been incorporated into people's daily lives, such as the abundant provision of data and conversations on social networking websites. These platforms enable users to manifest, produce, and share knowledge of interest to them. The network model overcomes the traditional rationale of information consumption, typical of mass media. The one-way hierarchical system, which polarized sender and receiver, gives way to a capillary and interactive mode, in which the surfer is capable of producing and consuming information.

By tracking information and conversational practices that circulate in these virtual spaces, we can understand the behaviors, interests, and feelings of human groups, that is, the social network denotes aspects of the sociocultural model in which we are inserted. Geographical, linguistic, and time boundaries have been broken, inaugurating dynamics in the communicative process that interfere with our perception of reality.

The statistics are indicative of how the digital social network has been incorporated into daily life, establishing new patterns of interaction that modify the way we relate. Almost half of the world's population is an active user of social networking sites, equivalent to 3.297 billion people, according to a report released in April 2018 by the *We are social* agency and the *Hootsuite* platform that analyze digital behavior. Facebook is the most popular social networking site in the world, with 2.234 billion users. Created in 2004, Facebook is the second most prolific traffic-generating website on the Internet, lagging behind Google's search engine (We Are Social Agency and Hootsuite 2018).

Facebook is an example of how the social network can create new dynamics, attracting the interest of more than 2 billion users who are willing to interact and share information. Surveys indicate that Brazilians spend 9 h a day surfing the Internet and are ranked third in the world. Brazil is featured in social networks with about 3 h of time spent on a daily basis. Facebook is the second most accessed social network in the country, lagging behind YouTube. One hundred thirty million Brazilians are connected to the social network and spend an average 13 min and 28 s per visit. They are the fourth most significant group of Facebook users in the world, behind India, the United States, and Indonesia (We Are Social Agency and Hootsuite 2018).

Numbers reveal the importance of this social network as a tool for sharing information, that is, an environment that provides interaction and generates dynamics that end up reconfiguring its uses. Conversation is one of Facebook's appropriations. Through new conventions and meanings created by users, the discursive practices among posters acquire their own shape (Recuero 2014).

If dialogue requires the attention of two or more interlocutors who interact verbally, in cyberspace, conversational practice consists in the appropriation of tools that establish new ways of communicating. As Recuero (2014) points out, the computer-mediated conversation is an adaptation of oral interaction to textual tools, whether synchronously, while speakers are connected at the same time, or asynchronously, when disconnected.

Social networking websites are platforms that allow for conversation. Personal profiles work as individual extensions, an extra presence that integrates the identity (Santaella 2013) and is expanded in the network. Facebook is one of the websites that has most influenced the Internet because it generates inter-profile connections. However, these linkages are less complicated, and the primary goal of social networking is the circulation of information (Recuero 2014).

Facebook tools allow users to create bonds that remain even when users are offline. Adding profiles or "friends" allows you to access a "friend's" published content on the network. Conversation, therefore, acquires a pervasive, public dimension, broadens in the social, and is capable of generating debates that interfere with peoples' opinions. This phenomenon is called network conversations (Recuero 2012).

Web-circulating content has characteristics that differ from face-to-face conversations. According to boyd[4,5,6] (2011), dialogue among networked audiences carries attributes of persistence, replicability, scalability, and searchability. Persistence is the characteristic of being extensible and occurs because knowledge is automati-

[4]The author writes her own name in lowercase.

[5]Data refer to May 2018.

[6]The Pinterest social network uses the letter "K" to indicate the number of thousand followers. Thus, as the site points out, there are 1.32 k followers in May 2018.

cally recorded and archived, acquiring breadth in the public space. Replicability consists of duplicating a message. “In the world of bits, there is no way to differentiate the original bit from its duplicate” (boyd 2011, 47). Scalability concerns the excellent potential for visibility of networked content, though it does not guarantee an audience. Finally, searchability is easy access to data provided by search engines.

The characteristics of online conversations involve dynamics that modify the way we establish social bonds and perceive reality. As Rheingold (1996, 28) points out, computer-mediated communication has the potential to change our lives because

> we will have perceptions, thoughts, and personalities (already formed by other communication technologies) that are affected by the way we use the medium and the way in which it uses us.

Thus, social networking sites have become strategic spaces for corporations to keep in touch with the public and influence consumer habits. It is possible to modify behaviors and to disseminate information, either through editorial content or advertising.

The *Melhor com Saúde* magazine fan page[7] is an example of the strategic use of information to engage users. It has 8.5 million followers on Facebook and is the webpage with the largest number of followers in Brazil that contains the word “health” in its title. Although there is no printed magazine associated with the site, the posts refer mainly to the homonymous virtual page, which is defined as a “blog about good habits and care for your health.”[8]

The blog provides free information on health but also operates as a vehicle for countless advertisements, including sponsored research, airline advertisements, clothes, and contact lenses, among others. *Melhor com Saúde* is also found in the following social networks: Google+, with 32,394 followers[9]; YouTube, with 9.4 thousand subscribers in its channel; and *Pinterest*, with 1.32 thousand followers.[10] Data indicates that the fan page generates significant user interest, while the other social networks are not as attractive. This is why studying the Facebook page and checking the Internet users’ perspectives vis-à-vis the subjects posted is important. Other studies may address other social networks and make further comparisons.

The blog’s content is geared to a female audience and divided into seven sections: *Good Habits*, *Natural Medicine*, *Curiosities*, *Beauty*, *Recipes*, *Weight Loss*, and *Sex and Relationships*. Health is based on the notion of well-being. The texts often use a pseudoscientific basis to support claims and offer credibility to what is promised in the title. The so-called journalistic approach reiterates the plausibility of narratives. Thus, the alleged promise of youth, bodily vigor, beauty, emotional and ecological balance, good relationships, nurturing spirituality, satisfying sex, and optimistic view toward life make up the health imaginary in postmodernity.

---

[7] “Melhor com Saúde” Facebook: https://www.facebook.com/melhorcomsaude

[8] “Melhor com Saúde” virtual page: https://melhorcomsaude.com.br/

[9] Data refer to May 2018.

[10] Data refer to May 2018.

We observe the mystical tone in some approaches that the condition of being healthy is related to spirituality. Illness, therefore, would be the result of a conflict with the world, and negative feelings would contribute to the occurrence of evils. Such a view, according to Terrin (1996, 185), would approach the shamanic conception in which health is a holistic fact, "it is the well-being of body and spirit in a balance between the forces of nature and spiritual forces [...]".

Dietetics is spread not only in the blogs' ads whose commercial appeal is notorious but in the dissemination of a lifestyle through the narratives posted online. The texts adopt a journalistic tone, although they lack clear and precise sources and data crucial to fact-based reporting. People seek information and advice about a quality and pleasurable life without the more significant concern of checking references or establishing the truth about the facts.

Digital media becomes effective because it divulges content in a continuous, replicable, insinuating, and playful way. Individuals, however, end up being accountable for the self-management of their bodies, emotions, and behaviors. These "welfare techniques" (Lipovetsky 2015) aim to provide the sensation of physical and psychic balance, modeling daily life in a seductive and pedagogical way. Before the whirlwind of information available on the network, it is necessary to approach, guide, and stimulate the reader to consume information.

The intense and continuous connection goes beyond the utilitarian nature of the information provided. The network empowers emotional attachment, restoring the importance of shared affections, experiences, and emotions that gather people, myths, and other narratives that transcend the purely rational realm. The newly established environment points to instability and urgency of the emotional and spiritual side. As Lyotard (2011) proposed, postmodernity is characterized by collapsing metanarratives, and science loses its primacy as legitimizing reality. Hence, there is the need for organic linkages, as a way to overcome modern mechanism: "[...] the rediscovery of the mystical world is a need for us not to be in the stifling world of computers and calculus at any cost. [...]" (Terrin 1996, 70).

Some data deserve attention concerning the fan page. In total, 8,670,115 people "liked" and 8,546,814 profiles are "following" the page.[11] These data justify the importance of studying *Melhor com Saúde* and verifying the stance of netizens vis-à-vis the subject matter posted online. Next, we highlight the videos that had the highest number of "likes" and "shares."

9.5 Videos of the Fan Page

We note that among the ten most commented posts, including sentences, texts, and videos, only one directly addresses the topic of disease, and it is titled: "Although facial paralysis may occur without being especially severe." The other posts refer to health only as it is related to the notion of well-being, such as nutrition and weight

[11] Data refer to May 2018.

loss. Other posts concern a holistic approach to health, such as attachment to spirituality and divine punishment, and issues such as the importance of nephews, calming a baby, and sleeping naked. Thus, we can observe that the topic of health acquires a pervasive dimension, associating itself with many daily issues and approaches that tend to attract attention due to the curiosity they trigger or the motivational and even mystical tone that they manifest.

Our study found that the fan page had 420 posts in the period from January 1 to March 1, 2018. We selected the two posts with the highest number of comments associated with the following videos: "Being left-handed is a privilege" with 18,842 comments and "Tequila has an interesting slimming effect," which obtained 6815 comments. We chose the first 50 comments from each video to perform categorical content analysis and analyze the views of users on the subjects posted.

The first post is a 41-s animation video[12] that addresses the difficulties of being left-handed, such as bullying suffered at school and maladjustment to some objects. The narrative states that many children are forced to use their right hand, are the subject of mockery, and feel left out at school because of the lack of left-handed objects and tools. The video states the following:

> Lefties are a minority in the population, and many children are required to use the right hand. They are subjects of jokes at schools and feel excluded because of the lack of objects and tools designed for them. However, one should not feel inferior for being left-handed … According to a study from St. Lawrence University, left-handed people are smarter than right-handed because their brain connections are faster and more sensitive. Also, they can generate ideas more quickly and effectively thanks to "divergent thinking." And they are less likely to suffer from Alzheimer's, ulcers, and arthritis. Feel happy to be left-handed!

The post refers to a study conducted by Alan Searleman and released at the annual conference of the American Psychological Association in 2000. According to an interview with the researcher: "Left-handed people have a more 'fluid' intelligence and better vocabulary than most of the population. Perhaps that is why there are more of them in creative professions like music, art, and writing" (Norton 2000). While the issue is quite controversial, the video is assertive in highlighting the qualities attributed to left-handed people.

The second post is a video titled "Tequila has an interesting slimming effect"[13] which received 6815 comments. The 51-s video shows pictures of people drinking at a bar and starts with the sentence "Tequila is so much more than something fun to drink with friends." The video claims that the American Chemical Society had conducted some experiments to find out how tequila could help people lose weight. The drink would slow down food digestion, thereby increasing the feeling of satiety and reducing appetite. The video says tequila comes from agave, a plant with nondigestible sugars that would lower blood glucose levels and help produce insulin. The drink could benefit people with diabetes since it is natural insulin. The video ends with the phrase: "Drinking is not always bad!"

[12] The video is available at https://www.facebook.com/melhorcomsaude/videos/768892306633606/

[13] The video is available at https://www.facebook.com/melhorcomsaude/videos/784733135049523/

The experiments mentioned in the video are summarized in a survey announced at the 247th National Meeting of the American Chemical Society and held by the Center for Research and Advanced Studies, Biotechnology and Biochemistry, Irapuato, Mexico. The study, released to the media (ACS 2014), includes a sweetener created from the plant used to make tequila, namely, agave, which could reduce glucose levels. The research does not discuss tequila, but the natural sweetener agavin that originates from the same plant used to produce the distilled drink. However, according to the researcher responsible for the study, this element is not found in tequila because it is converted into ethanol.

We note that the video posted on the page is not committed publishing results from scientific research; it only seizes the opportunity to produce easily assimilated content. It causes a stir because it focuses on a supposed benefit of an alcoholic beverage, contrary to commonly associated information that alcohol is harmful to health. According to the World Health Organization (WHO 2014), alcohol abuse has led to 3.3 million deaths worldwide in 2012 and cause more than 200 conditions of disease and injury.

9.6 Fan Page Comments

The video "Being left-handed is a privilege"[14] yielded 18,842 comments, and probably this interest was due to the social stigma that left laterality entails. The left-handed condition is historically devalued, associated with negative connotations, and viewed as sinister, awkward, and even related to the devil and witchcraft. According to McManus (2002), tradition relates the right-handedness to doing things, order, and significant achievements, while the left hand is just auxiliary, playing only a supportive role. In different cultures, the left hand is used for hygiene after defecation, and the right hand is used to take food to the mouth. Although prejudice toward them has declined, many left-handers have suffered discrimination or know stories of people who have experienced such discrimination.

Content analysis, in which we define the categories "agree" and "disagree" to check participant's views vis-à-vis the video, reveals that comments tend to agree with the content posted on the fan page. People comment on the advantages of being left-handed and prejudice they have experienced or witnessed. The benefits refer to the qualities associated with left-handedness, such as intelligence, privilege, and the sense of pride of this condition. "You must be smarter than her children. Certainly. Feel privileged." "I'm left-handed and my brother too, but I never had any problems because of that... We make a difference! Simple as that",[15] someone states in one of the comments.

[14] Video available at https://www.facebook.com/melhorcomsaude/videos/768892306633606/

[15] We reproduced the fan page comments as they were written, keeping the errors. As Recuero (2012) defines, it is a "verbalized" writing, the informal use of language adapted to use in social networks.

> I always suspected that left-handers were quicker in reasoning and problem-solving! When I was little, my father and mother tried to change me! They said I would suffer a lot in life, that the world was made for righties! In my mind, I always saw myself different from the others! Everyone in my room is right-handed and I'm the only left-handed! Once I even tried to change! I'm a very happy left-handed! We are a minority! We were selected! Today, I think it's beautiful to be left-handed! I'm a left-handed dentist with lots of love and pride!

Most of the comments highlight the prejudice faced by left-handers and relate to the experiences of Internet users, especially in childhood, as demonstrated in the video. Some comments address the stigma associated with the condition: "I am left-handed, and in my childhood they said that left-handed people were sorcerers (laughing)"; "My mother also had an ignorance similar to yours, but vis-à-vis her father. He said she was disabled for being left-handed! She was also a seamstress and is extremely intelligent!"

> I went through the same situation, but my mother had this thought that being left-handed was against God. I had to learn to write with the right hand, but I do the rest of the things with my left hand. I joke by saying that she confused my head as I don't even know whether I'm right-handed or left-handed anymore.

The vast majority of accounts mention abuse committed by teachers that forced students to be right-handed. "I also endured this situation, I was spanked, so I stayed three years in first grade…":

> My teacher forced me to write with my right hand … As a result, I am ambidextrous… I have both skills … I suffered a lot … I was punished with my nose on the wall behind the door in the classroom. My 5-year-old granddaughter is left-handed … and if I come to know that someone forced her to be otherwise… the brain is the boss… we have to let nature do her part and not force what is not meant to be…
>
> I also had a problem with a teacher because, in the beginning, my writing was very curved and I was tilted to the side and he thought I was cheating. That was in eighth grade, and he said I'm going to deduct half a point because you were cheating. So I scored 9.5 in mathematics and today I am a math teacher (laughing).

Some comments respond to the previous comment that mentions abusive experiences; they criticize and even mock the attitude of educators: "This teacher only had to study more"; "This teacher was crazy"; "Was she not the daughter of the devil instead?"; "Was she a teacher? Because to say that, not even I, as a child, think that. Crazy teacher."

Some comments refer to the difficulties faced in everyday life, for example, can openers and students' cards for left-handed people, forcing them to adapt to the world of right-handers. "I trained and I learned to use the opener with my right hand!"; "My buddy, I've been training at home and I'm good at it today. But, it was awful not to have a student card for lefties, and even today, when I do some exam, I go through this hassle."

The theme of the can opener elicited countless comments. Some use humor, as evidenced by the laugh: "(laughing), I'm left-handed, but I can open with both, it's a matter of training"; "(Laughing) I've already bent a lot! But then I found a big one of stainless steel! Beware of my strength (laughing)"; "I've never been able to open a can either…."

From the analysis of the first 50 comments, we observe that there is a tendency to reiterate the content of the video, that is, an agreement with the prejudice that left-handers face. The video urged netizens to recount their experiences of abuse. The reports drew comments from other members of the fan page, and some individuals' profiles were tagged to join the discussion. There is no disagreement with the post's fan page approach so that all comments can be listed in the "agree" category.

Reports about suffering tend to encourage other comments that share experiences of pain and, at the same time, empathetic statements that seek to be in solidarity with sufferers. Personal experiences are shared in the virtual space to attract the attention of Internet users who, synergistically, propose to comment. As Bauman (2013) points out, individual and atomized stories dominate the public space to the point of changing the boundaries between the public and private spheres.

The video "Tequila has an interesting slimming effect"[16] generated 6815 comments. From the analysis of category-related content performed in the first 50 comments, we have identified that most seem to agree with the content published. Some of them consider the benefits of the drink and take on a playful tone, referring to the numerous effects of alcohol.

Few comments seem to disagree with the content conveyed or are unrelated to the established conversation. The first one concerns the negative effects of tequila and adopts a joking tone: "My liver did not 'like' it… (smiling)." The following comment is a replica: "Much less mine"; and the third reiterates the statement: "That is true." The fourth review ruled out the possibility of drinking the tequila: "I was so happy, but I do not 'like' tequila, so I am only left with going on a diet…."

The following comment warns about alcoholism:

> And you may get addicted to other drugs, as well! People usually say that alcohol is not a drug! To make things worse, some people take some time to feel sick. In the first place, it upsets so much that the family gets sick instead!

The reply corroborates this comment, conceiving it as close to the real evil effects of alcohol. "I think this comment is more realistic […] (laughing)." One profile comments ironically: "[…] Of course, you lose weight… you just need to throw up your liver… and then you feel satiated…I'm joking… you feel sick and therefore you do not eat" (laughing). Another comment deviates from the context of the discussion but seems to disapprove of the tone of the conversation: "You cannot mock God, drink your *cachaça* and go to hell alone."[17]

Aside from the comments noted, the others tend to agree with the content of the video. They discuss the benefits or taste of the drink and weave in considerations about the excesses of alcohol consumption. "I love tequila! It's my favorite drink, but I've never felt sick. I've never even had a hangover. Isn't the problem excess?"; "But lady, you have to drink moderately and not fill the tank"; "I love the normal

[16] Video available at https://www.facebook.com/melhorcomsaude/videos/784733135049523/

[17] *Cachaça* is Brazil's most commonly drunk hard liquor and distilled from sugarcane.

way I drink [...]. It doesn't do any good for anyone. They said moderately, and I drink without moderation."

> You are wrong [...]. I drink because I like it, I appreciate it. I have never thrown up and I do not feel full, I know I drink a lot and I love it. Just one thing, I'm not sleeping and I don't even know why. But I don't give a damn; I keep on drinking.

The following comment gives a recipe on how not to get sick:

> Damn it! (laughing), is the only drink that doesn't hurt me. Of course, there are tequilas and tequilas... But I love it! I drink water in between if I drink more than two servings and I do not mix with anything else... And to play it safe, take Engov.

The video seems to promote alcohol intake by highlighting the supposed benefits of drinking, which we observe in the following comments: "Look [...] my desire to try this drink was my sixth sense telling me that there would be something good about it... (laughing)"; "[...] I always say that tequila helps to lose weight, let's organize and have some drinks, people"; "All right, ladies, I was drinking the wrong drink. Beer and sparkling wine? Never again. Just tequila, margaritas, mojito now (laughing)! Do you agree?"; "Look at the excuse to drink... Tequila: It makes you lose weight and is good for people with diabetes, not to mention that it's fun to be drunk! Let's do it [...]."

> Watch this [...]. After the benefits of wine, now its tequila's turn for its slimming properties. I've been thinking and have concluded that I'm going to get drunk instead of getting fit.

Many comments mark profiles so they can participate in the conversation. The posts of the profiles tend to reiterate the video posted on the page playfully. Few comments criticize or relativize the statements posted by fan page. The humorous tone reveals the ludic environment that is established on social networking sites, where the dynamics of relationships occurs from uncompromising, emotional, and empathic sharing.

9.7 Final Considerations

Disease is not the primary focus of the "*Melhor com Saúde*" fan page, but daily life issues that may affect body and spiritual balance. The themes arouse netizens' interest because they carry the promise of well-being, enhance the enjoyment of life, motivate, amuse, and still foment discussions that tend to generate a network of solidarity in relation to the subject matter.

By researching the most commented posts, we can infer how digital media reconfigures health. The subject – traditionally restricted to the scientific realm, to the doctor-patient relationship, or to the family sphere, among others – now transcends the private sphere and expands socially. Thus, interactions and practices create an atmosphere around the notion of health and tend to transform the ways of being/existing in the world.

We understand the new approach to health as a symptom of postmodernity, in which the crisis of metanarratives, as Lyotard (2011) pointed out, appropriates pseudoscientific knowledge to attract the attention of Internet users and impacts them. The synergy between the archaic (i.e., the feeling of belonging to a group) associated with the Internet (Maffesoli 1995, 2018) enables the organic amplification of experiences narrated in online comments. This creates a network of solidarity around topical themes without there being a definitive objective or concern with the truth of shared information. People participate with their comments, narrate experiences, and gain visibility in the social space.

Posts made by the fan page's administrators reveal their disinterest to correct published information since they refer to scientific research in a decontextualized and imprecise way. The first objective seems to be the production of engaging content in order to maintain website traffic and the consequent participation of netizens. A large number of posts in the period studied indicate an abundance of knowledge in circulation. People seem to seek information and advice on living well and pleasurably. The social networking site becomes effective because it disseminates content in a continuous, replicable, insinuating, and playful way.

The high number of comments reveals the aggregative character of the fan page. Contributors tend to comment on posts nonchalantly, establishing ephemeral links and natural conversations without a definite goal. This type of "emotional pact" (Maffesoli 1995, 2018) is characteristic of postmodern sociability, in which bonds are established through empathy but are revocable at any moment.

Most comments tend to agree with posts and reiterate the content, narrating experiences on the subject. In the case of the video about tequila, some comments disagreed with the content, warning readers about the harm derived from drinking. However, there is no post that questions whether the information conveyed in the post is correct. This phenomenon provides evidence about the emotional and ephemeral character of online manifestations that end up disinterested in the scientific validity of posts.

The reports assume a confessional nature (Bauman 2013) in narrating experiences, mobilizing other netizens to share experiences and opinions on the subject. The Internet becomes a kind of "magical" device, focusing on revelations capable of impacting readers, mitigating their concerns, and creating an ambiance that takes them beyond their immediate reality. Health would be associated with well-being and the hedonistic enjoyment of life. Beyond the rational, it is an ethos that is aesthetic, circumstantial, erected, and shared through network communication.

References

ACS – American Chemical Society. 2014. Tequila plant is possible sweetener for diabetics – helps reduce blood sugar, weight. https://www.acs.org/content/acs/en/pressroom/newsreleases/2014/march/tequila-plant-is-possible-sweetener-for-diabetics-helps-reduce-blood-sugar-weight.html. Accessed 7 Apr 2018.

Atkinson, Nancy L., Sandra L. Saperstein, and John Pleis. 2009. Using the internet for health-related activities: findings from a national probability sample. *Journal of Medical Internet Research* 11: e4. https://doi.org/10.2196/jmir.1035.

Bardin, Laurence. 2004. *Análise de conteúdo*. Lisboa: Edições 70.

Bauman, Zygmunt. 2013. *Vida a crédito*. Rio de Janeiro: Zahar.

boyd, danah. 2011. Social network sites as networked publics: affordances, dynamics, and implications. In *A networked self: identity, community, and culture on social network sites*, ed. Zizi Papacharissi, 39–58. New York: Routledge.

Davis, Erik. 2015. *Techgnosis: myth, magic and mysticism in the age of information*. Berkeley: North Atlantic Books.

Eysenbach, Gunther, and Georges Kohler. 2003. What is the prevalence of health-related searches on the World Wide Web? Qualitative and quantitative analysis of search engine queries on the internet. *AMIA Symposium Proceedings* 2003: 225–229.

Gomes, Denise Cristina Ayres. 2017. A saúde imaginada: jornalismo e imaginário do risco. *Intexto*. https://doi.org/10.19132/1807-8583201740.133-151

Le Breton, David. 2013. *L'adieu au corps: antropologie et société*. Paris: Editions Métailié.

Lévy, Pierre. 1995. *Qu'est-ce que le virtuel?* Paris: La Découverte.

Lipovetsky, Gilles. 2015. *De la légèreté*. Paris: Grasset.

Lyotard, Jean-François. 2011. *A condição pós-moderna*. Rio de Janeiro: José Olympio.

Maffesoli, Michel. 1995. *The time of the tribes: the decline of individualism in mass society*. London: Sage Publications.

———. 2016. L'imaginaire comme force invisible. *Imago* 5: 6–14.

———. 2018. *Être postmoderne*. Paris: Editions du Cerf.

Mcmanus, Chris. 2012. *Right hand, left hand: the origins of asymmetry in brains, bodies, atoms and cultures*. London: Weidenfeld & Nicolson.

Norton, Cherry. 2000. American Psychological Association: reports. *Independent*. https://www.independent.co.uk/life-style/health-and-families/health-news/left-handers-more-creative-but-forgetful-5370239.html. Accessed 7 Apr 2018

Recuero, Raquel. 2012. *A conversação em rede: comunicação mediada pelo computador e redes sociais na internet*. Porto Alegre: Sulina.

———. 2014. Curtir, compartilhar, comentar: trabalho de face, conversação e redes sociais no Facebook. *Verso & Reverso* 68: 114–124.

Rheingold, Howard. 1996. *La comunidad virtual: una sociedad sin fronteras*. Barcelona: Gedisa.

Santaella, Lucia. 2013. Intersubjetividade nas redes digitais: repercussões na educação. In *Interações em rede*, ed. Alex Primo, 33–47. Porto Alegre: Sulina.

Singh, Kultar. 2007. *Quantitative social research methods*. New Delhi: Sage Publications India.

Terrin, Aldo Natale. 1996. *Nova era: a religiosidade do pós-moderno*. São Paulo: Loyola.

We Are Social Agency, and Hootsuite. 2018. 2018 Q2 Global Digital Statshot. https://www.slideshare.net/wearesocialsg/2018-q2-global-digital-statshot-94084375?from_action=save. Accessed 7 May 2018

WHO – World Health Organization. 1946. *Constitution of the World Health Organization*. New York: World Health Organization.

———. 2014. *Global status report on alcohol and health*. Geneva: World Health Organization.

Part III
Internet and Health Challenges

Chapter 10
Evaluation of the Quality of Health Information on the Internet: An Analysis of Brazillian Initiatives

André Pereira Neto and Rodolfo Paolucci

Abstract Health information is produced on the Internet without evaluating its quality. Incomplete, contradictory, incorrect, or incomprehensible information can be harmful to health. But quality information can bring benefits to both citizens and health managers. This chapter analyzes Brazilian initiatives to evaluate the quality of health information based on the three systematic reviews on the subject. We found that the Brazilian academic production in this field does not follow international trends. Two Brazilian institutional initiatives are in place, namely, the "Regional Medical Council of São Paulo" and the "Internet, Health, and Society Laboratory" (LaISS) of the Oswaldo Cruz Foundation. LaISS made two evaluations that followed international literature and introduced innovative methods. We conclude that the pre-Internet communication culture seems to predominate among Brazilian health officials. Information and communication technologies are of secondary importance to public health managers and researchers.

10.1 Health Information on the Internet: A Contemporary Challenge

People's interactions with new information and communication technologies have promoted a series of transformations that are perceived in the way in which each one of us carries out his/her daily activities (Eysenbach 2001). Virtual resources increasingly mediate communication, financial transactions, transportation, food, and education. Thus, a growing number of people are communicating through Facebook and WhatsApp, buying and selling on sites like eBay and AliExpress, moving with Uber, feeding with iFood, and learning through massive open online

A. Pereira Neto (✉)
National School of Public Health, Oswaldo Cruz Foundation, Rio de Janeiro, Brazil

R. Paolucci
Support Foundation of the Rio de Janeiro State Technical School (FAETEC-RJ), Oswaldo Cruz Foundation, Rio de Janeiro, Brazil

A. Pereira Neto, M. B. Flynn (eds.), *The Internet and Health in Brazil*,
https://doi.org/10.1007/978-3-319-99289-1_10

courses (MOOCs).[1] These are few examples of the information accessed, produced, disseminated, and shared on the Internet.

Until recently, someone requiring some type of information had to have the purchasing power to buy a newspaper or go to an often distant and not very accessible library. Letters were sent by post and took some time to reach their final destination. New information and communication technologies provide a myriad of information to citizens in just a few seconds. Many of them would not be accessed at the same speed as before (Cheng and Dunn 2015). New information and communication technologies (NICTs) now provide unprecedented opportunities for both access and production and dissemination of information. Today, anyone can access, produce, and share information previously restricted to particular sociocultural groups. To do so, people must have the purchasing power to acquire an electronic communication device and have the technological conditions to access a network and the ability to handle these tools. The information available on the Internet is unlimited and covers any subject (Lee and Pang 2017). Given the amount of information available on the Internet, we have appropriated the biblical metaphor used by French philosopher Pierre Lévy to say that there is a "flood of information" on the Internet (Lévy 2001).

New information and communication technologies have become one of the main sources of health information around the world. In the area of health, public and private educational and research institutes, governmental and nongovernmental agencies, patient and professional associations, and individuals themselves have built virtual environments. The Internet allows health information to be published and shared without expert evaluation. Thus, incomplete, contradictory, incorrect, or even fraudulent information may be made available. Additionally, when correct and up-to-date, the way information is shown may hamper its understanding.

Access to low-quality information can have negative consequences. Misinformation can cause feelings of panic, anxiety, and paranoia (Lagan et al. 2011). Incorrect, incomprehensible, or obsolete information can rush citizens into decisions that harm their health (Powell et al. 2011). On the other hand, access to quality health information on the Internet can have positive consequences for citizens and managers of health systems. It can provide the development of skills that provide citizens with greater decision-making power over their health and self-care (Lagan et al. 2011; Albarrak et al. 2016). Quality information can also reduce costs of health systems (Park et al. 2015: Spoelman et al. 2016).

We are facing the following challenge: How do we address the issue of quality health information on the Internet?

Referring to the phenomenon of the "flood of information" promoted by the Internet, Lévy (2001) believes that it is necessary for each interest group to select or screen available information. Thus, he proposes that each group build an "ark." This metaphor of Lévy (2001) refers to the efforts needed to select quality sites and place them in a separate environment. He believes the selection and screening of available information would be an appropriate way of dealing with the problem of quality health information on the Internet.

[1] Chapter 15 addresses the theme of "massive open online courses" (*MOOCs*).

In our view, proposals to address this challenge can be gathered into three groups. The first covers search engines like Google, AltaVista, or Bing. When a subject is searched in these search engines, results are exhibited according to criteria of relevance, which are called page rank. These companies select the e-mail addresses they deem most relevant to their pages. The sites that usually appear at the top of the list are those belonging to sponsors. In addition, computational algorithms that combine several mechanisms such as personal information of users generate the list of results. These algorithms are capable of organizing increasingly larger amounts of information available on the Internet. In her book, Cathy O'Neil (2016) states that every day users provide an enormous amount of data that can be correlated, thanks to these algorithms, and that then can be mined, collected, and sold. This incidental information is not provided directly – it is indirect information. That is why people who analyze Twitter data can find out which politician a particular citizen should vote for or find out if that person is gay just by analyzing the posts they enjoy on Facebook, even if they do not say they are gay. Search engines also recognize the device utilized by the user. These technological resources gather this information and build user profiles that are then offered to large companies. With this information, businesses can identify where consumers of particular products or services are. Pariser (2011) explores the problem of algorithms and its consequences that, in their view, subject users to the economic interests of these companies. In *The Filter Bubble*, he shows how Google, Facebook, and Amazon build custom search filters for each user from their preferences. These filters prevent users from having access to the content of the entire Web, which hampers the construction of a broader understanding on a particular subject. According to Pariser (2011), personalization is based on a bargain. In return for the filtering service, we offer large corporations an enormous amount of data about our daily lives – data we often would not share with our friends. These companies are getting better at using this data to chart their trading strategies. Zhang et al. (2015, 2081) come to a similar position. They found several studies that identified that the page ranks of these search engines "were not reliable predictors of a site's overall content quality."

The second proposed group involves collective evaluation. It concerns assessment systems maintained by users engaged in providing information on the quality of institutions, business establishments, products, services, and so forth. Trivago and TripAdvisor are some examples of sites offering collective evaluation usually through information evaluation systems performed by users of these services. This type of evaluation greatly influences the decision-making of other consumers (Fritsch and Sigmund 2016). Analyzing this alternative of collective evaluation, Xiang et al. (2017) investigated the quality of user ratings on hotels in Manhattan from three tourism assessment sites. They concluded the research by stating:

> In this study, we showed that online review data drawn from three dominant platforms on a specific industry sector and from a specific geographic region could be considerably different in both content and structure. /…/ While our overall research design is based upon a specific case (i.e. Manhattan) using only three representative platforms in the U.S., our approach is valid since the goal was to show incongruences within the general assumption that it does not matter from which website a researcher draws the data (and how). (Xiang et al. 2017, 64)

Thus, collective evaluation does not follow any pattern and is guided by the subjectivity of the evaluator.

The third group encompasses public or private institutional initiatives to assess the quality of health information on the Internet. These efforts have been around for over 20 years. The first experiments are predominantly European and North American (Moreno et al. 2010). These initiatives have assumed, over time, different, simultaneous, and competing forms, such as technical recommendations, ethical principles or codes of conduct for site builders, and guidelines for users on aspects to be observed on sites. There are also more thorough evaluations, where professionals and users provide their opinion on information quality. Some of these initiatives give a quality seal to sites that meet their quality criteria. As a result, they ensure reliability to their visitors.

The main difference between the three groups of proposals lies, above all, in the objectives of the evaluation and in those responsible for assessing the quality of health information on the Internet. In the first group, there is clear commercial objective. Those responsible for the evaluation are private companies with marketing interests. In the second, the objective is similar to that of the first group, although users are the evaluators. In this case, the parameters used in the evaluation are too subjective because they do not follow precise quality indicators. Thus, the outcome of these assessments is unreliable. In the third case, the evaluation and recommendation of trusted sites are performed by professionals or institutions that meet specific quality criteria and are not guided by commercial interests.

This chapter analyzes Brazilian initiatives that evaluate the quality of information in health sites inserted in the third group mentioned above. Initially, the initiatives published in Brazilian journals submitted to double-blind peer-review process will be identified and analyzed. To do so, we used the Scientific Electronic Library Online (SciELO.br[2]), one of Brazil's open-access bibliographic databases.[3] In October 2017, a search was conducted using the word "Internet" in the subject index, which returned 479 results. Titles and abstracts of this sample were then read. Thus, we identified 21 studies[4] that analyzed the quality of health information on the Internet. While not very expressive, this sample seems to represent Brazilian

[2] The SciELO.org Portal offers more than 360 open-access journals. It is one of the main sources of Brazilian scientific information and encompasses a significant portion of the country's academic production.

[3] In Brazil, there are other open-access multidisciplinary bibliographic databases, such as Oasis. Br, LivRe, and BDTD or disciplinary-specific databases. There are also institutional repositories from several Brazilian research institutions.

[4] Studies selected were Silva et al. (2005), Barbosa and Martins (2007), Gondim and Falcão (2007), Souza et al. (2008), Santos et al. (2010), Silva and Gubert (2010), Leite and Correia (2011), Carlini et al. (2012), Gondim et al. (2012), Lins and Marin (2012), Cubas and Felchner (2012), Silveira et al. (2012), Del Giglio et al. (2012), Mori et al. (2013), Bastos et al. (2014), Pithon et al. (2014), Sousa et al. (2015), Chaves et al. (2015), Monteiro et al. (2016), Paolucci et al. (2017), and Pereira Neto et al. (2017).

academic studies on the topic, because it was obtained in this important open-access bibliographic database.

Institutional initiatives were then identified. In this case, we found initiatives by the São Paulo Regional Medical Council (CREMESP) and the Internet, Health, and Society Laboratory (LaISS), of the Oswaldo Cruz Foundation (Fiocruz),[5] a body linked to the Brazilian Ministry of Health. CREMESP is a federal, nonprofit authority founded on September 30, 1957, which regulates and supervises medical practice in the State of São Paulo (IBGE 2017). According to a study carried out in 2011, the State of São Paulo had 106,000 of the 371,000 doctors working in Brazil (Scheffer et al. 2011).

On March 9, 2001, the *Official Gazette of the State of São Paulo* published Resolution No. 097/2001, which established the *Manual of Ethical Principles for Medical and Health Websites* (CREMESP 2001). The preamble to this manual advocates that "the dissemination of information, the provision of services, and the sale of medical products on the Internet have the potential to promote health but can also harm Internet users and consumers." In the face of this evaluation, the manual establishes that organizations and individuals responsible for the creation and maintenance of health and medicine websites must "offer reliable, correct, and high-quality content, protecting the privacy of citizens and respecting the norms regulating the professional ethical practice of medicine." Its second paper states that:

> The doctors and health institutions registered in CREMESP are obliged to adopt the Manual of Ethical Principles for Medical and Health Websites for the purpose of idealization, registration, creation, maintenance, collaboration, and professional performance in Domains, Sites, Pages, or Portals on Medicine and Health on the Internet.

The Internet, Health, and Society Laboratory (LaISS) is linked to the Germano Sinval Faria Health School Center (CSEGSF), a department of the Sérgio Arouca National School of Public Health (ENSP) of the Oswaldo Cruz Foundation (Fiocruz). In the period 2012–2015, LaISS has developed experience assessing the quality of information on websites on dengue (2012–2013), tuberculosis (2013–2014), and breastfeeding (2014–2015). At the end of 2016, the LaISS obtained the right to certify health websites with the "Sergio Arouca Quality Seal"[6] from ENSP. For these reasons, the experiences of the LaISS will be analyzed in this chapter.

This chapter is divided into three parts. In the first, we will analyze 21 Brazilian academic studies evaluating the quality of health information on the Internet. In the second part, the characteristics of CREMESP's "Manual of Ethical Principles for

[5] The Oswaldo Cruz Foundation is one of the most important science and technology institutions in Latin America. It builds on the ideas of health promotion and social development, producing scientific and technological knowledge, and being an agent of citizenship. This is the official site: https://portal.fiocruz.br/en/content/foundation

[6] Physician Sérgio Arouca (1941/2003) provided theoretical insights and participated in the creation of the Unified Health System (SUS), a system that ensures comprehensive, universal, and equal access to the entire Brazilian population. It ranges from simple outpatient care to organ transplants (Law No. 8080 of 19 September 1990).

Medical and Health Websites") will be analyzed. Finally, attention will be paid to the experiences of LaISS. Before that, however, we will show the methodological procedure adopted.

10.2 Methods

In order to analyze Brazilian academic studies and institutional experiences, we will take into account the predominant criteria and evaluation processes assessing the quality of information of health websites found in the three systematic reviews[7] by Eysenbach et al. (2002), Zhang et al. (2015), and Paolucci (2015). Eysenbach et al. (2002) conducted the first systematic review on the topic. This paper, published in the *Journal of the American Medical Association* (JAMA), tabulated the methods and processes used for assessing the quality of health information on the Internet[8] in 79 studies published by 2001. Two results of this review are relevant to this chapter. One refers to the criteria used for evaluation. Another relates to the process by which each evaluation was performed. The second systematic review (Zhang et al. 2015)[9] was published 13 years later in the *Journal of the Association for Information Science and Technology* (JAIST). The authors' sample consisted of 165 different studies exclusively in English in the period 2002–2013 (Zhang et al. 2015).

The third systematic review was also published in 2015. This is Paolucci's (2015) Master's Thesis defended at the Institute of Scientific and Technological Communication and Information in Health (ICICT) of the Oswaldo Cruz Foundation, in Rio de Janeiro, Brazil. Paolucci (2015) performed a systematic review to update data found by Eysenbach et al. (2002) on the criteria and processes that evaluate the quality of information on health-related websites. To select his sample, he employed a search strategy similar to that applied in the first systematic review (Eysenbach et al. 2002). The period covered was from 2001 to mid-2014. Unlike Zhang et al. (2015), there was no restriction regarding the language of the studies found. The sample included 279 studies. This is a larger sample than that of Zhang et al. (2015), comprised of 165 titles, and that of Eysenbach et al. (2002), who examined 79 studies.

Let us look in more detail at the first systematic review.

This text by Eysenbach et al. (2002) shows two important contributions. One is the criteria used and the other is the process adopted in these evaluations.

---

[7] "A systematic review attempts to identify, appraise and synthesize all the empirical evidence that meets pre-specified eligibility criteria to answer a given research question. Researchers conducting systematic reviews use explicit methods aimed at minimizing bias, in order to produce more reliable findings that can be used to inform decision making" (Cochrane Library 2018).

[8] As of the writing of this chapter (October 2017), the *Web of Science* indicated that this article had been quoted about 800 times. It can therefore be considered the main reference in the field of evaluation of the quality of health information on the Internet.

[9] *Web of Science* indicates that this study published in 2015 was cited about 10 times (October 2017).

Eysenbach et al. (2002) identified 86 different quality criteria. To standardize such nomenclatures and show a methodological framework, they synthesized these 86 denominations into five quality criteria covering the realms of information used in the evaluation, namely:

1. Technical: a criterion related to the way in which the information is shown, including the authorship and/or origin of the information made available, the site's date of creation and last update, and the existence (or not) of commercial advertisement.
2. Design: criterion related to the site's aesthetic aspect, such as layout, colors, and ease of navigation.
3. Scope: criterion used to verify that all relevant information on a given topic is available on the site.
4. Accuracy: a criterion used to measure the level of agreement of information provided with the best evidence or one that is generally accepted by biomedical science.
5. Readability: a criterion that covers the level of reading of a document, that is, whether it is easy or difficult to understand.

The second important contribution relates to how the assessments identified were carried out. Authors stated "none of the studies conducted comprehension tests with current consumers or used judgments of literacy experts" (Eysenbach et al. 2002, 2695). In addition, they stressed that studies used technological resources to assess information readability. These authors argue that such formulas "do not reflect other factors that affect comprehension such as frequency and explanation of medical jargon, writing style [...] or use of culturally specific information" (Eysenbach et al. 2002, 2694).

Let us look at the second systematic review.

The study by Zhang et al. (2015) identified 11 evaluation criteria grouped into the categories of "content" and "design." The "content" category covers "accuracy," "completeness," "currency" (dates of updates), "credibility" (reference information), and "readability." The "design" category encompasses "accessibility," referring to the user's ease of access to a website's features and its appearance.

If we compare the categories submitted by Zhang et al. (2015) with the criteria shown by Eysenbach et al. (2002), we can say that the "content" category includes the criteria "technical," "accuracy," "scope," and "readability," while the "design" category approximates the criterion with the same name.

In relation to the evaluation process, Zhang et al. (2015, 2082) found that:

> [...] in all the studies included in the review, the evaluators were researchers or medical experts; few involved both domain experts and consumers themselves. Thus, limited knowledge was gained about differences between experts and general consumers in evaluating quality. Future research can fill this gap.

Therefore, Zhang et al. (2015) found that little had changed since its conclusions are close to those shown by Eysenbach et al. (2002): that is, in general, end users do not participate in evaluating the quality of information on health websites.

Table 10.1 Brazilian academic production per year

Year	2005	2007	2008	2010	2011	2012	2013	2014	2015	2016	2017	Total
n	1	2	1	2	1	6	1	2	2	1	2	21

Let us look at the third systematic review.

Paolucci (2015) checked whether the criteria used by Eysenbach et al. (2002) were still valid. He found that five criteria were used by most of the studies, in the following proportions: "accuracy" (64%), "readability" (38%), "scope" (27%), "technical" (24%), and "design" (17%). Moreover, he highlighted that the use of the "readability" criterion was significantly higher when compared to the first review (14%) (Eysenbach et al. 2002), showing a growing concern with this aspect of evaluating online information.

Paolucci (2015) was also concerned with identifying the profile of evaluators, grouping them into three categories: author, when the authors of the study carried out the evaluation; expert, when other professionals' participation was mentioned; and user, when a patient or a patient's relative participated in the evaluation. Authors were identified as evaluators in 79% of studies and experts in 9%. Users were found in only 5% of the studies.

Therefore, the low rates of experts and end users' participation, verified by Eysenbach et al. (2002), continued to predominate evaluation studies. In terms of "readability," most of the studies continued using formulas and other technological evaluation mechanisms as revealed by Eysenbach et al. (2002) 15 years ago.

In this chapter, we are interested in knowing the criteria and methods used by Brazilian efforts to evaluate health information on websites to verify to what extent they followed the results of these systematic reviews.

Let us first look at the criteria and methods adopted by Brazilian scholarly work.

10.3 Brazillian Academic Production

As mentioned previously, 21 studies evaluating the quality of health information on the Internet were identified in SciELO. Four comments deserve to be made on the profile of this sample before showing and analyzing the criteria and methods adopted by these Brazilian studies.

The first comment relates to the number of Brazilian academic publications per year on the subject. The first paper identified in this sample was published in 2005.[10] Most were published up to 2012 – year with the largest number of publications (6). At least one study was published in all subsequent years, making up the following Table 10.1:

[10] Most articles analyzed were published in English. The five papers mentioned below are published exclusively in Portuguese, namely, Souza et al. (2008), Silva and Gubert (2010), Cubas and Felchner (2012), Silveira et al. (2012), and Paolucci et al. (2017).

Table 10.2 Distribution of production by area of knowledge

Year	2005	2007	2008	2010	2011	2012	2013	2014	2015	2016	2017	Total
BIO	1	1		1		3		1	1	1		9
PH		1	1	1		2					2	7
H					1	1	1	1	1			5

We can come up with some interesting findings if we compare this table with the historical series of the two most recent systematic reviews on the subject.

Zhang et al. (2015) showed an increasing trend in the number of publications during the period between 2002 and 2013. Paolucci (2015) found a similar growth trend, considering that its sample is more comprehensive than that of Zhang et al. (2015). The two studies concluded that evaluation studies of health websites are growing, and Paolucci (2015) suggested that this growth is possibly related to streamlined Internet access and the academic and scientific concern with the health information published. However, Brazilian academic production on the subject does not follow the worldwide trend of growth in the quantity of publications.

The second comment refers to the areas of knowledge that journals publishing papers related to evaluation studies on the quality of online health information encompass. We found that the sample used for the elaboration of this chapter is spread over journals in biomedical sciences (BIO),[11] public health[12] (PH), and other health areas (H)[13] (Table 10.2).

Paolucci (2015) mapped the areas of the studies evaluating the quality of health sites. As with other Brazilian academic studies, he found that most of the studies were published in journals focused on specific medical subfields.

The third comment refers to the endogenous character of this production. What do we mean by that? These studies only evaluate sites in a specific area of knowledge, published in journals of the same area, aimed at readers who work and are interested in this field. For example, a paper published in the *Arquivo Brasileiro de Oftalmologia* evaluates the quality of information about myopia and photopsia (Barbosa and Martins 2007). Another, published in the *Revista Paulista de Pediatria*, analyzes the quality of information on child nutrition sites (Monteiro et al. 2016). This trend has been maintained among studies published in public health, as was the

[11] In the biomedical area, articles were published in the following journals: *Arquivos Brasileiros de Oftalmologia (1); International Archives of Otorhinolaryngology (1); Revista da Associação Médica Brasileira (1); Einstein, Instituto Israelita de Ensino e Pesquisa Albert Einstein (1); Revista Paulista de Pediatria (1); Revista Brasileira de Otorrinolaringologia (1); Revista Brasileira de Saúde Materno Infantil (1); Revista CEFAC, Associação Brasileira de Motricidade Orofacial (1);* and *Jornal de Pediatria (1).*

[12] In the public health area, papers were published in the following journals: *Revista de Saúde Pública (2), Ciências e Saúde Coletiva (2), Saúde em Debate (1), Trabalho Educação e Saúde (1),* and *Revista da Sociedade Brasileira de Medicina Tropical (1).*

[13] In the other health areas, papers were published in the following journals: *CoDAS, Jornal da Sociedade Brasileira de Fonoaudiologia (1); Revista Odonto Ciência (1); Acta Paulista de Enfermagem (1); Revista da Escola de Enfermagem da Universidade de São Paulo (1);* and *Dental Press Journal of Orthodontics (1).*

case of papers that evaluated the quality of information on tuberculosis and dengue sites, published, respectively, in the *Saúde em Debate* (Paolucci et al. 2017) and *Ciência & Saúde Coletiva* (Pereira Neto et al. 2017). In the same way, we showed this trend among papers of the other areas of health, as was the case of a nursing journal that published a paper evaluating first aid educational websites (Mori et al. 2013). A similar finding was found in the systematic review by Paolucci (2015), providing evidence of the same endogenous character in the worldwide scholarly production on the topic. He concluded by stating: "Among medical studies, most (64%) were written on subjects addressed by medical areas by doctors to doctors in medical journals" (Paolucci 2015, 71). It should be noted that human and social areas, such as communication and sociology, do not seem to be interested in this issue.

The 21 titles of this sample show studies evaluating a certain theme/issue of interest to a specific segment of researchers and/or health professionals, published in journals directed to this public. We can perceive that authors may have been interested in knowing the quality of the information on the Internet on the subjects they study and/or work professionally. Paolucci (2015, 71) proposed two explanations for this interest:

> [...] the need to alert colleagues about the quality of the information or to point out the problem of quality to reinforce their authority as a professional holder of health knowledge. At first, they would be trying to warn peers about the quality of online information. In the second, they would be concerned with reasserting their authority and disqualifying the Internet as a source of reliable health information.

The fourth comment we would like to make relates to the results found. The 21 studies that we analyzed, above all, reveal the problem of the quality of health information on the Internet. In the sample we used in this chapter, 934 sites were evaluated in all. Only four studies show positive results for the information evaluated, classifying sites as "good," "very good," or "positive" (Lins and Marin 2012; Bastos et al. 2014). Five had a score of average or variable quality (Silva and Gubert 2010; Gondim et al. 2012; Silveira et al. 2012; Mori et al. 2013; Pithon et al. 2014).

The remaining 12 revealed that the quality of information is poor, characterizing it as "non-compliant," "poor," "inadequate," "insufficient," "incorrect," "incomplete," and "negative." These results reiterate the need to address the problem of the quality of health information on Brazilian websites and on the Internet.

These four comments served to reveal to what extent the sample analyzed to elaborate this chapter follows or not the international trend observed in the systematic review carried out by Paolucci (2015) in his Master's Thesis.

In relation to the criteria used by Brazilian scholars, one fact surprised us: only 4 of the 21 papers cited in their bibliography the systematic review of Eysenbach et al. (2002). This aspect caused a stir, because this paper was published in *JAMA*, a journal of international circulation 3 years before the first national study available in our sample. These four papers were published, respectively, in 2011, 2014, and 2017. Let us see how they incorporate the study of Eysenbach et al. (2002).

Santos et al. (2010) developed a tool to assess information on the Internet about abuse of drugs to point out sites that simultaneously had good content, good accessibility, and credibility. In this case, the study by Eysenbach et al. (2002) does not seem to have influenced the establishment of the evaluation tool of these authors, since it was not mentioned, although it is included in the bibliography.

Pithon et al. (2014) used two criteria very similar to those shown in the systematic review by Eysenbach et al. (2002). The first one was called "quality assessment." It was defined as "the level of agreement between the information disclosed and the best evidence generally accepted in clinical practice" (Pithon et al. 2014, 87). The second was called "readability" and "measured by the reading skill an individual needs in order to understand what is written" (Pithon et al. 2014, 88). In this case, the study of Eysenbach et al. (2002) seems to have served as a reference because the first "quality assessment" resembles "accuracy" and "readability," as well as "intelligibility." However, Pithon et al. (2014) did not use the "scope," "technical," and "design" criteria in their evaluation.

Paolucci et al. (2017) and Pereira Neto et al. (2017) were the only two Brazilian studies that used the five criteria employed in the systematic review of Eysenbach et al. (2002). They appropriated these references and created others. The remaining 17 studies followed different paths. They were not based on nor quoted the systematic review of Eysenbach et al. (2002). We have grouped these studies according to the criteria adopted in the evaluations.

A first group, consisting of seven papers, used HONcode: an initiative of the Health On the Net Foundation – a Swiss nongovernmental organization.

HONcode consists of eight criteria,[14] namely, "authoritative," indicates the qualifications of authors; "complementarity," says that "information should support, not replace, the doctor-patient relationship"; "privacy," respects "the privacy and confidentiality of personal data submitted to the site by the visitor"; "attribution," "cites the source(s) of published information, date of medical, and health pages"; "justifiability," establishes that the site "must back up claims relating to benefits and performance"; "transparency," "site must have an accessible presentation and an accurate email contact"; "financial disclosure," "site must identify funding sources"; and "advertising policy," "clearly distinguishes advertising from editorial content" (HON 2010).

This is not the opinion of some of the authors who are part of our sample and used this code in their evaluation. For example, Del Giglio et al. (2012, 647) argue "the principles of the HONcode are the most traditional, reliable, and comprehensive for evaluating healthcare and medicine information available on the Internet."

Let us see in more detail how the seven Brazilian papers appropriated the HONcode.

Barbosa and Martins (2007) used a list of criteria based on the principles of HONcode. Carlini et al. (2012) built on five of HONcode's eight criteria. Leite and Correia (2011), Lins and Marin (2012), Silveira et al. (2012), and Cubas and

[14] The HONcode of Conduct for medical and health websites (HONcode): https://www.hon.ch/HONcode/Webmasters/Conduct.html

Felchner (2012) exclusively used the eight HONcode criteria. Del Giglio et al. (2012) associated the HONcode criteria with the "DISCERN Questionnaire" (DQ).

The DISCERN Project was developed by the Division of Public Health and Primary Health Care at the Institute of Health Sciences of the University of Oxford (Charnock and Shepperd 2004).[15] They provide an evaluation tool consisting of three sections: the first evaluates whether the publication is reliable.[16] The second one checks for any information that facilitates patients' choice of the most convenient treatment.[17] Answers are sorted in a Likert-scale type, where the evaluator responds no, partially, or yes. The third invites the evaluator to "rate the overall quality of the publication as a source of information about treatment choices."[18]

In the systematic review conducted by Paolucci (2015), we also identified studies that used HONcode and DISCERN as evaluation tools. These are the most used initiatives in studies evaluating the quality of health information on the Internet and have become international references. Paolucci (2015) contrasted the five criteria offered by Eysenbach et al. (2002) and those found in the initiatives in HONcode and DISCERN. He found that they did not use the "readability" criterion, and none simultaneously covered the five criteria synthesized by Eysenbach et al. (2002). We recall that these five criteria represent different aspects of information quality. Thus, the application of all is necessary for a more complete evaluation.

In our sample, four studies used other assessment tools.

One of them was the study by Mori et al. (2013) that combined three tools and evaluation models. Authors justify this choice as follows:

> Given the lack of a Brazilian website evaluation instrument that is translated and validated by consensus, the creation of one was necessary. This was made by using reference evaluation tools and models, such as Health-Related Web Site Evaluation Form, System Usability Scale, and Heuristic Evaluation. (Mori et al. 2013, 948)

They say that the first tool evaluated the site's structure; the second, the information; and the third, navigation. Bastos et al. (2014) make adaptions from the "Emory Health-Related Website's Evaluation Form" (EMORY): a questionnaire that includes as criteria "accuracy," "authorship," "updates," "public," "navigation," "links," and "structure." In addition, "content quality" about hearing issues was con-

---

[15] The DISCERN Instrument: http://www.discern.org.uk/discern_instrument.php

[16] The first section contains eight questions, namely: Are the aims clear? Does it achieve its aims? Is it relevant? Is it clear what sources of information were used to compile the publication (other than the author or producer)? Is it clear when the information used or reported in the publication was produced? Is it balanced and unbiased? Does it provide details of additional sources of support and information? Does it refer to areas of uncertainty?

[17] The second section contains seven questions, namely: Does it describe how each treatment works? Does it describe the benefits of each treatment? Does it describe the risks of each treatment? Does it describe what would happen if no treatment is used? Does it describe how the treatment choices affect overall quality of life? Is it clear that there may be more than one possible treatment choice? Does it provide support for shared decision-making?

[18] In this case, there are three options: "low, serious or extensive shortcomings"; "moderate, potentially important but not serious shortcomings"; and "high, minimal shortcomings."

sidered. Concerned with the question of readability, Souza et al. (2008) led a group of authors from Portugal in an evaluation that used the Next.Step Usability Questionnaire, a questionnaire that proposes a subjective evaluation demonstrating how the user feels when navigating a site.

Chaves et al. (2015) evaluated websites on newborn hearing screening in Portuguese by combining the "Flesch Reading Ease Score Formula" and the "Emory Health-Related Website's Evaluation Form." The "Flesch Reading Ease Score Formula" performs a "readability" classification of a text based on the number of syllables in a word and the number of words in a sentence. This was one of the few studies that emphasized readability of the information provided. In conclusion, it mentions that:

> [...] the sites differed in the aspects addressed because there is a need to revise the reading level of the content and quality of the technical aspects regarding the accuracy and timeliness of information, authorship, and links. (Chaves et al. 2015, 526)

In his systematic review, Paolucci (2015) found some studies that used the "Flesch Reading Ease Score Formula." Although "readability" was the second most commonly used criterion in the studies of his sample, almost all of them used formulas like this to determine whether a particular audience easily understood information. As we explained earlier, they do not consider subjective factors of language that could be perceived through human reading.

It should be noted that the criteria set out in the systematic reviews have not been fully utilized in these four papers. The other six papers were limited to evaluating the quality of information available on health sites using official documents or manuals of their respective areas of expertise.

This was the case of Silva et al. (2005), who evaluated sites on allergic rhinitis covered in the "Otorhinolaryngology Treaty of the Brazilian Society of Otorhinolaryngology." Gondim and Falcão (2007) evaluated Brazilian online pharmacies using regulation from the National Health Surveillance Agency (ANVISA), a body from the Brazilian Ministry of Health. In another paper, Gondim et al. (2012) analyzed the quality of drug information on Brazilian websites based on the World Health Organization and the Code of Ethics for Health and Services on the Internet. When analyzing the adequacy of information on visceral leishmaniasis available in Brazilian portals, Souza et al. (2008) confined themselves to checking whether information on disease transmission, reservoirs infected with Leishmania, control methods, symptoms, and clinical procedures related to the disease were correct. These authors used information contained in the *Normative Manuals of the Ministry of Health* and in the scientific literature. The parameter used for evaluating the quality of breastfeeding sites by Silva and Gubert (2010) was the *Food Guide for Children Under Two Years* published by Brazil's Ministry of Health (2010). When assessing the quality of nutritional information of children under 2 years on the Internet, Monteiro et al. (2016) also used the *Food Guide for Children Under Two Years*. The almost exclusive concern with information content, based on official manuals and documents, was also identified in 41% of the sample analyzed by Paolucci (2015).

To conclude the analysis of Brazilian academic production, let us see how these authors carried out the evaluation process.

The authors themselves were for the most part the evaluators of the studies that served as the basis for the research (12). Six other works included health professionals as evaluators, as was the case in studies involving nurses (Lins and Marin 2012), health and information technology professionals (Mori et al. 2013), childhood deafness experts (Bastos et al. 2014), and neonatal hearing experts (Chaves et al. 2015). The involvement of users as evaluators was identified in studies that included graduate students (Santos et al. 2010; Mori et al. 2013; Monteiro et al. 2016). In the study by Sousa et al. (2015), adolescents attending an obesity clinic evaluated information on weight control during adolescence on the Internet. Only two studies simultaneously adopted users and health professionals as evaluators. These are papers by Paolucci et al. (2017) and Pereira Neto et al. (2017).

As previously mentioned, only 4 of the 21 papers of this systematic review included Eysenbach et al. (2002) in their bibliographical references. Despite this, we can see that some Brazilian scholars sought to include end users as evaluators of information quality. Thus, a reality found by Eysenbach et al. (2002) that "none of the studies conducted comprehension tests with actual consumers or used judgments of literacy experts" may not be a predominant trend in Brazilian studies.

We will now analyze the Regional Council of Medicine of the State of São Paulo's experience evaluating the quality of online information.

10.4 CREMESP Manual

On March 9, 2001, the Regional Council of Medicine of São Paulo (CREMESP) published Resolution 97 accompanied by the *Manual of Ethical Principles for Medical and Health Websites on the Internet* (CREMESP 2001).[19]

In its preamble, this document considers that "the Internet conveys information, provides services, and sells products that have a direct impact on the health and life of citizens" (CREMESP 2001). In addition, it argues: "there is no specific legislation to regulate the use of the Internet or e-commerce in Brazil."[20] Thus, it considers that it is "necessary to encourage self-regulation of the sector to establish minimum standards of quality, safety, and reliability of Medical and Health sites" (CREMESP 2001).

As mentioned earlier, CREMESP's activities are restricted to the State of São Paulo. Despite this geographical limitation, it should remembered once again that São Paulo is the most populous state, with the highest per capita income and largest

[19] The manual, available in Portuguese, is available at this website: http://www.cremesp.org.br/?siteAcao=PublicacoesConteudoSumario&id=26

[20] The Brazilian Civil Rights Framework for the Internet was enacted in April 2014 through Law 12.965. Its passage is discussed in Chap. 2.

number of doctors in Brazil. In addition, this resolution was published in the Official Gazette of the Government of the State of São Paulo.[21]

It is a four-paper document. The first one shows "the seven principles" that Internet users have the right to demand from organizations and individuals responsible for health websites, which are *transparency*, *honesty*, *quality*, *informed consent*, *privacy*, *medical ethics*, and *responsibility and origin* (CREMESP 2001).

The second establishes that:

> Doctors and health institutions registered at CREMESP are obliged to adopt the "Manual of Ethical Principles for Medical and Health Websites" (annex) for the purpose of idealization, registration, creation, maintenance, collaboration, and professional performance in Medicine and Health Domains, Sites, Pages, or Portals on the Internet. (CREMESP 2001)

Thus, this Resolution is concerned with users and directly affects all physicians and health institutions operating in the State of São Paulo.[22]

The *Manual of Ethical Principles for Medical and Health Websites on the Internet* accompanying Resolution 97/2001 details each of the seven principles mentioned above.

We will now perform a comparison between the seven principles established in this manual and the eight HONcode[23] principles and the criteria to assess the quality of information on health websites identified in international literature by the last systematic review on the topic (Paolucci 2015).

The principle of *transparency* found in the manual considers it "mandatory to show the names of those responsible for the maintenance of, as well as the direct or indirect sponsors, of the site." Therefore, this first principle is close to the technical criterion mentioned by the last systematic review conducted about evaluating information quality on health sites (Paolucci 2015). The HONcode is also concerned with this realm of evaluation. The transparency principle found in the HONcode establishes that:

> [...] designers of this Web site will seek to provide information in the clearest possible manner and provide contact addresses for visitors that seek further information or support. The Webmaster will display his/her E-mail address clearly throughout the Web site. (HON 2010)

By mentioning the role of web designers in the transparency principle, the HONcode approaches the design criterion used by most of the international academic literature that analyzes the quality of health website information (Paolucci 2015).

---

[21] Resolution 97/2001 of CREMSP was published in the Official Gazette of the State of São Paulo (section 1 number 45) on March 9, 2001.

[22] The other two papers announce that the *Manual of Ethical Principles for Medical and Health Websites on the Internet* is annexed to this resolution and will become effective as of the date of its publication (March 9, 2001).

[23] The eight HONcode principles are authoritative, complementarity, privacy, attribution, justifiability, transparency, financial disclosure, and advertising policy. See https://www.hon.ch/HONcode/Webmasters/Conduct.html

The principle called *attribution* in HONcode can also be inserted in the technical standards exposed by the last systematic review (Paolucci 2015). This principle is as follows:

> Where appropriate, information contained on this site will be supported by clear references to source data and, where possible, have specific HTML links to that data. The date when a clinical page was last modified will be clearly displayed. (HON 2010)

CREMESP's *honesty* principle addresses the issue of the sale of health products or services over the Internet. According to this principle: "The objective of the educational or scientific content disclosed /.../ to advertise, promote, and sell must be clear" (CREMESP 2001). In the last systematic review, this is included in the technical criterion (Paolucci 2015). In the HONcode, it can be observed in two moments. This topic is included under the item financial disclosure and advertising policy. In the first, health sites should be "including the identities of commercial and non-commercial organizations that have contributed funding, services, or material for the site" (HON 2010). The second recommends: "If advertising is a source of funding, it will be clearly stated" (HON 2010).

The third principle of CREMESP's Manual is called *quality of information*. It establishes that information is "accurate, up-to-date, easy to understand, in objective language, and scientifically grounded" (CREMESP 2001). Therefore, this principle revives the aspects of accuracy and readability found in the last systematic review. The HONcode does not devote attention this information.

The fourth and fifth principles of CREMESP's Manual, called *informed consent* and *privacy*, are concerned with the preservation of confidential information provided by the patient in virtual environments. It establishes that:

> Sites should make clear storage and security mechanisms to prevent misuse of data through codes, passwords, software, and digital security certificates appropriate for all transactions involving users' personal medical or financial information. (CREMESP 2001)

Thus, once again, CREMESP's Manual focuses on website users. This time, it is concerned with the misuse of private information of citizens and spying on the Internet.[24] This issue was not among the criteria observed by the studies that carried out a systematic review. It is found, however, in the HONcode under the nickname of *privacy*. The HONcode states that:

> Confidentiality of data relating to individual patients and visitors to a medical/health Web site, including their identity, is respected by this Web site. The Web site owners undertake to honour or exceed the legal requirements of medical/health information privacy that apply in the country and state where the Web site and mirror sites are located. (HON 2010)

The sixth principle is called *ethics*. It is geared specifically to the practice of medicine via the Internet. It establishes that:

> The medical professionals and health institutions registered at CREMESP that have Internet sites must comply with the same codes and ethical norms regulating conventional professional practice. If the action, omission, misconduct, malpractice, negligence, or recklessness

[24] The issue of information security on the Internet is addressed in Chap. 11.

> of a physician, via the Internet, produces harm to the life or problems to the health of individuals, the professional will be liable for the violation of ethics at the Medical Council. Disciplinary penalties applicable after due process and judgment include a confidential warning; confidential censorship; public censorship in official publication; suspension of the professional practice for thirty (30) days, and cancellation of the professional practice. (CREMESP 2001)

In this case, systematic reviews and the HONcode do not mention ethics. However, HONcode grants the doctor the exclusive domain of "any medical or health advice provided and hosted on this site will" in its so-called *authoritative* criterion (HON 2010). The HONcode is concerned with the preservation of the hegemony of the physician in clinical practice in its principle called *complementarity*, which states that:

> The information provided on this site is designed to support, not replace, the relationship that exists between a patient/site visitor and his/her existing physician. (HON 2010)

The seventh principle of CREMESP's Manual is called *responsibility and origin*. Once again, it addresses the technical realm recommended by systematic reviews, since it proposes that sites make "explicit to users who they are and how to contact those responsible for the site and domain owners" (CREMESP 2001). In addition, the last principle states "the information must use, as professional sources, entities, universities, public and private bodies, and admittedly qualified institutions" (CREMESP 2001).

Finally, HONcode is concerned with something not found in CREMESP's Manual. The international agency considers relevant that "any claims relating to the benefits/performance of a specific treatment, commercial product, or service will be supported by appropriate, balanced evidence" (HON 2010).

Thus, "scope" was the only criterion found in the last systematic review (Paolucci 2015) that was not found in CREMESP's Manual or in the HONcode principles.

The most notable difference between these three evaluative parameters is related to how the evaluation process should be performed. Both the HONcode and CREMESP's Manual do not mention who the evaluators will be and how this evaluation will take place. Thus, CREMESP's *Manual of Ethical Principles for Medical and Health Websites on the Internet* does not show the method adopted to verify the adequacy of sites with its principles. Fifteen years into its enactment, we noted that the manual has not been updated. On the contrary, two papers continue to be in force in the Code of Medical Ethics of the Federal Medical Council (CFM 2010). Paper 37 establishes that the physician is prohibited to "prescribe treatment or other procedures without direct examination of the patient"[25] and, under Paper 114, to "consult, diagnose, or prescribe by any means of mass communication."

This manual, however, served as reference for one of the studies mentioned above. Silva et al. (2005) evaluated the quality of information found on sites on allergic rhinitis and published the paper in the *Brazilian Journal of*

[25] Sole paragraph of Article 37 establishes that: "Distance medical care provided as per telemedicine or of another method will be subjected to the regulation of the Federal Council of Medicine."

Otorhinolaryngology. The procedure adopted was to compare whether the information found on the sites complied with the definitions of each principle of CREMESP's Manual. Thus, despite its limitations, the *Manual of Ethical Principles for Medical and Health Websites on the Internet* has already been used in academic research.

We will now analyze the initiative of the Internet, Health, and Society Laboratory (LaISS) in evaluating the quality of information on health websites.

10.5 LaISS' Experiences

The Internet, Health, and Society Laboratory (LaISS) was inaugurated in December 2009 with support from the Foundation for Research Support of the State of Rio de Janeiro (FAPERJ). It is linked to the Germano Sinval Faria School Health Center – a primary care center of the Sergio Arouca National School of Public Health (ENSP), the Oswaldo Cruz Foundation, located in the neighborhood of Manguinhos in the city of Rio de Janeiro.

Manguinhos is a district with more than 36,000 inhabitants (IPP 2013). It is located in a mangrove area – a geographic condition that gave its name in the diminutive.[26] It encompasses 15 *favelas* (the local term to describe shantytowns or informal urban settlements) with similar sociodemographic profiles. In general, its population is unemployed or is engaged in temporary jobs (Fernandes and Costa 2013). There is no basic sanitation in most of the territory. Manguinhos has one of the worst human development indices in the city of Rio de Janeiro. About 80% of the population earns less than one minimum wage per month[27] (IPP 2013). The resident population is exposed to all kinds of infectious diseases (Lima 2010). Violence and armed conflict between drug traffickers, police officers, and militias[28] are frequent.

LaISS is linked to the Germano Sinval de Faria School Health Center that provides primary care services to this population.

Between 2012 and 2013, this laboratory developed a research project analyzing the quality of information on websites about dengue (Pereira Neto and Paolucci 2014). Tuberculosis sites were evaluated between 2013 and 2014 (Pereira Neto et al. 2016).

---

[26] In Portuguese, "Manguinhos" is the plural diminutive of the word "mangue," which means "mangrove" in English, thus, "small mangrove."

[27] The minimum wage is the lowest legally defined monetary payment that a worker must receive in a company for his services in Brazil for 1 month's work. The minimum wage amount is defined by a national law decree and is reassessed annually based on the current cost of living of the population. Currently, the monthly minimum wage in Brazil is 954 reais, approximately 297 US Dollars, or 10 US dollars per day.

[28] Militia is the generic name of military or paramilitary organizations, not legally recognized, composed of ordinary armed citizens who fight with drug traffickers and police over power in the favelas of various Brazilian cities (Misse 2011).

Dengue was chosen because it is a neglected tropical disease. According to the World Health Organization, neglected tropical diseases include:

> [...] a diverse group of communicable diseases that prevail in tropical and subtropical conditions in 149 countries – affect more than one billion people and cost developing economies billions of dollars every year. Populations living in poverty, without adequate sanitation and in close contact with infectious vectors and domestic animals and livestock are those worst affected. (WHO 2018)

Dengue fever has high rates of morbidity and mortality, especially in children and adults. It is a disease of worldwide importance that has accompanied humanity for years and has no prospect of being controlled in the short term. Quality information on the Internet can play an important role in preventing and treating this disease.

Tuberculosis is found in the sixth Millennium Goal[29]: "combatting AIDS, malaria, and other diseases." According to the "National Plan to End Tuberculosis" published in 2017:

> Brazil is one of the countries with the highest number of cases in the world, and since 2003, the disease is considered a priority in the political agenda of the Ministry of Health. Although it is a disease whose diagnosis and treatment is universal and free of charge through Brazil's Unified Health System (SUS), there are still access barriers and approximately 69,000 new cases and 4,500 deaths each year due to the basic causes of tuberculosis (Brasil 2017).

One of the main challenges facing tuberculosis is treatment abandonment. The treatment for healing is long and there are several socioeconomic and cultural reasons that hinder it. Many people start it but soon quit. Chirinos et al. (2017, 5) concluded:

> [...] there is a need for the appropriation of new scientific knowledge for people with TB, regarding both the disease and the treatment of tuberculosis, in an attempt to modify the representations and actions of abandonment.

Thus, information on the Internet can play an important role in TB treatment adherence and in the prevention of dengue.

The two experiences of assessing the quality of health website information developed in LaISS were largely guided by the conclusions in the systematic review of Eysenbach et al. (2002). They used and adapted the criteria stated by this study (technical, design, scope, accuracy, and readability). In addition, they sought to address the main shortcoming identified in the literature: the lack of participation of users and experts in the assessment. Thus, the two experiments developed in the LaISS did not use technological resources to evaluate the readability of the respective sites. In this case, a few residents of Manguinhos were the evaluators.

---

[29] The Millennium Goals were enacted through the United Nations Millennium Declaration adopted by the 191 member states on September 8, 2000.

We will show below how the participation of users and experts in each of these evaluations was developed and how they adapted the criteria set forth by Eysenbach et al. (2002).[30]

10.6 Evaluators, Researchers, and Citizens

The team that carried out the project decided to invite some Manguinhos residents to elaborate the evaluation questions and to play the role of evaluators of the quality of health information on the Internet on behalf of users. This choice is justified, since most of the Brazilian population and residents of Manguinhos live in the same socioeconomic conditions, where the monthly income not exceeding two minimum wages (IBGE 2017)[31] stands out. These residents had participated in a previous activity in LaISS. Thus, they were invited to join in these two evaluations. Experts' representatives were sensitized individually in different institutional settings, as will be described next.

The experience of evaluating dengue sites (2012/2013) was attended by 20 residents of Manguinhos – 17 women and 3 men. They had varying levels of schooling and ages between 30 and 60 years. Many had no basic computer skills or knowledge. Ten experts participated in the process: six women and four men. This group consisted of five primary care physicians working in the CSEGSF/ENSP/Fiocruz, a febrile disease researcher at the Evandro Chagas National Institute of Infectology (INI/Fiocruz)[32] and four newly trained physicians working in the Family Health Program.

In the case of the TB experience (2013–2014), the same 20 users from Manguinhos participated. The expert group of 19 people, all women, comprised of professionals/researchers from the Professor Hélio Fraga Reference Center (CRPHF), a TB specialized department of ENSP/Fiocruz, 5 professionals working in primary care at the CSEGSF/ENSP/Fiocruz, 1 researcher from the Oswaldo Cruz Institute (IOC/FIOCRUZ),[33] 6 professionals from the Laboratory of Regional

[30] This presentation will be based on the two research reports produced by the LaISS team (Pereira Neto and Paolucci 2014; Pereira Neto et al. 2016).

[31] The National Household Sample Survey – PNAD of the Brazilian Institute of Geography and Statistics (IBGE), a body linked to the Brazilian Federal Government, investigates on a quarterly basis a set of situational information on the trends and fluctuations of the labor force and, annually, structural themes relevant to understanding the Brazilian socioeconomic reality. In 2016, the PNAD revealed that 44.5 million Brazilians received on average R$ 747 (about US$200/May 2018) per month, less than the minimum wage. Meanwhile, the country's 889,000 highest paid people received an average of R$ 27,000 (about US$4000/May 2018) per month. That is, only 1% earns 36 times more than half the average worker does. The difference is evident when we find that the richest 10% keep 43% of all earnings.

[32] A Fiocruz unit focused on clinical research, teaching, reference services, and infectious diseases care.

[33] A Fiocruz unit that operates in the areas of research, technological development, and innovation, providing reference services for the diagnosis of infectious and genetic diseases and vector control.

Endemic Situations (LASER/ENSP/Fiocruz),[34] and 3 newly graduated professionals who are multiprofessional public health residency students.[35]

In both cases, Manguinhos' dwellers received a small financial stipend, while experts collaborated as volunteers.

In relation to users, the initial challenge was to familiarize these collaborators with the terms commonly used in the Internet universe such as site, homepage, website, link, download, send, and delete: foreign words that are generally unknown to a Brazilian population with limited schooling. Initially, activities were carried out to sensitize them about the structures and basic components of Web pages. Users could gradually learn more about the role of the Internet as a means of contemporary communication. The following year, when the experience of evaluating the quality of information on tuberculosis sites was carried out, the group of evaluators living in Manguinhos showed a greater proximity to the universe of computers and the Internet.

The representatives of users and experts participated in this process in two ways: building the quality indicators and conducting the evaluation, thanks to an online tool built for this purpose.

Let us see how the process of elaborating quality indicators occurred.

Throughout the process of constructing indicators to evaluate information on dengue, the LaISS team made efforts to have users' opinions considered for decision-making. For this purpose, the team incorporated Paulo Freire's (1976) theory of dialogical communication. Thus, users' representatives were able to appropriate the characteristics of criteria shown by Eysenbach et al. (2002).

LaISS' team fully incorporated the meaning of four of the five criteria submitted by this systematic review. The only one that underwent a minor change was the "design" criterion (Eysenbach et al. 2002), which was renamed "interactivity." Thus, communication channels between site managers and its users were valued among the users themselves. Therefore, this criterion was not limited to the visual aspects of the site as suggested by the Design criterion. One of the characteristics that distinguish a virtual communication medium from traditional ones is its ability to provide users with information exchanged between themselves and the managers. This characteristic is recognized in this criterion. A health website is complete if it enables users to communicate with each other and its manager to exchange information, ask questions, or make compliments or complaints. This proposed criterion ensures that the site under evaluation offer a means of communication such as "contact us," Facebook, Twitter, as well as basic navigation structures such as "menu" and "search engine." The page should also be attractive to the evaluators, whether users or professionals.

---

[34] LASER is "a research, education, and advisory unit that aims to institutionalize, disseminate, and update the evaluation and monitoring of endemic process control programs." For more information, see http://www6.ensp.fiocruz.br/laser/

[35] Residency aims to "promote the development of attributes for the higher education multiprofessional health team to work in the Family Health Teams and in the Family Health Support Centers (NASF)." For more information, see http://www.ensp.fiocruz.br/portal-ensp/ensino/cursos/index.php?idcurso=488&indtipo=2&menu=1213

The group of residents who participated in the process of building dengue quality indicators had been working at LaISS for 9 months. This period witnessed intense debates that allowed the construction of indicators for 4 criteria, each of which had a different number of indicators: technical (11 indicators), interactivity (5), scope (8), and readability (25). Thus, they began to play the role of citizen researchers and not just work collaborators or sources of information.

In the case of dengue, 2 medical researchers and disease researchers elaborated 14 indicators specifically related to this disease, within the criteria of accuracy. All quality indicators constructed for dengue were written in the form of evaluative questions.

In evaluating the quality of information on tuberculosis sites, the process was slightly different, especially in relation to the indicators for the "accuracy" criterion. The LaISS team realized that evaluative questions about accuracy should not be asked. Instead, statements should be made that contain the essential information on tuberculosis prevention, transmission, symptom, diagnosis, and treatment. In the second experiment, TB accuracy indicators were written differently. This decision was inspired by the Brazilian study by Souza et al. (2008) that evaluated the quality of sites through affirmative or negative sentences. In addition, in assessing information on dengue, the LaISS team found that some experts did not know how to answer all the questions about the issues addressed. Written in the form of an affirmation, evaluators were able to check whether the minimal contents on tuberculosis were available on the site or not. For example, instead of asking how tuberculosis can be prevented, the following statement was made: "Tuberculosis can be prevented in airy places" (Pereira Neto et al. 2016). Evaluators had to check whether this information was on the site under evaluation or not.

Twenty-one accuracy indicators were associated with tuberculosis and were elaborated with the participation of professionals from the Professor Hélio Fraga Reference Center (CRPHF/ENSP/Fiocruz). They did not work alone. Users' representatives also participated in the elaboration of the sentences related to the criterion of "accuracy." Researchers defined what information on tuberculosis should be listed on a website about this disease. For example, professionals elaborated the following sentence:

> While tuberculosis affects other organs (extra-pulmonary tuberculosis), the pulmonary and laryngeal forms of tuberculosis are those that transmit the disease. Most of the time, if treatment is performed correctly, within 15 days, the patient does not transmit anymore. (Pereira Neto et al. 2016)

This proposed sentence was taken to the residents of Manguinhos participating in the process. After a heated debate, this text was subdivided into two, with the following format:

1. Pulmonary and laryngeal tuberculosis transmit the disease.
2. Most often, if the treatment is performed correctly, within 15 days, the patient does not transmit anymore (Pereira Neto et al. 2016).

Information on extrapulmonary tuberculosis was considered secondary by citizen researchers. This new format was taken to the CRPHF/ENSP/Fiocruz researchers. They approved and agreed with the residents of Manguinhos: in the TB site, the two statements on the extrapulmonary aspect should determine the evaluation of the quality of information on tuberculosis sites.

Thus, the elaboration process of criteria and indicators for the evaluation of information of tuberculosis sites was different from that performed with information from dengue sites. Regarding tuberculosis, there was an effort to carry out, to a certain extent, "knowledge translation" (KT).

Clavier et al. (2012, 802) understand that KT:

> [...] is far from being a mechanical process: rather, it is the skilled crafting of cognitive, strategic and logistic practices that interweave the values, interests, and ideas of each partner.

There are different ways to name KT practitioners. Clavier et al. (2012) indicate that there are some "action researchers," "translators," "support staff," "leaders," and "knowledge brokers." KT is understood by Clavier et al. (2012) as:

> [...] a multifaceted, innovative practice that allows for multidirectional exchanges and the co-construction of knowledge among academics, community representatives, practitioners, and decision-makers. (Clavier et al. 2012, 792)

The group of residents who participated in the process of building TB quality indicators had been working at the LaISS for 9 months. Throughout this period, intense discussions were held that allowed the construction of indicators for each of the 5 criteria, each of which had a different number of indicators: technical (8 questions), interactivity (5 questions), scope (8 questions), and readability (20 questions). In this case, they also played the role of citizen researchers rather than just work as collaborators or sources of information. The 21 accuracy indicators were developed by researchers and users as affirmative or negative sentences.

Thus, for both dengue and tuberculosis, each criterion consisted of a different amount of evaluative questions or sentences.

Let us see now how the evaluation process was developed.

The process of evaluating dengue and tuberculosis sites began with questions and evaluative sentences at hand. An online assessment tool was devised for this purpose.

Sites linked to private and public institutions were evaluated. Some of them were intentionally chosen because they were sites from cities where disease incidence is greater. Twenty dengue sites and 12 tuberculosis sites were assessed. This research served to construct a preliminary diagnosis of the quality of information in these two areas and to test the evaluation tool.

The most important contribution of the LaISS initiative is related to the way in which the readability of the information available on these sites was evaluated. The LaISS team did not use the tools commonly used for this evaluation.

The LaISS team believes that a site with information on the prevention of tuberculosis or dengue is not enough. Questions were elaborated in which evaluators were asked to answer whether or not they had difficulty understanding what was

Table 10.3 Evaluators by criterion in the two experiments

Criterion	Dengue	Tuberculosis
Technical	User and expert	User
Scope	User and expert	User
Interactivity	User and expert	User
Readability	User	User
Accuracy	Expert	User and expert

written, whether they considered a sentence on this subject too long, or whether they found any words that were difficult to understand. Thus, for example, if a sentence was found difficult to understand by 18 of the 20 reviewers, it should be written in another way.

In both cases, only users' representatives evaluated the readability of information available on sites. Criteria evaluators varied according to experience, with the following set forth in Table 10.3:

The above table reveals that the LaISS staff made a major change in the evaluators. Users spearheaded the process! In the evaluation of the information of TB sites, experts evaluated only the accuracy. This change is justified because the LaISS team is more concerned about information being useful to ordinary users. With their higher education, experts have more resources to obtain information.

To conclude, we can state that, according to the analysis of specialized literature in the field of evaluation of the quality of health information on the Internet, the evaluation process used by the LaISS had two novelties that must be highlighted.

Firstly, it should be noted that the two LaISS experiments were attended by health professionals and end users in the construction of the evaluation tool and the evaluation process. The first systematic review on the subject (Eysenbach et al., 2002), nor in the following two revisions (Paolucci 2015; Zhang et al. 2015), identified such participation consisting of users and experts. In both cases, a negligible number of studies involving end users were identified in the evaluation, but not in the construction of the evaluation questions. Zhang et al. (2015), for example, have identified that almost all studies have had experts as evaluators and few have involved users. Paolucci (2015) generated even more evidence on the issue of evaluators. He identified that most studies relied on the authors themselves to evaluate health websites.

Secondly, it is important to emphasize how the readability assessment was performed. It was carried out using index-generating tools to represent levels of reading of documents based on the complexity and length of words and sentences. In 2002, no study had done this evaluation with real consumers of information or subject matter experts (Eysenbach et al. 2002). Paolucci (2015) demonstrated that these tools are still in force. In national and international academic production, many authors continue to use them when evaluating readability. In LaISS' experiment, ordinary citizens from the low-income population led the process – they did the evaluation.

The quality of LaISS work was recently recognized. In 2016, the LaISS became the first certifying agency of Brazilian health websites. It received the support of the Sergio Arouca National School of Public Health (ENSP/Fiocruz) to certify health

Fig. 10.1 Sergio Arouca's seal of quality health information on the Internet

sites with a quality seal. Since then, the health site certification service with the "Sergio Arouca Seal" has been provided to public sites or linked to Brazilian public agencies (Fig. 10.1).

10.7 Trends and Challenges

In Brazil, there is no news of any other public or private agency that is developing systematic activities to evaluate the quality of health information available on the Internet other than the Internet, Health, and Society Laboratory (LaISS/CSEGSF/ENSP/Fiocruz). Meanwhile, in the United States and Europe, government agencies, professional associations, and researchers have been evaluating information on health websites for more than two decades. Health On the Net (HON) and DISCERN are the most prominent. However, the work of LaISS differs from most academic studies and all existing institutional initiatives in the world.

The participation of experts and users to whom site information is intended is essential if sites are to reach people and provide the benefits of access to quality information. This participation can occur at all stages of research and certification processes of health websites. They can contribute as much to the building and validation of tools as in the evaluation of individual websites. Thus, it is possible to obtain more interesting results, from different perspectives of evaluators with different demographic, socioeconomic, and cultural backgrounds. Depending on the health issue you want to provide quality information on, it may be more interesting to involve specific profiles of experts and users.

Table 10.4 Results of the evaluation of Brazilian public sites on tuberculosis

Site	Technical (%)	Interactivity (%)	Scope (%)	Readability (%)	Accuracy (%)	Mean (%)
State Health Secretariat of São Paulo	44	77	83	41	72	63
National Tuberculosis Control Program	38	76	74	41	74	61
Municipality of Rio de Janeiro	52	79	66	40	47	57
Municipality of Porto Alegre	30	76	67	38	50	52
State Health Secretariat of Paraná	41	50	56	29	45	44
Brazilian Thoracic Society	44	80	39	20	23	41
Tropical Medicine Foundation (AM)	33	23	54	18	34	32

In academic terms, the number of published studies in the world on the subject has grown over the years, as the last two systematic reviews indicate. As we analyzed in this chapter, Brazilian scholarship in this area does not follow international trends.

Before the advances in telemedicine in Brazil and in the world, CREMESP's stance seemed to us quite reactive to the growth and availability of new information and communication technologies in people's lives, especially with regard to their health.

If we look at the results of the evaluation[36] carried out by the LaISS in the public sites of tuberculosis, we can see that none of them obtained more than 60% compliance with the criteria used (Table 10.4).

Thus, this sample reveals a problem with the quality of the information about tuberculosis provided by public sites.

Most surprisingly, of the 27 units in the federation, only 12 have a TB-dedicated website. Of the 5570 Brazilian cities, only 8 have TB sites. In Brazil, it is now common to find printed leaflets on tuberculosis distributed in health centers and other places. The pre-Internet communication culture seems to predominate.

We believe that the problems pointed out above, namely, both the low quality of current sites and the scarcity of sites, are directly related to degree of important public health managers and researchers; see information and communication on the Internet. The Brazilian political and intellectual elite seem not to have yet realized the role that new information and communication technologies play in societies around the planet.

[36]This information was retrieved from LaISS' website: http://laiss.ensp.fiocruz.br/pesquisa/buscar

The challenge now is to persuade health officials and intellectuals about the importance of assessing the quality of health information on the Internet.

References

Albarrak, Ahmed, Rafiuddin Mohammed, Nasriah Zakaria, Lujain Alyousef, Noura Almefgai, Hend Alqahtani, Hanan Alamer, and Ahlam Alsulaiman. 2016. The impact of obesity related websites on decision making among students in Saudi Arabia. *Saudi Pharmaceutical Journal* 24: 605–610.

Barbosa, Andréa Lima, and Elisabeth Nogueira Martins. 2007. Evaluation of Internet websites about floaters and light flashes in patient education. *Arquivos Brasileiros de Oftalmologia* 70: 839–843.

Bastos, Bárbara, Deborah Ferrari, Bárbara Guimarães Bastos, and Deborah Viviane Ferrari. 2014. Babies' portal website hearing aid section: Assessment by audiologists. *International Archives of Otorhinolaryngology* 18: 338–346.

Brasil. 2017. Plano nacional pelo fim da tuberculose. Ministério da Saúde. Secretaria de Vigilância em Saúde. Departamento de Vigilância das Doenças Transmissíveis. http://portalarquivos.saude.gov.br/images/pdf/2017/fevereiro/24/Plano-Nacional-Tuberculose.pdf. Accessed 12 Jan 2018.

Carlini, Beatriz Helena, Telmo Mota Ronzani, Leonardo Fernandes Martins, Henrique Pinto Gomide, and Isabel Cristina Weiss de Souza. 2012. Demand for and availability of online support to stop smoking. *Revista de Saúde Pública* 46: 1066–1081.

Charnock, Deborah, and Sasha Shepperd. 2004. Learning to DISCERN online: Applying an appraisal tool to health websites in a workshop setting. *Health Education Research* 19: 440–446.

Chaves, Juliana Nogueira, Ana Lívia Libardi, Raquel Sampaio Agostinho-Pesse, Marina Morettin, and Kátia de Freitas Alvarenga. 2015. Telessaúde: avaliação de websites sobre triagem auditiva neonatal na Língua Portuguesa. *CoDAS* 27: 526–533.

Cheng, Christina, and Matthew Dunn. 2015. Health literacy and the Internet: A study on the readability of Australian online health information. *Australian & New Zealand Journal of Public Health* 39: 309–314.

Chirinos, Narda Estela Calsin, Betina Hörner Schlindwein Meirelles, and Andréa Barbará Silva Bousfield. 2017. Relationship between the social representations of health professionals and people with tuberculosis and treatment abandonment. *Texto Contexto – Enfermagem* 26: 1–8.

CFM – Conselho Federal de Medicina. 2010. Código de Ética Médica – Atual. http://www.rcem.cfm.org.br/index.php/cem-atual#cap14. Accessed 28 Jan.

Clavier, Carole, Yan Sénéchal, Stéphane Vibert, and Louise Potvin. 2012. A theory-based model of translation practices in public health participatory research. *Sociology of Health & Illness* 34: 791–805.

CREMESP – Conselho Regional de Medicina do Estado de São Paulo. 2001. Regional Council of Medicine of the State of São Paulo. Resolução CREMESP n° 97, de 20 de fevereiro de 2001. São Paulo. http://www.cremesp.org.br/?siteAcao=PublicacoesConteudoSumario&id=26. Accessed 28 Jan.

Cochrane Library. 2018. About Cochrane reviews http://www.cochranelibrary.com/about/about-cochrane-systematic-reviews.html. Accessed 6 June 2017.

Cubas, Marcia Regina, and Paulo Cesar Zimmermann Felchner. 2012. Analysis of information sources about breast self examination available on the Internet. *Ciência & Saúde Coletiva* 17: 965–970.

Del Giglio, Adriana, Beatrice Abdala, Carolina Ogawa, Daniel Amado, Diego Carter, Fernanda Gomieiro, Fernanda Salama, Marina Shiroma, and Auro del Giglio. 2012. Quality of internet

information available to patients on websites in Portuguese. *Revista da Associação Médica Brasileira* 58: 645–649.
Eysenbach, Gunther. 2001. What is e-health? *Journal of Medical Internet Research* 3: e20.
Eysenbach, Gunther, John Powell, Oliver Kuss, and Eun-Ryoung Sa. 2002. Empirical Studies Assessing the Quality of Health Information for Consumers on the World Wide Web: A Systematic Review. *JAMA* 287: 2691–2700.
Fernandes, Tania Maria, and Renato Gama-Rosa Costa. 2013. As comunidades de Manguinhos na história das favelas no Rio de Janeiro. *Tempo* 19: 117–133.
Freire, Paulo. 1976. *Education, the practice of freedom*. London: Writers and Readers Publishing Cooperative.
Fritsch, Alexander, and Holger Sigmund. 2016. Review platforms in hospitality. In *Open tourism*, ed. Roman Egger, Igor Gula, and Dominik Walcher, 229–238. Heidelberg: Springer.
Gondim, Ana Paula Soares, and Cláudio Borges Falcão. 2007. Evaluation of Brazilian online pharmacies. *Revista de Saúde Pública* 41: 297–300.
Gondim, Ana Paula Soares, Davi Pontes Weyne, and Bruno Sousa Pinto Ferreira. 2012. Quality of health and medication information on Brazilian websites. *Einstein (São Paulo)* 10: 335–341.
HON – Health On the Net Foundation. 2010. HONcode: Guidelines – Operational definition of the HONcode principles. http://www.hon.ch/HONcode/Guidelines/guidelines.html. Accessed 8 Oct 2017.
IBGE – Brazilian Institute of Geography and Statistics. 2017. Brasil/São Paulo panorama. https://cidades.ibge.gov.br/brasil/sp/panorama. Accessed 12 Jan 2018.
IPP – Instituto Pereira Passos. 2013. Bairros cariocas. http://pcrj.maps.arcgis.com/apps/MapJournal/index.html?appid=096ae1e5497145838ca64191be66f3e3. Accessed 10 Nov 2017.
Lagan, Briege, Marlene Sinclair, and W. George Kernohan. 2011. What is the impact of the internet on decision-making in pregnancy? A global study. *Birth-Issues In Perinatal Care* 38: 336–345.
Lee, Helena, and Natalie Pang. 2017. Information scent – Credibility and gaze interactions: An eye-tracking analysis in information behaviour. *Information Research* 22: 20–23.
Leite, Filipa, and André Correia. 2011. Quality evaluation of websites with information on childhood dental caries in Portuguese language. *Revista Odonto Ciência* 26: 116–120.
Lévy, Pierre. 2001. *Cyberculture*. 1st ed. Minnesota: University of Minnesota Press.
Lima, Carla Moura. 2010. Vozes de quem sofre: discutindo a Saúde Ambiental na Bacia do Canal do Cunha. In *Território, participação popular e saúde: Manguinhos em debate*, orgs. Carla Moura Lima and Leonardo Brasil Bueno, 63–80. Rio de Janeiro: ENSP/Fiocruz.
Lins, Thaís Honório, and Heimar de Fátima Marin. 2012. Evaluation of a website on nursing care in the post anesthesia recovery room. *Acta Paulista de Enfermagem* 25: 109–115.
Misse, Michel. 2011. Crime organizado e crime comum no Rio de Janeiro: diferenças e afinidades. *Revista de Sociologia e Política* 19: 13–25.
Monteiro, Gisele da Silva Gomes, Maíra Macário de Assis, Maria Alvim Leite, Larissa Loures Mendes, Gisele da Silva Gomes Monteiro, Maíra Macário de Assis, Maria Alvim Leite, and Larissa Loures Mendes. 2016. Assessing the nutritional information for children younger than two years old available on popular websites. *Revista Paulista de Pediatria* 34: 287–292.
Moreno, Juan, José Manuel Morales Del Castillo, Carlos Porcel, and Enrique Herrera-Viedma. 2010. A quality evaluation methodology for health-related websites based on a 2-tuple fuzzy linguistic approach. *Soft Computing* 14: 887–897.
Mori, Satomi, Iveth Yamaguchi Whitaker, Heimar de Fátima Marin, Satomi Mori, Iveth Yamaguchi Whitaker, and Heimar de Fátima Marin. 2013. Evaluation of an educational website on First Aid. *Revista da Escola de Enfermagem da USP* 47: 950–957.
O'Neil, Cathy. 2016. *Weapons of math destruction: How big data increases inequality and threatens democracy*. New York: Crown.
Paolucci, Rodolfo. 2015. *Métodos para avaliação da qualidade de informação em sites de saúde: revisão sistemática (2001–2014)*. Master's thesis, Fundação Oswaldo Cruz, Rio de Janeiro.
Paolucci, Rodolfo, André Pereira Neto, and Rafaela Luzia. 2017. Information quality assessment on tuberculosis sites: Analysis of a participatory experience. *Saúde em Debate* 41: 84–100.

Pariser, Eli. 2011. *The filter bubble: What the internet is hiding from you*. New York: Penguin Books.
Park, Hayoung, Sang-Il Lee, Hee Hwang, Yoon Kim, Eun-Young Heo, Jeong-Whun Kim, and Kyooseob Ha. 2015. Can a health information exchange save healthcare costs? Evidence from a pilot program in South Korea. *International Journal of Medical Informatics* 84: 658–666.
Pereira Neto, André, and Rodolfo Paolucci. 2014. *Quality of information on dengue sites: Analysis of a innovative experience*. Rio de Janeiro: FIOCRUZ/ENSP.
Pereira Neto, André, Rafaela Luzia, Rodolfo Paolucci, Leticia Barbosa, and Otávio Porto. 2016. *Quality of information on tuberculosis sites: Analysis of second innovative experience*. Rio de Janeiro: FIOCRUZ/ENSP.
Pereira Neto, André de Faria, Rodolfo Paolucci, Regina Paiva Daumas, and Rogério Valls de Souza. 2017. Participatory evaluation of the quality of health information on the internet: The case of dengue sites. *Ciência e Saúde Coletiva* 22: 1955–1968.
Pithon, Matheus Melo, Elinailton Silva dos Santos, Matheus Melo Pithon, and Elinailton Silva dos Santos. 2014. Information available on the internet about pain after orthognathic surgery: A careful review. *Dental Press Journal of Orthodontics* 19: 86–92.
Powell, John, Nadia Inglis, Jennifer Ronnie, and Shirley Large. 2011. The characteristics and motivations of online health information seekers: Cross-sectional survey and qualitative interview study. *Journal of Medical Internet Research* 13: e20.
Santos, Vagner, Marcelle Maria Portal, Maristela Ferigolo, Denise Conceição Mesquita Dantas, Helena Maria Tannhauser Barros, and Carolina Sturm Trindade. 2010. Sites on drugs of abuse: Resources for assessment. *Trabalho, Educação e Saúde* 8: 575–585.
Scheffer, Mário, Aureliano Biancarelli, and Alex Cassenote. 2011. *Demografia médica no Brasil: dados gerais e descrições de desigualdades*. São Paulo: Conselho Regional de Medicina do Estado de São Paulo e Conselho Federal de Medicina.
Silva, Leonardo Victor España Rueda, João Ferreira De Mello Jr., and Olavo Mion. 2005. Evaluation of Brazilian web site information on allergic rhinitis. *Revista Brasileira de Otorrinolaringologia* 71: 590–597.
Silva, Rosângela Quirino, and Muriel Bauermann Gubert. 2010. The quality of information on maternal breast feeding and complementary feeding on Brazilian internet sites available for health professionals. *Revista Brasileira de Saúde Materno Infantil* 10: 331–340.
Silveira, Priscilla Carla Menezes, Antônia Eliana dos Santos Costa, and Cleone Cassemiro de Lima. 2012. Stuttering in the web: Quality of information. *Revista CEFAC* 14: 430–437.
Sousa, Pedro, Helena Fonseca, Pedro Gaspar, and Filomena Gaspar. 2015. Usability of an internet-based platform (Next.Step) for adolescent weight management. *Jornal de Pediatria* 91: 68–74.
Souza, Camila Luciano Narciso, Zélia Profeta Luz, and Ana Rabello. 2008. Analysis of the information on visceral leishmaniasis available through Brazilian portals of the worldwide web – Internet. *Revista da Sociedade Brasileira de Medicina Tropical* 41: 352–357.
Spoelman, Wouter, Tobias Bonten, Margot Waal, Ton Drenthen, Ivo Smeele, Markus Nielen, and Niels Chavannes. 2016. Effect of an evidence-based website on healthcare usage: An interrupted time-series study. *BMJ Open* 6: e013166.
WHO – World Health Organization. 2018. Neglected tropical diseases. http://www.who.int/neglected_diseases/diseases/en/. Accessed 4 Nov 2017.
Xiang, Zheng, Qianzhou Du, Yufeng Ma, and Weiguo Fan. 2017. A comparative analysis of major online review platforms: Implications for social media analytics in hospitality and tourism. *Tourism Management* 58: 51–65.
Zhang, Yan, Yalin Sun, and Bo Xie. 2015. Quality of health information for consumers on the web: A systematic review of indicators, criteria, tools, and evaluation results. *Journal of the Association for Information Science & Technology* 66: 2071–2084.

Chapter 11
Children and Adolescents on the Internet: A Current Profile of Risks in Brazil

Evelyn Eisenstein and Eduardo Jorge Custódio da Silva

Abstract Children and adolescents have changed their behavior due to access to digital technologies and the Internet. This fact is globally irreversible. Digital connections promote new opportunities but also more health risks. Messages of violence, discourses of hatred and intolerance, contacts with strangers, and online dependence can generate psychological distress and physical damage that are increasingly common. Apps and social networks accessed on smartphones are the primary vehicles for these aggressions and risks. In Brazil, 24.3 million young people (82%) between 9 and 17 years access the Internet through their smartphones (91%) or computers (60%), and 52% of parents did not know what contents are accessed through the Internet, according to the survey ICT Kids Online Brazil (2016). This chapter analyzes online health and safety problems, assess the protective factors, and highlight the importance of mediation by parents, educators, and health professionals in this context.

11.1 Introduction

Children and adolescents experience crucial stages of their growth, development, and brain-mental maturation, with their natural curiosity and impulsivity, and discover the current world more and more accelerated, superficial, noisy, and technostressing. Images of video violence and online games that are part of everyday technological challenges fill this context. Typing, clicking, and sliding fingers on smartphones, cell phones, notebooks, and computers are starting well before a child can tie shoelaces or even have the psychomotor ability to play with a ball. The cartoons and games available on devices inside homes replace playtime in the backyard.

E. Eisenstein (✉)
Faculty of Medical Sciences, State University of Rio de Janeiro, Rio de Janeiro, Brazil

E. J. C. da Silva
Pedro Ernesto Hospital, State University of Rio de Janeiro, Rio de Janeiro, Brazil

A. Pereira Neto, M. B. Flynn (eds.), *The Internet and Health in Brazil*,
https://doi.org/10.1007/978-3-319-99289-1_11

But, are these young people playing dangerous contests or transmitting nudes? Will everything be measured only by megabytes and by bitcoins that monetize fame and glamorization of young YouTubers who are the current celebrities?

Changes in behaviors and relationships between everyone in the family, parents, and children and also in school, between teachers and students, are part of the transformations of reality that no longer separates the virtual from the real. It is increasingly difficult to distinguish how media content influences the development of children and adolescents in their physical, mental, social, and now digital health.

The critical question seems to be this: How can we balance the benefits and opportunities that digital media offers while still avoiding risks and other damages in the future? This question has motivated a lot of research and study. The controversy is often related to the age that children should have access to social networks and the Internet, the time and duration of use, and what are the repercussions of this practice (Young and Abreu 2017).

In this chapter, we will present some relevant aspects related to the risks that children and adolescents face when accessing digital media. Also, we will reflect on the role of parents and educators in the social protection of children and adolescents. Our analysis will focus on the Brazilian reality, specifically the "Statute of the Child and the Adolescent" (Law 8,069/1990), especially articles 240 and 241, updated by Law 11,829 (2008), in its articles 26 and 29, and the recent Law 13,185/2015 establishing the "Program to Combat Systematic Intimidation" (Bullying)[1] assures the rights of this population. The recommendations of the *American Academy of Pediatrics* (AAP) (2016a) and the *Brazilian Society of Pediatrics* (SBP) (SBP 2016) will also serve as guiding principles for our chapter.

Children and adolescents who access the Internet, social networks, online games, and videos represent an important demographic group. We obtained the primary data and trends in the ICT Kids Online Brazil (2016) (CGI 2017) survey. It involved a population ranging from 9 to 17 years of age and their families and approximately 24.3 million people from different social classes of five Brazilian regions survey. This study found that 86% of people in urban areas are Internet users, while in rural areas the rate is 65%.

Eight out of ten connected youth exclusively use their cell phone to obtain access. Also, daily use is intense: 84% access the Internet more than once a day, 90% know how to connect to the Wi-Fi network, and 86% have a profile on social networks. In 31% of families, parents knew little about safety rules or knew anything about their children's activities, and 41% knew just a limited amount. These data show that more than half of families are experiencing security and privacy issues.

The ICT Kids Online Brazil (2016) (CGI 2017) research results also indicate that violence, intolerance, and hate speech in the network were shared by 41% of the sample, or 10 million, and 11% of children and adolescents had already experienced situations of embarrassment or discomfort. This rate reaches 52% in the case of adolescents between 15 and 17 years of age. These numbers and other evidence

[1]The issue of bullying and cyberbullying is discussed in Chap. 12.

presented throughout this chapter reveal that online risks can outweigh opportunities offered by the Internet. Therefore, this section will highlight the importance of parental mediation and educators in this process and the necessary awareness of health professionals and educators. Also, network security should be the goal of public policies in the areas of education and health as well as other governmental actions (NIC 2016).

The World Health Organization defines violence as the intentional use of physical force or threatened or actual power against itself or another person against a group or community that is highly likely to result in injury, death, and psychological harm, problems in development, ill treatment, or deprivation (WHO 2012). This definition does not distinguish actual acts from visual representations or recreations of violent acts online. Nor does it consider the sequels and repercussions associated with such actions, whether real or simulated or cybernetic and online, in the form of harassment or gender discrimination, among other types of intolerance and bigotry. They can result in increased vulnerability, distress, insecurity, depression, anxiety, and technostress. Also, they can retro-feed their violence into other more violent online reactions. Anonymity, fake news, biased news stories, and lack of security and privacy in social networks contribute to the naturalization of violence, especially in young people raised in dysfunctional, unstructured families, or complex political and cultural contexts (King et al. 2007; Livingstone and Palmer 2012; Luna 2013).

We divided this chapter into two parts. In the first part, we will present some aspects of the health of children and adolescents related to the excessive and uncontrolled use of new communication technologies. In this case, we will emphasize the following areas: growth and development, mental and behavioral health, and sexuality and sexual development.

In the second part, we list some of the most common health risks that children and adolescents can contract and the most common preventive measures suggested in specialized literature. In conclusion, some recommendations from the *American Academy of Pediatrics (AAP)* and the *Brazilian Society of Pediatrics (SBP)* are presented to prevent the harmful effects that often affect children and adolescents in the era of digital technologies.

Therefore, the risks will be described rather than analyzed in detail. Although we admit the existence of positive aspects in digital media, as discussed in Chap. 19,[2] this text aims to highlight the need to be alert to protect society's most vulnerable populations. The focus of our attention is on aspects related to the risks of compulsive and uncontrolled use of new information and communication technologies by children and young people.

[2] Chapter 20 addresses the issue of games in health.

11.2 First Part

11.2.1 Growth and Development

All children and adolescents are experiencing the crucial growth stages of their bodies and brains/minds. According to the criteria of the World Health Organization, we call children the people who belong to the age group from birth to 10 years of age and adolescents, people who are between 10 and 20 years of age. Many documents denominate youth the period from birth up to 24 years or until completing the university study. For us, it is more important to know how to differentiate between the gradual and final maturation of puberty (around 25) than to use criteria that are merely historical and legal frameworks for analyzing the issue of safety and social responsibility in different cultural and social contexts (Eisenstein 2005, Giedd 2008).

Factors such as sleep, eating, and physical exercise are essential in all these phases. Moreover, the positive stimuli of attachment, affection, and attention that are conditioning the construction of the personality of the individuals in their mental, emotional, and cognitive development are essential. The contextual and environmental conditions of parental and social protection, including the use of information and communication technologies, can contribute positively, generate different opportunities, or negatively promote risks. These can become social determinants of health and influence the development of these citizens, who have rights as subjects (WHO 2011; Eisenstein 2013).

Children and adolescents develop different practices in their daily routines that can compromise their health. These habits include unhealthy eating that promotes being overweight, obesity, and sedentary lifestyles. Additional challenges include sleep disorders, a tendency to experience violent or aggressive behaviors, mood disorders, depression and anxiety, disorders of image and body perception and self-esteem, hyperactivity, social and sexual conduct, smoking, and the more frequent use of alcoholic beverages and other drugs. Although these routines cannot be singled out as the only causal factor, recurrent, intense access to the video and digital media over the Internet for several hours of the day and night plays a vital role in all these risky behaviors (Strasburger et al. 2012).

Sleep disorders and sleeping difficulties, for example, are among the most frequent complaints of parents and legal guardians. In a review of the literature, involving 125,198 children and adolescents with a mean of 14.5 years of age, a consistent and robust association between the intensive use of the Internet and the inadequate amount of sleep time was apparent in several countries. Poor sleep quality and excessive daytime sleepiness/tiredness are also associated with the compulsive use of the Internet (Carter et al. 2016). Sleep disorders can lead to a drop in school performance because they impair concentration and memory, with increased irritability. Depression and constant complaints of a headache and dizziness are common with sleep disorders. Therefore, pediatric professional associations recommend that children and adolescents disconnect from digital media 2 h before bedtime (Dworak et al. 2007; AAP 2016b; SBP 2016).

It is paramount that children and adolescents have a healthy process of growth and development. To do this, parents must establish a balance between the time spent on online activities and other routine activities, such as playing outdoors, including exercise or sports, adequate feeding times, and sleeping patterns. Thus, the vicious cycles of the release of cortisol and dopamine, which affect the hormonal components of growth, will not be interrupted by stress (Silva and Ting 2013; Eisenstein and Silva 2016).

11.2.2 Mental and Behavioral Health

Excessive exposure to television programs, movies, or video games with violent content can lead to psychological damages. This habit may interfere with cognitive abilities, executive functions, language development, concentration, and long-term memory and increase aggressiveness and naturalize violence among children and adolescents. Some authors point out that abusive use of the Internet favors an increase in the prevalence of violence, hate, and intolerance networks and the risk of developing anxiety and depression, nightmares, sleep disorders, aggressive thoughts, and feelings of anger (Rich 2014). There is also an increase in rates of dangerous self-mutilation games and challenges such as incitement to suicide. Studies show that 10% of users have accessed content looking for ways to commit suicide. This figure increases to 13% in females (CGI 2017; Rich 2014).

Excessive time connected in online games and the use of social networking on the Internet are associated with the release of dopamine, a brain neurotransmitter acting on the reward system. With this, an observation of impulsive habits and attitudes in adolescence will shape the development of the executive and cognitive functions of the prefrontal cortex (NSCDC 2017; Siegel 2016).

Technological dependence can be the result of nonchemical interaction between man and machine, involving induction and behavioral reinforcement. This has given rise to new diagnostic proposals concerning individuals' reliance on the Internet as an "impulse disorder" (Young 1998; Young and Abreu 2011). Although the term "dependency"[3] is widely used, it still is not considered an acceptable medical diagnosis. For example, Rich et al. (2017) challenge the use of the term. So far, the *American Psychiatric Association's Diagnostic and Statistical Manual of Mental Disorders* (DSM-5) has only classified Internet gaming disorder as the only compulsive gambling disorder.

In this context, ICT Kids Online Brazil (2016) (CGI 2017) survey pointed out that 25% of Internet users from 11 to 17 years of age have tried unsuccessfully to spend less time on the network. Another 21% reported that they spend less time with the family because of excessive use of the Internet.

[3] Steven Johnson, in his book "Tudo que é ruim é bom para você" (Zahar, 2012), defends the idea that people who play video games are no worse or better than people who have a habit of reading. According to him, the practice of games stimulates the neurological and cognitive system and enables the development of abilities that past generations could never dream existed. This view is presented in Chap. 19, analyzing the role of the games in health practices.

The uncontrollable desire to be online, plugged in or connected all the time, unable to perform each task separately and with the proper attention and concentration, is being termed "technostress." In the initial stage, the frustration of not being able to access technology is the cause of stress. With persistence, the user can achieve his goal and is satisfied with himself for having managed to activate social networks. At an intermediate stage, there is the crisis of anger in the face of some impossibilities of dealing with applications, online games, devices, or technology equipment all the time. When these difficulties become more frequent, symptoms such as a headache and muscle tension begin to appear. In the last stage, the "technostress" becomes chronic through constant and intense use. At this moment, health becomes compromised due to the intense release of neurotransmitters such as corticotrophin and dopamine. These neurotransmitters influence the production of the hormone cortisol and a whole chain of reactions with repercussions on stress, causing brain dysregulation and various clinical and behavioral disorders, such as headaches and sleeping disorders already mentioned and the increase of anxiety depending on chronicity and intensity (Stratakis and Chrousos 1995). "Technostress" can be triggered by any technological incentives. It occurs when an individual experiences constant positive and negative technical stimuli and reacts in a stressed way because of the adaptations that must occur within themselves to accept such technological novelties in a rather short period.

According to a study conducted by the International Stress Management Association (ISMA) in Brazil, 60% of respondents declared themselves to be technostressed. Most of them reported physical symptoms of stress. Conducted in São Paulo and Porto Alegre, Brazil (ISMA 2001), with 1200 men and women aged 25–55 years, the ISMA study had the objective of identifying the most frequent causes and symptoms of "technostress." Most reported anxiety and distress as emotional effects. Also, behavioral changes were also diagnosed, such as increased alcohol and drug use, aggressiveness (e.g., throwing the cell phone on the floor), and excessive eating habits. The most interesting finding of this study was that 40% of the remaining people evaluated were suffering from "technostress," even without knowing (ISMA 2001).

There is also a syndrome called "induced attention deficit" first described by Edward Hallowell in 2002. It is a frequent diagnosis in adolescents who try to perform several tasks simultaneously, such as answering the cell phone in the middle of another conversation, opening emails, or replying and sending messages immediately. This deficit is also noticeable when someone writes on the cell phone during meals or walks with it on the sidewalks or crosses the streets looking at the cell phone without paying attention to their surroundings. The syndrome with a so-called multitask component can lead children and adolescents toward irritability, distraction, anxiety, and decreased school productivity. Because the human brain can only process one task at a time, this explains the number of mistakes made in school exams, according to the results of comparative tests with magnetic resonance imaging. Induced attention deficit also occurs as one of the leading causes of traffic accidents and the use of cell phones (Hallowell and Ratey 2014).

11.2.3 Sexuality and Sexual Development

New information and communication technologies have transformed not only new patterns of communication and social relationship but also the way in which one learns and manifests sexuality.

In the isolation and anonymity of your computer, in your bedroom or a lan-house, many teenagers begin their sexual acquaintance with information obtained freely on the Internet from people of all types and ages, whose real identities are often unknown. The sharing of *sexting* or *nudes* are observations of sexual experiences young people search with curiosity. So-called sexting involves the transmission of messages with sexual content or of the own self-image by webcam or so-called *selfies* on the Internet. The text messages that accompany sexting are short, simple, and direct, and are part of the new language used through the Internet and cell phones, in social relationship networks, even with strangers. Thus, videos with sexual content of children and adolescents are broadcast even though they are currently considered crimes in Brazil. The sending of videos with photos or sexual content, called *nudes*, is also part of everyday life, despite the Civil Internet Framework,[4] Articles 26 and 29, classifying them as crimes. In our opinion, the boundary line that separates the constructive and healthy versus the pathological use in sexual development is increasingly tenuous. The search for attention and affection on the Internet lies on a subtle and invisible division between health and the risks of future diseases (O'Keefe 2011).

According to the data presented in the ICT Kids Online Brazil (2016) (CGI 2017) survey, 23% of 15–17-year-olds in Brazil post and share sexually oriented videos and messages. On the other hand, 42% of the people surveyed had contact with other unknown people who initiated encounters through social networks (29%), of which only 22% met in person. There is also concern among scholars and family members about the risks of commercial sex exploitation and sexual trafficking networks embedded in many networks of relationships and "dating and sexual encounters on the Internet."

In this context, *grooming* has become more and more constant. It is a practice of seduction carried out through the Internet by pedophiles who try to win the adhesion of children and adolescents in social networks. These practices proliferate because of the absence of effective sexual education provided by parents and educators, compounded by the dearth of educational programs and applications appropriate for adolescents' understanding and engagement with social responsibility in media literacy (Haberland and Rogow 2015).

Easy access to pornography and age-inappropriate sexual content have been considered as risk factors for premature sexual experience, the exercise of unprotected sexuality, early pregnancy, and sexually transmitted diseases such as HIV/AIDS, HPV, and hepatitis C (Chandra-Mouli et al. 2015). Many videos are discriminatory, vexatious, perverse, or violent, inciting sexual, ethnic, or religious discrimination of minority groups of LGBTQ +, including extremist and defamatory contents.

---

[4] Chapter 3 reviews Brazil's Civil Internet Framework.

Pornography and online sexual abuse involving children and adolescents are the most frequent crime complaint in Brazil, according to current data from SaferNet Brasil[5] and INHOPE.[6]

11.3 Second Part

11.3.1 Health Risks

Children and adolescents are subject to taking risks with compulsive and uncontrolled use of new information and communication technologies. Some authors have classified the risks related to visual, auditory, postural, and alimentary issues.

As stated above, this chapter aims to present and analyze the risks that children and adolescents face with the use of new media. Although we acknowledge the existence of positive uses of the same media, we consider it fundamental to be alert to the health risk factors that children and adolescents face with the precocious, compulsive, and indiscriminate use of the Internet. We identified four types of risks: visual, auditory, posture, and eating disorders. Let's look at each one of them.

- *Visual risks: Monitors and screens emit excessive brightness and may cause phototoxicity, especially after prolonged use for many hours. Children or teenagers who play their video games with their eyes fixed on the screen and without blinking are more likely to get phototoxicity. The tears are essential to lubricate the cornea and keep it moist with its nutrients. Dry eye syndrome (DES), for example, is manifested by redness of the eyes, foreign body sensation, conjunctivitis, and keratitis (corneal infection), in addition to refractive errors such as myopia that may worsen during pubertal growth. Computer vision syndrome, whose symptoms are headache; eye discomfort; dryness, irritation, or burning sensation in the eyes; diplopia (double vision); and blurred vision due to convergence responses and ocular accommodation, has also been frequently diagnosed in children and adolescents (Rosenfield* 2011*). Changes in the biological clock and circadian cycle may be associated with sleep disorders and depression due to intense exposure (more than 6 h daily) and blue light waves from screens or LED lamps. This can cause suppression of melatonin and a decrease in HGH, a growth hormone, which is essential during the growth period in childhood and adolescence. It is recommended to reduce the use of computers and smartphones*

[5] SaferNet Brasil is a civil association of private law, with national, nonprofit or economic activity, without political party, religious, or racial bond. Founded on December 20, 2005, focusing on the promotion and defense of Human Rights on the Internet in Brazil. SaferNet Brasil: www.safernet.org.br

[6] INHOPE is an association created to facilitate cooperation between different Internet providers to combat child pornography and to protect children and adolescents of such crimes. INHOPE: http://www.safernet.org.br/site/institucional/redes/inhope

to improve sleep habits, in order to avoid the blue light from the screens 2 h before bedtime (Harvard Medical School 2015; *AAP* 2016b; *SBP* 2016*).*

- *Hearing risks: Continued use of high-power headphones can cause "noise-induced hearing loss" (NIHL). It is an irreversible problem because it compromises the hair cells of the inner ear (cochlea) that do not regenerate. The comfort level of noise for adults, according to the Environmental Protection Agency, is 80 dB. For children and teenagers, the safe level is 60 dB. Noise above 80 dB is considered to be harmful. The threshold for auditory pain is around 120 to 140 dB. The reception of the noise depends on hearing the music, the use of the equipment, and the greater or lesser proximity of the user to the source of the sound, sound box, or headphones. Other auditory symptoms may occur, such as tinnitus, which is an auditory illusion, a phantom sound that is produced in the absence of an external source of sound and interferes with human communication, especially in noisy environments (Carvalho* 2013*).*
- *Postural and osteoarticular risks: Children and adolescents may suffer from problems in the cervicothoracic-lumbar spine when connected with their portable and positioned devices or sprawled unevenly on chairs, armchairs, and sofas. Also, in many cases, school desks and home desks do not fit their size. Because the equipment manufacturers do not consider the physical and postural characteristics of youth, their desks do not fit. The most common changes are rectification or inversion of the cervical spine and the "neck-break" (now known as a "tech-neck") or the protruding head in front of the computer screen, torticollis. This torticollis is due to the neck and shoulders turned aside while answering the cell phone, sharp kyphosis (forward curve), and lordosis (backward curve). During the growth of the spine in adolescents, the deviations of the basin and the shoulders, besides the rotation of the trunk and the scoliosis (curve in "s" of the column), become frequent. "Repetitive strain injuries" (RSI), tenosynovitis and tendinitis, and cervicobrachialgia are also common – muscle pains radiated from the neck, shoulders, and arms after prolonged use of the computer and video games (Gentile et al.* 2004; *Del Peloso* 2013*).*
- *Eating disorders: Body worship and the unrealistic expectations of stereotypes of models and celebrities on digital screens get associated with eating disorders, diets and strict dietary restriction practices, use of anabolic steroids, excessive exercise or overweight/obesity, and chronic physical inactivity. In this case, many young people constantly access social networks and online technologies seeking treatment (Loucas et al.* 2014*). In the survey, ICT Kids Online Brazil (2016) (CGI* 2017*), the proportion of children and adolescents who accessed content on ways to stay very thin* via *the Internet in the last 12 months was 20%, and in the female sex a number that increased to 27% for those between 15 and 17 years old. Other risks exist and get associated with eating or behavioral disorders. Often these practices are associated with the use of drugs, anabolic steroids, or alcoholic beverages. E-cigarettes or electronic cigarettes are now on the scene. These are some warning signs of the health risks that children and adolescents face with the compulsive use of social networks.*

11.3.2 Risk Factors and Protection Factors

Technologies bring opportunities and risks for children and adolescents. In these circumstances, parental mediation is more of the primary challenge. Involvement and training of educators, teachers, and professionals dealing with children and adolescents, such as pediatricians and psychologists, are also significant. It is equally urgent to carry out continuing education and citizenship and digital literacy programs. Permissive practices versus restrictive practices, monitoring or technical mediation with supervision, or the shared use of information and communication technologies (ICTs) are issues that are the order of the day in this regard (Livingstone and Bulger 2013).

Faced with all these risk factors and online security and privacy issues, children and adolescents need to learn how to use passwords and block inappropriate and vexatious messages. They must especially be alert to any messages transmitted or shared with any content of discrimination, offensive messaging, or violence (NIC 2016).

It is crucial that parents take advantage of every possible moment to improve the opportunities to interact and exchange affection and attention in the daily life of the family rather than being each one typing messages on their cell phones at mealtimes or on weekends (Eisenstein et al. 2017). This same literature suggests that the moments of dialogue should be strengthened to reinforce resilience as to the relations of affection, support, and understanding. Living with family, friends, school, and community fosters the building of bonds of trust and respect and offers support, cohesion, and courage during routine activities.

The table below summarizes possible risk and protective factors within the family context. It is a scheme that relates the behavioral problems of children and adolescents to the use of information and communication technologies (Table 11.1).

Even so, online safety of children and adolescents requires an attentive professional network with diverse expertise and technical skills.

Morais (2013) compares the initiatives needed to deal with the risks associated with misuse of information and communication technologies to a "four-legged chair," which can be summarized as follows:

Table 11.1 Possible risk and protective factors within the family context

Risk factors in the family context	Protection factors in the family context
Lack of dialogue	Dialogue and responsible supervision with mediation
Affective abandonment without opportunities of coexistence	Affective bonds with frequent opportunities of coexistence
Lack of limits and appropriate rules	Positive identification models
Denial of inappropriate behaviors of the child	Development of ethical and humanistic family values
Family violence and/or dysfunctional family and/or drug use/alcohol	Protection and digital literacy

1. Regulatory approaches: Laws such as the Internet Civil Framework, the Statute of Children and Adolescents, and National and International Conventions and Documents provide for the appropriate use of technologies. In addition to being implemented, rules and laws need to be better known to all, in schools and families and society as a whole. Parents and children may also have rules of coexistence regarding the use of technologies, including the exchange of passwords, messages, information, photos, or videos. It is essential for everyone to know different privacy and public settings.
2. Educational approaches: Schools should guide students about the use of computers in research work. Teachers should, for example, direct students to check the veracity of the sources used and conduct a critical reflection on literacy and digital citizenship (Google 2013).
3. Parental approaches: Parents and grandparents must go offline and participate in the lives of their children or grandchildren. They should enjoy it and also learn with them. This way parents will have more opportunities to transmit family values that are also valid online. They will be able to remind their children that there are times when it becomes necessary to disconnect such as family mealtimes or joint activities on weekends, vacations, excursions or trips, and at family parties (Morais 2014).
4. Technological approaches: Everyone must keep up-to-date on the operating system of programs, applications, installations, and tools to avoid viruses and unwanted content in the use of the Internet and social networks. Currently, many instructional materials and booklets on these topics are now available online and free of charge (CERT 2016; NIC 2016; Rede E.S.S.E. Mundo Digital 2015).

11.4 Conclusion

UNICEF said in its 2017 report that, for better or worse, technology is now an irreversible fact in our lives and that one in three Internet users are children and adolescents connected in the digital world and that they are already leaving their tracks or "digital footprint" for the future (UNICEF 2017).

Medical societies dealing with the health of children and adolescents, such as the *American Academy of Pediatrics* (AAP)[7] and the *Brazilian Society of Pediatrics* (SBP), have produced some recommendations for adjusting to this new reality. These recommendations concerning the health of children and adolescents in the era of the digital technologies (AAP 2016a) and (SBP 2016) are even accessible online. The main recommendations of these two institutions are as follows:

1. Children younger than 2 years should not use screens as distraction.
2. Children between 2 and 5 years of age must have the total exposure time to media limit to not more than 1 h/day, always with supervision of parent/guardian.

[7] For more information, see https://www.aap.org/en-us/advocacy-and-policy/aap-health-initiatives/Pages/Media-and-Children.aspx

3. Children between 6 and 10 years of age should have total exposure time limited to not more than 2 h/day, always supervised by the parent/guardian.
4. Adolescents aged 11 years and above should have total media exposure time balanced with non-media open-space activities such as exercise or sports in hours/day and ensuring 8–9 h of sleep/night.
5. Parents should talk to children and young people about the rules of coexistence and conduct regarding the use of technologies. They should set time and clear limits and security settings and privacy and explain the risks of sharing photos, videos, or personal or family information. Avoid the use of webcams or virtual reality equipment at home.

The uninterrupted use of digital media also has a psychological dimension worth noting. Many teenagers expose themselves because they want to be celebrities or junior and juvenile YouTubers with endless views. This exposure is the way they know how to identify themselves and be recognized in social groups. This behavior mostly occupies empty spaces of time or results from distress concerning studies or uncertainties about the future. In this sense, Harari (2015) states:

> Without knowing where to go, letting algorithms always know where I am and where I want to go, is just a part of the flow of data. The individual is becoming a small chip within a gigantic system that, in reality, no one understands, and the degree in which the data processing system becomes omniscient and omnipotent, connecting to the system becomes the source of all meaning (Harari 2015, 388).

Encouraging the creation of social protection mechanisms and health education materials can be a valid alternative for the future. In these documents, the emphasis should be on questions about the rights of children and adolescents to health in digital networks. In recent times, school programs designed to develop critical and healthy thinking, as well as educational efforts and reflection about digital media, called "Literacy and Digital Citizenship," have gained strength and space on the Internet. One of them is developed by the Internet, Health and Society Laboratory of the National School of Public Health of the Oswaldo Cruz Foundation.[8]

Technology equipment and digital social networks have been progressively changing the way people relate. For this reason, some care should be taken to ensure the protection of children and adolescents during this period of growth and development. The compulsive and unrestricted use of digital media poses new challenges that must be addressed and studied by health and educational professionals.

References

AAP – American Academy of Pediatrics. 2016a. Media and Young Minds: Council on Communications and Media. www.pediatrics.aappublications.org/content/early/2016/10/19/peds.2016-2591. Accessed 8 June 2018.

———. 2016b. Media use in school-aged children and adolescents. *Pediatrics* 138: 1–6.

[8] For more information, see http://laiss.ensp.fiocruz.br/alfabetizacao/?s=apresentacao

Carter, Ben, Philippa Rees, Lauren Hale, Darsharna Bhattacharjee, and Mandar S. Paradkar. 2016. Association between portable screen-based media device access or use and sleep outcomes: A systematic review and meta-analysis. *JAMA Pediatrics* 170: 1202–1208.

Carvalho, Teresa Cristina R. 2013. Bbzzz, você está ouvindo? In *Vivendo esse mundo digital: impactos na saúde, na educação e nos comportamentos sociais*, ed. C.N. Abreu, E. Eisenstein, and S.G.B. Estefenon, 243–246. Porto Alegre: Artmed.

Chandra-Mouli, Venkatraman, Joar Svanemyr, Avni Amin, Helga Fogstad, Lale Say, Françoise Girard, and Marleen Temmerman. 2015. Twenty years after the international conference on population and development: Where are we with adolescent sexual and reproductive health and rights? *The Journal of Adolescent Health* 56: S1–S6.

CERT – Centro de Estudos, Resposta e Tratamento de Incidentes e Segurança no Brasil. 2016. *Cartilha de Segurança para Internet versão 4.0*. São Paulo: CGI.

CGI – Comitê Gestor da Internet. 2017. *ICT Kids Online Brazil: Survey on Internet use by children in Brazil 2016*. São Paulo: CGI.

Del Peloso, Denise. 2013. Alterações posturais e riscos futuros. In *Vivendo esse mundo digital: impactos na saúde, na educação e nos comportamentos sociais*, ed. C.N. Abreu, E. Eisenstein, and S.G.B. Estefenon, 247–258. Porto Alegre: Artmed.

Dworak, Markus Thomas Schierl, Thomas Bruns, and Heiko Klaus Strüder. 2007. Impact of singular excessive computer game and television exposure on sleep patterns and memory performance of school aged children. *Pediatrics* 120: 978–985.

Eisenstein, Evelyn. 2005. Adolescência: definições, conceitos e critérios. *Adolesc Saúde* 2: 6–7.

———. 2013. Crescimento biopsicosocial e virtual. In *Vivendo esse mundo digital: impactos na saúde, na educação e nos comportamentos sociais*, ed. C.N. Abreu, E. Eisenstein, and S.G.B. Estefenon, 207–220. Porto Alegre: Artmed.

Eisenstein, Evelyn, and Eduardo Jorge Custódio da Silva. 2016. Crianças e adolescentes e o uso intensivo das Tecnologias de Informação e Comunicação: desafios para a saúde. In *ICT Kids Online Brazil: Survey on Internet use by children in Brazil 2015*, ed. Comitê Gestor da Internet (CGI), 177–126. São Paulo: Comitê Gestor da Internet.

Eisenstein, Evelyn, Tito Morais, and Emmalie Ting. 2017. Resilience and preventing parenting. In *Internet addiction in children and adolescents: Risk factors, assessment and treatment*, ed. K. Young and C.N. Abreu, 161–175. New York: Springer.

Gentile, Douglas A., Charles Oberg, Nancy E. Sherwood, Mary Story, David A. Walsh, Marjorie Hogan, et al. 2004. Well child visits in the videoage: Pediatricians and the American Academy of Pediatrics guidelines for children's media use. *Pediatrics* 114: 1235–1241.

Giedd, Jay N. 2008. The teen brain: Insights from neuroimaging. *The Journal of Adolescent Health* 42: 335–343.

Google. 2013. Digital literacy tour. Google in Education. http://www.google.com/edu/resources/digital-literacy.html. Accessed 8 Sept 2017.

Haberland, Nicole, and Deborah Rogow. 2015. Sexuality education: Emerging trends in evidence and practice. *The Journal of Adolescent Health* 56: S15–S21.

Hallowell, Edward, and J. Ratey. 2014. *Driven to distraction: Recognizing and copping with attention déficit disorder from childhood through adulthood*. New York: Touchston.

Harari, Yuval Noah. 2015. *Homo Deus: uma breve história do amanhã*. São Paulo: Companhia das Letras.

Harvard Medical School. 2015. Harvard health letter: Blue light has a dark side. http://www.health.harvard.edu/staying-healthy/blue-light-has-a-dark-side. Accessed 8 Sept 2017.

ISMA – International Stress Management Association – Brasil. 2001. Homepage. http://www.ismabrasil.com.br. Accessed 8 June 2018.

King, Jonathan E., Carolyn E. Walpole, and Kristi Lamon. 2007. Surf and turf wars online, growing implications of internet gang violence. *The Journal of Adolescent Health* 41: 66–68.

Livingstone, Sonia, and Monica Bulger. 2013. *A global agenda for children's rights in the digital age*. Florence: UNICEF Office of Research.

Livingstone, Sonia, and Tink Palmer. 2012. *Identifying vulnerable children online and what strategies can help them*. Londres: UK Safer Internet Centre.

Loucas, Christina E., Christopher G. Fairburn, Craig Whittington, Mary E. Pennant, Sarah Stockton, and Tim Kendalla. 2014. E-therapy in the treatment and prevention of eating disorders: A systematic review and meta-analysis. *Behaviour Research and Therapy* 63: 122–131.

Luna, Cajetan. 2013. Uma *web* perturbada pela violência. In *Vivendo esse mundo digital: impactos na saúde, na educação e nos comportamentos sociais*, ed. C.N. Abreu, E. Eisenstein, and S.G.B. Estefenon, 60–71. Porto Alegre: Artmed.

Morais, Tito. 2013. Segurança na Net e a cadeira de 4 pernas. In *Vivendo esse mundo digital: impactos na saúde, na educação e nos comportamentos sociais*, ed. C.N. Abreu, E. Eisenstein, and S.G.B. Estefenon, 288–298. Porto Alegre: Artmed.

———. 2014. Projeto MiudosSegurosNa.Net. https://www.facebook.com/MiudosSegurosNa.Net/. Accessed 8 June 2018.

NSCDC – National Scientific Council on Developing Child. 2017. Construindo o sistema de "controle do tráfico aéreo" do cérebro: como as primeiras experiências moldam o desenvolvimento das funções executivas. https://46y5eh11fhgw3ve3ytpwxt9r-wpengine.netdna-ssl.com/wp-content/uploads/2017/08/estudo-func%CC%A7o%CC%83es-executivas-habilidades-para-a-vida-e-aprendizagem.pdf. Accessed 8 June 2018.

NIC – Núcleo de Informação e Coordenação do Ponto BR. 2016. Internet Segura: guias para crianças e adolescentes e para pais. https://internetsegura.br/. Accessed 8 June 2016.

O'Keefe, Gwenn Schurgin. 2011. *Cybersafe: Protecting and empowering kids in the digital world of texting, gaming and social media*. Elk Groove Village: American Academy of Pediatrics.

Rede E.S.S.E. Mundo Digital. 2015. Ética, segurança, saúde e educação para crianças e adolescentes. http://www.essemundodigital.com.br. Accessed 8 June 2018.

Rich, Michael. 2014. Moving from child advocacy to evidence-based care for digital natives. *JAMA Pediatrics* 168: 404–406.

Rich, Michael, Michael Tsappis, and Jill R. Kavanaugh. 2017. Problematic interactive media use among children and adolescents: Addiction, compulsion or syndrome? In *Internet addiction in children and adolescents: Risk factors, assessment and treatment*, ed. K. Young and C.N. Abreu, 3–28. New York: Springer.

Rosenfield, Mark. 2011. Computer vision syndrome, a review of ocular causes and potential treatments. *Ophthalmic & Physiological Optics* 31: 502–515.

Siegel, Daniel J. 2016. *Cérebro adolescente, a coragem e a criatividade da mente dos 12 aos 24 anos*. São Paulo: nVersos.

Silva, Eduardo Jorge Custodio, and Emmalie Ting. 2013. Tecnoestresse e cérebro em desenvolvimento. In *Vivendo esse mundo digital: impactos na saúde, na educação e nos comportamentos sociais*, ed. C.N. Abreu, E. Eisenstein, and S.G.B. Estefenon, 49–59. Porto Alegre: Artmed.

SBP – Sociedade Brasileira de Pediatria. 2016. Manual de Orientação, Saúde de Crianças e Adolescentes na Era Digital http://www.sbp.com.br/src/uploads/2016/11/19166d-MOrient-Saude-Crian-e-Adolesc.pdf. Accessed 8 June 2018.

Strasburger, Victor C., Amy B. Jordan, and Ed Donnerstein. 2012. Children, adolescents and the media health effects. *Pediatric clinics of North America* 59: 533–587.

Stratakis, Constantine A., and George P. Chrousos. 1995. Neuroendocrionology and pathophysiology of the stress system. *Annals of the New York Academy of Sciences* 771: 1–18.

UNICEF – United Nations Children's Fund. 2017. *The state of the world's children – 2017: Children in a digital world*. New York: Unicef.

WHO – World Health Organization. 2011. Declaração política do Rio sobre determinantes sociais da saúde. http://www.who.int/sdhconference/declaration/Rio_political_declaration_portuguese.pdf. Accessed 8 June 2018.

———. 2012. Violence prevention alliance: Definition and typology of violence. http://www.who.int/violenceprevention/approach/defintion/en/. Accessed 8 June 2018.

Young, Kimberly S. 1998. Internet addiction: The emergence of a clinical disorder. *Cyberpsychology and Behavior* 1: 237–244.

Young, Kimberly S., and Cristiano N. Abreu. 2011. *Dependência de internet: manual e guia de avaliação e tratamento*. Porto Alegre: Artmed.

Young, K.S. Abreu C.N. 2017. *Internet addiction in children and adolescents: Risk factors, assessment and treatment*. New York: Springer Pub Co

Chapter 12
Bullying and Cyberbullying: Conceptual Controversy in Brazil

André Pereira Neto and Leticia Barbosa

Abstract Bullying is generally defined as a violent, intentional, and repeated act in school environments based on an imbalanced power relationship. Cyberbullying is an aggressive and intentional behavior over the Internet against people who cannot easily defend themselves. The two phenomena may have negative consequences for the physical and psychological health of the victims. This chapter will provide a conceptual discussion about the definition of the two social phenomena: bullying and cyberbullying. To that effect, we searched international and Brazilian bibliographic databases with a view toward retrieving a sample of the academic work on this subject. National and international studies were categorized into three groups: those that attribute uniqueness to bullying, those who understand that the two phenomena have similarities, and those that give cyberbullying its specificity. This chapter reveals that Brazilian studies have analytical perspectives not addressed by specialized international literature.

12.1 Introduction

The Internet provides infinite and unprecedented possibilities in the areas of information and communication. Searching, having fun, and interacting with other people are increasingly frequent at any time and place online. These characteristics are generally advantageous, since they allow individuals to obtain and share knowledge and experiences in a way that their ancestors would find it hard to do (Foody et al. 2015). Internet use on mobile devices has reduced the cost of access and enabled written or verbal communication at all times due to its portability (Grigg 2010).

A. Pereira Neto (✉)
National School of Public Health, Oswaldo Cruz Foundation, Rio de Janeiro, Brazil

L. Barbosa
Institute of Scientific and Technological Communication and Information in Health, Oswaldo Cruz Foundation, Rio de Janeiro, Brazil

A. Pereira Neto, M. B. Flynn (eds.), *The Internet and Health in Brazil*,
https://doi.org/10.1007/978-3-319-99289-1_12

If this description suggests advantages, other experiences of using mobile technologies and the Internet seem to be devastating (Ybarra and Mitchell 2004). Thus, Tokunaga (2010) points out: "The constellation of benefits, however, has been recently eclipsed by numerous accounts of the Internet's undesirable social implications" (Tokunaga 2010, 277).

Cyberbullying is an example to that effect. This phenomenon is defined as an aggressive and intentional behavior carried out by an individual or a group, using the online medium, against someone who cannot easily defend himself. In these terms, the definition of cyberbullying is similar to that generally accepted for bullying (Ybarra et al. 2012; Slonje et al. 2013; Dredge et al. 2014).

In general, bullying is understood as a behavior that occurs when one is repeatedly exposed to a negative action of another person, due to the existence of an unequal relationship between the two (Juvonen and Gross 2008; Foody et al. 2015). Bullying manifests itself through physical, verbal, or psychological threats or abuse (Patchin and Hinduja 2010).

Bullying and cyberbullying have negative consequences on the physical and psychological health of victims. These practices reduce self-esteem, increase depression rates, and promote significant changes in the victim's social activity, including their isolation (Şahin 2012).

The emergence of cyberbullying has been attributed to the rapid development of new information and communication technologies and to the extensive penetration of virtual devices into the life of contemporary individuals: "online communication is not only anymore a daily way to work, but it is mostly used to communicate and interact with known and unknown people" (Baldry et al. 2015, 37).

Bullying and cyberbullying. These two terms have been increasingly used in recent times.[1] Identifying the similarities and differences in the definitions of these two phenomena is one of the great challenges facing scholars on the subject.

Some bibliographic analyses have described these phenomena in relation to their definition, effects, and intervention strategies (Grigg 2010; Tokunaga 2010; Selkie et al. 2016; Corcoran et al. 2015; Asam and Samara 2016; Zych et al. 2016; Olweus and Limber 2017).

This chapter aims to show some of similarities and differences between definitions of bullying and cyberbullying found in contemporary international literature. Next, we will verify whether Brazilian studies qualify bullying and cyberbullying in the same way as foreign authors. It is, thus, a conceptual study of comparative character.

To achieve this end, we conducted a bibliographic search to identify some international and national authors who are concerned with establishing conceptual definitions about these two social phenomena.

[1] "Bullying victim shoots and kills colleagues at school. A combination of humiliation with access to the firearm caused the crime. Son of a military police officer, a 14-year-old student took his mother's gun in his backpack, assassinated the main disaffection and then decided to shoot the others in his classroom, inspired by the massacres of Realengo and Columbine." Headline on the front page of Rio de Janeiro-based newspaper *Jornal O Globo* (10/27/2017).

12.2 Methods

In relation to international authors, the following methodological procedure was adopted.

We searched the ScienceDirect database using the following search strategy: "cyberbullying" and "concept" or "definition." We restricted the search of keywords "concept" and "definition" to journal articles' Abstracts. The word "cyberbullying" was applied to Title, Abstract, and Keywords fields. Thus, we retrieved scientific papers that specifically discussed the concept or definition of cyberbullying. This search strategy uncovered 21 titles. We also included in the bibliographic review the concept of cyberbullying works cited as references in the papers obtained in the survey. By removing the titles that appeared more than once, those that did not seem compatible with the interests of this work and those that were not scientific papers, we obtained 19 titles.[2]

Of the titles selected for the bibliographic review, two were published in 2010, two in 2012, two in 2013, three in 2014, six in 2015, two in 2016, and two in 2017. The search strategy of the selected database obtained no papers prior to 2010, nor papers published in 2011. Ten different scientific journals were identified among the titles in this sample as follows: *Aggression and Violent Behavior* (n = 5), *Computers in Human Behavior* (n = 5), *Journal of Adolescent Health* (n = 2), *Australian Journal of Guidance and Counselling* (n = 1), *Children and Youth Services Review* (n = 1), *Current Opinion in Psychology* (n = 1), *Internet Intervention* (n = 1), *L'Encéphale* (n = 1), *Psicología Educativa* (n = 1), and *Societies* (n = 1). They are grouped in the following areas: Multidisciplinary (n = 3), Psychology (n = 3), Interdisciplinary (n = 2), Psychiatry (n = 1), and Sociology (n = 1). Among the papers selected, 56 authors were identified, and 1 researcher is included in the authorship list of two papers. At the time of publication of the papers, these authors were associated with a group of 32 distinct institutions, located mainly in the United States and Western Europe.[3]

---

[2] Papers of the following authors were included in the bibliographic review: Seto (2002), Ybarra and Mitchell (2004), Gillespie (2006), Li (2007), Juvonen and Gross (2008), Grigg (2010), Patchin and Hinduja (2010), Tokunaga (2010), Şahin (2012), Ybarra et al. (2012), Slonje et al. (2013), Dredge et al. (2014), Baldry et al. (2015), Corcoran et al. (2015), Foody et al. (2015), Selkie et al. 2016, Asam and Samara (2016), Zych et al. (2016), and Olweus and Limber (2017).

[3] The institutions identified were Australian Catholic University (Australia), Center for Innovative Public Health Research (USA), Centers for Disease Control and Prevention (USA), Clemson University (USA), Dublin Business School (Ireland), Emory University (USA), Florida Atlantic University (USA), Freie Universität Berlin (Germany), Goldsmiths University of London (UK), Gothenburg University (Sweden), Karadeniz Technical University (Turkey), Kingston University (UK), KU Leuven (Belgium), Mykolas Romeris University (Lithuania), New York University (USA), Northeastern Illinois University (USA), Seattle Children's Research Institute (USA), Second University of Naples (Italy), Stockholm University (Sweden), Trinity College Dublin (Ireland), Universidad de Córdoba (Spain), Université Paris Ouest (France), Universiteit Antwerpen (Belgium), University of Arizona (USA), University of Cambridge (UK), University of Gothenburg (Sweden), University of Naples Federico II (Italy), University of North Texas (USA), University of Tartu (Estonia), University of Washington (USA), University of Wisconsin (USA), and

In addition to papers retrieved in the survey, we included texts by Ybarra and Mitchell (2004), Juvonen and Gross (2008), Patchin and Hinduja (2010), Seto (2002), Gillespie (2006), and Li (2007). These texts were mentioned in some of the selected publications and were included in our analysis because of their importance to the discussion of the results of the study.

In relation to Brazilian authors, a very similar methodological procedure was adopted. A survey was conducted in two open- and free-access Brazilian virtual libraries. Thus, we collected scientific papers published in Brazilian peer-reviewed journals that addressed cyberbullying as their research topic.

The first was the "Virtual Health Library" (BVS)[4]: a "virtual space for convergence on the Internet for cooperative work in scientific and technical health information" (Packer 2005, 250). It is an initiative promoted and coordinated by the Latin American and Caribbean Center on Health Sciences Information (BIREME) of the Pan American Health Organization (PAHO). It has an area dedicated to Portuguese-speaking countries, including Brazil.[5] Besides Spain, several Hispanic countries in Latin America are part of this portal.[6] One of BVS' main purposes is to promote the production, dissemination, and operation of information sources in multimedia formats, contributing to open-access scientific information. It can be accessed in English, Spanish, and Portuguese. It provides collections of information sources, which include, in addition to the databases produced by the BVS itself, scientific databases such as MEDLINE and other types of information (BIREME 2008; BVS 2017).

The second library consulted in our survey was the "Journals Portal" linked to the "Coordination for the Improvement of Higher Education Personnel" (CAPES), a government linked to the Brazilian Ministry of Education. This Portal aims to democratize, facilitate, and strengthen open access to scientific information produced at international and national levels. This tool provides remote access free of charge to more than 38,000 journals with full texts, databases of references and abstracts, theses, dissertations, reference works, patents, and several other types of electronic documents to students and researchers from Brazilian institutions (CAPES 2017).

The BVS and CAPES Journals Portal were the spaces chosen to conduct our survey due to the wide and diversified scientific collection of Brazilian open-access information. These tools enabled the free collection of scientific papers produced by researchers from institutions and different areas of knowledge on bullying and cyberbullying.

Washington State University (USA).

[4] For more information, see the portal in English located at http://bvsalud.org/en/

[5] In addition to Brazil, the Portuguese-speaking countries that are part of this portal are Angola, Cape Verde, Guinea-Bissau, Mozambique, Portugal, Sao Tome and Principe, and East Timor.

[6] The Latin American countries that integrate this portal are Argentina, Belize, Bolivia, Chile, Colombia, Costa Rica, Cuba, Ecuador, Guatemala, Guyana, Honduras, Mexico, Nicaragua, Panama, Paraguay, Peru, Puerto Rico, Trinidad and Tobago, Uruguay, and Venezuela.

To carry out the mentioned bibliographic survey, the following search terms were used: "cyberbullying" or "ciberbullying" or "bullying" or "assédio" or "intimidação" or "agressão" and "Internet" or "virtual" or "www" or "on-line" or "online" or "on line" or "rede social" or "mídia social."[7]

In the BVS database, the search strategy was limited to the title, abstract, and subject fields of the publications. At first, more than 5000 titles were obtained. We used two filters available in the library tool, "Bases de dados nacionais: Brasil" ["National Databases: Brazil"] and "Artigos" ["Articles"], to collect the most relevant results for the study. Thus, results, comprised only of scientific papers published in Brazilian journals and submitted for peer evaluation, returned 71 titles.

The same search strategy was employed in the CAPES Journals Portal and found only three titles. This quantity was insignificant to us, and, thus, we only used the words "cyberbullying" and "ciberbullying," restricted to the "Subject" field. We obtained more than 10,000 results. "Artigos" and "Idioma: Português" ["Language: Portuguese"] filters were used to select the most relevant results, which returned 19 titles.

The 90 titles retrieved in both platforms were exported and entered into Mendeley, which is a free tool that allows the management of bibliographic references. It enabled us to delete all duplicate results, leaving out 80 titles. Next, we analyzed authorship, title, summary, and keyword fields of each publication collected to verify their relevance to the study. In this process, only scientific paper publications evaluated by peers, with cyberbullying as the main theme and whose author was a professional linked to a Brazilian education and research institution, were included. Thus, the final academic production selected for analysis consisted of 12 scientific papers.[8]

Among the selected titles, one was published in 2010, five in 2012, one in 2013, four in 2014, and one in 2015. In the selected sample, no paper was found before 2010 or later than 2015. Moreover, no articles were published in 2011.

In this sample of papers, we identified 11 different Brazilian journals: *Boletim da Academia Paulista de Psicologia* (n = 1), *Ciberlegenda* (n = 1), *Movimento* (n = 1), *Nuances: estudos sobre Educação* (n = 1), *Nucleus* (n = 1), *Perspectivas online: humanas e sociais aplicadas* (n = 1), *Psicologia Clínica* (n = 1), *Revista Tecer* (n = 1), *Scientific Electronic Archives* (n = 1), *Temas em Psicologia* (n = 2), and *Texto Livre: linguagem e tecnologia* (n = 1). Such journals may be categorized in the

[7] We chose to consider two spellings for the term "cyberbullying" because some Brazilian scientific literature replaces the letter "y" with the letter "i" in the spelling of the term cyber. We also included synonyms for the term "cyberbullying," because it was deemed possible that Brazilian authors, while addressing this topic in their articles, would not specifically use the term imported from the English language to refer to aggressive, hostile, and harassing behaviors, as well as harassment by individuals or groups, through the Internet, aiming to cause harm or loss to third parties (Tokunaga 2010).

[8] Papers of the following authors were included in the bibliographical review carried out on the Brazilian studies: Aranha (2014), Azevedo et al. (2012), Barbosa (2014), Berto (2012), Dias et al. (2012), Gonçalves et al. (2014), Matte (2012), Schreiber and Antunes (2015), Stelko-Pereira and Williams (2010), Tognetta and Bozza (2012), and Wendt and Lisboa (2013, 2014).

following six areas: Psychology (n = 3), Multidisciplinary (n = 3), Interdisciplinary (n = 2), Communication (n = 1), Education (n = 1), and Physical Education (n = 1).

Nine journals are linked to higher education institutions with a postgraduate course.[9] Eight of them are located in states of the federation of the South and Southeast regions, where the population with the highest purchasing power of the country is concentrated. The other two journals are the responsibility of two scientific psychology societies: the Brazilian Society of Psychology and the São Paulo Academy of Psychology.

In the papers selected, 24 different authors were identified, of which 2 researchers signed 2 publications together – 1 in 2013 and another in 2014.[10] At the time of publication of the papers, this set of authors was associated with 14 different education and research institutions, all of them universities, 3 of which were foreign.

This chapter is divided into three parts: The first part will gather authors who identify characteristics to bullying. The second part will show those who admit that cyberbullying is no more than an extension of bullying, that is, cyberbullying would not preserve its specificity as a social phenomenon. In the third part, we will show the authors who give cyberbullying their singularity. Throughout this conceptual reflection, we will examine similarities of Brazilian authors' views analyzed to scholars from the international sample.

12.3 Bullying: A Unique Social Phenomenon?

Patchin and Hinduja (2010) published a paper in the *Journal of School Health* in which they show three characteristics that would give bullying the character of a unique social phenomenon. The first is associated with the fact that there is no mediation between aggressors and victims. Bullying would therefore be characterized by face-to-face contact between aggressors and victims. In addition, in bullying, aggressive behavior would have explicit and delimited geographical and time boundaries. For this reason, this practice would be confined mostly to schools, the arena of human interactions. Finally, bullying ends when the victim comes home, because direct contact was temporarily suspended (Patchin and Hinduja 2010).

Among Brazilian authors analyzed, Dias et al. (2012), Wendt and Lisboa (2014), and Schreiber and Antunes (2015) share a similar view to that of Patchin and Hinduja (2010), as they understand that bullying is a face-to-face contact practice.

[9]The Brazilian institutions of higher education identified are the following: Pontifical Catholic University of Rio de Janeiro (PUC-RJ), Educational Foundation of Ituverava, CENSA Higher Education Institutes, Federal University of Mato Grosso (UFMT), Methodist University Center Izabela Hendrix, Federal University of Minas Gerais (UFMG), Federal Fluminense University (UFF), State University of São Paulo (UNESP), and Federal University of Rio Grande do Sul (UFRS).

[10]Two papers by Guilherme Welter Wendt were identified in the sample. In the 2013 publication, he indicates the Pontifical Catholic University of Rio Grande do Sul as his institutional link, while in the 2014 publication, he mentions the University of London.

This aspect would define its uniqueness. This group of authors says that physical and verbal abuse, accusations, and threats would occur when aggressors physically find their victims.

Azevedo et al. (2012) emphasize that school is the physical space where bullying takes place. Their perspective follows the conception found in international literature. Selkie et al. (2016), for example, point out that traditional bullying tends to increase during the school years corresponding to primary and secondary education. Juvonen and Gross (2008, 497) show data that reinforce this view. They say "approximately 70% of youth report having experienced bullying at some point during their school careers."

According to Azevedo et al. (2012), bullying would be a typical old-school violence, where "bullies" oppress and threaten their victims for banal reasons, by imposing their "authority" (Azevedo et al. 2012). Matte (2012), Barbosa (2014), Wendt and Lisboa (2014), and Schreiber and Antunes (2015) agree with this viewpoint. Matte (2012) argues that bullying is greater in schools due to the identity construction process and the need for young people to be recognized by the generally restricted social circle they occupy in this closed environment. According to the Brazilian author:

> Bullying has appeared as a juvenile behavior in schools, at an age when social identity is underway, and thus when subjects are more vulnerable to provocations that exploit their 'failures' towards their socialization. (Matte 2012, 3)

It should be noted that Schreiber and Antunes (2015) admit that bullying can also take place at the workplace or within the family.

In these Brazilian papers, we could observe two important aspects that would characterize bullying. One of them refers to the fact that the categories of aggressors and victims of bullying are not necessarily antagonistic. In their work, Wendt and Lisboa (2014, 43) affirm that "when a teenager is both an aggressor and a victim, a profile can be outlined that characterizes him as an aggressor-victim." Barbosa (2014, 50) complements this idea by saying that "there is no necessary dichotomy between being a perpetrator and being a victim of bullying, because students can play both roles according to circumstances."

The second aspect found in the Brazilian literature that complements the definition of bullying identified in the international literature refers to the leisure experience that bullying can provide to its practitioners and spectators. In his study with adolescents from public schools in a small municipality in the Brazilian rural region, Barbosa (2014) identified that bullying was seen by young people as a form of "zoação," a Brazilian slang that means to mock someone jokingly. Aggressors interpret this "zoação" as a playful experience – a fun situation. Gonçalves et al. (2014, 965) argue that "bullying is a cruel behavior found in interpersonal relationships, in which the stronger person converts the more fragile into objects of enjoyment and pleasure." In their paper, Wendt and Lisboa (2014) also mentioned the extent of leisure in this practice. These authors point out that even those who do not commit bullying can view it as a form of entertainment, since they have fun while watching the aggressive situations experienced by a third person.

Let us have a look now at some authors who consider that bullying and cyberbullying are similar social behaviors.

12.4 Bullying and Cyberbullying: Similar Phenomena?

Some papers identified in our international sample admit that bullying and cyberbullying are similar social phenomena, since both carry the intention of an individual or a group to harm another person through a negative action. Ybarra et al. (2012), from Johns Hopkins Bloomberg School of Public Health, United States, point out that some authors consider cyberbullying as a type of bullying, equivalent to that which occurs in a physical space. Dredge et al. (2014, 13) affirm:

> The cyberbullying literature has consistently applied the definition of 'traditional' bullying to the realm of electronic media. Therefore, the most common definitions of cyberbullying are based on the three basic components of traditional bullying definitions, namely: repetition, deliberate intent to harm and power imbalance.

As Tokunaga (2010) admits:

> In many ways, traditional bullying and cyberbullying share considerable overlap in their core motivations. Individuals who cyberbully others wish to inflict harm on their targets and execute a series of calculated behaviors to cause them distress. (Tokunaga 2010, 278)

Thus, international authors mentioned above state that the concepts bullying and cyberbullying would have the same motivations, such as causing intentional harm – perceived as abuse; being based on the imbalance of power, where perpetrators are in a position superior to the abused; and promoting systematic and intentional humiliation. As flagged by Corcoran et al. (2015), bullying and cyberbullying manifest themselves when one is continuously subjected to negative or aggressive actions by a third person or group of people:

> Consistent with traditional bullying definitional criteria, […] cyberbullying was found to be characterised by intention to cause hurt and perception of the behaviour as hurtful (by the victim), *repetition of negative offline or online behaviours*, and a power imbalance […]. (Corcoran et al. 2015, 251, our italics)

A similar perspective is found in the paper by Slonje et al. (2013). The authors state that:

> Bullying is generally seen as intentional behavior to harm another, repeatedly, where it is difficult for the victim to defend himself or herself […], it is based on an imbalance of power; and can be defined as a systematic abuse of power […]. By extending the definition from traditional bullying, cyberbullying has been defined as 'an aggressive act or behavior that is carried out using electronic means by a group or an individual repeatedly and over time against a victim who cannot easily defend him or herself' […]. (Slonje et al. 2013, 26)

Thus, international authors mentioned above say that the two social phenomena would be conscious, intentional, permanent, and systematic acts of humiliation.

Some Brazilian authors share this view found in this international literature. Schreiber and Antunes (2015, 116) point out that both bullying and cyberbullying "aim to exclude and humiliate victims; thus, the two phenomena have similar characteristics." Tognetta and Bozza (2012, 163) point out that bullying and cyberbullying are practices that share an "intentional violence against another."

The view of some of these Brazilian authors coincides with that of international authors. Both affirm that intentional and conscious violence was an aspect common to both phenomena.

Dias et al. (2012) affirm that bullying and cyberbullying encompass "highly-aggressive attitudes and procedures that are constantly and consciously intentional and performed individually or in groups, resulting in pain, suffering and distress" (Dias et al. 2012, 40). Repetition would therefore be another common feature of bullying and cyberbullying (Tognetta and Bozza 2012). In works by Gonçalves et al. (2014) and Wendt and Lisboa (2014), bullying and cyberbullying share a resemblance since they involve systematically humiliating their victims. Gonçalves et al. (2014, 966) argue that such practice is "continuous, systematic abusive action… in which subjects who suffer this abuse are increasingly unable to defend themselves." Wendt and Lisboa (2014) say that, in addition to bullying and cyberbullying being repeated actions, they also occur when one seeks to intimidate, harass, or attack an individual or group: that is, acts of violence are not random but regular and orderly in order to constantly humiliate victims. Wendt and Lisboa (2014) reinforce this idea by stating that bullying and cyberbullying are not random jokes. According to Tognetta and Bozza (2012, 163), "bullying and cyberbullying agree on one feature that is intentional violence against another. […] Boys and girls of similar ages in both cases intimidate, humiliate, offend, threaten and disrespect their peers." In addition to continued abuse, individuals or a group committing bullying or cyberbullying intend to do so (Gonçalves et al. 2014). Thus, these are "consciously intentional" processes (Dias et al. 2012). They are not random; on the contrary, perpetrators' actions aim to humiliate and subjugate their victims.

Another common aspect indicated by international literature is related to the fact that the two behaviors are structured on an unequal power relation between victims and their offenders, called "imbalance of power" by Dredge et al. (2014), Corcoran et al. (2015), and Asam and Samara (2016). Dredge et al. (2014, 13) say that the "most common definitions of cyberbullying are based on the three basic components of traditional bullying definitions, namely, repetition, deliberate intent to harm, and power imbalance." Corcoran et al. (2015) point out that there is a consensus in literature about imbalance of power being one of the criteria that defines traditional bullying and that in research conducted with young students from Italy, Germany, Spain, Sweden, Estonia, and France, "intent and effect on the victim (as part of a power imbalance)" were also recognized as one of the defining criteria of cyberbullying (Corcoran et al. 2015, 5). According to Asam and Samara (2016, 128), "bullying is explained as a form of abuse that is based on imbalance of power." Authors note that the aspect of power imbalance is also found in the definitions of cyberbullying: "as previously defined, cyberbullying is summarized as an intentional aggressive and repeated behaviour that intends to harass, intimidate and threaten the victim via electronic means characterised by imbalance of power."

In the opinion of some Brazilian authors, an unequal power relationship between victims and their perpetrators would also be a feature that would draw bullying closer to cyberbullying.

Dias et al. (2012, 40) point out that "those who are stronger bully, threaten, oppress, frighten, and intimidate the weak." Stelko-Pereira and Williams (2010, 51–52) indicate that such imbalance may be related to several factors, such as "popularity, physical strength or physical stature, social competence, extroversion, intelligence, age, gender, ethnicity, and socioeconomic status" of offenders. Authors also point out that, in the case of cyberbullying, the unequal power relationship between aggressors and their victims may be based on the ability of each party to use digital technologies to harass, intimidate, and humiliate others:

> In cyberbullying, it is also assumed that the power gap between perpetrators and victims, whether assumed or actual, is configured by the different ability to use electronic technology to intimidate others and not necessarily in physical characteristics, popularity and more related to traditional bullying. (Stelko-Pereira and Williams 2010, 52)

This perspective discussed by Stelko-Pereira and Williams (2010) in the Brazilian journal *Temas em Psicologia* is consistent with that provided by Slonje et al. (2013, 27) in the *Scandinavian Journal of Psychology* who understand that "physical strength is not necessary for perpetration of cyberbullying, nor is strength of numbers. However, two other possibilities of power imbalance in cyberbullying are technical ability with ICTs and anonymity."

In a paper published in the Brazilian journal *Temas em Psicologia*, Wendt and Lisboa (2014) said this power imbalance puts victims in a situation in which they have little or no possibility of defending themselves. In the Brazilian journal *Perspectivas* online, Dias et al. (2012) affirm that victims feel intimidated and thus incapable of reacting to abuse, threats, and insults. Matte (2012, 3) points out that this inability to defend themselves becomes a kind of victory for perpetrators: "they win because they convince victims that they should defend themselves, and they also win because, in successful cases, victims are unable to defend themselves." The author argues that such incapacity occurs both in cases that are face-to-face and those mediated by digital technologies.

Another aspect that would bring bullying closer to cyberbullying is related to the fact that the two aggressions can affect the physical, psychological, and/or sexual spheres. The international authors who showed this perspective were Tokunaga (2010), Baldry et al. (2015), Şahin (2012), and Selkie et al. (2016).

Tokunaga (2010, 277) says bullying and cyberbullying can have negative consequences[11] for the victims: "cyberbullying victimization is associated with a host of negative problems similar to those of traditional bullying victims." Baldry et al. (2015, 37) show a similar perspective when they affirm that "the dark side of children's use of internet and associated technology is the risk of being bullied

[11] The issue of risks and health of children and adolescents on the Internet is discussed in Chap. 11.

online or bullying others, so called cyberbullying, leading to short and long term negative consequences [...] and ultimately even suicide or attempted suicide [...]." In a study with secondary school students, Şahin (2012) identified a positive relationship between loneliness and cyberbullying victims. The author affirms that: "cybervictims are not aggressive and do not provoke aggressive behaviors." This means that the high level of loneliness of cybervictims can be attributed to bad experiences they have with their peers (Şahin 2012, 836).

From a systematic review of the prevalence of cyberbullying among primary and secondary school students, Selkie et al. (2016, 131) highlight that "the range of CB prevalence found in this review suggests that CB may be a common occurrence among today's youth and could lead to other negative consequences outside the most severe cases."

This view has also been observed in some national studies. According to Azevedo et al. (2012), Berto (2012), Wendt and Lisboa (2014), and Barbosa (2014), acts of violence produce suffering for the victims, interfere in their development and social life, and promote low self-esteem, social panic, depression, aggression, eating disorders, drug abuse, and suicidal ideas (Berto 2012; Schreiber and Antunes 2015).

In addition, victims may also have their academic development compromised (Barbosa 2014). Matte (2012) emphasizes that the main characteristic of bullying, carried out both in physical space and the virtual environment, is not intimidation, but humiliation resulting from this practice. According to the author (2012, 7), "bullying can play with intimidation, but the main ingredient of abuse is ensuing humiliation; therefore, what is at stake is provocation: retaliate if you can." The author, who works under the theoretical-methodological matrix of semiotics, points out that:

> In the narrative plan, bullying involves two types of disputes: the clash between sender and recipient, in which the sender uses manipulation by provocation so that the sender accepts the framework of values according to which violence is a legitimate way of competing, and the clash between subject and anti-subject, in which the object would be this social integration [...]. (Matte 2012, 3)

Matte (2012, 4–5) clarifies that in semiotics, provocation is characterized as "a relationship between subjects in which a sending subject seeks to induce the addressee to an action based on a negative appreciation of this subject's being." Thus, the author adds an important dimension to the definition of bullying. In the semiotic perspective, bullying and cyberbullying would lead perpetrators to provoke victims, so that they would accept their frame of values as a way of socially integrating themselves.

Matte (2012, 3) states that offenders would be "doubly victorious" in this dispute. The first victory would be related to the victims' acceptance of the provocation and who thus would be convinced to defend themselves from the negative valuation that aggressors made of them. The second victory, in turn, would be related to situations where the perpetrators are successful and victims feel unable to defend themselves by accepting the frame of values imposed by aggressors.

Some international authors consider that cyberbullying is ultimately a type of bullying. Olweus and Limber (2017, 140) argue that there is a relationship between traditional bullying and bullying in the digital environment, so that "to put cyberbullying in proper perspective, it is in our view necessary to study it in the context of (traditional) bullying more generally." According to Juvonen and Gross (2008), cyberbullying could be understood as a bullying "extending the schools grounds." These teachers from the University of California, Los Angeles, argue that "cyberspace may not function as a separate risky environment but rather as an extension of the school grounds" (Juvonen and Gross 2008, 497).

In the analysis of the Brazilian papers, we identified authors that agree with this view. Wendt and Lisboa (2013, 75, our italics) state that cyberbullying is "a subtype of bullying with *specific characteristics*." According to these authors, the "specific characteristic" would be technological mediation. Thus, Wendt and Lisboa (2014, 42) affirm that "[…] the cyberbullying process can be understood as a specific type of bullying through technological instruments […]." Azevedo et al. (2012, 247) share this idea that cyberbullying would be a "digitized bullying." In addition, Barbosa (2014, 48) argues that cyberbullying would be the "most current form" of bullying among young students. Berto (2012, 30) says that cyberbullying would be "a bullying action in a virtual environment," that is, a type of bullying that happens from the resources facilitated by ICTs, which may include insults, abuse, and verbal and psychological broadsides. However, when using digital technologies, cyberbullying becomes a type of violence that transposes schools' physical barriers and can be seen as "a type of virtual bullying" (Tognetta and Bozza 2012, 165).

Linking cyberbullying to bullying was also found in the works of some Brazilian authors. Stelko-Pereira and Williams (2010, 52, our italics) state that "[…] cyberbullying is an *extension* of bullying […], which seeks to intimidate and harm an individual or group through the use of digital technologies." Gonçalves et al. (2014) analyzed three Brazilian communities on the Orkut digital social network. They concluded that humiliating actions, such as the use of pejorative nicknames, exposing intimate events, and negatively manipulating photographs begin in the classroom and move to young people's own virtual environments. One of the virtual communities investigated by the authors "is more explicitly aimed at making fun of the girl considered the 'ugliest' girl in school," and polls are posted in order to ridicule and humiliate a student considered by the members as excessively short on beauty standards. Authors describe an example of the practice of cyberbullying committed in the virtual environment. "In the question 'Why do you think she is the ugliest in school?', answers address the congenital realm: 'because she was born that way,' 'because she was born ugly,' or 'because she was always ugly'" (Gonçalves et al. 2014, 978).

Let us now have a look at some authors who consider that cyberbullying is a unique social behavior, different from bullying.

12.5 Cyberbullying: A Unique Social Phenomenon?

According to some authors found in the international and national literature, humiliation mediated by information and communication technologies confers singularity to cyberbullying. In bullying, aggression is direct. In cyberbullying, it is mediated by ICTs. In cyberbullying, harassment is not through actual physical presence; it does not presuppose direct face-to-face contact.

This is the view of some international authors consulted, such as Slonje et al. (2013), Zych et al. (2016), Selkie et al. (2016), Tokunaga (2010), and Corcoran et al. (2015).

Slonje et al. (2013, 26) point out that technology mediation characterizes cyberbullying, by affirming that "cyberbullying is a systematic abuse of power which occurs through the use of information and communication technologies (ICTs)." From a systematic review of studies in Spanish on cyberbullying, Zych et al. (2016) also identified the use of ICTs as an important aspect to define cyberbullying, stating that: "in general, the vast majority of the definitions stated that cyberbullying is perpetrated through electronic devices [...]" (Zych et al. 2016, 12).

Cyberbullying would bear no limits, no boundaries, and no constraints on the aggressors' action. Victims can be reached via mobile phone, email, and instant messaging anytime, anywhere, including their own home. Selkie et al. (2016, 125) state that cyberbullying "differs from 'traditional' forms of bullying [...] due to distinct features of the electronic medium. These include [...] minimal constraints on time and space in which bullying can occur." Tokunaga (2010, 278) underscores that "cyberbullying can occur through electronically mediated communication at school; however, cyberbullying behaviors commonly occur outside of school as well." In this perspective, due to the mediation of digital technologies, harm against victims does not imply physical interaction, as with bullying. Corcoran et al. (2015) also have this understanding: "cyberbullying mainly differs from traditional bullying in the reach of the offenders. Cyberbullies are able to extend the bullying beyond the school grounds and follow targets into their homes" (Corcoran et al. 2015, 246).

Some national authors are in tune with the international peers mentioned above. They also highlight the role played by ICTs in defining cyberbullying. Wendt and Lisboa (2013), of the Catholic University of Rio Grande do Sul, understand that derogatory content can be sent to victims through "[...] emails, text messages, dissemination of offensive photos and videos, manipulation of images, insults in chat rooms or on social networks" (Wendt and Lisboa 2013, 78).

Azevedo et al. (2012) ratify this point of view by stating that:

> Through the Internet, abusers can send abusive, obscene or defamatory messages via email, on social networking sites (such as Orkut, Facebook, Twitter) or using instant messaging programs (such as MSN and Google Talk). (Azevedo et al. 2012, 247)

Thus, according to this definition, in cyberbullying, victims would be reached regardless of time and place. Stelko-Pereira and Williams (2010) of the Federal University of São Carlos, São Paulo State, point out that abuse transposes the time-space relationship, reaching victims through messages, photos, and emails sent at any time of the day to wherever they are.

Azevedo et al. (2012) point out that the phenomenon of bullying usually occurs during the period that children and adolescents are in school. Cyberbullying, on the other hand, goes beyond this physical face-to-face aspect, allowing the victims to be reached even when they are no longer in or near the school environment. Wendt and Lisboa (2013, 2014) reiterate that cyberbullying does not have a circumscribed space, making the alternative escape or avoidance practically impossible for the abuse target. "A victim of cyberbullying, in general, has nowhere to go and is unable evade this violence" (Wendt and Lisboa 2014, 50). According to these authors:

> [...] victims of cyberbullying may never know the minute when they will be attacked again because the internet allows perpetrators to reach victims in countless ways and at any time by altering the contextual delimitations of bullying in school. Unlike bullying victims, who know they will be attacked when they arrive at school or fear recess, cyberbullying victims can receive threatening text messages even while they are asleep. (Wendt and Lisboa 2013, 78)

Thus, following this definition, harm in cyberbullying does not imply physical interaction. In bullying, the offender is in front of the victim. In general, one is the other's classmate at school. In cyberbullying, victims may not even know their abusers in person or find it difficult to recognize them over the Internet. The Internet would assure perpetrators a sense of anonymity when they commit their actions. The capillarity of social networks would allow humiliation and aggression to reach, with "likes" and "shares," an untold number of people. The use of social networks allows message senders not to be easily identified and the message to be widely spread. These two characteristics of Internet communication give cyberbullying its uniqueness.

We will analyze each of them below.

A first point highlighted by international authors is related to a *feeling* of anonymity related to Internet browsing. It is no coincidence that the word *feeling* is in italics. Some international authors in our literature address this aspect.

For example, Ybarra and Mitchell (2004, 330) claim that "the Internet is a tool for anonymous communication." They argue that "the *anonymity* associated with online interactions may strip away many aspects of socially accepted roles, leading the Internet to act as a potential equalizer for aggressive acts" (Ybarra and Mitchell 2004, 332). Foody et al. (2015, 236) corroborate with this idea, admitting that "one of the main distinguishing factors of cyberbullying is the *anonymity* of the crime, which can be executed in front of a large audience and at the same time, allow the perpetrator to remain unidentified." According to Slonje et al. (2013, 27, our italics), "two other possibilities of power imbalance in cyberbullying are technical ability with ICTs and *anonymity*." In the systematic review conducted by Zych et al. (2016), anonymity was identified as one of the aspects that distinguishes cyberbullying from bullying: "most of the definitions included also specific criteria such as possible *anonymity*" (Zych et al. 2016, 14).

Asam and Samara (2016, 128) reiterate the *feeling* of anonymity as a differentiated dimension of cyberbullying:

> […] It is easy to bully others in cyberspace; all that is required is access to an electronic device, such as a mobile phone or computer, and the details of the victim to whom the bullying will be directed, such as their mobile phone number, internet address or username. By using this method, perpetrators do not have to face their victims and therefore can remain anonymous; bullying can remain a cold attack on a person and perpetrators do not have to witness directly the consequences of their actions.

We said feeling of anonymity, because the computer from which the aggression started can ultimately be tracked. The interested party only requires discovering the Internet Protocol (IP) of the information-sending device. By making an analogy to Michel Foucault's book *Discipline and Punish: The Birth of the Prison* (1975), Silveira (2010) wrote an article entitled "Monitoring and Punishment: Communication and Control on the Internet." The Brazilian author emphasizes the persecutory and privacy-invasive role facilitated by the Internet.

According to him, on the Internet, citizens are free to decide what they want to watch, post, or share. However, it is possible to quickly find out through the IP address how many "netizens" have visited a particular site, with whom they communicate, and what is posted, bought, or sold. This is because it is "impossible to browse the Internet without an IP address and without accepting its basic communication protocols. Thus, when a computer accesses a website, it does so according to TCP/IP protocols" (Silveira 2010, 201). In another paper, the same author points out that, on the Internet, social relationships take place in a context governed by an information control system:

> Information transmission is almost always accompanied by its registration. Data are communicated generating data on the communication made, i.e. metadata are constantly being created. Records of what is done are based on these communication and control processes. (Silveira 2017, 28)

In fact, online activities leave a "digital trail" of users, producing data that is collected, aggregated, and monitored by technology companies and intelligence agencies. Many of them turn the data into money as they are sold to advertising agencies and companies interested in reaching their potential consumers (West 2017).

The Edward Snowden case has revealed to the world that US government espionage programs sift through the private lives of politicians, business owners, businesses, and ordinary citizens. This case revealed the limitations of anonymity in social networks. Governance, privacy, and Internet security have since become a problem that affects the citizenship rights of the men and women of the planet who access the Internet (Canabarro and Borne 2015).[12]

Silveira (2017) also points out that monitoring of online activities and collection of data transmitted in the network are not only for reasons related to national security but mainly because information has become a new and valuable commodity. With the emergence and popularization of cybernetic technologies and establishment of an information control system, a personal data market was created, whose

[12] This aspect is discussed in Chap. 3, which addresses the topic of Brazilian Civil Rights Framework for the Internet.

operation relies fundamentally on the violation of privacy of new information and communication technologies users:

> [...] Issuing the death certificate of privacy was a basic market need. The 21st Century information market needed to release its immense creativity for making money from the mass of data produced by the use of cybernetic technologies. Asserting that privacy is a right that should be abandoned for the greater benefits and new sensations provided by technologies was, and is, propitious to afford companies the safe conduct to collect and manipulate our information. (Silveira 2017, 65)

Either way, the average user who attacks the other through the Internet feels protected by this perceived anonymity. This false anonymity promoted by electronic measurement allows perpetrators not to be easily identified by victims.

Some international authors admit that the feeling of anonymity provided by the Internet allows perpetrators not to observe how their victims reacted to the humiliation, nor to know how aggressors behaved after offending someone. Foody et al. (2015, 236) affirm that "one of the main distinguishing factors of cyberbullying is the anonymity of the crime, which can be executed in front of a large audience and at the same time, allow the perpetrator to remain unidentified."

Part of the Brazilian academic literature analyzed believes that cyberbullying is different from bullying because it counts on anonymity in its practice of humiliation.

According to Berto (2012), a publicist in São Paulo, the resources available on the Internet allow perpetrators to create a "false profile as the purpose of defaming victims in a particular social network" (Berto 2012, 32). Dias et al. (2012), psychopedagogues in Rio de Janeiro, say that anonymity is not only an attraction for young people to feel freer to talk about their weaknesses. It also lets aggressors feel uninhibited to commit humiliation and aggression. These authors affirm that with anonymity "individuals will not be judged when using the computer, because they will not be exposed to others" (Dias et al. 2012, 43). Aranha (2014) points out that the feeling of anonymity facilitates writing and disseminating derogatory content that would not normally be expressed in face-to-face contact. Barbosa (2014, 51) corroborates this perspective by characterizing the virtual environment as a "space of impersonality and impunity."

Despite the caveats noted above, anonymity would be a hallmark of cyberbullying. In bullying, offenders are easily identifiable. On the Internet, abusers may use fake names or nicknames and cannot be easily recognized.

A second point that singles out cyberbullying is associated with the fact that the Internet allows humiliation and aggression to be far-reaching.

Some international authors share this view of which the work of Asam and Samara (2016, 128) stands out. These authors argue that "cyberbullying can be more repetitive with continual viewing/involvement of many individuals over varying periods of time, and due to its nature is more widely spread." Corcoran et al. (2015) and Grigg (2010) show similar perspectives. Corcoran et al. (2015, 246) point out that in cyberbullying "there is the potential for abusive or humiliating content to be disseminated to an audience of unknown size and location." Grigg (2010, 145) highlights that "offensive pictures and video clips are perceived as especially devastating, due to the breadth of audience who view these contents and the resulting psychological impact that these may pose to the targets [...]." Ybarra et al. (2012) follow the same argumentative rationale, by affirming that "it is possible to have a picture posted or rumor written once, yet shared with others over and over again. Although different in potential magnitude, this seems similar to a rumor scrawled once on a bathroom wall for many people to see repetitively" (Ybarra et al. 2012, 58). According to Baldry et al. (2015, 37):

> A single cyber-attack (a video, a comment, a picture) can remain online or in a mobile phone for quite some time, therefore prolonging the harm to the victims [...] and increasing access to potential cyberbystanders who can in turn share the attack, prolonging the victim's distress [...].

The disproportionate extent of humiliation is related to the characteristics of social networks. The ability to share information is one of the hallmarks of the so-called Web 2.0.[13] Social network goers play a central role in spreading humiliating content. Corcoran et al. (2015) and Baldry et al. (2015) say that this role is exercised when users share, like, comment, or even attach pictures and videos to the post made by the aggressor. Thus, according to some international authors, cyberbullying would have the potential to be seen by a much larger number of people than a face-to-face bullying (Asam and Samara 2016). Corcoran et al. (2015) and Grigg (2010) admit that Internet abuse can have a more harmful, severe, and lasting effect on victims than face-to-face, by sharing comments, photos, and videos with degrading content on third parties. In fact, according to these authors, cyberbullying gets out of the offender's hands. Once posted, humiliation gains social networks, becomes viral, and can reach people that the two parties involved neither know nor like.

The freedom and full availability of information on the Internet, as well as alleged anonymity, have recently been questioned. Google, for example, is one of the most popular search engines. It uses an algorithm that biases search results, favoring larger commercial sites to the detriment of smaller ones (Mager 2009). It also uses personal information and browsing habits of users to increasingly customize informative content, isolating individuals in bubbles that allow little or no access to opinions and interests divergent from theirs (Pariser 2011).

Either way, even if it is confined to a bubble, humiliation posted on social networks exceeds the abusers' control and reaches people who neither them nor victims know or relate personally or virtually. Some national authors clarify how this mechanism works.

Participants of perpetrators' social networks may, at any time, watch, like, and share texts and images offensive to a third person. Thus, discomfort can be disseminated on a large scale (Gonçalves et al. 2014). By liking a post aggressive to another

[13] In the early 2000s, according to many researchers, including O'Reilly (2005), Internet communication would have reached a new stage. "Web 2.0" would be characterized by new trends and practices centered on an architecture that favors/facilitates participation and sharing. To this end, technological resources such as social media, which facilitated the coproduction of content by users and increased the flow of interpersonal information, would be valued.

person on Facebook, users would be encouraging this practice and increasing the level of humiliation suffered. Thus, the rapid and extensive repercussion of abuse on social networks empowers aggressive practices (Schreiber and Antunes 2015). For this reason, following this definition, the effect of cyberbullying far surpasses the school's barriers. Countless users can perceive, and an uncontrollable number of sympathizers, with their likes and shares, can reproduce humiliation. Cyberbullying would therefore allow a greater number of onlookers witness the situation than those physically watching the bullying of a person. This is because the aggressive act can spread quickly. Tognetta and Bozza (2012, 163) recall that "once a comment is posted on social networks, the world is aware."

Wendt and Lisboa (2013, 78) were some of the Brazilian authors who contributed to this debate. They say that Web users' possibility to share disparaging content with regard to third parties gives this virtual practice a "permanence character." These same authors consider that individuals who share these posts are "supporters or promoters of the process" (Wendt and Lisboa 2014, 43). In their research, Tognetta and Bozza (2012) found that most cyberbullying onlookers share or disclose the cases they receive. Gonçalves et al. (2014) point out that pejorative nicknames, manipulated photographs, and exposure of intimacy quickly spread in virtual environments, and it is no coincidence that YouTube exposure is one of the most frequent types of cyberbullying.

Thus, thanks to the characteristics of the Internet, disparaging content in relation to third parties can be read, liked, and shared by individuals that neither the abuser nor the attacker knows personally or virtually. The aggressive or humiliating post can go viral, that is, spread rapidly like a virus, and without the parties directly involved having any responsibility in its dissemination.

> [...] *the use of information and communication technologies* - such as e-mail, mobile phones, instant message sending devices and programs, and personal websites - for the purpose of deliberately defaming or *supporting* behavior of individuals or group that somehow hurt others. (Schreiber and Antunes 2015, 111, our italics)

The Brazilian authors surveyed seem to have been more dedicated to defining this dimension of cyberbullying.

Dias et al. (2012, 42) point out that messages of humiliation, hostility, attack, and defamation bully young people, children, and adults and are "increasingly spread out on social networking sites such as Formspring, Tumblr, Twitter, or Facebook." Faced with so many alternatives of one person insulting or humiliating another through the different resources available on the Internet, some international authors have come to construct other denominations for referring variations of cyberbullying.

A few international authors have made this conceptual effort. Among them are Seto (2002) and Grigg (2010). Seto (2002) shows "cyberstalking" – a term that designates a type of violence in which a subject repeatedly invades another person's sphere of privacy by employing persecution tactics through social networks. Grigg (2010) refers to "sexting" and "happy slapping." "Sexting" is a contraction of "sex" and "texting" that refers to the dissemination of erotic and sensual content through cellphones, without the consent of victims. "Happy slapping," in turn, is a social behavior in which one or more people attack victims in order to record the abuse (usually with the camera of a smartphone) and later share the footage on social networks.

Some Brazilian authors share the same concern, among which Schreiber and Antunes (2015) stand out. They characterized "happy slapping" as follows:

> [...] Dissemination of videos showing scenes of physical aggression, where a victim may be intentionally or unintentionally chosen to be attacked on the street or on the way out of school, and perpetrated violence is recorded with cellphone cameras or camcorders and later posted on sites like YouTube or Google, aimed at spreading the aggression and humiliating the person attacked. (Schreiber and Antunes 2015, 116)

Gillespie (2006) showed the expression – "flaming" – that would be a hostile interaction between Internet users through offensive messages. Such messages are called flames and in most cases are published in responses to messages of content that are deemed provocative or offensive to the one who published the flame.

Aranha (2014) was one of the few national authors who participated in this terminological discussion. Featuring flaming and flame wars, he admits that these practices aim at promoting "online lynching," focusing more on humiliation toward, offense to, and discredit of the opponent than on combating the ideas themselves (Aranha 2014, 125). When the exchange of offenses between those involved becomes greater than the information that originated the discussion, the flame war begins. This term refers to the conflict of opinions that occurs in online discussion spaces, covering a vast amount of posts with pejorative content, which often deviate from the initial topic. Aranha (2014) emphasizes that these practices are not shaped by disagreement between parties that debate a certain subject, but by the disagreement to acquire huge proportions. He says:

> The terminology itself (*flame*) already evokes the idea of 'inflammable debate', since exacerbation is intrinsically related to the essence of the phenomenon. It is precisely in this extrapolation that the *flame war* gains its most worrisome bias, since there is a displacement of the debate around an idea towards the process moral lynching by the Internet. This can be done in a mutual or unilateral way. (Aranha 2014, 124)

Given the role played by ICTs and this diverse range of possibilities of Internet abuse, some Brazilian authors prefer not to use the term cyberbullying. They recognize the specificity of this phenomenon in the face of traditional bullying, but admit that the term cyberbullying is not compatible with the dimension of this social phenomenon. These authors sought to construct another denomination for this social practice. This was the case of Schreiber and Antunes (2015) and Wendt and Lisboa (2014).

Schreiber and Antunes (2015, 115) affirm that "increased studies on the phenomenon of cyberbullying have produced many definitions [...]." Wendt and Lisboa (2014) corroborate with this perspective, pointing out that there is still no consensus on the theoretical aspects of cyberbullying. They say that the lack of a precise definition of this phenomenon can be related to the proliferation of new technologies and the constant emergence of new behaviors and ways of acting in the virtual environment.

Criticisms made by Schreiber and Antunes (2015) and Wendt and Lisboa (2014) coincide with alternative definitions of the practice of abuse and insults in cyberspace provided by some foreign authors, such as Grigg (2010) and Corcoran et al. (2015).

Grigg (2010) points out that the term cyberbullying may not account for the diversity of negative acts on the Internet and proposes the term "cyber-aggression." According to the author, this term would define "intentional harm delivered by the use of electronic means to a person or a group of people irrespective of their age, who perceive(s) such acts as offensive, derogatory, harmful or unwanted" (Grigg 2010, 152). Grigg (2010) points out that, in addition to covering the range of online aggressive and hostile practices, the expression "cyber-aggression" would also extend to users of digital technologies who are onlookers of such practices. Corcoran et al. (2015) support Grigg's (2010) perspective. These authors state that the term "cyber-aggression" would be more appropriate, since cyberbullying can be confusing and does not address all the characteristics that single out and define the practice of online aggression.

For example, Tokunaga (2010) and Ybarra and Mitchell (2004) prefer to call this practice "online harassment," while others call this "insults and threats through electronic devices" (Juvonen and Gross 2008) or even "bullying perpetrated through electronic devices" (Li 2007). There are also those who have constructed the expression "cyberharassment," "cybervictimization," "online harassment," and "electronic bullying" (Grigg 2010).

12.6 Final Considerations

In the contemporary setting, the new ICTs have been increasingly imbricated in the personal and professional daily life of individuals, providing new and innumerable possibilities for interaction, knowledge exchange, entertainment, and trade. However, the opportunities and benefits brought by them coexist with various harmful practices, among which cyberbullying stands out. If individuals can talk to another person online on the other side of the world or instantly access a myriad of information sources, they can also suffer attack and aggressions through hostile messages, photos, and videos uploaded on websites, blogs, and digital social networks.

This chapter has carried out a bibliographical analysis of the international and national scientific literature that addresses the issue of cyberbullying. We identified the main issues in the international and national academic debate on this contemporary social phenomenon.

In the analysis of Brazilian scientific papers, we observed that Brazilian authors approach the international literature when discussing the similarities and differences between cyberbullying and bullying – a phenomenon that precedes the emergence of ICTs and is also characterized by the repeated and continuous exposure of victims to aggressions, threats, and insults. As in international publications, some Brazilian papers show cyberbullying as an extension or a specific type of bullying. They point to similarities between these two practices of exclusion and humiliation of victims: a continuous exposure of victims to abuse, repetitive and intentional acts, negative consequences for those involved, power imbalance between aggressors and victims, and violence between peers. The views of other Brazilian authors, by characterizing the specificities of cyberbullying and bullying, also converge with those found in the international literature. Some authors argue that bullying would be singled out for face-to-face contact, with explicit space-time boundaries and with a prevailing occurrence in schools. Cyberbullying would be characterized by the mediation of ICTs, incalculable repercussion, lack of physical interaction, and the feeling of anonymity. Both Brazilian and foreign authors discuss the different ways of cyberbullying.

While several points of convergence between national and foreign scientific literature have been identified, it is worth mentioning two points that distinguish Brazilian thinking analyzed in this study. One of them refers to questions about the characteristics of cyberbullying.

Matte (2012, 3) says the "virtual world is fallacy." She argues that the Internet is used as a means of provocation and humiliation among subjects who also relate and interact physically. This Federal University of Minas Gerais professor would find it hard to identify singularities in a bullying practiced in the digital environment. She has the following understanding:

> It would only make sense to me to speak about cyberbullying if relationships between the involved subjects happened exclusively on the web - which is of course possible. If the Internet, however, is only a resource used for provocation between individuals who relate in person and whose face-to-face relationship is the focus of the bullying in question, I see no use in thinking of cyberbullying. (Matte 2012, 4)

The author also discusses in her article whether the impact of online abuse and attacks would be greater or worse than those that occur face-to-face. She believes that bullying on the Internet would not necessarily be a greater threat to the victim than that occurring outside the virtual environment. If the immediate circle is not affected, the slanderous message becomes innocuous. She also contests the idea that offenses on the internet would be more lasting. She argues:

> Information on the internet only goes online forever if it is kept there. They can very easily be erased and remain there without being accessed, like a closed book that has never been read. Only an intentional action can ensure its permanence and focus, but also keeping information in focus is not an easy task nor is there even a formula that always works, neither in the web, nor in any other means of communication. (Matte 2012, 6)

Among the Brazilian papers analyzed, Matte's position (2012) seems to be the most critical in relation to the concept of cyberbullying. We did not find this line of questioning about the phenomenon of cyberbullying in the international literature consulted. It is worth mentioning that the discussion proposed by Matte (2012) opposes the more comprehensive debate, common in studies on cyberculture, which looks at the specificities and novelties of social phenomena when mediated by new communication technologies (Martino 2013). Some authors discussing the relationship between society and new ICTs say the Internet has introduced unprecedented forms of communication that have enabled global multidirectional communication flows that allow for the exchange of information and experiences, the production of multimedia content, and the generation of opportunities for cooperation between individuals from different parts of the planet (Fuchs 2007). Castells (2009, 2010), for example, points out that the Internet would have introduced a new type of communication, called mass self-communication, in which the message would have the capacity to reach a global audience. On the other hand, Lévy (2015) understands new ICTs as "molecular technologies" that would move away from massification, and be directed precisely to the "molecules" of the social fabric, that is, to the smaller and singular portions that compose a community. In discussing cyberbullying, Matte (2012) questions, to a certain extent, this perspective by highlighting the similarities that would exist between personally practiced bullying and bullying practiced through the Internet.

Another point in which Brazilian authors stand out in relation to international publications refers to proposed solutions to reduce or end cyberbullying.

Schreiber and Antunes (2015) emphasized that it would be up to schools to introduce this subject more intensely in the classroom. These authors explain that, although abuse can occur in online environments, school is the space where "these aggressive and transgressive behaviors become evident or aggravated most of the time" (Schreiber and Antunes 2015, 120). Tognetta and Bozza (2012), from the "Studies and Research Group on Moral Education" of the State University of Campinas (UNICAMP) propose the establishment of prevention and action programs in the school environment. These initiatives could stimulate respect in interpersonal (face-to-face or virtual) relationships of young people. Dias et al. (2012) say schools must involve the family in search for a solution to bullying and cyberbullying. However, these authors emphasize that this is not a simple task, since "tinkering with the structure of education consolidated in values divergent from those expected is a delicate matter and not an expected function of the school" (Dias et al. 2012, 43).

Others highlight the role of parents in coping with bullying and cyberbullying. For example, Wendt and Lisboa (2014) indicate that adequate parental control over the use of digital technologies can reduce risk behavior in the virtual environment. These authors also indicate that monitoring, assertive posture, and dialogue with children and adolescents can reduce these harmful practices.

In addition to school and family roles, other authors are concerned with finding ways to reduce or end cyberbullying.

Wendt and Lisboa (2013) and Schreiber and Antunes (2015) are some of them. They highlight the role that the State, through public policies, could play in coping with bullying and cyberbullying. Wendt and Lisboa (2013) point to the need for public regulation and policies that address the causes and consequences of these practices. On the other hand, Schreiber and Antunes (2015, 121) affirm that "in the legal world, laws and norms are still being developed when the subject is cyberspace."

The lack of a specific law does not prevent citizens' rights from being threatened with the practice of bullying and cyberbullying.

Regarding public policies aimed at combating and preventing bullying and cyberbullying, it should be noted that, after the publication of works by Wendt and Lisboa (2013) and Schreiber and Antunes (2015), Brazil passed Law 13.185/2015 that establishes the "Systematic Intimidation Control Program" at the national level (bullying). This program aims to prevent and combat bullying through a series of measures and actions that include the implementation and dissemination of educational campaigns, training of teachers and pedagogical staff, and the provision of psychological, social, and legal assistance to victims and aggressors. Although it refers to bullying, the program also covers cyberbullying, described in the text of the law as "systematic intimidation in the world computer network" (Brazil 2015).

It should be noted, finally, that this study conducted a bibliographic analysis of Brazilian scientific papers available in two virtual libraries. Other papers could have been found had we consulted other databases. The scope of our analysis could have been broader had we consulted gray literature. In addition, this chapter could have performed a comparative study between the scientific literature on cyberbullying in Brazil and in other countries with similar socioeconomic contexts. Empirical research on cyberbullying could also have been carried out, which focused on the possible singularities of aggressive practice, threats, and online insults in the Brazilian sociocultural context, or even analyze the relationships between cases of cyberbullying and bullying. The choice we made in conducting the study that culminated in this chapter makes readers of this book familiar with the conceptual problems inherent in social studies on this subject. In this chapter, readers were able to confirm that Brazilian studies are in tune with the concerns found in works carried out by foreign authors.

The phenomenon of cyberbullying covers a vast field of investigation. Studying the subject is a necessary undertaking in a setting in which the Internet and other digital technologies are increasingly present in daily life, especially among young people, a setting in which aggressions through ICTs can have serious consequences for the health of users of virtual networks.

References

Aranha, Glaucio. 2014. Flaming e cyberbullying: o lado negro das novas mídias. *Ciberlegenda* 31: 122–133.

Asam, Aiman El, and Muthanna Samara. 2016. Cyberbullying and the law: A review of psychological and legal challenges. *Computers in Human Behavior* 65: 127–141.

Azevedo, Jefferson Cabral, Fabiana Aguiar de Miranda, Fernanda Castro Manhães, and Carlos Henrique Medeiros de Souza. 2012. O ciberbullying e suas relações com as estruturas psíquicas. *Nucleus* 9: 241–252.

Baldry, Anna C., David P. Farrington, and Anna Sorrentino. 2015. Am I at risk of cyberbullying? A narrative review and conceptual framework for research on risk of cyberbullying and cybervictimization: The risk and needs assessment approach. *Aggression and Violent Behavior* 23: 36–51.

Barbosa, Carlos Henrique Macena. 2014. Cyberbullying and otherness at school: a study in social representations with students from São José dos Quatro Marcos, Mato Grosso. *Scientific Electronic Archives* 5: 47–52.

Berto, Matheus. 2012. O cyberbullying e a liberdade de expressão. Uma proposta de análise dos limites que garantem a manutenção do convívio social. *Revista Tecer* 5: 29–39.

BIREME – Latin American and Caribbean Center on Health Sciences Information. 2008. *Informe de Avaliação da BVS em seus 10 anos de operação*. São Paulo: BIREME/OPAS/OMS.

Brazil. Presidência da República. Casa Civil. 2015. Lei Federal n° 13.185, de 6 de Novembro de 2015. Institui o Programa de Combate à Intimidação Sistemática (Bullying). *Diário Oficial da República Federativa do Brasil*, 6 nov. 2015.

BVS – Biblioteca Virtual de Saúde. 2017. Sobre a BVS. http://brasil.bvs.br/vhl/sobre-a-bvs/. Accessed 28 June 2017.

Canabarro, Diego R., and Thiago Borne. 2015. The Brazilian reactions to the Snowden affairs: implications for the study of international relations in an interconnected world. *Revista Conjuntura Austral* 6: 50–74.

CAPES – Coordenação de Aperfeiçoamento de Pessoal de Nível Superior. 2017. Portal de Periódicos da CAPES. http://www.periodicos.capes.gov.br/. Accessed 28 June 2017.

Castells, Manuel. 2009. *Communication power*. Oxford: Oxford University Press.

———. 2010. *The rise of the network society: The information age: Economy, society, and culture*. Oxford: Wiley.

Corcoran, Lucie, Conor Mc Guckin, and Garry Prentice. 2015. Cyberbullying or cyber aggression?: A review of existing definitions of cyber-based peer-to-peer aggression. *Societies* 5: 245–255.

Dias, Danielle G., Shayane F. Santos, and Talita D.S. Ernesto. 2012. O esfacelamento da identidade do sujeito pós-moderno vulnerável ao novo e antigo mal: o bullying. *Perspectivas Online: Humanas e Sociais Aplicadas* 2: 33–38.

Dredge, Rebecca, John Gleeson, and Xochitl P. Garcia. 2014. Cyberbullying in social networking sites: An adolescent victim's perspective. *Computers in Human Behavior* 36: 13–20.

Foody, Mairéad, Muthanna Samara, and Per Carlbring. 2015. A review of cyberbullying and suggestions for online psychological therapy. *Internet Interventions* 2: 235–242.

Foucault, Michel. 1995. *Discipline and punish: The birth of the prison*. Nova York: Vintage Books.

Fuchs, Christian. 2007. *Internet and society: Social theory in the information age*. Hoboken: Taylor & Francis e-Library.

Gillespie, Alisdair A. 2006. Cyber-bullying and harassment of teenagers: The legal response. *Journal of Social Welfare & Family Law* 28: 123–136.

Gonçalves, Cynara, Giuliano Gomes Pimentel, and Beatriz Pereira. 2014. Escárnio de corpos, cyberbullying e corrupção do lúdico. *Movimento* 20: 965–988.

Grigg, Dorothy Wunmi. 2010. Cyber-aggression: Definition and concept of cyberbullying. *Australian Journal of Guidance & Counselling* 20: 143–156.

Juvonen, Jaana, and Elisheva F. Gross. 2008. Extending the schools grounds?: Bullying experiences in cyberspace. *The Journal of School Health* 78: 496–505.

Lévy, Pierre. 2015. *A inteligência coletiva*. São Paulo: Folha de S. Paulo.

Li, Qing. 2007. New bottle, but old wine: A research of cyberbullying in schools. *Computers in Human Behavior* 23: 1777–1791.

Mager, Astrid. 2009. A mediated health: Sociotechnical practices of providing and using online health information. *New Media & Society* 11: 1123–1142.

Martino, Luís Mauro Sá. 2013. Repensando a(s) teoria(s) da Cibercultura: articulações e tensões com as teorias da Comunicação. Questões Transversais. *Revista de Epistemologias da Comunicação* 1: 92–99.

Matte, Ana Cristina Fricke. 2012. A respeito da construção semiótica do sentido do bullying e do cyberbullying. *Texto Livre: Linguagem e Technologia* 5: 1–12.

Olweus, Dan, and Susan P. Limber. 2017. Some problems with cyberbullying research. *Current Opinion in Psychology* 19: 139–143.

O'Reilly, Tim. 2005. What's Web 2.0? Designing patterns and business models for the next generation of software. O'Reilly Radar Report. O'Reilly Media Inc. https://www.oreilly.com/pub/a/web2/archive/what-is-web-20.html?. Accessed 28 June 2017.

Packer, Abel Laerte. 2005. The collective construction of the Virtual Healthcare Library. *Interface – Comunic., Saúde e Educação* 9: 249–272.

Pariser, Eli. 2011. *The filter bubble: What internet is hiding from you*. Nova York: The Penguin Press.

Patchin, Justin W., and Sameer Hinduja. 2010. Cyberbullying and self-esteem. *Journal of School Health* 80: 614–621.

Şahin, Mustafa. 2012. The relationship between the cyberbullying/cybervictimization and loneliness among adolescents. *Children and Youth Services Review* 34: 834–837.

Schreiber, Fernando Cesar de Castro, and Maria Cristina Antunes. 2015. Cyberbullying: do virtual ao psicológico. *Boletim - Academia Paulista de Psicologia* 35: 109–125.

Selkie, Ellen M., Jessica L. Fales, and Megan A. Moreno. 2016. Cyberbullying prevalence among us middle and high school aged adolescents: A systematic review and quality assessment. *Journal of Adolescent Health* 58: 125–133.

Seto, Kimberly W. 2002. How should legislation deal with children as victims and perpetrators of cyberstalking? *Women's Law Journal* 9: 67–72.

Silveira, Sergio Amadeu 2010. Monitoring and punishment: Communication and control on the internet. In: *Survey on the use of information and communication technologies in Brazil:* 2005–2009, ed. CGI - Comitê Gestor da Internet no Brasil, 199–203. São Paulo: Comitê Gestor da Internet no Brasil.

———. 2017. *Everything about every@ne: Digital network, privacy and the personal data trade*. São Paulo: Edições SESC.

Slonje, Robert, Peter K. Smith, and Ann Frisén. 2013. The nature of cyberbullying, and strategies for prevention. *Computers in Human Behavior* 29: 26–32.

Stelko-Pereira, Ana Carina, and Lúcia Cavalcanti de Albuquerque Williams. 2010. Reflexões sobre o conceito de violência escolar e a busca por uma definição abrangente. *Temas em Psicologia* 18: 45–55.

Tognetta, Luciene Regina Paulino, and Thais Cristina Leite Bozza. 2012. Cyberbullying: um estudo sobre a incidência do desrespeito no ciberespaço e suas relações com as representações que adolescentes tem de si. *Nuances: Estudos Sobre Educação* 23: 162–178.

Tokunaga, Robert S. 2010. Following you home from school: A critical review and synthesis of research on cyberbullying victimization. *Computers in Human Behavior* 26: 277–287.

Wendt, Guilherme Welter, and Carolina Saraiva de Macedo Lisboa. 2013. Agressão entre pares no espaço virtual: definições, impactos e desafios do cyberbullying. *Psicologia Clínica* 25: 73–87.

———. 2014. Compreendendo o fenômeno do cyberbullying. *Temas em Psicologia* 22: 39–54.

West, Sarah M. 2017. Data capitalism: Redefining the logics of surveillance and privacy. *Business & Society* 1–22.

Ybarra, Michele L., and Kimberly Mitchell. 2004. Youth engaging in online harassment: Associations with caregiver-child relationships, Internet use, and personal characteristics. *Journal of Adolescence* 27: 319–336.

Ybarra, Michele L., Danah Boyd, Josephine D. Korchmaros, and Jay Oppenheim. 2012. Defining and measuring cyberbullying within the larger context of bullying victimization. *Journal of Adolescent Health* 51: 53–58.

Zych, Izabela, Rosario Ortega-Ruiz, and Inmaculada Marín-López. 2016. Cyberbullying: A systematic review of research, its prevalence and assessment issues in Spanish studies. *Psicología Educativa* 22: 5–18.

Chapter 13
Brazil and the US Internet-Based Medicines

Matthew B. Flynn, Tiago Coutinho, and Vera Lucia Luiza

Abstract Brazil and the United States share important commonalities and differences regarding Internet penetration, health literacy, and pharmaceutical coverage. In both countries, consumers are increasingly turning to the Internet in search of information and acquisition. Similarly, drug makers and distributors have used the Internet to advertise and market their products. Use and abuse of the Internet for prescription and over-the-counter drugs still differ due to government pharmaceutical policies that affect access and price, as well as the socioeconomic differences between the two societies. This chapter provides a review of the academic and gray literature about Brazil and US Internet-based medicine use, highlighting how the two cases compare and contrast in terms of access and appropriate use. Lastly, the chapter discusses the implications of these two countries' realities in terms of market characteristics, government regulations, and growing pharmaceuticalization through the use of new digital media.

13.1 Introduction

The consolidation of the Internet as the principal means of communication and information between individuals has significantly transformed daily life. With regard to the use of prescription drugs, the Internet and social media have profoundly altered the relationship between people and medicines. So-called new media, that is, media based on exchanging information over the Internet, provides important channels where it is possible to observe the pharmaceuticalization of society. In other words, society's growing dependence on pharmaceutical

M. B. Flynn (✉)
Department of Political Science and International Studies & Department of Sociology and Anthropology, Georgia Southern University, Statesboro, GA, USA
e-mail: mflynn@georgiasouthern.edu

T. Coutinho · V. L. Luiza
Department of Medicines and Pharmaceutical Services Policy, National School of Public Health, Oswaldo Cruz Foundation, Rio de Janeiro, Brazil

A. Pereira Neto, M. B. Flynn (eds.), *The Internet and Health in Brazil*,
https://doi.org/10.1007/978-3-319-99289-1_13

interventions for daily life results not only from the ease of obtaining pharmaceutical information but can also be observed by easier access with or without mediators to the products themselves. On the one hand, new technologies can simplify access, especially for those with chronic conditions and hard-to-reach populations, but on the other hand, they transform the traditional doctor-/pharmacist-patient relationship.

New information and communication technologies brought or driven by the Internet have given rise to the putative expert patient (Taylor and Bury 2007).[1] In looking at the influence of the Internet on doctor-patient relationships, Cabral and Trevisol (2010) affirm that access to technical-scientific information, together with increased educational levels of consumers, results in more patients seeking information about their illness, symptoms, medications, and hospitalization and treatment costs. Insomuch as information from this new media modifies or interferes in the doctor-patient relationship, the authors conclude that doctors are no longer the supreme holders of knowledge and are being questioned by patients who are increasingly informed (Cabral and Trevisol 2010).

Even more problematic is how the Internet can exacerbate a public health problem. One example is prescription drug abuse among young people through self-medication. A 2011 survey of nonmedical use of prescribed drugs (2013) found that adolescents used social networks as their main source of information on health and well-being, even if the credibility of such information is difficult to determine. The study also revealed that social networks provide information on all steps related to drug self-medication: face-to-face shopping, bartering, lending, sharing, stealing from friends or family, purchasing of medicines in illegal pharmacies, falsifying prescriptions, and searching for false doctors.

The Internet has not only given expert patient access to information but also a means to see drug approvals, substantial price differences, and marketing information across countries. As a disruptive force, online technologies thus challenge the traditional role of the state in regulating the operations of drug companies and distributors. According to Consumers International (2018), with the development and expansion of the Internet, the pharmaceutical industry has adopted new marketing strategies, such as chat groups and disease information pages, to promote their medicines. Despite its adoption in 1988, the World Health Organization's Ethical Criteria for Drug Promotion remains the paradigm in controlling the promotion of prescription medicines. The international health body's statement on drug marketing, though not anticipating the type of communication used in the digital universe, explicitly prohibits direct-to-consumer advertising.

In facilitating information about the substantial price differences of approved and unapproved medicines, digital technologies and media offer consumers and activist organizations greater awareness about the impact that exorbitant costs have on pocketbooks. Patients in the United States, seeking to sidestep one of the highest cost prescription drug markets in the world, use the Internet to find pharmacies that will accept their prescriptions and dispense medication across the Canadian border

[1] Chapter 6 delves into the topic of the "expert patient."

(Mangan 2014). Patient advocates like Doctors Without Borders (*Medecins Sans Frontieres*—MSF) employ online media to disseminate information and mobilize stakeholders for its Access Campaign for essential medicines. Since 2001, it has published *Untangling the Web of Antiretroviral Price Reductions* that demonstrates the differences in prices in branded, patent-protected AIDS drugs compared to far cheaper generic versions.

This chapter delves into these transformations by examining the benefits and drawbacks new online media provide in terms of access and prices, information and advertisements, and governance and regulatory issues. The first section considers the novel aspect of Internet-based medicines as a global phenomenon. Given the worldwide ubiquity of the web, the international reach of online pharmacies must be considered. The subsequent sections examine the cases of the United States and Brazil. Highlighting how online technologies intersect with both a mature and developing market reveals the challenges and trends that these countries' distinct health infrastructures and social realities present to policy makers as well as demonstrate growing phenomena of pharmaceuticalization across contexts. The information presented comes from a review of the academic and gray literature.

13.2 Internet-Based Medicines: Global Trends and Challenges

The Internet and related digital technologies facilitate the growth of the global prescription drug industry expected to reach $1.4 trillion in sales by 2020 (Berkrot 2015). There is no comprehensive data about the global scale, growth, and distribution of online pharmacies and transactions, not even from IQVIA, the health data consulting group that includes IMS Health, which aggregates data on worldwide pharmaceutical sales. Without any central registration database and due to the clandestine nature of some e-pharmacies, estimating the size of the online market, the number of venders, and the consumer base remains difficult. Still, systematic reviews of the academic literature, such as by Orizio et al. (2011), provide insight into some of these issues. They found various country surveys stating that 6% or less of the population had purchased drugs online—a number that has likely increased since the date of publication. In terms of access, the advantages of online pharmacies include 24-h access, a degree of privacy, access for the disabled and the housebound, the availability of practically every possible medicine, and discounted prices (Orizio et al. 2011).

The question of price varies, however, according to the type of drug, purchasing volumes, and issuance of prescription (Orizio et al. 2011). Larger orders often had lower per-unit costs among approved pharmacies. Comparisons between US retail prices and Canadian online pharmacies found the latter were less expensive for brand name drugs but not for generics. A few studies highlighting treatments for erectile dysfunction found consistently more expensive offerings from online venders than retail pharmacies. Additional costs with online pharmacies include membership fees, shipping costs, and whether a prescription is needed. Buying a drug without a prescription tends to increase its prices (Orizio et al. 2011).

When searching the Internet and medicines on academic databases, the peer-reviewed literature rarely mentions activist efforts to promote access to essential drugs. However, studies on the politics of providing AIDS medicines, especially in the developing world, highlight the importance of new digital technologies for political mobilization (t' Hoen 2009; Kapstein and Busby 2013). Besides the efforts of MSF mentioned above as well as price database maintained by Health Action International, some of the more prominent listservs for sharing information and coordinating advocacy efforts include IP Health, Health GAP, and the Global AIDS Alliance.

What has attracted the most attention from the media, government, and academics is the proliferation of illicit or so-called rogue pharmacies, which tend to operate across borders. Mackey and Nayyar (2016), in fact, warn that sites offering drugs at significantly lower prices tend to be associated with illicit operations. LegitScript (2016), a verification and monitoring service of online pharmacies worldwide, revealed that there were between 30,000 and 35,000 illicit online pharmacies currently in operation—a number that has fluctuated between 25,000 and 45,000 since the company began its operations in 2008. Although there was a decline in the number of sites from a few years ago, most of these websites operate in a "blatantly illicit manner," i.e., selling controlled medicines without a prescription. Furthermore, LegitScript emphasizes that there are 2000 to 3500 "primary actors (excluding webmasters and affiliate marketers)" who operate these websites. Since 82% of these sites are in English and 85% offer to ship to the United States, these illicit pharmacies focus on the US market (LegitScript 2016).

Numerous reports in the English-based academic literature have highlighted the risks associated with illicit online pharmacies. Many of these studies often conflate health risks associated with substandard medicines with the issue of counterfeit medicines—a concern regarding intellectual property. For example, the US Government Accountability Office (GAO 2013) states that "Rogue Internet pharmacies often sell unapproved prescription drugs—including those that are substandard, counterfeit, and have no therapeutic value or are harmful to consumers." Industry-affiliated groups in the United States, such as the Partnership for Safe Medicines, which opposes imports of prescription drugs from Canada, also have posts such as "SAFEMEDICINES Teaches You 5 Kinds of Poisons Found in Counterfeit Medicines." Lastly, Dukes et al. (2015, 147) state that "it seems likely that a fair proportion of drugs supplied [from Internet pharmacies] are either counterfeits having no medicinal value or are different from those ordered."[2]

Apart from the pharmaceutical industry's material interest to conflate counterfeit medicines with adulterated drugs, there are legitimate public health concerns with

[2] Similarly, the "European Alliance for Access to Safe Medicines study found that 62% of the products received were counterfeit, substandard, or unapproved medications (68% of these were generic and 32% were branded)" (Orizio et al. 2011).

illicit drugs sold online. Studies looking at chemical composition of medicines ordered online found that the percentage of tablets failing quality tests ranged from 0% to 10% of the total number of samples analyzed (Orizio et al. 2011). A more common problem concerns packing and labeling standards that failed to meet the US Food and Drug Administration (FDA) regulations in most of the orders made from online pharmacies, except for those originating in the United States and Canada (GAO 2005; Orizio et al. 2011). Another health risk is the availability of numerous products that had not received regulatory approval or were withdrawn from the market due to safety issues. Compared to onsite pharmacies which also sell unapproved medicines and engage in problematic marketing, traceability and reachability of online pharmacies present formidable challenges to enforcing regulations.

Direct-to-consumer (DTC) marketing and the problematic dissemination of prescription drug information over the Internet present another health risk. Choi and Lee (2007) found that more people are beginning to see the Internet as a more credible source of information compared to other media, but there were group differences with females more likely than males to use pharmaceutical websites to look up information, while older individuals are more likely to discuss with their physicians the drugs they see advertised.

Some companies require Internet users to select which country they reside in before sending consumers to webpages that adhere to national regulatory demands. Nonetheless, given the ubiquity of Internet-provided information, DTC ads through this medium are complicit in "internationalizing medicalization" (Conrad and Leiter 2008, 834). Regulators also lack the means to police content on social media like Facebook and Twitter, especially postings from illicit pharmacies compared to Internet sites linked to sellers (Mackey and Nayyar 2016). Studies have shown that content related to the top 20 prescription drugs came from illicit pharmacies on 17% of all Facebook pages, including dissemination through user-generated comments. Another study of tweets mentioning a generic drug name found that 77% of them came from a marketing company working on behalf of rogue pharmacies.

Most authors agree that Internet pharmacies are poorly regulated since online operations cross borders, while most legislative authority remains circumscribed by national boundaries. The complexity and international scope of Internet pharmacies, moreover, present significant challenges to enforcement agencies. One rogue pharmacy had a domain name registered in Russia, used services located in China and Brazil, processed payments in Azerbaijan, and shipped prescription drugs from India. Despite these challenges, INTERPOL annually conducts Operation Pangea involving more than 100 countries to seize illicit and counterfeit pills and remove illicit online pharmacies. The increasing growth of cryptomarkets using cryptocurrencies (e.g., Bitcoin) that employ online technologies for anonymous communication and for hidden transactions presents additional challenges for law enforcement (Bachhuber and Merchant 2017).

A country-level focus on the global reach and penetration of online pharmacies provides insight into the trends and challenges related to these new technologies.

13.3 An Overview of the US Internet-Based Medicine Market

The United States is the largest market for prescription drugs given its annual drug sales of $350 billion (QuintlesIMS 2016) and with 88% of adults who use the Internet (Pew Research 2017). Due in part to the ease of making online purchases, the United States is also the top online market for over-the-counter (OTC) medicines, (Kalorama Information 2018). Furthermore, previous surveys show that 72% of US adults have looked up health information online, 35% have used the Internet as a diagnostic tool, and 16% have read about drug safety and medicines they have seen advertised (S. Fox and Duggan 2013). A nonscientific survey conducted by the US Food and Drug Administration revealed that 23% respondents admitted to buying prescription drugs online (FDA 2013). While the majority said they used websites associated with their insurance provider, about 17% said they purchased medicines on websites not associated with their insurance or with a local pharmacy, and 15% said they would consider purchasing medicines online from sources outside the United States. Despite these estimates, calculating the number of people purchasing online medicines and the amount and/or volumes of sales conducted remains problematic (Orizio et al. 2011).

With regard to the profile of online drug shoppers, a recent study based on 2002–2010 panel survey data from the United States found that most online consumers tend to be older and have more prescriptions, higher health costs, and greater morbidity rates than non-online users, as well as are likely being privately insured, white, married, and more educated (Brown and Li 2014). The authors also found that those with insurance are also more likely to seek treatments for chronic conditions, while those seeking potential drugs of abuse (i.e., narcotic analgesics, antidepressants, narcotic analgesics, and sedatives) are less likely to purchase through the Internet. In terms of age groups and contrary to expectations, youth were not more likely to purchase medicines online than older people (Mazer et al. 2012). However, both age and sex determinants vary depending on the drug. One review about online recreational drug users found that they tend to be highly educated, avid Internet users, in their 20s, and white males who use the Internet for privacy in order to protect their professional status (Orsolini et al. 2015). Despite efforts to characterize the online population, Mackey and Nayyar (2016, 122) conclude that "there may not be a 'single' profile for an online pharmacy customer and that users are as diverse as the medications they seek out."

There are several factors why people in the United States use online pharmacies, which offer medicines of every therapeutic class, to purchase drugs. For legal pharmacies, the main factors include convenience, lower cost, privacy, and patient autonomy (Orizio et al. 2011; Mazer et al. 2012; Brown and Li 2014; Mackey and Nayyar 2016; Smith et al. 2017). A survey of women who ordered the emergency contraception ulipristal acetate, for example, found that 58.9% of the respondents preferred ordering the drug online because they found it easier to complete the online medical eligibility questions, which are then reviewed by a physician, than having to order from a doctor, clinic, or pharmacy (Smith et al. 2017). People ordering online tend to use more cardiovascular drugs, respiratory treatments, statins, antidepressants, antidiabetic agents, sedatives, contraceptives, and erectile dysfunction medications compared to non-online users (Brown and Li 2014). Lastly, online communities also play a key role encouraging the online purchase and consumption of drugs and medicines, especially for those who live in remote locations or use unusual psychedelic drugs (Orsolini et al. 2015).

For the so-called rogue pharmacies, the chief factor driving people to risk purchasing from these sites is their desire to reduce health costs, lack of insurance coverage, interest in illicit drugs, limited trust in medical professionals, and preference to sidestep prescription barriers (Cicero and Ellis 2012; Brown and Li 2014; Orsolini et al. 2015; Mackey and Nayyar 2016). Health costs include not just the prices of online medicines but also the expenses associated with seeing a physician. An online survey of people seeking the opioid analgesic tramadol also revealed that price considerations were not the only important factor but also the perception that their needs were not appropriately addressed through official health channels as well as insufficient doses of the drug to relieve pain (Cicero and Ellis 2012). Self-diagnosis also leads people to seek out online pharmacies, thereby sidestepping the role of physicians and pharmacists (Mackey and Nayyar 2016). Many sites include medical questionnaires that have neither been standardized nor validated, as well as "cyberdoctors" that use patient information to fill prescriptions virtually.

A comprehensive study of five national data sets found that purchasing medicines at illegal online sites is relatively small (Inciardi et al. 2010). For example, the surveys revealed that between 0.5% and 3% of survey respondents purchased prescription opioids online. Still, generalizing to the entire population, this could potentially represent up to nine million people. Additionally, those using Internet pharmacies to acquire opioids represent less than one percent of the US population (Brown and Li 2014). The main reason why the Internet is not used more is because of the cheaper prices from dealers or family/friends, concerns about online scams, and worries of law enforcement. Another study of common psychotropic drugs used to treat mental disorders found 30 online pharmacies supplying the medication with or without a prescription. Of these 57% were classified as rogue (Monteith et al. 2016). Orsolini et al. (2015, 313) note the following factors limit the use of Internet pharmacies for sourcing recreational drugs: fear of extra costs, fear of nondelivery, fear that products can be counterfeit/not approved/illegal, the possibility to be traced by the authorities in doing the purchase itself, lack of availability from the web, and the advice from a "real-world" health professional.

Given the attention to health risks associated with illicit pharmacies, it is expected that there would be stronger data to back up the concerns. However, most of the health problems come not from surveys but from clinical case reports. Mackey and Nayyar (2016, 122) surmise that "case reports are a crude measure of incidence, with the majority of Internet pharmacy-related cases likely left unreported, even if resulting in an adverse outcome." One exception is the study by Cicero and Ellis (2012) that found people using the opioid pain medication tramadol from non-prescription pharmacies experienced a significantly greater number and severity of adverse events, including life-threatening seizures, compared to those in a traditional doctor-patient-pharmacy model.

In terms of information and marketing, the United States is one of the few countries allowing pharmaceutical companies to conduct direct-to-consumer (DTC) advertising. For pharmaceutical companies, the Internet fulfills FDA guidelines about multichannel disclosures of information. In fact, the medium is likely to see the greatest increase in DTC advertising, which totaled $4.9 billion in 2007, 30% of that amount went to Internet publicity (H. Kim 2011). Research on DTC advertisement can be classified into two types: first are studies conducted by scholars of advertising who often take an instrumental approach concerning the efficacy of DTC ads online (Huh et al. 2005; Choi and Lee 2007; Fogel and Novick 2009; H. Kim 2011) and second, those who take more of a public health perspective on the problematic nature of DTC marketing (Conrad and Leiter 2008; Ebeling 2011; Mintzes 2012; Dukes et al. 2015).

Advertising scholars have analyzed trust, credibility, and subsequent health actions of those who see online ads in the United States. One survey in the southeast United States concluded that most respondents accept online information to a certain extent but overall trust levels are low. When trust is significant, it is associated with trust in other media and is often followed by certain ad-promoted behaviors, such as discussions with doctors and others about the drugs (Huh et al. 2005). Another study using undergraduates by Kim (2011) found that online information provided by a corporate pharmaceutical company (i.e., Pfizer) was viewed equally credible to content from a government agency (i.e., National Institutes of Health). Furthermore, DTC ads online, according to Fogel and Novick (2009), motivated US college students to seek out more information about the pharmaceutical products compared to other media.

In contrast to advertising researchers, studies by sociologists and public health researchers emphasize the material interests behind DTC advertising. According to Mintzes (2012), the websites of top brand pharmaceutical companies and heavily advertised medicines fail to explain how a treatment is likely to work, require more "clicks" in order to see information about risks, and rarely mention the cost of treatments. In fact, average per patient retail cost was $1559 for which cheaper alternatives typically existed. Ebeling (2011) highlights how the top-ten, best-selling prescription drugs used symptom checklists for self-diagnosis in order to promote the use of the drugs. To extend the patent for the drug, Eli Lilly rebranded fluoxetine (i.e., from Prozac to Sarafem) as a treatment for premenstrual dysphoric disorder. The drug company then employed the same clinical psychiatrist who was instrumental in first classifying the health condition as a treatable depressive disorder to develop the new online symptom checklist for the rebranded drug (Ebeling 2011).

In the United States, there are agencies at both the federal and state levels responsible for enforcing laws governing the sale and marketing of drugs over the Internet (GAO 2013). The Food and Drug Administration (FDA) oversees every facet of prescription drugs including testing, manufacturing, labeling, safety, efficacy, and marketing. Since the arrival of Internet pharmacies, the FDA has had to work in collaboration with various agencies, private companies, and international organizations to police online markets (Chandra and Cupps 2002).

The Ryan Haight Online Pharmacy Consumer Protection Act of 2008, named after an 18-year old who died from overdosing on Vicodin purchased online, regulates the distribution and dispensing of controlled substances (about 10% of the US prescription drug market) on the Internet. The law mandates that all businesses selling controlled substances online be registered and authorized by the Drug Enforcement Agency (DEA), which is responsible for the enforcement. The Ryan Haight Act also forbids businesses located outside the United States from obtaining registrations, makes it illegal for consumers to import controlled substances, and stipulates what constitutes legal prescriptions. The law, for instance, stipulates the requirements for telemedicine-based prescriptions. The Customs Border Patrol (CBP) is the enforcement agency for seizing illegally imported goods, including unauthorized prescription drugs, and other controlled substances. At the state level, pharmacists and pharmacies must have a license to operate, as well as abide by rules and regulations outlined by state pharmacy boards.

While lacking the power of the law, there are also private-based forms of regulation (GAO 2013). The National Association of Boards of Pharmacy (NABP) established the Verified Internet Pharmacy Practice Sites (VIPPS), an accreditation program designed to assist the public in identifying legitimate online pharmacies. In 2013, they created a new top-level domain name *.pharmacy* for accredited websites. LegitScript allows consumers to enter website addresses to determine whether they adhere to NABP's standards. The Federation of State Medical Boards has also developed guidelines for how electronic technology should support instead of replace the doctor-patient relationship. Lastly, the Center for Safe Internet Pharmacies and the International AntiCounterfeiting Coalition have worked with supporting companies, such as Internet registrars, search engines, credit card companies, and payment processors, to deny services to rogue pharmacies. The Ryan Haight Act appears to have led to a decline in controlled substances sold illicitly over the Internet (GAO 2013; LegitScript 2016). Some successes include FDA investigations of rogue pharmacies that have resulted in 219 convictions and $76 million in fines.

US regulators have also investigated legitimate companies for disseminating unapproved information (GAO 2013; Dukes et al. 2015). The FDA reached a $500 million settlement with Google for accepting advertisements from Canadian pharmacies offering to sell drugs to US customers. The agency also issued warnings to Novartis for sharing information about its leukemia drug Tasigna (nilotinib) on social media without communicating health risks and for providing "false and misleading" information about another brand name cancer drug Gleevec (imatinib).

13.4 An Overview of Brazil's Internet-Based Medicine Market

In 2015, Brazil became the seventh largest pharmaceutical market in the world with estimated sales of R$45 billion reais (about US$ 13 billion) and is expected to be ranked 5th by 2020. Increased consumption is linked to several factors. In addition to some more structural variables, such as an aging population and broader access to consumer goods, self-medication is one of the factors influencing increased consumption (Interfarma 2016).

Brazil's government census bureau (IBGE, Brazilian Institute of Geography and Statistics) reported that 57.5% of households are connected to the Internet (IBGE 2017). The growing number of Internet users has been leading to an increase in demand for virtual Brazilian pharmacies (Gondim and Falcão 2007). There is no information about how many consumers adequately use health information or data about how many drug purchases are actually made through the Internet with a physician's prescription.

Despite extensive regulation in the sector, there are significant problems in the sale and purchase of medicines. To begin with, there is uncertainty about the number of pharmacies throughout the country, with estimates varying from 60,000 to 70,000 (Valor Econômico 2014). Other problems include the presence of substandard medicines with poor quality and pharmacies that do not fully comply with market legislation. Difficulties include oversight of local pharmacy establishments, which is the responsibility of municipal health authorities, who face political and financial problems and insufficiently trained inspection teams. Despite these problems, information about how to conduct Internet sales procedures for entrepreneurs (SEBRAE 2015a, b; ANFARMAG 2017) as well as for patients (IDEC 2017) is readily available.

Gondim and Falcão (2007) highlight that increased purchasing of drugs online can lead to easier access to unregistered drugs and less control over the sale of controlled drugs, thus facilitating the inappropriate and indiscriminate use of medications. Inadequate use may expose people to various health risks such as therapeutic ineffectiveness, concerns over drug safety, adverse reactions, poisoning, and dangerous interactions. The authors point out the growing need for better regulation of this new modality in the commercialization of medicines (Gondim and Falcão 2007).

Academic studies about the retail prescription drug trade and consumer habits and practices, as well as on corruption that could potentially explain various related problems, are rare in Brazil. In particular, there is very little about the use of the Internet to purchase medicines. However, there has been an overall increase in online sales (G1 2016). Regarding online purchases, in addition to the advantages found in other countries about the convenience of reduced travel and the possibility of shopping at any time, there is also the issue of access to products not available in the country.

The media, nonetheless, have reported on several cases of tax fraud as well as substandard and falsified health products (Jornal i 2013; Folha de Londrina 2015; UOL Notícias 2015; Jornal de Notícias 2016; Diário de Amapá 2017; Portal Correio 2017; Jornal de Notícias 2017). It is known that violations against legislation regulating health products are common, resulting in the sale of overdue products, prescription medicines without a prescription, falsified goods, and products that do not meet the quality standards required by law. In the same vein, Silva Luiz (1997) reports a series of illegal practices, such as the intentional selling of low-quality or expired pharmaceutical products.

Thus, it is not difficult to imagine that the sale of online medicines also breaches established norms. It is usually fairly easy to buy prescription drugs without prescriptions, and it is very hard to know who to speak to if you seek advice from the pharmacist. In fact, a study that analyzed 18 virtual pharmacies found irregularities in 15 of them (Gondim and Falcão 2007).

Brazilian laws governing pharmaceutical trade and health surveillance date back to 1973 (Brazil 1973). The legislation defines the types of establishments in the wholesale and retail trade, their organization, activities, and types of products that each would be allowed to market (e.g., allopathic, homeopathic, industrialized, or manipulated according to the needs of specific consumers). Although this law remains in force, several more recent regulatory efforts have sought to update different aspects of the country's legal framework. In this sense, it is important to mention the Law 13021/2014 (Brazil 2014), which regulates pharmaceutical services. These are defined as "the set of actions and services aimed at ensuring comprehensive therapeutic care and the promotion, protection and recovery of health in public and private establishments that carry out pharmaceutical activities, having the medicine as an essential input and aiming at its access and its rational use."

The regulatory framework related to medicines and pharmaceutical services is determined, in this decreasing hierarchical order, by the laws and decrees passed by the legislature and sanctioned by the executive, the regulations of the National Agency of Sanitary Surveillance (ANVISA), and those of the Federal Council of Pharmacy. Some approaches or interpretations of regulations enacted by these bodies sometimes conflict, and it takes the same effort to harmonize them.

It is worth mentioning some specific features of the country's prescription drug landscape. One is the magnitude of drugs dispensed free-of-cost to end users in public health units, either in specific establishments for the dispensation of medicines or, more commonly, located within health facilities. Thus, outpatient dispensing of drugs can occur in units of different levels of complexity. Another issue is the size and diversity of these dispensaries. Thus, pharmaceutical establishments include, for example, drug stations—units of small size and complexity and even airplanes and boats serving remote areas. Applying the country's laws governing medicines always raises questions if the requirements are applicable to all types of establishments, whether public or private.

Like the United States, drugs must be sold with a prescription, except those listed as permissible as over-the-counter (OTC). The law defines specific regulations for both groups, including the size of the sales package, package inserts, free samples, and the prohibition of advertising to the lay public for prescription drugs.

In 2009, ANVISA established Good Pharmaceutical Practices (Brazil 2009) related to regulations governing the operation, dispensation, and commercialization of products and the provision of pharmaceutical services in pharmacies and drugstores. Some of these aspects have been present in legislation since 1973, but ANVISA defined them in the 2009 rules. For example, pharmacies and any other places dispensing medicines must have a pharmacist present whom should provide pharmaceutical services to support users in the appropriate use of medicines.

This same legislation (Brazil 2009) regulates for the first time the remote sale of medicines (i.e., telephone, facsimile, and Internet), a practice already used by some pharmacies at the time (E-Commerce News 2015). In these cases, there is no physical proximity between the buyer and the seller of medicines. The rules state that only companies with physical stores can sell drugs through these means and they are not allowed to sell products subject to special control. In addition to psychoactive products, other drugs such as antibiotics, retinoids, and anabolics are subject to special control at the different stages of the drug chain (i.e., production, distribution and commercialization, or dispensation). The law also stipulates that sellers must have a pharmacist responsible for the user, embed the delivery costs in the retail price, provide adequate conditions for transporting medicines, maintain the confidentiality of consumer data, and not use consumer information to send advertisements.

In comparison to the US market that allows companies to establish prices, Brazil has far more extensive controls on prices. ANVISA establishes maximum prices for consumer sales (*Preço Máximo ao Consumidor*—PMC) for each product. As demonstrated by a consumer protection organization, IDEC (2012), in addition to the huge price variation from one establishment to another, the vast majority of venders practice values below the PMC. The authors conclude that this reveals a flaw in the legislation, since it would place PMCs too high by giving pharmaceutical companies too much room to set prices to the detriment of the consumer. Because of information asymmetry, the consumer generally does not have sufficient knowledge for proper research. Brazil's law on generic medicines mandates that these drugs be marketed by their international nonproprietary names (INN) and that, even in branded medicines, the INN must be presented on the outer packaging in visible size. However, vast social inequality and deficient health literacy hinders the proper use of this information by users. Nonetheless, online purchasing and price research allow consumers to find better prices with little effort on their part.

Another important use of the Internet in Brazil is price research, a tool also employed by government bodies purchasing medicines. There are public databases as well as private databases. SIASG is a public one, made available by the federal government[3] where it is possible to see purchase prices of completed transactions. Some private enterprises, like the Price Bank (or *Banco de Preços* in Portuguese),[4] sells access to price information in a supposedly easy-to-use-platform.

In Brazil, self-medication is widespread (Servidoni et al. 2006). Nevertheless, nationally representative data remains scarce. National survey data developed by the Ministry of Health, one of the few published studies with national coverage, has made it possible to evaluate the situation of self-medication in the country as a relevant issue, given the inherent risks (e.g., drug intoxications and adverse reactions) and possible increases in associated health expenditures. The general prevalence of self-medication was 16.1%, ranging from 11.4% to 23.8%, respectively, in the South and Northeast regions of the country (Arrais et al. 2016).

[3] For more information, see http:// dados.gov.br/dataset/compras-publicas-do-governo-federal

[4] For more information, see https://www.bancodeprecos.com.br

According to Souza et al. (2008), among the causes of the indiscriminate use of drugs among the population, especially self-medication, are the multiplicity of pharmaceutical products on the market and their massive advertising, the low-income population's barriers to medical services, the limited campaigns to raise awareness about the health problems of self-medication, and the role of the mass media including the Internet in disseminating information about medicines. The authors also point out that websites and discussion groups, especially those aimed at discussing diseases, are primarily responsible for promoting self-medication on the Internet. Often, information such as indication and posology is available, allowing an individual to initiate treatment without prior consultation with a physician or even a correct diagnosis. The authors also report a survey conducted among university students from Rio Grande do Sul state who use drugs to improve their cognitive ability, highlighting that the Internet is increasingly influential in this process and is listed as the fifth factor by the interviewees as being decisive in their decision to self-medicate. Still, the survey revealed that information collected in the virtual world is less influential than information from family, friends, or other users regarding the use of medicines without the supervision of a doctor. Nonetheless, the results indicate that the Internet has been gaining more and more space because many of the factors considered influential by the interviewees are mediated by the virtual world (Souza et al. 2008).

Gondim et al. (2012) compared the quality of information on websites about health in general and websites specific to medicines. Except for the category of "visibility of a publication or revision date" in which medicine information websites ranked worse, they were similar in the criteria of "access, appearance, and organization." But, medicine information websites performed worse according to the criteria of "honesty, transparency, and accountability."

In addition to access to medication and pharmaceutical information by lay people, the Internet has brought some changes to the lives of health professionals who work with medicines in their daily lives. Pereira et al. (2016) followed the implementation of a smartphone application that assists nurses in calculating medicines given to their patients. The study concluded that the use of applications in the operationalization of nursing work presented satisfactory results for encouraging learning by student nurses. The authors emphasize the optimization of the use of time, although they reinforce the importance of students learning how calculations are made and how the formulas are devised.

Within the subject of "medicine and the Internet," research concerning the relationship between drugs and social networks remains limited. Only two papers addressing this issue have been published in Brazil. The first one analyzes non-therapeutic virtual communities of Benflogin® among adolescents in the Social Network Service [or *Serviço de Rede Social* in Portuguese] online social network. The product, an anti-inflammatory drug with the active ingredient benzydamine, has been used recreationally by adolescents for its hallucinogenic effect in high doses. The authors concluded that a virtual community organized around the discussion of the non-therapeutic use of a drug can contribute to its promotion, especially in young people (Souza et al. 2008).

The other study analyzes the relationship between methylphenidate and social networks, collecting data through the application of data extraction software from social networks (Facebook) in order to map information about the use of this drug in this network. The content, publicly accessible, was analyzed and categorized by anchoring the literature on the topic of pharmaceuticalization. The data map showed that Facebook offers important virtual spaces for the circulation of information, with a reach of approximately 600,000 people. The spaces represent discussion forums where the main controversies about the uses of methylphenidate are posed: diagnosis, attention-deficit/hyperactivity disorder (ADHD) identity, resistance to drug use, acquisition, etc. Considering the main points raised by this study, it is possible to affirm that, in the case of the consumption of methylphenidate, its use presents aspects of the pharmaceuticalization of daily life (Coutinho et al. 2017).

13.5 Digital Commonalities but Distinct Realities of Internet-Based Medicines

The cases of the United States and Brazil reveal the growing use of the Internet to mediate information, access, and use of drugs, both prescription and OTC drugs, by consumers and suppliers. To date, the scholarly literature on the subject is much more extensively focused on the United States than in Brazil. Still, there are distinct differences between the two countries given their size, medical infrastructures, and market particularities. One major difference is the amount of attention in the US literature on illicit, or "rogue," online pharmacies. While fraud and substandard medicines along with dispensing drugs without a prescription remain a concern in Brazil, the US's emphasis on illegal cyber pharmacies draws attention to the unique characteristics of the US market.

With some of the highest drug prices in the world and gaps in insurance coverage, access remains a problem in the United States. In contrast, as mentioned above, a lot of medications are distributed free-of-charge in Brazil's public health system. Access is also a problem throughout Brazil, but the country offers important lessons to the United States for addressing this issue. Most US literature about online pharmacies suggest more informational campaigns to educate the public and health-care providers about the risks involved with illicit pharmacies (FDA 2013; LegitScript 2016). Oddly, universal coverage of essential medicines that would guarantee access and eliminate most of the black market occupied by rogue pharmacies rarely appears as a policy prescription in the literature. Even in the retail market, Brazil regulates prices on new medicines entering the market—a practice that also could be adopted in the United States in order to reduce consumer preferences for cheaper options from dubious online sellers. One study demonstrating the lower prices of Canadian online pharmacies to Medicare beneficiaries even suggested the use of these online dispensaries as a way to address cost barriers (S. H. Kim et al. 2017). Of course, safety is a very important issue (Livingstone 2011; Gondim et al. 2012), and studies on access to the Internet must be followed by the ones on appropriate use of medicines, quality of information, and Internet literacy.

Differences between the United States and Brazil also extend to regulating the sale of drugs online. While both countries have robust and comparable legal frameworks for governing the prescription, sale, and dispensation of medicines, they differ in terms of commercialization of controlled drugs that have the potential for abuse (e.g., psychoactive, anabolic, and retinoid drugs). Brazil restricts sales of controlled medicines by phone, fax, or the Internet. In contrast, the US Ryan Haight Act specifies the conditions for their sale, including the use of telemedicine. Moreover, there is extensive focus in US legislation and law enforcement for combatting illicit pharmacies.

Another major difference between the United States and Brazil is the intersection of the Internet with direct-to-consumer advertising, legal and widespread in the United States but illegal in accordance with WHO guidelines in Brazil. Huh et al. (2005, 712) summarize the three benefits that advocates make for online prescription drug information:

1. It empowers consumers by improving their understanding of health-related subjects and their ability to actively participate in health care.
2. It delivers a wide range of health information with privacy and immediacy.
3. It allows relative anonymity, where consumers can retrieve, send, and discuss information on illnesses, treatments, and drugs.

These benefits have merits to the extent that information is presented in order to educate the public about both risks and benefits of using prescription drugs.[5] The problem is that digital opportunities to democratize information, in effect, result in reproducing power disparities in society through DTC marketing and in promoting a medicalized or, better yet, pharmaceuticalized model toward addressing everyday concerns.

In terms of discursive power, the Internet exacerbates what Brody and Light (2011, 399) call the "inverse benefit law" or in other words "the ratio of benefits to harms among patients taking new drugs tends to vary inversely with how extensively the drugs are marketed." Extending this concept to the online world, the Internet offers marketers additional means to promote medicines that could result in more adverse drug reactions. In fact, studies of Internet-based medicines suggest that consumers have more difficulty making drug selections due to the way information is provided and dearth of details about efficacy and negative consequences (Huh et al. 2005, 712). The use of online diagnostics that channel users to drug treatments is a poor substitute since this type of consumer "is precisely the type of customer pharmaceutical marketers seek to enroll" (Ebeling 2011, 826). The result is "Digital Iatrogenesis" (Mackey and Liang 2014) since most new medicines offer no or limited improvements over existing treatments yet expose populations to significant adverse risks resulting in an estimated 3.75 million hospitalizations worldwide and over 100,000 deaths annually just in the United States (Light 2009).

[5] Chapter 10 in this book evaluates the quality of health information on different websites.

The worldwide extension of the web presents significant regulatory challenges to policing information for public health objectives (N Fox et al. 2006; Dukes et al. 2015). With DTC advertising legal in the United States (and New Zealand), consumers everywhere are susceptible to questionable and biased sources of information about prescription drugs. "To date no satisfactory means has been found of excluding improper and masked promotion from the Internet, especially when it emanates from other countries, without impairing the medium's value in rendering possible the free availability of genuine information," concludes Dukes et al. (2015, 145). Digital delivery systems also extend to doctors to whom most advertisers hope to reach. Now more than half of marketing outreach to doctors occurs through digital, nonpersonal communication, according to a recent survey (Snyder Bulik 2016).

Even when there were adequate controls about drug promotion, the Internet will continue to facilitate a deeper cultural predisposition for easy pharmaceutical interventions to address everyday maladies. In this regard, both the United States and Brazil have this trait in common. As the uptake in Internet use increases, and people turn toward this medium for information about their personal issues, the biomedical search for solutions will likely increase. Such pharmaceuticalization also extends to so-called expert patients, as illustrated by the biomedical discourses of overweight people and their reliance on the weight-loss drug orlistat in online forums (N Fox et al. 2005). Along these lines, social media venues permit the circulation of information in a much more dynamic and thus further challenging the "scientific knowledge" previously monopolized by physicians and other medical professionals.

13.6 Conclusion

While the Internet offers unique advantages for people to gain knowledge about disease and medicines, the medium also presents a number of challenges. Online opportunities can disrupt traditional distribution networks as well as flows of information. With the digital technologies offering new possibilities and risks for access, patient and consumer advocacy groups continue to mobilize. In their *Brussels Principles on Medication Sales over the Internet*, these groups reaffirm that access to safe and effective medicines is part of the human right to health (KEI et al. 2017). While acknowledging problems with fraudulent online pharmacies, it is worth highlighting a few principles outlined in their *Brussels Principles*:

- Consumers should be able to use the Internet to order and have delivered through the mail safe and affordable medications.
- Policies that affect online access to medication should be consumer-focused, patient-centered, and evidence-based and created with the understanding that prices often prohibit access.

These groups tend to focus on differential access to treatment due to individuals' and countries' income levels compounded by exorbitant differences in prices found in different national markets.

Missing in the *Principles*, however, is the importance of adequate levels of pharmaceutical care. Even here, there are interesting innovations provided over the Internet, including the ePharmaCare platform that shifts the focus from the sale of prescription drugs to the provision of services (Lapão et al. 2017, 12). Yet, even in these cases, it is important that Internet-based technologies for pharmaceutical service address health communication disparities between sociodemographic groups (DeLorme et al. 2010; Moreno et al. 2016).

More research is needed to understand the various impacts of the Internet and social media on access to and appropriate use of essential medicines. This need is especially apparent in middle- and low-income countries where the Internet is rapidly penetrating into the daily lives of new social groups. This literature review delineated the new digital pharmaceutical reality in comparing the United States and Brazil by highlighting the differences and similarities in terms of access, information flows, and regulatory challenges.

References

ANFARMAG – Associação Nacional de Farmacêuticos Magistrais. 2017. Dispensação Remota de Produtos Farmacêuticos. http://portal.crfsp.org.br/images/stories/2016/06_16/anfarmag.pdf. Accessed 20 June 2017.

Arrais, Paulo Sérgio Dourado, Maria Eneida Porto Fernandes, Tatiane da Silva Dal Pizzol, Luiz Roberto Ramos, Sotero Serrate Mengue, Vera Lucia Luiza, Noemia Urruth Leão Tavares, Mareni Rocha Farias, Maria Auxiliadora Oliveira, and Andréa Dâmaso Bertoldi. 2016. Prevalence of self-medication in Brazil and associated factors. *Revista de Saúde Pública* 50: 50. https://doi.org/10.1590/s1518-8787.2016050006117.

Bachhuber, Marcus A., and Raina M. Merchant. 2017. Buying drugs online in the age of social media. *American Journal of Public Health* 107: 1858–1859.

Berkrot, Bill. 2015. Global drug spending to hit $1.4 trillion in 2020: IMS. *Reuters*, November 18. https://www.reuters.com/article/us-health-ims-drugspending-idUSKCN0T70GQ20151118. Accessed 20 June 2018.

Brasil. Anvisa. Agência Nacional de Vigilância Sanitária. Diretoria Colegiada. 2009. *Resolução-RDC No 44, de 17 de agosto de 2009. Dispõe sobre Boas Práticas Farmacêuticas para o controle sanitário do funcionamento, da dispensação e da comercialização de produtos e da prestação de serviços farmacêuticos em farmácias e drogarias e dá outras providências*.

Brasil. Presidência da República. Casa Civil. 1973. *Lei Federal nº. 5.991, de 17 de dezembro de 1973. Dispõe sobre o Controle Sanitário do Comércio de Drogas, Medicamentos, Insumos Farmacêuticos e Correlatos, e dá outras Providências*. Vol. 17 de dezembro de 1973.

———. 2014. *Lei 13021 de 8 de agosto de 2014. Dispõe sobre o exercício e a fiscalização das atividades farmacêuticas*. Diário Oficial da União, 11 de Agosto de 2014.

Brody, Howard, and Donald W. Light. 2011. The inverse benefit law: How drug marketing undermines patient safety and public health. *American Journal of Public Health* 101: 399–404.

Brown, Joshua, and Chenghui Li. 2014. Characteristics of online pharmacy users in a nationally representative sample. *Journal of the American Pharmacists Association* 54: 289–294.

Cabral, Rodrigo Viana, and Fabiana Schuelter Trevisol. 2010. A influência da internet na relação médico-paciente na percepção do médico. *Revista da AMRIGS* 54: 416–420.

Chandra, Ashish, and Stephen Cupps. 2002. E-regulation and Internet pharmacies: Issues and dilemmas. *Clinical Research & Regulatory Affairs* 19: 67.

Choi, Sejung Marina, and Wei-Na Lee. 2007. Understanding the impact of direct-to-consumer (dtc) pharmaceutical advertising on patient-physician interactions: Adding the web to the mix. *Journal of Advertising* 36: 137–149.

Cicero, Theodore J., and Matthew Stephen Ellis. 2012. Health outcomes in patients using no-prescription online pharmacies to purchase prescription drugs. *Journal of Medical Internet Research* 14: e174.

Conrad, Peter, and Valerie Leiter. 2008. From Lydia Pinkham to Queen Levitra: Direct-to-consumer advertising and medicalisation. *Sociology of Health & Illness* 30: 825–838.

Consumers International. 2018. Consumers and the Internet of things: One connection too many? Divulgação cientifica. https://www.consumersinternational.org/news-resources/blog/posts/20170313-consumers-and-the-internet-of-things-one-connection-too-many/. Accessed 20 June 2017.

Coutinho, Tiago, Angela Fernandes Esher, and Claudia Garcia Serpa Osorio-de-Castro. 2017. Mapeando espaços virtuais de informação sobre TDA/H e usos do metilfenidato. *Physis: Revista de Saúde Coletiva* 27: 749–769.

DeLorme, Denise E., Jisu Huh, and Leonard N. Reid. 2010. Evaluation, use, and usefulness of prescription drug information sources among Anglo and Hispanic Americans. *Journal of Health Communication* 15: 18–38.

Diário de Amapá. 2017. Prefeitura de Macapá e Anvisa interditam seis farmácias durante fiscalização. Diário do Amapá. http://www.diariodoamapa.com.br/2017/06/22/prefeitura-de-macapa-e-anvisa-interditam-seis-farmacias-durante-fiscalizacao/. Accessed 1 July 2017.

Dukes, Graham, John Braithwaite, and J.P. Moloney. 2015. *Pharmaceuticals, corporate crime and public health*. Cheltenham: Edward Elgar Publishing.

Ebeling, Mary. 2011. "Get with the Program!": Pharmaceutical marketing, symptom checklists and self-diagnosis. *Social Science & Medicine (1982)* 73: 825–832.

E-Commerce News. 2015. Comércio eletrônico de medicamentos enfrenta barreiras na legislação. E-Commerce News. https://ecommercenews.com.br/artigos/cases/comercio-eletronico-de-medicamentos-enfrenta-barreiras-na-legislacao. Accessed 20 June 2017.

FDA – Food and Drug Administration. 2013. BeSafeRx: Know your online pharmacy – Survey highlights. Food and Drug Administration. https://www.fda.gov/Drugs/ResourcesForYou/Consumers/BuyingUsingMedicineSafely/BuyingMedicinesOvertheInternet/BeSafeRxKnowYourOnlinePharmacy/ucm318497.htm. Accessed 15 May 2017.

Fogel, Joshua, and Daniel Novick. 2009. Direct-to-consumer advertisements of prescription medications over the internet. *Health Marketing Quarterly* 26: 347–371.

Folha de Londrina. 2015. Vigilância intensifica fiscalização em farmácias. Folha de Londrina. http://www.folhadelondrina.com.br/geral/vigilancia-intensifica-fiscalizacao-em-farmacias-907767.html. Accessed 1 July 2017.

Fox, Susannah, and Maeve Duggan. 2013. Information triage. Pew Research Center: Internet, Science & Tech. http://www.pewinternet.org/2013/01/15/information-triage/. Accessed 22 June 2018.

Fox, N., K.J. Ward, and A.J. O'Rourke. 2005. The 'expert patient': Empowerment or medical dominance? The case of weight loss, pharmaceutical drugs and the Internet. *Social Science & Medicine* 60: 1299–1309.

Fox, Nick, Katie Ward, and Alan O'Rourke. 2006. A sociology of technology governance for the information age: The case of pharmaceuticals, consumer advertising and the Internet. *Sociology* 40: 315–334.

G1. 2016. Vendas pela internet devem dobrar até 2021, diz pesquisa do Google. Economia. October 17. http://g1.globo.com/economia/noticia/2016/10/vendas-pela-internet-devem-dobrar-ate-2021-diz-pesquisa-do-google.html. Accessed 18 July 2017.

GAO – Government Accounting Office. 2005. *Internet pharmacy and drug importation: Exploring risks and benefits : Hearing before the Special Committee on Aging, United States Senate, One Hundred Ninth Congress, first session, Washington, DC, January 26, 2005*. S. Hrg.: 109–23. Washington, DC: U.S. Government Printing Office.

———. 2013. *Internet pharmacies: Federal agencies and state face challenges combating rogue sites, particularly those aboard: Report to congressional committees*. [Washington, DC]: United States Government Accountability Office.
Gondim, Ana Paula Soares, and Cláudio Borges Falcão. 2007. Avaliação das farmácias virtuais brasileiras [Evaluation of Brazilian online pharmacies]. *Revista de Saúde Pública* 41: 297–300.
Gondim, Ana Paula Soares, Davi Pontes Weyne, and Bruno Sousa Pinto Ferreira. 2012. Qualidade das informações de saúde e medicamentos nos sítios brasileiros [Quality of health and medication information on Brazilian websites]. *Einstein (São Paulo)* 10: 335–341.
t' Hoen, Ellen F.M. 2009. *The global politics of pharmaceutical monopoly power*. Diemen: AMB.
Huh, Jisu, Denise E. DeLorme, and Leonard N. Reid. 2005. Factors affecting trust in on-line prescription drug information and impact of trust on behavior following exposure to DTC advertising. *Journal of Health Communication* 10: 711–731.
IBGE – Brazilian Institute of Geography and Statistics. 2017. Mais de 100 milhões de brasileiros já acessam a internet, diz IBGE. Estadão. http://link.estadao.com.br/noticias/cultura-digital,mais-de-100-milhoes-de-brasileiros-ja-acessam-a-internet-diz-ibge,10000090597. Accessed 2 July 2017.
IDEC – Instituto de Defesa do Direito do Consumidor. 2012. Matéria - Diferença além da conta. Idec - Instituto Brasileiro de Defesa do Consumidor. http://www.idec.org.br/em-acao/revista/diferenca-que-incomoda/materia/diferenca-alem-da-conta/pagina/73. Accessed 1 May 2017.
IDEC – Instituto Brasileiro de Defesa do Consumidor. 2017. Dicas & Direitos - conheça as regras para venda de medicamentos em farmácias. Idec - Instituto Brasileiro de Defesa do Consumidor. http://www.idec.org.br/consultas/dicas-e-direitos/conheca-as-regras-para-venda-de-medicamentos-em-farmacias. Accessed 20 June 2017.
Inciardi, James A., Hilary L. Surratt, Theodore J. Cicero, Andrew Rosenblum, Ahwah Candice, J. Elise Bailey, Richard C. Dart, and John J. Burke. 2010. Prescription drugs purchased through the internet: Who are the end users? *Drug and Alcohol Dependence* 110: 21–29.
Interfarma – Associação de Indústria Farmacêutica de Pesquisa. 2016. Guia 2016 : Dados de Mercado. https://www.interfarma.org.br/guia/guia_2016/dados_de_mercado/. Accessed 1 July 2017.
Jornal de Notícias. 2016. Duas farmacêuticas e seis médicos acusados de corrupção e burla. Jornal de Notícias. October 11. http://www.jn.pt/justica/interior/duas-farmaceuticas-e-seis-medicos-acusados-de-corrupcao-e-burla-5436438.html. Accessed 1 July 2017.
———. 2017. Farmacêutica detida por fraude. Jornal de Notícias. February 9. http://www.jn.pt/justica/interior/farmaceutica-detida-por-fraude-5657902.html. July 1 2017.
Jornal i. 2013. Buscas a farmácias. Sete detidos por suspeitas de corrupção. *Ionline*. https://ionline.sapo.pt/371563. Accessed 20 June 2018.
Kalorama Information. 2018. Global Over-the-Counter (OTC) drug markets : Market research report. January 23. https://www.kaloramainformation.com/Global-Counter-OTC-Drug-11401855/. Accessed 20 June 2018.
Kapstein, Ethan B., and Josh Busby. 2013. *AIDS drugs for all*. Cambridge: Cambridge University Press.
KEI, Prescription Justice, EFF, and Public Citizen. 2017. Brussels principles on medication sales over the Internet. June 27. https://www.keionline.org/node/2817. Accessed 29 June 2017.
Kim, Hyojin. 2011. Pharmaceutical companies as a source of health information: A pilot study of the effects of source, web site interactivity, and involvement. *Health Marketing Quarterly* 28: 57–85.
Kim, Sean Hyungwoo, Young Joo Ryu, Na-Eun Cho, Andy Eunwoo Kim, and Jongwha Chang. 2017. Prescription drug price paradox: Cost analysis of Canadian online pharmacies versus US medicare beneficiaries for the top 100 drugs. *Clinical Drug Investigation* 37: 957–963.
Lapão, Luís Velez, Miguel Mira da Silva, and João Gregório. 2017. Implementing an online pharmaceutical service using design science research. *BMC Medical Informatics and Decision Making*. 17: 31. https://doi.org/10.1186/s12911-017-0428-2.
LegitScript. 2016. The Internet pharmacy market in 2016. http://www.safemedsonline.org/wp-content/uploads/2016/01/The-Internet-Pharmacy-Market-in-2016.pdf. Accessed 20 June 2017.

Light, Donald W. 2009. Bearing the risks of prescription drugs. In *The risks of prescription drugs*, 1–39. New York: Columbia University Press.

Livingstone, Sonia. 2011. Internet literacy: Young people's negotiation of new online opportunities. *Matrizes*. https://doi.org/10.11606/issn.1982-8160.v4i2p11-42.

Luiz, Silva. 1997. *Farmáfia: falcatruas nos balcões de farmácias*. Foz do Iguaçu: Imed Editora.

Mackey, Tim K., and Bryan A. Liang. 2014. Digital Iatrogenesis: Policy advocacy to prevent patient harm from access to dangerous drugs online. *Harvard Health Policy Review* 14: 11.

Mackey, Tim K., and Gaurvika Nayyar. 2016. Digital danger: A review of the global public health, patient safety and cybersecurity threats posed by illicit online pharmacies. *British Medical Bulletin* 118: 110–126.

Mangan, Dan. 2014. Patients cross borders for online deals on medications. *CNBC*, May 23. https://www.cnbc.com/2014/05/23/patients-cross-borders-for-online-deals-on-medications.html. Accessed 2 Feb 2018.

Mazer, Maryann, Francis DeRoos, Frances Shofer, Judd Hollander, Christine McCusker, Nicholas Peacock, and Jeanmarie Perrone. 2012. Medications from the web: Use of online pharmacies by emergency department patients. *The Journal of Emergency Medicine* 42: 227–232.

Mintzes, Barbara. 2012. Advertising of prescription-only medicines to the public: Does evidence of benefit counterbalance harm? *Annual Review of Public Health* 33: 259–277.

Monteith, Scott, Tasha Glenn, Rita Bauer, Jörn Conell, and Michael Bauer. 2016. Availability of prescription drugs for bipolar disorder at online pharmacies. *Journal of Affective Disorders* 193: 59–65.

Moreno, Gerardo, Elizabeth Lin, Eva Chang, Ron Johnson, Heidi Berthoud, Cam Solomon, and Leo Morales. 2016. Disparities in the use of internet and telephone medication refills among linguistically diverse patients. *Journal of General Internal Medicine* 31: 282–288.

Orizio, Grazia, Anna Merla, Peter J. Schulz, and Umberto Gelatti. 2011. Quality of online pharmacies and websites selling prescription drugs: A systematic review. *Journal of Medical Internet Research* 13: e74–e74.

Orsolini, Laura, Giulia Francesconi, Duccio Papanti, Arianna Giorgetti, and Fabrizio Schifano. 2015. Profiling online recreational/prescription drugs' customers and overview of drug vending virtual marketplaces. *Human Psychopharmacology* 30: 302–318.

Pereira, Francisco Gilberto Fernandes, Joselany Afio Caetano, Natasha Marques Frota, and Maguida Gomes da Silva. 2016. Use of digital applications in the medicament calculation education for nursing. *Investigación y Educación en Enfermería* 34. https://doi.org/10.17533/udea.iee.v34n2a09.

Pew Research. 2017. Internet/broadband fact sheet. Pew Research Center: Internet, Science & Tech. http://www.pewinternet.org/fact-sheet/internet-broadband/. Accessed 15 May 2017.

Portal Correio. 2017. Saúde encontra fraude em 40% das solicitações de remédios do "Farmácia Popular". Portal Correio. https://portalcorreio.com.br/saude-encontra-fraude-em-40-das-solicitacoes-de-remedios-do-farmacia-popular/. Accessed 1 July 2017.

QuintlesIMS. 2016. IMS Health Study: U.S. Drug Spending Growth Reaches 8.5 Percent in 2015. IMS Health. November 7. http://www.imshealth.com/en/thought-leadership/quintilesims-institute/news-and-press. Accessed 19 May 2017.

SEBRAE – Serviço Brasileiro de Apoio às Micro e Pequenas Empresas. 2015a. As regras para as farmácias online. Sebrae. http://www.sebrae.com.br/sites/PortalSebrae/artigos/as-regras-para-as-farmacias-online,f7e99e665b182410VgnVCM100000b272010aRCRD. Accessed 20 June 2017.

———. 2015b. Boas Práticas em Saúde Online - Dicas e orientações sobre o e-commerce de produtos e serviços de saúde. http://www.bibliotecas.sebrae.com.br/chronus/ARQUIVOS_CHRONUS/bds/bds.nsf/ceba8421b82be1b7ee7335c4fd3d7e7b/%24File/5777.pdf. Accessed 20 June 2017.

Servidoni, Alexandre Barbosa, Liliane Coelho, Marcos de Lima Navarro, Fernanda Gobbi de Ávila, and Raquel Mezzalira. 2006. Self-medication profile of ENT patients. *Brazilian Journal of Otorhinolaryngology* 72: 83–88.

Smith, Nicole K., Kelly Cleland, Brandon Wagner, and James Trussell. 2017. "I don't know what I would have done." Women's experiences acquiring ulipristal acetate emergency contraception online from 2011 to 2015. *Contraception* 95: 414–418.

Snyder Bulik, Beth. 2016. Pharma's digital contact with docs now surpasses sales rep visits: Survey. Fierce Pharma. https://www.fiercepharma.com/marketing/pharma-digital-contact-doctors-now-surpasses-sales-rep-visits-survey-finds. Accessed 4 June 2017.

Souza, João Fábio R. de, Carmem L.C. Marinho, and Maria Cristina R. Guilam. 2008. Medicine consumption and the internet: Critical evaluation of a virtual community. *Revista da Associação Médica Brasileira* 54: 225–231.

Taylor, David, and Michael Bury. 2007. Chronic illness, expert patients and care transition: Chronic illness, expert patients and care transition. *Sociology of Health & Illness* 29: 27–45.

UOL Notícias. 2015. Esquema de corrupção distribuía remédio vencido em 20 cidades do PR, diz TV. Cotidiano. https://noticias.uol.com.br/cotidiano/ultimas-noticias/2015/08/02/esquema-de-corrupcao-distribuia-remedio-vencido-em-20-cidades-do-pr-diz-tv.htm. Accessed 1 July 2017.

Valor Econômico. 2014. Valor: Análise setorial: Farmácias e Drogarias. Valor Econômico. https://setorial.valor.com.br/produto/194/farmacias-e-drogarias. Accessed 20 June 2018.

Part IV
Internet and Health Education

Chapter 14
E-*Learning* and Problematizing Pedagogies: A Brazilian Experience in Monitoring and Evaluation Teaching

Elizabeth Moreira dos Santos, Gisela Cardoso, and Dolores Abreu

Abstract The present chapter analyzes three E-learning initiatives developed by the Evaluation Laboratory (LASER) at the Sergio Arouca National School of Public Health, Fiocruz, Rio de Janeiro, Brazil (ENSP/FIOCRUZ), highlighting the challenges of using current pedagogical methodologies for monitoring and evaluation (M&E) teaching. The research is based on three classes of a specialization course in health evaluation in the online distance learning (ODL) format, as part of a technical cooperation agreement between ENSP/FIOCRUZ and the Brazilian Ministry of Health (MS). The initiatives suggest E-learning facilitates access to information and training. The experience indicates that E-learning in M&E in health makes an essential contribution in M&E practices and knowledge, among professionals working in Brazil's Unified Health System (SUS). However, critical theoretical and practical challenges persist, either from a pedagogical approach, specificity of content in M&E, the information and communication technologies (ICT) involved, or institutional factors.

14.1 Introduction

This chapter describes the Brazilian experience with E-learning[1] in training of monitoring and evaluation (M&E) through innovative pedagogical approaches. The utilized approach includes the development of new professional skills, enabling conditions to create knowledge transfer operations (Clavier et al. 2011), build socio-technical networks (Latour 1996), and act critically in the transformation of social

[1] Chapter 15 addresses the theme of "massive open online courses" (MOOCs).

E. M. dos Santos (✉)
National School of Public Health, Fundação Oswaldo Cruz, Rio de Janeiro, Brazil

Institute of Studies in Collective Health, Federal University of Rio de Janeiro, Rio de Janeiro, Brazil
e-mail: bmoreira@ensp.fiocruz.br

G. Cardoso · D. Abreu
National School of Public Health, Fundação Oswaldo Cruz, Rio de Janeiro, Brazil

A. Pereira Neto, M. B. Flynn (eds.), *The Internet and Health in Brazil*,
https://doi.org/10.1007/978-3-319-99289-1_14

reality in the search for *social betterment* (Mark et al. 2000). This chapter focuses on analyzing the experience of developing and implementing the Laser/ENSP/Fiocruz specialization course in the distance learning modality conducted in three classes. For some, the specialization courses in E-learning in Brazil would be better classified as semi-synchronous courses, since the legal provisions in the country (Resolution of the National Education Council) require for this modality to have at least three real-time meetings for the tests and course completion term (Ministry of Education 2007).

M&E is a priority for improving health systems due to the decreasing volume of resources destined to the implementation of public health interventions in Brazil (Brazil 2014), the need to monitor performance and effectiveness in response to the impositions of public accountability (OECD 2016) (ordinance of May 2016), and the demands of increasingly well-informed and demanding users. The complexity of health problems and interventions requires integrated responses consistent with current daily practices, technological innovations, and new values and rights in health. M&E as a reflexive tool is indispensable to respond to dynamic health scenarios and complexity of interventions.

Online distance learning (ODL) is a comprehensive term used to designate the physical separation between teacher and student in the teaching-learning process. This definition refers to the origins of distance learning using printed material, understood as correspondence teaching. Today it combines teaching-learning experiences based on both diverse technologies and human interaction, like telephone calls, video conference, CD-ROMs, and teleconferences involving different computer mediations (Ruhe and Zumbo 2009). With the development and consolidation of the World Wide Web, new information and communication technologies have improved the architecture of teaching and learning, marking the overlap between E-learning and distance learning (Ruhe and Zumbo 2009).

E-learning refers to forms of learning in virtual environments.[2] It describes, therefore, a set of initiatives mediated by information and communication technologies (ICT) including presential, semi-presential, and distance learning experiences (Struchiner and Carvalho 2014). They also allow different sectors of the population to dominate information and communication technologies to access and share a particular type of knowledge at any time and place. *E-learning* also involves processes of digital inclusion, since the problematization of mobilizing themes leverages interests and abilities of social groups in a situation of restricted access to computing and quality information (Paolucci et al. 2017).

Public health E-learning programs are part of Brazil's strategy to strengthen M&E by upgrading human resources at the different levels of management of the Unified Health System (SUS), the country's integrated health system. We share the assumption that E-learning increases access to information and knowledge about M&E, thereby promoting the use of these tools and consequently facilitating their institutionalization.

[2] Chapter 16 discusses digital innovation for medical training.

14.2 A Little of Context and History

In Brazil, distance learning started at the end of the nineteenth century with correspondence courses (Mugnol 2009; Menelau 2010). By the 1940s, broadcasting began as a means to improve literacy among youngsters and adults, mainly in the North and Northeast regions of the country. The beginning of the 1960s marked the introduction of television in distance learning aimed at 5th to 8th grade students of elementary school (Menelau 2010).

In the 1990s, the Internet and the growth of information and communication technologies (ICT) led to the emergence of formal online distance learning (ODL) programs. Municipal and state education secretariats supported these programs targeting first the continuing education of public school teachers, such as some initiatives in Recife and São Paulo (Mugnol 2009; Menelau 2010). In 1996, Brazil's National Council for Scientific and Technological Development (*Conselho Nacional de Desenvolvimento Científico e Tecnológico*—CNPq) launched a pilot project to create new forms of didactic interaction for the computer environment. Since 1998, the number of public and private teaching institutions interested in implementing ODL courses has increased (Menelau 2010). In particular, ODL rose from 1993 to 2003 through the more intense use of ICTs in courses offered.

Following the publication of Decree No. 5,622 of December 2005 regulating the authorization and accreditation of ODL courses in Brazil, the number of offerings has expanded and increasingly focused on specific market niches (Alonso 2014; Petry et al. 2014). It is necessary to emphasize that this regulation occurred in a context of expanding access to education, especially to higher education, that was the goal of many public policies. Several authors (Santos 2011; Sguissardi 2008) consider the importance of the conjuncture of the time, whereby efforts to align Brazilian economic policy with the international one occurred simultaneously with the commitment toward incorporating civil and social rights as reflected in the choices and implementation of numerous social policies. Changes in these efforts over the last 12 years have continuously influenced the profile of federal education initiatives, including those of related to ODL in the country.

In this context, Brazil's distance learning expanded during a time of significant change in the role in the state in education. The government went from treating educational projects as a public initiative and citizenship right to that of private law dictated by competition and subjected to the efficiency requirements of the private sector, thus establishing new relations with the collective and social subjects (INEP 2017).

Considering that ODL seeks to improve course offering and increase access to knowledge, the rollout of ODL occurred unevenly, with more courses in the Southeast and South regions of Brazil (Alonso 2014). According to the 2016 Census of the Brazilian Association of Distance Education (*Associação Brasileira de Educação a Distância*—ABED), based on a sample of institutions offering ODL and who voluntarily participated in the survey, the highest number of institutions is in the Southeast (42%) and South (27%). Both account for 61% of the ODL offer in Brazil.

In 2016, nearly three million students enrolled in undergraduate higher education[3,4] courses, of these, 82.3% in private institutions. Between 2015 and 2016, the number of new attendees grew by 2.2%, mainly because the distance modality increased more than 20% between these 2 years, whereas the number of new attendees in presential courses decreased by 3.7% (INEP 2017). Thus, the findings of Petry et al. (2014) are not surprising. According to these authors, there were 37,849 face-to-face graduation courses and 10,163 ODL courses (21.2%) in Brazil in 2014. Private institutions offered 71.4% of the in-class courses and 90.3% of the distance learning offers. The research findings also point out that the ODL modality accounts for 44.4% of courses for technologists, 34.5% for undergraduates, and 21.1% for graduates, in direct contrast with face-to-face classes that account for 54.8% of baccalaureate students, 23.8% of graduates, and 20.3% of technologists. Also, 38% of institutions offering different ODL classes said that modality accounts for 76–100% of the institute's revenue (ABED 2017). Adding to changes in the state's role in education from being a regulator to that of a competitor in the market (Laval and Dardot 2016), this distribution of courses suggests for accommodating arrangements of Brazilian educational system toward reducing public spending, increasing work insecurity and cost compression, and transitioning toward regressive policies in terms of social distribution and solidarity (Miranda 2014).

Regarding areas of knowledge and the supply of *lato* sensu graduate courses[5] that are the focus of this article, the data provided by the ABED census focuses on the humanities (250 courses) and applied social sciences (218), but there are course offerings in practically all the other areas of knowledge. ODL health courses still represent a small portion of this total; that is, of the 1098 sessions entirely ODL, 67 are in the area of health sciences, and out of the 109 semi-presencial ones, 55 are in a similar field.

[3] The Census of Higher Education conducted annually by Instituto Nacional de Estudos e Pesquisas Educacionais Anísio Teixeira (Inep) is an important tool for obtaining data to support the formulation, monitoring, and evaluation of public policies, as well as being an important element for the development of studies and research on the sector. The Census collects information on higher education institutions (HEIs), on graduation and sequential courses of specific training, and on the students and teachers linked to these courses.

[4] The results collected contribute to the National System of Higher Educational Assessment (Sistema Nacional de Avaliação da Educação Superior—Sinaes), in calculating the Preliminary Course Concept (CPC) and General Course Index (IGC) indicators, as well as supplying information on the number of registrations, enrollments, and graduations, among others. Comparing different survey years, statistics can analyze student trajectories from their enrollment in a given undergraduate course and consequently creation of indicators on the follow-up and flows in higher education.

[5] In Brazil, it is customary to divide the postgraduate programs into two types: *stricto* sensu and *lato* sensu. The *stricto* sensu postgraduate course comprises master's (for 2 years) and PhD (for 4 years) programs with a workload of 360 and 540 h per year, respectively. To complete the course, the candidate must submit a thesis that will be defended before a public assessment bank. The *lato* sensu postgraduate course comprises specialization and MBA courses (for a year, with a minimum workload of 360 h) and residencies in the health area (for 2 years, with a minimum of 2800 and a maximum of 3200 h per year). The completion of these courses is not necessarily conditional on the presentation of written work and defended before a public assessment bank.

Among the leading challenges pointed out by ABED, there is growing concerns about innovation in pedagogical approaches, which is at the top of the list in 2016 (ABED 2017). The literature discusses the need to broaden the debate about the training processes in health, especially those using the distance learning modality with the professionals that enable the student's autonomy in the continuity of their professional training and practice.

A review of the literature by Vargas et al. (2016) based on 21 studies identified the main theoretical and pedagogical characteristics of ODL in the area of health. The authors divided the pedagogical approaches into four categories: theoretical references in constructivist educational perspectives, theoretical and pedagogical concepts of Paulo Freire, continuing education in health, and theoretical conceptions of ODL. In this chapter, we will not expand upon the typology used by these authors, as their empirical nature is not very reflexive, in that it is not related to the critical and noncritical ethico-political beliefs that have informed the training of health professionals in Brazil, and even less so the training processes of professional academic associations (Ramos 2001; Saviani 2007).

Thus, this chapter seeks to describe a Brazilian experience in ODL in the area of M&E in health and analyze this process and use of active and problematizing pedagogies.

14.3 The Case of Online Distance Learning: Specialization in Evaluation and Health

In 2003, the Evaluation Laboratory (Laboratório de Avaliação—LASER) of Oswaldo Cruz Foundation (Laser/Ensp/Fiocruz) and the *Centers for Disease Control and Prevention* (CDC) along with the Ministry of Health's Department of AIDS and Viral Hepatitis conducted a situational diagnosis. The initiative identified low operational capacity and little value given to M&E within the governmental sphere, with these functions linked primarily to auditing and knowledge production, more specifically as a form of academic research aimed at answering specific thematic issues. M&E was not institutionalized as a management tool but as a form of research and study.

Back then, besides evaluative research, there were some federal efforts responding primarily to demands of international partners, as in the case of the National STD/AIDS Program of the Brazilian Ministry of Health (MoH), whose central partnership in M&E was with the CDC, and the Department of Primary Care of the Ministry of Health (DAB/MS), with financing from the World Bank.

The situational diagnosis made it possible to identify the need to train MoH technical staff to incorporate a standard operational language into M&E, learn about the uses of M&E as a management tool, and promote its institutionalization. We then proceeded to develop integrated initiatives adapted to respond to identified needs, taking into account two premises: a pedagogical approach based on active pedagogies and the promotion of a socio-technical network of internal evaluators as the interface for the translation of knowledge (Ministry of Health 2004; Santos 2005).

Some integrated strategies were then chosen to address the problem, i.e., the need to train MoH technical staff in M&E. The decision was to structure training and education programs to institutionalize M&E as an initiative to foster the interaction of socio-technical networks (Santos and Natal 2007; Latour 1996), covering different levels of complexity of strategic discourses and practices in M&E, namely, workshops (presential and in virtual environment) to improve actions dissemination, specialization courses and professional master's degree for the creation of a community of practices, and specific trainings conducted by national and international experts involving critical partners on topics considered essential to the MoH's M&E. The latter involved theory and practice in economic evaluation as well as time and space sampling methodologies, including national and international seminars and events to jointly train networks of researchers and highly qualified MoH professionals in methods and techniques applied to M&E. The table below summarizes the training activities conducted by Laser/Ensp/Fiocruz between 2004 and 2017 (Table 14.1).

The *lato* sensu graduate programs comprise specialization programs for graduates in higher education diploma courses. The *stricto* sensu graduate courses contain master's and doctorate programs for graduates in higher education courses.

Table 14.1 Synthesis of graduate-level initiatives (*lato e strictu senso**) Laser/Ensp/Fiocruz

Initiatives	Modality	Year	Institutions involved
Specialization course in M&E of programs for endemic process control.		2004–2005 2005–2006	Laser/ENSP/Fiocruz, CDC, HIV/AIDS/MoH Program, Tulane University
Since 2007 it is called specialization course in health evaluation	Face-to-face	2007–2008	Laser/Ensp/Fiocruz, SVS/MS, HIV Program/AIDS Program/MoH, Tulane University
Specialization course in M&E in health	ODL (Viask)	2011–2012	Laser and ODL/Ensp/Fiocruz, SVS and Dep. HIV/AIDS/VMSCDC
		2013–2014 2015–2016	Laser and ODL/Ensp/Fiocruz, Demas/MoH
Professional master's course in M&E and health	Face-to-face	2005–2007 2007–2009 2009–2011 2015–2017	DST/Aids/MoH Program SVS/MS Demas/MoH

CDC Centers for Disease Control and Prevention, *DEMAS/MS* Department of Monitoring and Evaluation of SUS/Ministry of Health, *Laser/Ensp/Fiocruz* Laboratório de Análise de Situações Endêmicas Regionais/Sérgio Arouca National School of Public Health/Osvaldo Cruz Foundation, *SVS/MS* Department of Health Surveillance/Ministry of Health, *VIASK* Virtual Institute of Advanced Studies Knowledge

It is important to highlight that the change in the name of graduate course depicted in the template responds to the adaptations of content (object) to the demand profile of its financiers and its participants. External resources finance the course initially, but it gradually becomes technically and financially sustainable by national resources. From the mid-2000s, family health strategy and the primary healthcare system in Brazil began to integrate actions to prevent and control endemic diseases. At the same time, there was a national movement regarding the need for transparency in public management and mechanisms of social regulation, inducing the implementation of institutional arrangements in M&E, thereby encouraging training initiatives. Table 14.2 presents the summary of the short-term, updated improvement initiatives developed by Laser/Ensp/Fiocruz in this context.

Table 14.2 Summary of the short-term training initiatives developed and implemented by the Laser/Ensp/Fiocruz

Initiatives	Modality	Years	Institution involved
Short workshop for M&E AIDS	Presential	2005–2007	MoH, Laser/ENSP
Short workshop for M&E pharmaceutical assistance	Presential	2006	PAHO, NAF, Laser/ENSP
Short AIDS workshop for M&E leprosy	Presential	2008	PAHO, Laser/ENSP
M&E workshop for health actions	Presential	2009–2012	Laser/ENSP/Canal Futura/ Roberto Marinho Foundation
Short workshop for M&E and tuberculosis	Presential	2010	PNCT/SVS/MS and Fundo Global, Laser/Ensp
Short workshop for M&E QualiSUS-Network	Presential	2012–2013	Depart. Health Economics/ MS, Laser/Ensp
Short workshop for M&E urgency and emergency	Presential	2013	MS, Laser/ENSP
Short workshop for M&E and prison health	Presential	2013–2014	MS, Laser/ENSP
Short workshop for M&E integrated to strategic planning of SVS/MS	Presential	2013	DEMAS/MoH and SVS/MS, Laser/ENSP
Short workshop integrating strategic planning and M&E for the MoH	Presential	2016	Demas/MS Laser/Ensp
Short integration workshop between strategic planning and PNH < 0	Presential	2017	PNH/SAS/MS, Laser/ENSP
Online workshop in M&E integrated to strategic planning of SVS/MoH	*Online* (interactive pdf)	2017	SVS/MS, Laser/ENSP and ODL/ENSP

Source: Laser Files and Document Analysis

DEMAS/MoH Department of Monitoring and Evaluation of SUS, *Laser/Ensp/Fiocruz* Analysis of Regional Endemic Situations Laboratory/Sérgio Arouca National School of Public Health/Osvaldo Cruz Foundation, *NAF* Center for Pharmaceutical Assistance; *MoH* Ministry of Health, *PAHO* Pan American Health Organization, *PNCT* National Program for Tuberculosis Control, *PNH* National Policy on Humanization, *QualiSUS-Rede* Project on Training and Quality Improvement of the Health Care Network, *SAS/MoH* Department of Health Care/Ministry of Health, *SVS/MS* Department of Health Surveillance/Ministry of Health

These workshops represented a strong effort toward dissemination and agreement of operational terminologies in M&E applied to the health system in Brazil, as well as inculcating the evaluative way of thinking. For example, workshops offered with support from the Department of HIV/AIDS Department at Brazil's MoH conducted from May to December 2007 benefited more than 4800 participants from the 329 Brazilian municipalities in priority need for actions to prevent and control the HIV/AIDS epidemic (Paranaíba 2008). The workshops related to leprosy were carried out between 2007 and 2008 and involved the participation of 465 professionals (Cruz et al. 2009). Those carried out from 2009 to 2012 as part of the "Health Action" Project in the state of Maranhão were a unique experience of participatory teaching methodology (Santos et al. 2013).

Professionals who work in SUS comprised the majority of the participants in these initiatives. These participants who come from a variety of professional backgrounds actively integrated the Brazilian public healthcare system in various political and administrative positions and exercised their professional abilities in the multiple care networks of the healthcare system. However, both for the master's degree and for the face-to-face and distance specializations, once the priority demands complied, the professionals were absorbed from nongovernmental institutions, some of them without an institutional link at the time of selection.

The development and implementation of training processes considered the following premises:

1. Translation operations as essential to creating connections within M&E technical and social networks as the basis for the institutionalization of M&E practices
2. The use of a virtual interaction platform for the exchange of health M&E knowledge and experiences by mediating between the professional evaluators and the researchers in M&E
3. Management and mobilization of knowledge for the promotion of M&E culture, its practices as a reflection for change, using participatory learning based on problematization and the principles of emancipatory education developed by Paulo Freire (1987) as the pedagogical support

14.4 Methods

This article involved a narrative review of the literature and the documentary analysis of all the material developed by Laser/Fiocruz for the creation of the initiatives in electronic media.

Literature was reviewed by searching the databases of two platforms, PubMed and SciELO, selecting only articles published since January 2012, that is, the period of the last 5 years so as to focus on the most literature on the subject. In SciELO, the search terms were *distance learning* and *health evaluation* in English, Spanish, and Portuguese. In PubMed, the terms used were *evaluation* or *health evaluation* or *evaluation capacity building* and *distance learning* or *distance education* or *E-learning*, in the title and abstract fields in English. We also searched for websites offering distance learning courses in M&E in the Google search tool. The work of some participants who are in professional master's course consisted some important initiatives, and these contributions were considered (Assis 2011; Paranaíba 2008).

There is a variety of online M&E courses offered around the world. Some examples include the courses offered by institutions such as *Canadian Evaluation Society*, *American Evaluation Association*, *Global Fund*, *Ontario Council for International Cooperation (Canada)*, and *Public Health Foundation of India*, universities such as *University of North Carolina (USA)*, and some South African universities such as *University of Pretoria*, *University of Estellenbosh*, *University of Cape Town*, and *University of the Witwatersrand.*

Despite these various offerings, we found few publications analyzing these experiences of distance learning in M&E in our bibliographic review. Most of the articles found were about the evaluation of distance learning courses in general, or about the development of methods, including tools for student's assessment.

The documentary analysis included the examination of the documents available in the LASER and EAD/ENSP archives and presentations at various national and international congresses. The material available comprised (a) course program, didactic material, participant manual, and final reports of academic course management; (b) reports of three evaluation workshops, one for each course carried out, with representatives of students, tutors, coordinators, ODL team, and financier; (c) several statements and comments made by students during the course; (d) reports of systematic meetings between coaches, tutors, and pedagogical and evaluation support services; and (e) memories of meetings between the course coordination, ODL team, and IT support.

14.5 Teaching-Learning in Health Evaluation: A Political Pedagogical Process

The pedagogical framework employed in the specialization course is based on a critical perspective of knowledge construction aimed at transformative action. Its assumptions include participants' autonomy to manage their learning processes, as well as mobilizing and articulating various forms of knowledge and tools for the development of flexible and innovative professional practices.

Since its conception, the initiative involves reflexive sharing across a network of work processes. This action is critically linked to the transformative processes of health realities aligned with the principles of SUS, thus, developing the logical links of the pedagogical activities related to the practical and reflexive experiences and everyday and formal knowledge that goes beyond the understanding of technical-scientific fundamentals. This includes the sociohistorical and cultural context that leads to unequal productive processes and appreciation of rights and of life. The pedagogical organization of the course clearly expresses the pragmatic view that knowledge is a function of question-positing reality and of processes that explain or resolve issues in a public, legitimate, and shareable language.

To invest in the proper training of a professional evaluator, we chose to adopt a proposal that dynamically combines work and teaching, practice and theory, and teaching and community. The relationships between employment and education and problems and alternatives to solve them must always have the sociocultural characteristics of the environment in which this process develops and the commitment to social improvement as the background (Mark et al. 2000).

The organizing axes of the course involve approaching the context as well as the health and technology policies in Brazil, the contents in monitoring and in monitoring systems, the evaluation with emphasis on evaluation processes and evaluation synthesis, and the ethical practices carried out in networks applied to the M&E activities of healthcare practices.

The proposal articulating teaching, practice, and theory is based on two pillars: critical problematization and the operations of translating knowledge. Critical pedagogy based on problematization considers that in a world of rapid changes what is important is not knowledge, nor the incorporation of skills, but rather increasing subjects' ability to detect real problems and flexibly mobilizing knowledge and technologies in search of original and creative solutions. The main issue of problematization is to propose important dimensions of individuals' reality for discussion, systematization, and transformation, that is, teaching to build the "viable novelty," working the limits between "being and being more" (Freire 1987). Problematization involves a constant dialogue in which experts and participants examine their experiences to produce a new understanding of a problem and consider possible solutions that may be implemented (praxis). The four operations of translation explored in this dialogue articulating the inherent unity between teaching and learning include problematization, sensitization, mobilization, and entanglement (Hartz et al. 2008).

Pedagogy using problematization reverses the cognitive cycle of traditional teaching from theory to practice. It starts with the problematized practice, and then we systematize the divergences related to it through sensitization processes and mobilization of the actors involved in the transformative action. Their insertion in a knowledge-for-action approach, in theory, enables the confrontation of systematized controversies (i.e., practice) with those approaches that make their solution possible through different translation operations that are potentially productive for their materialization in context. Thus, a new practice for the various human and non human actors occurs in situ (action). The assumptions are based on the idea that people experience spatial-time conditions marking them (TO BE), and they also mark these situations (TO DO) and their possibilities to critically reflect on their historical situation. That is, the "to do" in a situation announces the dimension of KNOWLEDGE and valuing the TO BE dimension of the evaluator's role and ethical profile (Santos and Natal 2005). Thus, one learns to learn how to learn.

Learning and teaching are overlapping processes in which "human and non human actors" hybridize in the operations of problematization, motivation, and mobilization, the latter understood as a precondition for the construction of connections and alliances in work networks. The training of professional evaluators was understood as a process of training actors in knowledge management for modulating action in a knowledge society, aimed at participatory organizational development and social change. Clavier et al. (2011) have explored the role of intermediary mechanisms in participatory processes of knowledge production, suggesting that they occur through translation operations (problematization, motivation, mobilization, and alliance construction) in three domains of mediation: cognitive, strategic, and logistical. For the authors, the cognitive area involves the multidirectional circulation of knowledge; the strategic one implies the mobilization of procedures aimed at developing new meaning aligned to the different interests of various actors (human) and players (nonhumans), and the logistic one is linked to the implementation of actions and processes to guarantee connections between partners, such as channel communications, meetings, memories, and minutes of meetings (Abreu et al. 2017). Considering the evaluator as a modulator of policies, programs, and processes, we used the proposed referential for training, understood as a process to improve translation operations in the aforementioned domains.

It is important to emphasize the radical difference between this conception of translation and those approaching the transfer of knowledge as a unidirectional flow between those who know and those who do not. In other words, they are based on conceptions that consider teaching and learning as processes of mere transfer of knowledge.

The understanding of the evaluator as an actor in a socio-technical network necessarily coexists with the construction of connections. In this sense, an integrated curriculum underlines and facilitates in its pedagogical units the operations of translation. In other words, problematization, motivation for change, enrollment, and the construction of alliances are expected to occur as shown in Fig. 14.1.

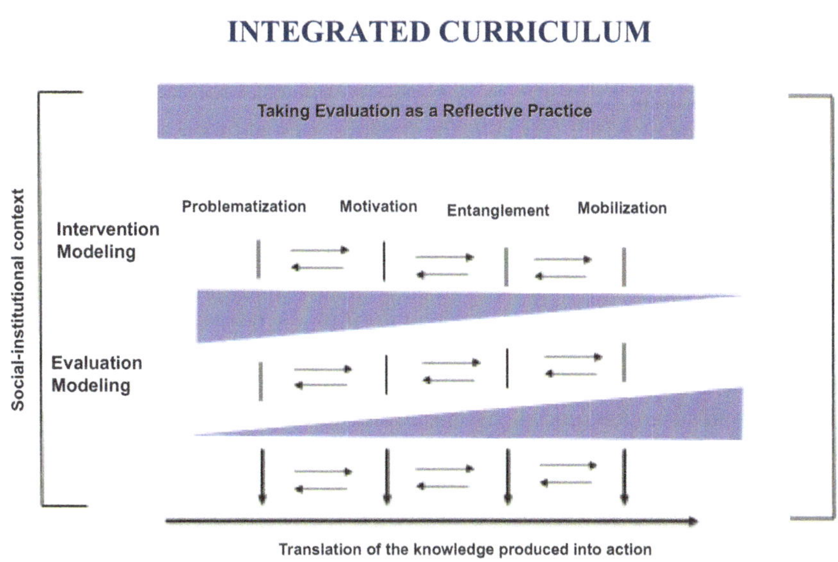

Fig. 14.1 Integrated curriculum of the health evaluation course, ODL

Table 14.3 Instructional arrangement: specialization course in evaluation and health

Instructional arrangement: specialization course in evaluation and health			
Modules: cognitive dimensions	Pedagogical units	Sequence of activities	Transversal subjects

The contents of the health evaluation course, ODL, are organized into an integrated curriculum, with a total workload of 420 h and a duration of 14 months divided into modules with broad subjects (cognitive dimensions) in order to allow the problematization of specific competencies (pedagogical units and sequence of activities) including the development and critical reflection on the evaluation proposal under construction (transversal content).

Each pedagogical unit and its sequence of activities detailed by tutor and participant are organized following the modeling of Maguerez (apud Bordenave and Pereira 1989) according to the phases of (1) observing reality, (2) identifying key thematic points, (3) theorizing the problem, (4) building hypotheses and choosing solutions, and (5) implementation to reality. Table 14.3 presents the instructional arrangement of the specialization course.

The curriculum is organized in seven modules structured in pedagogical units through which the problematization of participants' practice is made feasible. That is, the thematic contents in the field of M&E point toward ways of systematizing as well as solving controversies and problematized points, in the context of their work relations. Each module includes a different number of sequences of activities corresponding to the contents addressed by the pedagogical units. All modules include at least one educational unit and detail the sequences of activities related to the preparation of the final project of the course based on at least one of the participants' practical experience. The final coursework can be either the design of a monitoring system; an M&E plan; an evaluative research project related to their practices, such as a strategic assessment; or an efficiency appraisal of a given intervention.

Module I, "Taking Evaluation as a Reflective Practice," considers three pedagogical units to learn M&E concepts, the possible uses and focuses of evaluation, stakeholder's analysis, and their possible conflicts of interest. Module II, "Modeling the Intervention," comprises the following units: interventions and contexts; a description of the intervention, that is, its theory of change and its theory of functioning; and the practical steps of evaluation. Module II expects the participant to be able to describe and develop the steps of an evaluation study. Module, "Evaluation Models and Methods," includes the study of the different approaches in monitoring and evaluation and their possible application to the student's proposal. Modules IV and V, "Understanding the Theory of Change" examine, respectively, strategic analysis and implementation, encompassing evaluation questions, evaluation design, and the appreciation process. Module VI, "Managing and Implementing Evaluation," discusses the main communication channels and the dissemination of results. Finally, Module VII, "Evaluating Evaluation: The Meta-evaluation," analyzes the quality of an evaluation, the concepts and principles of meta-evaluation, and the ethical principles of the evaluation practices. Before launching, the course content was approved by specialists in evaluation and education and developed entirely online, in the virtual learning environment (VLE) using VIASK (*Virtual Institute of Advanced Studies Knowledge*) software. VIASK is an E-learning environment allowing interactive models of content from different actors and collaborative tools (Pedroso 2002). It allows students to navigate course content, access activities, participate in discussion forums and chats, as well as evaluate individual student performance, consult, and archive of documents in the virtual library. The platform also gives tutors, course administrators, and the ODL support team to send information (Santos et al. 2015).

Participants' discussions occur mainly through the aid of the tutor, who acts as mediator in the pedagogical relationship and facilitator of the teaching-learning process, stimulating participants to think critically and to carry out assigned activities. Although the primary interaction tool is the VIASK platform, communication between the tutor and participant takes place by other means, as needed, such as telephone, email, Skype, and WhatsApp. The tutor is responsible for evaluating the participants, suggesting readings, and proposing adjustments in the execution of the activities. Each tutor is responsible for 15 participants, with small variations in the three classes. For each group of three tutors, there is a support learning coach. The learning coach is a professional with previous experience in ODL tutoring and expertise in the subject. The course coordination team has regular meetings with the tutors and learning coaches, usually at each change of module, to support the group solving possible difficulties in the teaching-learning process and to clarify doubts at new subject's introduction. There are also meetings with the ODL/ENSP academic-pedagogical team for follow-up.

According to Brazilian legal requirements, the course has three presential moments: at the beginning, for tutor-student introductions, course proposal, didactic material, and the virtual learning environment (VLE); in the middle, for the first presential test and presentation of the draft monitoring or evaluation plan; and at the end, for the second test and presentation of the final course work. The course's main objective is to obtain diploma as a specialist in health evaluation by Brazil's Ministry of Education.

14.6 The M&E/ODL Training Processes: Inducing the Socio-technical Network

So far, three versions of the course were appropriately carried out for the target audience and requesting Ministry of Health units, the National STD/AIDS Program, and the Department of Monitoring and Evaluation of SUS. The first version for the National STD/AIDS Program began in August 2011 with 75 students enrolled. The students' profile consisted of health professionals and related areas with interest in monitoring and evaluation, from governmental or nongovernmental organizations and practicing in the health system and services. An undergraduate university degree recognized by the Ministry of Education was required. The course started

Table 14.4 Description of the ODL courses: course version, year, initial enrollment, number of students who started and finished the course, and percentage of attrition

Course	Year	Requesting	Initial enrollments	Started the course	Graduated[a]	Attrition (%)[b]
1st version	2011	PNDST-Aids/MS	75	69	50	27.5
2nd version	2013	DEMAS/MS	300	253	153	37.9
3rd version	2015	DEMAS/MS	100	88	58	30.7
Total	NSA	NSA	475	410	261	34.6

[a]Graduates: number of students who actually enrolled who completed all modules successfully and completed the final course work
[b]Attrition: consisting of students who dropped out of the course

with 69 students divided into the five tutors-teachers and ended with 50 specialists trained by the completion of the course in October 2012, as shown in Table 14.4.

The second version of the course began in November 2013, with an initial enrollment of 300 students from the Department of Monitoring and Evaluation of SUS (DEMAS) divided between 20 tutors. Students consisted of professionals with university degrees, who work at the Ministry of Health active or not in the area of M&E. In this class, 253 students started the course, and by January 2015, 153 specialists finished their training in evaluation. Due to the continued partnership with DEMAS, a third course was carried out. This last version selected higher-level professionals working in M&E at the Ministry of Health, however included professionals working in the same area in any of the three levels (i.e., federal, state, or municipal) involved in SUS's administration. There were 100 enrollment vacancies, and the course started in September 2015 with 88 students divided among six tutors. By November 2016, 58 health experts completed the training.

There were interesting differences in the professional profile of those completing the course based on which course offered. Whereas the first and second versions of the course had a considerable number of trained nurses, the last version had an important number of professionals from business administration. In the first version, a majority of graduates, or 54% of the total, were nurses. The other 23 graduates (46%) were professionals from 13 different areas. In the second version, 72 graduates (47%) consisted of 52 nurses (34%) and 20 pharmacists (13%). The other 81 graduates (53%) had 22 distinct professional backgrounds. In the third version of the course, 25 (43.1%) are concentrated in two professions: nursing 13 (22.4%) and business administration 12 (20.7%). The other 33 graduates (56.9%) were from 24 different professional categories.

There are two important facts in Table 14.4. The first one is the difference between the number of participants who registered for the course and those who are enrolled. In this group, the losses are due to two identifiable problems. First, a significant part of the students did not complete their enrollment because they do not fulfill the necessary conditions, either they could not prove their graduate status or they could not get financial support for participating in the initial presential meeting, a necessary condition of enrollment. The second problem emphasized in the table is the degree of attrition observed. Considering that the estimated rate of distance learning incompletion varies between 10% and 30% (Almeida 2008; Comarella 2009; Pacheco 2007), the second and third versions of the course had higher values than expected. These values are also higher than the attrition rate of the ODL courses offered by Brazil's Sergio Arouca National School of Public Health between 1998 and 2014, which is around 25.9% (Ribeiro 2015).

Distance learning is, above all, an education organized model in which the student plays the role of subject, (re)building knowledge through their own experience. At ODL/ENSP, this model is put into practice using innovative principles and methodologies. These include the virtual learning environment, tutoring system, didactic material, and educational pedagogical follow-up, all guided by the implementation of a dialogical educational process. With the three presential moments and the course evaluation workshops, it was possible to identify the facilitating aspects and challenges that we will describe below.

The political and pedagogical proposal adopted that departed from the presentation and completion of activities emerging from everyone's experience prior to the discussion of the conceptual content confused a significant part of the participants, generating discomfort mainly in the initial phase of the course ("I think the practice of first implementing the activity and then explaining the content should be reviewed. They should at least explain what it is about") (Participant, version 3). Some participants reported realizing little by little that after each unit's activity, the "solution of the problem" was presented, making them often to move forward in reading the material to access the responses before the performance of the task. Some even questioned whether there was any "mistake" in the development of the course. The role of the tutors was essential, but both tutors and participants suggested "clarifying and strengthening with examples at the very beginning of the course explanations of the problem-solving methodology"(tutor who participated in the three versions remark). In the presential courses, the pedagogical processes experienced by the participants in critical active methodologies are continuous objects of elaboration by the facilitator. In ODL, the challenge still involves developing solutions that need analysis and practical solutions.

From the point of view of curricular organization, according to participants, tutors, and learning supervisors, the organization in modules/pedagogical units/sequence of activities contributed to the completion of the course objectives and to the development of the student's expected skills ("the material used allowed for in-depth knowledge of the field of evaluation, and made possible a strong understanding of the subject") (Participant, version 1).

Some cognitive contents were identified as more complex than others. For example, several students pointed out that it was difficult to differentiate between modeling of intervention from modeling of evaluation. Some emphasized difficulties with the description of the object undergoing evaluation and the evaluation assessment itself.

A recurrent reported difficulty was the apprehension of valuation (judgment) processes and the related functions of the evaluator. It should be emphasized that this point is complex even in presential evaluation teaching experiences and usually is relegated to a balance between teacher's previous experience and scientifical criteria In *E-learning*, this balance requires alignment with the political and philosophical choices made by course developers. For the teaching and learning process in M&E on health policies and programs, this is a critical point. It has implicit and explicit repercussions on the evaluation conceptions being used, the possible functions of the evaluator, and indeed the sustainability of the initiative itself. This content needs additional maturation from the point of view of the course's pedagogical and political affiliation, and creative virtual solutions should be considered.

A second cognitive content that students reported as "difficult" concerns the definition of public health problems based on context analysis. This point is expressive of two components, that is, the mixed composition of the demand for course content and the contradictions inherent in the organization of Brazil's health system (*Sistema Unico de Saude*). In Brazil, training in public health is predominantly epidemiologic. In evaluation and health, there is a greater emphasis on evaluation research as compared to studies focusing on management, administration, and public governance, all mandatory requirements for the jobs occupied by the participants. Job profile, regardless of the participant's professional profile, was an essential factor to determine changes in the courses' practical exercises and content. The course's second and third cohorts required the incorporation of topics on regulation, routine administration processes, and principles of accountability of the Brazilian state. In the third version of the course, content on strategic planning and health planning tools from the three management instances of SUS were included. Despite the participants' suggestions, the expansion of this subject was made gradually and in a way to differentiate legal auditing processes from those of M&E. Balancing these approaches was particularly necessary to respond to the different functions expected for social regulation, legal compliance, and organizational learning related to the transparency of management, implementation, and public policy principles in Brazil (Januzzi 2016).

Despite participants' insistence to broaden the content of research methodologies, the course coordinators chose to emphasize only case study design and mixed methods. Both are the basic approaches related to M&E applied to management and organizational development. The quoted student request is associated with the view that evaluation is academic research, a Brazilian institutional culture.

Even though there is a step-by-step guide in the student's handbook, participants also requested to have a more structured outline for final course work (TCC). One suggestion was to have one more presential meeting during the course to address the preparation of the TCC before its presentation. Students' expectation that an evaluation plan is a research plan lies in their difficulty of aligning it with the guidelines of the evaluation plan proposed in the student's handbook (page 78). These issues point to the tension between becoming a professional evaluator and becoming a researcher. This demonstrates the need for the course to enable ways for supporting an organic professional identity with greater engagement. This may result in less attrition and may strength self-identification and professional networked practices.

In spite of these comments, most of the participants, in the three course versions, considered that the topics and course contents instigate interest and motivation in the field of evaluation ("I think I am ready to evaluate") (Participant, Course 3rd version).

In the evaluation carried out, tutors and learning supervisors requested the inclusion of texts to guide participants on how to do a literature review and bibliographical research. They also included didactic material and a document on personal accountability in the case of academic plagiarism, a problem frequently detected in the products presented. One of the assumptions defended by Paulo Freire is that the learning process is not divisible into teaching and learning, that is, one learns while teaching, and one teaches while learning. Knowledge emerges from the dialogue between learning subjects immersed in situations significant for the transformative professional ethical experience. In this sense, the active participation of tutors was significant, "The tutor was always available and helped a lot in the process" (Participant, Course 2nd version), besides the exchange with the colleagues through forums, WhatsApp groups, and presential moments.

Regarding the logistics of the course, participants complained about the large number of activities, as well as the short time for completing the most complex assignments. Some pointed out that the statements about some activities were not very clear ("I had a hard time understanding what the activity called for. The propositions seemed somewhat vague and not very explanatory...") (Participant, Course 3rd version).

Throughout various versions of the course, some tutors and supervisors highlighted the importance of defining more precise criteria for monitoring participants' development and their retention in the course. The problem of deadlines and limits in handling activities, as well as the time for their correction, appears as a very important topic that concerns tutors. They all stressed the importance of keeping regular meetings between the tutor, learning supervisor, and coordination for the possibility of exchange and methodological alignment. Tutors and supervisor discussed with the course coordinators the possibility of holding a "short workshop" with M&E content during the first presential meeting to problematize the course approach. In the third version of the course, there were connectivity problems that made it difficult to access the VIASK platform and, in many cases, navigate it. The use of the communication tools WhatsApp and e-mail was mandatory for pedagogical mediation, not only to keep the students' encouragement but also to enable prompt and timely communication, especially for submitting assignments. Using WhatsApp audio made it easier to explain complex concepts and clear doubts and worked as a good substitute for the digital platform on numerous occasions.

Due to the impossibility of copying text contents using *flash* software, participants suggested leaving some video lessons available for key content such as logic models' judgment matrices and evaluation synthesis. Several participants in the third version of the course were MoH workers in distant regions of the country, without or with limited access to the Internet. In these cases, a printed version of the course content would make it easier for them to complete assignments by due dates, as well as to send them via a digital platform. Another suggestion was to have a link in the course library organized by module with the used references.

14.7 Final Considerations

Critical pedagogical practice in health is not exempt from addressing the social dimensions that can influence health understood as the full existence of life with quality. Thus, it should provide learners not only with the conditions to know the scientific and the technical bases of their practice but also the social and historical ones. In the Brazilian case that encompasses inequalities in living conditions and the constitutional right to health, the link between the training of evaluators for SUS, especially its principle of universal health, is the axis that enhances M&E processes beyond mere cognitive, strategic, and logistic contents in technology and method. The challenges faced by this pedagogical practice in monitoring and evaluation are even greater, since these practices often include face-to-face criticism and sometimes antagonistic policy formulation, implementation, and regulation recommendations.

The implementation of a specialization course in health evaluation in its three versions in a quickly changing Brazilian conjuncture that directly influences public policies implied a challenging experience. It included an almost on time systematization of methodology and materialization of content adaptation for practically each one of the three versions, although the structural elements of the pedagogical proposal, the integrated curriculum, and the virtual platform remained the same.

An important aspect of the teaching-learning process which was appreciated by those involved was the centrality of problematization. Despite the polarization between "learning by problematizing everyday work," that is, in situation, and "learning to solve work problems," or in other words, learn before and apply afterward, there was an agreement concerning the positive force of work as a productive educational principle. Since problematization does not offer the certainty of "right and wrong," but the complexity of the provisional, the tutor and the sharing forums play a prominent role in mediating the dialogue between everyday knowledge, technique, and science. The problems of the real world of health work are complex. They usually happen in an environment of continuous technical and political tension marked by the centrality of reflection and learning. The teaching-learning process focuses on the problematization of the daily work, establishing its relations with the scientific, technical knowledge mobilized for its transformation.

Students frequently emphasized that the instructional material and notably the platform played the leading role as influencing factors in the implementation of the course. The tutors and the means of interaction and communication configure motivation and mobilization mechanisms, as they include actions and practices contributing to motivate and define the function-identity of each "actor" of the network (Oliveira et al. 2017), enabling possible alliances. The challenge is to shift these practices from cognitive components of the course to professional evaluative practices. The institutionalization of evaluation as a profession is still incipient in Brazil, and the activities required for a professional are much closer to a "compliance verifier" than to a modulator of "values" or to a skilled manager and translator of knowledge.

Regarding tutors and coaches, the learning strategies of supervision, continuous training, and coordination in response to the needs of the students have worked satisfactorily. Participants evaluated positively the coordinated action of tutors. However, attrition has pointed out the need to improve articulations with the world of work, especially the MoH. It seems necessary not only to define the adequacy of learning activities but also the career profiles and the insertion of qualified professionals.

The initiative aiming to create the network of health evaluators consists of three main axes: training through an integrated program, professionalization, and institutionalization. The health evaluation course is only one piece of the initiative by the Ministry of Health and ENSP to train evaluators. Planning of a variety of training activities continues to be carried out by ENSP and other respected teaching and research institutions in Brazil. They seem to have affected professional capacity-building and diffusion of M&E in the health area, promoting the expansion of a socio-technical network of evaluators. There is some evidence of an increased professionalization and institutionalization of evaluation, such as the first M&E professional hiring by the Ministry of Health (2014), the recent creation of the Work Group to elaborate the National M&E Policy (Ministry of Health 2017), and the creation of the Brazilian Monitoring and Evaluation Network.[6]

References

ABED – Associação Brasileira de Educação a Distância. 2017. *Censo EAD.BR: relatório analítico da aprendizagem a distância no Brasil 2016*. Curitiba: InterSAberes.

Abreu, Dolores, Elizabeth Santos, Gisela Cardoso, and Elizabeth Artmann. 2017. Usos e influências de uma avaliação: translação de conhecimento? *Saúde em Debate* 41: 302–316.

Almeida, Onília Cristina de Souza. 2008. Evasão em cursos a distância: análise dos motivos de desistência. *14° Congresso Internacional ABED de Educação a Distância*, Santos.

Alonso, Katia Morosov. 2014. A EAD no Brasil: sobre (des)caminhos em sua instauração. *Education Review* 4: 37–52.

Assis, Ana Maria. 2011. *Avaliar a institucionalização: o estudo de caso da formação em monitoramento e avaliação da Secretaria de Vigilância em Saúde*. Master's thesis, Oswaldo Cruz Foundation, Rio de Janeiro.

Bordenave, Juan, and Adair Pereira. 1989. *Estratégias de ensino aprendizagem*. Petrópolis: Vozes.

Clavier, Carole, Yan Sénéchal, Stéphane Vibert, and Louise Potvin. 2011. A theory-based model of translation practices in public health participatory research. *Sociology of Health & Illness* 34: 791–805.

Comarella, Rafaela Lunardi. 2009. *Educação superior à distância: evasão discente*. Master's thesis, Universidade Federal de Santa Catarina, Florianópolis.

Cruz, Marly, Maria Aparecida Patroclo, Elizabeth Moreira dos Santos, Thaís Coutinho de Oliveira, and Olga Maria de Alencar. 2009. A experiência brasileira de formação profissional em monitoramento e avaliação do programa de controle de hanseníase. *Cadernos Saúde Coletiva (UFRJ)* 17: 115–129.

Freire, Paulo. 1987. *Pedagogy of the oppressed*. New York: Continuum Publishing.

Hartz, Zulmira, Jean Louis Denis, Elizabeth Moreira, and Alvaro Matida. 2008. From knowledge to action: Challenges and opportunities for increasing the use of evaluation in health promotion policies and practices. In *Health promotion evaluation practices in the Americas: Values and research*, ed. V. Mcqueen David and Louise Potvin, 101–120. New York: Springer.

[6] Brazilian Monitoring and Evaluation Network: http://redebrasileirademea.ning.com/site

INEP – Instituto Nacional de Estudos e Pesquisas Educacionais Anísio Teixeira. 2017. *Censo de Educação Superior 2016: notas estatísticas*. Brasília: MEC.

Januzzi, Paulo de Martino. 2016. Eficiência econômica, eficácia procedural ou efetividade social: três valores em disputa na Avaliação de Políticas e Programas Sociais. *Desenvolvimento em Debate* 4: 117–142.

Latour, Bruno. 1996. On actor-network theory: A few clarifications. *Soziale Welt* 47: 369–381.

Laval, Christian, and Pierre Dardot. 2016. *A nova razão do mundo: ensaio sobre a sociedade neoliberal*. São Paulo: Boitempo.

Mark, Melvin, Gary Henry, and George Julnes. 2000. Social betterment through evaluation. In *Evaluation: An integrated framework for understanding, guiding, and improving policies and programs*, 3–104. San Francisco: Josey-Bass.

Menelau, Sueli. 2010. Fundamentos do ensino a distância no Brasil. *Revista Cocar* 4: 62–74.

Ministry of Education. 2007. Resolução CNE/CES n°1 de 8/6/2007. http://portal.mec.gov.br/cne/arquivos/pdf/rces001_07.pdf. Accessed 17 Jan 2018.

Ministry of Health. 2004. *Programa Nacional de DST e Aids: Monitor Aids*. Brasília: Ministério da Saúde.

———. 2014. Concurso público para provimento de vagas em cargos do plano de carreiras de ciência e tecnologia nas carreiras de planejamento, gestão e infraestrutura e desenvolvimento tecnológico. Edital n° 4, Funcab.

———. 2017. Portaria n° 1.535, de 16 de junho de 2017. http://bvsms.saude.gov.br/bvs/saudelegis/gm/2017/prt1535_20_06_2017.html. Accessed 12 Mar 2018.

Miranda, Alcides S. 2014. Discursos práticos sobre valores sociais, bens e serviços públicos de saúde, em viés ideológico de pragmatismo utilitário. In *25 anos do direito universal à saúde*, ed. Maria Lucia Rizzoto and Ana Maria Costa, 103–131. Rio de Janeiro: Cebes.

Mugnol, Marcio. 2009. A educação à distância no Brasil: conceitos e fundamentos. *Revista Diálogo Educacional* 9: 335–349.

Oliveira, Egléubia A., Gisela Cordeiro Pereira Cardoso, Elizabeth Moreira dos Santos, Margareth Martins Oliveira, and Marly Marques Cruz. 2017. O apoiador local como ator estratégico na implementação do QualiSUS-Rede: engenheiros de conexão? *Saúde em Debate* 41: 275–289-289.

OECD – Organization for Economic Cooperation and Development. 2016. *Supreme audit institutions and good governance: Oversight, insight and foresight*. Paris: OECD.

Pacheco, Andressa Sasaki Vasques. 2007. *Evasão: análise da realidade do curso de graduação a distância da Universidade Federal de Santa Catarina*. Master's thesis, Universidade Federal de Santa Catarina, Florianópolis.

Paolucci, Rodolfo, André Pereira Neto, and Rafaela Luzia. 2017. Avaliação da qualidade da informação em sites de tuberculose: análise de uma experiência participativa. *Saúde em Debate* 41: 84–100.

Paranaíba, Nádia. 2008. *Análise de implementação das oficinas de avaliação com foco na melhoria dos programas municipais de DST/AIDS*. Master's thesis, Oswaldo Cruz Foundation, Rio de Janeiro.

Pedroso, Eva. 2002. *Interfaces gráficas em ambiente de e-learning: caso VIASK*. Master's thesis, Universidade Federal de Santa Catarina, Florianópolis.

Petry, Jonas, Gustavo da Rosa Borges, and Maria José Carvalho de Souza Domingues. 2014. Ensino a distância: um panorama da expansão na região norte do Brasil. *Revista Eletrônica de Estratégia & Negócios* 7: 114–138.

Ramos, Marise. 2001. *Pedagogia das competências: autonomia ou adaptação*. São Paulo: Cortez.

Ribeiro, Antônia. 2015. *EAD/Ensp em números: uma expressão dos desafios em 16 anos*. Rio de Janeiro: CDEAD/ENSP/Fiocruz.

Ruhe, Valerie, and Bruno Zumbo. 2009. *Evaluation in distance learning and e-learning*. New York/London: The Guilford Press.

Santos, Boaventura V. 2011. *A crítica da razão indolente: contra o desperdício da experiência*. São Paulo: Editora Cortez.

Santos, Elizabeth M. 2005. *Plano Nacional de Monitoramento e Avaliação - Programa nacional de DST e AIDS: Assessoria de Monitoramento e Avaliação*. Brasília: Ministério da Saúde.

Santos, Elizabeth M., and Sônia Natal. 2005. *Dimensão sócio-histórica: unidade didático pedagógica - educação permanente comunicação*. Rio de Janeiro: Abrasco.

———. 2007. *Dimensão técnico-operacional.: unidade didático pedagógica - educação permanente comunicação*. Rio de Janeiro: Abrasco.

Santos, Elizabeth, Egléubia Oliveira, Marly Cruz, Aline Gonçalves, Aline Macedo, and Carlos Cunha. 2013. Institutionalization of monitoring as a reflexive managerial practice. *The EES Newsletter Evaluation Connections* 1: 20–24.

Santos, Henriette, Gisela Cardoso, Dolores Abreu, and Elizabeth Santos, eds. 2015. *Caderno do aluno: curso de avaliação em saúde*. Rio de Janeiro: EAD/ENSP.

Saviani, Dermeval. 2007. Pedagogia: o espaço da educação na universidade. *Cadernos de Pesquisa* 37: 99–134.

Sguissardi, Valdemar. 2008. Modelo de expansão da educação superior no Brasil: predomínio privado/mercantil e desafios para a regulação e a formação universitária. *Education and Society* 29: 991–1022.

Struchiner, Miriam, and Rodrigo Carvalho. 2014. Reflexões sobre os conceitos e fundamentos de pesquisa em educação a distância. In Educação a Distância e Tecnologias Digitais: reflexões, saberes, contextos e processos, eds. Aline Reali e Daniel Mill, 127–148. São Carlos: EdUFSCar.

Vargas, Francisca Maria de Almeida, Mônica Cristina Nunes da Trindade, Gisele Damian Antonio Gouveia, and Mareni Rocha Farias. 2016. A educação a distância na qualificação de profissionais para o Sistema Único de Saúde: meta-estudo. *Trab. educ. saúde* 14: 849–870.

Chapter 15
Massive Open Online Health Courses (MOOCs): Brazilian Initiatives

Liara Saldanha Brites and Cristianne Maria Famer Rocha

Abstract *Massive open online courses* (MOOCs) are open and massive courses provided in virtual learning environments that allow participants to share experiences, knowledge, and information. This chapter aims to map out Brazil's academic literature on MOOCs in health using dissertations and theses on MOOCs and from governmental initiatives in health that are similar to MOOCs. This is a qualitative study based on the documental analysis of the websites of the Brazilian Ministries of Health and Education, the MOOC-List.com, and the "Brazilian Digital Library of Theses and Dissertations." While not adopting the MOOC nomenclature, Brazil invests in massive, online, and open-learning initiatives. The academic work on Brazil's MOOCs in health is incipient. There is potential to be explored, including permanent and continuing education of health professionals and exchange of information between researchers, professionals, and users of the Brazilian health system.

15.1 Massive Open Online Courses (MOOCs)

New information and communication technologies have changed in our living and work environments. All around us, we see that we are surrounded by computers, smartphones, tablets, notebooks, and other mobile devices that continue to evolve all due to rapid product development. These devices have become integral parts of our daily lives, both as individuals making use of health services and as health professionals. Users engage in brief research on a health issue on websites or applications, update their knowledge, or even clarify concerns when contacting professionals or other health services users. We considered this dynamic scenario when we decided to write this chapter about the most obvious and potent combination of themes "Internet" and "health": online education.

L. S. Brites (✉) · C. M. F. Rocha
School of Nursing, Federal University of Rio Grande do Sul, Porto Alegre, Brazil

A. Pereira Neto, M. B. Flynn (eds.), *The Internet and Health in Brazil*,
https://doi.org/10.1007/978-3-319-99289-1_15

Distance learning (DL – which is analyzed in another chapter of this book)[1] is known to Brazilians and has been keeping pace with information technology. There was a time when students received their materials by physical correspondence and attended classes through television. Today, they all have technological devices and the Internet.

In this context, we invite readers to consider analyzing the novel phenomena of massive open online courses (MOOCs) in Brazil, especially in the field of health.

MOOCs are a type of online course that fall under the category of distance learning (DL), but they also go beyond DL because, as their name implies, they involve open education, the free and open access to materials along with the flexibility that is unusual for DL's formal character (Marques, 2015). They can also approach other concepts, such as online education or education without distance (Tori, 2010), given the countless possibilities for immediate interactions. However, this definition is hampered by the short time of existence of MOOCs and, consequently, of studies on this questioning.

The open-access movement, which is closely related to MOOCs, is present in Brazil and in health. In the case of the promotion of free scientific literature and without access fees, there have been a growing number of digital repositories since 2009. Currently, Brazil has 48 institutional repositories, including the LUME (from the Federal University of Rio Grande do Sul – UFRGS) and ARCA (of the Oswaldo Cruz Foundation – Fiocruz), known for the publication of public health research in Brazil.

Open education appears mainly in open universities that admit, for example, students without proof of prior knowledge and that facilitate the establishment of study courses of their own, which can be attractive to adults who have well-defined learning objectives. Students receive course certificates either at the end of each module or after completing a minimum number of credits (Inamorato, 2009). In Brazil and in health, the Open University (UAB) and the Open University of the Unified Health System (UNA-SUS), by governmental initiatives, through the Ministry of Education and the Ministry of Health, respectively, in partnership with several higher education institutions, all offer open education programs. Because of their similarity to MOOCs, these government initiatives will be discussed in this study.

MOOCs originated in Canada. Dave Cormier first coined the acronym which was first used in 2008, when alluding to the open-access course Connectivism and Connective Knowledge by George Siemens and Stephen Downes who taught it online to the 2300 people who registered, although only 25 of them have paid a fee to receive a certificate at the end of the course (Yuan and Powell, 2013).

MOOCs are usually short (usually 3–12 weeks) and are provided free of charge to anyone with Internet access. Renowned educational institutions typically promote and coordinate them through virtual learning platforms that offer various options such as paid certificates in different areas of knowledge (Dal Forno et al., 2013) to anyone who so desires. However, due to diverse courses, platforms,

[1] Chapter 14 addresses the issue of health e-learning in Brazil.

pedagogical methods, institutions, and business models that already characterize the universe of MOOCs, some definitions of MOOC as always being an open, massive, online course are not extended to all existing experiences. In some cases, fees are charged for certificates, and there is a growing trend of payment to access MOOCs, such as in universities in the United States, where there is already a movement for MOOCs to be recognized and validated as part of undergraduate or graduate degree programs. Many courses advertised as MOOCs also require registration and the student participates in a closed platform. In addition, not all materials have open source or are open education resources, since many are protected by some kind of intellectual property (Mattar, 2013).

Despite these variations, it is interesting to explore how the implementation of MOOCs is taking place in Brazil and how they are being used in the public health system (known as SUS – Unified Health System), such as through professional training modules. SUS is a model for the rest of the world, mainly for constitutionally ensuring free and universal access to health for all citizens (regardless of belief, color, or social class) (Brazil 1988, 1990a, b). Brazil's Constitution also stipulates that SUS oversee the development of human resources in health, as well as increase health-related scientific and technological development (Brazil, 1988).

In a brief Internet search, one can access dozens of MOOC platforms and select only those categorized as health courses. In addition to these platform sites, information is available from thousands of MOOCs on the MOOC-List.com website (MOOC-List, 2017). It is an English-speaking directory of MOOCs that publishes open-access courses available to 90 providers, while also allowing for the option to pay for a certificate or examination. One can find MOOCs using various filters available in a search tool, such as areas of knowledge, new courses, courses starting soon, suppliers, universities, duration, categories, estimated weekly study time, language, country, and list of keywords.

MOOCs address content from different areas of knowledge, albeit equally. When searching on sites of large MOOC platforms/providers (such as Coursera, Udacity, Veduca, edX, and MiríadaX), it is possible to notice that Science, Technology, Engineering, and Mathematics stand out, which may be attributed to the fact that, historically, the first MOOCs are from these areas and also the large partner universities with these platforms began in these fields. Few MOOCs were seen in the area of health. Concurrently, there are few academic studies in Brazilian Theses and Dissertations on the subjects "MOOC" and "health."

It is difficult to collect data on similar MOOCs' experiences (with regard to the main characteristics of MOOCs: online, open, and large-scale courses) developed in Brazil, since there is no directory that centralizes this information. This becomes more problematic when narrowing the search to the area of health.

MOOCs have a huge potential in the field of health education, adherence to medications, the influence of genetics on cancer development, and the availability of beginners' guides about cardiovascular health (Spring, 2016); for example, they could be offered in this modality to allow access to hundreds or thousands of participants, at no cost to them. In addition, MOOCs are important in educating health professionals and health service users, who could benefit from supportive communities and access to up-to-date knowledge (Hoy, 2014).

In this context, based on the MOOCs and questions about their use in Brazilian health education, this chapter aims to map out what dissertations and Masters theses have studied about MOOCs and MOOC-like initiatives by governmentin the area of health.

15.2 Methodology

This exploratory, mixed-approach study included a number of steps. In order to get to know the international reality of MOOCs in health and how Brazil appears in this setting, a database (in the form of a table) was created to analyze the courses by searching on the *MOOC-List.com* website. First, among the 32 categories (available search options on the site by specified theme), only the so-called health and society was selected on the site. Thus, 376 courses were located and are shown briefly on the website. In the *MOOC-List.com*, each course name contains a hyperlink to a new virtual page with the course details (i.e., name, provider, educational institution, instructors, category, course start date, duration, prerequisites, final assignment type, language, country, and educational resources used). These elements were collected individually and aggregated in a table/database. All courses available in the directory (regardless of their end or start date) as of May 22, 2016 (date of the last collection) were included, and none of the 376 selected courses were excluded from the analysis. Once the summary table of MOOCs was drawn up, we surveyed the number of times courses were offered for further analysis and categorization.

Based on this research, the MOOC platforms/providers with the most health-related course offerings were *Canvas Network*, *Coursera*, *edX*, *France Université Numérique* (*FUN*), *FutureLearn*, *MiríadaX*, and *TELELAB* and Brazil's *Veduca*. A content analysis stage up to June 12, 2017, was then carried out from the sites of these platforms to seek information on partnerships of said engines with Brazilian institutions and organizations. In this same period, a content analysis of Brazilian dissertations and theses on MOOCs was carried out through the *Brazilian Digital Library of Theses and Dissertations* (BDTD) – a search portal that gathers theses and dissertations defended throughout Brazil and by Brazilians abroad. The search was performed using the subject "MOOC" and included all dissertations and theses found until June 12, 2017.

Data collected in the above steps are discussed based on the content analysis of MS and MEC sites, with a search by subject "MOOC." In addition, an analysis of the UAB websites (a MEC initiative containing health courses) and UNA-SUS, the Virtual Learning Environment in the SUS (AVA-SUS), the Community of Practices (CdP), and Distance Learning (DL) of the Sérgio Arouca National School of Public Health ENSP/Fiocruz (MS initiatives that produce health courses) was performed. Searches on these institutional sites were conducted in October 2017.

15.3 Results and Discussion

15.3.1 Health MOOCs Worldwide

Before delving into data on Brazilian health-focused MOOCs, we first want to highlight that worldwide health-related courses have limted representation in the universe of MOOCs compared to other areas of knowledge.

From the *MOOC-List.com* search, we found that the 376 courses identified in the "health and society" category accounted for only 8.19% of the 4593 courses available in the MOOCs directory. One can observe the recent establishment and gradual growth of MOOCs in health over the years.

Interestingly, while MOOCs began in 2008, and 2012 is considered "the year of MOOCs" (Pappano, 2012) (due to the rapid growth and visibility of the courses that year, both by the number of students enrolled and renowned educational institutions that started supplying courses through provider platforms), no MOOC was found in the field of health those years. The first ones began in 2013, when eight courses were made available. The 376 health courses pertain to 25 of the 90 platforms listed on MOOC-List.com. US-based *Coursera* ranks first in the number of health courses offered (37.77%), followed by British *FutureLearn* (15.69%), United States' *edX* (14.36%) and *Canvas* (7.18%), Iberian American *MiríadaX* (5.32%), and the French *France Université Numérique* – FUN (4.79%).

Platforms provide MOOCs with content developed by partner educational institutions. Thus, the three platforms with the highest number of MOOCs have partnerships with institutions experienced in the area of health. In a study about the view of US and Brazilian specialists on MOOCs, Jacoski (2015) pointed out that *Coursera* has more institutions and more courses and has been growing significantly, which may also explain its leadership in health courses. According to *Coursera's* website, it currently has partnerships with 150 institutions from 29 countries (Coursera, 2017), among them, some with renowned technical and scientific productions in the field of health, such as the *Johns Hopkins Bloomberg School of Public Health*, *Stanford University*, *University of Copenhagen*, *Yale University*, *University of Michigan*, and *University of Manchester*. Among *FutureLearn's* partnerships are the *University of Birmingham*, *London School of Hygiene & Tropical Medicine*, *University of Leeds*, and *Taipei Medical University* (FutureLearn, 2017). Meanwhile, *edX* has the renowned *Harvard University*, *University of Toronto*, and *Boston University*, among others (edX, 2017).

Information related to the country and language of origin of each MOOC is also closely linked to partnerships between institutions and platforms. In general, a Brazilian university, for example, will produce MOOCs in at least the native language (Portuguese, with translation into other languages), and this will be made available on the partner platform of this institution.

The United States leads in the production of health-related MOOCs (43.62%), followed by the United Kingdom (18.35%), France (5.85%), Spain (5.59%), and Australia (5.05%). Brazil ranks sixth, with 3.19% of the courses. This data is compatible with languages through which MOOCs are taught. English is predominant and is present in 81.35% of the courses provided, followed by Spanish (6.99%), French (5.18%), and Portuguese (3.37%). These results concide with the study by Finardi and Tyler (2015), who found 2326 courses in English (83%) among the 2800 MOOCs analyzed.

The leadership of universities that provide MOOCs in English is also associated with the ranking of the best universities in the world and has been the subject of discussion about the role and relationship between globalization and foreign languages in the process of higher education's internationalization (Finardi et al., 2016). When analyzing the World Reputation Rankings (2016), one can observe in Table 15.1 that eight US institutions are among the ten best universities in the world (all English-speaking), have partnerships with Coursera and edX, provide health courses, and produce MOOCs predominantly in English.

These findings highlight that some knowledge of English and digital literacy is required to access information online and to actively participate in the globalized world and that English still predominates online content (Finardi and Tyler, 2015). Nonetheless, Altbach (2014) warns that these facts also imply the possible knowledge of control. He contends that the course content in MOOCs build off of US academic experiences and pedagogical ideas, and even when trying to diversify with translations into other languages, US or European contexts tend to prevail, since they dominate scientific literature and have renowned professors who lecture

Table 15.1 Ranking of the best universities in the world, country and partner platforms

Institution	Country	Main language	2016 ranking	MOOC platform
Harvard university	United States of America	English	1	edX
Massachusetts institute of technology	United States of America	English	2	edX
Stanford university	United States of America	English	3	Coursera
Cambridge university	United Kingdom	English	4	Provides online courses that are not considered MOOCs
Oxford university	United Kingdom	English	5	Provides online courses that are not considered MOOCs
University of California, Berkeley	United States of America	English	6	edX
Princeton university	United States of America	English	7	Coursera
Yale university	United States of America	English	8	Coursera
Columbia university	United States of America	English	9	edX and Coursera
California institute of technology	United States of America	English	10	Coursera

Source: Authors elaboration (2017)

and conduct research in prestigious universities. Thus, Boal and Stallivieri (2015) suggest that MOOCs should consider curricular internationalization and look at different viewpoints, including different worldviews.

15.3.2 Where Are Health MOOCs in the Brazilian Scenario?

The first evidence of MOOCs in Brazil date back to 2012 (Marques, 2015), but the availability of Brazilian universities' courses in US portals began only 2 years later, in September 2014, through an agreement between the State University of Campinas (UNICAMP) and the University of São Paulo (USP)[2] with *Coursera*. At the time, the institutions committed themselves to producing and making MOOCs available in several subject areas, in Portuguese, but with translation into other languages (Souza and Cypriano, 2016).

Since then, the production of MOOCs for health in Brazil has been growing. As of June 2017, some of the platforms that produce health MOOCs are reported the most. Table 15.2 lists current partnerships between 13 Brazilian institutions and organizations to produce MOOCs:

The *Canvas Network*, *edX*, *FUN*, and *FutureLearn* platforms do not yet have any records of partnerships with Brazilian institutions.

Although not listed in Table 15.2, because it does not yet produce health MOOCs, it is important to mention that Brazil already has a platform internationally known in the world of MOOCs, namely, *Veduca*.

This Brazilian engine started activities in 2012 with a collection of classes from the best universities in the world (such as the Massachusetts Institute of Technology

Table 15.2 Partnerships of MOOC platforms and Brazilian educational institutions

MOOC platform	Brazilian educational institution
Coursera	University of São Paulo (USP) State University of Campinas (UNICAMP) Lemann foundation Institute of Higher Education and Research (Insper) Technological Institute of Aeronautics (ITA) Institute of Administration Foundation
MiríadaX	Pontifical Catholic University of Rio Grande do Sul (PUCRS) Regional University of Blumenau Foundation (FURB) Anhembi Morumbi university Vale do Rio dos Sinos university (UNISINOS) Universidade de São Paulo (USP) Federal University of Rio Grande do Sul (UFRGS).
TELELAB	Federal University of Santa Catarina (UFSC)

Sources: Authors elaboration (2017)

[2] Chapter 16 analyses the experience of University of São Paulo in digital innovation for medical training.

(MIT), Harvard, Yale, Stanford, and USP), with video lessons in Portuguese. In 2013, it launched the first MOOC in Latin America and offered certificates for its completion. Currently, in addition to USP faculty members, it works with professionals from the University of Brasília (UnB), State University of São Paulo (UNESP), Lemann Foundation/Península Institute, UFSC, UNISINOS, and UNICAMP (Ding et al., 2014; Silva, 2014; Veduca, 2016).

When calculating the representativeness of Brazilian institutions in health-related MOOCs during our search through the *MOOC-List*, only 12 courses were found when using the filter "health and society" to the country "Brazil." Ten are offered through the *TELELAB* platform and are produced by UFSC; one at *Coursera*, produced by USP; and one in *MiríadaX*, produced by PUCRS. There are only a few institutions who participate: 3 higher education institutions out of the 2850 currently registered with Brazil's Ministry of Education.

With the exception of *Coursera* and *MiríadaX* MOOCs, those at *TELELAB* focus on pathologies (identification, monitoring, treatment, and care), have self-instructional learning characteristics, estimated 1-hour weekly dedication, have exams, and provide certificates of completion. These characteristics may be related to the profile of the institution that produces the MOOCs for this platform (UFSC) and to the demands of the Ministry of Health, which is the maintainer of TELELAB, "a continuing education program of the Ministry of Health that provides free courses targeting health professionals" (TELELAB, 2017).

MOOCs vary as to their format (i.e., methodology, technology, and pedagogy), since, in addition to the profile of the MOOC provider platform and of the institution that assists in the production of contents, the choice of a MOOC is imbricated with the type of construct desired for the course. For example, in the analysis of the four pioneering Brazilian experiences in MOOCs – such as "Classroom journal" (developed from *Veduca*), the "Law of Guidelines and Baselines of Brazilian Education" (developed from *Moodle*), "MOOC Tutoring" (developed from Moodle), and "MOOC EAD" (developed from a blog) – each had its own characteristics. The pedagogical assumptions used in the experiments were not uniform, and the formats of these MOOCs were not standardized with respect to methodology, technology, and pedagogical approach (Marques, 2015).

Considering the productions of dissertations and theses, the Brazilian academic work on MOOCs is poorly explored in Brazilian universities. While more frequent since 2015, considering the BDTD collection of 351,831 Masters theses and 130,660 doctoral dissertations from a hundred Brazilian academic institutions, only 11 papers from 8 universities were found, of which 10 Masters theses and 1 doctoral dissertation, all in Portuguese. No health-related publications were found. Work in the disciplines of education (one doctoral dissertation and eight Masters theses) and science (two Masters theses) focuses on discussing methods and opinions of authors with regard to the MOOCs produced, showing that MOOCs were effective and positive and converging with a recent Brazilian study. Six papers on health MOOCs were evaluated by an integrative review. A small number of scientific publications on the development of MOOC were found, and most of them discussed the methodology and opinion of authors with regard to the courses, indicating that MOOCs were effective and positively affecting health teaching-learning (Almeida et al., 2017).

Government sites give MOOCs little visibility. The Ministry of Health website does not mention the term MOOC. The Ministry of Education signals an investment through technical cooperation signed in May 2017 with the TIM Institute. Initially, 25 MOOCs will be provided through the e-Tec Brasil Network (an initiative that is an integral part of the actions of the National Program for Access to Technical Education and Employment – Pronatec) on programming languages, databases, websites, game design, and design of interfaces (Brazil, 2017). The TIM Institute was founded in 2013 and currently has 25 MOOCs, and 5 more will be available soon (TIM, 2017). However, none of them are about health.

15.3.3 Online, Massive, and/or Open Courses: Are There Governmental Initiatives in Health MOOCs?

Even with the aforementioned search, the issue as to whether Brazil's online health courses produced were MOOCs and the degree from which they fall short of or draw closer to MOOCs remains to be seen.

While Brazil shows little experience in the production of MOOCs, there are important institutional initiatives that must be highlighted in the movement of online health courses, such as those provided by UAB, linked to the Ministry of Education and the Ministry of Health initiatives: UNA-SUS, AVA-SUS, and the Community of Practice (CdP). These experiences and their characteristics are described below.

The UAB is a system comprised of public universities that provides higher education courses for people that have difficulty accessing university education through distance learning. Target audiences are teachers, managers, people in leadership positions, and those who work in basic education. It works as an instrument for the universalization of access to higher education and for faculty requalification in other disciplines, strengthening school in the interior of Brazil, minimizing the concentration of undergraduate courses in large urban centers, and avoiding the migratory flow to big cities. It was created in 2005 and, currently, 105 institutions are part of UAB (UAB, 2017).

The UNA-SUS System (UNA-SUS, 2017) is somewhat more recent than the UAB. It was created in 2010 to meet the training and continuing education needs of health professionals working in SUS. UNA-SUS consists of the collaborative network of higher education institutions, the Collection of Educational Resources in Health (ARES), and the Arouca platform. In order to facilitate access for health professionals, all the courses are free and follow the distance-learning modality. Course offerings have a practical focus, based on health professionals' needs and daily routines, and certificates are issued at various levels of training according to the workload. Online tests and issuance of certificates in the Arouca platform detail the knowledge acquired in these courses. ARES provides free access to all its contents and educational resources.

Courses can be developed both by the 35 universities that are part of the collaborative network and the UNA-SUS Executive Secretariat. By accessing courses and platforms, one can observe that results in various formats and enrollment possibilities based on prior training, according to the institution and the course's objectives. Some, for example, target a specific audience; other courses are "open" only to a level of education that is self-instructional, with tutors and limited spots, with a requirement to fulfill activities in order to obtain a certificate, and with start/end dates.

As of June 2017, UNA-SUS has 31 courses on its website (of which 25 are closed), which deal with practical matters of daily life and the needs of health professionals (in particular SUS) and clinical cases. These courses have characteristics common to massive online courses, but while the institution disseminates them as open, some are restricted to certain professional categories or only to professionals (which prevents, e.g., access by the general public).

Not all UAB and UNA-SUS courses are massive. There is mostly a need for registration and the number of spots is limited. These platforms have recently invested in mass and open courses, just like MOOCs, but the institutions do not use this nomenclature.

In September of 2015, the Ministry of Health, in partnership with the Federal University of Rio Grande do Norte (UFRN), launched yet another open education strategy to SUS professionals, namely, AVA-SUS. It is an environment developed for health professionals and students, whose main objective is to improve SUS training, management, and care. With government funding, educational modules prepared by UNA-SUS and facilitated by the institutions are available. They consist of several resources (such as texts, audios, and videos) addressing clinical issues and the organization of the work process in the SUS.

AVA-SUS is Moodle-based, since most UNA-SUS partners use this free software-based distance-learning platform. However, the UFRN team has developed a layout that seems more intuitive and attractive than Moodle, as well as responsive (its appearance adapts to mobile devices). Visual work is also perceptible as it shows a menu of courses and materials based on a user profile, mapped according to users' data (such as profession, areas of interest) and access. Participants are allowed to choose their courses, select specific modules geared toward their interests, and face no deadlines for completing work as modules are always available. A free course certificate is issued for each completed educational module, and certification at the level of improvement is possible (after having completed at least 180 h of educational modules) (AVA-SUS, 2017).

Apparently, AVA-SUS meets the requirements of online and massive courses. There only difference to MOOCs is restricted access. Considering the suggestion of the institutes of higher education that elaborated the contents and ethical issues involved, courses are restricted to certain professions and/or schooling level. When registering, users must provide a code from the Brazilian occupation registry, which directs them to specific courses. For example, a course related to medical clinical care is not viewed by a community health worker[3] (CHW). For the same reason, this impediment can also be observed in some UNA-SUS courses.

In addition to the educational courses available in AVA-SUS, the system encourages the use of other Ministry of Health learning tools, such as the community of practice (CdP, 2016). Established in 2012 and financed with public resources, CdP is a virtual space where health managers and workers, especially those working in primary healthcare, can meet and share experiences. Setting up such a collaborative network aims at improving working conditions and quality of healthcare for the population. With more than 45,000 subscribers, the community has chat rooms, case reports, and spaces for thematic discussions created by participants and a free online course environment.

The first course was launched in February 2014 and, by 2016, it had 11 free online courses. Despite having relatively few participants (altogether, 29,688), compared to the other virtual environments mentioned above, all courses are massive and open. The most sought-after course, "Self-Care: How to Provide Support to People with Diabetes – Higher Level," for example, has 6281 participants. This course is different from those offered at UNA-SUS or AVA-SUS. It has no limitation on participants and no deadline for completion, is always available, and, despite being indicated for higher education professionals, can be accessed by anyone.

Although Petra et al. (2000) and the Ministry of Health do not categorize the courses offered at CdPs as MOOCs, they are the ones that are closest to the main characteristics of MOOCs (online, massive, and open). The CdP courses are coinstructional, open, and without limits on class size or use of tutors. Materials are available, but participant contributions are appreciated, especially in asynchronous interaction spaces. They are based on open education resource modality and use a Creative Commons license, allowing students to redefine materials by downloading, modifying, and reproducing materials in other environments. When a course is completion, the Ministry of Health issues a certificate, which is not be recognized in public examinations or in selections by educational institutions, but provides a record of health professional training (Petra et al., 2015).

The EAD/ENSP/Fiocruz is an initiative for distance training and qualification of professionals who work in health and health-related areas. It has a multidisciplinary team of professionals with expertise in several areas of activity. Created in 1998, it has 59,793 graduates, 100,942 students enrolled, and 2247 teachers/tutors trained during its 59 courses in the categories of specialization, improvement, updating, and continuing education. Its courses are not characterized as MOOC. While online, most do not have open access nor are they massive, as they restrict access by inclusion/training criteria, include a selection process for a limited number of spots available and have a limited duration. In June 2017, only one of the courses (called "Training for Technicians Responsible for Transfusion Agencies," at refresher level) can be completed, but only with prior selection approval and for a restricted number of spots (Fiocruz, 2017).

[3] The digital inclusion of community health workers is discussed in Chap. 17.

Even with the analysis of these initiatives of the Brazilian government of online health courses, it is not possible to ensure that UNA-SUS, AVA-SUS, UAB, EAD/ENSP/Fiocruz, and CdP courses are MOOCs. This is not only due to the variability of their characteristics (e.g., the massive and open-access criteria vary within the same initiative as well) but also a more global situation: the difficulty of defining MOOCs themselves, since they differ in their construction and learning process. Marques (2015) states that the incipient MOOCs carry with them many uncertainties in the field of scientific research.

At this moment, we can only affirm that there are Brazilian initiatives in the way of the MOOCs. All courses are online, so they share the potential offered by Internet connectivity to bring health knowledge to several locations and enable a broad exchange of experiences. They are all produced in Portuguese (the official Brazilian language), which allows Brazilians to understand them, but can be an impediment toward expanding international access to these courses and to widely disseminating what is being produced by the country's health education institutions.

The MOOC is a new tool in health and can expand the scope of educational and training opportunities for professionals and future professionals in the field (Parkinson, 2014). This has been the priority of the Ministry of Education and Ministry of Health's initiatives. It positively fulfills the constitutional commitments envisaged for the training of professionals but, in contrast, ends up limiting access to the general population. This restriction may be based on professional impediments (e.g., for ethical reasons, teaching clinical procedure cannot be widely available, under penalty of risk to health, and this may only be possible for people with specific training to that effect). However, it limits other (nonprofessional) citizens from accessing educational content and information on health-related issues, especially public/collective health.

15.4 Brazilian Health MOOCs: Challenges and Trends

While this chapter does not cover all MOOCs, since there may be courses not listed on MOOC-List.com or not found on the institutional sites searched, we aimed to identify what Brazil produces in terms of MOOCs or what initiatives have been produced in the country for health with online, massive, and/or open courses features.

It was not possible to affirm that there are health MOOCs encouraged by the Brazilian government, but one can identify initiatives in the way of MOOCs, which can contribute with reflections and discussions about the planning and implementation of new MOOCs for participants and institutions interested in health.

Studies in Brazil on Brazilian MOOCs and their potential for health-related education are lacking, perhaps because the subject is too recent or not gained the interest of academics or educational institutions. The greatest health challenge in MOOCs may be the one posed by their innovative characteristics. MOOCs require on financial investment for preparing, maintaining, and facilitating platforms that allow thousands of people to access quality content. The country's current economic recession, however, has curtailed the flow of economic resources and, consequently, investment in scientific research.

In addition, MOOCs promote a change of attitude, especially in the traditional Brazilian teaching institutions that are attached to a classroom-teaching model, requiring completion of a module/content in order to access another module and the importance of a certificate. This MOOC movement also requires students to adapt to a technology and accept being able to choose their formative courses, since they are faced with an education model that makes use of the Internet and is most of the time self-instructional and without a teacher/tutor. These factors may be challenges, but also represent interesting advances in a new approach to learning, if they are overcome.

In the field of health, unlike other science-focused subjects that pioneered the development and use of MOOCs, ethical and corporate issues are also important challenges. The academic community, professional councils (Brazilian bodies that represent professional categories and, among other functions, conduct ethical oversight), and MOOC providers (whether governmental or not) must advance discussions of what content may or may not be disseminated and taught broadly to the population and initiate productions of courses that go beyond the clinical perspective, such as making health education modules for the entire Brazilian population.

However, the combination of education, technology, and health promoted by MOOCs is an important advancement to be enjoyed by thousands of people. Developing MOOCs require intense work and dedication, planning, knowledge of technologies, and methodology to guide production – something institutional partnerships enable.

Finally, we suggest that MOOCs in the health area in the world and in Brazil mainly involve the permanent and continuing education of workers; the exchange of experiences among students, practitioners, and users from different parts of the world (where, e.g., the same pathology or even an epidemic may manifest itself differently); and the spread of knowledge in order to strengthen individual autonomy and to improve population health. A country where online tool-mediated education is already being used, with a large number of health workers and millions of people accompanied by one of the largest public health systems in the world, seems to signal an albeit little-known demand and a favorable setting rarely explored in the use of MOOCs.

References

Almeida, Lisiane M., Simone T. Canabarro, and Helena T.H. Silva. 2017. Ferramenta de ensino-aprendizagem na área da saúde Massive Open Online Courses. *Revista Emrede – Revista de Educação à Distância* 4: 130–142.

Altbach, Philip G. 2014. Moocs as neocolonialism: Who controls knowledge? *International Higher Education* (75): 5–7.

AVA-SUS. 2017. Ambiente virtual de aprendizagem do SUS. https://avasus.ufrn.br. Accessed 10 June 2017.

Boal, Helena M. C., and Luciane Stallivieri. 2015. Os MOOCs e o processo de internacionalização das instituições de ensino superior. *XV Colóquio Internacional de Gestão Universitária – CIGU – Desafios da gestão universitária no século XXI*, Mar del Plata.

Brazil. 1988. Constituição da República Federativa do Brasil de 1988. http://www.planalto.gov.br/ccivil_03/constituicao/constituicao.htm. Accessed 5 Nov 2017.

———. 1990a. *Lei n° 8.080, de 19 de setembro de 1990. Dispõe sobre as condições para a promoção, proteção e recuperação da saúde, a organização e o funcionamento dos serviços correspondentes e dá outras providências*. Diário Oficial da União, 20 Setembro 1990.

———. 1990b. *Lei n° 8.142, de 28 de dezembro de 1990. Dispõe sobre a participação da comunidade na gestão do Sistema Único de Saúde (SUS) e sobre as transferências intergovernamentais de recursos financeiros na área da saúde e dá outras providências*. Diário Oficial da União, 31 Dezembro 1990.

———. 2017. Ministério da Educação. Ensino Médio: MEC fecha parceria para oferecer cursos técnicos gratuitos online. http://portal.mec.gov.br/busca-geral/211-noticias/218175739/49331-mec-fecha-parceria-para-oferecer-cursos-tecnicos-gratuitos-online. Accessed 15 June 2017.

CdP – Comunidade de Práticas. 2016. https://cursos.atencaobasica.org.br/comunidades. Accessed 26 May 2016.

Coursera. 2017. https://pt.coursera.org/. Accessed 17 June 2017.

Ding, Yang, Meng Wang, Yao He, Adam Yongxin Ye, Xiaoxu Yang, Fenglin Liu, Yuqi Meng, Ge Gao, and Liping Wei. 2014. "Bioinformatics: Introduction and methods," a bilingual Massive Open Online Course (MOOC) as a new example for global bioinformatics education. *PLoS Computational Biology* 10: e1003955.

EDX. 2017. https://www.edx.org/. Accessed 29 May 2017.

Finardi, Kyria Rebeca, and Jhamille R. Tyler. 2015. The role of English and technology in the internationalization of education: Insights from the analysis of MOOCs. *7th International Conference on Education and New Learning Technologies – IATED* 1: 11–18.

Finardi, Kyria Rebeca, Jane Santos, and Felipe Guimarães. 2016. A relação entre línguas estrangeiras e o processo de internacionalização: evidências da coordenação de letramento internacional de uma universidade federal. *Interfaces Brasil/Canadá* 16: 233–255.

Fiocruz – Fundação Oswaldo Cruz. Educação a distância da Escola Nacional de Saúde Pública. http://www.ead.fiocruz.br/. Accessed 29 May 2017.

Forno, Dal, Josiane Pozzatti, and Graziela Frainer Knoll. 2013. Os MOOCs no mundo: um levantamento de cursos online abertos massivos. *Nuances: estudos sobre educação* 24: 178–194.

FutureLearn. 2017. https://www.futurelearn.com/. Accessed 29 May 2017.

Hoy, Matthew B. 2014. MOOCs 101: An introduction to Massive Open Online Courses. *Medical Reference Services Quarterly* 33: 85–91.

Inamorato, Andreia. 2009. O conceito de abertura em EAD. In *Educação a distância: o estado da arte*, ed. F.M. Litto and M. Formiga, 290–296. São Paulo: Pearson Education do Brasil.

Jacoski, Claudio A. 2015. *Técnicas de aprendizagem e MOOCs: uma visão de especialistas do Brasil e Estados Unidos da América*. INPEAU/UFSC: Mar del Plata.

Marques, Paula Fogaça. 2015. *Massive Open Online Course (MOOC): uma análise de experiências pioneiras*. In *Maste's thesis, Universidade Federal do Rio Grande do Sul*. Porto: Alegre.

Mattar, João. 2013. Aprendizagem em ambientes virtuais: teorias, conectivismo e MOOC. *Teccogs* 7: 20–40.

MOOC List. 2017. https://www.mooc-list.com/. Accessed 10 June 2017.

Pappano, Laura. 2012. *The year off the MOOCs*. *The New York Times*. http://www.nytimes.com/2012/11/04/education/edlife/massive-open-online-courses-are-multiplying-at-a-rapid-pace.html. Accessed 1 Sept 2016.

Parkinson, Denis. 2014. Implications of a new form of online education. *Nursing Times* 110: 15–17.

Petra, Thiago, Fernanda Marcolino, Aline Corso, and Felipe Cavalcanti. 2015. EaD Colaborativa no SUS: uma proposta da Comunidade de Práticas para os trabalhadores da Saúde. *VII*

Congresso Internacional de Ambientes Virtuais de Aprendizagem adaptativos e acessivos, Novo Hamburgo.
Silva, Siony. 2014. MOOC como ambiente de aprendizagem? *Sinergia* 15: 121–125.
Souza, Rodrigo, and Elysandra Figueredo Cypriano. 2016. MOOC: uma alternativa contemporânea para o ensino de astronomia. *Ciência & educação* 22: 65–80.
Spring, Hannah. 2016. Online learning: The brave new world of massive open online courses and the role of the health librarian. *Health Information & Libraries Journal* 33: 84–88.
TELELAB. 2017. http://telelab.aids.gov.br/. Accessed 10 June 2016.
TIM – Instituto TIM. 2017. Cursos. https://cursos.timtec.com.br/courses. Accessed 15 June 2016.
Tori, Romero. 2010. *Educação sem distância*. São Paulo: Senac.
UAB – Universidade Aberta. 2017. http://www.capes.gov.br/uab. Accessed 10 June 2016.
UNA-SUS – Universidade Aberta do Sistema Único de Saúde. 2017. https://www.unasus.gov.br/cursos. Accessed 10 June 2016.
Veduca. 2016. http://www.veduca.com.br/. Accessed 10 June 2016.
World Reputation Rankings. 2016. The Times Higher Education. https://www.timeshighereducation.com/world-university-rankings/2016/reputation-ranking#!/page/0/length/25/sort_by/rank_label/sort_order/asc/cols/rank_only. Accessed 30 July 2016.
Yuan, Li, and Stephen Powell. 2013. *MOOCs and Open Education: Implications for higher education*. JISC CETIS Publications. http://publications.cetis.org.uk/2013/667. Accessed 20 Nov 2015.

Chapter 16
Digital Interactive Education and Educational Resources for Enhancing the Training of Health Professional: 20 Years of Experience in the Discipline of Telemedicine in the Pathology Department at the University of São Paulo Medical School (1997–2017)

Lung Wen Chao and Maíra Lie Chao

Abstract Telecommunication and computing have evolved at a rapid pace, changing how people interact with each other through mobile devices with social networks, instant messaging, and so on. Considering that use of these technologies will be increasingly present in our daily life, it is imperative that education and health care keep up with the evolution of digital society by innovating and updating current approaches. Since its creation in 1997, FMUSP's Telemedicine Discipline (DTM) has been researching, developing, and implanting health education models and resources that transcend Brazil's geographical barriers. DTM has been a reference in structuring research networks and technological centers through videoconference infrastructure, connecting disparate locations across the country with the concept of connected education, and sharing educational and laboratory infrastructures. DTM explores new health education methodologies, called Metacognitive Interactive Education 4.0 model, integrated with an educational platform with exclusive resources for health teaching, such as a digital microscopy room, directed dynamic communication in computer graphics, and 3D printing (Virtual Human Project), Digital Objects, Doubts Voters, and Opinion Voters (Design Thinking), webmeeting rooms, videos in 360°, etc.

L. W. Chao (✉) · M. L. Chao
Medical School, University of São Paulo, São Paulo, Brazil
e-mail: chao@usp.br

A. Pereira Neto, M. B. Flynn (eds.), *The Internet and Health in Brazil*,
https://doi.org/10.1007/978-3-319-99289-1_16

16.1 Introduction

The rapid transformation of the electronics, telecommunications, and computing fields during the last 15 years has been facilitating access to resources and services that had not been possible to the vast majority of population due to their high costs. As mobile devices (i.e., smartphones, tablets, smartwatches), cloud computing, and digital social networks became more popular, the way people, especially youngsters, interact has been changing significantly.[1] This transformation is going to increase in the next years, owing to the rise of 5G broadband for cellphones, rising processing power of smartphones and tablets, the emergence of new applications and support devices, improvements and innovations in social network services, diffusion of virtual and immersive realities, and, soon enough, the creation of a new generation of electronic devices based on graphene technology (that is going to replace silicon). Informatics and interactive technology will be part of our day even more. That said, education and health care will have to innovate and update its work models to keep up with socio-technological evolution, including in emerging countries such as Brazil (Kifle et al. 2010).

16.2 Brief Background

In Brazil, the Discipline of Telemedicine in the Pathology Department at the University of São Paulo Medical School[2] (DTM-FMUSP) can be considered a milestone in the area. In addition to being the first in the country, the purpose of its creation has been to keep abreast with the current times, given the consolidation of mobile technology use, mixed reality, cloud processing, use of biosensors to monitor biosignals, automatic systems supported by artificial intelligence, and the perspective of a fourth Industrial Revolution, i.e., creating society 4.0.

The university's Faculty Congregation created DTM-FMUSP in October 1997 to offer undergraduate and graduate degrees. The first course, which began in 1998, used a discussion list as the main educational tool for reflexive cognitive development and for graduate-level students to interact (Chao et al. 2000). Since then, the Discipline has been developing activities in education, assistance, research, and university extension, along with an optional undergraduate course, a graduate course with 120 h of workload, and university extension courses. A key milestone in DTM-FMUSP's trajectory occurred in October 2003, when a student presented and defended the first Associate Professorship thesis in telemedicine. It was titled, translated from Portuguese, "Virtual ambulatory (cyberambulatory) model and electronic

[1] The issue concerning young people and "digital natives" will be the theme of Chap. 7.

[2] The University of Sao Paulo (USP) is one of the biggest and most important public institutions, free of charge, of higher education and research in Brazil. It is funded by the São Paulo State government, offering many undergraduate and postgraduate courses and extension activities, researches, and innovation. For more information, see http://www5.usp.br/english/?lang=en.

tutor (cybertutor) for application in medical inter-appointment and distance learning via technology" (Chao 2003). It was the first time an integrated concept between an educational platform and a digital didactic ambulatory clinic, both based in the Internet, had been defended. The work also proposed integrating clinical-practical approaches and education; it can be considered as the precursor of educational tele-assistance and formative second opinion (Haddad et al. 2015) in Brazil. Wen (2003) also developed the basis for the Telemedicine Project "Digital Medical Station – Implementation Strategy and Telemedicine Spread in Brazil – Digital Medical Station (EDM, acronym in Portuguese)" for the Millennium Institute Program of the National Scientific Development Council, part of the Ministry of Science, Technology, Innovation and Communication from 2005 to 2008, which had nine participating institutions coordinated by the USP Medical School.

This chapter will describe some of the most significant initiatives in the first 20 years of DTM-FMUSP (1997–2017) and its innovations in the field of education. This presentation is an initial report of the most relevant issues, organized in chronological order, that made all the telemedicine infrastructure possible, including its educational activities, followed by digital interactive education activities and interactive educational resources.

16.2.1 Technological Infrastructure

The first important step was building an infrastructure with equipment and an effective communication network that could meet the institution's needs and make it the best in Brazil's field of telemedicine.

Another milestone was the foundation of the FMUSP Teaching and Research Network (EPesq) that connects the medical school's building – including its many laboratories and sectors – to its teaching hospital (*Hospital das Clínicas*), the São Paulo State Secretary of Health, the USP Public Health Faculty, the Paula Souza Health Centre, the USP School of Nursing, the Institute of Medicine and Law, and the Rebouças Convention Centre. The construction of the network, occurring between 2004 and 2007, used a fiber-optic cable, connecting laboratories for education, an amphitheater, surgical centers, the Death Verification Service (SVOC), surgical technique, walk-in clinics, emergency rooms, health centers, the Institute of Medicine and Law, and other assistance and educational structures. In 2006, FMUSP's EPesq network was connected to the Telemedicine University Network (RUTE) and to USP-Net, which made it possible to connect USP's campus, located in São Paulo, with and other cities in the state, such as USP Dentistry Faculty in Bauru,[3] the Hospital for Rehabilitation of Craniofacial Anomalies (HRAC/Centrinho), and the Ribeirao Preto campus.[4]

[3] Bauru is a Brazilian city located in State of Sao Paulo countryside, with about 350,000 habitants. It is 330 km from Sao Paulo City, the state capital.

[4] Ribeirao Preto is a Brazilian city located in State of Sao Paulo countryside, with about 600,000 habitants. It is 315 km from Sao Paulo City, state capital.

From 2003 to 2005, videoconference infrastructure was modernized with the acquisition of lots of equipment, including portable models, furniture for a surgical center, intensive care unit (ICU) and amphitheater, a camera for documents, micro-cameras, a tele-emergency set based on colored palmtops, voice over internet protocol (VoIP) devices, data servers, and videostreaming servers. This equipment was used for streaming sessions based on an innovative educational model, such as telepathology (anatomic-pathological discussion based on a live-streamed autopsy at SVOC), teletraumatology, telegeriatry, etc., and the creation of Future Classroom models using tablets (2004). This modernization process made it possible to build many "technology centers" (or CETECs) at FMUSP/HC.[5]

The first CETEC was inaugurated in October 2002 at USP Medical School. It represented a milestone for the development of telemedicine at this institution and became a role model for videoconferencing rooms during the first phase of RUTE's development. After being upgraded in 2004, this CETEC, located in the second floor of USP Medical School, was named the CETEC-TelePorto-Studio because it had videoconferencing equipment with a medical care unit, microcomputers, tablets, high-performance Wi-Fi, auxiliary cameras (videodermatoscopy and micro-cameras), document cameras, PTZ (or pan-tilt-zoom) cameras, encoding equipment for videostreaming events, infrastructure for webconference, 360° multicamera, and other resources.

Through CETEC-TelePorto, DTM-FMUSP hosted many interactive activities for educational purposes at the USP Medical School, for the Clinics Hospital of FMUSP, and other USP units, and also for national and international institutes. Until this moment, telepathology (created in 2002) is considered one of the most comprehensive models for the education of medical investigative reasoning.

16.2.2 Interactive Tele-education

With the organization of the technological structure in place, many networked events were launched (like courses; meetings; congresses; surgical, clinical, and practical demonstrations; etc.), and also many interactive proof of concepts using technology teaching-learning methods in health could be applied (Chao 2010), such as the educational platform called Cybertutor (based on ASP/DotNet) in dermatology (Soirefmann et al. 2010) and Assistential Cyberambulatory that was used for didactic education in dermatology (Chao 2003).

Some of the following activities must be highlighted because of their historic importance:

(a) The first cardiology course streamed to the Amazon region by videoconference. This activity was streamed from CETEC-TelePorto for students from the first class of a new medical course in Rio Branco, Acre (July 2003). This 1-week

[5] For more information, see: http://www3.fm.usp.br/en/institucional/the-fmusp.

course also held the first telepathology-based autopsy session streamed live to the Amazon in Brazil's history.

(b) The completion of continuous telepathology sessions with the development of investigative reasoning from USP Death Verification Service (SVOC), which is Brazil's largest[6]. Between 2004 and 2008, permanent streaming sessions for many institutions in São Paulo State (in partnership with the Regional Medical Council of São Paulo), Regional Medical Council of Parana, and other institutions in the country (Garcia et al. 2009) were made.

(c) Teletraumatology began in 2004 and since then has performed real-time trauma surgical demonstrations from USP's SVOC. The unit also has produced interactive videos based on graphic computation to demonstrate various medical procedures, such as intubation, cricothyrotomy, thoracic puncture, thoracic drainage, intubation of difficult airways, etc.

(d) TeleGero is a Geriatric Multicentric Clinical Meeting that, since 2005 until now, has been carrying out monthly activities. Nowadays, it has ten partner institutions using videoconference assistance, including an institution in Portugal.

(e) The creation of a permanent telemedicine unit in Parintins City, in Amazonas State, based off a partnership between DTM-FMUSP, Amazonas State University (UEA), and Intel, in September 2006. This partnership made some permanent educational and assistance activities by videoconference between Sao Paulo, Manaus, and Parintins possible. This action enhanced the practical development of students at a rural boarding school in the Federal University of Amazonas and UEA.

(f) University extension courses based on an interactive educational platform, which we may highlight:

- *Clinic Microbiology Specialization course by USP Dean of Culture and Extension that takes place over 18 months using a blended model (*i.e.*, practical abilities during face-to-face classes and cognitive learning based on the educational platform). This paid course was well received by participants and resulted in a PhD thesis* (Andreazzi et al. 2011).
- *A course on leprosy using hybrid education in the Amazon* region (Paixão et al. 2009a, b).
- *Elderly Health Care course (2 editions, 1500 students) and Pregnant and Puerpera Health Care course (1200 students) in partnership with the São Paulo State Health Secretariat.*
- *Integration of Competencies of the Performance of Judiciary Activities course with users and drug users and addicts (15,219 students), with the Justice Ministry.*

---

[6] Since 2002, for 15 years uninterrupted, it has been made anatomopathological discussions based on autopsies, by videoconference, to FMUSP students and to dozens of other medical schools of São Paulo State and other faculties from other states in the country. More than 450 sessions were streamed so far.

- *Motorcyclists' Accident Prevention course (2 editions, 2000 students), with the São Paulo State Health Secretariat and the Fire Department.*
- *Care of At-Risk New Born course (2 editions – 22,000 students), with Fiocruz health complex.*
- *Caregiver for Physical Disability People (900 students), with São Paulo State Secretary of Disability People Rights.*
- *Gynecological Oncology, Telepsychiatry for Primary Care, electrocardiogram course, and others.*

16.3 Digital Interactive Education

Training of health professionals has been changing, focusing on graduating professionals capable of problem solving, acting in multiprofessional teams, and recognizing social needs, including subjective and biological aspects of the health/disease process. More specifically, professionals must be able to develop treatment strategies in a biosocial approach, building bonds and taking responsibility in dealing with patients' cure, rehabilitation, and reintegration. To achieve this, some change will be necessary in training methodologies in order to achieve more articulation in the biological, psychological, and social fields and also more integration between theory and practice and more quality in evaluation geared toward learning.

Education is a complex and multifactorial process, and the use of interactive technology resources might enhance the teaching-learning process. In countries with an extensive landmass, like Brazil, interactive technology will probably be the best way to provide high-quality education, continuing educational courses for professionals, and to build collaborative networks between institutions in order to develop content (i.e., generate knowledge) made available through the cloud (i.e., Health Cloud) (Anisimova and Krasnova 2015) (Fig. 16.1).

Frenk et al. (2010) published an article in which they present the main challenges facing health systems in this century, including the epidemiologic and demographic transition, population demands, professional differentiation, and technological innovation. To face these challenges, they suggest that every health professional throughout the world must be educated to mobilize knowledge and to get involved in critical reasoning and ethical conduct in order to be competent to participate in health systems centered on patients and in the population as team members who are locally agile and globally connected (Frenk et al. 2010). For this, they proposed some instructional and institutional reforms that could promote transformative learning and interdependent education. They also mentioned that learning must be formative through the acquisition of knowledge and skills in the way that socializes students to values and be transformative in order to develop the attributes of leadership with the purpose of creating agents of change.

The organization of an adequate system to evaluate educational yield (cognitive knowledge, reasoning, decision-making capacity, behavior, practical abilities, etc.)

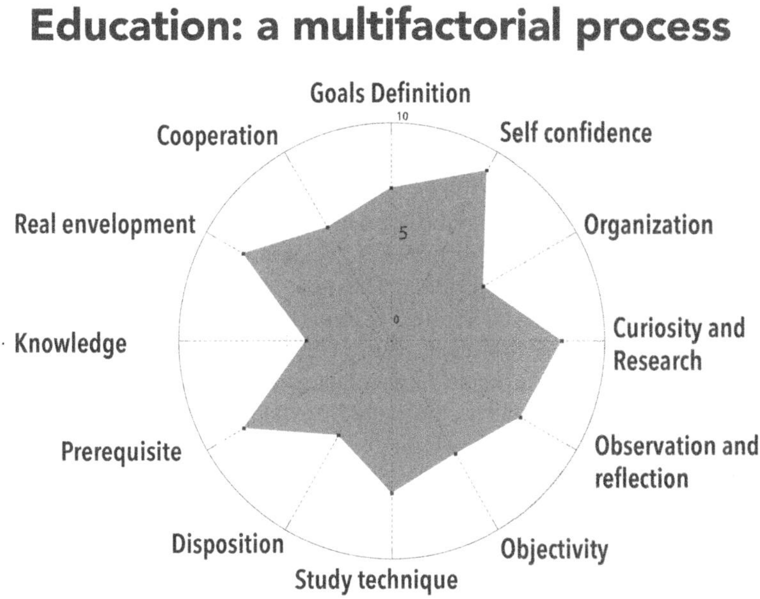

Fig. 16.1 Aspects involved in students and professional graduation

is an aspect that deserves highlighting in modernizing all educational processes. Choosing an evaluation methodology is not an easy task and always represents a challenge to educators. This choice might be made based on, whenever possible, a technique that is, at the same time, valid, reliable, viable, and acceptable for all participants involved in an evaluation. Evaluation validity is related to "what" to evaluate, while reliability is "how" we evaluate. Evaluation fulfills the criteria of validity when it involves significantly important tasks capable of being carried out at the level of difficulty compatible with the level of difficulty of a student's training in a context that best represents daily practices.

Despite being common, the separation of distance learning from conventional education, DTM-FMUSP had always been working in the strand of "technology-supported education" (Selwyn 2016) and had begun to develop, since 2014, a new educational model to substitute interactive tele-education (Chao 2009a) for a model called digital interactive education. In this new format, instead of dividing the two types of education, the objective was to combine the best resources and methods from both models in order to enhance learning with the use of interactive technology (i.e., learning objects, knowledge units, serious games, clinic simulators, interactive eBooks, immersive reality, augmented reality, 3D print, and digital microscopy room) combined with new communication strategies (educational communication design) and new educational formats including video and audio, mind maps, and infographics, among others.

16.4 The *Interactive Learning Environment*[7]: Developing the Inovalab Digital Medical Station

Since 2011, DTM-FMUSP started to develop and implement an educational platform based on open-source Moodle, whose resources were enhanced with many custom modules specially projected to combine concepts of the Future Classroom, allowing more interaction in face-to-face activities or connected ones, with individual monitoring of students' performance. Modern resources also included new graphic and dynamic communication. The new platform was called Inovalab (Innovation Laboratory) Digital Medical Station (EDM, in Portuguese) because its building was concluded in the scope of the USP Graduation Dean Pró-Inovalab Project (2013). After that, the name was shortened to Inovalab EDM.[8] Moodle was chosen due to its popularity and use by many Brazilian universities, including USP; therefore, the choice would facilitate the platform's adoption by many professors, reduce training costs, and make content compatibility and interchange between other Moodles possible, if it were necessary to make interoperability between courses. For the purpose of making the Moodle platform adequate to meet the demands for DTM-FMUSP's educational, new resources were developed and implemented, besides some improvement in navigation interface (usability). After the implementation of the Inovalab EDM platform, it has been used extensively in graduation, postgraduation, extension courses, medical residency, miltiprofessional residency, and social activities such as the Young Doctor Project.

All 12 resources described below were designed, specifically, to facilitate different educational methods aimed at flexible and meaningful learning.

(1) Recurrent Doubts Voter. A module that can be used in both presential and distance-connected classes. It increases interaction between teachers and students during activities. It can also be used as a complementary resource for studies in groups or by the individual. In the group dimension, this voter can help identify the most common and meaningful doubt in a class. It improves interactivity between students and teachers, letting each student know the common doubt in his/her class in the issue under study. There are several

[7] We do not use the expression *Virtual Learning Environment* (VLE), because it is an old terminology and because it does not correctly express our ideas in the face of modern technology. Modern platforms are not "virtual." The word "virtual" suggests a derogatory understanding. Nowadays, we do not use expressions like virtual bank or virtual commerce; these were replaced by digital banks or Internet banking (in the first case) and electronic commerce or e-commerce (in second case). Good educational platforms are real, digital, and interactive. They are not just content repositories but great tools for management and monitoring students' performance; its resources are flexible, improving the learning process by means of providing the professor the possibility to adopt different educational methods. Besides, platforms need to incorporate resources that, beforehand, were only available through physical and face-to-face meetings. An example of this case is microscopy learning with digitized slides. Therefore, we use the term *interactive learning environment*. We also strongly believe that very soon it will have modules using artificial intelligence to improve students' development.

[8] For more information, see http://edm.org.br/portal/plataforma-educacional-inovalab-medusp-digital/.

advantages of the tool. It makes it possible to increase the scale of the course without the need to increase the number of teachers proportionally. The voter can be applied to small sizes classes of 25 students or to large classes of 10,000 students without damaging the quality of interaction with students. This resource also promotes "doubt brainstorming" between participants, as it amplifies students' perception of the issue. That is, a student may find an interesting doubt that, until this moment, he/she had not thought about. So, he/she can vote in this doubt, and also he/she can be inspired by this particular doubt and come up with other questions that may be interesting for other students.

(2) Opinion Voter grouped by category. The purpose of this tool is to develop reflective team activities by making it easy to identify the impost important aspects of a subject. It is one of the more efficient tools for mental mapping of a group. The most common categories used in this module are the "most important aspects," "do not forget aspects," and "may be improved aspects."

(3) Digital Microscopy Room (Digital HistoPatho). The purpose of this tool is to effectively train people in microscopy without a microscope. This module allows for the management of a collection of microscopic slides that were digitized by a slide scanner, allowing students access to contents via 3G or digital subscriber line (DSL), from anywhere. This resource moves learning beyond the physical limits of faculty microscopy labs. Besides, this module also allows microscopy slides to be associated with short, 3-minute tutorial videos, an educational guide, and reinforcement tests for each slide. It enhances microscopy learning and can be used in histology, pathology, mycology, and parasitology, among others.

(4) Digitally enlarged imaging room. Using resources similar to the digital microscopy room, this module allows students to not only enlarge an image but also store sequentially cut images, which makes visualization of layers possible. The purpose of the tool is to visualize clinical or radiological images or in sequential frames in order to navigate them by layer.

(5) 360° visualization. A playlist of 360° videos. The purpose is to allow students to get used to all situations in which it is necessary to learn an entire environment, like examination rooms, surgical rooms, ICUs, emergency rooms, and emergency simulations, among others.

(6) Computerized test with automated assessment and feedback. The purpose is to make testing a teachable movement, because it gives professors the possibility to debate material after each test through immediate feedback.

(7) Drag and Drop evaluation. Its purpose is to examine students' skills of observation and identification of anatomical structures or the association of these structures with exam images (radiography, tomography, resonance, ultrasound, etc.) and with histology slides. This resource can be used in assessment as part of the objective structured clinical examination through the development of an online module.

(8) Decision-making simulation evaluation. This lets professors develop clinical reasoning in stages, during face-to-face classes, and identify decision-making and individual- and team-based behavior.

(9) Radiological images and tutorial library. This stores radiological images, clinical radiological videos, and tutorials. This allows students to learn diagnostic skills using images and permits professors to prepare classes.
(10) Virtual Human Library. The library contains more than 400 thematic videos of 3D graphic computing for instruction in various subject areas.[9] Nowadays, this area is called a Video Interactive Learning Object or VILO for short. It is characterized for being compact (1–3 min long), encompassing a large amount of information, and transmitting knowledge through dynamic graphic computing. The library also trains students in observation skills. Its purpose is to facilitate knowledge transmission and use as a study guide for students.
(11) Virtual Human Project Digital Objects Library. These are applications that can be installed in tablets and smartphones and allow students to manipulate virtual human structures as if they were physical objects, being able to add or subtract structures. This resource may be used with virtual human physical structures, produced with a 3D printer. This resource is also called MILO (Mobile Interactive Learning Object). Examples of Virtual Human MILO include airways and thoracic drainage, respiratory systems, heart dynamic functioning, electrophysiology correlation to ECGs, female pelvis anatomy, brain and central nervous system, abdominal organs, and liver segmentation. Students can install the apps in their devices, increasing the interaction time with educational materials.
(12) Digital rooms for online meetings. There are 7 rooms that can host 100 participants each for synchronous meetings via web or audio conferences. They allow for recordings, online surveys, chats, whiteboards, summary notes, and screen sharing, among other resources. The purpose is to enhance interactivity between professors and teacher-students and to provide webinars that compliment educational materials.

16.5 The Assistential Cyberambulatory Platform

The Assistential Cyberambulatory Platform is a complementary platform that can be connected to Inovalab EDM's platform. It is composed of a central nucleus designed for teleattendance and connected to complementary modules of didactic class, drug interaction, medicine bank, reference articles, management reports, and epidemiological surveillance. The cyberambulatory platform trains students in telepropaedeutics and is also a way doing a supervised internship through distance learning.[10]

---

[9]Virtual Human videos are carefully developed. Each one of them lasts 1–4 min and usually is equivalent to about 50 pages of text.

[10]Due to its characteristics, the concept became part of the Telemedicine Project of the Millennium Institutes Program and later included in the Brazilian Ministry of Health's Telehealth Network Program as the Second Formative Opinion.

16.6 Interactive Education 4.0 Metacognitive Model Application Experience

In the context of training students, integrated learning has always been one of the most debated questions of our times. Where did this proposal come from? The distribution of subjects according to curriculum in different grades with more thematic subdivisions is considered one of the difficulties for integrating knowledge when educating students. Students, in general, are usually subjected to a learning dynamic compartmentalized into separate classes with just a few moments to achieve the integration of knowledge during limited periods of work that involve carrying out various set activities. Besides, owing to large amount of students, many classes that should have been practical, with such insufficient resources, are becoming just moments of clinical and surgical observation and demonstration.

Nowadays, there are many educational models looking to solve those problems. Each one has its specific characteristics with strong and weak points. It is worth highlighting that none of them has been able to cover all the aspects involved in graduate-level education in health and medicine. With the goal of increasing interactive educational possibilities, DTM-FMUSP created and applied in 2017 a new method called Interactive Education 4.0 Metacognitive. It is based on meaningful learning through participatory activities, reflective thinking, and critical analysis so that students become capable of identifying and solving problems using Inovalab EDM's platform and resources.

This approach integrates five educational models that are the following: "Structured Learning," "Problem-Based Learning," "Team-Based Learning," "Meaningful Learning," and "Project-Based Learning." This model encourages interaction and reflective thinking among students, and between students and teachers, with the aim toward identifying problems and also developing solutions (i.e., practical contextualization) via teamwork and the integration of different kinds of knowledge (metacognition). This dynamic received the name of Problem-Solution Project-Based Learning.

This system was applied in an USP Medical School's Telemedicine graduate course that lasted 8 weeks (120 h) and had 94 students. This course had six parts and includes one professor, two part-time professionals for technical support, and one part-time communication professional. Student satisfaction for the course was high (Fig. 16.2).

First of all, course contents were divided into four thematic blocs (each 25% of the total) and made available on the platform structured in such a way that each bloc of study and learning lasted 2 weeks. In the study period, there were two online meetings lasting 45 min that complemented the course material.

This course began with an interactive face-to-face class, using Recurrent Doubt Voter and Digital Room for simultaneous distance participation. At least once a week, each student had to participate in Doubt Voters, Opinion Voters, and Discussion Lists in their four groups with their respective teams. To facilitate transversal monitoring of the specific activities among the four groups, a weekly news synthesis highlighting the six most relevant issues was sent for debate to each of the four thematic blocs. For this, two graduate students were chosen as editors for this work in conjunction with the professor and journalist.

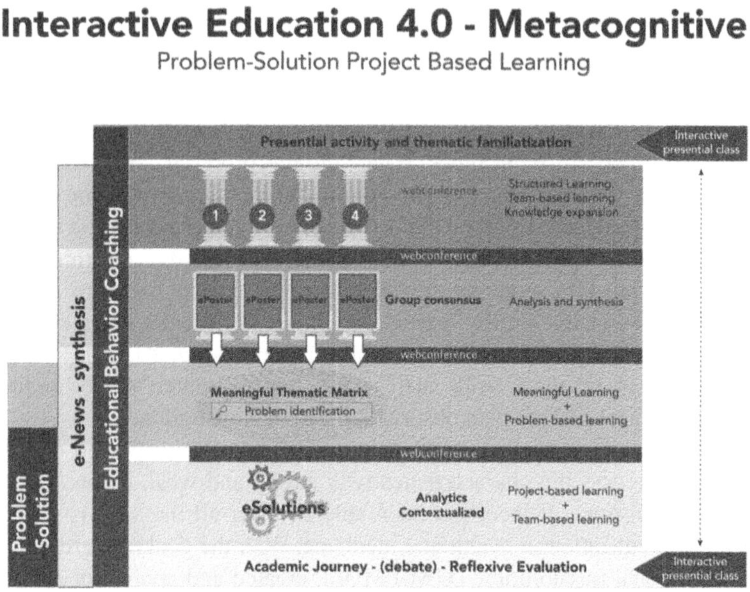

Fig. 16.2 Problem-Solution Project-Based Learning model employed in the graduate-level telemedicine course

Student assignments included the submission of three individual syntheses, one at the beginning of the course (magna class), one at the end of the thematic structured learning period (phase 2 at the end of the third week), and the last one at the end of the course (phase 6 in the 8th week). In team activities, each group indicated three people (writer, reporter, and debater) responsible for developing presentations, an ePoster, with meaningful content in their respective thematic blocks and also presenting a solution for the most voted problem (eSolution). Each group's eSolution was made available for each student's individual evaluation pointing out explicitness in problem exposure, problem relevance, solution originality, the coherence of the solution's presentation, and its feasibility. The last phase was a face-to-face activity to end the debates and the development of a general consensus.

For monitoring and carrying out the course, just one part-time professor who assumed the role of collaborative content debater/reviewer and as performance coach (i.e., monitoring goal achievement) was necessary. Besides, a part-time educommunication professional (or communication coach) who interacted with two student volunteers as thematic editors and two IT professionals for report development was also necessary.

Course activities generated:

- *184 doubts with 2266 votes*
- *1587 forum posts and 50,880 words*
- *83,324 platform accesses of which 4.763 occurred early in the morning*
- *44 videos watched 2154 times.*

According to student feedback on the course, 92% considered the weekly e-news synthesis very important as a way of transmitting the most important knowledge in each of the blocs, and 95% considered that this educational model had changed their attitude. Additionally, 89% gave grades of 9 and 10 (on a 10-point scale) for ending the course symposium as a method for consolidating the most important aspects in the course, and 86% gave 9 and 10 for the course format.

It was possible to apply this model with a small team and also provide instruction oriented toward project development requiring solutions to problems. Its characteristics included multiprofessional participation, interdisciplinarity, articulation, and instigation so that students could identify a problem and experience easy, feasible, developed solutions, which was a motivational factor for learning. Problem-Solution Project-Based Learning made cognitive-practical learning with new methodologies, upheld by interactive mobile technology, a reality.

16.7 Educational Communication Design

Many studies have sought to deepen our knowledge about the impact of interactive media in science museums on the development of youngsters. One study evaluated the effectiveness of the Smithsonian Institution's National Postal Museum (Smithsonian Institution 2009). Content published on the Museum's website made it easy to deepen information learned during visits and to facilitate visitors' involvement in face-to-face activities. The report's results basically suggest that interactivity increases young people's participation in the museum. This indicator has shed some light on youngsters' interest in the use of new information and communication technology. The fact that the Museum has integrated information exposed physically with the website deepened knowledge and awakened young people's interest in the subject matter.

An interesting aspect of interactivity is the possibility of a user/participant applying his/her new knowledge. Interactivity used in information streaming makes the learning process easier, turning it into something fun and enjoyable. This is the main positive point for using interactivity in education: it allows the subject to have fun and to learn at the same time.

Alexander et al. (2001), from John Hopkins University (USA), questioned if it is necessary to spend time looking over pedagogical models or if it would be better to think about offering good complementary learning during "extra formal education," through cultural activities. They considered culture an important element in developing citizen knowledge and ideal way of providing it was through experimentation.

In this area, DTM-FMUSP began the formation of a group called "educational communication design," which includes journalists, filmmakers, audiovisual professionals, illustrators, public relation, and psychologists, among others. This team's objective is to plan the use of communication media to improve the transmission of health information to a target audience in order to improve knowledge retention. Using the objective and competence matrix, the multimedia matrix, and script-writing technique, the team developed new videos and audios to achieve fluid knowledge transmission. They also developed many instructional modules using infographics.

Besides improving educational professionalization, the team was also responsible for the creation of health-related exhibits in museums, libraries, and cultural spaces.[11]

For the development of diverse audiovisual materials, the "Digital Production Center" was created. For example, the unit developed multiprofessional material about milking and breastfeeding techniques that include the medical aspects of breastfeeding (i.e., pediatrics and gynecology); the view of nurses concerning mother-child care; a speech therapy perspective about the development of oropharyngeal muscles developed in the process of child communication; and the dentists' perspective about teeth development and nutrition.

Besides producing audiovisual content, the team also created new ways of spreading knowledge using a "health cloud" where educational material are grouped, including interactive eBooks with multimedia, such as videos, audios, 3D computing, expandable images, and easy bookmarks, with bidimensional navigation and platform integration.[12]

16.8 Virtual Human Project and Learning Objects

One of the areas that deserve attention in educational technology is the use of learning objects to help professors in the educational process and students in learning. One example is the "Virtual Human Project,"[13] which uses visual communication resources through 3D computer graphics to transmit knowledge in a visual and dynamic way. Because they are flexible units and can be used in different ways by educators, the Virtual Human is also designated as "learning objects."

The "Virtual Human Project" is considered a method of dynamic and directed communication. It consists of graphically representing a large amount of specialized information in a pleasant, interactive, dynamic, and objective way. The learning objects created from the "Virtual Human Project" facilitate the understanding of complex subjects with the help of scripted communication. Therefore, they become an accurate translation of scientific knowledge, based on a communication strategy appropriate for the target audience (Chao 2009b). More than 3D anatomy, the "Virtual Human Project" is an instrument that provides detailed visualization of physiological processes, causes and effects of diseases, drug efficacy, and surgical procedures. Examples include the visualization of the hepatitis virus' invasion of a liver cell, the gait of a normal person and an amputee, the phonation and dynamics of the vocal cords, and the functioning of the temporomandibular joint. This tool, whose conception started in 2003 by DTM-USP, helps to train health professionals, teach students in the area, orient patients, and promote the health of the general public. Through it, the sequences of the lower limbs can be observed when a normal

---

[11] For further details, see http://jovemdoutor.org.br/.

[12] In this new modality, interactive voice eBooks were produced and registered in the National Library-Ministry of Culture, having obtained the ISBN numbers. Complete work: ISBN – 978-85-92510-00-08. Voz: Medicina e Fonoaudiologia volume 1 – ISBN 978-85-92510-01-5. Voz: Medicina e Fonoaudiologia volume 2 – ISBN – 978-85-92510-02-2

[13] Further details, see http://homemvirtual.org.br/.

person is walking and muscles that would need to be strengthened with the use of prosthetics (Chao 2016). From then on, the development of these dynamic and three-dimensional iconographic models became continued and extended to diverse areas of health. Currently, the "Virtual Human Project" is organized in modules. They include more than 450 sequential topics, 60 structures to use in 3D printers, 75 units of knowledge, and 6 digital objects. If this intellectual patrimony, equal to 120,000 work-hours of work, were to be assembled, it amounts to a major collection of 3D scientific computer graphics about health, which is continuously updated by the DTM-Faculty of Medicine at USP.

The construction of the "Virtual Human Project" is the result of integrating specialists in certain subjects such as telemedicine and digital designers. Unlike classic computer graphics productions, the "Virtual Human Project" details each of the scientific steps. This tool can be made available in schools, libraries, and cultural spaces throughout the country in order for teachers to use it as an educational instrument, optimizing class time, and facilitating teacher-student communication. In addition, students themselves can consult the material in libraries to complement the knowledge acquired in the class.

The recent developments of computing technologies have made access to new types of equipment possible, such as 3D printers. With the use of photosensitive resins, plastic filaments, plaster, wax, or other substances, these devices are able to construct physical objects with great detail if there is a digital matrix previously developed in 3D computer graphics. This resource has opened a variety of perspectives for students who can study, analyze, enhance, customize, and alter anatomical objects if they have access to computer graphics equipment with the 3D anatomical libraries of the "Virtual Human Project." This activity may allow them to produce 3D physical objects of anatomical parts. This new dynamic can stimulate learning based on collaborative works, and it may improve the capacity of observation.

The "Virtual Human Project" collection is not used only in learning anatomy, as it was originally intended. It is also designed for holistic and integrated morphofunctional understanding of various subjects involving anatomy, physiology, and physiopathology and/or microscopic or biomolecular mechanisms of action. The effort included the development of six digital interactive applications of the "Virtual Human Project" for tablets and smartphones, as a digital correspondent for anatomical structures printed in 3D.[14] Moreover, the themes produced in the "Virtual Human Project" cover several health sciences besides medicine, like nursing, dentistry,[15] speech therapy, and physiotherapy, among others (Fig. 16.3).

[14] These six applications attend to the following areas: (1) anatomy of the heart, structures, and functional dynamics, nerve beam, and electrical stimulation processes with corresponding ECG representations; (2) the skull, brain, central nervous system, and 12 cranial pairs; (3) male pelvis and male genitourinary anatomy; (4) female pelvis and female genitourinary anatomy; (5) thorax and respiratory system; and (6) anatomy of the liver, with segmentation, vascularization, and correlation with organs of the abdomen.

[15] In the scope of dentistry, several "learning objects" were produced in 3D computer graphics such as the dysfunction of the temporomandibular joint (TMJ), dental structure, atraumatic restorative treatment (ART), applying anaesthesia, and the "International Caries Detection and Assessment System" (ICDAS).

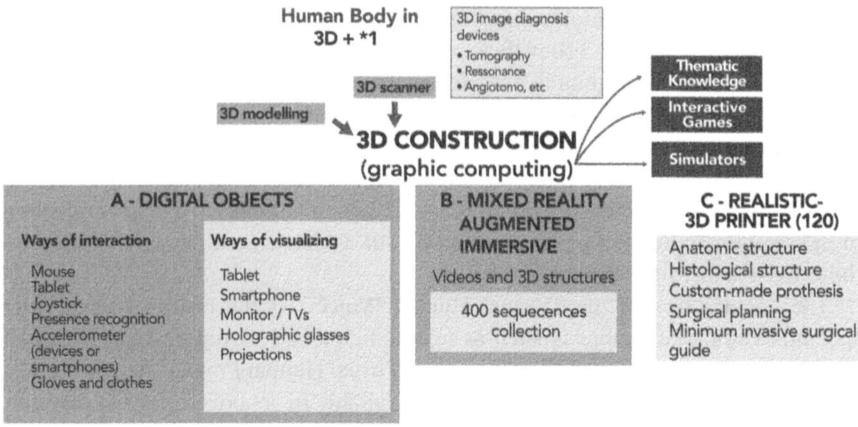

Fig. 16.3 Diagram demonstrating Virtual Human Project applications

16.9 Conclusions and Challenges

Faced with the changes, resulting from the incorporation of digital resources in the daily life and the perspective of the fourth Industrial Revolution, the modernization of education is urgent and imperative. Not only for informing and providing content, but it is necessary for developing new skills, entrepreneurship, and a sense of innovation, as well as for identifying problems and promoting continuous improvement, group work, and the perception of a continuous learning, based on the cloud of knowledge and networked education.

The training of future physicians and health professionals depends on the efficient integration of technologies with the use of new educational models that can develop multifactorial training.

The main challenge is to promote changes in a structured and continuous manner in all educational institutions and to collectively organize with governmental and regulatory bodies continuous plans with 5-year strategies for the introduction and consolidation of new forms of education, including trainings for human resource teams to provide support. Education should follow actions similar to those in the film industry, i.e., effective professionalization with an investment in the production chain that is scripted and efficient.

Digital interactive education cannot be seen as the use of devices and platforms. It should be understood as the creation of a new learning ecosystem, where research and educational innovations are permanently pursued, seeking to incorporate new methods and to associate the foundations of neuroscience, psychopedagogy, and neurolinguistics.

References

Alexander, Karl L., Doris R. Entwisle, and Linda S. Olson. 2001. Schools, achievement, and inequality: A seasonal perspective. *Educational Evaluation and Policy Analysis* 23: 171–191.

Andreazzi, Denise B., Flávia Rossi, and Chao L. Wen. 2011. Interactive tele-education applied to a distant clinical microbiology specialization university course. *Telemedicine and e-Health* 17: 1–6. https://www.ncbi.nlm.nih.gov/pubmed/21749260

Anisimova, Tatyana Ivanovna, and Lyubov Alekseevna Krasnova1. 2015. Interactive technologies in electronic educational resources. *International Education Studies* 8: 186.

Frenk, Julio, Lincoln Chen, Zulfiqar Bhutta, Jordan Cohen, et al. 2010. Health professionals for a new century: Transforming education to strengthen health system in an interdependent world. *Lancet* 376: 1923–1958.

Garcia, Maria Lucia, L.F.F. Silva, Chao Lung Wen, and György M. Böhm. 2009. Telepatologia: raciocínio de investigação diagnóstica baseada em autópsia. In *Medicina USP/HC-Faculdade de Medicina da USP*, ed. M.A. Martins, vol. 3, 885–887. São Paulo: Editora Manole.

Haddad, Ana Estela, Mary Caroline Skelton-Macedo, Verônica Abdala, Caren Bavaresco, Daniele Mengehel, Camilla Abdala, and Erno Harzheim. 2015. Formative Second Opinion: qualifying health professionals for the Unified Health System through the Brazilian Telehealth Program. *Telemedicine and e-Health*. https://doi.org/10.1089/tmj.2014.0001.

Kifle, Mengistu, Fay Cobb Payton, Victor Mbarika, and Peter Meso. 2010. Transfer and adoption of advanced information technology solutions in resource-poor environments: The case of telemedicine systems adoption in Ethiopia. *Telemedicine Journal and E-Health* 3: 327–343.

Paixão, Maurício Pedreira, Hélio Amante Miot, Pedro Elias de Souza, Ana Estela Haddad, and Chao Lung Wen. 2009a. A university extension course in leprosy: Telemedicine in the Amazon for primary healthcare. *Journal of Telemedicine and Telecare* 15: 64–67.

Paixão, Maurício Pedreira, Hélio Amante Miot, and Chao Lung Wen. 2009b. Tele-education on leprosy: Evaluation of an educational strategy. *Telemedicine Journal and E-Health* 15: 552–559.

Selwyn, Neil. 2016. *Education and technology: Key issues and debates*. London: Bloomsbury Publishing.

Smithsonian Institution. 2009. Visitors to the National Postal Museum. Office of Policy and Analysis Smithsonian Institution. https://repository.si.edu/bitstream/handle/10088/23037/09.06.NPMSpringVisitors.Final.pdf. Accessed 13 June 2018.

Soirefmann, Mariana, Juliana Catucci Boza, Cristiane Comparin, Tania Ferreira Cestari, and Chao Lung Wen. 2010. Cybertutor: A teaching tool in Dermatology. *Anais Brasileiros de Dermatologia* 85: 400–402.

Chao, Lung Wen. 2003. Modelo de ambulatório virtual (cyber ambulatório) e tutor eletrônico (cyber tutor) para aplicação na interconsulta médica, e educação à distância mediada por tecnologia. PhD diss., Universidade de São Paulo, São Paulo.

———. 2009a. Homem Virtual. Clínica Médica. In *Medicina USP/HC-Faculdade de Medicina da USP – vol. 1*, ed. M.A. Martins, 988–991. São Paulo: Editora Manole.

———. 2009b. Segunda Opinião Especializada Educacional. In *Medicina USP/HC-Faculdade de Medicina da USP – vol. 6*, ed. M.A. Martins, 777–779. São Paulo: Editora Manole.

———. 2010. *Telemedicina e Telessaúde: a experiência da Universidade de São Paulo. Sistemas e Tecnologias de Informação na Saúde*. Porto: Universidade Fernando Pessoa.

———. 2016. Homem Virtual (Ser Humano Virtual 3D): a integração da computação gráfica, impressão 3d e realidade virtual para aprendizado de anatomia, fisiologia e fisiopatologia. *Revista de Graduação USP* 1: 7–15.

Chao, Lung Wen, Paulo Sérgio Panse Silveira, Raymundo Soares Azevedo, and György Miklós Böhm. 2000. Internet discussion lists as an educational tool. *Journal of Telemedicine and Telecare* 6: 302–304.

Chao, Lung Wen, Tânia F. Cestari, Lucio Bakos, Marcela Rocha de Oliveira, Hélio A. Miot, and György Miklós Böhm. 2003. Evaluation of an Internet-based tedermatology system. *Journal of Telemedicine and Telecare* 9: 9–12.

Chapter 17
Digital Inclusion of Health Workers in Goiás State: An Account of an Educational Initiative

Ana Valéria M. Mendonça, Elizabeth Alves de Jesus Prado, Natália Fernandes Andrade, Donizete Moreira, João Paulo Fernandes da Silva, and Maria Fátima de Sousa

Abstract This chapter provides an account of the Community Health Workers' Digital Inclusion Project concerning the knowledge management and capacity building in their skills and attitudes for preventing, caring, and promoting health of individuals, families, and communities. Distance learning was the pedagogical-didactic approach adopted for the training of these health workers, building on the technological setting using the Moodle online platform. Results achieved so far suggest that participants are still alien to the universe of information and communication technologies, despite their mid-level of schooling and the scope of digital inclusion in Brazil. Transforming these workers into managers of information they acquire or generate is to promote social justice through technological inclusion as well as improve the quality of work they provide focused on improving population health. Initiatives like this one directly influence access to information and consequently assistance to users of the public health system in their areas. Participants' feedback recognized the merits of the ongoing project. Strategies of this nature should be adopted by municipal health managers especially given Brazil's complex economic, political, and sociocultural characteristics.

17.1 Introduction

Some affirm that digital inclusion in Brazil has been overcome.[1] We would instead say it has been minimized. It has not met the needs for information management and knowledge in a country so diverse in its political, economic, and sociocultural realms, with complex organizational processes of municipal health systems,

[1] Chapter 17 discusses a pioneering Digital Inclusion project in Brazil.

A. V. M. Mendonça (✉) · N. F. Andrade · D. Moreira · J. P. F. da Silva · M. F. de Sousa
Faculty of Health Sciences, University of Brasília, Brasília, Brazil

E. A. de Jesus Prado
UnB Faculty in Ceilândia, University of Brasília, Brasília, Brazil

A. Pereira Neto, M. B. Flynn (eds.), *The Internet and Health in Brazil*,
https://doi.org/10.1007/978-3-319-99289-1_17

especially those opting for primary healthcare, as the starting and circulating point of the organization of healthcare and services. Furthermore, digital inclusion also has not included Community Health Workers (CHWs) and family health strategies as the possible pathway in the processes of health-disease care, toward integrated networks, in a universal, decentralized, public, and quality health system. These options constitute the strategies in the organization and structuring of the Brazilian health system.

The Brazilian health system, namely, the unified health system (or SUS according to its Portuguese acronym) presupposes health as a social right. Thus, the Brazilian healthcare model should promote actions and unwavering health services, so its primary healthcare (PHC) was decided as the care coordinator. This means that PHC should monitor individuals, promote long-term care, and refer patients seeking health services to other levels of complexity and specialized care by coordinating care.

PHC is an alternative that transforms the rationale of health practices, based on family and household interventions (Ministry of Health, 2006). In PHC, the understanding of the illness-cure process (or health-disease process) is understood comprehensively and in a multicausal way, as well as seen as determined by the individual, family, social, and environmental factors. In this regard, the Brazilian health system, in implementing PHC as the coordinator of care to reach individuals considering their economic and social context, focuses on so-called family health teams consisting of a physician, nurse, nursing technician, and Community Health Workers (CHWs) who are individuals residing in the territory and are responsible for conducting home visits and monitoring individuals and families and for being the communication link of health needs in the area. This initiative is called the family health strategy.

In 2007, we started the Digital Inclusion Project of Community Health Workers in the states of the Brazilian Federation, because we understood that, in such a diverse and complex country, including professionals who first knock at health's door is urgent and necessary.

From the positive results achieved in this initiative and, above all, recognizing that these professionals could not stay on the sidelines of new technological revolutions, the state of Goiás saw us as preferential partners in the development of a strategic Digital Inclusion Project targeting CHWs in all the state's municipalities. In this regard, the Center for Public Health Studies, the Faculty of Health Sciences of the University of Brasília (UnB), and the State Health Secretariat of Goiás signed an agreement to develop the quality improvement project of Community Health Workers.

What is this all about? It is about a certain number of health workers from Brazil's central-west region who took online distance-learning modules, but who did not have the knowledge, skills, or attitudes to use these information and communication technologies (ICTs). Thus, in this chapter, we reflect on this initiative, as well as the sociodemographic characteristic and ICT use of these professionals, their difficulties, and how we worked together to help these health workers climb one step further toward digital and informational inclusion, so that they could be more successful in their service training.

However, we should recall that the Community Health Workers program created in 1991 is a strategy to promote health and improve the quality of life of individuals, families, and communities, each of whom are linked to a multi-professional team working in specific urban and rural areas (Ministry of Health 2009; Brazil 2011). Subsequently expanded and consolidated into the family health program, these efforts propose a new healthcare model, which improves healthy environments, protects people against health threats, and enables communities to increase their development capacities and opportunities (Mendonça et al. 2017).

By the end of 2017, Brazil had 257,872 Community Health Workers (CHWs). Of these, 8132 were located in the state of Goiás (Ministry of Health 2018).

17.2 *Capacita CHWS/CEWS*: Online Information and Knowledge

The online training course *Capacita*[2] for CHWs and Community Endemic Workers (CEWs) aims to build professionals' capacities to work together with their multi-professional teams, to improve the quality of their work in providing care, and to promote health for individuals and social groups at the household and community level. The course has a workload of 220 h and is carried out in Virtual Learning Environments through a distance-learning modality. It started in December 2016 and is expected to be completed by the end of 2018.

Eight hundred eighty-one workers enrolled in the first module of the first of 14 classes planned until the end of the project. The second and third class had 764 and 1700 enrolled, respectively. In total, the course had 3345 active participants. More than 11,000 workers are expected to complete the course.

The participants were selected by the State Health Secretariat of Goiás. An e-mail invitation was sent to them that contained a link to an electronic form with questions about their social, professional, and technological backgrounds. Let us have a look at some information about those who enrolled.

17.3 Profiles of Distance-learning Course Participants

In the social profile, we highlight "Gender," "Bearer of special needs," "Schooling," and "Household income." Of the 3345 enrolled in the first three groups, 2566 (76.7%) were female and 779 (23.3%) were male.

Sixty-three workers (1.9%) reported a disability. For these, in the questionnaire, the question included the type of disability, whether visual, intellectual/cognitive, or other.

---

[2] *Capacita* comes from the Portuguese word *capacitar* which means to build capacity, to train, or to enable.

Regarding schooling, prevalence of high school education (58.36%) between CHWs and CEWs was followed by college education (17.43%), incomplete college education (11.36%), incomplete secondary education (4.93%), complete elementary education (3.35%), incomplete elementary education (1.49%), and postgraduate studies (3.08%). This information provides evidence about the academic level of workers, mainly when it refers to the percentage of these with college-level degrees vis-à-vis those who do not.

Regarding household income, 97.7% of those enrolled reported earnings up to four minimum wages in Brazil, which corresponds to US$ 1163 (as early 2018).

Concerning the professional profile, we highlight questions concerning the following topics: "Works as a CHW"; "Professional link with the municipality"; "Length of service as a CHW"; "Completed the professionalization course to work as a CHW"; "Participated in training courses to be a health worker"; and "Municipality of service".

Of the total of 524 enrollees, only 4.4% had a formal work contract with the health secretariat. This fact shows an elevated rate of poor work relationships facing CHWs.

Regarding the length of service as a CHW, 27.1% of the enrollees had 9–11 years of service, 15.3% had 12–14 years, and 16.8% 15–18 years. This information demonstrates that they are experienced professionals, since 63.5% of the enrollees have 9 years or more of service.

Still in relation to participants' professional profile, workers were consulted regarding the CHW professionalization course and whether they had completed job training lessons. As for the professionalization course, 17.8% said they did not do it, and with respect to training, 22.1% also said they did not do it. These results draw attention to the number of CHWs who did not complete the professionalization course or subsequent training courses. This may reveal a weakness in professional training, as well as the inadequate information and communication in the health management process that is attributed to and expected of them.

Lastly, enrollees also had a question about the municipality they work. A total of 80 municipalities were identified, with the largest number of CHWs from Anápolis (428 enrolled), Águas Lindas de Goiás (258), Aparecida de Goiânia (248), Luziânia (189), Rio Verde (174), and Planaltina de Goiás (131). The others had less than 100 enrollees per municipality.

17.4 The Technological Profile

In this session of the questionnaire, we asked about the respondents' frequency of use of ICTs. The questions concerned access to technologies such as computers, tablets, and smartphones, all with Internet access. The frequency consisted of "1–3 times a week", "4–6 times a week", "daily," and "I have no access."

Regarding the use of computers, tablets, and smartphones, 24.9%, 83.1%, and 24% of enrollees said they did not have access, respectively. The data showed that

25% of the enrollees did not have access to the two types of widely used ICTs, a proportion that increased in regard to tablets. Also, in the case of Virtual Learning Environments course, this number becomes even more significant, since access to technologies is a fundamental prerequisite in the learning process.

Following questions about access to ICTs, the next one tried to identify the location of access. We observed that 90% of enrollees with access to the Internet do so at home or work.

To finalize the technological profile and the questionnaire, we sought to find out whether CHWs/CEWs knew about distance-learning platforms and, for those who said they did, whether they had already attended a distance-learning course. In the questionnaire, 43.8% said they knew about distance-learning platforms, and of those who said they did, 59.5% had already attended some distance-learning course through these platforms.

Considering the issue of access and lack of workers' knowledge about distance-learning platforms, the Laboratory of Education, Information and Communication in Health and Center for Public Health Studies/UnB, with the support of State Health Secretariat, scheduled digital inclusion workshops targeting CHWs and CEWs who are experiencing greater difficulties in accessing these technologies. This demand arose after evaluating data collected on student enrollment in the first class, where we observed that, in three municipalities, a large number of CHWs/CEWs said that they did not have access compared to the number of those enrolled in their location.

The municipalities that drew the most attention with this problem were Posse, with 38 workers of the 81 enrolled; São Miguel do Araguaia, with 29 of 58; Cavalcante, with 26 of 34; São Domingos, with 16 of 31; and São Simão, with 15 of 50. Therefore, with 48.8% stating that they did not know about distance-learning platforms, only the first class showed the need for workshops that enabled CHWs/CEWs to make use of ICTs, not only to follow the course but also to be able to include themselves in the virtual universe in a way that could consolidate access to information for absorbing and managing knowledge (Mendonça 2009; Mendonça et al. 2009). Given this reality, the training needs of these professionals became central for the course in understanding the role of the educator and goal of overcoming the challenges at hand (Mendonça 2007). Thus, we will describe the profile of the workshops that were conducted, as well as how these were put into practice.

17.5 The Participants' Profile in the Digital Inclusion Classes

The digital inclusion (DI) workshop is an 8-h workload practicum and theoretical activity to provide ICT skills to CHWs and CEWs who are not digitally experienced in the use of smartphones, notebooks, tablets, computers, and other devices. The theoretical content seeks to provide CHWs/CEWs the skills necessary to take the *Capacita* CHWs/CEWs training course.

Workshop participants who declared that they are not digitally included answered a new semi-structured questionnaire at the beginning of the lesson in which they reported their main difficulties regarding the use of ICTs. The analysis informed the elaboration of participants' profile for the workshops and directed the application of theoretical contents addressed during the group study sessions. The profile described below sought to identify which ICTs the workers had more familiarity with and ease of handling on a daily basis, whether for personal use or at work.

The digital inclusion workshop is aimed at professionals registered in the course platform, installed from the free Moodle software. However, not all those enrolled in the course participated in the workshop. The first activity was carried out in a municipality of Goiás state, and six other seminars took place in other municipalities throughout the state from August to November 2017.

By the end of December 2017, 524 professionals were included in the program, with the purpose of familiarizing themselves with the platform and later acting as local facilitators. The workshops' initiative aims to provide autonomy to participants either for social mobilization in their work processes or empowerment as citizens (Freire 2002; Toro and Werneck 2004).

The questionnaire contained 12 questions concerning which ICTs are most commonly used by CHWs, whether they had access to the Internet or some online activity (Facebook, Instagram, Twitter, blog, etc.), and finally the main difficulties they faced in accessing the Internet. The questions were based on the course's needs since it is a distance-learning course.

The participation of CHWs (364) was higher than CEWs (154), which is because there is a larger number of CHWs than CEWs in the Brazilian state of Goiás.

The questionnaire started by asking workers whether they used any ICT device, such as a computer, cellphone (smartphone), or tablet. In total, 476 questionnaires were analyzed, of which 82% (393) answered that they use one of the listed technologies, 12% (56) said they did not, and 6% (27) did not respond.

Most make use of some ICT device. When questioned about which devices are most commonly used, cellphones prevailed with 63% (277) of the respondents, followed by notebooks, with 14.5% (55), and tablets, with 7% (31).

The mainstreaming of smartphones results from the fact that cellphones are the most commonly used devices, which is due, among other things, to having more known and useful functions (CGI 2016).

In activities of this nature, it is ideal for the participant to dedicate about 1 h a day to the course, reading the available material, completing assignments, and consulting complementary references for greater mastery of the content. The difficulty in accessing the course may reflect the dropout rate (Silva 2016). To identify such difficulties, workers were asked to list the main difficulties they face when using the Internet. Many reported problems in typing, accessing a site, performing a search, and accessing e-mail, but safety was not an issue. This is related to the fear of damaging something; one participant stated: "We are all afraid to access programs and delete the rules."

Access to the Internet can be more straightforward if the user is already familiar with the tool. Many of them do activities online, but they do not realize that they are using the Internet through social media, such as Facebook, Twitter, Instagram, blogs, and other programs, which are also connected to the Internet (Mendonça et al. 2009). So, we asked them if they did any activities online (blog, Twitter, Facebook, etc.) and, if so, what they were. Of the 370 agents who answered this question, 73% (271) do some type of activity on the Internet, and then we asked them which one. The most common uses were Facebook and the WhatsApp messaging application. Also included were Instagram, YouTube, e-mail, and LinkedIn.

In summary, the profile of the participants of in the DI workshops reveals that workers perceive themselves as digitally excluded although they own and use cell-phones and develop activities through social media. Also, the most significant issues refer to safety and fear of using ICTs.

Next, we shall describe the organizers' reflection and participant's feedback regarding the digital inclusion workshops. The goal in this report is that we can target and identify the potential of these sessions to increase workers' knowledge, disseminate understanding, and affect participants' perception. We also observe how their expertise in information management has advanced and how use of ICTs has improved their quality of life and work.

17.6 What Does This Experience Teach Us?

The face-to-face digital inclusion courses for CHWs were carried out from the enrollment questionnaire of the *Capacita* CHWs course, which at the time showed that 25% (837) of the workers were not experienced with digital technologies.

The first insight of the workshop organizers' group was that it was necessary to get to know the participants of the courses using ICTs. Although common sense points out that, ideally, everyone participating in the Virtual Learning Environment courses knows at a minimum how to handle and use the ICTs. The reality may be that the students want to join in distance-learning courses, but do not have sufficient knowledge to follow in the course, as was identified in the *Capacita* CHWs course.

We should then reflect on the following: will these digitally challenged professionals ever have the necessary perquisite skills for entering the digital environment? Also, will they always be on the sidelines for skill training and professionalization training when they are in Virtual Learning Environment? Thus, the starting point chosen in *Capacita* CHWs was to provide these professionals the skills so that they could continue in the course.

The digital inclusion (DI) workshops generally took place on Saturdays in strategically located municipalities that would maximize the number of participants, lasted for 8 h, and consisted mainly of practical activities. In principle, these municipalities should have been in a location that would favor student travel to and from locations and have spaces with sufficient technological infrastructure to accommodate the largest number of participants. The size of the state of Goiás, located in the center-west region of Brazil, has a surface area of more than 340 thousand km^2, slightly larger than Finland, has a population estimated at 6.7 million inhabitants

(IBGE 2017), and consists of 246 municipalities grouped in 17 health regions. Regarding access to ICTs, Goiás state ranks higher than the means in relation to the percentage of households with access to the Internet, mobile phone, and computer. According to the 2016 PNADC – Access to Internet and Television and Ownership of Cellphone for Personal Use (IBGE 2016) – the state of Goiás has 71.8% of households with Internet access (compared to 69.3% in Brazil), 95.6% have cellphones (Brazil 85.5%), and 46.7% have computers or tablets (Brazil 45.3%).

The DI training sessions included material about computing concepts, knowledge of computer parts and pieces, operating systems, software programs, basic operations in the digital graphics environment, text editors, browsers, and even the presentation of the Virtual Learning Environment platform where the DI course would be provided, helping them access the Internet for the first time. Course instructors adjusted content according to participants' level of knowledge. For example, in the municipality of Posse, where the first workshop was held, most of the workers had never used a computer and could not even switch it on. In Goianésia, one-third of the workers had never touched a computer, while the others already knew how to switch them on but felt insecure and unable to operate them.

The DI workshop revealed several realities. In all the locations, there were no problems related to participant attendance. Instead, some of the challenges concerned the limited availability of the physical spaces requested in some municipalities. Also, none of the seven locations had an infrastructure that covered the demand for workshops. Sites with the best conditions were in the following cities that had universities: Luziânia (Federal Institute of Goiás – Luziânia Campus), Anápolis (Evangelical University), and Aparecida de Goiânia (Federal Institute of Goiás – Aparecida Campus), all of which stood out for the number of operating computers with access to the Internet.

Once classes started, we observed that the primary challenge was physical, that is, getting people to just touch the computer. When we saw participants in the room, we noticed some misbelief and fear of approaching the devices in their faces. Gradually, with practical exercises, encouraging them and grabbing their hands to touch the mouse together, we got them to switch on the computers and start the proposed activities. This very moment was the first icebreaker: workers rejoiced at every folder of documents they created and sentence finished in the Word editor that began to make sense to them.

Workers that participated in the workshops were mostly in the C and D social classes,[3] as well as in the 25–65 years age group, concentrated mainly in the 35–45 years age group. Most did not have a computer at home, and those who had one did not use the device, reporting that their children used it.

[3] IBGE, the federal government's census bureau, classifies social classes based on the official minimum monthly salary. At the time of this publication, the minimum monthly salary was R$ 954, which is approximately US$ 300. Therefore, who makes between two to four minimum salaries (i.e., about US$ 600 to US$ 1200 a month) would be in the D class, from 4 to 10 minimum salaries in class C, from 10 to 20 minimum salaries in class B, and above 20 salaries in class A.

The DI workshop is based on a constructivist educational model, in which the subject is active and jointly responsible for his/her learning[7]. At the outset, we noticed several situations in which people never had contact with the computer, while others who had access to technologies did not know how to use them but were very eager to learn. Many revealed insecurity for fear of breaking the machine or damaging the operational system, erasing something, or even destroying the computer. In turn, all the class exercises were explained, showing their importance and practical applicability, both for the completion of the course and in their current work, as well as to facilitate their personal life activities.

Therefore, the workshop moved from acquiring basic knowledge of how to operate the computer, editing texts, and accessing the Internet and later starting the DI course in the Moodle platform. Practical activities performed in the virtual learning platform included participation in discussion forums and sending files (the same ones they produced earlier on). We repeated, as many times as necessary, computer commands and how to complete them. We also distributed a guide manual, with all the necessary steps taught in the classroom and with other teachings on basic computer science for everyday life.

Finally, CHWs were encouraged to become active and intuitively search for new functionalities on the teaching platform and the computer. We realized that the most significant challenge was not teaching them in the few practical hours everything they could possibly accomplish using a computer but to induce them to critically recognize themselves as computer operators. The exchange between classroom practice and the online functions in participants' work and personal activities contributed, in this regard, toward improving the session's results, not only for online learning but also for applying it to their jobs.

In this context, DI actions are of paramount importance for individuals. Although pre-workshop questionnaires showed that 82% use smartphones with Internet access and social media activities, they did not consider themselves to be part of the digitally included. A cellphone is currently a device for social inclusion, and its users are often unaware of what they can accomplish with them beyond ordinary activities.

The DI workshops were not and are not only for these workers a lesson but also an active space of self-knowledge and trust since these classes allow them to begin the process of overcoming their fears and barriers vis-à-vis of what is new and novel that stems from technological progress. The fear of damaging or erasing something, the feeling of inability, as well as insecurity are gradually replaced by "I can," "I am now even going to buy a computer," "I'll show my son that I already know how to use the computer," and "I will now study again all there is in the manual so that I don't forget."

In spite of the several adverse settings in this experience, such as the short period for digital inclusion workshops, rooms with obsolete physical capacity, and inadequate access to the Internet, initiatives such as these are of paramount importance to give new meaning to the role of education. And here we come to the main highlight of our experience – educating is a living process that concerns the feasibility of the other's learning process, learning how to teach and giving new meaning to the content studied (Vasconcelos 2010; Zitkoski 2006). The student will only be included in this process if this transformation has meaning in his/her life: it is not just about accessing information but about being the manager of information (Demo 2005).

Thus, the knowledge consolidated in these workshops values the use of technologies in workers' everyday lives. They built, with the group of workshop organizers, possible ways of implementing these technologies in their work. Making these subjects managers of their information contributes to the promotion of social justice.

17.7 Evaluating the Processes

Participants were given the option to evaluate the course through a semi-structured interview and a questionnaire at the end of the class.

Students could rate classes as Very Good, Good, Fair, Bad, or Very Bad. In general, the classes received positive evaluations from 404 participants who answered the assessment, and 76% (307) of the participants rated classes as Very Good, 21% (83) Good, 2% (10) Fair, and only 1% (4) Bad or Very Bad.

The first evaluation point covers what the course meant to participants and what their expectations were at the outset. The main takeaway was that the course had exceeded expectations. They were surprised with the knowledge they acquired and their advances in the workload provided (8 h, carried out in a single day), as highlighted in the section:

> [...] I arrived at this municipality 14 years ago. Participating in this course as I see it is very gratifying and vital. I'm enjoying it and am absolutely certain that all my friends are also satisfied. This course should have been given to us a long time ago. I believe so, also because I was kind of inexperienced with this stuff and for me, today, incredibly, these little minutes and hours will be very important for us who are in the working class. (Interview 7)

Another relevant aspect is the fact that workers, while having on average 9 years as employees of the Municipal Health Secretariat, had no previous training in the use and access of ICTs. This showed us two participants' wishes: the first concerns the need for complementary training, in particular, incorporating themes related to the use of health technologies; and the second refers to work computerization and replacing paper with technological devices, as can be seen in the following account:

> This was excellent news to me; it was fascinating because I have been a Community Health Worker for 23 years. In all my years as a Community Health Worker, I have never seen anything like this so focused on helping people even at work. [...] I live in a rural area, 100 km from here and I came exactly because I found it interesting. It is going to contribute a lot. I still see myself as a CHW working without paper, because, you know, the world is headed toward eliminating as much paper as possible. And now, with this course, this expectation increases even further, because that's what we've been waiting for. (Interview 8)

The previous report corresponds to another question: what are the classes' contributions to the participant? They emphasized that learning added meaning to their lives, both for improving their performance at work and in their personal lives. The main positive aspects mentioned by participants are computer use, Internet browsing, and the use of application tools in general. It is noteworthy that they felt they were unable to learn to use ICTs and felt scared. Thus, another positive aspect was the class's contribution toward instilling self-confidence and new skills.

The interviews also highlight the didactics used by teachers. According to the participants, workshop organizers acted transparently and patiently, respecting the learning pace of each of the groups:

> When I came to this course, I was "unmotivated". Because all the other courses we did, they really did not yield what we expected. And this course now, today, is captivating, you know? It stimulates people to complete the course, to know how it is going to be. The class is very dynamic...I believe it will be very interesting, mainly because, from what I saw, from the colleagues there, it made them feel like learning how to use computers. Many said [...] "I do not like to fiddle with a computer, with this machine", and now that it works, I want to have one now. As soon as class began, the staff were already very interested. I think it really is "stimulating". [...] In the end, everyone will benefit from it. It is worth it. (Interview 12)

This feedback highlights that DI initiatives are still required today, despite Silva (2016) already pointing out that half of the Brazilian households have access to the Internet, representing 32.3 million households in the country. The last ICT Households Survey, conducted in 2015 by the Internet Steering Committee in Brazil (CGI.br), included 67,038,766 households. The survey provides evidence that, in the center-west region of Brazil, where Goiás is located, only 48% of households have Internet access, ranking third after Brazil's south and southeast regions. We understand that access to information through the use of ICTs remains a challenge for the Brazilian population (CGI 2016).

In addition to feeling incapable, as mentioned in the previous account, workers considered themselves displaced by generational differences for this type of learning, affirming that a "computer is a young person's thing." At the end of the day, there was a change in their discourse, which showed that the knowledge they acquired motivated them. One interviewer stated: "I saw that it is never late to learn" (Interview 17). It is, therefore, essential for health educators to realize that digital inclusion initiatives of currently active professionals are of paramount importance for improving working conditions and quality of life.

Regarding the negative points, the primary factor is the class workload. According to students, the course should be even longer. Also, the infrastructure was also a displeasing issue to participants, because, in some municipalities, students worked in pairs sharing the same computer, which, according to them, impaired learning and took a little more time to accomplish the assigned tasks.

17.8 The Roads Ahead: The Task

The commitment of the Brazilian health system toward achieving a decentralized, comprehensive, and universal public health system necessarily furthers the democratization of health. Thus, it strengthens and increases the potential of CHWs and primary healthcare, as an organizer and coordinator of local health systems, in the provision of healthcare that is affectionate, binding, and circumscribed to the real health needs of individuals, families, and communities who are then able to assume responsibility in health prevention and promotion[4] in their living, work, and life environments. Configuring access to health services, according to Sousa (2007), establishes connections between individuals, families and communities, managers, and family health program teams permeated through social bonds and co-responsibility. It is through this permanent exercise of creating opportunities and capabilities among subjects in the processes of caring for health-illness-death that leads to expressions of respect, autonomy, and participation.

Making these people managers of their own information, whether acquired or produced, is to promote social justice through technological inclusion, as well as to subsidize improvements in the quality of their work. Because they are in direct contact with the population and because they are residents of their territory, these individuals become vital players in community health promotion. Therefore, initiatives such as these have a direct influence on access to information and, consequently, caring for SUS users in the areas under their responsibility. Training these individuals in ICTs sustains a communication model that promotes the health of the population and strengthens Brazil's healthcare model.

Digital inclusion initiatives for these individuals are, therefore, necessary actions. The gains from technological advances are immeasurable, especially as regard to preventing injuries and recovery of individual health. Still, the benefits are not any less when we refer to health promotion of individuals and the training of professionals to work together along these fronts in which technology-mediated education is highlighted.

However, it is necessary to make this model of education feasible. In addition to offering technology, we need to know how to use it. Technologies without meaning are just devices that are underutilized, so we need to make them palpable, usable, and useful.

Brazil is a country of continental dimensions and marked by inequalities across regions, levels of education, and access information. Initiatives such as DI workshops take on meaning and importance in the current context and, therefore, as a way of promoting knowledge management and multiplying know-how.

During the preparation of this chapter, the evaluation commission of the Innovation in Education Laboratory of the Brazilian Ministry of Health and the Pan American Health Organization (PAHO) selected our project out of the 251 applicants in the Permanent Education in Health. We desire that this experience is recognized thanks to the results it has achieved, since its objective is not only to facilitate digital inclusion but also to promote the autonomy of CHWs in their work, overall through the development of continuous educational projects to improve their skills. We also hope that this experience transforms these workers into educators and health promotors in their community, thus contributing toward healthy environments.

---

[4] Chapter 19 addresses the theme of ICTs and Health Promotion.

References

Brazil. 2011. *Portaria MS/GM no 2.488, de 21 de outubro de 2011. Aprova a Política Nacional de Atenção Básica, para a Estratégia de Saúde da Família (ESF) e o Programa de Agentes Comunitários de Saúde (PACS)*. Diário Oficial da União 22 out. 2011; Seção 1.

CGI – Comitê Gestor da Internet. 2016. *Survey on the use of information and communication technologies in brazilian households: ICT households 2015*. São Paulo: Brazilian Internet Steering Committee.

Demo, P. 2005. Inclusão digital: cada vez mais no centro da inclusão social. *Inclusão Social* 1: 36–38.

Freire, Paulo. 2002. *Extensão ou comunicação?* Rio de Janeiro: Paz e Terra.

IBGE – Brazilian Institute of Geography and Statistics. 2016. Pesquisa Nacional por Amostra de Domicílios Contínua – PNAD Contínua – Acesso à Internet e à televisão e posse de telefone móvel celular para uso pessoal. https://www.ibge.gov.br/estatisticas-novoportal/multidominio/condicoes-de-vida-desigualdade-e-pobreza/17270-pnad-continua.html?edicao=19937&t=sobre. Accessed 25 June 2018.

———. 2017. Brasil/ Goiás Panorama. https://cidades.ibge.gov.br/brasil/go/panorama. Accessed 25 June 2018.

Mendonça, Ana Valéria M. 2007. *Os processos de comunicação e o modelo todos-todos: uma relação possível com o Programa Saúde da Família*. Brasília: Editora do Departamento de Ciência da Informação e Documentação da Universidade de Brasília.

———. 2009. O processo de comunicação Todos-Todos e a produção de conteúdos: desafios à Gestão do Conhecimento. In *Gestão do Conhecimento em Saúde no Brasil: avanços e perspectivas*, ed. J. Moya, M.E. Santos, and Ana Valéria M. Mendonça, 18–24. Brasília: Organização Pan-Americana da Saúde.

Mendonça, Ana Valéria M., Maria Fátima de Sousa, Ronaldo Nunes Linhares, Júlio César Cabral, and Pablo Boaventura Sales Paixão. 2009. Inclusão digital dos agentes comunitários de saúde no Brasil: novas formas de aprender em rede. *Tempus – Actas de Saúde Coletiva* 3: 28–37.

Mendonça, Ana Valéria M., Grasiela S. Pereira, Mariella S. Oliveira-Costa, and Maria de Fátima Sousa. 2017. Fala Agente! Saberes e práticas comunicacionais nos territórios de atuação. In *Mediações comunicativas da saúde*, ed. Igor Sacramento, 119–133. Rio de Janeiro: Editora Multifoco.

Ministry of Health. 2006. *Política Nacional de Atenção Básica*. Brasília: Ministério da Saúde.

———. 2009. *O trabalho do Agente Comunitário de Saúde*. Brasília: Ministério da Saúde.

———. 2018. Sala de Apoio à Gestão Estratégica. http://sage.saude.gov.br/#. Accessed 6 Feb 2018.

Silva, João Paulo Fernandes. 2016. Programa de inclusão digital dos conselheiros de saúde: o uso das tecnologias de informação e comunicação auxiliam no controle social? Master' thesis, University of Brasília, Brasília.

Sousa, Maria Fátima. 2007. *Programa Saúde da Família no Brasil: análise da desigualdade no acesso à atenção básica*. Brasília: Editora do Departamento de Ciências da Informação e Documentação da Universidade de Brasília.

Toro, José Bernardo, and Nisia Maria D. Werneck. 2004. *Mobilização social: um modo de construir a democracia e a participação*. Belo Horizonte: Autêntica.

Vasconcelos, Eymard M. 2010. Redefinindo as práticas de Saúde a partir de experiências de Educação Popular nos serviços de saúde. *Interface Comunic, Saúde* 5: 121–128.

Zitkoski, Jaime J. 2006. *Paulo Freire e a educação*. Belo Horizonte: Autêntica.

Part V
Practical Applications of Digital Health Technologies

Chapter 18
mHealth: Smart Wearable Devices and the Challenges of a Refractory Context

Thiago Augusto Hernandes Rocha, Nubia Cristina da Silva, Allan Claudius Queiroz Barbosa, Cyrus Elahi, and João Ricardo Nickenig Vissoci

Abstract The development of smart wearable devices has strengthened a new area: mHealth. This is characterized by the use of mobile technologies for the diagnosis, monitoring, and intervention of health conditions. When inserted into the wider universe comprising the Internet of Things, mHealth solutions emerge with real-world applications. The myriad of mHealth-based applications already draws a scenario in which these new technologies will be responsible for changing the current logic of healthcare delivery. Nevertheless, there are numerous challenges for mHealth before its full potential can be realized. The Brazilian context is marked by peculiarities regarding the challenges for the dissemination of mHealth. There are few professionals, resistance to adopting new health technologies, an inexistent regulatory framework, regional inequalities, the absence of guidelines for protecting personal data, and difficulty associated with communication networks. Such aspects are discussed throughout this work together with components relating to the current status of development linked to mHealth.

18.1 Introduction

Today we live in a connected world. There are about 5 billion mobile phones in the world, roughly 1 for every person over 15 years old (Slovensky and Malvey 2015). Wireless connectivity allows us to access information and communicate anywhere and at any time. These characteristics of the modern world have contributed to

---

T. A. H. Rocha (✉) · N. C. da Silva · A. C. Q. Barbosa
Department of Business Administration, Faculty of Economics, Federal University of Minas Gerais, Belo Horizonte, Minas Gerais, Brazil

C. Elahi
Duke Global Health Institute, Duke University, Durham, NC, USA

J. R. N. Vissoci
Division of Emergency Medicine, Department of Surgery, Duke University, Durham, NC, USA

A. Pereira Neto, M. B. Flynn (eds.), *The Internet and Health in Brazil*,
https://doi.org/10.1007/978-3-319-99289-1_18

changing the way we work, play, and live. The impact of the Internet has irreversibly reconfigured our way of life. The implications of these innovations, associated with the possibility of unlimited communication, also resonate with health, clearing the way for the spread of mHealth. This term, coined over 20 years ago by Robert Istepanian, summarizes the new possibilities for the supply and consumption of health services facilitated by ubiquitous connectivity (Istepanian et al. 2010). Despite the many definitions of the term, it can be understood as the provision of medical services and/or public health, which use the technological support of mobile devices such as cell phones, sensors, and other smart wearable devices directly connected to the user, for monitoring or the administration of health interventions (WHO 2011). Smart wearable devices are used in equipment adjacent to the body, which are able to monitor various health parameters as well as perform health interventions.

The concept of mobile health (*mHealth*) is intricately related to the unfolding of another technology called the Internet of Things[1] (*IoT*, acronym in English). *IoT* refers to the use of devices with Internet connection capability, allowing them to interact with other devices, services, and/or people with large scale-up possibilities (Mukhopadhyay 2014). The term *IoT* was first proposed in 1999 by Massachusetts Institute of Technology (MIT). At the time, the definition was understood as the extension of communication skills to things, allowing them to communicate with each other and with people (Ashton 2009). Put differently, *IoT* allowed devices and equipment that were once isolated to interact with each other and with the Internet in an integrated fashion. Thanks to the large number of devices and applications, by 2030 *IoT* is expected to exceed people as the largest producer of information on the Internet (Evans 2011).

The concepts of the *IoT* and mHealth cluster together under a broader term linked to health: eHealth. This refers to the provision of health services remotely, built on technologies such as the Internet, smart wearable devices (SWDs), electronic medical records, telehealth, *cloud computing*, and smartphones. *mHealth* is an integral part of this ecosystem by bridging mobile solutions and *IoT* technologies services via smart wearable devices.

The applications of mHealth-based solutions are diverse and have the potential to revolutionize the way health services are performed. During the next coming years, the traditional ways of providing health services will be profoundly modified. For example, the ubiquitous availability of medical records is possible thanks to cloud storage solutions (*cloud computing*). Health professional consultations may be held electronically, with diagnostic and therapeutic information as readily available as current in-person consultations. Specific laboratory tests are no longer required since "electronic testing devices at the point of care" (DTPC) are able to collect laboratory data. This noninvasive approach possesses the same accuracy as traditional methods and can be used repeatedly. Preventive interventions, based on

[1] This aspect is also discussed in Chap. 21, which addresses the topic of the Internet of Things (IoT) applied to health in Brazil.

models of artificial intelligence, will be prioritized to prevent the occurrence of acute episodes. These are only some of the numerous possibilities.

When discussing the elements that characterize the concepts of mHealth and the *IoT*, it is crucial to understand the challenges that govern the Internet of Things. These obstacles impact the spread of mHealth solutions, especially in the Brazilian context. Therefore, it is necessary to examine the current state of both issues in relation to each other. The task of mapping the state of mHealth is challenging given the relevance the topic has received in the last 10 years. Initial attempts to trace the literature on the subject allowed us to understand the complexity of the subject and the breadth of the current scientific literature at the global level. Nevertheless, the topic is emerging within the Brazilian context. Thus, to contextualize the discussion, we decided to carry out a literature review to map out existing studies. This allowed us to better comprehend the use and development of mHealth solutions. From this, it was possible to approach the Brazilian reality in its nascent state regarding the use and development of mHealth-based applications.

After delineating the existing state of the field of mHealth, the different roles of multiple agents that operate in this field will be analyzed. Additionally, we will examine the developments already materializing in the field of mHealth which will have the potential to modify the logic of providing health services over the next few years. We will also address the challenges present in Brazil's local reality and how they relate to the prospects of incorporating solutions based on mHealth.

18.2 An Overview on Health Mobile Technology (mHealth)

Given the recent nature of the studies dedicated to mHealth, it can be said that research groups, universities, companies, and other *stakeholders* in this ecosystem occupy relatively nascent positions. A *stakeholder* is an individual, group, institution, or organization with the ability to affect the operations and success of the other agents inserted in a given ecosystem. They are also likely affected by the decisions and actions of other agents in this ecosystem (Slovensky and Malvey 2015). The relationships between the different *stakeholders* in health are much more reciprocal than unidirectional. In this sense, the evidence on the impact, degree of relevance, and relative importance in the field are still scattered or in the consolidation phase. There are several agents producing information about mHealth albeit not as a unified front. Nevertheless, it is already possible to identify countries, researchers, and centers starting to collaborate in the area.

To provide an overview of key *stakeholders* in the context of mHealth, we draw on a recent study conducted by Sweileh et al. (2017) who performed a bibliometric analysis of everything that has been produced on mHealth between the years 2006 and 2016. With this, it was possible to identify the key players leading the development of the field, their location, affiliated institutions, and partner networks.

Bibliometrics can be understood as a statistical method used to evaluate the quality and quantity of literature produced in a given context (Santha kumar and

Kaliyaperumal 2015). It also helps to identify trends, impact analysis of works by citations, and national and international contributions to a body of work in a field of study (Fatehi and Wootton 2012). Specifically, Sweileh et al. (2017) analyzed the following dimensions within mHealth: growth in the number of publications, contribution of each country, international collaboration, analysis of impact through citations, main authors and universities, and main communication channels on the subject. The data were extracted from *Scopus*; 5,464 papers were summarized. From this study, it can be seen that the volume of work has increased significantly in the 10 years analyzed. The number of papers published per year has increased almost tenfold, which points to the growing debate on mHealth and its potential applications. The increase of available data, greater propensity of *stakeholders* for the development of pilot projects, and dissemination of the importance of proper information management for designing strategies aimed at problem solving may be considered *proxies* for increasing work on the subject.

Additionally, the main topics covered in each study were processed and categorized to allow for network analysis (Sweileh et al. 2017). Creating the networks allows for an analysis of related themes, main categories, and relationships between the different actors.

As for the themes related to the papers, it is possible to highlight the management of chronic conditions as well as applications related to mental health, disease prevention, and physical activity. For chronic conditions such as diabetes, self-management was a recurrent topic in the works analyzed. Adherence to treatment was a cross-cutting topic that was related to disease prevention and also for the control of chronic conditions such as diabetes and hypertension. Solutions for the cessation of tobacco use and applications related to mental health were addressed by several of the studies considered in the analysis. Finally, there is a need to highlight issues associated with weight control, physical activity, and health promotion. Several important topics related to prevention have yet to be satisfactorily addressed by previous studies. These include the health of workers and neglected diseases. This gap suggests there is a potential niche for further discussions and for contextualized propositions that are currently lacking.

Canada, the United States, the United Kingdom, Australia, South Korea, India, Germany, China, Spain, France, the Netherlands, Switzerland, and Sweden have made major contributions to the study of mHealth. The two biggest contributors were the United Kingdom and the United States. These two countries have established themselves as leaders in the production of scholarly studies on mHealth, responsible for producing more than 40% of all studies reviewed by Sweileh et al. (2017).

There is significant overlap between the countries with the most published studies on mHealth and the location of the most outstanding institutions. Prominent research centers in mHealth are mostly located in the United States and Canada. Nine of the top 10 centers are located in these two countries. Another topic of interest is the major presence in the list of research centers in the world, mainly by universities. The main channels of communication on mHealth are the leading scientific journals. The most influential channel on mHealth is the *Journal of Medical Internet Research*. Others with considerable influential are *Artificial*

Intelligence in Medicine, JAMA, American Journal of Preventive Medicine, Lancet, and PloS One. There is also a prevalence of international journals, renowned in other areas, serving as consolidated media outlets on advances relating to mHealth.

The international studies on mHealth are extensive and have been taking place for a few decades. In the Brazilian context, however, there are studies on the subject. For one, there are few studies on the subject published in Portuguese (Rocha et al. 2016). A January 2018 survey, performed on Brazilian publications registered in the electronic database SciELO (standing for Scientific Electronic Library Online), found only two papers addressing the theme of mHealth. In addition, there is a refractory stance by institutions, academics, and policy makers on the subject. The best journals in Brazilian healthcare lacked publications on mHealth until the latter portion of 2017. The pioneering nature of this type of technology, coupled with the lack of debate in the Brazilian context, has relegated the discussion of mHealth's potential in Brazil to a secondary level (Rocha et al. 2016).

In Brazil, the overall scenario, despite the occasional initiatives, is the lag time of local scholars in relation to the level of debate that exists in the international context. The scientific communication streams in Brazil, especially those in the health field, are marked by a traditionalist stance and resistant to debates on innovations. In addition, corporatism restricts researchers from discussing innovative and unexplored themes in national literature. Thus, the stance adopted by Brazilian media outlets screens out new debates and discussions that are not part of what is traditionally discussed in the national scientific scenario. The result is a self-absorbed debate, with little propositional capacity, which seeks to legitimize itself to ensure its perennial character.

The current position of the popular science media delays more fruitful discussions that have a great disruptive potential. This eventually affects the formation of new opinions in the Brazilian context, hinders the dissemination of innovative technologies, slows the inclusion of innovative themes in the context of health policies, and fosters dependence on foreign knowledge. Only in the last 2 years do we see debates on mHealth-based applications and projects discussed on the national scene. Few of the initiatives by research groups are dedicated to examining the impact of mHealth solutions on health in the Brazilian context.

Despite the refractory academic context, there is a thriving reality regarding startups. There are several companies working in the mHealth sector that are trying to produce solutions to manage the challenges of caregiving in the context of the *IoT*. There are initiatives dedicated to including electronic medical records, management of medical services, development of *devices*, genomics, population management, engagement of patients, Big Data, developing *apps*, telemetry, wellness, and health marketing (Belle et al. 2015; Bissonnette and Bergeron 2017; Gatzoulis and Iakovidis 2007; Grossglauser and Saner 2014; Handel 2011; Martin 2012; Nicholas et al. 2015; Soh et al. 2013; Srivastava et al. 2015; West 2012).

The next two decades will witness an unprecedented revolution in the way health services are delivered. Their impact on the provision of health services will vary to differing degrees. It is expected that there will be an improvement in health conditions observed today. We will examine the central agents of this process and their associated limitations and potential.

18.3 Role in Disruptive Technologies in Health: Key Stakeholders Involved in the Development of mHealth Solutions

A first step to better understand the *stakeholders* active in a given context is to classify them according to similarity of activity or source of power. In a simplified way, the sources of a *stakeholder's* power come from one or more of the following: control over necessary resources, mastery of critical skills for the design and operation of processes, position as required service provider, holds political influence, has veto power, and is responsible for large volumes of purchases or financial transactions. We can construct the environment for mHealth by taking into account these sources. The main *stakeholders* in this scenario would be: patients, either as individuals or organized into groups; doctors and other health professionals; institutions providing care; agents responsible for care cost coverage, such as government and healthcare operators; pharmaceutical corporations; technology companies; and providers of communication services (Slovensky and Malvey 2015). All these agents act interdependently, contributing to the characterization of the mHealth ecosystem. This typology of *stakeholders* involved in the mHealth ecosystem is only an approximation in defining categories for the main agents operating in this ecosystem.

18.3.1 Patients

The main items valued by patients seeking health services, with respect to mHealth, are healthcare solutions that simplify the resolution of current problems. Complex solutions that increase the difficulty of monitoring biomedical parameters, release impertinent warnings, and/or have a high learning curve are classically abandoned by end users (Slovensky and Malvey 2015). Patients are faced with a very large volume of smart wearable devices, medical information, and *apps* for monitoring health conditions. Nevertheless, those solutions with empowering features that simplify the troubleshooting process associated with obtaining care and improving access to medical care get a higher degree of acceptance (Siau and Shen 2006).

18.3.2 Doctors and Other Health Professionals

Historically, doctors and health professionals have assumed been spokespersons regarding therapeutic strategies and the provision of health-related information. Technology has changed these roles and empowered healthcare consumers with information not previously available. mHealth will only encourage this trend, since not only clinical information will be more accessible but also reliable data for diagnosis. The availability of accurate information that will allow the patients themselves to be guided by the nuances of differential diagnoses will require a reconfiguration of the roles played by health professionals.

Medicine is an area resistant to the incorporation of new technologies. Not only will the relationship with patients be adjusted but also the way professionals perform their daily activities. It will no longer be necessary to have backup diagnostic and therapeutic support services in the manner that exists today. Professionals will be able to test and examine multiple diagnostic possibilities with data from biomedical markers directly in their offices. Especially for simpler questions, doctors will not need to develop third-party services. The increased use of smartphones in the clinical setting is already a proxy for this trend (Nerminathan et al. 2017). A study conducted by a research institute in Florida found accessing electronic medical records by primary care physicians on their *tablets* or smartphones has increased significantly, indicating that professionals have chosen to get access to their patients' medical information using a cloud platform. This type of platform is similar to those that mHealth telemetry centers can provide.

Stakeholders interested in the development of mHealth solutions must be prepared to overcome the obstacles that are still present, especially in relation to resistance by health professionals in using technology-based solutions. Evidence from recent studies show an emerging trend for the dissemination of solutions based on mHealth. This scenario, however, is not yet completely set, and the resistance of some professional groups represents a hurdle. Slovensky and Malvey (2015) pointed out that among the medical specialties, those most resistant to the incorporation of new technologies are orthopedists, ophthalmologists, and otolaryngologists. Moreover, these authors pointed out that government incentives to encourage new technologies in the workplace have been effective in raising the awareness of previously resistant groups on the importance of adopting new solutions. This may be a way to facilitate the spread of mHealth applications.

18.3.3 Care Providers and Health Systems

Health service providers are strongly vested players in the massification of mHealth solutions. Initiatives have been undertaken with the objective of increasing the use of mHealth applications, as these have the potential to improve the quality of life of patients with a concomitant reduction in healthcare provision costs.

The ability to monitor biomedical markers continuously and link the results to electronic medical records with unique identifiers opens the possibility of implementing *healthcare analytics* solutions for performing predictive analysis. Such analyses can be used to stratify the risk of a given population or user profile, design interventions for health promotion and disease prevention, and prevent medical complications from acute episodes such as stroke, heart attacks, or amputations.

Many companies have taken advantage of this niche. The development of predictive solutions dedicated to minimize care supply costs has been met with euphoria by the market and has spurred the development of startups. Companies like Weltok[2] have adopted an aggressive procurement policy to cover the widest possible range of services associated with providing predictive healthcare solutions in the United States.

In Brazil, initiatives of this nature are limited, but there are already some startups such as Hekima[3] and Pyron[4] health seeking to develop solutions in the health arena.

For health systems, the benefits are even greater due the volume of care and the potential benefits that can be earned for the population as a whole. In terms of spending, the potential savings as well as improvement in people's quality of life are significant.

In Brazil, a solution for electronic medical records has been in development for some years, the SUS card (Ministry of Health 2015). The idea is to provide a national health record number to each user of the public system in order to monitor patient demands more accurately. This type of health data management device opens the possibility of developing population health monitoring applications for injury prevention capabilities and health promotion.

The health minimum data set (CMD[5]) unites nine systems within SUS: Outpatient Production Bulletin (BPA), Outpatient Procedure Authorization (APAC), Registration of Ambulatory Health Actions (RAAS), Hospitalization Authorization (SISAIH01), Collection Communication Hospital Information and Outpatient (CIHA01), Outpatient Information System (CIS), Hospital Information System (HIS), Hospital Information Communication Processing and Outpatient (CIHA 02), and Regulation System, Control and Evaluation (SISRCA) (Ministry of Health 2017). All public and private health facilities in the country will record information for the minimum data set. The data can be sent through the existing systems that will be integrated into DATASUS. The availability of such data will create opportunities for new applications developed for SUS such as solutions based on predictive analytics.

18.3.4 Institutions

The pharmaceutical industry is considered an important agent in the context of mHealth due to its heavy investments in research and the substantial volumes of financial resources involved (Slovensky and Malvey 2015).

The development of innovative solutions for the treatment of diseases passes through research on new drugs and the use of nanotechnology to a more effective model of drug administration (Reddy and Aggarwal 2015; Rodrigues et al. 2016). The disruptive potential of these solutions is immense, and the way medicines are

[2] Welltok, Inc.: https://welltok.com/analytic_services/.

[3] Hekima: http://www.hekima.com/.

[4] Piron: https://piron.co/.

[5] All system acronyms are in Portuguese.

discovered, prescribed, marketed, and managed will change substantially over the next few years due to innovations associated with mHealth. There are already smart wearable devices that can deliver drugs in response to metabolic changes in real time. In addition, there is a whole range of innovative solutions in health supported by nanotechnology. Clinical protocols have been impacted as drug treatments are reinvented. Thus, drug therapies will be modified in light of new possibilities for drug administration and dosage control.

18.3.5 Technology and Private Business Investors

The environment for developing new applications anchored in information technology requires its own logic. The creation of startups, applications, and platform solutions or services usually receives support from incubators and accelerators looking to equip entrepreneurs with the skills needed to increase the chances of business success.

There are several funds dedicated to financing good ideas in health. There are global initiatives in this direction with possibilities on almost every continent. The study on the action plan designed for the *IoT* in Brazil contains an entire section analyzing and comparing research funding initiatives in *IoT* worldwide (National Development Bank 2017). In Brazil, there are government-based financing initiatives with the National Development Bank (BNDES) and Finep Startup Program (as known as the Funded Studies and Projects).

The quest to make the ideas developed in the startup environment more concrete has produced some interesting results, especially in solving practical problems in a scalable way. Some startups have been devoted to the development of hardware solutions with quite impressive results. Bragi[6], a German startup, is a prime example. A challenge for disseminating smart wearable devices is the ability to capture multimodal biomedical parameters. This type of capture allows data from multiple sensors to be collected simultaneously, creating new monitoring possibilities. Few smart wearable devices have this ability, and it is critical toward improving quality of information generated by *IoT* devices dedicated to health. The potential associated with mHealth cannot transcend the realm of promises without this kind of data capture since interoperability between solutions is an obstacle. Bragi developed a headset with multimodal capability, long battery life, and superb ergonomics at reasonable price. The device, called DASH, embodies what smart wearable devices need to be in conceptual terms. Thus, some initiatives are already providing real-world solutions with the potential to capture the promise associated with mHealth.

The role of private investors and technology companies within mHealth is to address and overcome challenges in hopes of achieving the full potential of the field. There are numerous technology giants such as Google, Amazon, IBM, Oracle, Samsung, and Apple with health initiatives. The epidemiological transition process

[6] Bragi: https://www.bragi.com/.

across the globe has increased attention dedicated to health as a potential source of financial gains.

Finally, a challenge that is still present is demonstrating the potential to monetize innovations associated with mHealth. Because it is a new technology, there are still no validated business models. As a result, some investors prefer to adopt a more conservative stance with orders placed for mHealth solutions. The ability to prove profitability is linked to demonstrating results that can add value to the *stakeholders* involved. This is another peculiarity related to the issue of private investment (Slovensky and Malvey 2015).

18.3.6 Providers of Communications Services

mHealth depends fundamentally on a solid communication infrastructure. Without it, the possibility to transmit data reliably and in real time is lost and, with it, one of the main benefits from this type of technology. The role associated with communication service providers is crucial to enable the spread of mHealth.

The infrastructure available in most parts of the globe is precariously positioned to support the transit of information according to the standards required by *IoT* solutions. Overall, there are still issues to be addressed in order to provide an adequate environment for reliable data transmission. Without proper management of these circumstances, the widespread dissemination of mHealth applications will be constrained by barriers related to access and the quality of communication services.

The evolving situation is complex, marked by multiple agents shaped by several determining factors. It is critical to understand how different *stakeholders* adjacent to mHealth are intertwined in order to establish partnerships, select trends to monitor, and mentor opinion leaders. Knowing the different *stakeholders*, their aspirations, importance, and networks is fundamental for creating more favorable conditions in the management of an unstable environment as seen with mHealth.

It is possible to envision a series of modifications to the provision of healthcare resulting from the influence of the aforementioned agents. So, we will examine how the technologies linked to mHealth can make changes and analyze the different *devices* for intelligent monitoring of health conditions.

18.4 Potential Associated with the Smart Wearable Devices: New Perspectives of Care

The current provision of health services will change considering the ongoing diffusion of smart wearable devices. From a population perspective, SWD can facilitate the dissemination of health information, improve epidemiological surveillance aspects, and expand the volume of data available for research. They will also encourage improvements in the organization of healthcare networks, service utilization profiles, and access parameters that can be modeled in real time based on geolocation data.

Interventions for health promotion and disease prevention can be made based on predictive information from the analysis of patients' biomarkers. Such an approach will help to minimize the negative consequences of acute events such as complications associated with diabetes, hypertension, and acute coronary syndrome. In addition, patients may take a more active role with their care. Data collected by smart wearable devices can empower patients leading to more precise management of chronic conditions. Doctors will be able to monitor their patients continuously, leveraging time series data. This is an upgrade from intermittent laboratory tests which do not allow accurate situational monitoring. Additionally, thanks to telemetry monitoring, patients being transported in emergency mobile units can be received in the emergency centers with backup infrastructure already adjusted for their health needs.

Salient procedures for the diagnosis of diseases can be performed directly in health facilities, or even in homes, since there are already devices that can monitor noninvasive biomarkers. The use of nanosensors will contribute to expanded diagnostic possibilities. They can be performed in real time, involving diseases such as cancer or infectious affections. Lifestyle patterns can be linked to biomedical markers assisting professionals and patients in outlining the best strategies for chronic disease management.

Figure 18.1 highlights four main areas and the different existing capacities related to smart wearable devices with respect to mHealth's potential.

In the second half of 2017, 406 *devices* from 273 different companies were mapped as smart wearable devices for external use only. Of this group of 273 companies,

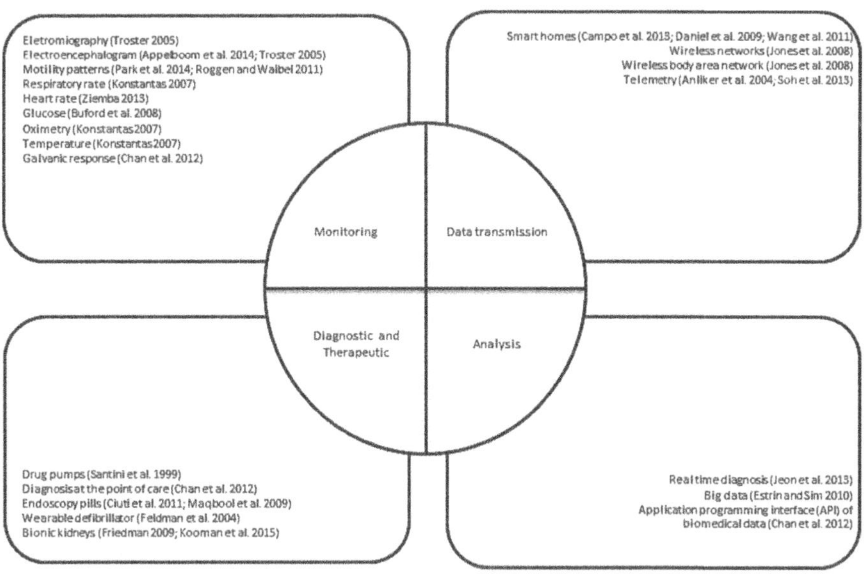

Fig. 18.1 Established possibilities for smart wearable devices. (Source: Rocha et al. (2016))

51 manufacture more than 1 device. The complete list of *devices* currently available can be accessed at: https://vandrico.com/wearables/list. This list of devices has been built collaboratively and has a satisfactory coverage mapping out solutions and updating data. The list provided in this website is extensive, but not exhaustive. There are few systematic initiatives that map out all the devices due to the industry's rapid production of new products, which makes it difficult to maintain a current central repository. There are some works, such as Chan et al. (2012), which sought to provide an overview of existing technologies and manufacturers. This work, however, is becoming dated given the rapid innovations within the field.

These innovations represent the initial steps of the revolution that will be promoted by the expanding use of mHealth solutions. The main advantage associated with this type of technology is linked to the use of information. mHealth creates the basis for the development of *healthcare analytic* solutions by making continuous data capture possible. Part of an incipient scientific field called data science, the domain of *healthcare analytics*, brings together knowledge of computer science, statistics, epidemiology, and public health to transform health data to an effective substrate for care management based on evidence (Reddy and Aggarwal 2015).

The application of analytical solutions has the potential to transform healthcare delivery from being reactive to a proactive approach. The analysis of clinical data based on this set of techniques facilitates the identification of hidden patterns in the data allowing patients to improve their health, professionals to develop unique and more effective therapeutic programs, and managers to organize health systems based on the assumptions provided therein (Porter and Lee 2013).

A new set of techniques is required for proper data management in order for the potential of the Information Age to be reached. Dedicated tools to extract nonobvious patterns from large data volumes belong to the field of "artificial intelligence," particularly from the subsection called "machine learning." This subspecialization allows computer systems to infer patterns from data and can then execute automated activities (Ali et al. 2016). Intrinsically linked to the area of machine learning is another field that deals with the realization of predictive models. Predictive modeling is simply the prediction of future behavior for a particular object of analysis based on past behavior. For this, it relies on data mining techniques and statistical modeling (Shmueli and Koppius 2011).

The adoption of *healthcare analytic* techniques carries the potential to modify existing forms of organization and healthcare provision. There are countless possibilities to capitalize on information and communication technologies in health. At first glance, the benefits to clinical care appear limited to the individual level. However, the mass use of these solutions allows potential advances to expand to the population realm and macro-level management. Despite the potential, the challenges to consolidate this type of technology loom large. There are numerous issues that need to be addressed to allow the dissemination of this set of technologies when examining a global scenario.

The challenges are even greater when one considers the Brazilian context. We will examine the current existing bottlenecks that are slowing the expansion of these innovations.

18.5 The Locoregional Challenges of the Brazilian Context

The Brazilian locoregional challenges that will be presented below are based on the research carried out, with the support of "National Bank for Economic and Social Development" (BNDES), examining the challenges that underlie the country's reality. The ongoing diagnosis by the BNDES highlighted several technological challenges of *mHealth* specific to Brazil: the lack of infrastructure, legal complexity, and lack of skilled labor. So the obstacles to mHealth applications in Brazil are permeated by additional determinants related to our local and regional characteristics.

The first element addressed is about the infrastructure of local communication networks. Currently there are few companies operating in this sector in Brazil, and there is a need for investments aimed at improvements. There is no high-speed Internet coverage throughout the country, and there are regions without any coverage. Expansion is fundamental to enable designs based on mHealth (McKinsey & Company 2016).

Opening the sector to private companies accelerated the process of infrastructure improvement, but not enough to ensure the necessary support for the operational development of *IoT* applications. Current sectoral regulation determines the provision of telecommunication services through grants. Thus, there are unanswered questions about who should receive the grants for *IoT packaged* services. International data roaming is another issue. *IoT* solutions and the associated data traffic do not respect national geographical boundaries (McKinsey & Company 2016). The question of taxation in relation to the services provided is still an unanswered question. The issue of infrastructure will be a bottleneck for the traffic of high-speed information intrinsic to the IoT unless we rethink the current legal framework and construct actions to stimulate communication.

Another critical element pervades the quality of services. *IoT* applications have different requirements in terms of transmission quality, speed, latency, and bandwidth. There is a need to reflect on what niches will demand what type of transmission pattern and with what type of quality. The definition of a single quality standard does not seem appropriate in the *IoT* context, and it will be necessary to differentiate the telecommunication connections and services that will operate as *IoT* infrastructure.

The use of a radio frequency in Brazil requires prior government authorization. Some applications of *IoT* require this scarce good, and it will be necessary to think about strategies to relax the limits of applications for unlicensed frequencies, make use of *white spaces*, and consider the possibility of promoting the relocation of tracks (McKinsey & Company 2016) .

The approval of equipment also limits the adoption of telecommunications solutions in Brazil. The work of the National Telecommunications Agency (ANATEL) only allows approved equipment to be marketed. The advent of *IoT* is expected to produce a significant increase in the amount of applications to be examined for approval. This process, which can take months, represents a bottleneck for adopting new solutions. There is a need to rethink this process, maintain speed, and ensure security and interoperability levels (McKinsey & Company 2016).

As for IP systems, migration from IPv4 to IPv6 is not yet fully complete in Brazil. IPv6 is essential for the connection of *IoT* devices (McKinsey & Company 2016). It is important to examine what obstacles remain and take measures to overcome them. The volume of devices to be registered will constantly increase in the coming years with no prospect that they level off.

Interoperability standards are another key point in the Brazilian reality. Standard requirements are often based on an attempt to avoid lock-in practices. However, agents have been left to themselves to define the standards to be used. This has fostered an environment of competition and no standardization. The lack of standardization hinders integration of solutions between different manufacturers, making the development of applications difficult. The regulatory standards are not healthy, and the lack of intervention has resulted in obstacles for the development of integrated applications in Brazil.

The Brazilian legal scenario adds another nuance to an already complex context: the absence of specific legislation on personal data protection. The absence of this regulation creates an unsafe environment for users and companies that can negatively impact the development of *IoT* applications. The need to develop a framework that protects users without stifling the industry is a technical and political challenge still unresolved (McKinsey & Company 2016). Government regulation has emerged as a constricting factor of innovation. Barriers erected by laws, agencies, and regulations have hindered faster adoption of *IoT* solutions and, as result, mHealth.

From the business point of view, there are no tested and validated models relating to mHealth which could serve as a guide for investors and entrepreneurs. There is little evidence of the ability to monetize the technologies, gaps in consumer perception persist, and there are no studies demonstrating the effectiveness of mHealth-based solutions (Slovensky and Malvey 2015). Another characteristic feature of the health sector is resistance to adopt disruptive technologies (Christensen et al. 2000). Slovensky and Malvey (2015) show that the average time for an innovation to become a clinical standard is 17 years. This culture reflects the stance of the medical professional community, who tend to take a more conservative position when adopting innovations (Slovensky and Malvey 2015).

mHealth solutions are commonly made using a top-down approach. Changes are promoted by a person with hierarchical authority with the purpose of ensuring that health professionals adopt policies, protocols, and preestablished workflows. As such, many programs miss an opportunity for improvement by leaving out health professionals and patients in the design of projects and implementation. Adaptability increases when end users are part of the process (Whittaker et al. 2012). Brazil is not immune to these problems as there is resistance from local agents on the incorporation of technologies associated with mHealth and *IoT* (POETAS.IT 2016).

Finally, the biggest challenge existing in the Brazilian reality is human. Applications of eHealth and *mHealth* have great promise to improve global health. As these projects develop, managers need to be aware of the need for an adequate labor force that enables its implementation and understand healthcare, information technology, communication channels, the people involved, and the organizational challenges.

Despite these needs, what we see is a labor shortage. According to the *World Health Report* of 2006, a health workforce deficit was documented in 57 countries, the worst scenario being in Southeast Asia (Adibi 2015). According to some national estimates, the world needs more than four million doctors, nurses, pharmacists, laboratory technicians, midwives, community health workers, and other frontline health professionals (Bollinger et al. 2013). In Brazil, the health professional category with the largest deficit is medical. The ratio of physicians per thousand inhabitants in Brazil is close to 2 per 100,000.[7] There are also major internal variations as to the proportion of doctors per capita. The north and northeast regions, which are those of lower economic development in the country, have lower medical rates per capita, while the most developed region has nearly 4 physicians per 100,000 inhabitants (Biffi and Tuissi 2017).

The lack of human resources in the health sector is an identified bottleneck to achieving universal access to quality healthcare. However, there is also lack of training, guidance, and continued educational opportunities for quality healthcare professionals interested in innovation-related training programs (Hersh et al. 2010). More specific health labor market research is needed to better characterize the necessary workforce, along with the roles, skills, and great education levels of workers (Hersh et al. 2010).

The context of the IT professional labor market is similar to that of doctors but with an aggravating factor; they are among the professions with severe professional shortages in the Brazilian and world market. The situation regarding a new category called data scientist specialists is even more delicate.

Brazil has a great need for data scientists, with fewer than 200 professionals across the country. These individuals are capable to handle large volumes of data (*Big Data*), integrate databases, analyze structured and unstructured data, and develop predictive models. All these skills are indispensable features for working with *mHealth*. It is clear that these shortages can interfere with project and program implementation since the competition for this business is fierce (Pereira 2017).

A good data scientist is expert in at least four areas of knowledge: (i) communication, (ii) statistics, (iii) programming, and (iv) business. Demand for data scientists worldwide will exceed the volume of professionals being trained. Moreover, this kind of talent is hard to produce, taking years of training for someone with intrinsic math skills (Manyika et al. 2011).

The remuneration will naturally be an aggravating factor in disseminating the potential associated with the work of data scientist. Moreover, an informal survey of data scientists' priorities revealed something even more important: this professional wants to be the "central command." Considering how difficult it is find and hold onto data scientists, one would assume that a good strategy is to hire them as consultants. Most consulting firms, however, do not have many of these professionals. Even the large companies – Accenture, Deloitte, IBM Global Services – struggle when it comes to supporting *Big Data* projects for their clients. Resources from data

[7] Europe's rate was 3.3 in 2014 (WHO 2015).

scientists who are already part of the team are being applied primarily to more conventional quantitative analysis problems (Davenport and Patil 2011).

Such shortage drives competition for data scientists culminating in many of the professionals opting for large corporations. Microsoft alone has more data scientists than all of Brazil. Countries in distress cannot fill this workforce gap by simply importing talent or changing the graduate requirements and waiting for people to be trained with more skills (although these may be important actions to take). It will be necessary to recycle a significant amount of talent on the spot and invest in education to address the adequacy of professionals in the market.

In short, the *IoT* and mHealth scenario is complex and involves multiple stakeholders. Its complexity is itself part of the object to which the whole context seeks to address. Health problems, too, are complex and multifaceted. Developing solutions to these problems requires coordinated work between different *stakeholders* to create value for both those who consume services and for those responsible for providing care. The challenges associated with technological development of *IoT*, and therefore mHealth, have not yet been fully addressed. Regarding this aspect, Mukhopadhyay (2014) argues that some of the main issues to be addressed are miniaturization, availability of the Internet, the development of sensors for wireless sensor networks (WSN) and radio-frequency identification (RFID), improvement of security and privacy standards, need for cheaper components, fault tolerance, consumption and energy saving, user acceptance, and training of specialists. These issues still present obstacles that have not been completely overcome and that, in some context, end up limiting the potential associated with *IoT* and mHealth solutions. Another key point is the ubiquitous availability of the Internet. Generally speaking, the observed situation is that of a challenging state that requires further ripening.

18.6 Future Directions: What the Future Holds for mHealth Solutions

Despite more than 20 years exploring this concept, we still cannot say for sure where the spread of mHealth will take us. Any such attempt is speculative at best due to the sector's inherent complexity and challenges. What is known is that mHealth is a disruptive innovation, marked by immense potential, since it creates possibilities to reorganize the way health has previously been treated. Despite its recent development, it can be said that addressing the challenges related to mHealth is not done linearly. The structure is more like a ladder in which there are periods of stagnation, followed by abrupt progress (Slovensky and Malvey 2015).

Fitbit applications, for example, emerged as a device for monitoring training. However, recently, with the incorporation of some sensors, they were redirected to follow up variations of blood pressure and heart rate for patients undergoing cardiac surgery (Alharbi et al. 2016). The path that has been trodden by mHealth is no different from those already covered by other innovations that have an impact on health. In the early twentieth century, the logic of visiting doctors by patients was modified considering the invention of the car (Slovensky and Malvey 2015). Hospitals have become the main locations of complex surgeries, thanks to the availability of support services and diagnostic anesthesia (Slovensky and Malvey 2015). All these changes took time and were gradually incorporated into health frameworks.

The gradual incorporation of new innovations is a hallmark of healthcare. At the beginning of the early 1980s, computers were used in hospitals to perform accounts payable processing procedures and other financial features. The incorporation of such technology to support care was performed only in a second instance. In order to incorporate a technology together with the health services delivery system, there is a need for evidence on the positive impact on improving health outcome indicators, promoting healthier behaviors in the population, increasing patient engagement with the treatment guidelines provided, and improving the efficiency of care delivery (Slovensky and Malvey 2015). For many items, mHealth is still a promise without solid evidence. Nevertheless, the search for such evidence has been increasing, once there is an enlargement of the debate on mHealth and its unfoldings (Sweileh et al. 2017).

Systematic adjustments are needed to catalyze the necessary changes to realize mHealth's proclaimed potential benefits. The first change is related to developing a culture of innovation. This is different from the mere incorporation of innovations (Slovensky and Malvey 2015). A culture of innovation allows simultaneous consideration of the different aspects necessary for a solution to reach maximum potential. This means reinventing the logic of providing care so that it takes into account a different supply system, new roles associated with the players acting in this system, a new operational infrastructure, and any misunderstandings that will be committed throughout the process of improvement.

The future of mHealth is seen today as something fluid, tenuous, and dependent on multiple factors. Nevertheless, the new possibilities arising from this mobility are a trend with no return. Mobility associated with healthcare provides the opportunity to address disparities in care, especially among minorities and disadvantaged populations (Slovensky and Malvey 2015). The strengthening of mobile connectivity solutions related to health is something that will crystalize over the next few years. For the other aspects of this technology, the only certainty is uncertainty.

The Brazilian context and prospects waiting on the horizon are challenging. Overcoming obstacles that exist in our local reality will require coordinated efforts in multiple areas and sectors to allow the design of an environment conducive to the development of mHealth solutions. Aware of the size of this challenge, the first point to address would be to dilute resistance that leaves the Brazilian context refractory to the use and incorporation of new technologies. The health sector has some formidable views, predominantly among professionals, who occupy positions of power. This ultimately leads to the mantra of resistance to change. The unfounded resistance to new changes, given the volume of international evidence, seems to be based on the need to maintain an already outdated agenda. This stance is only capable of supporting projects and resources in already solidified areas and to the benefit of those in positions of power. Overcoming this first hurdle may create more suitable conditions for disruptive applications to be developed in the Brazilian context.

References

Adibi, Sasan. 2015. *Mhealth: Multidisciplinary verticals*. Boca Raton: CRC Press.

Alharbi, Muaddi, Adrian Bauman, Lis Neubeck, and Robyn Gallagher. 2016. Validation of Fitbit-Flex as a measure of free-living physical activity in a community-based phase III cardiac rehabilitation population. *European Journal of Preventive Cardiology* 23: 1476–1485.

Ali, Anwaar, Junaid Qadir, Raihan ur Rasool, Arjuna Sathiaseelan, Andrej Zwitter, and Jon Crowcroft. 2016. Big data for development: Applications and techniques. *Big Data Analytics* 1: 2.

Anliker, Urs, Jamie A. Ward, Paul Lukowicz, Gerhard Tröster, et al. 2004. AMON: A wearable multiparameter medical monitoring and alert system. *IEEE Transactions on Information Technology in Biomedicine* 8: 415–427.

Appelboom, Geoff, Elvis Camacho, Mickey E. Abraham, Samuel S. Bruce, Emmanuel Dumont, et al. 2014. Smart wearable body sensors for patient self-assessment and monitoring. *Archives of Public Health* 72: 28.

Ashton, Kevin. 2009. In the real world, things matter more than ideas. *RFID Journal*. http://www.rfidjournal.com/articles/pdf?4986. Accessed 9 May 2018.

Belle, Ashwin, Raghuram Thiagarajan, S.M. Reza Soroushmehr, Fatemeh Navidi, Daniel A. Beard, and Kayvan Najaria. 2015. Big Data analytics in healthcare. *BioMed Research International* 2015: 1–16.

Biffi, Carlo A., and Ausonio Tuissi. 2017. Stato dell'arte sulle tecniche di produzione additiva per metalli. *Metallurgia Italia* 1: 5–10.

Bissonnette, Luc, and Michel G. Bergeron. 2017. Portable devices and mobile instruments for infectious diseases point-of-care testing. *Expert Review of Molecular Diagnostics* 17: 471–494.

BNDES – National Development Bank. 2017. Benchmark de iniciativas e políticas públicas: relatório final. https://www.bndes.gov.br/wps/wcm/connect/site/48fff464-7a3c-442b-98c3-aa4634ad08d8/Relatorio-de-benchmark-fase-1-20170516_Produto_Frente_1_Benchmark_ENTREGA_FORMAL_FinalRevisado.pdf?MOD=AJPERES&CVID=lNGCXmw. Accessed 16 May 2018.

Bollinger, Robert, Larry Chang, Reza Jafari, Thomas O'Callaghan, Peter Ngatia, Dykki Settle, Jane McKenzie-White, et al. 2013. Leveraging information technology to bridge the health workforce gap. *Bulletin of the World Health Organization* 91: 890–892.

Buford, Randall Jean, Eric C. Green, and Melanie J. McClung. 2008. A microwave frequency sensor for non-invasive blood glucose measurement. IEEE Sensors Applications Symposium 2008: 4–7.

Campo, Eric, D. Hewson, C. Gehin, and N. Noury. 2013. Theme D: Sensors, wearable devices, intelligent networks and smart homecare for health. *Irbm* 34: 11–13.

Chan, Marie, Daniel Estèvea, Jean-Yves Fourniols, Christophe Escriba, and Eric Campo. 2012. Smart wearable systems: Current status and future challenges. *Artificial Intelligence in Medicine* 56: 137–156.

Christensen, Clayton M., Richard Bohmer, and John Kenagy. 2000. Will disruptive innovation cure health care? *Harvard Business Review* 78: 102–112.

Ciuti, Gastone, Arianna Menciassi, and Paolo Dario. 2011. Capsule endoscopy: From current achievements to open challenges. *IEEE Reviews in Biomedical Engineering* 4: 59–72.

Daniel, Kathryn M., Carolyn L. Cason, and Sherry Ferrell. 2009. Emerging technologies to enhance the safety of older people in their homes. *Geriatric Nursing(Minneap)*. 30: 384–389.

Davenport, Thomas H., and D. J. Patil. 2011. Data scientist: The sexiest job of the 21st century. Harvard Business Review. https://hbr.org/2012/10/data-scientist-the-sexiest-job-of-the-21st-century. Accessed 9 May 2018.

Estrin, Deborah, and Ida Sim. 2010. Health care delivery – Open mHealth architecture: An engine for health care innovation. *Science* 330: 759–760.

Evans, Dave. 2011. The Internet of Things: How the next evolution of the internet is changing everything. CISCO. https://www.cisco.com/c/dam/en_us/about/ac79/docs/innov/IoT_IBSG_0411FINAL.pdf. Accessed 9 May 2018.

Fatehi, Farhad, and Richard Wootton. 2012. Telemedicine, telehealth or e-health?: A bibliometric analysis of the trends in the use of these terms. *Journal of Telemedicine and Telecare* 18: 460–464.

Feldman, Arthur M., Helmut Klein, Patrick Tchou, Srinivas Murali, W. Jackson Hall, Donna Mancini, John Boehmer, Mark Harvey, et al. 2004. Use of a wearable defibrillator in terminating tachyarrhythmias in patients at high risk for sudden death: Results of WEARIT/BIROAD. *PACE – Pacing and Clinical Electrophy* 27: 4–9.

Gatzoulis, Loukianos, and Ilias Iakovidis. 2007. Wearable and portable eHealth systems. *IEEE Engineering in Medicine and Biology Magazine* 26: 51–56.

Grossglauser, Matt, and Hugo Saner. 2014. Data-driven healthcare: From patterns to actions. *European Journal of Preventive Cardiology* 21: 14–17.

Handel, Marsha J. 2011. mHealth (mobile health): Using apps for health and wellness. *Explore: The Journal of Science and Healing* 7: 256–261.

Hersh, William, Alvaro Margolis, Fernán Quirós, and Paula Otero. 2010. Building a health informatics workforce in developing countries. *Health Affairs* 29: 274–277.

Istepanian, Robert S.H., Swamy Laxminarayan, and Constantinos S. Pattichis, eds. 2010. *M-Health: Emerging mobile health systems*. New York: Springer.

Jeon, Byungkook, Jundong Lee, and Jaehong Choi. 2013. Design and implementation of a wearable ECG system. *International Journal of Smart Home* 7: 61–70.

Jones, V.M., R. Huis in't Veld, T. Tonis, et al. 2008. Biosignal and context monitoring: Distributed multimedia applications of Body Area Networks in healthcare. *IEEE 10th Workshop on Multimedia Signal Processing:* 820–825.

Konstantas, Dimitri. 2007. An overview of wearable and implantable medical sensors. *Yearbook of Medical Informatics:* 66–69.

Kooman, Jeroen P., Jaap Joles, and Karin G. Gerritsen. 2015. Creating a wearable artificial kidney: Where are we now? *Expert Review of Medical Devices* 12: 373–376.

Manyika, James, Michael Chui, Brad Brown, Jacques Bughin, Richard Dobbs et al. 2011. *Big data*: The next frontier for innovation, competition, and productivity. *McKinsey Glob. Inst.* https://bigdatawg.nist.gov/pdf/MGI_big_data_full_report.pdf. Accessed 9 May 2018.

Maqbool, Sabba, Henry P. Parkman, and Frank K. Friedenberg. 2009. Wireless capsule motility: Comparison of the SmartPill GI Monitoring System with scintigraphy for measuring whole gut transit. *Digestive Diseases and Sciences* 54: 2167–2174.

Martin, Thomas. 2012. Assessing mHealth: Opportunities and barriers to patient engagement. *Journal of Health Care for the Poor and Underserved* 23: 935–941.

McKinsey & Company. Internet das Coisas: um plano de ação para o Brasil [Internet]. Brasília; 2016.

Ministry of Health. 2015. *Sistemas de informação da atenção à Saúde: contexto históricos, avanços e perspectivas no SUS*. Brasília: Ministry of Health.

———. Brazil. 2017. Conjunto Mínimo de Dados. http://datasus.saude.gov.br/noticias/atualizacoes/1033-ministerio-da-saude-avanca-nainformatizacao-do-sus. Accessed 17 Dec 2017.

Mukhopadhyay, Subhas Chandra. 2014. *Internet of Things applications: Challenges and opportunities*. New York: Springer.

Nerminathan, Arany, Amanda Harrison, Megan Phelps, Karen M. Scott, and Shirley Alexander. 2017. Doctors' use of mobile devices in the clinical setting: A mixed methods study. *Internal Medicine Journal* 47: 291–298.
Nicholas, Jennifer, Mark Erik Larsen, Judith Proudfoot, and Helen Christensen. 2015. Mobile apps for bipolar disorder: A systematic review of features and content quality. *Journal of Medical Internet Research* 17: e198.
Park, Jin-Tae, Hyun-Seo Hwang, and Il-Young Moon. 2014. Study of wearable smart band for a user motion recognition system. *International Journal of Smart Home* 8: 33–44.
Pereira, Tiago. 2017. Cientista de dados: por onde começar em 8 passos. Data Science Academy. http://datascienceacademy.com.br/blog/cientista-de-dados-por-onde-comecar-em-8-passos/. Accessed 9 May 2018.
POETAS.IT. 2016. IoT: uma estratégia para o Brasil. www.cesar.org.br/poetas.it/visionstatement. Accessed 9 May 2018.
Porter, Michael E., and Thomas H. Lee. 2013. The strategy that will fix health care. *Harvard Business Review*. https://hbr.org/2013/10/the-strategy-that-will-fix-health-care. Accessed 9 May 2018.
Reddy, Chandan, and Charu Aggarwal. 2015. *Healthcare Data Analytics*. New York: CRC Press.
Rocha, Thiago, Luiz Augusto Fachini, Elaine Thumé, Núbia Cristina da Silva, et al. 2016. Saúde Móvel: novas perspectivas para a oferta de serviços em saúde. *Epidemiol. e Serviços Saúde* 25: 1–10.
Rodrigues, Jose, Fernando Paulovich, Maria Oliveira, and Osvaldo de Oliveira Jr. 2016. On the convergence of nanotechnology and Big Data analysis for computer-aided diagnosis. *Nanomedicine* 11: 959–982.
Santha kumar, R., and K. Kaliyaperumal. 2015. A scientometric analysis of mobile technology publications. *Scientometrics* 105: 921–939.
Santini, John T., Michael J. Cima, and Robert Langer. 1999. A controlled-release microchip. *Nature* 397: 335–338.
Shmueli, Galit, and Otto Koppius. 2011. Predictive analytics in information systems research. *Management Information Systems Quarterly* 35: 553–572.
Siau, Keng, and Zixing Shen. 2006. Mobile healthcare informatics. *Medical Informatics and the Internet in Medicine* 31: 89–99.
Slovensky, Donna J., and Donna Malvey. 2015. *Mhealth: Transforming Healthcare*. London: Springer.
Soh, Ping Jack, Bertold Van den Bergh, Hantao Xu, Hadi Aliakbarian, et al. 2013. A smart wearable textile array system for biomedical telemetry applications. *IEEE Transactions on Microwave Theory and Techniques* 61: 2253–2261.
Srivastava, Shilpa, Millie Pant, Ajith Abraham, and Namrata Agrawal. 2015. The technological growth in eHealth services. *Computational and Mathematical Methods in Medicine* 2015: 1–18.
Sweileh, Waleed, Samah W. Al-Jabi, Adham S. AbuTaha, Sa'ed H. Zyoud, Fathi M.A. Anayah, and Ansam F. Sawalha. 2017. Bibliometric analysis of worldwide scientific literature in mobile-health: 2006–2016. *BMC medical informatics and decision making* 17: 72.
Troster, Gerhard. 2005. The agenda of wearable healthcare. *Yearbook of Medical Informatics* 1: 125–138.
Wang, Liang, Tao Gu, Xianping Tao, Hanhua Chen, and Jian Lua. 2011. Recognizing multi-user activities using wearable sensors in a smart home. *Pervasive and Mobile Computing* 7: 287–298.
West, Darrell. 2012. How mobile devices are transforming healthcare. *Brookings Education* 18: 1–38.
Whittaker, Robyn, Sally Merry, Enid Dorey, and Ralph Maddison. 2012. A development and evaluation process for mhealth interventions: Examples from New Zealand. *Journal of Health Communication* 17: 11–21.
WHO – World Health Organization. 2011. *MHealth: New horizons for health through mobile technologies*. Switzerland: World Health Organization.

———. 2015. Density of physicians (total number per 1000 population, latest available year). http://www.who.int/gho/health_workforce/physicians_density/en/. Accessed 16 May 2018.

Ziemba, Meaghan. 2013. Qardio's smart, wearable solutions provide users daily, continuous heart and health monitoring. https://www.wirelessdesignmag.com/article/2013/10/qardio-monitoring-system-smarter-healthcare. Accessed 10 May 2018.

Chapter 19
The Use of Information and Communication Technologies in Health Promotion: Brazilian Initiatives

André Pereira Neto, Celita Almeida Rosário, Zélia Andrade, and Lise Renaud

Abstract Health promotion is a behavioral, political, and social practice aimed at meeting the individual and collective needs and aspirations of citizens. Since the Ottawa Charter (1986), new information and communication technologies (NICTs) have been understood as an integral part of health promotion and are found in international documents that establish priorities for this topic. This chapter analyzes Brazilian academic work on the use of NICTs in health promotion by surveying publications in the "Brazilian Digital Library of Theses and Dissertations" – an open and free-access portal. Six PhD dissertations and 18 master's theses were found and were thematically grouped. This chapter concluded that, in the Brazilian studies analyzed, new information and communication technologies (NICTs) are applied in cases of specific pathologies or particular age groups. Brazilian studies in this field reinforce individualistic and biomedical perspective that is far from the wider social parameters defined by international conferences on health promotion.

19.1 Introduction

Health promotion is a concept associated with the idea that health is a behavioral, political, and social practice focused on meeting individual and collective needs and aspirations. To achieve this, citizens and communities must be able to cope with and change the environment around them (WHO 1986).

The Ottawa Charter enacted in 1986 under the auspices of the World Health Organization is a milestone in the historical process that led to the establishment of this concept and social practice. This event was preceded by others, such as Alma Ata's "International Conference on Primary Health Care" (1978) and the

A. Pereira Neto (✉) · C. A. Rosário · Z. Andrade
National School of Public Health, Oswaldo Cruz Foundation, Rio de Janeiro, Brazil

L. Renaud
Department of Social and Public Communication, Universite de Quebec à Montreal, Montreal, QC, Canada

A. Pereira Neto, M. B. Flynn (eds.), *The Internet and Health in Brazil*,
https://doi.org/10.1007/978-3-319-99289-1_19

"Black Report on Health Inequalities" (Townsend and Davidson 1982). The importance of the Ottawa Charter lies in the fact that this document offers a vision that goes beyond the individualistic understanding of lifestyles as responsible for health and disease conditions and instead highlights the importance of social environments and policies crucial for individual and community health. In fact, it emphasizes the context and meaning of health actions and the social determinants that enable people to be healthy or not (Kickbusch 2003).

The Ottawa Charter is divided into three parts. The first part seeks to define the concept of "health promotion"; the second establishes the means to achieve and exercise it; and the last one indicates the commitments needed to make these ideas come true.

The first part consists of four items, namely, "health prerequisites," "advocate," "mediate," and "enable." Among the prerequisites for health are "peace, shelter, education, food, income, a stable ecosystem, sustainable resources, social justice, and equity." According to this document, mediation must be carried out by different social segments such as (non-)governmental organizations and "by local authorities, industry, and *the media*" (our italics). For people to reach their full potential, the Ottawa Charter stipulates "a secure foundation in a supportive environment, *access to information*, life skills, and opportunities for making healthy choices" (our italics).

Thus, the 1986 document lists the role played by various media and mentions access to information as integral parts of the definition of health promotion.

The second part of the Ottawa Charter, dedicated to possible health promotion actions, is subdivided into five items. The first one aimed to put "health on the agenda of policy makers in all sectors and at all levels, directing them to be aware of the health consequences of their decisions and to accept their responsibilities for health." The second is concerned with establishing "living and working conditions that are safe, stimulating, satisfying, and enjoyable." The third emphasizes the importance of community action. It states "at the heart of this process is the empowerment of communities, their ownership, and control of their own endeavors and destinies." According to the same document, "this requires full and continuous *access to information*, learning opportunities for health, as well as funding support" (our italics). The fourth highlights the role of developing personal skills "by *providing information*, education for health, and enhancing life skills" (our italics). The last item values the reorientation of health services that must "open channels between the health sector and broader social, political, economic, and physical environmental components."

Thus, access and provision of information are two of the possibilities for actions related to health promotion, this time accompanied by the notion of empowerment.

In the third part, the Ottawa Charter shows the commitments assumed by the 38 document signatory countries,[1] among which are as follows: to enter the arena of

[1] The Ottawa Charter was signed by representatives from the following countries: Antigua, Australia, Austria, Belgium, Bulgaria, Canada, Czechoslovakia, Denmark, Eire, England, Finland, France, the German Democratic Republic, the Federal Republic of Germany, Ghana, Hungary, Iceland, Israel, Italy, Japan, Malta, the Netherlands, New Zealand, Northern Ireland, Norway, Poland, Portugal, Romania, St. Kitts and Nevis, Scotland, Spain, Sudan, Sweden, Switzerland, Union of Soviet Socialist Republics, the United States, Wales, and Yugoslavia.

public health policy by advocating the principle of equity in all sectors; to fight against products, environments, and foods that are harmful to health; to focus on issues related to pollution and occupational and housing hazards; to recognize that the community is the essential voice in terms of health, living conditions, and well-being; and to share power with other sectors and other disciplines and, most importantly, with people themselves.

In the end, the Ottawa Charter (WHO 1986) establishes that:

> The Conference is firmly convinced that if people in all walks of life, nongovernmental and voluntary organizations, governments, the World Health Organization and all other bodies concerned join forces in introducing strategies for health promotion, in line with the moral and social values that form the basis of this charter, Health for All by the year 2000 will become a reality.

Soon after its enactment, some authorities and intellectuals expressed their support to the Ottawa Charter.

According to Breslow (1999), with the Ottawa Charter, health became a "daily living resource." Since then, health promotion is understood as something that moves beyond health care. Its meaning became increasingly associated with a commitment to social reform and equity. Thus, George Alleyne, director of the Pan American Health Organization from 1995 to 2003, stated that: "for a health organization such as ours, the main health promotion strategies can be applied in almost all aspects of our work" (Alleyne 2001). Since then, the Ottawa Charter has exerted significant, direct, and indirect influence on the debate on public health, health policy formulation, and health promotion practices in many countries (Kickbusch 2003).

Nearly 40 years after the enactment of the Ottawa Charter (WHO 1986), the objectives set in 1986 are far from being achieved. In recent years, several authors have debated the meaning of this document.

Paraphrasing the analogy proposed by Kickbusch (2006), Potvin and Jones (2011) understand health promotion not as a tree but as a rhizome – a type of stem that grows horizontally, usually underground, but which may also have aerial segments. These authors argue that the emergence of new challenges in the field of health promotion reinforces the relevance of the Ottawa Charter. They state that:

> Health Promotion is actively being defined through practice taking place across the globe. To use Kickbusch's (2006) analogy, the roots of health promotion are spreading as a rhizome. The emergence of new challenges for the field does not negate the relevance of the Ottawa Charter. On the contrary, the significance of the Ottawa Charter lies in its longevity as a mouthpiece for the field of health promotion. It continues to confirm a vision, orient action, and underpin the values that compromise health promotion today. Building capacity of workforce, organizations and infrastructures for health promotion will be the crux for assessing the next round of achievements. (Potvin and Jones 2011, 247)

Labonté (2016) also analyzed the intentions of the Ottawa Charter. He believes that the current economic and ecological crisis and inequality are very complex and embedded in a multipolar world. He says this reality poses different challenges from those experienced in 1986. At the time, the neoliberal austerity was only beginning, and the world was split between the capitalist and communist matrix. Labonté (2016) emphasizes that the current reality is quite different. He argues that:

> [...] we have a rampant inequality in which the ever-shrinking 0.000.000 .01% of humanity – just 62 people – now hold as much global wealth and the resources and political power it commands as the rest of the planet's 7.4 billion residents. (Labonté 2016, 675)

In view of this picture, Labonté (2016) "exhorted health promoters to support social movements and civil society activists working at national and global scales to pressure economic reform and ecological salvation" (Labonté 2016, 680).

The Ninth Global Conference on Health Promotion was held in China at the end of 2016. The "Shanghai Declaration on Health Promotion in the 2030 Agenda for Sustainable Development" (WHO 2016) was approved during this event.

The "Shanghai Declaration," as it became known, ratified an agenda containing the 17 "Sustainable Development Goals by 2030" defined by the United Nations in September 2015. The official website of the United Nations states that:

> The new goals are unique in that they call for action by all countries, poor, rich and middle-income to promote prosperity while protecting the planet. They recognize that ending poverty must go hand-in-hand with strategies that build economic growth and addresses a range of social needs including education, health, social protection, and job opportunities, while tackling climate change and environmental protection. (The United Nations 2015)

Since then, the United Nations has come to recognize health and well-being as essential conditions for achieving sustainable development, defined as follows:

> Ensuring healthy lives and promoting the well-being for all at all ages is essential to sustainable development. Significant strides have been made in increasing life expectancy and reducing some of the common killers associated with child and maternal mortality. Major progress has been made on increasing access to clean water and sanitation, reducing malaria, tuberculosis, polio and the spread of HIV/AIDS. However, many more efforts are needed to fully eradicate a wide range of diseases and address many different persistent and emerging health issues. (The United Nations 2015)

With regard to information and communication, the 2015 United Nations Resolution establishes that:

> The *spread of information and communications technology* and global interconnectedness has great potential to accelerate human progress, to bridge the digital divide and to develop knowledge societies, as does scientific and technological innovation across areas as diverse as medicine and energy. [our italics] (The United Nations 2015)

With this document, access to information and communication technologies was now seen as an instrument capable of accelerating human progress and developing societies throughout different areas of knowledge.

The "Shanghai Declaration" emphasizes some aspects of health that we consider fundamental. It understands that health promotion is found in all the Sustainable Development Goals, insofar as all of them can be considered social determinants of health. Thus, the "Shanghai Declaration" refers to the quality of water, hunger, unemployment, and so forth. In addition, inequality in access to health services is unacceptable and requires political action in various sectors and regions. In this case, the document suggests prioritizing good governance, local action in cities and communities, and empowering people through access to health information. While not written in this way, we can admit that the promotion of health literacy can be performed through different devices available in social networks.

There are also some public commitments made by signatories of the "Shanghai Declaration," among which we highlight a part that addresses the problem of health in urban centers, "where people live, love, work, shop, and play." The same Declaration establishes that "it will not accept that city residents in poor areas suffer ill-health disproportionately and have difficulty accessing health services." With regard to information and communication technologies, the "Shanghai Declaration" signatories commit themselves to:

> prioritize policies that create co-benefits between health and wellbeing and other city policies, making full use of social innovation and *interactive technologies* [our italics] increase citizens' control of their own health and its determinants, through harnessing the potential of *digital technology*. [our italics] (WHO 2016, 2)

Thus, we notice that information and communication technologies are on the agenda of the international documents that define the priorities for sustainable development and health promotion since the Ottawa Charter (WHO 1986).

In Brazil, Ordinance N° 687, of the Ministry of Health, established the "National Health Promotion Policy" in 2006 (Brazil 2006). This policy comprises part of the "Unified Health System," which ranges from simple ambulatory care to organ transplantation, providing comprehensive, universal, and free access to the entire Brazilian population. The National Health Promotion Policy (PNPS) aimed to promote equity and improved conditions and ways of living, enhancing the potential of individual and collective health. It also sought to reduce vulnerability and health risks from social, economic, political, cultural, and environmental determinants.

In 2014, this Ordinance was revoked and the National Health Promotion Policy (PNPS) established. The National Health Promotion Policy (PNPS) was then based on values and principles that should guide actions in the field of health promotion, namely:

> (a) it recognizes the subjectivity of people and collectives in the process of attention and care to protect health and life;
> (b) it considers solidarity, happiness, ethics, respect for diversity, humanization, co-responsibility, justice, and social inclusion as founding values in the process of its implementation;
> (c) it adopts as principles equity, social participation, autonomy, empowerment, intersectoriality, intrasectoriality, sustainability, integrality, and territoriality. (Brazil 2015, 10)

Among the specific objectives, it is worth highlighting item IX, which looked "to establish media strategies aimed at strengthening the principles and actions in Health Promotion and advocacy of healthy public policies" (Brazil 2015, 23).

Also in the operational axes, information and communication are shown as important themes for the operationalization of the promotion policy. They are the following:

> VIII – production and dissemination of knowledge, as a stimulus to a reflexive and resolutive attitude on community problems, needs, and potential in collecting, sharing, and disseminating results broadly with the community;
> IX – media, as the use of the various formal and popular communication expressions to favor the listening and voicing of the different groups involved, including information about the planning, execution, results, impacts, efficiency, efficacy, effectiveness, and benefits of the actions. (Brazil 2015, 11)

After more than 10 years, the "National Health Promotion Policy" (PNPS) has been the subject of analysis by different authors. In Brazil, most academic studies are linked to graduate programs, mainly through research groups registered in the Directory of the National Council for Scientific and Technological Development (CNPq). In his master's thesis, Minowa (2016) identified 102 research groups in health promotion in Brazil. Yamaguchi et al. (2016) carried out a similar effort by conducting a study of the national and international academic literature on the PNPS in two bibliographic bases and identified 88 publications related to the "National Health Promotion Policy." Thus, the debate on the evaluation of the "Health Promotion Policy" has mobilized different institutions, research groups, government agencies, and sectors of civil society (Carvalho et al. 2007).

However, as Hartz et al. (2014) pointed out, the use of multi-strategic approaches to assessing health promotion initiatives and programs, such as theory-based evaluation, is still limited. This is why we understand that this policy requires evaluations that are more consistent. A critique by Pinto (2008), in his master's thesis, about the first version of the Health Promotion Policy (Brazil 2006) emphasized that:

> [...] it maintains the traditional emphasis on the orientation for the modification of behaviors, highlighting the individual dimension, and it does so in a vertical and authoritarian way. This perspective, by making the subject responsible, contributes to depoliticizing the concept of health. (Pinto 2008, 6)

Minowa (2016) and Yamaguchi et al. (2016) did not identify or analyze Brazilian academic studies on the use of new information and communication technologies (NICTs) in health promotion.

In international literature, we found the work by Lintonen et al. (2008) who surveyed 15 different international journals to address this issue. They identify 1352 articles published between 2003 and 2005. Of these, only 56 papers contained content related to the use of NICTs in health promotion. They say that this number reveals that research in this field is just beginning.

Lintonen et al. (2008) grouped these 56 titles into four groups that represent different ways in which NICTs can be applied to health promotion. The first one includes papers in which information technology is used as an "intervention medium." Of the 56 articles analyzed, 20 were included in this group, among which we highlight the one published by Irvine et al. (2004) that analyzes the effectiveness of an interactive multimedia program to influence eating habits. Another paper in the same group evaluates the acceptance of an internet-based smoking cessation campaign (Parlove et al. 2004). Yet another work evaluates a computer-developed project encouraging physical activity (Vandelanotte and Bourdeaudhuij 2003).

The second group gathered 12 of the 56 titles analyzed. In this case, papers address the "use of information technology as a research tool, either in data collection or in reaching research subjects" (Lintonen et al. 2008, 563). It includes works on assessing the quality or usability of health information available online, such as that of Charnock and Shepperd (2004) and Ragon (2004), who explore ways in which people use information technology to seek information about health problems.

Ten papers are part of the third group created by Lintonen et al. (2008). This group includes works where technological information is seen as a research tool either in the search for data or research themes such as the case of De Vet et al. (2005), who conduct a study using the Delphi method. Lintonen et al. (2008) state that this group of works is justified because:

> Application of electronic survey forms to gather health-related data in the WWW is becoming popular as Internet access has become widespread in the industrialized world. (Lintonen et al. 2008, 563)

The fourth group includes papers that analyze the role of NICTs in professional development. In this group, authors found 14 titles, some of which are geared to distance learning, such as the work by Bernhardt et al. (2003). Moreover:

> Theoretical and conceptual issues related to the use of information technology in promoting health were studied and discussed in several papers. (Lintonen et al. 2008, 563)

Lintonen et al. (2008) have built a figure that summarizes the work of classification of the academic production that they realized on the use of NICTs in health promotion, as follows (Fig. 19.1):

A similar effort will be made in this chapter. We carried out a bibliographic survey of Brazilian academic literature to identify studies that address different possibilities in applying and appropriating health promotion information and communication technologies. The classification schema we employ follows the effort by Lintonen et al. (2008).

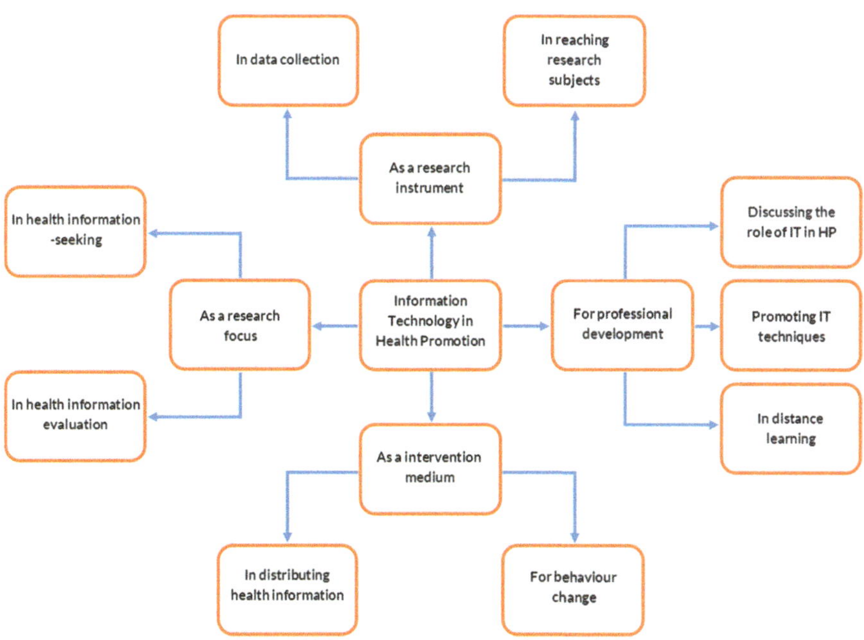

Fig. 19.1 The use of information technology in health promotion – analysis of published research articles. (Adopted from Lintonen et al. (2008))

19.2 Methodology

The bibliographic survey carried out for the elaboration of this chapter was undertaken in the "Brazilian Digital Library of Theses and Dissertations".[2] This open-access Brazilian portal collects doctoral dissertations and master's theses defended throughout Brazil and by Brazilians abroad, in all areas of knowledge. The Brazilian Institute for Science and Technology Information (IBICT), with the support of the Funding Authority for Studies and Projects (FINEP), a Brazilian public company linked to the Ministry of Science, Technology and Innovation, conceived and maintained the portal. The "Brazilian Digital Library of Theses and Dissertations" was conceived under the "Brazilian Digital Library Program" and became available on the Internet at the end of 2002. It follows the precepts of the "Open Archives Initiative" (OAI), thus adopting the model based on interoperability standards. The "Brazilian Digital Library of Theses and Dissertations" is a distributed network of information systems that manage full-text theses and dissertations. Its management is possible thanks to the existence of two main stakeholders: the data providers, who manage submissions and publications, exposing metadata for harvesting, and service providers, who provide information services based on metadata collected from data providers. Thus, educational and research institutions act as data providers, and the IBICT provides information services on this metadata and offers them for collection to other service providers.

The portal provides access to master's and doctoral studies of the 6470 sensu stricto[3] graduate programs available and recognized by the Ministry of Education throughout the national territory. Thus, the "Brazilian Digital Library of Theses and Dissertations" is considered the most complete database of Brazilian theses and dissertations.

In order to carry out the bibliographic survey, we combined the Portuguese-equivalent expressions "health promotion" and "new information and communication technologies" (NICTs), as well as other related terms such as "Internet," "social networks," "web," and "Facebook."

For this research only the term "health promotion" was chosen as the key word. We are aware that this term is recent and that health communication practices and health education practices are in fact achievements in health promotion. This is a research bias that underestimates the actual number of academic articles related to health promotion.

---

[2] Brazilian Digital Library of Theses and Dissertations: http://bdtd.ibict.br

[3] In Brazil, it is customary to divide the postgraduate programs into two types: sensu stricto and sensu lato. The sensu stricto postgraduate course comprises Master's programs (for 2 years) and PhD (for 4 years) with a workload of 360 and 540 h per year, respectively. To complete the course, the candidate must submit a thesis that will be defended before a public assessment bank. The sensu lato postgraduate course comprises specialization and MBA courses (for a year, with a minimum workload of 360 h) and residencies in the health area (for 2 years, with a minimum yearly of 2800 and a maximum of 3200 h per year). The completion of these courses is not necessarily conditional on the presentation of written work and defended before a public assessment bank.

Table 19.1 General result of the bibliographic survey

Terms	NICTs	Internet	Social networks	Web	Facebook	Total
Thesis	4	10	7	5		26
Dissertation	11	26	14	24	3	78
Total	15	36	21	29	3	104

The result of this first survey was the following (Table 19.1).

Without revealing the sources researched, Lintonen et al. (2008) inform that they did the research in 15 "relevant journals between 2003 and 2005." They also did not report the keywords used in the search, which found 1352 titles, "of which 56 contained content related to the use of information technology in the context of health promotion" (Lintonen et al. 2008, 560). Thus, of the total sample obtained, they only analyzed 4.1% of their initial results.

In our case, 104 titles were found. To make our second selection, we followed recommendations by Lintonen et al. (2008). Thus, from the studies initially found, duplicates were discarded and abstracts read. We decided on 24 titles to be analyzed in this study (see Annex 1). Thus, we included 23% of the total sample initially obtained in our analysis.

We selected 6 doctoral dissertations and 18 master's theses. Some general comments should be made about this collection.

Of the 24 studies, only 2 were defended in graduate programs outside the axis of the south/southeast regions of the country, where the population with the highest purchasing power and with the highest educational level in Brazil resides. These data do not coincide with the results found by Cirani et al. (2015) on the evolution of sensu stricto graduate programs in Brazil during the 1998–2011 period. These authors found, in general, that there was a trend toward a regional homogenization of graduate studies.

In our sample, only two studies were linked to private education institutions, and of the 24 studies, women wrote half of them. In this case, data found in our sample coincide with the study by Cirani et al. (2015), which found that the sensu stricto graduate courses in Brazil focus on public institutions, linked either to state governments or the federal government. They also found that Brazil joined the select group of countries that achieved gender equality at the highest level of education.

To classify these 24 studies, we adopted an individual and collective procedure. Initially, we began to familiarize ourselves with the works by reading their abstracts. Next, we sought to identify individually the information and communication technology analyzed in each of the 24 texts. Finally, we attempted to insert these studies in the classification proposed by Lintonen et al. (2008). In order to complete this classification work, we held a meeting in which we discussed the results of the classification schema each of us devised until we reached a consensus.

Therefore, the procedure employed for this study was similar to that adopted by Lintonen et al. (2008) because it:

> [...] was executed in a consensus process involving two researchers to decrease the role of subjective evaluations. The identification and condensation addressed themes of factual

> nature - this made achieving consensus relatively straightforward. The result of the analysis is a pattern of descriptive categories generated from the data. (Lintonen et al. 2008, 562).

Thus, the results shown below are the result of a consensus among the three authors of this chapter.

19.3 Results

As mentioned before, this chapter will verify whether the classification parameters of academic papers used by Lintonen et al. (2008) are valid for the selected Brazilian sample.

These authors established "four broad thematic application areas," namely:

> use of information technology as an intervention medium, use of information technology as a research focus, use of information technology as a research instrument and use of information technology for professional development. (Lintonen et al. 2008, 560)

The classification of the dissertations and theses that we construct follows, in general lines, the one suggested by Lintonen et al. (2008), with some changes. These authors identified four groups of topics where papers were assembled. In our case, we identified three groups of studies. Two are similar to those mentioned by Lintonen et al. (2008). But, our third one differs. Similar to Lintonen et al. (2008), we could not identify papers that analyzed the use of NICTs as a research tool in professional training either.

In our study, we ended up grouping studies into three categories: In the first one, we collected papers that analyzed NICTs as a means of intervention in health promotion. In the second, there are studies in which NICTs were the object of research. In the third, we gathered studies concerned with the search profile of health information on the Internet and its impact on people's behavior.

Let us explore the first group.

This first group is similar to that of the study by Lintonen et al. (2008): "use of information technology as an intervention medium." In the sample selected for this study, 8 of the 24 Brazilian academic papers used NICTs as a means of intervention for health promotion. Two of them submitted specific health-related interventions, and the remaining six proposed not only interventions but also assessed their impacts.

The two works are the master's theses of Bevilaqua (2012) – "Digital television and health: proposal for content production" – and Sant'Ana (2012), "Establishing a hypermedia tool for the Promotion of Hearing Health in young users of individual portable sound devices."

The work by Bevilaqua (2012) was defended in the professional master's of the "Media and Technology Graduate Program" (PPGMiT) of the Júlio de Mesquita Filho São Paulo State University (UNESP). In her thesis, Bevilaqua (2012) sought to submit a structure for the production of health content "based on the possibility of audience participation and convergence between digital platforms" (Bevilaqua 2012, 69). The author argues that health was chosen because it is a subject of great interest among Brazilians who seek information and because television does not prioritize the dissemination of healthy habits and practices. She therefore aimed to "develop a structure for the production of health content that meets the principles of promotion to help citizens adopt healthy habits and recognize when it is necessary to seek medical help" (Bevilaqua 2012, 121). Thus, we can say that this work meets one of the "priority issues" of the "National Health Promotion Policy" (2015), namely, to promote "adequate and healthy food" (Brazil 2015, 22–23).

The second thesis using technological information as a means of intervention was defended by speech therapist Nicolle Sant'Ana (2012) at the Faculty of Dentistry of the University of São Paulo (USP) in 2012. She aimed to create a hypermedia tool for the promotion of hearing health in young users of individual portable sound devices. She argued that hearing loss induced by high sound pressure levels stems from the advent of amplified music and the increasing popularity of individual portable sound devices among children and adolescents.

Her master's thesis aimed to develop hypermedia[4] material about individual portable sound devices and their consequences on hearing health. Thus, her work can be seen as an initiative in the field of education and sensitization of children and adolescents. She chose CD-ROM as the media. It has been programmed to be applied with earphones to demonstrate proper use of individual portable sound devices.

We observed that these two works are based on a health promotion vision associated to the idea of individual, and not community, health habits and practices. Both are problem-specific (feeding and hearing) and are biomedical model-centered.

The other six scholarly works included in this first group used information and communication technologies as an intervention tool and at the same time made an evaluation of this initiative.

This was the case of Silva (2009a) in his master's thesis defended in the Public Health Graduate Program of the São Paulo School of Medicine of the Federal University of São Paulo (UNIFESP). He constructed and evaluated an Internet radio model that included 30 radio programs available to the public. The evaluation counted on the participation of students from the Open University for the Elderly[5] of UNIFESP. Silva argued that Radio UNIFESP did not become a portal with radio programs. The radio had a continuous program with vignettes, programs, and breaks with the participation of live listeners. He concludes by affirming that:

> The proposed web radio model stands out as a prototype open to all possible improvements, which must be constant, taking into account the experience of the communication and health professionals involved and the technological advances arising thereof. (Silva 2009a, 81)

[4] Hypermedia, according to Gosciola (2007), is a group of means that allow simultaneous access to texts, images, and sounds in an interactive as opposed to a linear way, allowing users to make links between elements in the media, control navigation of content, and even extract text, images, and sounds whose sequencing will constitute a personal version developed by the user.

[5] The "Universities for the Elderly" are found in different parts of the world. In Brazil, they began to be organized in the 1970s. They are based on interdisciplinary actions committed to the insertion of the elderly as an active citizenry in society. They aim to contribute to the promotion of the physical, mental, and social health of the elderly, making use of the opportunities available at the universities. Brazil has over 150 programs of this nature (Veras 2012).

The evaluation indicated that this initiative has high levels of credibility, clarity, usefulness, and usability.

Two other initiatives for the production and evaluation of information and communication technologies for health promotion were aimed at the elderly.[6]

The first was developed by Arakawa (2015) in her PhD defended at the Faculty of Dentistry at the University of São Paulo (USP). She created and evaluated a website[7] with information on Alzheimer's disease. To build this website, Arakawa (2015) collected information from books and scientific papers. She took great care with the language used, trying to make it simple, clear, and concise. The group of evaluators consisted of 16 elderly people, 12 elderly caregivers, and 28 speech therapists. The website's content was rated "excellent" and achieved the corresponding percentile of "easy" under the Flesch readability index.[8]

The second was produced by Moreira (2016). He developed his master's thesis in the Applied Informatics Postgraduate Program (PPGIA) at the University of Fortaleza. This study includes different information and communication technologies for health promotion, namely, a mobile application, a web application, an interactive primer, and a virtual environment. These initiatives were aimed at oral health promotion and prevention among the elderly. To validate the proposed technologies, four dentists used and evaluated the tools in order to identify their advantages and disadvantages. Moreira (2016) concluded his work by stating that the technologies developed could sensitize and guide the elderly population with regard to the procedures and techniques appropriate for oral health promotion and prevention.

The interest in health promotion for the elderly population found in these three works has practical implications. The Brazilian Institute of Geography and Statistics (IBGE) published a synthesis of social indicators in 2016 and concluded that, in the period 1950–2000, the proportion of elderly people in the Brazilian population was below 10.0%. This percentage was similar to that found in less developed countries. In 2010, this indicator is close to that projected in developed countries. The proportion of the Brazilian elderly population is estimated at 35.0% for the year 2070, an indicator higher than expected for all developed countries (IBGE 2016).

The next three scholarly works that have produced and at the same time evaluated information and communication technologies for health promotion are aimed at specific audiences, namely, beauty professionals (Vieira Junior 2014), health promoters (Silva 2009a), and people with psychiatric disorders (Bittencourt 2012).

---

[6] Chapter 8 discusses access and use of information and communication technologies to promote active aging.

[7] Website address: http://portaldosidososaceite.lecom.com.br/portaldosidosos/Portugues/index.php

[8] Rudolf Flesch devised the readability index for the English language. It calculates a readability score based on mean word and sentence sizes along with reading ease. The adaptation to Portuguese of the index proposed by Flesch was carried out by a team of researchers from the University of São Paulo, São Carlos campus (USP-SC), also responsible for the development of the Portuguese Language Writing Program. Further information can be found in Nunes MGV, Oliveira Jr ON. The ReGra grammar proofreader development process (available from http://www.niee.ufrgs.br/eventos/SBC/2000/pdf/semish/semi001.pdf).

Vieira Junior (2014) defended his PhD at the medical school of the University of São Paulo (USP) where he submitted and evaluated a course for the training of professionals who work in beauty parlors using "interactive teleducation".[9] His research project emerged from the problem he stated as the following:

> Many diseases are transmitted when proper hand hygiene practices and sterilization of materials are not followed in activities that can cause injury or trauma to the skin, such as in parlors. / ... including sexually transmitted diseases, such as warts, hepatitis B and C, and HIV. (Vieira Junior 2014, X)

The course was designed from an array of goals and competencies and embedded in a Moodle-based educational platform, with interactive learning environments and an educational management tool. Fifty-five beauty professionals enrolled in the course, namely, 46 females and 9 males. To evaluate the knowledge of beauty professionals, he developed a practical situation simulator based on daily practices that can transmit diseases. The success of this experience led the University of São Paulo to turn it into a distance-learning course.

The other work was aimed at health promoters. It was developed by Ana Cláudia Silva (2009b) in her PhD thesis entitled "Technology-based Education: developing and evaluating learning resources for the training of health promoters," defended at the Faculty of Medicine of the University of São Paulo (USP). Silva constructed and evaluated two NICTs: a blog[10] and a group of emails – both geared to training health promoters. Her proposal was based on the idea that "due to their interactive, asynchronous, and geographic barrier-free capacity, the addition of online resources in face-to-face courses can be seen as a potential facilitator of health professionals' continuing education[11]" (Silva 2009b, IX). Her study involved 211 students in health promotion refresher and specialization courses during the 2006, 2007, and 2008 editions. The author concluded her thesis affirming that:

> Although the use of the blog and group of e-mails increased during the study, the progressive inclusion of NICTs in Health Promotion Education did not significantly alter the gain of knowledge and abilities, nor did it trigger effective changes in the students' professional or personal behavior. (Silva 2009b, X)

---

[9] According to Vieira Junior (2014), teleducation or distance learning is a way of educating without requiring the learner's physical presence in 100% of the course. This practice predates the advent of the Internet. "Interactive teleducation" is the careful association of computer and telecommunication resources based on educational models that stimulate the constant participation of learners and educators through means of communication that favor the sharing of knowledge (Wen 2003).

[10] Website address: http://promosaude2007.blogspot.com.br/

[11] "Continuing education in health" is an ethical-political-pedagogical effort by the federal government that aims to improve health care through constant training processes and pedagogical practices. Brazil's Ministry of Health established the "National Permanent Education Policy" (PNEPS) in 2004. It is part of the strategy for improving the services provided by the Unified Health System (SUS). Thus, the training and development of health professionals seek to integrate teaching, service, and community. In addition, it assumes the regionalization of SUS management as a basis for the development of qualified initiatives to meet the needs and difficulties for the full functioning of SUS (Health Portal – Ministry of Health) (available from http://tinyurl.com/y845p3z8).

This conclusion seems important to us, since it emphasizes the idea that information and communication technologies do not necessarily promote changes in behavior patterns in individuals.

The third paper was submitted by Bittencourt (2012). She revealed that developing a blog by people in psychological distress could lead to behavioral changes. Bittencourt defended her master's thesis at the Faculty of Education of the Federal University of Alagoas (UFAL). She showed and analyzed a creative experience of promoting mental health, using information and communication technologies. She sampled four people with psychiatric problems who attended a "psychosocial care center" (CAPS)[12] that allowed them to build their own blogs. This activity occurred over 6 months and included 12 face-to-face meetings. Bittencourt (2012) concluded her study stating that:

> Making blogs allowed patients to realize their creative abilities in demonstrable ways to both family members and CAPS health professionals. The blog was a space for expressing what was significant to them, as well as showing their feelings about the desire for change in behavior and in the attitudes of society that see them with fear, prejudice, and discrimination. The activities provided shared learning, exchange of experiences, socialization, interaction, companionship, satisfaction and the strengthening of bonds between all participants. (Bittencourt 2012, 91)

The studies that have analyzed the use of information and communication technologies as a means of intervention are, therefore, far removed from the primacy of health promotion. We could not identify a single study in this first group that evaluated the contribution of NICTs to end misery and unemployment, for example, as stated by the "Shanghai Declaration" (WHO 2016).

Let us have a look at the second group.

The second group of papers uses NICTs as a research object in the area of health promotion. In this case, studies evaluate the quality of virtual environments or digital tools available on the web. This second group is similar to that found in Lintonen et al. (2008): "use of information technology as a research focus." We have identified nine studies for this purpose. One evaluates the quality of videos (Moraes 2004); five are concerned with portals, virtual libraries, and sites; two dedicate themselves to evaluating games; and one carries out a review of the literature on educational programs of health promotion for children and adolescents. The ninth study examines the application of NICTs in the area of health surveillance.

Let us have a look at each one of them in detail.

In her PhD thesis defended in the Information Science Program at the School of Communication, Federal University of Rio de Janeiro/Institute for Science and Technology Information (UFRJ/IBICT), Moraes (2004) evaluates the quality of the finalist videos of the project "III National Exhibition of Health Videos," promoted by the Oswaldo Cruz Foundation (Fiocruz), held in Rio de Janeiro in 1998 – a time

---

[12] According to Brazil's Ministry of Health, "psychosocial care centers" (CAPS) are bodies linked to Brazilian municipal health secretariats that provide free care to users with severe and persistent mental disorders, people who suffer from and/or have mental disorders in general, and even people with substance abuse problems like the use of crack, alcohol, or other drugs.

when the Internet was not as widespread as it is today. The author states that informational action in disease prevention and health promotion can trigger individual behavioral changes. In these videos, she identified different informational strategies that she defines as discursive, communicational, cognitive, sociocultural, educational, and power-related. She concludes her work recommending the simultaneous use of more than one of the strategies in the production of future videos.

Five studies evaluated the quality of information[13] available in portals, virtual libraries, and health websites.

One of them was developed by Lemos (2009) in her master's thesis defended in the Graduate Program in Social Communication at the Methodist University of São Paulo (UMESP). She analyzes the latent (insinuated) content, the manifest language, the presentation of the layout, and the usability in two national portals of the scientific societies: "Cardiol" and "Diabetes." The author concludes that the "two cases analyzed indicate that statements, understood as units of discursive communication, reveal how web editors write as specialists and, in doing so, present their work as scientific."

The other study was submitted by Berbel (2012) in the Graduate Program in Science, Technology and Society of the Federal University of São Carlos (UFSCar). In his paper entitled "Communicating Science in Online Health Campaigns: A Case Study of the Health Portal," Berbel investigated how campaigns about healthy eating, vaccination, and medication[14] dialogue with the public. The author concludes the study by stating that "despite available resources, online campaigns still preserve a model that favors the context of medical and scientific authority, the provision of information and behavior modeling" (Berbel 2012, 7).

The third study concerned about evaluating the quality of information available online in health promotion was by Lourenço (2013), who defended his master's thesis in the Information Science Postgraduate Program of the School of Communication of the Federal University of Rio de Janeiro and the Brazilian Institute for Science and Technology Information (UFRJ/IBICT). In his work, Lourenço (2013) sought to understand the potential of communicational interactivity between a virtual health library and low-income lay users. He concluded by pointing out "users' difficulties, barriers, and expectations regarding search activity in the virtual library" (Lourenço 2013, 7).

The fourth work of this second group was submitted by Picolini (2011) in her master's thesis defended at the Faculty of Dentistry of the University of São Paulo (USP). She used the cybertutor teaching tool to measure the effectiveness of a training program on genetic syndromes available on the "Young Doctor Program"[15] website. The study was carried out in two elementary schools, one from the public system and another from the private one. In all, this research involved 21 students, of both genders, between the ages of 13 and 14. The results indicated high levels of participant satisfaction with "interactive teleducation."

[13] The issue of quality of online health information is addressed in Chap. 10.

[14] Chapter 13 discusses the issue of Internet-based medicines.

[15] Young Doctor Program: http://jovemdoutor.org.br

As we previously announced, two studies focused on evaluating games available on the Internet. One was by Finco (2010) and another by Vasconcelos (2013).

Finco (2010) defended his master's thesis in the Human Movement Science Post-Graduation Program at the Physical Education School, Federal University of Rio Grande do Sul (UFRGS). His study does not stem from a problem, but a finding. Finco (2010) says that video games are one of the most important currents in the entertainment industry. Its presence is felt in physical education, where some "new digital artifacts" enable corporal interaction, among which the video game Wii Fit stands out. His study evaluates how users share the healthy life precepts conveyed by this video game. Finco (2010) concludes his work by stating "not only does the Wii Fit game promote the practice of regular physical activities, but also allows users to become aware of their quality of life" (Finco 2010, 8).

In his doctoral thesis, Vasconcelos (2013) investigated the potential of "massively multiplayer online role-playing games" (MMORPGs) for communication and health from the perspective of health promotion. The author states that traditional media (print, radio, and TV):

> [...] have limitations due to their communicational matrix, which produces a practice characterized by a normative and prescriptive approach and centralized production, with the consequence of not attending to the diversity and specificities of the multiple cultural and health contexts of a country like Brazil, besides establishing a unidirectional communicative standard, without space for dialogue with citizens. (Vasconcelos 2013, 8)

He concluded his study, defended in the Health Information and Communication Postgraduate Program of the Oswaldo Cruz Foundation (ICICT/Fiocruz), confirming the potential of the "massively multiplayer online role-playing games" for health promotion.

Daniel dos Santos (2012) completed a bibliographic analysis on educational programs for the promotion of hearing health for children and adolescents in his master's thesis in the Program for the Promotion of Hearing Health for Children and Adolescents at the Faculty of Speech and Hearing Therapy, Catholic Pontifical University of São Paulo (PUC-SP). His study included clinical trials, literature reviews, abstracts, monographs, dissertations, theses, books, and websites. Therefore, he searched electronic databases such as "Index of scientific and technical literature of Latin America and the Caribbean – LILACS" (lilacs.bvsalud.org/); the PubMed, engine with free access to the MEDLINE database of citations and abstracts of biomedical research papers (https://www.ncbi.nlm.nih.gov/pubmed/); and the "Scientific Electronic Library Online" (SciELO), an electronic library covering a selected collection of Brazilian scientific journals. He concluded his study by stating:

> [...] some programs have perfected the techniques and structures of others. Unfortunately, what is lacking are more published studies on the effectiveness and efficacy of the revised programs. (Santos 2012, 8)

The ninth study of this second group considers the application of NICTs in the area of health surveillance. This is the master's thesis of Patrick Ribeiro (2013) defended in the Information Science Postgraduate Program at the School of

Communication of the Federal University of Rio de Janeiro and the Brazilian Institute for Science and Technology Information (UFRJ/IBICT). This is another theoretical study that based on a systematic review to understand the production of papers on the topic in order to see how they address the issue of information systems integration.

Studies in this second group have an essentially theoretical nature. They have not evaluated public policies that have generated well-being nor the use of digital technologies that increase citizens' control over their own health, strategies that have been articulated since the Ottawa Declaration (WHO 1986) and are recently found in the Brazilian PNPS (2015) and the "Shanghai Declaration" (WHO 2016).

The third group of studies identified in the survey did not find any similarities with the work of Lintonen et al. (2008).[16] These are six studies concerned with the search profile for health information on the Internet and its impacts on people's behavior.

One of them was submitted by Moretti (2012), in his PhD thesis defended at the Federal University of São Paulo (UNIFESP). Moretti (2012) sought to understand users' profile and search trends for health information on the Internet. His research was conducted with 1828 individuals who answered an electronic questionnaire made available in a commonly accessed health portal. He concluded that there is a predominance of female users seeking information for their own health (90%). Most of them use the Internet as the main source of health information (86%). They spend 5 to 35 h on the web per week (62%). Moretti (2012) concluded that the "Internet has been shown to be a source of health information of great relevance to the population." He argued: "the certification of sites is a strategy to be considered for improving the quality of information and promoting public health" (Moretti 2012, 16).

The second study in this third group was written by Giacomini (2011). In his master's thesis, defended in the Health Information and Communication Postgraduate Program at the Oswaldo Cruz Foundation (ICICT/Fiocruz), the author analyzed the interactions among people living with HIV/AIDS (PLHA) in virtual communities on the Internet. He aimed to understand to what extent interaction in these communities can make them into virtual spaces of community mutual assistance and promote individual behaviors of self-care and health promotion. Giacomini (2011) concluded his study affirming that:

> We observed the potential of virtual communities as spaces for Health Promotion and incentivizing self-care, which are fundamental to adhering to follow-up medical care and antiretroviral treatment of PLHA in follow-up care and health care services. (Giacomini 2011, X)

The theme of care with the elderly reappeared in our sample with the studies by Carleto (2013) and Miranda (2009).

[16] The third group of the study by Lintonen et al. (2008) gathered studies that use technological information as a research tool.

Carleto (2013) defended his master's thesis in the Bioengineering Postgraduate Program of the University of São Paulo (USP). His study examined how access to information and communication technologies (ICT) affects the generational relationships among the elderly. The convenience sample consisted of 160 subjects, specifically 80 elderly participating in digital inclusion programs, 40 elderly individuals not participating in digital inclusion programs, and 40 family members from the cities of Uberaba, Minas Gerais state, and Ribeirão Preto, São Paulo state, both located in southeast Brazil. He concluded by stating that NICTs exert a positive influence on the intergenerational relationships of the elderly. According to him, "the mastery of these technological resources in daily life tends to favor a feeling of self-efficacy among subjects and consequently affect their self-esteem, increasing their participation in this technological society and allowing new social roles and the experience that they continue being a part of society" (Carleto 2013, 7).

Miranda (2009) developed her master's thesis in the Physical Education Post-Graduation Program of the Federal University of Santa Catarina (UFSC). She investigated the contribution of the website *Saber + Saúde* (*Knowledge + Health*) in promoting healthy living habits for the elderly population. Her research, conducted over 4 months, involved 40 people (22 women and 18 men) over 60 years old who are Internet users and were not practicing physical activity. Many of the respondents reported using the Internet 4–7 times a week for about 21 min to 1 h. Miranda (2009) concluded that "a website that aims to inform and intervene about physical activity and health, personalized for the elderly population, can be effective and obtain good results" (Miranda 2009, 7).

Thus, these two studies do not evaluate any websites or their impact on the promotion of healthy life habits for the elderly population. Thus, they were placed in this third group of works.

Another recurring issue is living a healthy lifestyle. Freitas (2012), who studied in the Pediatrics Post-Graduation Program of the São Paulo School of Medicine at the Federal University of São Paulo (UNIFESP), identified this topic in her doctoral dissertation. Freitas' objective was to describe the social, economic, and epidemiological characteristics and lifestyles of those registered in the *Portal Estilo de Vida Saudável*.[17] A little more than 10% of those registered in this Portal participated in this cross-sectional study. She found that, "while there is still limited evidence that internet use can influence education about nutrition, it is an innovative and promising tool to motivate people to live healthier lives" (Freitas 2012, 9).

The doctoral thesis of Fraga (2005) was also concerned about healthy lifestyle. He transformed his study into a book, published the following year (Fraga 2006). His work, defended in the Education Post-Graduate Program of the School of Education of the Federal University of Rio Grande do Sul (UFRGS), discusses the strategies employed by information and communication technologies to persuade subjects that the accomplishment of daily 30 min of moderate physical activity "makes the difference."

[17] Portal Estilo de Vida Saudável: http://www.saude.br/index.php

He analyzes how the promotion of physical activities incorporates different strategies for governing bodies. In doing so, these practices construct a network for disseminating information that transforms the active life into a valuable object for the education of bodies, the regulation of health, and self-government.

According to Goellner (2009) who reviewed this book, Fraga (2006) "refers to Foucauldian genealogy to analyze how the construction of what he calls the 'machinery of agitation' and Deleuze's formulations on the control society to understand how, today, bodies are subject to a network of techniques, procedures, and knowledge that regulate lifestyles" (Goellner 2009, 673).

Finally, the master's thesis by Caran (2015) concerned the visually impaired. He investigated which factors facilitate and hinder access to information for the visually impaired. The realization of this work, defended in the Information Science Postgraduate Program of the School of Communication at the Federal University of Rio de Janeiro and the Brazilian Institute for Science and Technology Information (UFRJ/IBICT), relied on the participation of Facebook "Low Vision" group members. Caran (2015) concluded that "the general results of the research pointed to a varied set of intervening factors in the access to information that are multidisciplinary, overlapping, and interrelated" (Caran 2015, 10).

19.4 Final Considerations

The review by Lintonen et al. (2008), which served as reference for our study, analyzed papers published in academic journals and underwent peer evaluation. The empirical basis of our study is doctoral dissertations and master's theses published in Brazil. This is a first distinction between the two studies.

In this regard, it is worth mentioning a difference between our work and that of Lintonen et al. (2008) in relation to the construction of the sample. They did not make it clear which were the "15 relevant journals" they selected nor the reasons that led them to choose these journals specifically. It was also not clear how they adopted their search. In our research, the bibliographic database consulted, the search terms employed, the results of our search, and the list of the dissertations and theses analyzed were explained.

In our case, as in the study by Lintonen et al. (2008), the conclusions are provisional because the sample is not representative.

> In any case, it is likely that some relevant papers have been missed and, as a result, the observed extent of information technology use is an underestimate. (Lintonen et al. 2008, 563)

Although tentative, some reflections deserve to be made.

Firstly, it should be noted that the exponential growth of information and communication technologies in the lives of citizens was not reflected, in both cases, in the number of papers that associate this innovation with health promotion. In addition, the term health promotion was the only one used to cross-reference our data

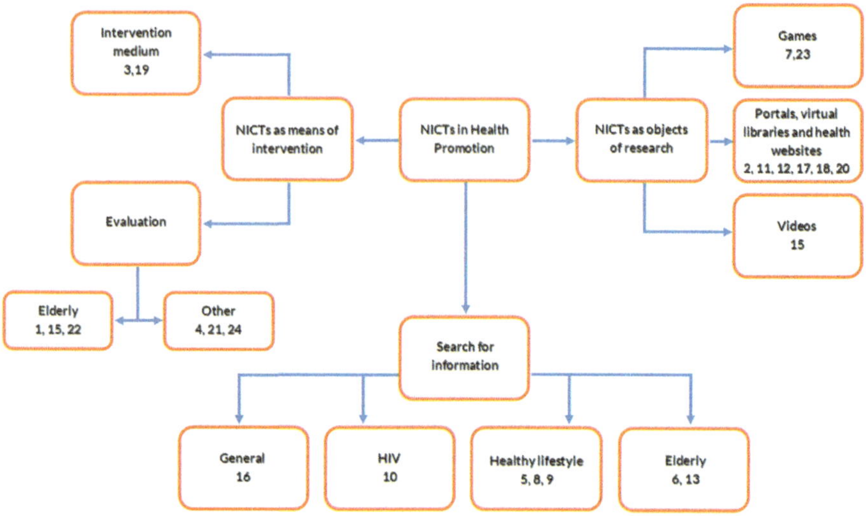

Fig. 19.2 The use of NICTs in health promotion – analysis of Brazilian academic production. Intervention medium; Games; NICTs as means of intervention; NICTs as objects of research; Portals, virtual libraries and health websites; Evaluation; Elderly; Other; Information and communication technologies in health promotion; Videos; Search for information; General; Elderly; HIV; Healthy lifestyle. (Source: Authors)

with information and communication technologies. But in a context where practices are realized in other words as communication for health or health education, it is likely that some academic articles have escaped our research.

As Lintonen et al. (2008) have noted, there were few critical studies. In our case, the work by Fraga (2005) is an exception. It reveals that the primacy of "lifestyles," so recurrent in the literature on health promotion, can be analyzed as a transitional strategy of the "disciplinary society," present in Foucault's (1975) thought, and the "control society" by Deleuze (1990).[18]

Lintonen et al. (2008) grouped the 56 titles found in their bibliographic survey into four groups (see Fig. 19.1, page 8). Each of them classifies an area where NICTs can be used in health promotion.

Our work has taken advantage of two of these groups and suggests the establishment of a third one aimed at evaluating users in relation to the impact of information and communication technologies on citizen health promotion, as shown in the figure below (Fig. 19.2).

One last comment deserves attention in order to conclude this chapter.

In our opinion, a good part of the Brazilian studies followed a biomedical logic and moved away from the parameters defined by international health promotion conferences. Some studies focused on specific pathologies and others in particular

[18]The influence of Foucault's contributions in the fields of social medicine and public health in Brazil is very large. For more details, see Rodrigues (2016).

age groups. The five items in the Ottawa Charter could not be observed in the studies found. For example, we did not identify a single study concerned with the construction of public policies aimed at the social determinants of health such as those focused on community action or a more healthy environment. We also did not find works that sought to emphasize the reorientation of health services, including their social, political, and environmental dimensions.

Thus, our study reached similar conclusions to those of Lintonen et al. (2008) insofar as it identified works whose "main use seems to have been to support interventions targeting individual persons" (Lintonen et al. 2008, 563).

Largely, Brazilian studies are attached to an individualistic understanding of lifestyle as responsible for people's health and disease condition. Few point out the importance of environments and social policies in health for individuals and communities. In addition, the context in which health actions supported and/or mediated through new information and communication technologies are inscribed has not been sufficiently recognized.

Thus, the challenge for Brazilian academic studies concerned with the impact that information and communication technologies have on health promotion is to include in the research agenda those aspects exhaustively voiced in the numerous international health meetings. These conferences preach that theory and practice of health promotion be associated with the idea of "living and working conditions that are safe, stimulating, satisfying, and enjoyable." We hope these ideas will translate into future studies and become a new trend.

Annex I List of Dissertations and Theses

List of dissertations and theses – in alphabetical order
1. Arakawa, Aline. 2015. *Portal dos idosos: desenvolvimento e avaliação de um website com informações sobre a doença de Alzheimer e suas conseqüências para a comunicação.* PhD diss., Universidade de São Paulo, São Paulo.
2. Berbel, Danilo. 2012. *A comunicação da ciência nas campanhas de saúde online: um estudo de caso do Portal da Saúde.* Master's thesis, Universidade Federal de São Carlos, São Carlos.
3. Bevilaqua, Leire. 2012. *Televisão digital e saúde: proposta para a produção de conteúdos.* Master's thesis, Universidade Estadual Paulista, São Paulo.
4. Bittencourt, Ivanise. 2012. *O processo de habilitação psicossocial de pessoas em sofrimento psíquico na interface com produção de blog.* Master's thesis, Universidade Federal de Alagoas, Maceió.
5. Caran, Gustavo. 2015. *O acesso à informação pelo deficiente visual e suas implicações para a Promoção da Saúde.* Master's thesis, Universidade Federal do Rio de Janeiro, Rio de Janeiro.
6. Carleto, Daniel. 2013. *Relações intergeracionais de idosos mediadas pelas tecnologias de informação e comunicação.* Master's thesis, Universidade de São Paulo, São Paulo.

List of dissertations and theses – in alphabetical order
7. Finco, Mateus. 2010. *Wii fit: um videogame do estilo de vida saudável*. Master's thesis, Universidade Federal do Rio Grande do Sul, Porto Alegre.
8. Fraga, Alex. 2005. *Exercício da informação: governo dos corpos no mercado da vida ativa*. PhD diss., Universidade Federal do Rio Grande do Sul, Porto Alegre.
9. Freitas, Anna Helena. 2012. *Estilos de Vida de Internautas Participantes de um Portal de Prevenção de Doenças Crônicas não Transmissíveis*. PhD diss., Universidade Federal de São Paulo, São Paulo.
10. Giacomini, Paulo. 2011. *Constelações sociais no ciberespaço posithivo: as comunidades virtuais como espaços de Promoção da Saúde das pessoas que vivem com HIV/AIDS*. Master's thesis, Fundação Oswaldo Cruz, Rio de Janeiro.
11. Lemos, Lúcia. 2009. *Discursos e práticas comunicacionais: saúde na web*. Master's thesis, Universidade Metodista de São Paulo, São Bernardo do Campo.
12. Lourenço, Regina. 2013. *Biblioteca virtual temática em saúde: interatividade com usuário leigo*. Master's thesis, Universidade Federal do Rio de Janeiro, Rio de Janeiro.
13. Miranda, Letícia. 2009. *A Internet enquanto ferramenta de orientação de atividade física na Promoção da Saúde do idoso*. Master's thesis, Universidade Federal de Santa Catarina, Florianópolis.
14. Moraes, Alice. 2004. *O uso de estratégias na transferência de informação nos vídeos em saúde*. PhD diss., Universidade Federal do Rio de Janeiro, Rio de Janeiro.
15. Moreira, Rafael. 2016. *Promoção e prevenção da saúde bucal de idosos baseados em um aplicativo mobile e realidade virtual*. Master's thesis, Universidade De Fortaleza, Fortaleza.
16. Moretti, Felipe. 2012. *Uso da internet para saúde. Tendência, perfil e comportamento de usuários*. PhD diss., Universidade Federal de São Paulo, São Paulo.
17. Picolini, Mirela. 2011. *Teleducação interativa na capacitação de estudantes do ensino fundamental em síndromes genéticas*. Master's thesis, Universidade de São Paulo, São Paulo.
18. Ribeiro, Patrick. 2013. *Redes Sociais online e dispositivos tecnológicos: sua utilização na vigilância e Promoção da Saúde*. Master's thesis, Universidade Federal do Rio de Janeiro, Rio de Janeiro.
19. Sant'ana, Nicolle. 2012. *Criação de uma ferramenta hipermídia para a Promoção da Saúde auditiva em jovens usuários de dispositivos sonoros portáteis individuais*. Master's thesis, Universidade de São Paulo, São Paulo.
20. Santos, Daniel. 2012. *Programas Educacionais de Promoção da Saúde Auditiva para Crianças e Adolescentes: Revisão da Literatura*. Master's thesis, Pontifícia Universidade Católica, São Paulo.
21. Silva, Rilvanda. 2009a. *Rádio UNIFESP Web: construção e avaliação de um modelo para a disseminação do conhecimento em saúde baseado em rádio na internet*. Master's thesis, Universidade Federal de São Paulo, São Paulo.
22. Silva, Ana Cláudia. 2009b. *Educação apoiada em tecnologias: desenvolvimento e avaliação de recursos didáticos para a formação de promotores de saúde*. PhD diss., Universidade de São Paulo, São Paulo.
23. Vasconcelos, Marcelo. 2013. *Comunicação e saúde em jogo: os vídeo games como estratégia de Promoção da Saúde*. PhD diss., Fundação Oswaldo Cruz, Rio de Janeiro.
24. Vieira Junior, Elso. 2014. *Modelo de curso para o treinamento dos profissionais que atuam nos salões de beleza usando a teleducação interativa*. PhD diss. Universidade de São Paulo, São Paulo.

References

Alleyne, George. 2001. The director's message. Annual Report of the Director – 2001. http://publications.paho.org/english/OD302_prelim.pdf. Accessed 02 June 2017.

Arakawa, Aline. 2015. *Portal dos idosos: desenvolvimento e avaliação de um website com informações sobre a doença de Alzheimer e suas conseqüências para a comunicação*. PhD diss., Universidade de São Paulo, São Paulo.

Berbel, Danilo. 2012. *A comunicação da ciência nas campanhas de saúde online: um estudo de caso do Portal da Saúde*. Master's thesis, Universidade Federal de São Carlos, São Carlos.

Bernhardt, Jay, Carol Runyan, Ingird Bou-Saada, and Elizabeth Felter. 2003. Implementation and evaluation of a Web-based continuing education course in injury prevention and control. *Health Promotion Practice* 4: 120–128.

Bevilaqua, Leire. 2012. *Televisão digital e saúde: proposta para a produção de conteúdos*. Master's thesis, Universidade Estadual Paulista, São Paulo.

Brazil. Ministério da Saúde. Secretaria de Vigilância em Saúde. Secretaria de Atenção à Saúde. 2006. *Política Nacional de Promoção da Saúde: PNPS*. Brasília: Ministério da Saúde.

———. 2015. *Política Nacional de Promoção da Saúde: PNPS: revisão da Portaria MS/GM n° 687, de 30 de março de 2006*. Brasília: Ministério da Saúde.

Breslow, Lester. 1999. From disease prevention to health promotion. *JAMA* 281: 1030–1033.

Bittencourt, Ivanise. 2012. *O processo de habilitação psicossocial de pessoas em sofrimento psíquico na interface com produção de blog*. Master's thesis, Universidade Federal de Alagoas, Maceió.

Caran, Gustavo. 2015. *O acesso à informação pelo deficiente visual e suas implicações para a Promoção da Saúde*. Master's thesis, Universidade Federal do Rio de Janeiro, Rio de Janeiro.

Carleto, Daniel. 2013. *Relações intergeracionais de idosos mediadas pelas tecnologias de informação e comunicação*. Master's thesis, Universidade de São Paulo, São Paulo.

Carvalho, Antônio Ivo, Marcia Westphal, and Vera Lúcia Lima. 2007. Health promotion in Brazil. Promotion & Education 14 supl. 1: 7–12.

Cirani, Cláudia, Milton Campanario, and Helóisa Helana Silva. 2015. A evolução do ensino da pós-graduação senso estrito no Brasil: análise exploratória e proposições para pesquisa. *Avaliação (Campinas)* 20: 163–187.

Charnock, Deborah, and Sasha Shepperd. 2004. Learning to DISCERN online: Applying an appraisal tool to health websites in a workshop setting. *Health Education Research* 19: 440–446.

De Vet, Emely, Johannes Brug, Jascha De Nooijer, Arie Dijkstra, and Nanne De Vries. 2005. Determinants of forward stage transitions: A Delphi study. *Health Education Research* 20: 195–205.

Deleuze, Gilles. 1990. *Pourparlers*. Paris: Les Éditions de Minuit.

Finco, Mateus. 2010. *Wii fit: um videogame do estilo de vida saudável*. Master's thesis, Universidade Federal do Rio Grande do Sul, Porto Alegre.

Fraga, Alex. 2005. *Exercício da informação: governo dos corpos no mercado da vida ativa*. PhD diss., Universidade Federal do Rio Grande do Sul, Porto Alegre.

———. 2006. *Exercício da informação: governo dos corpos no mercado da vida ativa*. Campinas: Autores Associados.

Freitas, Anna Helena. 2012. *Estilos de vida de internautas participantes de um portal de prevenção de doenças crônicas não transmissíveis*. PhD diss., Universidade Federal de São Paulo, São Paulo.

Foucault, Michel. 1975. *Discipline and punish: The birth of the prison*. New York: Random House.

Giacomini, Paulo. 2011. *Constelações sociais no ciberespaço posithivo: as comunidades virtuais como espaços de Promoção da Saúde das pessoas que vivem com HIV/AIDS*. Master's thesis, Fundação Oswaldo Cruz, Rio de Janeiro.

Goellner, Silvana. 2009. Exercício da informação: governo dos corpos no mercado da vida ativa. *Ciênc. saúde coletiva* 14: 673–674.

Gosciola, Vicente. 2007. A linguagem audiovisual do hipertexto. In *Hipertexto e Hipermídia: as novas ferramentas da comunicação digital*, ed. Pollyana Ferrari et al., 107–120. São Paulo: Contexto.

Hartz, Zulmira, Carmelle Goldberg, Ana Cláudia Figueiró, and Louise Potvin. 2014. Multiestratégias na Avaliação de Intervenções Comunitárias em Promoção da Saúde. In *Avaliação em Promoção da Saúde: uma antologia comentada da parceria entre Brasil e Cátedra de Abordagens Comunitárias e Iniquidades em Saúde (CACIS) da Universidade de Montreal de 2002 a 2012*, ed. Z. Hartz, L. Potvin, and R. Bodstein, 22–138. Brasília: Conselho Nacional de Secretários de Saúde.

IBGE – Brazilian Institute of Geography and Statistics. 2016. *Síntese de indicadores sociais: uma análise das condições de vida da população brasileira*. Rio de Janeiro: IBGE.

International Conference on Primary Health Care. 1978. Declaração de Alma-Ata. 1978. http://cmdss2011.org/site/wp-content/uploads/2011/07/Declara%C3%A7%C3%A3o-Alma-Ata.pdf. Accessed 1 Aug 2017.

Irvine, Blair, Dennis Ary, Dean Grove, and Lynn Gilfillan-Morton. 2004. The effectiveness of an interactive multimedia program to influence eating habits. *Health Education Research* 19: 290–305.

Kickbusch, Ilona. 2003. The contribution of the World Health Organization to a new public health and health promotion. *American Journal of Public Health* 93: 383–388.

———. 2006. Health promotion: Not a tree but a rhizome. In *Health promotion in Canada*, ed. M. O'Neill, A. Pederson, S. Dupéré, and I. Rootman. Toronto: Canadian Scholars' Press.

Labonté, Ronald. 2016. Health promotion in an age of normative equity and rampant inequality. *International Journal of Health Policy and management* 5: 675–682.

Lemos, Lúcia. 2009. *Discursos e práticas comunicacionais: saúde na web*. Master's thesis, Universidade Metodista de São Paulo, São Bernardo do Campo.

Lintonen, Tomi, Anne Konu, and David Seedhouse. 2008. Information technology in health promotion. *Health Education Research* 23: 560–566.

Lourenço, Regina. 2013. *Biblioteca virtual temática em saúde: interatividade com usuário leigo*. Master's thesis, Universidade Federal do Rio de Janeiro, Rio de Janeiro.

Minowa, Evelyn. 2016. *Produção científica dos grupos de pesquisa em Promoção da Saúde no Brasil: perfil e discussão de uma amostra nacional*. Master's thesis, Universidade de São Paulo, São Paulo.

Miranda, Letícia. 2009. *A Internet enquanto ferramenta de orientação de atividade física na Promoção da Saúde do idoso*. Master's thesis, Universidade Federal de Santa Catarina, Florianópolis.

Moraes, Alice. 2004. *O uso de estratégias na transferência de informação nos vídeos em saúde*. PhD diss., Universidade Federal do Rio de Janeiro, Rio de Janeiro.

Moreira, Rafael. 2016. *Promoção e prevenção da saúde bucal de idosos baseados em um aplicativo mobile e realidade virtual*. Master's thesis, Universidade De Fortaleza, Fortaleza.

Moretti, Felipe. 2012. *Uso da internet para saúde: tendência, perfil e comportamento de usuários*. PhD diss., Universidade Federal de São Paulo, São Paulo.

Parlove, Amy, Joan Cowdery, and Sarah Hoerauf. 2004. Acceptability and appeal of a web-based smoking prevention intervention for adolescents. *The International Electronic Journal of Health Education* 7: 1–8.

Picolini, Mirela. 2011. *Teleducação interativa na capacitação de estudantes do ensino fundamental em síndromes genéticas*. Master's thesis, Universidade de São Paulo, São Paulo.

Pinto, Elzimar. 2008. *Promoção da Saúde: uma nova política pode alterar um paradigma?*. Centro de Ciências Humanas e Naturais, Universidade Federal do Espírito Santo.

Potvin, Louise, and Catherine Jones. 2011. Twenty-five years after the Ottawa Charter: The critical role of health promotion for public health. *Canadian Journal of Public Health* 102: 244–248.

Ragon, Bruce. 2004. The use of technology by students at an HBCU. *The International Electronic Journal of Health Education* 7: 63–68.

Ribeiro, Patrick. 2013. *Redes Sociais online e dispositivos tecnológicos: sua utilização na vigilância e Promoção da Saúde*. Master's thesis, Universidade Federal do Rio de Janeiro, Rio de Janeiro.

Rodrigues, Heliana Conde. 2016. *Ensaios sobre Michel Foucault no Brasil: presença, efeitos, ressonâncias*. Rio de Janeiro: Lamparina.

Sant'ana, Nicolle. 2012. *Criação de uma ferramenta hipermídia para a Promoção da Saúde auditiva em jovens usuários de dispositivos sonoros portáteis individuais*. Master's thesis, Universidade de São Paulo, São Paulo.

Santos, Daniel. 2012. *Programas Educacionais de Promoção da Saúde Auditiva para Crianças e Adolescentes: Revisão da Literatura*. Master's thesis, Pontifícia Universidade Católica, São Paulo.

Silva, Rilvanda. 2009a. Rádio *UNIFESP Web: construção e avaliação de um modelo para a disseminação do conhecimento em saúde baseado em rádio na internet*. Master's thesis, Universidade Federal de São Paulo, São Paulo.

Silva, Ana Cláudia. 2009b. *Educação apoiada em tecnologias: desenvolvimento e avaliação de recursos didáticos para a formação de promotores de saúde*. PhD diss., Universidade de São Paulo, São Paulo.

The United Nations. 2015. Resolution adopted by the General Assembly on 25 September 2015. Transforming our world: The 2030 Agenda for Sustainable Development. http://www.un.org/ga/search/view_doc.asp?symbol=A/RES/70/1&Lang=E. Accessed 30 June 2017.

Townsend, Peter, and Nicholas Davidson, eds. 1982. *Inequalities in health: Black report*. Middlesex: Penguin Books.

Vandelanotte, Cornnel, and Ilse De Bourdeaudhuij. 2003. Acceptability and feasibility of a computer-tailored physical activity intervention using stages of change: Project FAITH. *Health Education Research* 18: 304–317.

Vasconcelos, Marcelo. 2013. *Comunicação e saúde em jogo: os vídeo games como estratégia de Promoção da Saúde*. PhD diss., Fundação Oswaldo Cruz, Rio de Janeiro.

Veras, Renato. 2012. Experiências e tendências internacionais de modelos de cuidado para com o idoso. *Ciênc. saúde coletiva* 17: 231–238.

Vieira Junior, Elso. 2014. *Modelo de curso para o treinamento dos profissionais que atuam nos salões de beleza usando a teleducação interativa*. PhD diss. Universidade de São Paulo, São Paulo.

Wen, Chao Lung. 2003. *Modelo de ambulatório virtual (cyber ambulatório) e tutor eletrônico (cyber tutor) para aplicação na interconsulta médica e educação à distância mediada por tecnologia [livre docência]*. PhD diss., Universidade de São Paulo, São Paulo.

WHO – World Health Organization. 1986. Ottawa charter for health promotion. Charter presented at: International conference on health promotion. http://www.phac-aspc.gc.ca/ph-sp/docs/charter-chartre/pdf/charter.pdf. Accessed on 29 June 2017.

———. 2016. Shanghai declaration on health promotion in the 2030 agenda for sustainable development. http://www.who.int/healthpromotion/conferences/9gchp/shanghai-declaration/en/. Accessed 24 Aug 2017.

Yamaguchi, Mirian, Marcelo Bernuci, and Gilberto Cezar Pavanelli. 2016. Produção científica sobre a Política Nacional de Promoção da Saúde. *Ciênc. saúde coletiva* 21: 1727–1736.

Chapter 20
Games and Health Communication: Brazilian Players' Point of View

Marcelo Simão de Vasconcellos, Flávia Garcia de Carvalho, and Inesita Soares de Araujo

Abstract This chapter discusses how online digital games could address shortcomings in traditional health communication strategies, namely, their centralized production, normative tone, and unidirectional diffusion, without space for dialogue with the population. Games could be used to present health content in attractive formats, fostering an active stance in seeking such content and even enhancing population's social participation. To this end, we analyze theoretical perspectives of meaning production in games like the concepts of serious games, procedural rhetoric, and games as participation. Our research methods include interviews with 22 players of a popular online digital game in order to draw conclusions about their views about the potential of digital games to communicate health themes and illustrate collective health issues. The research results allow us to conclude that participating in games and the fact that games generally bring participants together are decisive elements of the potential digital games for health.

20.1 Introduction[1]

Health communication is an important element to public health policies and is essential to democratic access to health services and to the improvement of the quality of life of the population. Brazil's public health system, known as SUS (Unified Health System), one of the largest in the world, manages public health and most of the health communication in Brazil, based on the principle that health is a right for every person and a duty of the state. SUS adopts an expanded concept of health, encompassing not only physical and mental well-being but all social, economic, cultural, ethnic, psychological, and behavioral factors, which influence the

[1]The findings presented in this chapter were originally presented as a paper in the Third International Conference on Serious Games and Applications for Health – SeGAH 2014, occurred in Rio de Janeiro, Brazil. The present chapter updates and further expands that paper.

M. S. de Vasconcellos (✉) · F. G. de Carvalho · I. S. de Araujo
Institute of Scientific and Technological Communication and Information in Health (ICICT), Oswaldo Cruz Foundation (Fiocruz), Rio de Janeiro, Brazil

A. Pereira Neto, M. B. Flynn (eds.), *The Internet and Health in Brazil*,
https://doi.org/10.1007/978-3-319-99289-1_20

occurrence of health problems and their risk factors in the population (Buss and Pellegrini Filho 2007).

SUS aims to provide comprehensive, universal preventive, and curative care, providing health services to the entire population and promoting community participation at all administrative levels (Victora et al. 2011). Consequently, the Brazilian government places a lot of importance in health communication strategies, using printed media, large health campaigns on radio and television, and, lately, websites and social media to provide the population with information about disease prevention, epidemics, and guidelines for a better quality of life (Victora et al. 2011).

However, such initiatives, particularly the big health communication campaigns, typically falter due to their centralized production and inability to cater to specific subpopulations. Moreover, they use an impersonal style, devoid of cultural references, that is unidirectional and focused on diffusing norms and encouraging behaviors for people to adopt. Such characteristics are inadequate in a country as diversified as Brazil and alienate several groups in society, limiting the efficacy of those campaigns (Araujo and Cardoso 2007; Araujo et al. 2009).

Even when dealing with new media like websites for vaccination campaigns, Facebook profiles for public health sectors, and specialized Twitter accounts dealing with major health topics, like AIDS, dengue fever, and Zika, public health communication initiatives still reproduce old practices, thus limiting themselves to spreading messages to the public and providing little opportunity for citizen dialogue. At the end of the day, this approach to public health communication runs the risk of reducing the amazing potential of the Internet to a mere electronic bulletin board (Araujo et al. 2009; Vasconcellos 2013).

This trend is clearly visible in many public health messages for AIDS prevention among youth. There is plenty of information available for teenagers, but the number of new HIV cases continues to grow. Data from the Brazilian Ministry of Health shows that while 97% of the population between 15 and 24 years old recognizes the importance of prophylactics, only 60.9% used them in their first sexual encounter (Santos 2010).

As an example, previous studies conducted by our institution a few years ago in a poor neighborhood in Rio de Janeiro support the Ministry of Health's data concerning knowledge about AIDS. The research confirmed that health information is widely available, but adolescents failed to appropriate the health concepts for their own lives. Study respondents complained about the dry style of health information about AIDS, its emphasis on the prescription of clinical measures, and its disconnection from other parts of life (e.g., love, friends, social status, etc.). They also complained about the type of language used in educational material, too removed from their local culture. Finally, they were annoyed with the constant repetition of such (to them) meaningless messages that ultimately became a factor toward rejecting them. As a result of these problems, the study detected a disregard about HIV risk among adolescents who considered official health communications as exaggerations, fictions, or something that was a risk only to other people (Cardoso and Lerner 2009).

Therefore, it is important to look for alternatives for communicating health content to diverse populations, particularly the younger generations,[2] in a way that connects effectively with their lives, creates possibilities for dialogue, and fosters their active search for information. We argue that online digital games, combining the appeal of games with the reach and ubiquity of the Internet, can be more effective in engaging the population in order to more actively learn about health.

Game media is based on players' agency, and players soon learn to be more active not only in the game but in real life as well (Yee and Bailenson 2007). Perhaps this has the added benefit of contributing to a more participatory approach in society. In its broadest aspect, participation refers to citizens exerting influence through political organization, consumption, and production. In the field of media, participation means the public's or audience's ability to contribute and influence the media production apparatus (Schäfer 2008). The fact that citizen participation in building public health policies is one of the principles of SUS, as mentioned before (Victora et al. 2011), further emphasizes such importance. Such qualities can contribute to filling the gap left by the traditional media and the old ways of health communication.

A 2010 survey ranked Brazil as the fourth world market for digital games, with approximately 35 million people (of the country's current population of 195 million inhabitants) playing routinely (Newzoo 2011). This population is not limited to children and adolescents. The majority of Brazilian players are between 25 and 34 years old, evenly distributed on both sexes (Pesquisa Game Brasil – 2017 2017). Another study reported that 90% of children from 5 to 9 years had their first experiences on computers and the Internet playing online games (Brazilian Internet Steering Committee 2011).

Games are not just popular, but they present a rich combination of text, audio, graphics, and interaction, allowing greater flexibility for presenting health content in interesting ways. Interactivity, perhaps the most typical characteristic of games, stimulates the user to take action instead of passively receiving information. Online gaming intensifies such interaction, creating many kinds of social connections through a digital medium. These characteristics could provide dialogue with the public that the conventional media lack. Games also tailor their contents to each player according to his/her skill, knowledge, and actions in game. At the same time, it is possible to measure players' responses to the game, informing the game designers about opportunities for its improvement (Lieberman 2001).

There are innovative projects applying digital games for educational purposes like Quest Atlantis (Barab et al. 2005) and even online games to aid in treating depression such as the game Sparx (Leasca 2012; Merry et al. 2012). Our objective with this work is to explore the potential for similar initiatives in Brazil, questioning whether digital games can represent a more effective form of health communication for contemporaneity, contributing to overcoming the limitations of more traditional media, focused on the diffusion of content.

[2] Chapter 7 addresses the issue of digital natives and health.

In order to answer this question, we will discuss the kind of games that aim to convey more than entertainment, called serious games, their definitions, and applications. Then, we will present procedural rhetoric, the main theory to explain how digital games convey meaning. We will also raise some potential issues coming from an exaggerated focus on this theory, proposing a more prominent position of the player concerning serious games' effects. We adopt the concept of games as a kind of participatory media culture. Then, we will present our research consisting of interviews with players of the online video game World of Warcraft. From the data analysis, we present conclusions about players' participation in the game and the potential of online games for health communication in Brazil.

In addition, despite dealing with the potential of online digital games for public health communication strategies in Brazil, the findings described here potentially apply to other scenarios and societies. We believe that discussing the use of online games as part of greater public health policies for the benefit of a country's whole population is relevant, since most of the literature about using games for health tends to focus more on content-delivering aspects and far less on player's agency and participation that are enhanced by the mix of digital games and online connections.

20.2 Serious Games for Health

Many researchers and educators defend the use of games for education, training, and other purposes. They argue that digital games make students develop an active problem-solving approach, allowing a progression of the content that is adaptable to the student's performance and able to simulate workplace situations, being more useful to real life than memorizing information (Gee and Shaffer 2005; Prensky 2004).

In the health field, digital games emerged in different areas, and in the last 20 years, they have been used in professional training, therapy, self-care, health promotion, and health communication (Papastergiou 2009). In 2006, the game Re-Mission became a notorious example of the great potential of digital games for health – demonstrating success in promoting knowledge and self-esteem in young cancer patients while enhancing their adherence to their treatment (Kato et al. 2008).

Games used for other purposes beyond entertainment are called serious games which, despite presenting educational content, tend to focus more on entertainment values than traditional educational games (Michael and Chen 2006). Since the emergence of the term serious games, both its supporters and its critics have struggled to reach consensus on its definition (Ritterfeld et al. 2009). Raessens (2010) argues that "Serious games are games that are designed and used with the intention or purpose of addressing the most pressing issues of our day and of having real-life consequences" (Raessens 2010, 95). Such a definition is useful for the purpose of health communication since it makes clear the correlation between the game and the player's active experience, suggests that topics addressed by serious games have social relevance, and highlights a connection between the game and the physical world beyond. Connecting the virtual and real worlds is an essential trait for serious games for health since players must carry the game's effects into their daily lives. Hence, it is important to understand how the player produces meaning from playing a serious game and what the specific contribution of game media is to build such meaning (Raessens 2005).

Bogost (2007) presented the concept of procedural rhetoric as the main form of meaning production in digital games, claiming that despite games' reliance on text, images, sounds, and other kinds of representation formats, their unique characteristic is their ability to communicate through processes and rules, creating dynamic metaphors for real-world processes. Similar to the Aristotelian concept of enthymeme, a syllogism that hides one of the premises and delegates to the listener filling the blank to complete the argument, the meanings of a serious game emerge when the player interacts with its rules. Under this view, a game consists of procedural enthymemes that the player completes by interacting with the game system, thus uncovering the game's message. Such interaction follows parameters and rules previously defined by the game designer, and the player's role is to fill the gap between game rules and her individuality, which Bogost calls "simulation gap." By reconstructing the meaning embedded in the rules, the player would "solve" or "win" the game and be persuaded (Bogost 2007). It follows from this approach that a serious game requires careful planning to build a procedural argument with the correct simulation gaps in order to convey the correct message to the player.

Procedural rhetoric states that the meaning of a game is contained in its rules, forcibly assuming a player who plays the game in a predictable manner without space for deviations or additions of her contributions to the game (Sicart 2012). However, despite procedural rhetoric's importance for Game Studies, an exclusive or exaggerated emphasis on its tenets raises some problematic implications. First, confining the meaning of a video game to its rules disregards narrative elements that give meaning to rules and mechanics, thereby making the game designer the main responsible for the game and devaluating other professionals who participate in its creation, like writers, artists, musicians, animators, and others. Second, the emphasis on procedural rhetoric promotes a deterministic view of the game media, since often the player's role is relegated to connecting the dots previously laid out by the game designer (Ferrari 2010). The game risks becoming instrumental, determined by reason and subject to rigid rules, objectives, and systems, too removed from the act of playing (Sicart 2012). It also states that there is a "right way" to experience a game, defined by the authority of the game designer, and thus creating digital games with strict paths, assuming that adequate reception of the game supposedly would result in a perfect transfer of knowledge (Vasconcellos 2013). Ultimately, this disregards the creative potential of the players. As many empirical studies about experiencing games confirmed, there is plenty of room for imperfections, distortions, and co-creation in the players' appropriation of game content. Players often ignore the rules or play inefficiently on purpose and even subvert said rules for their amusement (Ferrari 2010). However, we shouldn't see this as failures but as a legitimate act of active appropriation of games by the players and, therefore, a confirmation of the expressive potential of the medium by acknowledging players as co-creators of the playful experience (Vasconcellos 2013).

This personal aspect of the production of meaning is even more visible in multiplayer games. The impact of the Internet on the field of games cannot be overstated. When games started to allow connections between players, a range of new possibilities for playing emerged. Online games now could provide not only online fun but contact with fellow players all around the world. Often, online games' rules become mere excuses for social interaction with other players (Sicart 2012). Thus, any process of production of meaning in digital games must necessarily take into account the intervention of the player, since the experience of playing a video game will result from the interrelationships between rules, players, and culture (Vasconcellos 2013). In this regard, Raessens argues that participation is a distinctive characteristic of digital games, describing not only their specificity but also the media culture around them (Raessens 2005).

Related to participation is participatory culture, which operates in an environment of social participation, presents low barriers to civic and artistic expression, fosters mentorship, and places value in sharing, contribution, feedback, and social connection (Jenkins et al. 2006). The digital games' culture shares many of these characteristics, which allows their classification as participatory media culture, facilitating or promoting public participation in three aspects: interpretation, reconfiguration, and construction (Raessens 2005).

Interpretation refers to how the player perceives the media of digital games. Although similar to the interpretation that occurs in other media such as television and film, it is also active and participatory. Interpretation is socially situated, incorporating three reading strategies, which in terms of games are dominant-hegemonic (accepting a game according to the dominant ideology), oppositional (playing it against such ideology), and negotiated (with varying degrees of adaptation) (Raessens 2005).

Reconfiguration exists in two forms in games. The first is the freedom that the player has to explore a game. Different from media such as film, where the viewer follows the narrative from a fixed point, a digital game provides the player with a wide range of means to analyze strategically and reposition her point of view to discover new interpretations like walking, checking character's attributes, weapons, and the score. The second form of reconfiguration means manipulating elements of the game to get some effect, like building a farm, firing a gun, or pressing a button to open a door. Reconfiguration is related to the act of closing the "simulation gap" (Bogost 2007), and perhaps it is the most typical type of participation in digital games. However, it happens within a space of possibilities created by the game designers, and these possibilities are fixed, programmed in the code that gives shape to the video game (Raessens 2005). In digital games, interpretation and reconfiguration tend to happen together most of the time, since the player is continually interacting with the changes in the game systems.

Construction is the third domain of participation in digital games, meaning the addition of player-created elements to the game. It encompasses a range of activities that include alteration of narrative aspects and rules of a game; the addition of objects, interfaces, systems, or functions; and even reusing parts of digital games to create new games from different genres. According to Raessens (2005), construction depends mostly on programming skills. Thus, given the necessary ability to intervene successfully in the structure of the internal code of the video game, such participation tends to be much less common than interpretation and reconfiguration. Despite its reliance on technical aspects, construction often is part of social and cultural movements, when, for example, a player reprograms the game to change the protagonist's gender as a political statement (Johnston 2012).

Another example from 2 years ago perhaps can better convey the impact of construction practices in a social context. Several games today allow the use of "mods," small pieces of code that can significantly alter a game's rules, even adding new content. These mods are given for free by their creators (called "modders"), but in 2015, Steam, the biggest online game retailer, decided to allow the creators of mods for the very popular game Skyrim to charge for their creations (Campbell 2015). Suddenly, a violent debate took place, with many players condemning this practice and questioning its ethical aspects. Perhaps the most interesting aspect of this conflict was the "protest mods," mods that violently denounced the sale of mods, by mocking Steam's founders, having a price tag of thousands of dollars or merely being blatantly useless (Chalk 2015; Grayson 2015). This way, players appropriated one of the game functions to create protests against mod charging inside the very game that was charging them. The procedural rhetoric of Skyrim's inner workings was subverted by players to fuel their activist initiatives.

Although Raessens defines construction as changing the game by means of programming, we believe that other creative players' behaviors could also fall in this category. This type of construction would add to the digital game without necessarily relying on programming. It includes, among other practices, role-playing events in online games like collective reenactments parties, marriages between characters, guilds, politics, and even the creation of characters' background story (Vasconcellos 2013). Similarly, the search for loopholes in the rules and game system, and even cheating for personal gain, also could be considered examples of construction (Glas 2010). Thus, in addition to the programming form of construction, it is possible to infer that there is also a construction form that happens socially, which for many players is one of the greatest appeals of online games.

While many digital games for health tend to focus on the interpretation domain by presenting health information to the player, we believe that reconfiguration and construction are the most promising domains for health communication in games. Reconfiguration provides greater freedom to the public to learn about health in a gradual, personalized way, engaging the player in an active pursuit of knowledge while she is playing the game. Construction, although more difficult to be fostered, could be even more effective, since it allows players to share their ideas and creativity. We believe that this domain of participation, in particular, could be a unique contribution to the digital game media to foster a more socially participant society, especially in the field of health communication.

20.3 Methods

In order to confirm if the theoretical findings corresponded to actual practices in the virtual world of an online game, we conducted interviews with players from Rio de Janeiro, who mainly played online games. Our intent was to assess their opinions about using games for other objectives beyond fun, how they used them as means of communication, and if and how they engaged in participatory activities (interpretation, reconfiguration, and particularly in construction domains). The interviews were conducted in person and digitally recorded. This research was approved by the Ethics Committee of the Polytechnic School of Health Joaquim Venâncio of Oswaldo Cruz Foundation.

Conditions for participating in this study were being a resident in the state of Rio de Janeiro, being of legal age (18 years old in Brazil), and being a player of the online game World of Warcraft. This game was selected because it is the online game with the largest community in Brazil and is the only massively multiplayer online role-playing game (MMORPG) completely translated and adapted to Brazilian language and culture (Vasconcellos 2013).

World of Warcraft is the biggest MMORPG in the world, peaking at 12 million players in 2010 (VG247 2013). Its popularity fostered a large number of related products like action figures, board games, books, toys, and many fan-created productions. Players of the game share a magical fantasy world populated with humanoid races and monsters. The setting is inspired by previous fantasy games and literary works, but the game designers gradually added elements from other sources like science fiction and pop culture. Each player creates a character (his avatar) and with it explores the world, interacts with the environment, creatures, and other players. Combat is prominent in the game, and players can cooperate in battle against the enemies controlled by the game or can fight among themselves. Like most MMORPGs, its virtual world is persistent and three-dimensional and hosts many player communities and groups within it (Glas 2010).

Several scholars in the field of Game Studies recommend that video game researchers acquire some gaming experience of the titles that they are researching in order to know what questions to ask and understand the context of the game, reaping benefits from a direct experience even when not specifically working with participant observation or other ethnographic methods (Glas 2010; Aarseth 2003). Thus, we devoted 3 months to explore many facets of the game, playing with different characters, exploring several game strategies, and taking part in several activities. This experience allowed us to understand better the answers that resulted from the interviews.

Concerning the subjects, key members of the local chapter of International Game Developers Association (IGDA) suggested the first names, followed by a snowball sampling of other gamers referenced by the first respondents. We contacted the selected subjects by phone or e-mail, and once they agreed to participate in the study, they signed a consent form. Confidentiality was assured for all the subjects. In total, 22 participants were interviewed.

The interviews were semi-structured, and the questions concerning the present study were in three categories: experience with games, opinions about serious games and health games, and behavior within the game and with other players. The questions were:

A. **Experience with games**

1. How long have you played digital games?
2. How long have you played online games?
3. How long have you played World of Warcraft?
4. Have you played with more than one character?

B. **Opinions about serious games and health games**

5. What is your opinion about serious games?
6. Do you think it is possible to use digital games for health communication?
7. How do you imagine these games?
8. What would attract you to play such games?

C. **Behavior within the game and with other players**

9. How is your relationship with other players? Are you part of regular groups or a guild?
10. Have you ever met someone in a game who you later contacted online or face to face?
11. Do you participate in forums, blogs, or websites about World of Warcraft?
12. Do you use or create mods?
13. Do you engage in cheating, "ganking," or "griefing"?[3]
14. Have you ever created some media related to the game (like a post in blogs or social networks, drawing, cartoon, comic, video, or "machinima")?[4]

When analyzing the answers, we focused mainly on the aspects of reconfiguration and construction reported by the players. Since the different aspects of participation do not happen in a neutral way but imply factors like the player, her cultural heritage, and the environment that surrounds her, we also used in our analysis concepts from a game model that emphasizes the social aspects of communication and participation.

The "Model for Relational Analysis of Games: Contexts, Participation, and Apparatus" – MoRAG – describes the main relations between the game as an object, the player, and, through her, other players, under a participatory view. It understands the game as an activity that is socially inserted and that in turn reverberates throughout society (Vasconcellos et al. 2017).

[3] "Ganking" is using a very powerful character to defeat another that is clearly less powerful. "Griefing" is causing distress, irritation, or anger to another player on purpose.

[4] "Machinima" comes from machine + animation, meaning animations and movies made inside a game.

Under MoRAG's perspective, an amalgamation of several contexts conditions the way a player produces meaning from game media. It is possible to define four contexts, mutually constituted in a dynamic and continuous process. The "existential context" refers to the individuality of the player, his background, and personal history. "Situational context" concerns a player's position in society in a given moment, also called "place of interlocution." "Intertextual context" includes references to other texts, previously integrated into the private background of each individual or group. Finally, the "technological context" describes all technological aspects surrounding the experience within a digital game as technological competence, hardware capabilities, Internet connection, game controls, and even abusive practices like the use of unauthorized programs for cheating (Vasconcellos et al. 2017). These contexts helped us to understand participants' answers better.

20.4 Results and Discussion

20.4.1 Serious Games and Health Games

When asked about serious games, the players at first misunderstood the term as a synonym for educational games and were very critical of these kinds of games. Several participants stressed that educational games were boring, poorly executed, and ineffective. In their view, any game, even for educational purposes, must be fun and engaging. This misconception is understandable, since "serious games" is still a recent expression. Nevertheless, the players' strong rejection of educational games confirmed a widespread perception that games focused on education and other purposes like health are dull and ineffective for learning, even when made with the best of intentions.

One of the reasons participants suggested they received educational games negatively was the overly direct approach and even imposition of educational content onto the players without first winning their interest. Another reason was the often poor adaptation of thematic content, transplanted directly into the game, making educational games similar to textbooks in disguise. They also complained of the disregard of games' fun and engagement and finally the amateurism of such productions, as well as their inferior originality, story, graphics, and rules in relation to entertainment games. Several respondents suggested abandoning terms like "educational" and "educative" due to the previous failures of many low-quality products.

In their view, one way to correct these problems would be making the educational content implicit in the game, giving the player a chance to discover it for herself. They also stressed the importance of providing a proper context to health information both in terms of the rules and in terms of the story presented in the game, such as including well-developed characters with credible lives in the game, allowing players to experience health issues through their perspectives.

Concerning the use of digital games for health communication, all respondents stated their belief that games could be very effective, due to their ability to put players in different situations, allowing them to train new skills and to gather knowledge and experience about other life situations, providing relaxation, and socializing as well. These advantages would make digital games far superior to traditional media when adequately applied to instructional purposes.

While acknowledging the high cost of consoles and personal computers in Brazil, especially taking into account the population's income levels, participants still did not believe that digital games are economically inaccessible to the general public. The constant cheapening of equipment and Internet connections and the emergence of new digital inclusion public initiatives[5] have contributed to the growth of the adoption of digital games, even among poor population. The proliferation of Internet cafes in low-income areas and the ability to rent computers with Internet access at very low prices are important factors of digital inclusion in Brazil. Finally, the consolidation of mobile platforms like smartphones and tablets as game platforms also contribute to increasing the potential public for digital games (Brazilian Internet Steering Committee 2010).

Concerning their ideas for health games, some respondents suggested scenarios where the player should identify diseases or deal with epidemics, similar to medical TV shows. Others suggested teaching notions of health to players through historical scenarios, like a game occurring during the black plague. What was common in these answers was the reliance of these hypothetical health games on strong stories and narratives as means to ensure the player's immersion in the subject, an aspect that many participants considered essential to attract players to such games.

Some participants also suggested strategies not confined to the virtual world, as combinations of digital games, card games, and board games, expanding them into the physical world. Similarly, one subject suggested games with tasks in both online and in the physical world, like combining Internet research about health with visits to hospitals, health research centers, and poor communities, thereby putting the players in touch with more realistic situations and even contributing social benefits to a game.

Although there are diseases in the game World of Warcraft, the term usually refers to magical effects, and there is no intention to create any similarities with real diseases. The representation of the "health" of a character is abstract, in the form of a horizontal bar that decreases with hits in combat and when it ends, the character dies. Death, however, has negligible implications for the player: his character resurrects in a cemetery nearby and returns to the game. Nevertheless, participants actively seek to enhance the physical power and well-being of their characters, since situations of disability (loss of movement, strength, or skills) are common in the game. While players considered death a mere inconvenience, they avoided any limitations or disabilities on their characters at all costs.

Paradoxically, the most realistic representation of disease in the game happened because of a defective game system, the Corrupted Blood event, in September 2005.

[5] Chapter 4 discusses "Piraí Digital," a digital inclusion project in Brazil.

This so-called plague originated from a common life-draining magical effect in the game that went out of control, transmitted to vulnerable characters, originating a virtual epidemic that killed the characters of millions of players. Later, two groups of epidemiologists reported that the behavior of players during the event had striking similarities with behaviors reported in human populations during real outbreaks, suggesting that virtual worlds could function as dynamic laboratories for epidemiological studies (Balicer 2007; Lofgren and Fefferman 2007).

One of the participants experienced this epidemic and narrated in detail the moments of perplexity; he experienced finding big cities in the game deserted, with hundreds of corpses littering the floor. Once contaminated, he experienced a constant struggle for preserving his character's life while impotently watching people around him dying by dozens. Later, thinking about the event, he concluded that contracting a degenerative disease inside World of Warcraft somehow made him understand better the experience of his deceased father, who died after a long battle with cancer.

20.4.2 Social Activities

Social activities are an inherent part of online games. In World of Warcraft, there is a distinction between combat with enemies controlled by the game (player vs. environment – PvE) and combat with other players (player vs. player – PvP), but participants reported that in both cases it is common for players to cooperate to achieve their goals. Many subjects reported that playing in a group was essential to enjoy the game, and two participants reported never playing alone. Thus, despite group play being developed as a way to overcome the challenges of World of Warcraft, for many participants, playing in a group has less to do with goals and more with the interaction inside the virtual world, with some of them explicitly declaring this was their main reason to be online.

While some participants reported starting friendships in World of Warcraft, and sometimes meeting these people in physical world afterward, respondents mostly played the game with friends or acquaintances from the "real" (physical) world. In this sense, World of Warcraft becomes less like a hub for new friendships and more like a new social space for a group of friends, integrating the routine of the group's social activities. Similarly, many subjects do not communicate much with players outside their circle of friends, with the exception of members of their guilds. In some cases, this was made on purpose, aiming to avoid contact with players not proficient in game or who lack politeness, which could result in situations that hinder the smooth progress of gaming sessions. Overall, participants feel that groups formed by strangers experience less cohesion, as group bonds break easily and the experience is less enjoyable.

Player guilds were introduced in World of Warcraft as a means to structure bigger groups of players in a more stable form. Typically, the individual player relates to his closest friends, plays with a small group, and finally tends to belong to a guild. Although guild affiliation relates to game objectives, as time passes the relationship between guild members becomes more personal. The participants mentioned episodes where they formed temporary groups with strangers in order to win specific challenges, but most of their relationships occurred at the individual level between offline friends or guild members. Thus, the guild is the main community space in World of Warcraft. Additionally, while the term "community" is very frequently used to describe the population of players in an online game like World of Warcraft, it is important to keep in mind that this community is not necessarily an integrated whole, since several small enclaves, represented by the guilds, maintain little or no contact with other guilds.

Many participants reported developing a sense of duty to their guild, modifying their behavior in the game in many ways in order to help the guild collective. In addition, cases of mentoring are common, when a more experienced player helps a beginner, providing guidance in learning the rules, giving items or resources, or even assisting her in battles. This sense of duty acts as a fulcrum for many players, and participants pointed out the relationship with friends in the game as the main reason that kept them playing World of Warcraft. Crossing between physical and virtual often occurs in the collective context too, with groups and guilds of players organizing meetings in bars and restaurants for socializing or even combining joint game sessions in cyber cafes.

Thus, concerning social activities, it was observed that most of the contacts between players in World of Warcraft transferred from the physical world. Once the player has friends and becomes part of a guild in the game, he tends to focus his social relationships in this social group. Although it is not possible to say that all communities in World of Warcraft exist because of groups of offline friends, this seems to be a significant factor. The importance of the social element for keeping the players in World of Warcraft aligns with other research about online games conducted in other societies (Nardi and Harris 2006).

20.4.3 Construction in World of Warcraft

Among the domains of participation in digital games, probably the one which has more potential for application in public policies of health communication is the construction domain. While interpretation and reconfiguration often occur together, construction happens in fewer and more marked instances.

World of Warcraft is designed primarily for the interpretation and reconfiguration domains of participation, but it is possible for players to create "add-ons" or pieces of code that affect the game's behavior. While radical changes in the operation of World of Warcraft are not possible, since the core game runs on secure servers, "add-ons" can be quite versatile tools to customize the game experience, allowing the reorganization of the game's interface, which can have significant effects on players' performance. There are "add-ons" to help group leaders organize their missions, to mark treasures found on the map and to do many other activities.

Subjects reported frequent use of "add-ons," but just two respondents were interested in creating them, given the specific programming knowledge they require.

Although the domain of construction in the games defined by Raessens (2005), as changing the code of a video game through programming, there is a wide range of practices that are related to creative aspects while not directly affecting the gameplay mechanics, and it seems appropriate to categorize them as subtypes of construction.

A common practice is taking screenshots during playing, capturing awkward or funny scenes, inspiring scenes, poses of victory over powerful enemies, and even images that subvert immersion in the game, such as bugs that cause bizarre events. These images are shared on websites or social networks, recording significant events at the individual or social level and also showing to others the adventures in the game. Two participants, a young couple in the physical world, created a "photo album" in Facebook, containing only pictures of their characters together in different regions of World of Warcraft, as a memento of their relationship.

More sophisticated creative activities were also mentioned. Some people wrote biographies for their characters, trying to give them motivations and existential dramas, while others wrote stories about events experienced in the game, like wars in which they participated. There is also creation of cartoons, comics, illustrations, and funny photomontages. Participants also recorded videos during play, for sharing online or turning into "machinimas," short movies made inside the game. One of the participants, who also enjoyed playing board games, even created a board game about World of Warcraft as a tribute to the game. In general, they were not concerned with gain beyond personal satisfaction and mentioned that these activities were just ways to enjoy more of World of Warcraft.

In these examples, players enhance their experiences of World of Warcraft, helping to maintain the illusion of a collectively experienced dynamic world. Even when they record bugs and failures, breaking the epic tone of the game, it is possible to note their familiarity with the environment, like being comfortable enough to play with the elements of the game without fear of breaking the spell. It is perhaps a way to have fun with a well-established virtual daily routine.

Creative participation with more structured contours involves making text and video tutorials that teach beginners to play the game; guides detailing professions, classes, regions, or races; and other articles explaining aspects of World of Warcraft. In addition, subjects reported participating in forums, seeking help, or answering newbies' questions about the game. In these spaces, participation goes beyond the limits of the virtual world, and research shows that at least 30% of players participate in discussions about World of Warcraft, a high number compared with typical rates of participation among fan cultures (Glas 2010). It is possible to say that a whole ecosystem of websites, forums, blogs, fan pages, YouTube channels, and other forms of communication has emerged around World of Warcraft, greatly expanding its influence, even when players are not actually playing the game (Vasconcellos 2013).

There is also another type of participation that adds elements to the game without manipulating its code. This aspect of construction happens through social contact between players, who create procedures and customs, working within the general rules of the video game and generating specific practices inside it. Examples found in the interviews range from simple moments of dramatic interpretation of a character to complex simulations of social events performed in a game, such as diplomatic parties and weddings.

This type of construction is not always ethically oriented, and many players develop behaviors that violate the game experience as planned by the game designers. These acts include cheating (using illegal programs), "ganking" (repeatedly attacking a weaker player), and general "griefing" that includes stealing, harassing, mocking, insulting, scamming, or otherwise disrupting other players' activities for fun. Only one participant reported using programs for cheating, while another one reported doing "ganking" often. Yet, most of the participants were very critical of these borderline behaviors.

Although such acts are condemned by many players, they can sometimes lead to curious developments. One participant reported an occasion when he and a group of friends started a war between major factions of the game through a complex sequence of lies, intrigues, and subterfuges. The war went on for weeks with widespread conflicts between the two factions, until coalitions of guilds from both sides met in a council and decided to make a peace treaty. According to him, what started as a joke became a world conflict and subsequently was solved in a political way. Months after these events, people still recounted their "war stories," and the participant felt he has contributed to making the game more memorable to everyone.

Politics is often present in relations between players. Many participants reported taking part in elections to choose leaders for their guilds or voting to decide activities or missions. In addition, there is a whole range of interpersonal relations necessary to win allies or influence other players, whether in a guild or outside it. Thus, the game systems that form World of Warcraft can be seen as a kind of raw material or prop where players organize themselves to create innovations in the social aspects of the game, often building sophisticated social and political structures. This can be an example of Huizinga's view of how the game is socially agreed (Huizinga 1955). Although the rules and game mechanics that form World of Warcraft's systems are technologically coded, players fill in the gaps, building their own systems and content over the basic rules in order to create their particular meanings for the experience of playing the digital game.

20.5 Conclusion

The complaints about educational games concerning their excessive focus on content and lack of adaptability echo the previously mentioned complaints from youngsters regarding health communication about AIDS. This strong rejection of the static content and lack of fun in educational games should guide future initiatives in order to not repeat such mistakes. Digital games can be much richer for health communication than mere channels for disseminating content. Games allow players to experience other life stories and rethink their health, as the mentioned example of the player who gained a new understanding of his father's death after experiencing disease in the game. Thus, this study confirms that games encourage players' actions not as operators but as active participants, engaging themselves far beyond the rules of the game. This is particularly true for online games, where Internet connections make interactions with many other people possible, creating opportunities for cooperation, organized action, and political activism, as well as fostering the creation of communities and even a feeling of citizenship within a game world.

It was also possible to expand the original definition of construction to include players' cultural and social productions inspired by or based on a given game. One result of this participatory culture is the dissolution of boundaries between producer and consumer, making players more emancipated, creative, and community-oriented. They create content both within the game through their actions and outside the game as well. Such contributions are essential to the amplitude of the video game and a fundamental part of the richness of the gaming experience. Participatory acts of construction represent innovative ways for appropriating the virtual world, by which players continually produce meanings for themselves. Through these activities, each player develops new ways of having fun, interacting with each other in the game, improving the gaming environment, and taking ownership of aspects of the virtual world.

Despite the danger of an exaggerated faith in the benefits of participatory culture, construction in its various aspects is a crucial part of the potential of digital games for health. It is a movement of player empowerment, as participants become co-producers of games and contributors to a community. Both aspects align with the tenets of health promotion. This way, a hypothetical online video game for health promotion would foster players' protagonism, creating a dynamic and participant society in the virtual world, in which players could contribute with proposals and strategies on health, bringing these ideas to public debate and encouraging such players to be more active in society. Thus, such a game could foster health communication by giving voice and opportunity for action to the population. The health managers themselves could enter the virtual world to communicate with the public and learn from their cultural production and activism.

Our research also confirmed how the game works as a social aggregator among participants. More than a game to be won, World of Warcraft, as the name suggests, is an environment, not only because of its geography and history but also mainly due to its communities. The connections between the virtual and physical world are constant, allowing the migration of relationships made inside the game to other areas of life and vice versa. In the social aspect, construction can be even richer for communication initiatives in public health, since it highlights the collective aspect of health promotion.[6] Interacting with other players through competition, cooperation, or combat, a player would verify firsthand that in society everyone has a role and some level of influence. Responsibility with others, companionship in the face of

[6]Chapter 19 discusses the use of information and communication technologies in health promotion.

danger and disease, collaboration to effect changes, and public debate to define strategies are activities that potentially could show players new ways for understanding public health, where the health of an individual is not a personal and isolated matter anymore but part of a larger whole.

Finally, digital games dedicated to health communication would be versatile enough to model many situations and scenarios in order to challenge players' conceptions about individual and collective health. Such situations would not be limited to epidemiological issues, as happened in World of Warcraft's epidemic, but they could include political and social aspects, making the game a fertile space for virtual experimentation and rehearsing of new approaches to public health policies. Although perfect health communication is not only dependent on the population but an integral part of broader political processes, the use of online games in health communication could make an enormous contribution toward enhancing information flows. This includes citizens' interest in actually participating in public health policies, from the identification of health priorities until their deployment and reception, thereby making these games an innovative option for health communication. It is our hope that new advances in the use of online digital games for health communication will foster the participation of gamers on many levels, allowing lessons about health learned in the virtual world to be fruitfully used within its physical counterpart, for the benefit of all of society.

References

Aarseth, Espen. 2003. Playing research: Methodological approaches to game analysis. http://www.bendevane.com/VTA2012/wp-content/uploads/2012/01/02.GameApproaches2.pdf. Accessed 7 June 2018.

Araujo, Inesita S., and Janine M. Cardoso. 2007. *Comunicação e saúde*. Rio de Janeiro: Editora Fiocruz.

Araujo, Inesita S., Janine M. Cardoso, and R. Murtinho. 2009. A comunicação no Sistema Único de Saúde: cenários e tendências. *Revista Latinoamericana de Ciencias de la Comunicación* 6: 104–115.

Balicer, Ran D. 2007. Modeling infectious diseases dissemination through online role-playing games. *Epidemiology* 18: 260–261.

Barab, Sasha, Michael Thomas, Tyler Dodge, Robert Carteaux, and Hakan Tuzun. 2005. Making learning fun: Quest Atlantis, a game without guns. *Educational Technology Research and Development* 53: 86–107.

Bogost, Ian. 2007. *Persuasive games: The expressive power of videogames*. Cambridge: The MIT Press.

Brazilian Internet Steering Committee. 2010. *Survey on the use of information and communication technologies in Brazil – ICT LANHOUSES*. São Paulo: Brazilian Internet Steering Committee.

———. 2011. *Pesquisa TIC Crianças 2010: Pesquisa sobre o uso das Tecnologias de Informação e Comunicação no Brasil*. São Paulo: CGI.

Buss, Paulo M., and Alberto Pellegrini Filho. 2007. A saúde e seus determinantes sociais. *PHYSIS: Rev Saúde Coletiva* 17: 77–93.

Campbell, Colin. 2015. Facing extreme abuse, Skyrim modders defend paid work. Polygon. https://www.polygon.com/2015/4/27/8504939/facing-extreme-abuse-skyrim-modders-defend-paid-work. Accessed 22 June 2017.

Cardoso, Janine, and Katia Lerner. 2009. Young people and the discourse on AIDS: From the centrality of context to the appropriation of sense. *RECIIS* 3: 66–74.

Chalk, Andy. 2015. Fake "protest mods" hit the Steam Workshop. PCGamer. http://www.pcgamer.com/fake-protest-mods-hit-the-steam-workshop/. Accessed 22 June 2017.

Ferrari, Simon. 2010. *The judgement of procedural rhetoric*. Master's thesis, Georgia Institute of Technology, Atlanta.

Gee, James P., and David W. Shaffer. 2005. *Before every child is left behind: How epistemic games can solve the coming crisis in education*. Madison: Wisconsin Center for Education Research.

Glas, René. 2010. *Games of stake: Control, agency and ownership in World of Warcraft*. PhD diss., University of Amsterdam, Amsterdam.

Grayson, Nathan. 2015. Steam's most popular Skyrim mod is a protest against paid mods. Kotaku. http://steamed.kotaku.com/steams-most-popular-skyrim-mod-is-a-protest-against-pai-1700486550. Accessed 22 June 2017.

Huizinga, Johan. 1955. *Homo ludens: A study of the play-element in culture*. Boston: The Beacon Press.

Jenkins, Henry, et al. 2006. *Confronting the challenges of participatory culture: Media education for the 21st century*. Cambridge: The MIT Press.

Johnston, Casey. 2012. "I am no man": For Zelda-playing daughter, dad gives Link a sex change. http://arstechnica.com/gaming/2012/11/i-am-no-man-for-zelda-playing-daughter-dad-gives-link-a-sex-change/. Accessed 20 Nov 2012.

Kato, Pamela M., Steve W. Cole, Andrew S. Bradlyn, and Brad H. Pollock. 2008. A video game improves behavioral outcomes in adolescents and young adults with cancer – A randomized trial. *Pediatrics* 122: e305–e317.

Leasca, Stacey. 2012. SPARX: New video game designed to help combat teen depression. Globalpost. http://www.globalpost.com/dispatch/news/health/120731/sparx-new-video-game-designed-help-combat-teen-depression. Accessed 4 Mar 2013.

Lieberman, Debra A. 2001. Management of chronic pediatric diseases with interactive health games: Theory and research findings. *The Journal of Ambulatory Care Management* 24: 26–38.

Lofgren, Eric T., and Nina H. Fefferman. 2007. The untapped potential of virtual game worlds to shed light on real world epidemics. *The Lancet Infectious Diseases* 7: 625–629.

Merry, Sally N., Karolina Stasiak, Matthew Shepherd, Chris Frampton, Theresa Fleming, and Mathijs Lucassen. 2012. The effectiveness of SPARX, a computerised self help intervention for adolescents seeking help for depression: Randomised controlled non-inferiority trial. *BMJ* 344: e2598. https://doi.org/10.1136/bmj.e2598.

Michael, David, and Sande Chen. 2006. *Serious games: Games that educate, train, and inform*. Boston: Thomson Course Technology.

Nardi, Bonnie, and Justin Harris. 2006. Strangers and friends: Collaborative play in World of Warcraft.In *20th anniversary conference on computer supported cooperative work (CSCW '06)*, Alberta.

Newzoo. 2011. Gap closing between emerging and western game markets. https://newzoo.com/about/press/press-releases/gap-closing-between-emerging-and-western-games-markets-globalcollect-version/. Accessed 1 June 2011.

Papastergiou, Marina. 2009. Exploring the potential of computer and video games for health and physical education: A literature review. *Computers in Education* 53: 603–622.

Pesquisa Game Brasil – 2017. 2017. Pesquisa Game Brasil 2017: o perfil do gamer brasileiro. https://www.pesquisagamebrasil.com.br/. Accessed 18 June 2018.

Prensky, Marc. 2004. *Digital game-based learning*. New York: McGraw-Hill.

Raessens, Joost. 2005. Computer games as participatory media culture. In *Handbook of computer game studies*, ed. J. Raessens and J. Goldstein, 373–389. Cambridge: The MIT Press.

———. 2010. A taste of life as a refugee: How serious games frame refugee issues. In *Changes in Museum practice: New media, refugees and participation*, ed. H.L. Skartveit and K. Goodnow, 94–105. New York/Oxford: Berghahn Books.

Ritterfeld, Ute, Michael Cody, and Peter Vorderer, eds. 2009. *Serious games: Mechanisms and effects*. London: Routledge.

Santos, Débora. 2010. Casos de Aids entre jovens devem aumentar, diz Ministério da Saúde. Globo.com. http://g1.globo.com/ciencia-e-saude/noticia/2010/12/casos-de-aids-entre-jovens-devem-aumentar-diz-ministerio-da-saude.html. Accessed 3 Feb 2012.

Schäfer, M. T. 2008. *Bastard Culture! User participation and the extension of cultural industries*. PhD diss., Utrecht University, Utrecht.

Sicart, Miguel. 2012. Against procedurality game studies. *The International Journal of Computer Game Research* 11.

Vasconcellos, Marcelo. S. 2013. *Comunicação e saúde em jogo: os video games como estratégia de promoção da saúde*. PhD diss., Oswaldo Cruz Foundation, Rio de Janeiro.

Vasconcellos, Marcelo S., Flávia G. Carvalho, and Inesita S. Araujo. 2017. Understanding games as participation: An analytical model. *Cibertextualidades* 8: 107–118.

VG247. 2013. Acti-Blizz Q4 FY13: Digital nets $1.54B, WoW subs slide. VG247. http://www.vg247.com/2013/02/07/activision-blizzard-q4-fy13-net-revenues-of-4-86-billion/. Accessed 14 Feb 2013.

Victora, Cesar G., Mauricio L. Barreto, Maria do Carmo Leal, Carlos A. Monteiro, Maria Ines Schmidt, et al. 2011. Health conditions and health-policy innovations in Brazil: The way forward. *The Lancet* 377: 2042–2053.

Yee, Nick, and Jeremy Bailenson. 2007. The Proteus effect: The effect of transformed self-representation on behavior. *Human Communication Research* 33: 271–290.

Chapter 21
"Move and Be Healthy!": Performative Sensibility and Body Experiences Mediated by Wearable Devices in Brazil

André Lemos and Elias Bitencourt

Abstract In this chapter we reflect on the role played by the agency of performative sensibility (PS) in the association between bodies and wearable technologies. We explore this particular form of algorithmic agency (PS) in bodies by mapping user experiences with wearable devices in Brazil. A total of 121 responses from a digital questionnaire were analyzed. The findings indicate that although these technologies are sustained by a discourse that values a healthy lifestyle, the behaviors acquired by the users suggest that the latter are motivated more by a desire to produce data for the system. The results also show that the data visualization interfaces support a narrative of "healthy" based on the amount of general "body movement." We argue that PS acts as a "rhetorical communicational device" that translates the practice of physical activity by separating body performance from the context of the action.

21.1 Introduction

This study focuses on transformations observed in the field of body experiences mediated by wearable technologies and the consequences of these changes. As offshoot of the Internet of Things (IoT), wearables are part of a broader category of computational tools for individual quantification known as personal informatics (Lupton 2014, Rapp and Cena 2016). More specifically, they are particular objects with info-communicational properties (Lemos 2013) that can extract detailed information about users' bodily patterns, provide individual algorithmically constructed narratives, and invite the body to participate in the same sociotechnical network of which the wearable is a part. We call this sentient characteristic of objects that is a part of IoT as performative sensibility (PS) (Lemos 2016). This general aspect of the IoT is also a feature of wearable devices (Lemos and Bitencourt 2017a, b) and

A. Lemos (✉)
Communication Department, Federal University of Bahia, Salvador, Brazil

E. Bitencourt
Department of Design, Bahia State University - UNEB, Salvador, Brazil

A. Pereira Neto, M. B. Flynn (eds.), *The Internet and Health in Brazil*,
https://doi.org/10.1007/978-3-319-99289-1_21

makes datafication of body experiences possible (Smith 2016; Sumartojo et al. 2016). PS, therefore, extends the properties of wearable computing beyond merely making information regularly available to the user as initially proposed by Steve Mann (1998), attributed with the first definition of this model of computing.

Among the many categories of devices available on the market, wearables designed specifically for health monitoring (fitness trackers) have been the main drivers of growth in the sector. According to the most recent IDC (2016) survey, fitness trackers accounted for 85% of the growth in the sector in 2016, with 23 million units sold in the last quarter of that year alone. The last Tractica (2016) report forecasts an increase in shipments of this type of wearable from 2.5 million units in 2016 to 97.6 million in 2020.

Designed to extract body data regularly in exchange for guidance on a healthier lifestyle, fitness trackers have also been gaining prominence in the digital health market (Chung et al. 2016; Mercer et al. 2016). This distinction is primarily because of their growing relevance to public policies that promote individual responsibility for preventing disease and developing a healthy body (De Vogli 2011; Ayo 2012). The European Commission Green Paper on mobile health (European Commission 2014) projected that the global mobile health[1] market would reach US$ 23 billion in 2017. According to the Commission, remote monitoring treatment solutions accounted for 60% of the European mobile health market at the time. The article also noted that these technologies could help save € 99 billion in healthcare costs in the EU in 2017, with the most significant savings being in wellness/prevention and treatment/monitoring, for which the potential economies were estimated at € 69 billion and € 32 billion, respectively.

There have been similar forecasts made for Brazil and Mexico. Tripathi et al. (2013) suggest that the use of mobile health could provide access to healthcare for an additional 28 million people in Brazil and 15 million in Mexico without any other investments in physicians. They also estimate that implementation of remote health management could reduce public and private costs in the sector by up to US$ 14 billion in Brazil and US$ 3 billion in Mexico. Logicalis Inc. (2012) suggests that 75% of wearable users in emerging economies, including Brazil, Russia, India, the UAE, and Malaysia, demonstrated strong propensity to let their employers use personal data from their wearables in the workplace in exchange for discounts on corporate health programs, a practice known as BYOD (bring your own device).

In the literature, advocates of wearable computing include Springbuk (2016), who support reduced health insurance costs for users of wearables; Raj and Ha-Brookshire (2016), who argue that wearables give users "superpowers"; and other authors who suggest that symptoms can be prevented by means of the algorithmic predictions made by these devices (Aalbers et al. 2015; Pellanda and Pellanda 2016; Rahman and Demith 2017). Authors who are more critical of wearables, however, question the effectiveness of the information provided and the models of engagement they promote. The most common arguments are the very high percentage of individuals who stop using the devices in the first 6 months (Ledger 2014, 2016;

[1] Chapter 18 addresses the theme of mHealth.

Ledger and McCaffrey 2014); the poor reliability of the data (Hilts et al. 2016); declining engagement over time (Schaefer et al. 2016); the enormous effort involved in recording data (Choe et al. 2014); the limited integration with daily activities; the limited relevance of the information provided by the interfaces and the difficulty interpreting it (Rapp and Cena 2016); and the lack of tools to allow users to get answers to specific questions using the stored data (Li et al. 2011).

Although wearable computing has aroused international interest, there is a shortage of literature on the subject in Brazil. A search in the CAPES portal—the most extensive database of indexed journals in the country—for peer-reviewed articles in Portuguese over the last 20 years[2] identified only six papers. In just four of these, wearables are the primary focus. The most recent studies view wearables as technologies that play a fundamental role in preventing risk factors for heart disease (Pellanda and Pellanda 2016) and reflect on the changes in the way communications is produced, accessed, and consumed as the consequences of wearable computing make themselves felt in the techno sphere (Squirra 2016). Articles published before 2012 characterized interfaces that place body action and performance at the center of the data input procedure as inactive (Donati 2008) and debated the definition of wearables and their potential to reconfigure the body and space (Donati 2004).

Nevertheless, none of the four studies referred to above include an empirical investigation based on users' experiences with devices available on the market. The only study of this kind in Brazil is a field study of 505 individuals by Carenet Longevity (2015), which found that 79% (399) knew what the term "wearables" meant, and of these only 27% (108) had already bought this type of equipment to track their physical activity. Of the 292 subjects who did not yet have a wearable, 91% (265) were prepared to pay for one, although 57% (143) of these potential buyers mentioned price as the main obstacle to acquiring such a device. Indeed, in a recent interview[3], the CEO of Carenet, Immo Oliver, attributed the limited popularity of wearables in Brazil to the high taxes in the country and the absence of major international retail chains.

In this paper, we therefore seek to contribute to the theoretical and empirical study of wearables in Brazil by reflecting on the info-communicational agency of these devices on the body and mapping users' experiences of this type of technology in Brazil. We were interested in understanding the inner body transformations observed by users, and the possible relations between these changes and action programs promoted wearable systems. We collected the data with the aid of an electronic questionnaire made available on Facebook[4] and Twitter and electronic mailing lists. In all, 121 valid completed surveys were received between December 20, 2016,

[2] The search was performed on May 30, 2017, using the search terms "wearables" and its Portuguese translation *vestíveis*. This result, although based on a representative source, cannot be considered a comprehensive search of all Brazilian articles on the subject.

[3] During the data collection stage, an unstructured interview was held with the CEO of Carenet. At the time of writing, Carenet Longevity is the largest Brazilian company in the wearable technologies sector.

[4] The issue of health and Facebook is addressed in Chap. 9.

when the questionnaire was released, and March 16, 2017. The data represent a non-probabilistic sample and were analyzed with Atlas.ti so that we could compare the responses of different groups of users.

21.2 What Is Not a Wearable Device: Sensible Objects vs. Sentient Objects

Initially defined as "a computer that is subsumed into the personal space of the user, controlled by the user, and has both operational and interactional constancy" (Mann 1998), wearable computing became famous as a tool for making information instantly available. Initially, this model of personal computing was intended to free up both a user's hands and provide rapid access to information for industry and the military (Viseu 2003). More recently, with the increasing use of microprocessors and evermore pervasive connections to communications networks, wearable computing has become defined metonymically regarding, for example, responsivity and sensibility (Viseu 2003), digital companions (Özcan et al. 2016), and a second skin (Donati 2004). As Lupton notes (2016a), wearables have become repositories of users' communications with others and not only for exchanging information but also to interpret the bodies with which they are coupled (Lupton 2012).

The interpretative capability of wearables, however, is not restricted to the object but distributed throughout the platform of which it is part. We argue that wearable devices are actor-networks (Latour 2005; Lemos 2013). Consequently, they cannot be defined merely by the attributes of the object—having a sensor, providing information continually—and use on the body. The peculiarity of wearables lies precisely in their ability to extract body data and exchange and produce information and performative actions by using shared processing. Wearables are therefore characterized more by their ability to circulate, process, interpret, and provide body information in a network than by the presence of electronics and embedded sensors in the materiality of the object. They differ from other electronic devices dedicated to the body in four fundamental regards: sentience, body-oriented materiality, the model-platform ecosystem, and PS.

Wearables are sentient as they do not only react to stimuli (a property which would characterize all other automated-only objects as "sensible"). They have a numerical identity, they identify their position on the network, and they perceive their surroundings by extracting data through sensors and computer processing. This autonomous perception, however, depends on their second characteristic, connectivity. It is the existence of physical and software interfaces that allow wearables to be connected to a broader information processing network, making them autonomous in relation to the user. The autonomy of wearables depends on a network connection and is not guaranteed merely by the presence of embedded computing.

Wearables also differ from other mobile devices in that their materiality is oriented primarily toward the body, be it in the form of performance-oriented protocols or interfaces that allow them to couple with the body. Although a smartphone can detect movements and biometric data, wearable devices are designed to extract specific information related to body patterns (circadian rhythms, glycemic indexes, stress, temperature variations, etc.). Unlike electronic devices that are merely sensible, wearable computing depends on a platform (Gillespie 2010) to process large amounts of data and produce information based on observed patterns. It uses the platform to expand the computational properties of objects, constructs narratives, and makes decisions to be taken based on an extensive network of objects, companies, and third parties.

The characteristics mentioned above are directly linked to the last peculiarity of wearables, PS (Lemos 2016). Since a wearable is an actor-network, the sensibility we attribute to it is different from the rest of the sensitive properties pertaining to sensors embedded in the object. In the case of wearables, PS is an assemblage of algorithmic sensibility and performance made possible by the networked processing and interpretation of information extracted from the environment and the body. We say, therefore, that PS is a sensibility whose performativity is distributed and acts in a network. It is not only located in the device but produces informational agencies by means of it (Lemos and Bitencourt 2017a).

Hence, without the network, the device is only a sensible object, no different from a wristband thermometer, a blood pressure monitor, or a blood glucose monitor, for example. And without the purpose, the platform cannot "feel" the body. When they are connected, however, the body-object-platform network is activated by the PS, making information circulate and producing discourses (about the body, health, the object, the company, etc.) systemically. In this sense, PS works like a medium, a communicational device that not only directs narratives but also produces them through its network-based algorithmic procedurality. Wearable computing can thus be understood not so much regarding the specific material characteristics of the object (hearables, ingestibles, implantables, patches, etc.) but more so regarding the way in which the PS of wearable devices translates users' body experiences. In other words, we argue that wearables are sentient, networked objects with a (physical and digital) materiality aimed at autonomous body datafication that act through the PS distributed in the economic platform of which they are part.

21.3 Data Collection and Analysis Procedures

The data collection instrument used was a survey, and we determined the study population through non-probabilistic sampling. The questionnaire[5] consisted of 37 questions, of which 13 were multiple choice, 17 single choice, 3 Likert scale questions, and 4 open-ended. The questions were divided into four groups: user demographic profile, personal monitoring practices, capture of personal data, and consequences of using wearables. We published the questionnaire on individual and

[5]The questionnaire used in the survey can be found at https://goo.gl/forms/jqVtkY8g9UsEQAqk1

institutional (Lab404) profiles on Facebook and Twitter and electronic mailing lists. When we first posted the survey, we used the "sponsored link" feature with a target audience of Brazilians between 18 and 60 years of age who had an interest in topics related to well-being, physical activity, and technology. We also published the questionnaire in Facebook communities and groups where people share information about wearables and devices sold by the most famous global brands—Apple, Fitbit, Garmin, Samsung, and Xiaomi (IDC 2016).

In all, 124 completed questionnaires (of which 121 were valid) were received between December 20, 2016, when the survey was released, and March 16, 2017, the end of the data collection period. We stress that there are, to our knowledge, no official data on the number of users of wearables in Brazil. Although three of the five largest global brands mentioned by respondents sell devices in Brazil (Garmin, Apple, and Samsung), there is no official information on shipments or market share in the country. Despite the prominence of wearable computing in the Rio Olympic Games (Alvarez 2016; Comstock 2016), global reports on the subject provide little information about the number of devices sold in Brazil. Of the few reports available, the study by Carenet Longevity (2015) found that of 505 interviewees, only 107 had used a wearable device. Thus, although the present study involves a more extensive population sample (n = 121) and focuses only on wearables, our limited knowledge about users of this type of technology in Brazil prevents the findings from being generalized.

We tabulated the data from the survey and imported it into Atlas.ti, a qualitative data analysis software package. We categorized the different answers of the 37 survey questions into categories, grouping responses for subsequent analysis. The data analysis aimed to characterize users' experiences with wearable technology based on the following parameters: the length of use, the intensity of use, positive consequences observed, and habits acquired after using the tool (Table 21.1).

21.4 Profile of the Users

Most of the users in the sample were males (83.5%), approximately half (47%) were between 26 and 40 years old, and slightly under two-thirds (59.5%) had a monthly income of more than R$ 5000 (US$ 1200). Most were from the southeast (40.5%) or northeast (31.4%) of the country, used the Apple operating system (50.4%), and also used other mobile apps to monitor their health (95.3%). The replies to the questionnaire indicated that the most popular devices were activity trackers (73.7%) and smartwatches (53.4%). Smart earphones and clips accounted for only 6.8% and 5.9%, respectively, of devices chosen by participants (Fig. 21.1). Only 18% of the population sample stopped using wearables, a lower percentage than the 33% reported in the studies by Ledger (2014, 2016) and Ledger and McCaffrey (2014).

The most popular brands among respondents do not mirror the ranking of the market leaders identified by IDC (2016). While Fitbit had the highest worldwide sales, followed by Xiaomi, Garmin, and Apple, Xiaomi (38%) was the preferred

Table 21.1 Details of the categories used for the analysis based on the results of the questionnaire

Group	Category[a]	Variable	Definition	Users per response	Total no. of respondents	Type of question
Parameters used for the analysis	Length of time using the wearable	Up to 6 months	Used for between 1 and 6 months	33	119	Single choice
		Up to 1 year	Used for between 6 and 12 months	21		
		More than 1 year	Used for between 13 and 24 months	32		
		More than 2 years	Used for more than 24 months	33		
	Intensity with which the wearable was used	Moderate to intense	Only removes the wearable to sleep, have a shower, or charge it (depending on the limitations of the device)	77	119	Single choice
		In particular circumstances or intermittently	Only uses the wearable when he/she is training or doing physical activity or intermittently	14		
		Stopped using it	Only used it occasionally and then stopped	5		
Experience with the device and interactivity	Engagement	Active	Still using it	88	120	Single choice
		Stopped using it	Stopped using it	21		
		Device lost or stolen	Stopped using it for external reasons	8		
Body experiences	General self-perception after using the device	Pays attention to his/her body	Users start to become concerned about sleep, food, weight, and a sedentary lifestyle	70	115	Multiple choice
		Motivated to do physical activity	Users feel more motivated and inclined to do sports or some physical activity	70		
		Under pressure to achieve goals	Users start to feel under pressure to achieve goals and statistics determined by the system	39		
		Frustrated without the device	Users feel frustrated without the device. Activities that are not recorded seem to lose their meaning (walking, sleeping, eating, etc.)	12		

(continued)

Table 21.1 (continued)

Group	Category[a]	Variable	Definition	Users per response	Total no. of respondents	Type of question
	Habits acquired after using the device	Behavior	Eating habits, users move more, sleeping habits	80	120	Multiple choice
		Interactivity	Checks graphics and data, tries to achieve goals, tries to do extra steps	76		
		Perception	Body limit based on the system, decides based on data, assesses his/her own general well-being, assesses his/her stress and emotions	51		
		Body	Lost weight, developed nervous tics related to the device	36		
	Positive consequences observed in daily life	Sport	Users start to do sports or improve their performance	65	119	Multiple choice
		Health	Users improve their medical indexes, such as blood sugar level and cholesterol	64		
		Behavior	Users start to sleep or eat better	35		
		Self-image	Users feel "cooler" or more fashionable	33		

[a]The categories used in the analysis were based on the reasons behind each question in the questionnaire

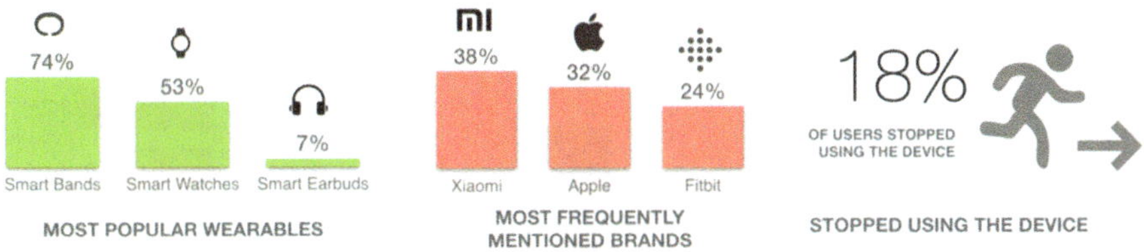

Fig. 21.1 Most popular wearables, most frequently mentioned brands, and percentage of users who gave up

brand among respondents, ahead of Apple (31.6%) and Fitbit (24%). Interestingly, of the names mentioned by respondents, Xiaomi devices are the least expensive—the Mi Band 2 costs R$ 250 (US$ 55) including import duties[6]. In contrast, products from Brazilian suppliers such as Netshoes and Carenet accounted for only 3.3% and 2.5%, respectively, of devices used by respondents. In addition, although a survey by Carenet Longevity (2015) found that 35% of respondents had a Polar wearable and 24% an All4One device, only one user (0.8%) in our study mentioned the Polar brand. There was no mention of All4One.

The most appreciated features offered by the wearables were the possibility of getting to know your body better (65% of respondents), the feeling of power derived from receiving instantaneous information about your health (60%), and optimization of training and physical health (47.1%). The most important information provided by the devices was deemed to be the number of steps taken (72.7%) and the user's heart rate (72.7%) and sleep patterns (65%). The rewards for achieving goals were considered significant by only 10% of respondents.

With regard to the flow of the data, approximately two-thirds of respondents (67%) admitted to knowing very little or not having any information about the company's data management and storage policies. Furthermore, in the collective imagination of 54% of the respondents, only the brand and the user would have access to the information and body patterns recorded. Only 32% of the users were aware that individual data are shared with the brand's partner companies, corporate clients, and government bodies. However, despite not being aware of how personal data are processed in the wearable platform, 95% of users consider the data to be an advantage; 80% believe the information about their bodies they receive from their devices is credible; 65% are not interested in cases involving leaks of personal data from the brand name devices they use; 9% are entirely familiar with the company's privacy policies; and only 5% are aware of the main points on the network through which data pass (Fig. 21.2).

[6]Xiaomi had a presence in Brazil between 2015 and 2016. However, Xiaomi wearables are no longer available locally and must be imported (Mari 2016).

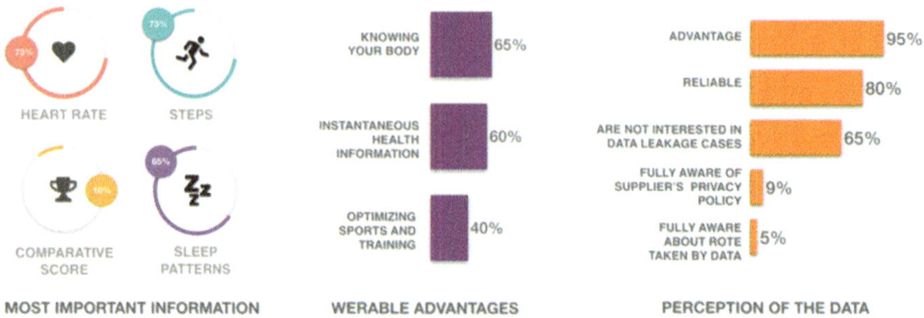

Fig. 21.2 Users' perceptions of the most important information provided by the interface, the importance of using wearables, and the digital data itself

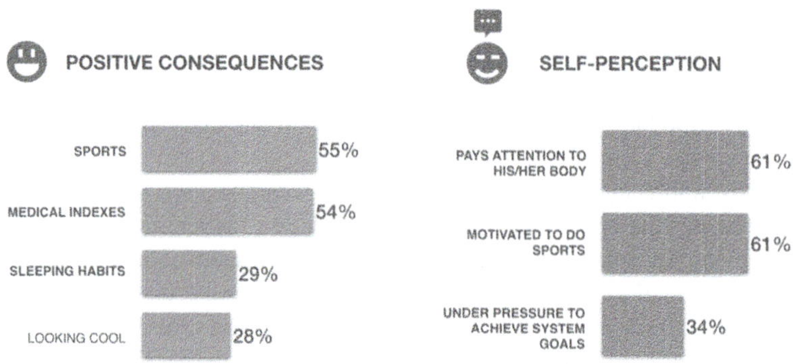

Fig. 21.3 Positive consequences and users' self-perception after using wearables

21.5 Mapping Users' Experiences

We analyzed responses in three main areas: positive consequences observed in daily life, general self-perception, and new habits acquired after using the device. We addressed these closely related areas in different ways in the questionnaire (Table 21.1).

In general terms, the data indicate that the primary positive consequences reported by users were in the areas of sports, health, behavior, eating, sleep, and personal image. Around 54.6% of respondents reported improved performance when doing sports; 53.7% noticed improved blood sugar levels, cholesterol levels, etc.; 29.4% said they had changed their attitude toward sleeping and eating; and 27.7% attributed an enhanced personal image to the wearable, which they felt made them seem modern or "cool" (Fig. 21.3). Slightly under two-thirds of respondents (60.8%) noticed that they paid more attention to their body and sleep patterns and felt more motivated to do physical activities. The third most significant change was the newly acquired feeling by users that they were under pressure to achieve goals stipulated by the systems associated with the wearables (33.9%).

As any assessment of habits acquired must take into account the patterns of engagement between user and wearable, we combined the responses in this category with two other groups: intensity of use and length of time using the device. We divided the detailed findings into two areas: habits acquired as a function of depth of use and habits obtained as a function of the length of use.

For this analysis, users were grouped according to intensity of use as follows: (1) moderate or intense use, user only takes off the wearable to have a shower or charge the battery or sleep (if the device was not designed to wear while sleeping); (2) used in particular circumstances or intermittently, the wearable is worn only for training or intermittently; and (3) stopped using it, user stopped using the device because it got lost or stolen or he/she gave up. According to these criteria, 84% of the respondents make moderate or intense use of the wearable, 11.7% wear it only when they are training or sporadically, and 4% stopped using it.

Among those who make intense use of the wearable, the most significant changes reported were increased movement (64%), motivation to achieve system goals (52%), and frequent checking of graphics (51%). For individuals who only use the device in specific circumstances, increased movement and routine checking of graphics were still very prominent (57% and 29%, respectively). In this category of user, weight loss and checking of graphics had the same values (29%). Although weight loss had a similar value (30%) for users who make intense and moderate use of the wearable, it was less significant concerning the other classes of variables reported by this group (moving more and watching graphics). Regardless of the intensity of use, 21% of subjects indicated that they started to develop behaviors aimed at increasing the number of steps they took to enhance their statistics.

In other words, subjects who made intense use of the device acquired habits involving interaction with the system: of the three most notable changes, two are associated with procedures related to achieving goals and visualizing graphics (Fig. 21.4). These changes are more striking than, for example, changes in eating habits (reported by 18%) or sleep patterns. The same is true for individuals who

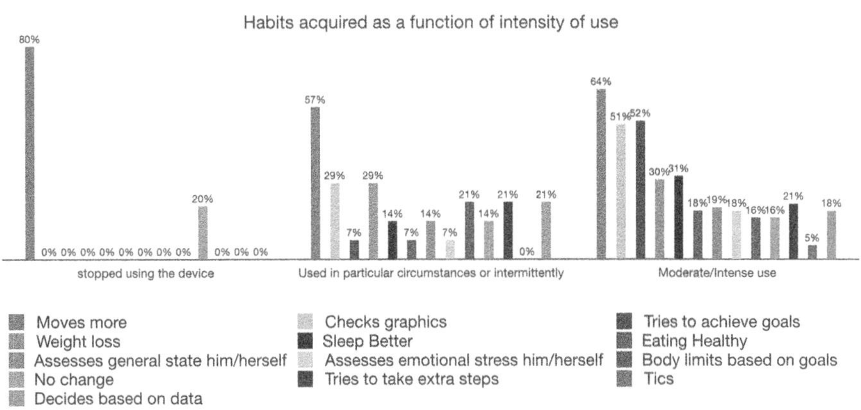

Fig. 21.4 Habits acquired as a function of intensity of use

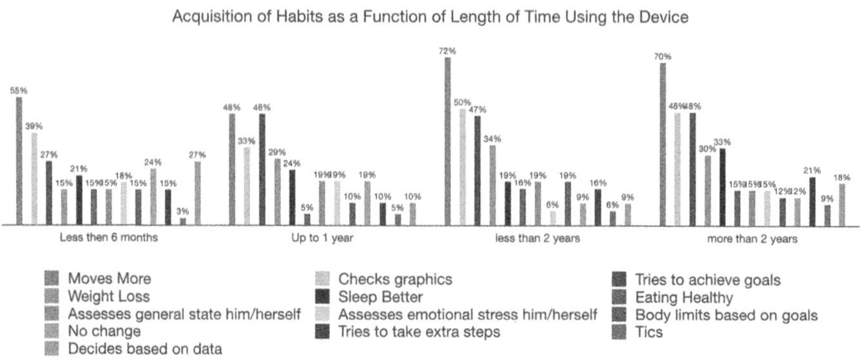

Fig. 21.5 Habits acquired as a function of length of time using the device

make more moderate use of the device. Participants reported that increased movement and checking of graphics had a higher percentage of users than improved eating habits (7%) or sleeping patterns (14%). Even among users who stopped using the device, the two changes observed relate to increased movement (80%) and a focus on achieving system goals (20%).

When broken down by the length of time using the device, the study population was relatively evenly distributed: 27.7% of the subjects had been using the device for less than 6 months; 17.6% had been using it for up to 1 year; 26.8% for more than 1 year and less than 2 years; and 27.7% had over 2 years' experience with the technology (Fig. 21.5). During the first year of contact with the wearable, users tend to overestimate the changes they observe in their habits from their established routines to their more recently acquired habits. Individuals who had been using the device for up to 6 months mainly reported that they had started to move more (55%) and check graphics frequently (39%). For this group, the third most commonly observed changes were "decides based on the data" (27%) and "tries to achieve system goals" (27%).

Those who had been using the technology for between 1 and 2 years also noticed an increase in activity (72% reported that they had started to move more), a higher tendency to check graphics regularly (50%), a tendency to meet system goals (47%), and a loss of weight (34%). For those with more than 2 years' experience, the increased movement continued to be the most frequently observed habit (70%), followed by checking of graphics (48%), the need to meet goals (48%), improved sleep (33%), and weight loss (30%).

Interestingly, a perception that they were acquiring habits related to interactivity (watching graphics, achieving goals) was more common among users who had been wearing the devices longer: 59% of those who reported this type of change had been using the wearable for between 1 and 2 years or more than 2 years. However, a more significant percentage of less experienced users (those with less than 6 months of use) (23%) than of individuals who had been using the device for more than 1 year (19%) reported acquiring habits related to interactivity. We expected to find a higher number of first-time users indicating that they had learned habits aimed at producing data, since this is when they need to supply the system in return for valuable information. However, we only observed this pattern of behavior was among more experienced users. Still, no significant increase in other habits associated with the promotion of physical and emotional well-being was found among these more experienced subjects.

21.6 The Generalization of Movement and the Agency of Performative Sensibility as a Rhetorical, Communicational Device

As noted in the previous section, increased movement was the change most frequently mentioned by respondents. Around 62% of all the users reported that they started to move more, and 80% of those who stopped using the device also acknowledged that they had moved more while they had been using it. Although these findings may initially appear to underscore the health gains produced by this type of technology, the development of habits associated with interaction with the systems (achieving goals and visualizing data) accompanies the growth in the percentage of users taking more steps with increasing length of use.

Furthermore, although health and sport are the main areas in which participants identified transformations after they started using a wearable, most new habits relate primarily to body performances aimed at interaction with the systems associated with the device. More specifically, users mentioned the practice of looking at personal graphics very frequently (44%), more often than weight loss (26.6%), changes in sleeping habits (24%), general assessment of physical well-being (17.5%), or emotional well-being (15%) (Fig. 21.6).

The same is true for the practice of trying to achieve step goals (42.5%) or of taking extra steps to satisfy the system's demands (17%), which were mentioned more often than new eating habits (14%) or achieving goals that were intended to correspond to the physical limits of the body itself (15%). Although having a more active routine is endorsed by the World Health Organization, merely moving more is in itself no guarantee of a healthier lifestyle. The findings infer that the notable general increase in habits related to movement is not accompanied by effective increases in other areas related to general well-being. Rather, too much importance is attached to the production of steps as an absolute indicator of an individual's state of health.

Although the data visualization interfaces in the devices most frequently mentioned in the survey include analyses of sleep, calorie gains, and eating habits, movement continues to be the action for which wearables, users, and the platform place most emphasis. As seen earlier, although 65% of the study population identified "the possibility of knowing one's body better" as the main advantage of using a wearable, the information most valued by users (72%) is the number of steps and heart rate. Added to this finding is the fact that most of the users observed benefits

Fig. 21.6 Users' perceptions of changes in their habits after they started using wearables

in the areas of sports (54.6%) and health (53.7%), although the behavior they developed emphasized the production of steps and data visualization.

These findings suggest a possible translation (Latour 2005) in the perception of health mediated by discourses that value quantification of the body, as pointed out by Nascimento and Bruno (2013) and Nascimento (2014). However, in the case of wearables, the monitoring of improvements in physical health suffers the direct agency of the PS that characterizes wearable computing. The dashboard interfaces, visualization graphics, and prizes are the real face of a narrative of self, built by PS through the algorithmic assemblage of data generated by the sensors and processed according to the action programs that guide the heuristics of the wearable computing platform.

In an earlier study, Fritz et al. (2014) noted that fitness tracker users tended to attach more importance to activities that the device accounted for and that this was to the detriment of other fitness practices; the focus on accumulating steps made weight-lifting sessions less attractive than walking in the mall, for example. Research by Li (2009) showed that an excessive emphasis on the quantification of movements displayed through the wearable interface does not help users to relate their physical activity to the context in which the action is carried out.

Both the literature discussed here and the results of the present study support the thesis of a rhetorical mediation by PS that tends to promote an informational entanglement between the wearable and user. This entangling is based on the development of narratives of the body that are constructed from user data, filtered by the system heuristics and favored by the platform. In this sense, increased movement can be considered a common denominator that satisfies the demands of the main actors involved in the association. A body in the process of instauration (Latour 2013) that seeks to perfect itself through control, training, and exercise (Foucault 1990); an object whose instauration involves extracting and sharing data; and a political-economic platform that produces value from data circulating in the network are some examples.

In this process, each actor requires suitable conditions to take part in the network. The body seeks detailed information about its health to use the wearable; the wearable depends on the body moving through space to work appropriately; the platform needs the body data extracted by the wearable to achieve financial equilibrium. This implies acknowledging that there are at least three forms of expression (Deleuze and Guattari 1988) of movement that need to be considered. For the body, movement is a physical activity; for the object, it is displacement of the body in space; and for the platform, it is a heuristic commodity.

Wearable computing only exists in this dispute. As Latour (2013) observes, what defines wearable devices are the conditions for subsistence in a network that makes the instauration of wearable computing possible. We suggested previously that wearable computing is made possible through a negotiation between the different interests of the trajectories of instauration involved—body, object, and platform. In the network, what each actor achieves matters less than that all the actors can obtain what they need to continue existing as a network. Wearable computing establishes itself by requiring that the body remains motivated to monitor, the object continues extracting and sharing data, and the platform continues generating value from the procedural narratives. In other words, the body must perceive the benefits of increased physical activity, so the object continues extracting body data, and the platform continues providing services and making profiling predictions.

We argue that PS operates precisely as a communicational device that makes the different regimes of expression of "movement"[7] (Deleuze and Guattari 1989) compatible with each other, ensuring that the wearable actor-network functions correctly. The narratives of PS are procedural; they obey a nonrepresentational model, a text in which "words do[ing] things" (Thrift 2005, 241). The substrate of the syntax of PS resides in the heuristic categories that guide the protocols used in the network algorithms. This implies that the heuristic narrative of PS ensures that "movement" is compatible with the different representational regimes involved: PS presents "movement" to the user in terms of the subject's own regime of expression

[7] For Deleuze and Guattari (1989, 89), "just as there are asemiotic expressions, or expressions without signs, there are asemiological regimes of signs, asignifying signs, both on the strata and on the plane of consistency." In this sense, "assemblages are necessary in order for the unity of composition enveloped in a stratum, the relations between a given stratum and the others, and the relation between these strata and the plane of consistency to be organized rather than random" (Deleuze and Guattari 1989, 92).

(visual discourse), classifying it as "physical activity," and adopts narratives favored by science (statistics, trend lines, graphics) presented in a personal interface in which information about the user's movement is a condition for self-knowledge.

A consequence of this rhetorical agency of PS is that the perception of physical activity becomes divorced from its performance context. Users in the population sample studied here perceived benefits in the areas of health and sports as they moved more. However, rising physical activity (62%) was accompanied not by the development of other healthy routines but by the acquisition of habits related to visualizing and increasing movement according to the parameters established by the wearable platform—44% of users started to watch the graphics frequently, and 42% started to try to achieve goals.

In an earlier study carried out with members of the Fitbit community, we found a similar failure by users to associate steps with the action of walking, so that activities were rated positively according to the number of steps they allowed the user to accumulate in the system (Lemos and Bitencourt 2017b). In a related study, we also found that subjects tended to associate any activity that resulted in an increased step counts as fitness (Bitencourt 2017). Similarly, Ruckenstein (2014) and Pantzar and Ruckenstein (2015) observed that users reassigned meaning to their domestic chores based on heart rate monitors according to the extent to which these activities enhanced their statistics.

Hence, one can say that by separating the body's activities from the context of its actions, PS creates the necessary conditions for the body, object, and platform to cooperate, allowing the body-wearable actor-network to exist. On the one hand, PS enables the wearable platform to read body movements using the logic of data categorization employed by the network, while on the other, it filters all the user's bodily attitudes and presents them according to a regime of expression that associates "healthy" with any movement that prioritizes the system's heuristics.

Consequently, body data tend to be considered quite reliable—80% of users surveyed deemed the information they received from the wearable credible—and very helpful for self-management (95%). This contrasts with a significant lack of awareness of the processes involved in the translation of "movement" into narratives that relate more movement to "healthy practices" or "self-care": only 9% of those surveyed were fully aware of the company's privacy policies, and only 5% were aware of the main points on the network the data passes through. PS simplifies the process of developing a healthy body and summarizes the conditions required for the network to operate based on the argument that "all you need to do to be healthy is move."

21.7 Final Considerations

We analyzed the responses of 121 users of wearable technologies to a questionnaire shared on Facebook, Twitter, and electronic mailing lists between December 26, 2016, and April 21, 2017. We imported the data into the Atlas.ti software package in order to examine the results for combinations and co-occurrence. The findings showed that, although most of the individuals surveyed reported that there had been improvements in fields of sports (54.6%) and health (53.7%), the most commonly reported newly acquired habits were increased movement (61.6%), a tendency to visualize graphics and statistics frequently (44%), and a need to meet the step goals determined by the system (42.8%). The percentages of respondents reporting changes in sleeping habits (24%), eating habits (14%), or management of emotions (15%) were significantly lower. The results, therefore, show that movement was an essential element for perceiving healthy body attitudes.

We propose a definition of wearable computing that views the wearable as an actor-network limited neither to the sensor nor to the ergonomic characteristics of the materiality of the object; rather, the definition stresses the importance of the interfaces, the autonomous datafication procedures, the economic model underlying the platforms, and the agency of PS as characteristics that distinguish wearables from merely sensible electronic devices. We argue that the agency of PS on the body is central to understanding the communicational processes involved in the production of procedural narratives in the body and the perception of bodies in terms of this information constructed algorithmically in the network.

Although the data analyzed here do not allow the results to be generalized, the paths they reveal lead us to argue that PS acts as a "rhetorical communicational device" responsible for ensuring that the different regimes of expression (Deleuze and Guattari 1988) of "movement" for the user, wearable, and platform are compatible. We have shown that it is not "movement" that is at stake but the different forms of expression of "movement"—physical activity, displacement, and heuristics. Negotiations between these different regimes by PS translate the practice of physical activity for users, separating body performance from the context of the action. We argue, therefore, that PS operates as a discursive, rhetorical key moving between these different regimes (Deleuze and Guattari 1988) and respecting the laws of expression in each territory to ensure the conditions required for each of the actors involved in the association to exist.

Finally, we recognize that although the possibilities for health and body management afforded by the Internet of Things constitute an expanding market (Chung et al. 2016; Mercer et al. 2016) and are arousing increasing interest among researchers in the digital humanities (Gina and Nafus 2016; Nafus 2016; Lupton 2016b; Cheney-Lippold 2017), there remain challenges to be overcome in the Brazilian context. Among the most obvious of these are the high cost of the devices due to import duties and the absence of retail chains, preventing widespread adoption of the technology and its subsequent use in many different sectors of society.

In the field of theory, approaches based on the new materialities (Miller 2005; Bennet 2010; Dourish 2017; Finn 2017), object-oriented ontology (Harman 2011; Harman 2016), and the social nature of nonhuman agency (Dourish 2004; Latour 2005, 2013; Lemos 2013) have yet to gain more significant support from scholars in the applied social sciences. Together, limited access to empirical objects and epistemological disputes in the field of theory constitute some of the limitations to—yet at the same time indicate possible trends in—studies of health and the Internet of Things in Brazil.

References

Aalbers, Teun, Maria Baars, Li Qin, Annet de Lange, Roy Kessels, and Marcel Olde Rikkert. 2015. Using an eHealth intervention to stimulate health behavior for the prevention of cognitive decline in Dutch adults: A study protocol for the brain aging monitor. *JMIR Research Protocols* 4: e130.

Alvarez, Edgar. 2016. Wearable tech will be everywhere at this year's Olympics. https://www.engadget.com/2016/07/29/olympics-wearable-tech/. Accessed 20 June 2018.

Ayo, Nike. 2012. Understanding health promotion in a neoliberal climate and the making of health conscious citizens. *Critical Public Health* 22: 99–105.

Bennet, Jane. 2010. *Vibrant matter: A political ecology of things*. London: Duke University Press.

Bitencourt, Elias Cunha. 2017. *Step addicts: Bodily practices guided by data in Fitbit user community*. Salvador. Working Paper.

Carenet Longevity. 2015. *Primeiro estudo de wearables no Brasil*. São Paulo: Carenet Longevity.

Cheney-Lippold, John. 2017. *We are data: Algorithms and the making of our digital selves*. New York: NYU Press.

Choe, Eun Kyoung, Nicole B. Lee, Bongshin Lee, Wanda Pratt, and Julie A. Kientz. 2014. Understanding quantified-selfers' practices in collecting and exploring personal data. In *Proceedings of the 32nd annual ACM conference on human factors in computing systems – CHI '14*, 1143–1152.

Chung, Arlene, Asheley Skinner, Stephanie Hasty, and Eliana Perrin. 2016. Tweeting to health: A novel mHealth intervention using fitbits and twitter to foster healthy lifestyles. *Clinical Pediatrics* 56: 26. https://doi.org/10.1177/0009922816653385.

Comstock, Jonah. 2016. Olympians turn to wearables, virtual reality and other digital health tools for an edge in Rio. MobiHealthNews. http://www.mobihealthnews.com/content/olympians-turn-wearables-virtual-reality-and-other-digital-health-tools-edge-rio.

De Vogli, Roberto. 2011. Neoliberal globalisation and health in a time of economic crisis. *Social Theory & Health* 9: 311–325.

Deleuze, Gilles, and Félix Guattari. 1988. *A thousand plateaus: Capitalism and schizophrenia*. Bloomsbury Publishing.

Donati, Luisa Paraguai. 2004. Computadores vestíveis: convivência de diferentes especialidades. *Conexão: Comunicação e Cultura* 3: 93–102.

———. 2008. Interfaces multisensoriais: espacialidades hibridas do corpoespaço. *Revista Famecos* 15: 54–60.

Dourish, Paul. 2004. *Where the action is – The foundations of embodied interaction*. Cambridge: The MIT Press.

———. 2017. *The stuff of bits: An essay on the materialities of information*. Cambridge: MIT Press.

European Commission. 2014. Green Paper on mobile Health ("mHealth"). https://ec.europa.eu/digital-single-market/en/news/green-paper-mobile-health-mhealth. Accessed 20 June 2018.

Finn, Ed. 2017. *What algorithms want: Imagination in the age of computing*. Cambridge: MIT.

Foucault, Michel. 1990. *The history of sexuality: The care of the self*. Vol. 3. London: Penguin.

Fritz, Thomas, Elaine Huang, Gail Murphy, and Thomas Zimmermann. 2014. Persuasive technology in the real world: A study of long-term use of activity sensing devices for fitness. In *Proceedings of the SIGCHI conference on human factors in computing systems*. https://doi.org/10.1145/2556288.2557383.

Gillespie, Tarleton. 2010. The politics of "platforms". *New Media & Society* 12: 347–364.

Gina, Neff, and Dawn Nafus. 2016. *Self tracking*. Cambridge: MIT Press.

Harman, Graham. 2011. *The quadruple object*. Hants: Zero Books.

———. 2016. *Immaterialism: Objects and social theory*. Cambridge: Polity Press.

Hilts, Andrew, Christopher Parsons, and Jeffrey Knockel. 2016. Every step you fake: A comparative analysis of fitness tracker privacy and security. Open Effect Report. https://openeffect.ca/reports/Every_Step_You_Fake.pdf. Accessed 20 June 2018.

IDC – International Data Corporation. 2016. Worldwide quarterly wearable device tracker report. https://www.idc.com/tracker/showproductinfo.jsp?prod_id=962. Accessed 20 June 2018.
Latour, Bruno. 2005. *Reassembling the social: An introduction to actor-network-theory*. Oxford: Oxford University Press.
———. 2013. *An inquiry into modes of existence. An anthropology of the moderns*. Vol. 1. Cambridge: Harvard University Press.
Ledger, Dan. 2014. Inside wearables – Part 2. Endeavor Partners. https://blog.endeavour.partners/inside-wearables-part-2-july-2014-ef301d425cdd. Accessed 20 June 2018.
———. 2016. Inside wearables – Part 3. The rocky path towards personalized, insightful wearables. https://www.slideshare.net/d99n/inside-wearables-the-rocky-path-towards-personalized-insightful-wearables. Accessed 20 June 2018.
Ledger, Dan, and Daniel McCaffrey. 2014. Inside wearables: How the science of human behavior change offers the secret to long-term engagement. Endeavor Partners. https://blog.endeavour.partners/inside-wearable-how-the-science-of-human-behavior-change-offers-the-secret-to-long-term-engagement-a15b3c7d4cf3. Accessed 20 June 2018.
Lemos, André. 2013. *A comunicação das coisas: teoria ator-rede e cibercultura*. São Paulo: Annablume.
———. 2016. Sensibilités Performatives: les nouvelles sensibilités des objets dans les métropoles contemporaines. *Societes* 132: 75–87.
Lemos, André, and Elias Bitencourt. 2017a. Sensibilidade performativa e comunicacao das coisas: explorando as narrativas algorítmicas na fitbit. In *Anais da Compós 2017*, São Paulo.
———. 2017b. "I feel my wrist buzz": Smartbody and performative sensibility in FitBit devices. *Galaxia* 1: 5–17.
Li, Ian. 2009. Beyond counting steps: Using context to improve monitoring of physical activity. https://pdfs.semanticscholar.org/presentation/c9ed/54b29636cfec345034e22ced1587bae3b85f.pdf. Accessed 20 June 2018.
Li, Ian, Anind K. Dey, and Jodi Forlizzi. 2011. Understanding my data, myself. In *Proceedings of the 13th international conference on ubiquitous computing – UbiComp '11*. https://doi.org/10.1145/2030112.2030166.
Logicalis Inc. 2012. Logicalis commissions white paper study into BYOD. https://www.logicalis.com/news/logicalis-commissions-white-paper-study-into-byod/. Accessed 20 June 2018.
Lupton, Deborah. 2012. M-health and health promotion: The digital cyborg and surveillance society. *Social Theory & Health* 10: 229–244.
———. 2014. Self-tracking cultures: Towards a sociology of personal informatics. In *Proceedings of the 26th Australian computer-human interaction conference on designing futures: The future of design*. https://doi.org/10.1145/2686612.2686623.
———. 2016a. Digital companion species and eating data: Implications for theorising digital data-human assemblages. *Big Data & Society* 3: 1–5.
———. 2016b. *The quantified self*. Malden: Polity Press.
Mann, Steve. 1998. Definition of "wearable computer" – Taken from Prof. Mann's Keynote speech of 1998 international conference on wearable computing. http://wearcam.org/wearcompdef.html. Accessed 20 June 2018.
Mari, Angelica. 2016. Xiaomi downsizes Brazil operations. ZDNet. http://www.zdnet.com/article/xiaomi-downsizes-brazil-operations/. Accessed 31 May 2017.
Mercer, Kathryn, Melissa Li, Lora Giangregorio, Catherine Burns, and Kelly Grindrod. 2016. Behavior change techniques present in wearable activity trackers: A critical analysis. *JMIR mHealth and uHealth* 4: e40.
Miller, Daniel. 2005. *Materiality*. Durham: Duke University Press.
Nafus, Dawn. 2016. *Quantified: Biosensing technologies in everyday life*. Cambridge: MIT Press.
Nascimento, Liliane da Costa. 2014. O auto-conhecimento através dos números: as práticas de auto- monitoramento dos quantified selves. PhD diss., Universidade Federal do Rio de Janeiro, Rio de Janeiro.
Nascimento, Liliane da Costa, and Fernanda Bruno. 2013. Quantified selves: contar, monitorar e conhecer a si mesmo através dos números. In *Anais da 22 COMPÓS*, Salvador.

Özcan, Beste, Daniele Caligiore, Valerio Sperati, Tania Moretta, and Gianluca Baldassarre. 2016. Transitional wearable companions: A novel concept of soft interactive social robots to improve social skills in children with autism spectrum disorder. *International Journal of Social Robotics* 8: 471–481.

Pantzar, Mika, and Minna Ruckenstein. 2015. The heart of everyday analytics: Emotional, material and practical extensions in self-tracking market. *Consumption Markets & Culture* 18: 92–109.

Pellanda, Eduardo Campos, and Lucia Campos Pellanda. 2016. Primordial prevention and wearable health devices: The wearables in cardiology. *Arquivos brasileiros de cardiologia*. https://doi.org/10.5935/abc.20160094.

Rahman, Cindy, and Ken Demith. 2017. Artificial intelligence automatically detects atrial fibrillation using apple watch's heart rate sensor. Heart Rhythm Society. https://www.hrsonline.org/News/Press-Releases/2017/05/Artificial-Intelligence-Automatically-Detects-AFib. Accessed 20 June 2018.

Raj, Deepika, and Jung E. Ha-Brookshire. 2016. How do they create "superpower"? An exploration of knowledge-creation processes and work environments in the wearable technology industry. *International Journal of Fashion Design, Technology and Education* 9: 82–93.

Rapp, Amon, and Federica Cena. 2016. Personal informatics for everyday life: How users without prior self-tracking experience engage with personal data. *International Journal of Human – Computer Studies* 94: 1–17.

Ruckenstein, Minna. 2014. Visualized and interacted life: Personal analytics and engagements with data doubles. *Societies* 4: 68–84.

Schaefer, Sara, Cynthia Carter Ching, Heather Breen, and J. Bruce German. 2016. Wearing, thinking, and moving: Testing the feasibility of fitness tracking with urban youth. *American Journal of Health Education* 47: 8–16.

Smith, Gavin. 2016. Surveillance, data and embodiment: On the work of being watched. *Body & Society* 22: 108–139.

Springbuk. 2016. Wearable technology: Unlocking ROI of workplace wellness contents – An employer case study in health care cost management. https://d39a28rhl1iwx3.cloudfront.net/sa/wearable%20technology_unlocking%20roi%20of%20workplace%20wellness.pdf. Accessed 20 June 2018.

Squirra, Sebastiao Carlos. 2016. A tecnologia e a evolução podem levar a comunicação para a esfera das mentes. *Revista Famecos*. 23: 21275. https://doi.org/10.15448/1980-3729.2016.1.21275.

Sumartojo, Shanti, Sarah Pink, Deborah Lupton, and Christine Heyes LaBond. 2016. The affective intensities of datafied space. *Emotion, Space and Society* 21: 33–40.

Thrift, Nigel. 2005. Beyond mediation: Three new material registers and their consequences. In *Materiality*, ed. Daniel Miller, 231–256. Durham: Duke University Press.

Tratica Inc. 2016. Healthcare wearable device shipments to reach 98 million units annually by 2021. Tractica. https://www.tractica.com/newsroom/press-releases/healthcare-wearable-device-shipments-to-reach-98-million-units-annually-by-2021/. Accessed 20 June 2018.

Tripathi, Shashank, Mohammad Chowdhury, Rana Mehta, David Wijeratne, and Lokesh Khanna. 2013. Socio-economic impact of mHealth: An assessment report for Brazil and Mexico. https://www.pwc.in/assets/pdfs/consulting/strategy/socio-economic-impact-of-mhealth-brazil-and-mexico.pdf. Accessed 20 June 2018.

Viseu, Ana. 2003. Social dimensions of wearable computers: An overview. *Technoetic Arts* 1: 77–82.

Chapter 22
The Future of Healthcare: The Impact of Digitalization on Healthcare Services Performance

Luís Velez Lapão

Abstract Healthcare systems are facing many challenges, from demographics to multi-morbidities that are associated with increasing the demand for more services. New technologies are thought to be a solution to these problems. However, to address these problems with digitalization of healthcare will imply the combination of properly using technologies, aligned with integrated working processes and skilled professionals. The first section of this chapter highlights the challenges associated with the digitalization of healthcare, the next the implementation of digital services, considering a method to design online service, and then the impact of digitalization on healthcare workforce performance. Finally, the discussion examines the challenges of digitalization for the future. Proper digitalization of healthcare will enable changes in the paradigm of healthcare delivery as well as in the mechanism for patients' participation and engagement. The sustainability of healthcare will depend on how efficient we will make digital service design.

22.1 Introduction

Healthcare systems need to be strengthened to face the challenges that lie ahead. Demographics seem to be increasing the demand for more services. The resulting comorbidities are also making the system costlier. The new technologies are thought to be a positive contribution to mitigate today's problems. The digital revolution is transforming society every day, yet this transformation in health seems to be lagging behind (Jorgenson 2001; Lapão 2018). There is a disconnect between the appealing launch of innovative services and measures of their economic impact and ability to create employment (McAfee and Brynjolfsson 2017).

Among experts, two ideas predominate, each opposing the other. From one side, there are those who depict a skeptical picture about the payoff of digital health and

L. V. Lapão (✉)
Global Health and Tropical Medicine, Instituto de Higiene e Medicina Tropical, Universidade Nova de Lisboa, Lisbon, Portugal
e-mail: luis.lapao@ihmt.unl.pt

A. Pereira Neto, M. B. Flynn (eds.), *The Internet and Health in Brazil*,
https://doi.org/10.1007/978-3-319-99289-1_22

the need to deal with healthcare reorganization due to low level of economic growth and increasing demand for services. Digitalization shows potential impact on unemployment from change in healthcare services (Gregório et al. 2014). Other authors are, however, more convinced of the promise of innovation in healthcare, believing that the economic gains from the digital revolution are still to come (Ahern 2007).

Amidst ongoing debates, the Internet and related digital technologies are producing a significant growth of information in healthcare. Emerging evidence provides support for some beneficial effects of interactive digital systems (Lapão et al. 2017), although many challenges remain with respect to understanding approaches to methodology, implementation, and evaluation to address real health challenges (Ahern 2007).

Healthcare reorganizations are trying very different approaches: reorganizing processes and skill-mix strategies, staff education, and training; implementing appropriate performance-based pay and reward systems; and designing new digital services. Health digital services are expected, as in the banking sector, to be an effective way to improve services (Eysenbach 2001). But, a large gap exists between the promises and evidence with demonstrated benefits (Black et al. 2011); there is still much to learn and study about overcoming the barriers that limit this "transformational" process.

Understating the effects of digitalization of healthcare services on the reorganization of healthcare is essential. Moreover, we need to study how eHealth, or mHealth, implementations can increase the availability, accessibility, aceptability, and quality (AAAQ) of workforce (WHO 2013), and thereby enabling the scaling-up of capacity to deliver more efficient services.

Chronic diseases are the main causes of mortality throughout Europe, with a prevalence and impact on the cost of care that is threatening the sustainability of health systems (Casalino et al. 2003). Chronic diseases are becoming a challenge for middle- and low-income economies due to the demographic and epidemiological transitions taking place (WHO 2010). The increasing prevalence of chronic diseases is inducing health system reforms with interprofessional collaboration in primary care emerging as a model of integrated healthcare service provision (WHO 2008; Rothman and Wagner 2003). This is an extraordinary ground for digital innovation.

The goal of a multidisciplinary model is to transform the daily care of chronic patients, engaging physicians but also assigning major roles for non-physicians, such as community pharmacists (CP) and nurses (Cranor et al. 2003; Makowsky et al. 2009; Bodenheimer et al. 2002). The focus on multidisciplinary models of care and the consequent primary healthcare reforms are encouraging in terms of rethinking the roles of both nurses and community pharmacists (Kennie-Kaulbach et al. 2012). For instance, the community pharmacy orientation toward a patient-centered practice has become the new paradigm of pharmacy practice, supported by the development of a clinical role for community pharmacists and a more active role for patients in their own disease management (Chisholm-Burns et al. 2010). This new paradigm has led to the development of new concepts about "pharmaceutical services" (Moullin et al. 2013). On the side of the primary care center, nurses are increasingly mediating chronic diseases patients with physicians.

Good communication between professionals is essential in multidisciplinary practice, making Information Systems and Technologies (IST) a prerequisite underpinning healthcare services in future health systems (Katz and Moyer 2004). The continuous development of IST led to the onset of eHealth that can be defined as "the utilization of IST to support health service provision, complying with the needs of citizens, patients, health professionals and other providers" (Callens 2015). IST in healthcare has been used primarily to improve administrative management. However, implementation of eHealth services has the potential to promote better access to information by patients and providers, improve the quality and safety of healthcare services, and encourage healthier lifestyles (Bates and Gawande 2003; Neuhauser and Kreps 2010; Piot 2012). Investing in IST and modernizing the architecture of healthcare services (e.g., pharmacies) is considered a necessary and critical step toward the diffusion of new forms of practice (Gregório et al. 2014).

eHealth services may develop in the next few years to harvest the full potential of healthcare services, enhancing their role in the care network and supporting their activities in chronic disease management (George et al. 2010). However, difficulties in eHealth implementation are frequently reported (Kreps and Neuhauser 2010; Kuhn et al. 2007). Most of these difficulties are frequently attributed to managerial and behavioral factors (Petrakaki et al. 2012). To resolve these difficulties, some authors propose that a user-centered approach should be promoted to be certain that eHealth services will satisfy users' needs (Armstrong and Powell 2008). The user-centered approach also reinforces users' ownership of the system leading to higher compliance and ongoing use of the system (Thursky and Mahemoff 2007; Paulo et al. 2017). The complex characteristics of the problems affecting health systems worldwide, aiming at more responsive healthcare services, demand new ideas and innovations (Christensen et al. 2000).

The implementation of multidisciplinary-service models requires proper planning and management, especially when innovative experience and patient knowledge is lacking. For instance, digital services required the assessment of the potential of eHealth in the provision of clinical services by actively enabling the interaction with patients and promoting their education. Furthermore, the project is expected to address the use of eHealth supporting health services, establishing its acceptability, feasibility, sustainability, and adaptability to future changes.

In order to achieve these objectives, an online health service can be conceived, designed, developed, demonstrated, and evaluated by using the design science research methodology (DSRM) (Peffers et al. 2007; Hevner et al. 2004; Lapão et al. 2017). A service can be considered as an artifact for DSRM, and it would support, for instance, the patients' disease and therapeutic monitoring.

In the next section, I highlight the challenges associated with the digitalization of healthcare; then the implementation of digital services will be addressed considering the use of a method for designing, demonstrating, and evaluating online service design (Peffers et al. 2007). Next, the impact of digitalization on healthcare workforce will be analyzed, considering its many challenges. The final section provides a more detailed analysis on the impact of digital services on the performance of the health workforce. The discussion section examines the challenges of digitalization in more detail. The paper then closes with a conclusion that includes the main lessons learned plus future work.

22.2 Digitalization of Healthcare

Digitalization is comparable to the advent of steam power and electrification as examples of general-purpose technologies, i.e., technologies with broad application across an economy that changed the production paradigm. Moore's Law allows for improvements and reductions in costs of digital technologies (McAfee and Brynjolfsson 2017). As a result, healthcare organizations are likely to find even wider use than previously expected for sensors and medical devices, opening up services to new categories of workers. A different prospect could emerge from the potential of machine-to-machine communication, allowing devices to interact with each other and respond to new conditions without human intervention (WHO 2016). A scenario where there is the digitization of all healthcare processes would produce a stream of data that makes a ubiquitous "Internet of things" possible and eventually provide the necessary information for continuing improvement in healthcare processes (Lapão 2016).

The three dimensions of digitalization of healthcare services include the following: the significant domain of the new technologies and what is their potential and bottlenecks (Marques et al. 2017); the domain of the working processes as continuous improvement organizational cycles (e.g., comprehensive use of management tools like LEAN systems (Lapão 2016) and clinical governance guidelines); and, last but not the least, the existence of a digitally qualified workforce (Lapão et al. 2017).

Technology is an important factor but only when properly aligned with a (integrated) healthcare process. New technologies like big data, Internet of things, artificial intelligence (AI), and 3-D printing are very relevant but also require some evidence of their usefulness. Big data, combined with AI in the future (let's say in 10–20 years), will allow for better understanding of health systems (e.g., patient behavior, service utilization, the emergence of epidemics) patterns allowing for better use of resources and increased creation of valuable knowledge. IBM and Google are investing huge amounts of money into the combination, but so far the results have not yet reached significant value for health systems. The Internet of things in healthcare brings other challenges (Marques et al. 2017). The quality of data and the sustainability of credible network of health sensors are among the most important ones. However, integration with proper healthcare services (e.g., ePharmacare) and the accreditation of sensors and mobile apps could represent important breakthroughs. Interestingly, 3-D printing is a great success in healthcare, for instance, the use of 3-D printing in education (e.g., Prof. Chao Wen in São Paulo University[1]) and use of new materials for surgical implants.

Nonetheless, the key for successful digitalization is the existence of highly qualified professionals. A digitally qualified professional will know how to address the care team in using digital tools that are implemented as a way to improve quality and reduce costs. One main area of activity for these professionals is the development of new online care channels (Lapão et al. 2017).

22.3 Innovation by Implementing New Digital Services

The digitalization of health depends on the implementation of innovative digital health services. The development of new digital services is a way to the future and a new area of research. The case of ePharmacare service will be used as an example of how one should develop new services (Lapão et al. 2017). The operation of DSRM's six steps produced an online pharmaceutical service which is explained below. This online service is a good example as it implies the interaction between health professionals (e.g., pharmacists and physicians) in a collaborative way and patients (i.e., chronic patients).

Step 1: To Identify the Real Problem and Motivation to Address It

The problem identification activity is crucial to help focus the DSRM and to guarantee user involvement. Three complementary approaches were used to help define the problem: a scenario exercise (e.g., strategy), an online survey (e.g., market analysis), and an observational study (e.g., understanding the organizational processes).

(a) Scenario exercise: The scenario analysis highlighted that the development of a new role for community pharmacists is dependent on the economic and legislative environment in which these professionals operate and also of their inner ability to innovate and develop new services. In a scenario where online pharmaceutical services would be a reality across the country, new health regulations have to be in place alongside a more competitive pharmacy market. Besides that, an innovative approach by pharmacy managers and practicing CP will be needed.

(b) The online survey helped to identify the two main issues: the lack of financial incentives for online pharmaceutical services implementation and lack of support and guidance from professional organizations.

(c) Observational study: In order to understand the working processes, an observational study took place in the community pharmacy. About 54 min of free or idle time per pharmacist was found. Regarding the provision of pharmaceutical services, 29.9% of pharmacist time was spent dispensing prescriptions and 13.2% dispensing over-the-counter (OTC) medicines. Also of relevance is the 4.3% of

[1] See Chap. 16 in this volume.

pharmacist time that was spent counseling patients without dispensing any medicine. The IST was used to support sales, detecting possible interactions and identifying adverse effects of the dispensed medicines.

(d) Costing study: In general, pharmaceutical services costs in the participant pharmacies were similar. The costing study also identified the costliest activities in pharmaceutical service provision (Gregório et al. 2017). In these pharmacies, validation and dispensing of the prescription and the managing of inventory and other records were found to be the highest-cost activities. These activities are main targets to innovation.

Step 2: Define Objectives of a Solution

DSRM proposes the definition of objectives for a solution. When people were asked about new desired pharmacy services, the home delivery and Internet ordering of medicines were the most referred services, followed by integrating pharmacy services with primary care (e.g., gatekeeping, scheduling of GP consultations, patient follow-up).

Supported by the results from these studies, the main targets for the new service could be defined. The online pharmaceutical service should allow the pharmaceutical care of chronic patients without overloading community pharmacists' workload, at a cost comparable to a screening service. This service should address the monitoring of patients' therapy (covering medication reviews, medicine interactions, adherence, and medication management), alongside features that aimed to test service integration with the primary healthcare (e.g., emission of reports to the GP).

Step 3: Design and Development

From the insights obtained in the previous activities, the design of a disease management platform to support online pharmaceutical care services for chronic patients can be proposed. The platform was called ePharmacare. The core of the platform is the storage of patient's treatment information and the possibility to improve that information by allowing both pharmacists and patients to enter new valuable information on the platform. Once pharmacists have their patients registered in the platform, it is possible to provide disease management on several levels: estimation of "refill dates," providing the pharmacist with a prevision of when a re-stock and refill of medicines is needed for a specific patient; monitoring of therapeutic results; and early detection of adverse reactions, addressing minor ailments or other queries reported by patients.

Allowing real-time monitoring of patient's parameters such as blood pressure or glycemia levels is another important aspect of the platform. Currently, pharma-cists monitor and register their patient's therapeutic progress on paper (or not at all). ePharmacare allows patients and pharmacists to enter and store these data in a database. Pharmacists can then see, edit, organize, and interpret the data in a more convenient way. For patients, the potential of this feature lies in the possibility of accessing their own therapeutic and disease management data outside of the pharmacy, thus greatly improving their own decision-making.

Step 4: Demonstration
Pharmacists held monthly meetings with patients, observing, discussing, and registering clinical data. These meetings finished with an information session about different health themes but usually in the context of chronic diseases, such as the proper use of medications, interactions of medicines and herbal products, etc. The online information exchange between patients and pharmacist was related to questions of therapy modifications, self-administration of medicines, or self-medication with OTC medicines and herbal products. Among the collected parameters, blood pressure and postprandial glycemia showed significant improvements.

Step 5: Evaluation
To help in assessing the usability of the web platform, eye-tracking glasses were used. It was found that a CP took an average of 7:38 min to perform the tasks. This is an important finding since it fits within the free time found in activity one. Nevertheless, it is more important to highlight that to really use this free time in an efficient way, some reorganization of pharmacies' internal working processes and role definition among professionals must be done. For patients, the time to perform a set of tasks was considered less relevant since patients can use the platform whenever it is most convenient. The difficulties in using IST are common among this age group and are usually addressed in usability field studies (Kaufman et al. 2003).

Step 6: Communication
This step is responsible to sharing the results of the implementation of the new online service as a positive solution to the initial problem. Both the researchers and the pharmacists presented the results in several technical workshops and conferences, as well as publishing on both scientific and professional journals (Lapão et al. 2017).

The development of a new online pharmaceutical service could be an important contribution to efficient chronic diseases' management. Of importance, the close monitoring and sharing of information allows for the detection of early signs of adverse reactions or potentially dangerous interactions between medicines and non-prescription products. By the end of the demonstration, the patients were so engaged that they asked if it was possible to continue to use the platform for data registration because they were already familiar with its functioning. This is a vision of the future. This perspective implies a new way of working in community pharmacies. Some authors argue that it is necessary to create new organizations to embrace digital services and to incorporate them into their business models (Albanese et al. 2010).

On patients and caregivers' side, an integrated system may improve professionals' needs assessment, while providing tailored information through more frequent communication for low-cost service, yielding high-value disease management. Innovation is a process implying the transformation of ideas about a perceived problem into a new product, process, or service. Innovation in healthcare has usually a direct impact on the quality of care services and on the life of patients. The challenges posed by the rising prevalence of chronic diseases demand new strategies toward health innovation (Gardner et al. 2007). The ultimate goal of technology and innovation is to improve the quality of life. Yet, all too often, introduction of new tools is decided by policymakers and experts without genuinely involving future users and those experiencing the potential risks. However, good business model designs are likely to be context dependent, and both the design and implementation processes are likely to involve iterative processes (Teece 2010).

22.4 Digitization Impact on Health Workforce

Most health digital services studies have focused narrowly on text messaging systems for patient behavioral change, and few studies have examined systems for digital services strengthening (Lapão 2016, 2018). There is limited literature on clinical effectiveness, costs, and patient acceptability, and none on equity and safety issues. There were only four papers on digital skills requirements for professionals (Tsiknakis and Kouroubali 2009; Christiansen et al. 2014; Quaglio et al. 2016; Tian et al. 2017). Despite the bold promise of digital tools to improve health, much remains unknown about whether and how this will be fulfilled.

Furthermore, it was identified clinical trial protocols of large-scale, multidimensional digital interventions, suggesting that the current limited evidence base will expand in the coming years.

The literature suggests that eHealth/mHealth can be used as tools to meet the challenges of healthy ageing and universal access to healthcare services in the context of the increasing burden of chronic diseases (Gregório et al. 2014). More specifically, they have showed the capacity to:

- Promote the adoption of healthy lifestyles and self-care (Tsiknakis and Kouroubali 2009).
- Improve access to a wide range of healthcare services, covering conditions such as mental illness, heart and cerebrovascular disease, diabetes and cancer.
- Services such as radiology and rehabilitation have also benefited (van Deursen and van Dijk 2011; Bashshur et al. 2009).
- Enhance efficiency in clinical decision-making and prescribing, through easier communication between healthcare providers (Gregório et al. 2014; van Deursen and van Dijk 2011).
- Promote individualized, patient-centered care at a lower cost (Bashshur et al. 2009).
- Increase the effectiveness of chronic disease management in both long-term care facilities and at home (Gregório et al. 2014; van Deursen and van Dijk 2011; Bashshur et al. 2009).

The European Commission adopted a policy to encourage the development of eMedicine (EM) (Eysenbach 2001). It identified the ways in which EM services might assist patients, particularly those living in remote areas or experiencing conditions that might not be treated as often as needed. It is also cited specific benefits such as improving access to healthcare by giving access to specialists who are not available locally and at the organizational level helping to shorten patient waiting lists, optimizing the use of resources, and enabling productivity gains. In the last decade, a number of European initiatives have been launched in support of the development of EM under the Competitiveness and Innovation Programme, in particular its Policy Support Programme, and its pilot experiments or European FP7 projects such as Renewing Health, United4Health, and Digital Agenda for Europe. Major policy actions, such as Horizon 2020, the European Innovation Partnership (e.g., Active and Healthy Ageing), and the 2012 European eHealth Action Plan, have highlighted the value of using technologies, such as EM. The EHTEL Sustainable Telemedicine offers paradigms for future-proof healthcare by proposing good practices in the use of ICT in integrated care (WHO 2016). The deployment of eHealth is already the objective of several European initiatives. Currently, EM exists through three main types of services:

- Diagnosis: The results of x-ray, ultrasound, etc. exams are sent digitally from a diagnostic device to the appropriate health professional who in turn make a diagnosis that is sent digitally to the referring physician or diagnostic clinic.
- Monitoring: Data derived from devices measuring patient vital signs are tracked by a monitoring center or individual clinician. Embedded algorithms, written guidelines, or professional judgment all support this process. If an unusual event occurs, the monitoring process generates a response in the form of an alert, contact with a clinician, or some form of guidance to the patient.
- Consultation: When a virtual visit or dialogue takes place instead of, or in addition to, a face-to-face encounter.

22.5 The Impact of Digital Services on the Performance of the Health Workforce

Digital services should improve health workforce performance. However, literature remains scarce about how these new services affect the health workforce. We examine what the literature indicates about the AAAQ (availability, accessibility, acceptability, and quality) dimensions of the workforce:

Availability The more general literature indicates that the utilization of EM augments the productivity of clinicians thanks to time-saving practices, less paper work, and more rapid access to information. Higher productivity translates into increased availability and capacity to provide services to more users, even if the absolute numbers of health professionals remain constant (Tsiknakis and Kouroubali 2009; Christiansen et al. 2014).

Accessibility Accessibility improves as providers intervene at a distance, with the capacity to diagnose problems and monitor patient conditions through devices (van Deursen and van Dijk 2011). Specialists, who typically concentrate in urban areas and hospitals, become accessible as they interact with their colleagues or directly with patients, irrespective of distance. This has the potential to enable the expansion of homecare and service integration (Tian et al. 2017).

Acceptability EM services make communication with patients easier and more direct and adapted to each individual need, thereby potentially enhancing the acceptability of providers. This is more likely with younger persons who are more familiar with the utilization of computers and mobile devices, but strategies to facilitate their use by older patients may therefore be needed (Gregório et al. 2014; Bashshur et al. 2009).

Quality EM give providers rapid access to valid information, second opinions, and guidelines, all of which contribute to scaling up the competencies and compliance with professional standards, thereby improving patient safety (WHO 2013; Tsiknakis and Kouroubali 2009; Christiansen et al. 2014).

The use of the AAAQ framework is relevant to detail how one can use digitalization of healthcare to improve health workforce performance. Therefore, every digitalization project should consider the proper evaluation of the impact of the online services on the efficiency of health professionals and teams.

22.6 Discussion

Digital services are already changing how many sectors of the economy function, but they are relatively new in healthcare (McAfee and Brynjolfsson 2017). The experts agreed that this raises questions about what can facilitate their utilization and which barriers need to be overcome to make real the potential performance gains of health workers and services. Healthcare digitalization is not a panacea, but it offers significant opportunities to improve access to care, contain costs, and scale up quality. The experts helped identify facilitators and barriers, including individuals, such as patients, providers, and managers; professional associations; provider organizations; and the institutional and regulatory environment.

The recent evolution of IST (e.g., big data, artificial intelligence, and chronic care sensors) is an important opportunity toward the integration of new roles for online services, while allowing a more active role from patients in their disease management. The use of platforms, like ePharmacare or Google Health, presents a possible turning point in the way business is done within primary care, by reaching out to new channels and shifting the focus from the sale of products to the provision of services. The patterns of a pharmacist's time usage, the costing studies, and the patterns of service provision and demand reflect a need to reorganize pharmacies management and acquire additional skills in order to enable online pharmaceutical services provision.

The ePharmacare platform is able to offer pharmacies and physicians a way to better monitor their patients and therefore increase the quality of their therapy.

By bringing to life a needed tool, the platform fulfills the detected need for IST in pharmaceutical services provision, offering patients a new way to interact with their data and be part of their own therapy as active members on disease management.

The quality and usability of the platform is critical. But the platform is not everything. Developing and implementing online services takes properly trained and motivated professionals. Online pharmaceutical services need to be more integrated in the current daily practices and some communication and marketing efforts need to be done, to recruit and demonstrate value to the chronic patients. A rethinking of the community pharmacy business model in order to effectively and coherently integrate community pharmacies services into the future health system models, where patients will have an increasing role in disease management, is paramount.

The acquisition or development of digital skills by health workers is critical. This has implications for the education of health workers, the management of health services, policymaking, and research. Proper digital service implementation requires adjustments in service delivery and in how work is organized. Competencies to work in a digitalized environment have already been identified as among the core competencies that health professionals must have to deliver the services that meet the current and future needs of populations. The policy challenge is for educational institutions to adapt the contents of curricula and learning strategies to prepare future professionals for new ways of practicing; it also includes the need to help the existing workforce acquire digital skills, which did not exist when they were initially educated. The impact of digitalization on the provision of services will affect the availability of the health workforce, depending on the type of service. In some instances, it may lead to a reduction of needs if productivity increases and demand remains constant. More likely, it will generate additional and new needs, such as health data analysts. As professionals are now able to monitor patients remotely, more physicians and nurses will be needed to respond to a demand in rapid growth from a population of patients with chronic condition or mental impairment. New categories of professionals in tele-nursing, smart decision-making, etc. will also be needed. Most experts consider that most facilitators and barriers to the diffusion of digital services are not very different from that of other innovations.

Factors such as engaging stakeholders in implementing change, the visibility of its advantages and user-friendliness, the leadership of respected so-called champions, access to training, the commitment and support of managers and decision-makers, good planning, and an enabling financial and legal environment can all play a positive role. A typical barrier involving the resistance of older workers could become less of an issue as new tools become more user-friendly and as their utility for the worker and patients is almost immediately apparent. Another argument is that the technology seems to be changing more rapidly than the organizational and institutional environment. Issues linked to legal responsibility, the definition of scopes of practice, remuneration and reimbursement, and the standardization of tools are starting to be addressed. However, these are particularly difficult in a context such as that of the EU where the mobility of workers and patients is a fundamental right. Another challenge is planning for the future health workforce in a context of rapid technological, demographic, epidemiological, economic, and social change. How we will use and manage digital tools to face the health challenges is a fundamental health policy and research question to be addressed in the next years.

22.7 Conclusion

Healthcare online services are complex endeavors that can benefit from implementation methodologies. The use of DSRM to implement an innovative online healthcare service offers a higher involvement to the stakeholders enabling the proper alignment with both processes and workforce skills. This involvement shows the potential to develop a tailored information system. The new models of collaborative work also bring up the need for innovation in the healthcare workforce where the inclusion of nurses can be beneficial for the efficiency of care.

New technologies are critical; however it requires excellent knowledge of functionalities and costs to appropriately integrate them into the health professionals' working processes. It also benefits from a co-design approach, whereas the health professionals will lead and assume the utilization of the new technologies.

For these reasons, the uptake of digital services is taking some time. Its benefits will not come spontaneously. Policymakers will be interested in the economics of the utilization of healthcare digital services; direct costs may be low, and there may be savings from less visits and hospitalizations, but indirect costs also need to be assessed, whether it is for training or through increased demand induced by the greater accessibility facilitated by the technologies. Planning for a positive impact of digitalization of healthcare services on health workforce performance is essential, whereas a rigorous evaluation of healthcare services should be executed as a continuous process of improvement. The digitalization of healthcare will support the changes in the paradigm of healthcare delivery as well as in the mechanism for patients' participation and engagement. The sustainability of healthcare will depend on how efficient we will make the design of new digital health services.

References

Ahern, David. 2007. Challenges and opportunities of eHealth research. *American Journal of Preventive Medicine* 32: S75–S82.

Albanese, Nicole Paolini, Michael Rouse, and Marissa Schlaifer. 2010. Scope of contemporary pharmacy practice: Roles, responsibilities, and functions of pharmacists and pharmacy technicians. *American Journal of Health-System Pharmacy* 50: e35–e69.

Armstrong, Natalie, and John Powell. 2008. Preliminary test of an Internet-based diabetes self-management tool. *Journal of Telemedicine and Telecare* 14: 114–116.

Bashshur, Rashid L., Gary W. Shannon, Elizabeth A. Krupinski, Jim Grigsby, Joseph C. Kvedar, Ronald S. Weinstein, Jay H. Sanders, et al. 2009. National telemedicine initiatives: Essential to healthcare reform. *Telemedicine and e-Health* 15: 600–610.

Bates, David W., and Atul A. Gawande. 2003. Improving safety with information technology. *The New England Journal of Medicine* 348: 2526–2534.

Black, Ashly D., Josip Car, Claudia Pagliari, Chantelle Anandan, Kathrin Cresswell, et al. 2011. The impact of eHealth on the quality and safety of health care: A systematic overview. *PLoS Medicine* 8: e1000387. https://doi.org/10.1371/journal.pmed.1000387.

Bodenheimer, Thomas, Edward H. Wagner, and Kevin Grumbach. 2002. Improving primary care for patients with chronic illness: The chronic care model, Part 2. *JAMA* 288: 1909–1914.

Callens, Stefaan. 2015. The EU legal framework on e-health. In *Health systems governance in Europe: The role of EU law and policy*, ed. Elias Mossialos, Govin Permanand, Rita Baeten, and Tamara K. Hervey, 561–588. Cambridge: Cambridge University Press.

Casalino, Lawrence, Robin R. Gillies, Stephen M. Shortell, Julie A. Schmittdiel, Thomas Bodenheimer, et al. 2003. External incentives, information technology, and organized processes to improve health care quality for patients with chronic diseases. *JAMA* 289: 434–441.

Chisholm-Burns, Marie A., Joshua S. Graff Zivin, Jeannie Kim Lee, et al. 2010. Economic effects of pharmacists on health outcomes in the United States: A systematic review. *American Journal of Health-System Pharmacy* 67: 1624–1634.

Christensen, Clayton M., Richard M.J. Bohmer, and John Kenagy. 2000. Will disruptive innovations cure healthcare? *Harvard Business Review* 78: 102–112.

Christiansen, Ellen, Eva Henriksen, Lise Jensen, et al. 2014. *Towards a personalised blueprint – For doers, by doers: European momentum for mainstreaming telemedicine*. Brussels: European Commission.

Cranor, Carole W., Barry A. Bunting, and Dale B. Christensen. 2003. The Asheville project: Long-term clinical and economic outcomes of a community pharmacy diabetes care program. *Journal of the American Pharmaceutical Association* 43: 173–184.

Eysenbach, Gunther. 2001. What is e-health? *Journal of Medical Internet Research* 3: e20.

Gardner, Charles A., Tara Acharya, and Derek Yach. 2007. Technological and social innovation: A unifying new paradigm for global health. *Health Affairs* 26: 1052–1061.

George, Pradeep P., Joseph A. Molina, Jason Cheah, Soo Chung Chan, and Boon Lim. 2010. The evolving role of the community pharmacist in chronic disease management – A literature review. *Annals of the Academy of Medicine, Singapore* 39: 861–867.

Gregório, João, Afonso Cavaco, and Luís V. Lapão. 2014. A scenario-planning approach to human resources for health: The case of community pharmacists in Portugal. *Human Resources for Health* 12: 58.

———. 2017. How to best manage time interaction with patients? Community pharmacist workload and service provision analysis. *Research in Social and Administrative Pharmacy* 13: 133–147.

Hevner, Allan R., Salvatore T. March, Jinsoo Park, and Sudha Ram. 2004. Design science in information systems research. *MIS Quarterly* 28: 75–105.

Jorgenson, Dale W. 2001. Information technology and the US economy. *American Economic Review* 91: 1–32.

Katz, Steven J., and Cheryl A. Moyer. 2004. The emerging role of online communication between patients and their providers. *Journal of General Internal Medicine* 19: 978–983.

Kaufman, David R., Vimla L. Patel, Charlyn Hilliman, Philip C. Morin, Jenia Pevzner, et al. 2003. Usability in the real world: Assessing medical information technologies in patients' homes. *Journal of Biomedical Informatics* 36: 45–60.

Kennie-Kaulbach, Natalie, Barbara Farrell, Natalie Ward, Sharon Johnston, Ashley Gubbels, et al. 2012. Pharmacist provision of primary health care: A modified Delphi validation of pharmacists' competencies. *BMC Family Practice* 13: 27.

Kreps, Gary L., and Linda Neuhauser. 2010. New directions in eHealth communication: Opportunities and challenges. *Patient Education and Counseling* 78: 329–336.

Kuhn, K.A., D.A. Giuse, L. Lapão, and S.H.R. Wurst. 2007. Expanding the scope of health information systems: From hospitals to regional networks, to national infrastructures, and beyond. *Methods of Information in Medicine* 46: 500–502.

Lapão, Luís Velez. 2016. The future impact of healthcare services digitalization on health workforce: The increasing role of medical informatics. *Studies in Health Technology and Informatics* 228: 675–679.

———. 2018. Digitalization of healthcare: Where is the evidence of the impact on healthcare workforce's performance? *Studies in Health Technology and Informatics* 247: 646–650.

Lapão, Luís Velez, Miguel Mira da Silva, and João Gregório. 2017. Implementing an online pharmaceutical service using design science research. *BMC Medical Informatics and Decision Making* 17: 31.

Makowsky, Mark, Theresa Schindel, Meagan Rosenthal, Katy Campbell, Ross Tsuyuki, and Helen Madill. 2009. Collaboration between pharmacists, physicians and nurse practitioners: A qualitative investigation of working relationships in the inpatient medical setting. *Journal of Interprofessional Care* 23: 169–184.

Marques, Rita, João Gregório, Fernando Pinheiro, Pedro Póvoa, Miguel Mira da Silva, and Luís Velez Lapão. 2017. How can information systems provide support to nurses' hand hygiene performance? Using gamification and indoor location to improve hand hygiene awareness and reduce hospital infections. *BMC Medical Informatics and Decision Making* 17: 15.

McAfee, Andrew, and Erik Brynjolfsson. 2017. *Machine, platform, crowd: Harnessing our digital future*. New York: WW Norton & Company.

Moullin, Joanna C., Daniel Sabater-Hernandez, Fernando Fernandez-Llimos, and Shalom Benrimoj. 2013. Defining professional pharmacy services in community pharmacy. *Research in Social and Administrative Pharmacy* 9: 989–995.

Neuhauser, Linda, and Gary Kreps. 2010. eHealth communication and behavior change: Promise and performance. *Social Semiotics* 20: 9–27.

Paulo, Marília Silva, Tom Loney, and Luís Velez Lapão. 2017. The primary health care in the emirate of Abu Dhabi: Are they aligned with the chronic care model elements? *BMC Health Services Research* 17: 725.

Peffers, Ken, Tuure Tuunanen, Marcus Rothenberger, and Samir Chatterjee. 2007. A design science research methodology for information systems research. *Journal of Management Information Systems* 24: 45–77.

Petrakaki, Dimitra, Nick Barber, and Justin Waring. 2012. The possibilities of technology in shaping healthcare professionals: (re/de-)professionalisation of pharmacists in England. *Social Science & Medicine* 75: 429–437.

Piot, Peter. 2012. Innovation and technology for global public health. *Global Public Health* 7: S46–S53.

Quaglio, Gianluca, Claudio Dario, Panos Stafylas, Madis Tiik, Sarah McCormack, Pēteris Zilgalvis, et al. 2016. E-Health in Europe: Current situation and challenges ahead. *Health Policy and Technology* 5: 314–317.

Rothman, Arlyss A., and Edward H. Wagner. 2003. Chronic illness management: What is the role of primary care? *Annals of Internal Medicine* 138: 256–261.

Teece, David J. 2010. Business models, business strategy and innovation. *Long Range Planning* 43: 172–194.

Thursky, Karin A., and Michael Mahemoff. 2007. User-centered design techniques for a computerised antibiotic decision support system in an intensive care unit. *International Journal of Medical Informatics* 76: 760–768.

Tian, Maoyi, Jing Zhang, Rong Luo, Shi Chen, et al. 2017. Mhealth interventions for health system strengthening in China: A systematic review. *JMIR* 5: e32.

Tsiknakis, Manolis, and Angelina Kouroubali. 2009. Organizational factors affecting successful adoption of innovative eHealth services. *International Journal of Medical Informatics* 78: 39–52.

van Deursen, Alexander, and Jan van Dijk. 2011. Internet skills performance tests: Are people ready for eHealth? *Journal of Medical Internet Research* 13: e35.

WHO – World Health Organization. 2008. *World health report – Primary health care: Now more than ever*. Geneve: World Health Organization.

———. 2010. *Global status report on non-communicable diseases*. Geneve: World Health Organization.

———. 2013. *Health 2020: A European policy framework & strategy for the 21st century*. Copenhagen: WHO Europe.

———. 2016. *Global strategy on human resources for health: Workforce 2030*. Geneva: WHO Document Production Services.

Index

A. Pereira Neto, M. B. Flynn (eds.), *The Internet and Health in Brazil*,
https://doi.org/10.1007/978-3-319-99289-1

H

I

The manufacturer's authorised representative in the EU is Springer Nature Customer Service Centre GmbH, Europaplatz 3, 69115 Heidelberg, Germany. If you have any concerns regarding our products, please contact ProductSafety@springernature.com

Printed and bound by CPI Group (UK) Ltd, Croydon, CR0 4YY
30/09/2026
02225655-0014